ATLA BIBLIOGRAPHY SERIES
edited by Dr. Kenneth E. Rowe

1. *A Guide to the Study of the Holiness Movement,* by Charles Edwin Jones. 1974.
2. *Thomas Merton: A Bibliography,* by Marquita E. Breit. 1974.
3. *The Sermon on the Mount: A History of Interpretation and Bibliography,* by Warren S. Kissinger. 1975.
4. *The Parables of Jesus: A History of Interpretation and Bibliography,* by Warren S. Kissinger. 1979.
5. *Homosexuality and the Judeo-Christian Tradition: An Annotated Bibliography,* by Tom Horner. 1981.
6. *A Guide to the Study of the Pentecostal Movement,* by Charles Edwin Jones. 1983.
7. *The Genesis of Modern Process Thought: A Historical Outline with Bibliography,* by George R. Lucas, Jr. 1983.
8. *A Presbyterian Bibliography,* by Harold B. Prince. 1983.
9. *Paul Tillich: A Comprehensive Bibliography . . .,* by Richard C. Crossman. 1983.
10. *A Bibliography of the Samaritans,* by Alan David Crown. 1984.
11. *An Annotated and Classified Bibliography of English Literature Pertaining to the Ethiopian Orthodox Church,* by Jon Bonk. 1984.
12. *International Meditation Bibliography, 1950 to 1982,* by Howard R. Jarrell. 1984.
13. *Rabindranath Tagore: A Bibliography,* by Katherine Henn. 1985.
14. *Research in Ritual Studies: A Programmatic Essay and Bibliography,* by Ronald L. Grimes. 1985.
15. *Protestant Theological Education in America,* by Heather F. Day. 1985.
16. *Unconscious: A Guide to Sources,* by Natalino Caputi. 1985.
17. *The New Testament Apocrypha and Pseudepigrapha,* by James H. Charlesworth. 1987.
18. *Black Holiness,* by Charles Edwin Jones. 1987.

THE NEW TESTAMENT APOCRYPHA AND PSEUDEPIGRAPHA:

a guide to publications, with excursuses on apocalypses

by

JAMES H. CHARLESWORTH

with

James R. Mueller

assisted by many, especially
Amy-Jill Levine, Randall D. Chesnutt,
and M. J. H. Charlesworth

ATLA BIBLIOGRAPHY SERIES, NO. 17

The American Theological Library
Association and
The Scarecrow Press, Inc.
Metuchen, N.J., and London • 1987

Library of Congress Cataloging-in-Publication Data

Charlesworth, James H.
    The New Testament apocrypha and pseudepigrapha.

    (ATLA bibliography series ; no. 17)
    Bibliography: p.
    Includes index.
    1. Apocryphal books (New Testament)--Bibliography.
2. Apocryphal books (New Testament)--Criticism,
interpretation, etc. I. Mueller, James R. II. Title.
III. Series.
Z7772.Z5C45 1987   [BS2840]   016.229'9   85-18350
ISBN 0-8108-1845-0

for Lois and Art

with whom I heard the Bible read

by Art and Jean

CONTENTS

III.   THE CONTINUUM OF JEWISH AND CHRISTIAN
      APOCALYPSES: TEXTS AND ENGLISH TRANSLATIONS

IV.   BIBLIOGRAPHY

EDITOR'S FOREWORD

The American Theological Library Association Bibliography Series is designed to stimulate and encourage the preparation of reliable bibliographies and guides to the literature of religious studies in all of its scope and variety. Compilers are free to define their field, make their own selections, and work out internal organization as the unique demands of the subject require. We are pleased to publish James Charlesworth's impressive guide to the New Testament Apocrypha and Pseudepigrapha as number 17 in our series.

James H. Charlesworth is a Phi Beta Kappa graduate of Ohio Wesleyan University and Duke University, where he took the M.Div. degree and the Ph.D degree in Biblical studies. Following post-doctoral study at the École Biblique de Jérusalem Dr. Charlesworth began his teaching career at Duke University. Since 1984 he has been the George L. Collord Professor of New Testament Language and Literature at Princeton Theological Seminary. A Fulbright Fellow, Thayer Fellow of the American School of Oriental Research and Fellow of the American Council of Learned Societies, Dr. Charlesworth has published many articles and several monographs, including the definitive two volume work The Old Testament Pseudepigrapha, 1983-1985.

Kenneth E. Rowe
Series Editor

Drew University Library
Madison, NJ 07940

PREFACE

The preparation of this work has taken over five years. My work
on the Pseudepigrapha and Modern Research with a Supplement and
decisions related to the preparation of The Old Testament Pseudepigrapha inevitably led me into a fairly intense study of the New Testament Apocrypha and Pseudepigrapha (NTAP). It soon became clear
to me that James' The Apocryphal New Testament and Hennecke,
Schneemelcher, and Wilson's New Testament Apocrypha were not complete and definitive editions of the NTAP. Many documents I had
read were not included or even mentioned in these standard collections; soon I had compiled a large collection of xeroxed texts and
translations. Each new discovery led to other writings, previously
unknown to me. With the invaluable help of my assistants I began
to systematize my random forays into the byways of the canon. The
first card index tray was filled with cards in less than a year; another one was purchased, then another--finally cards filled six trays.
The typescript grew to more than 600 pages and 6,000 entries. It
has been exceedingly difficult to organize these thousands of publications; revision followed revision. Now the work is before you in
the best form I can presently obtain; yet I fear there may be far
more chaos still in the creation.

I am indebted to many individuals who helped me during the
five years of this project. Marie Smith proved to be a loyal typist;
Ann Rives typed many of the additional entries.

Deep appreciations are warmly extended to Elizabeth Larocca,
who began helping me with this task in 1979, and to my other assistants over the years, namely Melanie McKittrick, who helped with
the publications in Russian, and Jean H. Charlesworth, who indefa-
tigably searched for obscure publications.

To be singled out for special recognition are Randall D. Chesnutt and Amy-Jill Levine who helped me significantly, and to James
R. Mueller who worked closely with me the last year of the project;
he went with me to New York City to correct entries, and even
helped me polish the introductory chapters.

Stefan M. Pugh of the Duke University Department of Slavic
Languages and Literatures corrected and translated the entries in
East European languages. The work has also been assisted by my

colleagues in the Duke University Divinity School Library and in Perkins Library. Emerson Ford, head of the Interlibrary Loan Office, was a constant friend and valued colleague. Donn Michael Farris, Harriet Leonard, Linda K. Gard, and the other members of the Duke Divinity School Library staff provided continuing advice and assistance.

Wanda C. Camp of the Department of Religion helped with payrolls and guided me through a maze of bureaucratic rules and regulations. The preparation of the work was funded by a generous grant from the Duke University Research Council. The Dean of the Divinity School, Thomas A. Langford, graciously provided space in which to prepare and complete this work. Also, I am most grateful to my colleagues, here and abroad, who counseled me and sent me their books and offprints.

I am especially indebted to Professor J.-D. Kaestli, le Directeur de l'Institut des Sciences bibliques of the Université de Lausanne, for working through the final draft and sending me a list of corrigenda. He is a remarkable scholar, and knows more than I do about the NTAP. His long hours of work on behalf of scholarship significantly improved the following bibliography. His selfless service and meticulousness deserve special commendation. He receives my deep words of appreciation.

While many have helped me prepare this publication, I alone am responsible for the introduction; these should not be taken to represent a <u>consensus communis</u>.*

James H. Charlesworth

---

*After completing this work a major source book for the study of apocalyptic thought in antiquity appeared: D. Hellholm (ed.) <u>Apocalypticism in the Mediterranean World and the Near East</u> (Tübingen, 1983).

PART I: INTRODUCTION

A REPORT ON RESEARCH

The work published here began in the mid-seventies; since that time
there has been an unparalleled international interest in the New Testament Apocrypha and Pseudepigrapha (NTAP). About the year
1965 we entered into a new phase of intensive interest in and research upon the NTAP. Scholarly research may be divided into four
phases.

The first phase of interest in the NTAP began sometime during
the Middle Ages with the increased interest in the apocalypses and
the antichrist (see Part II). Among the documents in the NTAP
the one signaled out for most attention was the Protevangelium Jacobi, today renamed the Birth of Mary, according to the title in the
Greek papyrus. Three major tendencies marked this phase: the
assessment of the NTAP in light of the superiority of the canon,
the preoccupation with dogma, and ironically the judgment that many
apocryphal writings are reliable and authentic. The first phase continued through the eighteenth century. The hallmark of this phase
is the publication of J. A. Fabricius' monumental Codex Apocryphus
Novi Testamenti (2 vols., Hamburg, 1703, 1719[2]).

The second phase basically encompasses the nineteenth century.
The first two tendencies in phase one continued unchanged; but
the rise of rationalism, the pervasive critique of traditions, and the
search for knowledge according to the post-Enlightenment and post-
Kantian mood caused a gradual collapse of the third tendency. The
apocryphal writings were almost all regarded as false; some were
even scandalously misinformed and misleading. There were highs
and lows during the nineteenth century, representing successively
the critique of the canonical gospels and dogma by F. C. Baur and
the Tübingen school, the effects of revolutions in 1848, the pervasive influence of Hegel and criticisms of him, and the expanding
horizons and additional manuscripts obtained by first France's and
then Britain's conquests in the Near East. Of the many hallmarks
that could be listed only three will be mentioned briefly: J.-P.
Migne's Dictionnaire des Apocryphes, ou collection de tous les livres
apocryphes (2 vols., Paris, 1856-58); K. Tischendorf's volumes--
especially his Acta Apostolorum Apocrypha (Leipzig, 1851), Apocalypses Apocryphae (Leipzig, 1866), and Evangelia Apocrypha (Leipzig,
1876)--and A. Resch's Aussercanonische Paralleltexte zu den Evangelien (4 vols.; TU 10:1, 2, 3, 4; Leipzig, 1893-96).

1

The third phase commences about the beginning of the twen-
tieth century. The first tendency, seeing the NTAP in light of the
superiority of the canon, continues; the second tendency, a preoccupation with dogma, wanes markedly. A. Harnack's Lehrbuch der
Dogmengeschichte (3 vols., Tübingen, 1909[4]) is a product of the
nineteenth century; each Vorwort is dated 1885, 1887,[2] 1893,[3] and
1909.[4] The third tendency, judging the apocryphal writings as authentic, has passed.

A new, fourth tendency emerges, reflected in the labors of
Resch, but now sparked to a new level of interest by the discovery
of the Oxyrhynchus papyri; it is a keen interest in lost gospels and
"forgotten" sayings of Jesus. The new tendency, foreshadowed in
Resch's books, breaks into the open in four publications by B. P.
Grenfell and A. S. Hunt, namely Sayings of Our Lord from an Early
Greek Papyrus (London, 1897), New Sayings of Jesus and Fragment
of a Lost Gospel from Oxyrhynchus (with L. W. Drexel, London,
1897, repr. 1904), Fragment of an Uncanonical Gospel from Oxyrhynchus (Oxford, 1908), and Papyrus d'Oxyrhynque 849 (6 vols., London, 1980). This interest in the agrapha or lost sayings of Jesus
was made popular by many scholars, especially J. Jeremias in his
Unbekannte Jesusworte (Zürich, 1948, 1951[2], 1963[3]; ET in 1957 and
1964[2]).

Three hallmarks of the third phase are W. Bauer's two master-
pieces Das Leben Jesu im Zeitalter der neutestamentlichen Apokryphen
(Tübingen, 1909, repr. 1967) and the paradigmatically important
Rechtgläubigkeit und Ketzerei im ältesten Christentum (BHT 10; Tü-
bingen, 1934, 1964 [2d. ed. with appendices by G. Strecker]; for
ET see 1.38), E. Hennecke's Handbuch zu den Neutestamentlichen
Apokryphen (Tübingen, 1904) and Neutestamentliche Apokryphen
(Tübingen, 1904, 1924[2]; expanded to 2 vols. in 1959[3] and 1964[3] with
W. Schneemelcher; for ET see 1.228), and finally M. R. James' The
Apocryphal New Testament (Oxford, 1924, repr. 1926-1969). Hen-
necke's collection of the NTAP, as the successive editions and the
English translation indicate, simply dominated the field; and the real
interest was in volume one subtitled, Gospels and Related Writings.

Beginning around 1965 there was a worldwide renewal of interest in the NTAP. The tendency to see these writings only in light
of the superiority of the canon begins to wane. This awakening
frees them for appreciation, as reflected in the Introduction to the
New Testament by H. Koester (as we shall see). It also helps re-
move the canonical straitjacket into which the NT writings had been
forced, allowing sensitive scholars to judge, as L. Keck has argued
(cf. no. 4.77), that the New Testament really is not a separate field
of study. We have entered into a new era, characterized by a wider
appreciation of early Christian writings: Why should scholars feel
apologetic about being interested in the apocryphal writings when
their colleagues are content to read the apostolic fathers? Why should
a historian, a biblical scholar, or a history-of-religions specialist

treat one document differently than another, the Didache in a different manner from the Odes of Solomon, the Gospel of John from the
Gospel of Thomas? The only possible answer is the confessional com-
mitment to a closed canon. And this answer reveals a deep-seated
bias that tends to vitiate the truthfulness of our own best work.

The first tendency has only begun to wane; and we can report
this advance by viewing the curricula at only our best universities
and the interests of distinguished colleagues throughout the world.
Their publications are listed--perhaps hidden--in the thousands of
publications cited in the following pages. The second tendency,
a preoccupation with dogma, has ceased. The third tendency, judging the apocryphal writings as authentic, has also concluded. The
"new" or fourth tendency--a search for lost sayings of Jesus--continues
and is a characteristic of some of the most recent erudite publications.
Koester (1.280-82, 5.151) has been foremost on this side of the At-
lantic, for appealing to the early and reliable nature of some of Jesus'
sayings in the NTAP. For many scholars the search for the ipsissima
verba Jesu (certainly not the bruta facta) will now include a more
appreciative awareness of the sayings of Jesus in the apocryphal
documents.

N. Walter, in a letter dated 9 August 1982, expressed the opinion that the Gospel of Peter derives not from the synoptic gospels
but from pre-synoptic traditions (see 71.100). After the completion
of the present bibliography, two articles on this subject were published.

In the first of these, C. W. Hedrick argues insightfully for
the possible authenticity of numerous sayings about the Kingdom
of Heaven in the gnostic Apocryphon of James. See his "Kingdom
Sayings and Parables of Jesus in the Apocryphon of James: Tradition and Redaction," NTS 29 (1983) 1-21.

In the second article, S. L. Davies exaggerates the importance
of the Gospel of Thomas for recovering Jesus' authentic words. He
treats too cavalierly the possible gnostic focus of many of the sayings; it is certainly unfair and unrepresentative to report that scholars have concluded the Gospel of Thomas is gnostic because it was
found among gnostic documents. As the present bibliography reveals,
over 400 publications have appeared on this document. Many of these
conclude correctly that the present shape of this gospel is gnostic.
Davies also misrepresents the facts when he claims that this gospel "may be our best source for Jesus's teachings. And then
again, it may not be" (p. 9). See S. L. Davies, "Thomas: The
Fourth Synoptic Gospel," BA 46 (1983) 6-9, 12-14. (Also see his
"A Cycle of Jesus's Parables," BA 46 [1983] 15-17; and The Gospel
of Thomas and Christian Wisdom [New York, 1983].)

Putting exaggerations and possible hyperboles aside, I think

one must now admit that some of the gospels recovered during the
last 100 years have been judged harshly, and only in light thrown
on them from the canon. The so-called apocryphal writings have
been shaped by later communities; however, nothing is clearer from
our recent research than the fact that the Gospels of Matthew, Mark,
Luke and John have been heavily redacted. None of them preserve
an unedited recording of Jesus' words. Redactions are characteristic
of our received traditions, whether they are inside or outside the
canon. Yet, I am convinced that the search for Jesus' authentic
words is not futile and that the best research in this area of scholarship will demonstrate that the search for ipsissima verba Jesu must
no longer be limited to the canonical documents.

   Turning from the fourth tendency to the hallmarks of the new
or fourth phase, we must single out the appearance of two impressive
collections of the NTAP. In chronological order they are M. Erbetta's
Gli Apocrifi del Nuovo Testamento (3 vols.--actually 4, vol. 1 is
in two books--Turin, 1966-75) and L. Moraldi, Apocrifi del Nuovo
Testamento (2 vols., Classici delle Religioni, sezione 5; Turin, 1971).
Each of these is in the great tradition of Fabricius, Migne, James
and Hennecke-Schneemelcher-Wilson; moreover, they are informed
and inclusive of documents many scholars have not yet read.

The Series Apocryphorum of the
Corpus Christianorum

   In the late fall of 1983, when this work was already in final
draft, I accepted an invitation from the Faculté de Théologie of the
Université de Lausanne to speak about my work on the NTAP to the
members of the team in Switzerland who are contributing to the Series Apocryphorum of the Corpus Christianorum. It soon became
clear that they were defining the corpus of the so-called NTAP in
a way appreciably different from the way I have done in the present
work. I have followed the age-old method used by Fabricius, Migne,
James, and Hennecke-Schneemelcher-Wilson. This approach seeks
to define the corpus of the NTAP in terms of the canonical New Testament, and also, of course, in terms of the other collections (like
the Apocrypha and Pseudepigrapha of the Old Testament) which receive their definition or description primarily in relation with and
reflections on the canonical Old Testament. Preparing the works
for the Series Apocryphorum is a team, founded in 8 October 1981,
which is called L'Association pour l'Étude de la Littérature Apocryphe
Chrétienne. This team intentionally avoids the term "New Testament"
and calls the collection the "Christian Apocryphal Literature." Note
the following official description of the project:

> This [the Series Apocryphorum] includes essentially what
> are usually called the New Testament apocrypha (the gos-
> pels, acts, epistles, apocalypses). But to relate these works
> only to the New Testament is to underestimate the variety of

this literature. Its scope is wider: it embraces pseudepi-
graphs or anonymous texts of Christian origin where the
main subject is characters named in the Bible or present at
events described in biblical texts. Texts such as the Ascension of Isaiah or the Apocalypse of Zachariah belong to
this literature insofar as they have become gradually chris-
tianized, although they concern characters of the Old Testament and build on Jewish traditions.

The need to break with the classical definition of a NTAP and to
collect all the Christian apocryphal literature into one series is de-
fended by E. Junod in "Apocryphes du NT ou Apocryphes Chrétiens
Anciens?" (Études théologiques et religieuses 3 [1983]:409-21). Now
for the first time in one series we will have texts, translations, and
reliable introductions to the "littérature apocryphe chrétienne." The
President of L'Association, F. Bovon, in "Vers une nouvelle édition
de la littérature apocryphe chrétienne: La Series apocryphorum du
Corpus christianorum" (Aug 23 [1983] 373-78) describes the format
for the series as follows:

> Chaque livre aura l'allure et le format d'un volume du Cor-
> pus Christianorum, mais la structure d'un ouvrage des
> Sources Chrétiennes, car nous tenon--étant donné la variété
> et l'importance des versions anciennes--à accompagner le
> texte d'une traduction en langue moderne dite internationale.
> Vu la complexité des problèmes d'introduction et d'interpré-
> tation, une large place sera faite aussi aux commentaires et
> à l'annotation [p. 373].

Significant works have already appeared. Besides F. Bovon (no.
3.9) see the following publications:

F. Bovon, "Pratiques missionnaires et communication de L'Évangile dans le christianisme primitif," RTP 114 (1982) 369-81.

E. Junod and J.-D. Kaestli, L'Histoire des actes apocryphes
des apôtres du IIIe au IXe siècle: Le cas des Actes de Jean
(Cahiers of the RTP 7; Geneva, Lausanne, 1982).

J.-D. Kaestli, "Le rôle des textes bibliques dans la genèse et
le développement des légendes apocryphes," Aug 23 (1983)
319-36.

E. Junod and J.-D. Kaestli, Acta Iohannis (Corpus Christianorum, Series Apocryphorum 1-2), 2 vols. Turnhout, 1983.

The classical and the new approaches to the "NTAP" are not
contradictory but complementary. Both of us exclude the Nag Hammadi Codices, because they are superbly handled in separate collections and series. Both of us see the need to move beyond the fourth
century in search of apocryphal documents. The classical approach

has the advantage of collecting into one corpus literature similar to
and derivative from the New Testament; the new approach has the
advantage of bringing together in a series all Christian apocryphal
literature. The former is more conducive for specialists in the New
Testament and Christian Origins; the latter is more helpful for Patri-
istic scholars and historians of the early Church.

The members of the team in attendance voiced the need for the
present work, and stated that it would be a major reference work.
I was shown some pages of M. Geerard's Clavis apocryphorum, and
a xerox copy of the present work was mailed to him for consultation
in the preparation of the Clavis. Letters from Geerard disclose that
he is finding the following bibliography invaluable; he plans to have
his Clavis at the publisher, Brepols, Turnhout near the end of 1984.

DESCRIPTION

The NTAP is a modern collection of Christian extra-canonical
writings, dating from the early centuries, perhaps from around 125
to 425, or from the decades in which the latest writings in the New
Testament were composed until one century after Christianity became
the state religion of the Roman Empire and the New Testament was
widely considered closed. Documents later than the fifth century
are included only because of the early traditions they may preserve
or because they are organically related to the early compositions
in the NTAP. The major characteristic of the documents in the NTAP
is that they purport to be apostolic and scriptually equal to the 27
New Testament documents. In fact they are almost all imitations
of the gospels, acts, letters, or the apocalypse in the New Testament; hence, the forms of the documents in the NTAP are similar
to those in the New Testament. To call these documents "apocryphal" does not mean to discard them or label them as unorthodox,
inauthentic, or derivatively secondary to the New Testament scriptures. It is unwise to push this description or apply it strictly.[1]

EXCLUDED DOCUMENTS

In the bibliography I have tried to cite the publications on
the New Testament Apocrypha and Pseudepigrapha. Excluded are
six types of documents.

(1) Apostolic Fathers

An early group of documents are categorized as "the Apostolic
Fathers." A convenient and reliable edition of the Greek and English
was published by K. Lake (The Apostolic Fathers with an English
Translation; 2 vols. LCL. Cambridge, Mass., London, 1912; repr.
from 1914 through 1965). It contains the following:

(Vol. 1)	(Vol. 2)
1 Clement	Shepherd of Hermas
2 Clement	Martyrdom of Polycarp
Ignatius	Epistle to Diognetus
Polycarp	
Didache (Teaching of the Apostles)	
Epistle of Barnabas	

Some collections of the NTAP include one or more of these documents.
Of this group, three writings--the Didache, the Epistle of Barnabas,
and the Shepherd of Hermas--can make an impressive claim to belong
within the NTAP. The last two are included in Codex Sinaiticus,
one of the oldest Greek manuscripts of the Bible.[2]

(2) The Nag Hammadi Codices

Also excluded are the 52 tractates found in the Nag Hammadi
Codices. Many of these have titles similar to, even at times identical with, documents in the NTAP; but these documents are correctly
gathered together in one group, both because they were found together in an ancient collection of documents and because almost all
of them are gnostic, and hence distinguishable from most of the writings in the NTAP.[3] To be distinguished from similarly titled documents in the NTAP are the following Nag Hammadi tractates:

Apocryphon of James	Apocalypse of Paul
Gospel of Truth	First Apocalypse of James
Apocryphon of John	Second Apocalypse of James
Acts of Peter	Acts of Peter and the Twelve Apostles
Gospel of Philip	Apocalypse of Peter
Book of Thomas the Contender	Letter of Peter to Philip
Gospel of the Egyptians	Gospel of Mary

To avoid confusing these documents with similarly titled ones in the
NTAP, I have referred to them with prefixed qualifying parentheses;
hence, the (Nag Hammadi) Apocalypse of Paul is clearly distinguishable from the Apocalypse of Paul, a document in the NTAP.

(3) The Old Testament Pseudepigrapha

Excluded from the NTAP are writings now included in the OTP.
Among the latter collection are some writings that are clearly Christian in the final and present form.[4] Worthy of special note are the
following:

Apocalypse of Sedrach	Testaments of the Twelve Patri-
	archs

Greek Apocalypse of Ezra	Testament of Isaac
Vision of Ezra	Testament of Jacob
Questions of Ezra	Testament of Adam
Revelation of Ezra	Martyrdom and Ascension of Isaiah
Apocalypse of Elijah	History of the Rechabites
Apocalypse of Daniel	Odes of Solomon

It is not always easy to explain why these documents belong in the
OTP and not in the NTAP. Four good reasons may be offered: 1)
They are originally Jewish writings or are heavily influenced by Early
Judaism. 2) They are attributed to Old Testament men or groups.
3) They are often related in form to writings in the Old Testament
or OTP, or are derived from one of them, and thus belong to cycles
of literature in the OTP. 4) The custom among scholars has been
to place them in the OTP; and here I must emphasize that these literary categories are really modern conventions for organizing texts.

(4) Early Syriac Writings

        Some early Syriac documents, besides those included in the
NTAP--for example, the Acts of Thomas--should not be included
in the NTAP. The main reason for this decision is that they fail
to contain the major characteristic of a document in the NTAP; that
is, they do not claim to be apostolic and spiritually equal to the New
Testament writings. Excluded are the following:

    Extracts from Various Books Concerning Abgar the King and
        Addaeus the Apostle[5]
    The Teaching of Addaeus the Apostle
    The Teaching of the Apostles

The titles of these works indicate that they should be included in
the NTAP; but a mere cusory reading of them should convince the
attentive reader that they are paradigmatically dissimilar to the New
Testament writings. They are etiological legends by the Christians
at Edessa, reflecting their desire to have roots going back to Addaeus,
or Thaddaeus, "one of the seventy-two apostles" (Extracts 6), who
--they say--was sent by the resurrected Jesus through the apostle
Thomas to convert the citizens of Edessa. These writings are related
to but categorically different from the Letters of Christ and Abgarus
(category 19 in the Bibliography).

(5) Earliest Versions of the New Testament

        A. D. Nock, in his assessment of Hennecke's third edition,
lamented that "Tatian" should have received "more attention."[6] Certainly there are ancient and apocryphal traditions preserved in the
earliest versions of the New Testament, especially in the Old Syriac
Gospels (in particular the Syrus Sinaiticus) and the Old Latin, as

I have discussed elsewhere (1.100); however, to add Tatian's so-
called Diatessaron or any of the versions to the NTAP would confuse
the already loose consistency of this corpus of literature. The har-
mony was produced by Tatian; it is neither an apocryphon nor a
pseudepigraphon.

These brief remarks accentuate the fact that the study of the
NTAP must go hand in glove with the examination of other non-
canonical, but not apocryphal, writings. At least six categories
other than the NTAP must be consulted: the canon itself, the apostolic fathers (Patristics), the early Syriac Literature, the Nag Hammadi codices (and the other gnostic works such as the Pistis Sophia),
the early versions of the New Testament, and alia (e.g., the Secret
Gospel of Mark; see the publications by Morton Smith).

(6) Fakes

Emphatically to be excluded from the NTAP are the modern forgeries. Almost all of these fakes were completely unknown to me, as
they are to most scholars, and were brought to my attention--as I
now learn was also the case for E. J. Goodspeed[7]--by students and
curious individuals. Unworthy of scholarly attention, they are here
merely noted in passing. Unfortunately, more fabricators should
have come forward, as did Signor Gino Gardella[8], and admitted that
the fiction had been concocted to advertise some event or publication.
Many of these forgeries were discussed by Goodspeed in his Strange
New Gospels and are now similarly criticized by P. Beskow in Strange
Tales About Jesus.[9]

Foremost among these spurious works is The Archko Volume,
or the Archeological Writings of the Sanhedrin and Talmuds of the
Jews; These are the Official Documents Made in These Courts in
the Days of Jesus Christ, "Translated by Drs. McIntosh and Twy-
man" (Philadelphia, 1913). Mr. W. D. Mahan, who claims to have
obtained this "volume" from the Vatican, was, to be polite, a clever
novelist; to be frank, he was "found guilty of falsehood and of pla-
giarism, and suspended from the ministry for one year" (Goodspeed,
Strange New Gospels, p. 56). Professor Goodspeed's judgment is
fair: "The whole work is a weak, crude fancy, a jumble of high-
sounding but meaningless words, and hardly worth serious criticism.
It is difficult to see how it could have deceived anyone" (p. 48).
The work is in many prestigious libraries--it is in the Duke Divinity
School Library--and can easily confuse the curious. In the twenties
M. R. James, in The Apocryphal New Testament (Oxford, 1924; p.
90), had to label it "a ridiculous and disgusting American book...."
And in the seventies, R. L. Anderson, a professor at Brigham Young
University, lamented that "some Bible believers accept the Archko
documents so that the book is often stocked in religious bookstores
and periodically quoted to church audiences as containing 'factual
accounts' of those who came in contact with the Lord." Anderson,

of course, labeled it "a modern forgery," noting that "perversions
of fact contaminate virtually every page of the book, so that anyone
with basic knowledge of ancient history can multiply Goodspeed's
random samples of blunders it contains."[10]

Enough has been said about modern hoaxes;[11] attention should
not be drawn to them. They belong in no way to the ancient documents in the NTAP.

(7) Possible Candidates

Numerous documents have come before me recently as either
new discoveries or not sufficiently examined writings. Most of these
date too late to be included in the NTAP. Those that might be candidates for inclusion are the following:

The Gospel of Judas [lost]. (Though early, perhaps from
the second century, it is excluded because it is an example
of gnostic perversion of the truth; Judas, alone of the
apostles, acted rightly; he was inspired).[12]

Jesus Pseudepigraph. (See J.-P. Migne, "Jésus-Christ. [Éc-
rits attribués ou relatifs à Jésus-Christ.]," Dictionnaire 2.
Cols. 365-400.)

Passion of Ananias. (See A. de Santos Otero, Altslavischen
Apok. Vol. 1, pp. 138f.)

Quaestiones Apostolorum. (See A. de Santos Otero, Altslavischen Apok. Vol. 1, p. 210.)

Didascalia Domini. (See A. de Santos Otero, Altslavischen
Apok. Vol. 2, pp. 233-36.)

De Arbore Crucis. (See A. de Santos Otero, Altslavischen
Apok. Vol. 2, pp. 129-47.[13])

The Rebellion of the Angels.[14]

Gospel of Barnabas.[15]

Gospel of the Simonians. (Lost; but mentioned in the Arabic
preface to the Council of Nicea.)[16]

Gospel of Thaddeus. (Lost; but mentioned in the Decretum
Gelasianum.[17])

The Eternal Gospel.[18]

The Life of St. Anna.[19]

The Gospel of Apelles.[20] (This document, attributed to the
disciple of Marcion, is early, perhaps dating from the second century. Epiphanius [Haer. 44] quoted an agraphon
from it. The reasons to exclude it from the NTAP are that
it is gnostic and not attributed to a figure in the New Testament.)

The Teaching of Peter.[21] (Little is known of this document.
It is not to be confused with the Preaching of Peter. I have
listed publications on it under the Peter cycle. Perhaps it
deserves to be included in the NTAP.)

The Dialogue Between Christ and the Devil.[22] (This document
is difficult to exclude from the NTAP. It is similar to the
Christian expansion of the History of the Rechabites. It
is early enough [III-V cent.]; however, it appears not to
be an apocryphon [a writing similar in literary form to the
NT writings, e.g., gospels, acts, letters, apocalypses], but
a homily on humanity's fate, Christ's conquest of the devil,
and the end of the world based on the NT accounts of the
temptation and the transfiguration.)

The Apocalypse of Philip.[23] (This lost work, used perhaps
by the author of the Irish work titled The Evernew Tongue,[24]
was probably not an apocalypse.)

These observations may help set the stage for a long overdue
scholarly discussion of the contents of the NTAP.[25] The brief, perhaps too opinionated comments should help clarify that it is difficult
to distinguish an apocryphon from a legend or a homily (and this
fact reveals that our study of the history and thought of early Christianity must be more carefully atuned to the NTAP). The list of
documents placed in the NTAP as a result of my research is much
longer than in any published collection; yet, without a doubt, other
documents also should be considered for possible inclusion in the
NTAP. It is impossible to develop and explain a set of criteria that
will define definitively what documents should be included in the
NTAP. The history of Christianity, and its canonical concerns,
cover far too many centuries and territories to enable us to arrive
at anything more than a reliable approximation of the contents of
this corpus.

INTRODUCTIONS

Introductions to the NTAP are listed among the more than 550
entries under the first category in the following bibliography (e.g.,
General: 1. Studies, Text Editions, Translations). I have profited
from far too many introductions to list them all now. Attention will
be drawn to those that are most reliable and recent. The classical
works are, of course, the volumes by Fabricius, Migne, James, and

Hennecke-Schneemelcher-Wilson. É. Amann (1.6) published a thorough,
erudite and reliable introduction; since it was published in 1928,
it is now somewhat dated. H. T. Andrews (1.10) and P. Bigaré
(1.52) have published convenient up-to-date introductions.   The
best major introductions, with translations, are the multi-volumed
works by Erbetta (1.148) and Moraldi (1.353). Of singular significance is a recent publication by a master of the apocryphal writings.
This magnificent introduction appeared when the work on the bibliography was completed and the present book was about to go to the
publisher. I am referring to H. Koester's Introduction to the New
Testament. Volume One: History, Culture, and Religion of the Hellenistic Age. Volume Two: History and Literature of Early Christianity (Hermeneia; Berlin, New York, Philadelphia, 1982; the German
original appeared in 1980). This introduction centers upon the New
Testament, but--as the title to volume two clarifies--many of the
documents in the NTAP receive significant discussion. Koester clearly
appreciates the apocryphal writings and does not see them only in
light of the New Testament. How refreshing it is to read his following words:

> It seems quite unlikely that any of the apocryphal texts
> was written during the apostolic period, but some of these
> writings may have been composed as early as the end of
> I CE and a very large number are products of II CE.   The
> NT Apocrypha are therefore sources for the history of early
> Christianity which are just as important as the NT writings.
> They contain many traditions which can be traced back to
> the time of the very origins of Christianity. They provide
> us with a spectrum that is much more colorful than that of
> the canonical writings and permit insights into the manifold
> diversity of early Christian piety and theology, in short, a
> perspective which the polemical orientation of the canon of
> the NT often obstructs or seeks to limit [vol. 2, p. 13].

Perhaps the first tendency of research on the NTAP--the perception
and judgment of the NTAP in light of the superiority of the canon
--has finally begun not only to wane but to disappear. If so, it
will be typical of only the best scholars for some time.

PURPOSE

In this publication we have attempted to accomplish eight goals:

- to clarify the nomenclature in this field of research;

- to order and describe the contents of the NTAP;

- to publish a full and organized bibliography on this corpus;

- to point to the vast number of publications and the lack of
  consensus in this area of study;

- to intimate the significance of the NTAP;

- to draw attention to the continuum of apocalypticism and apocalypses;

- to encourage and facilitate research on the NTAP;

- to lay the basis for the preparation of an edition of the NTAP similar to Doubleday's The Old Testament Pseudepigrapha.

Preparing and completing this publication has been more demanding and time-consuming than accomplishing the analogous work for The Pseudepigrapha and Modern Research with a Supplement. The major reason for this discrepancy is because of the lack of nomenclatural clarity and the complicated transmission histories of many of the NTAP.

NOTES

1. W. Schneemelcher (in 1.228) also warned that a "strict application" of his definition of the New Testament Apocrypha would reveal that "many of the writings assembled there [in "the first and second editions of the present" work] could not be considered New Testament apocrypha" (vol. 1, p. 27). His definition is similar to the description now offered; see his scholarly opinion that a definition "may perhaps" be offered as follows:
> The New Testament Apocrypha are writings which have not been received into the canon, but which by title and other statements lay claim to be in the same class with the writings of the canon, and which from the point of view of Form Criticism further develop and mould the kinds of style created and received in the NT, whilst foreign elements certainly intrude. (vol. 1, p. 27)
E. Amann (in 1.6. Cols. 460-65) discusses the problems in defining the NTAP. He affirms what I see is the major characteristic of the documents in the NTAP; he states, "Pour nous catholiques, est apocryphe, par définition, tout livre qui affiche, plus ou moins ouvertement, la prétention d'être une écriture sacrée, de s'équiparer aux livres reconnus par l'Eglise comme inspirés, et qui, pourtant, n'a été officiellement reçu dans le canon des Livres saints" (col. 461). Recently, R. E. Brown (in 1.70), observing that "some ancient subapostolic works," like the Didache, 1-2 Clement, Hermas, and the Epistle of Barnabas, "treated as Scripture by early Church writers" are "patristic writings"; hence, the NTAP is "used in a narrower sense to refer to noncanonical books more closely related in form or in content to NT writings" (p. 544).
2. Hermas is missing some leaves in Codex Sinaiticus. See K. Lake and H. Lake (eds.), Codex sinaiticus petropolitanus: The New Testament, the Epistle of Barnabas and the Shepherd of Hermas Preserved in the Imperial Library of St. Petersburg, Now Reproduced in Facsimile from Photographs (Oxford, 1911). Codex Sinaiticus dates

from the fourth century; some missing leaves have been recovered
recently in St. Catherine's Monastery. The major portion of the
codex is now preserved in the British Museum. Clement of Alexandria thought some quotations in the Epistle of Barnabas derived from
the apostle Barnabas himself. Origen, as the compiler of Codex Sinaiticus, thought the epistle was canonical. Jerome considered it one
of the books in the NTAP. Most scholars abide by the consensus
and leave it among the Apostolic Fathers. Scholars' opinions are
less certain about the proper place for the Shepherd of Hermas.
J. Quasten, for example, in his Patrology (Westminster, Maryland,
1962) claimed the following: "Although numbered among the Apostolic Fathers, the Shepherd of Hermas belongs in reality to the apocryphal apocalypses" (vol. 1, p. 92). Hermas is included in my list
in Part III. P. Vielhauer (in 1.531) called Hermas a "Pseudoapoka-
lypse" (p. 522). D. Hellholm (in 2.32) seeks to describe more ac-
curately the genre of an apocalypse by examining the interrelation-
ships between form, content and Sitz im Leben of Hermas.

    3. My comments are not intended to be categorical; many doc-
uments in the NTAP were considered "gnostic" by the early Church
Fathers. The exact relationship between the documents in the NTAP
and gnostic works is complex and deserves a separate full examination. A convenient English edition of the Nag Hammadi codices is
published under the editorship of J. M. Robinson, The Nag Hammadi
Library in English (New York, London, 1977). Also see the discussion of these apocalypses in Part III. R. H. Charles and W. O.
E. Oesterley listed items in the NTAP writings that they admitted
are "mainly gnostic"; this procedure would now add confusion. See
their "Apocryphal Literature," Encyclopaedia Britannica (1956), vol.
2, pp. 105-08.

    4. I include only documents heavily redacted by Christians,
not those with interpolations. For a distinction between redaction
and interpolation, see J. H. Charlesworth, "Reflections on the SNTS
Pseudepigrapha Seminar at Duke on the Testaments of the Twelve
Patriarchs," NTS 23 (1977) 296-304.

    5. English translations of these documents are found in ANF
8, but the introductions and notes are not reliable or informed; see
the translations by B. P. Pratten in ANF 8, pp. 655-75. I do include
under LetCAb and AcThaddeus certain works on Doctrine of Addai.

    6. A. D. Nock, "The Aprocryphal Gospels," JTS N.S. 11
(1960) 63-70.

    7. E. J. Goodspeed, Strange New Gospels (Chicago, 1931),
pp. vii-viii.

    8. See Goodspeed, Strange New Gospels, pp. 96f. Also see
Goodspeed's Modern Apocrypha (Boston, 1956) and his Famous Biblical Hoaxes (Grand Rapids, Mich., 1956).

    9. P. Beskow has made the modern forgeries the subject of
his Strange Tales About Jesus: A Survey of Unfamiliar Gospels
(Philadelphia, 1983).

    10. R. L. Anderson, "The Fraudulent Archko Volume," Brig-
ham Young University Studies 15 (1974) 43-64.

    11. Another hoax, probably plagiarized from PsMt, InfGosTh,

and Arabic InfGos, is the following: C. Mendès, L'Évangile de la jeunesse de Notre-Seigneur Jésus-Christ d'après S. Pierre (Paris, 1894; with Lat. text and trans.); H. C. Greene, The Gospel of the Childhood of Our Lord Jesus Christ (London, 1904).

12. See S. Baring-Gould, "The Gospel of Judas," The Lost and Hostile Gospels (London, 1874) pp. 299-305; A. de Santos Otero, "Judas," Altslavischen Apok. Vol. 2, pp. 119-28; F. A. Brunklaus, Het Laatste Testament, Het Evangelie van Judas, Het Hooglied van Maria Magdelena, de Openbarung van de Apostel Thomas (Maastricht, 1969); E. Amann, "Évangile de Judas," DBSup. 1. Col. 479; Fabricius, "Evangelium Judae Ischariothae," Cod. Apoc. NT. 1, pp. 352f; F. Repp, "Untersuchungen zu den Apokryphen der Österr. Nationalbibliothek: Die russische kirchenslavische Judas-Vita des Cod. slav. 13," Wiener Slavist. Jahrbuch 7 (1957) 5-34.

13. Other works, far too late for the NTAP, and perhaps Slavic compositions, are included in A. de Santos Otero's Altslavischen Apok.

14. See A. van Lantschoot, "Un texte palimpsest de Vat copte 65," Muséon 60 (1947) 261-68.

15. Two very different works receive the name the "Gospel of Barnabas." One is very early and was condemned by the Gelasian Decree (see the Bibliography). This pseudepigraphon is lost. Another "Gospel of Barnabas" appeared in Italian, but it dates from perhaps as late as the fifteenth century. For publications on this document, which is too late for inclusion in the NTAP (unless it proves to contain remnants of earlier works), see the following: S. Abdul-Ahad and W.H.T. Gairdner, The Gospel of Barnabas: An Essay and Inquiry (Hydarabad, India, 1975); W.E.A. Axon, "On the Mohammedan Gospel of Barnabas," JTS 3 (1902) 441-51; O. Bardenhewer, "Der sog. Barnabasbrief," GAL. 1, pp. 103-16; H. Bergema, "Het 'Evangile naar Barnabas,'" Christusprediking in de wereld, studien J. H. Bavinck (Kampen, 1965); L. Cirillo, L'Évangile de Barnabé, 3 vols. (Paris, 1975); idem, Évangile de Barnabé: Recherches sur la composition et l'origine (Paris, 1977); idem, "Le Pseudo-Clementine e il Vangelo di Barnaba della Biblioteca nazionale di Vienna," Asprenas 18 (1971) 333-69; idem, "Un nuovo vangelo apocrifo: Il Vangelo di Barnaba," Rivista di Storia e Letteratura Religiosa 11 (1975) 391-412; idem, "Les sources de l'Évangile de Barnabé," RHR 189 (1976): 130-35; idem, "Les 'Vrais Pharisiens' dans l'Év. apocryphe de Barnabé," RHR 191 (1977) 121-28; idem and M. Frémaux, Évangile de Barnabé (Paris, 1977); H. Corbin, "Theologoumena iranica," Studia Iranica 5 (1976) 225-35; F.P. Cotterell, "The Gospel of Barnabas," Vox Evangelica 10 (1977) 43-47; M. de Epalza, "Sobre un posible autor español del 'Evangelio de Barnabé,'" Al-Andalus 28 (1963): 479-91; M. Erbetta, "Vangelo di Barnaba," Apoc. del NT, 1.2, pp. 225f.; J.E. Fletcher, "The Spanish Gospel of Barnabas," NovT 18 (1976) 314-20; G. Jeffery, The Gospel According to Barnabas (London, 1975); J. Jomier, "Une énigme persistante: L'Évangile dit de Barnabé," Mélanges de l'Institut Dominicain d'Étude Orientales 14 (1980): 271-300; idem, "L'Évangile selon Barnabé," Mélanges de l'Institut Dominicain d'Étude Orientales 6 (1959-61) 137-226; M.F. Kermāni,

Enjil-e Barnābā (Teheran, 1968); J.M. Magnin, "En marge de l'ébion-
isme: L'Évangile de Barnabé," Proche-orient chrétien 29 (1979) 44-
64; M. Philonenko, "Une tradition essénienne dans l'Évangile de Barnabas," Mélanges d'histoire des religions offerts à Henri-Charles Puech,
eds. P. Lévy and E. Wolff (Paris, 1974), pp. 191-95; L. Ragg, The
Gospel of Barnabas (Oxford, 1907); idem, "The Mohammedan 'Gospel
of Barnabas,'" JTS 6 (1905) 424-33; A. de Santos Otero, "Evangelio
de Bernabé (el Italiano)," Evangelios Apócrifos, pp. 24f.; J. Slomp,
"The Pseudo-Gospel of Barnabas," Bulletin du Secretariatus pro non
Christianis 11 (1976) 69-77; idem, "The Pseudo-Gospel of Barnabas:
Muslim and Christian Evaluations," Al-Mushir 18 (1976)*; F. Stegmüller, Repertorium Biblicum, vol. 1, p. 108, vol. 8, pp. 80f.; R.
Stichel, "Bemerkungen zum Barnabas-Evangelium," Byzantino-Slavica
43 (1982) 189-201; H. Suasso, "Some Remarks on the 'Gospel of Barnabas,'" Orientasi 3 (1971) 78-86; R. McL. Wilson, "Barnabas, Gospel of," ZPEB, vol. 1, p. 479.
     16. See Migne, Dictionnaire. 2. Cols. 953f.
     17. See Migne, Dictionnaire. 2. Cols. 959f.
     18. See Fabricius, "Evangelium Aeturnum," Cod. Apoc. NT.
1, pp. 337f.
     19. This document on the mother of "the Virgin" is actually
a legend and not an apocryphon, but those two categories considerably overlap. It seems too late for inclusion in the NTAP. See
Migne, Dictionnaire 2. Cols. 105f.; also see Migne, Dictionnaire
des légendes du Christianisme (Paris, 1855), col. 1220; and P.V.
Charland, Les trois légendes de madame sainte Anne (Montreal, 1898).
     20. See Migne, Dictionnaire. 2. Col. 112.
     21. See B. P. Pratten, "The Teaching of Simon Cephas in
the City of Rome," ANF. 8, pp. 673-75; and W. Cureton (ed.),
"Acts of Simon-Kepha in the City of Rome," Ancient Syriac Documents Relative to the Earliest Establishment of Christianity in Edessa
and the Neighboring Countries (London, 1864), pp. 35-41.
     22. See especially the introduction, Greek texts and English
translation by R. P. Casey and R. W. Thompson, titled "A Dialogue
Between Christ and the Devil," JTS N.S. 6 (1955) 49-65. Also
see, in chronological order, the following erudite publications: A.
N. Pypin, False and Dismissed Books (Moscow[?], 1862), pp. 86-
88 [Russian]; N. S. Tikhonravov, Monuments of Dismissed Russian
Literature (Moscow, 1863), pp. 282-88 [Russian]; A. Vassiliev, Anecdota graeco-byzantina (Moscow, 1893), pp. 4-10; S. Novaković, "Apo-
krif o prepiranju Isusa Hrista sa djavolom," Starine 16 (1884) 86-
89; G. Polívka, "Opisi i izvodi...," Starine 21 (1889) 200-03*; N.
Bonwetsch, in Harnack, Gesch. altchrist. Lit. (1893), p. 910; M. R.
James in AA 2, p. 154; I. Franko, Apocrypha and Legends (L'vov,
1898), vol. 2, pp. 196-203 [Russian]; K. F. Radčenko, Zametki o
pergamennom (Moscow [?], 1903), pp. 175-211; K. F. Radčenko,
"Etjudy po bogomil'stvu," Izbornik Kievskij v čest' T. D. Florinskogo
(Kiev, 1904), pp. 28-38; R. Strohal, Stare hrvatske apokrifne (Bjelovar, 1917), pp. 54-56; J. Ivanov, Bogomilski knigi i legendi (Sofia,
1925), pp. 248-57; É. Turdeanu, "Apocryphes bogomiles et apocryphes
pseudobogomiles," RHR 138 (1950) 194-99; E. Georgiev, Literatura

na izostreni borbi v srednovekovna Bŭlgariya (Sofia, 1966), pp. 194-97; A. de Santos Otero, "Diaboli cum Jesu Contentio," Altslavischen Apok. 2, pp. 156-60.

23. This so-called "apocalypse" is lost; it probably was not an apocalypse. See the comments in part III, "Documents Often Considered to Be 'Apocalypses,'" regarding this document.

24. For this Irish apocryphon see the impressive and learned work by M. McNamara titled The Apocrypha in the Irish Church (Dublin Institute for Advanced Studies; Dublin, 1975), pp. 115-18, 132. McNamara, in his discussion of Tenga Bithnua (The Evernew Tongue), refers to the possibility that "the Apocalypse of Philip" was used by the redactor of the Irish work, but wisely states that it "is difficult to determine what sources the author used" (p. 115). Also see M. Erbetta, "Apocrifi Irlandesi (medioevo)," Apoc. del NT. 3, p. 483.

25. A full list of excluded works would move our whole discussion of the NTAP off center and into medieval and even later literature. Many writings with titles similar to those of documents in the NTAP are simply medieval compositions. For example, the Epistle Concerning the Life and Passion of Our Lord Jesus Christ is far too late for the NTAP. See M. Hedlund, Epistola de Vita et Passione Domini Nostri: Der Lateinische Text mit Einleitung und Kommentar (Kerkhistorische Bijdragen 5; Leiden, 1975).

PART II: THE APOCALYPSE OF JOHN--
ITS THEOLOGY AND IMPACT ON
SUBSEQUENT APOCALYPSES

INTRODUCTION

The Apocalypse of John is a frightening enigma for many today.
In light of wild claims by non-specialists to explain it and in antici-
pation of the apocalyptic enthusiasm that will surely accompany the
ending of the second millennium, it seems prudent first to attempt
an assessment of scholarly research on the Apocalypse, viewing its
relationship to the numerous apocalypses contained in The Old Testament Pseudepigrapha,[1] and second to seek a perception of its ef-
fect upon the apocryphal apocalyses subsequent to it.

THE APOCALYPSE AND ITS THEOLOGY

In a recent publication concerning contemporary research on
the Gospel of John, D. Moody Smith voiced the opinion that some
readers may have "the impression that scholars, like so many pro-
verbial horsemen, are riding off in different directions through a
trackless morass."[2] Certainly, the same impression would be given
were I to attempt to summarize all scholarly work now available on
the Apocalypse. There are, however, some significant points of
agreement among modern scholars if we focus upon the most carefully
controlled research, overlooking speculative reconstructions, such
as the claim by J.M. Ford that the Apocalypse derives from the circle
of John the Baptist,[3] or the attempts to unravel the complexities
in the Apocalypse by methods that are not yet refined, as--for example
--the use of structuralism in the Apocalypse.[4] I am convinced that
some of the fog has begun to lift from some parts of the Apocalypse.

(1) Historical Methodology

Critical scholars today are in solid agreement that the Apocalypse must be seen historically as the product of one particular period
in history. The major error committed by non-scholars is to ignore
the historical forces that produced the writing, to focus solely upon
present crises, and to resolve them by an eisegesis of the Apocalypse.
Such discussions frequently take the form of a prophetic proclamation

that announces the meaning of the Apocalypse both for the present
and the near future. Self-proclaimed prophets call into question
their own credibility and method, because the "prophecies" change
with the times, which disprove the prediction. Critical scholars have
come to agree that the Apocalypse was written sometime after the
destruction of Jerusalem in 70 C.E. and before the defeat of Bar
Kokhba in 135 C.E. The recent works by G. Mussies[5] and N. Turner[6] have demonstrated that the author of the Apocalypse wrote in
Greek but often thought in Hebrew or Aramaic. Scholars have de-
bated whether the Apocalypse is essentially a Jewish writing that
has been edited by a Christian or a Christian composition. This
debate has tended to conclude with the recognition that the author
was a Christian who was fundamentally and profoundly influenced
by Jewish apocalypticism, especially its cosmology, concept of two
worlds, eschatology, and metaphorical images.[7] It is clear that both
the author and his readers lived in western Asia Minor. Biblical
scholars, therefore, agree that an attempt to understand the Apocalypse must derive from a historical examination of the period from
70 to 135 C.E., and focus upon the early Christian communities in
Asia Minor.

(2) Other Apocalypses

There is a growing recognition among specialists that the Apocalypse must be seen in relation to the numerous apocalypses that
preceded it or were contemporaneous with it. Today we are confronted
with a rich abundance of apocalypses and apocalyptic literature from
1 Enoch in the Old Testament Pseudepigrapha and Daniel in the Old
Testament to 4 Ezra or 2 Baruch, that is, roughly speaking, from
the third century B.C.E. until the last decades of the first century
C.E.

The history of that period is important for an understanding
of the development and essence of Jewish apocalypticism. P.D. Hanson[8] correctly argues that Jewish apocalyptic thought originated out
of late prophetic movements, especially those reflected in Isaiah 56–
66 and Zechariah 9-14. It is important for an understanding of
Jewish apocalypticism, however, to observe that almost all of the
Jewish apocalypses were written during the period from 230 B.C.E.
to 135 C.E.[9]

At least three major factors help us understand the flowering
of Jewish apocalypticism. First, Jewish apocalypticism was enriched
by the impregnation of Judaism by languages and ideas foreign to
Palestinian Jews, especially from Greek, Egyptian, and Iranian perspectives. Second, Jewish apocalypticism may have evolved out of
prophetic thought, but its development was significantly influenced
by the wisdom tradition.[10] Third, Jewish apocalypticism was shaped
on the anvil of successive conquests and persecutions of Palestinian
Jews. In 198 B.C.E. Palestinian Jews were subjugated by the Seleucid

Syrians who later prohibited the practice of the ancient Jewish traditions and laws, including circumcision and the observance of the
Sabbath. The Seleucids murdered Jews who refused to worship Zeus
or eat pork. In 167 there was a dynamic resurgence of Jewish na-
tionalism and loyalty to traditions under the guidance and leadership
of the Maccabees. In 165 the revolt achieved such success that the
Temple that had been profaned was rededicated; this festival is hon-
ored yearly and called Hanukkah. The Maccabean movement lost
its religious fervor and in 63, the Romans began to control Palestine
either indirectly or directly. In 66 C.E. the Jews exploded in full
rebellion against Rome. The war was long and extremely costly:
the Temple was destroyed in 70, but the final flickers of the revolt
were not stamped out until 74 at Masada.[11]

Thousands of Jews were put to death under these successive
pogroms. Recently archeologists discovered just north of Jerusalem
at Givat ha-Mivtar the grim reminder of Roman domination and persecution. The skeletal remains of these Jews reflected the hardships
of individuals who lived during the time, and in the land, in which
Jewish apocalypticism was then full blown. At Givat ha-Mivtar, skel-
etons revealed the following story: a little boy died from an arrow
wound to the skull, an old woman succumbed when her skull was
smashed, a teenaged boy was probably burned to death on the rack,
and a man in his thirties suffered crucifixion.[12]

Jewish apocalypticism produced the apocalypses: I have become
convinced that the apocalyptic literature was produced by the oppressed
and the persecuted. It was squeezed out of individuals who could
see no hope or meaning in contemporary events. The Jewish apoca-
lyptists perceived that meaning cannot come from the present or the
past; it must come from the future through a divine intervention
from the world above or the age to come. Here we see the reason
for Jewish apocalypticism's need for a dualism of two worlds and
of two ages. Thus, according to 4 Ezra, Ezra is told that this "present world is not the end ... the day of judgment will be the end of
this age and the beginning of the immortal age to come ..." (4 Ezra
7:112f. OTP).

Today we are fortunate to have extant no fewer than nineteen
Jewish apocalypses, or Jewish writings closely related to them, that
predate or are roughly contemporaneous with the Apocalypse of John.
A chronological listing of these nineteen documents might be as follows:

Classical Jewish Apocalypses and Related Documents
(c. 200 B.C.E. to c. 135 C.E.)

1.	1 Enoch (clearly composite)	(III B.C.E.-I C.E.)
2.	Daniel 7-12	(II B.C.E.)
3.	Testament of Moses[13]	(II B.C.E.-I C.E.)
4.	Jubilees 23	(II B.C.E.)

5.	Sibylline Oracle Book 3	(II B.C.E.)
6.	Ascension of Isaiah 1:1-3: 12, 5:1-14 (= Martyrdom of Isaiah)	(II B.C.E.)
7.	Testaments of the Twelve Patriarchs (esp. TLevi 2-5, 14-18; TJudah 21-24; TDan 5:7-13)	(II B.C.E.)
8.	Treatise of Shem[14]	(I B.C.E.)
9.	Sibylline Oracle Book 4	(I C.E.)
10.	Testament of Abraham	(I-II C.E.)
11.	4 Ezra	(I C.E.)
12.	2 Baruch	(I-II C.E.)
13.	3 Baruch	(I-II C.E.)
14.	2 Enoch	(I C.E.)
15.	Apocalypse of Abraham	(I-II C.E.)
16.	Sibylline Oracle Book 5	(II C.E.)
17.	Apocryphon of Ezekiel	(I B.C.E.-I C.E.)
18.	Apocalypse of Zephaniah	(I B.C.E.-I C.E.)
19.	Apocalypse of Adam (?)	(I-IV C.E.)

To group these nineteen writings together as Jewish apocalypses or related writings does not mean that we have a clear definition of a Jewish apocalypse or that it represents a coherent genre. Today we are confounded by inabilities to define precisely what we mean by the noun "apocalypse." As we seek a definition of this term, it seems certain that we should not start with an a priori definition and then search for documents that fit it. Neither can we appeal to a selection of writings chosen as apocalypses by ancient writers--the early Jews never defined the term "apocalypse"; hence, we must begin by gathering together writings that most scholars today judge to be apocalypses (see part III, "Description of an Apocalypse").

This is the method employed by a team of scholars organized by J.J. Collins, who after examining many of the apocalypses is impressed by a common core of constant elements and defends the following definition: "'Apocalypse' is a genre of revelatory literature with a narrative framework, in which a revelation is mediated by an otherworldly being to a human recipient, disclosing a transcendent reality which is both temporal, insofar as it envisages eschatological salvation, and spatial insofar as it involves another, supernatural world."[15] Although this definition must be taken seriously and is a significant contribution to scholarship, it should not be taken as definitive for the present or concretized. It is wise to observe that Collins has focused on the Jewish apocalypses. Future research will judge whether he and his team are correct in isolating a "common core of constant elements,"[16] whether he has included in his survey all the necessary writings, whether he has adequately balanced the content and form of the apocalypses, whether he has erred in over-emphasizing the elements in some of the apocalypses, and whether

he has failed to give sufficient attention to the emotional and theological tone of the apocalypses.

In contrast to Collins,[17] H. Anderson has argued in favor
of a recognition of the attitude or tone of so-called apocalyptic literature, claiming "that since not by any means all of the books desig-
nated "apocalyptic" have a uniform literary structure (compare the
Book of Daniel with Jubilees or the Book of Revelation with the Testaments of the Twelve Patriarchs), the term "apocalyptic" may perhaps
be more appropriately taken to denote not a specific literary genre
but a particular religious posture characterized by a peculiar preoccupation with the End-time or the Last Days of the world."[18]

Collins certainly has provided us with much to discuss and
has achieved some significant breakthroughs in perceiving the narrative structure of some apocalypses; but he has gone too far in
the direction of defining an "apocalypse" as a literary genre with
a "common core of constant elements." Not only are the apocalypses
far more varied than Collins suggests, but also--and more importantly
--the essence of an apocalypse cannot be grasped by looking at parts
of it or elements in it. I would argue that the tone of an apocalypse
is fundamental; any included elements are apocalyptic because of
the tone, not the tone because of the elements. This tone, granted,
is to a certain extent impossible to define, but it is not elusive or
amorphous. It derives from the author's certainty of having received
a new revelation that contains a perspective in discontinuity with
Heilsgeschichte (the Israelite claim that God meets Israel in history
and guides her through events in history to the proper way and
telos). The apocalyptist is one who claims--either through vision
or audition--to have been introduced to unseen or unheard of things.
He or she often claims to have visited the world above or the future
age, and subsequently lives, and urges others through writing to
live, in terms of the eternal that is becoming eschatologically real.
The apocalyptist's meaningless terrestrial world receives meaning
through redefinitions of essential concepts by an "indwelling" of a
meaningful celestial world.

We biblical scholars have still much to do in polishing a definition of such terms as "apocalypse," "apocalyptic thought," "apocalyptic eschatology," and "apocalypticism." It has become transparent
to the historian, however, that Jewish apocalypticism was not rele-
gated to the exotic fringes of Palestinian Judaism, as many scholars
thought earlier in this century.[19] Jewish apocalypticism influenced
practically every stratum of Jewish society, including the Pharisees,
as argued recently by most scholars.[20] This perspective has evolved
slowly: first, out of a careful examination of the documents listed
above as apocalypses or related apocalyptic writings; second, from
the recovery and continued study of the Dead Sea Scrolls, which
are probably writings of an Essene religious community whose thought
was pervasively shaped by apocalypticism;[21] and third, from the
recognition that the Mishna, Tosephta and Talmud--though exceedingly

important for an understanding of the religious customs of Palestinian
Jews prior to the destruction of the nation and Temple in 70--do not
mirror the widespread interest in apocalypticism during that early
period because apocalyptic elements were edited out systematically
by their compilers.[22] It is evident that the editors and compilers
of this rabbinic material were less concerned with preserving pre-70
Palestinian traditions than with eliminating from Jewish tradition the
literature and ideas that, on the one hand, were volatile and had
led to the great revolt of 66 to 70 (or 74) and the second major revolt of 132 to 135, and on the other hand, portrayed the nonterres-
trial or extraworldly perspective and dreams that helped to shape
early Christianity. This editorial process helped to define Judaism
in distinction from political revolutions and from Christianity.

        These insights and conclusions help us to assess the indebted-
ness of the Apocalypse to the earlier and contemporaneous Jewish
apocalypses. The Apocalypse inherits from Jewish apocalypticism
much of its tone, which centers upon a pessimistic evaluation of the
events occurring in the present age and world, and upon an enthus-
iastic endorsement of the events that are about to happen on earth
and that are transpiring even now in the world above (or in the
age to come that is already dawning in the present). Also, the Apocalypse inherits from Jewish apocalypticism its images, symbols, metaphorical language, and tendency toward bizarre narratives. Yet,
it also clearly distinguishes itself from the Jewish apocalypses by
the central function of Christ in the scenes and narratives, by the
nonpseudonymous nature of the writing--it is clearly connected with
John[23]--and by the traditions that derive ultimately either from earlier Christians or perhaps even from Jesus himself.

        Having acknowledged the Apocalypse's dependence on and in-
dependence from the Jewish apocalypses, we should emphasize that
the Apocalypse does not quote any extant apocalypse,[24] nor has
it been influenced directly by any of the many Jewish apocalypses.[25]
There is still a possibility, nevertheless, that the author of the Apocalypse knew and was influenced slightly by 4 Ezra, which had been
completed by a Jew only a few years before the Apocalypse was composed.[26]

(3) A Unity

        The Apocalypse is not an unintelligible collection of earlier
apocalypses, as R. H. Charles maintained;[27] rather, it appears to
be a coherent unity reflecting the thoughts of one author. Granted,
this author was influenced by many earlier writings, and although
he did not quote from them he certainly inherited early Jewish traditions. Nonetheless, successive scholarly examinations of the Apocalypse have undermined the positions supporting the hypothesis that
the Apocalypse was composite; for example, it is now clear that the
Semitisms of the Apocalypse are not derived from sources but are the

product of the author himself, who wrote in Greek but thought in
Semitic.[28] Likewise, it is now recognized that the repetitious nature
of the Apocalypse does not reflect separate sources, but indicates the
tendency of apocalyptic writers to recapitulate (as Victorinus of Pettau argued in the first commentary on the Apocalypse).[29]

    One of the last of the earlier arguments to fall pertains to
the origin of the hymns that are sprinkled throughout the Apocalypse.
For some time, it seemed highly probable that these hymns were derived from the early Jewish or Christian liturgy.[30] It is now widely
acknowledged that most of the hymns in the Apocalypse were written
by the author himself and betray his characteristic vocabulary and
use of images.[31] The author of the Apocalypse composed most of
the poetic sections, inserting them into his narrative in order to
illustrate a theological position with the terms and phrases that echo
and reinforce those employed in contiguous verses. There are only
a very few exceptions to this situation; yet, I think we should admit
the possibility that there may be some hymns in the Apocalypse that
were inherited by the author from his own community and that these,
having shaped his thought, eventually were used to illustrate it.
Future scholarly research on the hymns in the Apocalypse will certainly help us to understand better the origin and function of these
poetic sections; such research should also recognize that the Apocalypse was intended to be read aloud within the Christian community
and was itself related to the life of Christian worship. Thus, I am
persuaded that ho anaginōskōn (Ap. 1:3) should not be translated
"one who is reading," but rather "one who is reading aloud" in public. It is significant that Luke, when he describes Jesus reading
the scripture in the Synagogue, uses this very same verb (Luke
4:16, also cf. Hermas, Vision 1.3.3).

(4) Martyrdom

    The Apocalypse reflects a particular social setting; the Chris-
tian communities behind it are certainly suffering persecution and
facing martyrdom. The opening three chapters of the apocalypse,
which contain the Letters to the Seven Churches,[32] refer both to
impending suffering (viz. 2:10) and to past martyrdom (viz 2:13).
Repeatedly the author[33] exhorts his hearers to persevere and to
conquer (2:11, 17, 26; 3:5, 12, 21); note, for example, the mixture
of exhortation and promise which reputedly comes from Christ through
an angel to the church in Laodicea: "He who conquers, I will grant
him to sit with me on my throne, as I myself conquered and sat down
with my Father on his throne" (3:21 RSV). The meaning of this
verse has been understood for years; for example, in 1940, M. Kid-
dle in his commentary on The Revelation of St. John, stated that
"just as Christ was rewarded with authority through His sacrificial
death, so His martyrs will be allowed to share in this authority,
in the 'rule of the saints' which is to follow the great battle with
the armies of evil (xix. 19, xx. 4)."[34]

The anguish of anticipated martyrdoms by his fellow Christians
and perhaps the piercing memory of those who have already died
have shaped the pictorial narrative in at least three major passages
(cf. also Ap. 17:1-6). In 6:9-11, the author describes how when
the Lamb "opened the fifth seal, I saw under the altar the souls
of those who had been slain for the word of God and for the witness they had borne; they cried out with a loud voice, 'O Sovereign
Lord, holy and true, how long before thou wilt judge and avenge
our blood on those who dwell upon the earth?' Then they were each
given a white robe and told to rest a little longer, until the number
of their fellow servants and their brethren should be complete, who
were to be killed as they themselves had been" (6:9-11 RSV).

In 7:9-17, the author describes in graphic detail the multitude
of martyrs who gathered before the throne of God: "These are they
who have come out of the great tribulation; they have washed their
robes and made them white in the blood of the lamb" (7:14 RSV).

In 14:1-5, the author says that he saw standing on Mt. Zion
not only the Lamb but also with him 144,000 individuals. This crowd
is to be identified with "the dead who die in the Lord" (14:13); and
though it is conceivable, as G.R. Beasley-Murray has argued,[35] that
this verse refers to any Christian who dies, whether martyred or not,
it is probable that the author of the Apocalypse is again thinking
specifically about those who have suffered martyrdom. I would tend
to read 14:13 in terms of 13:15, wherein we hear about those who
have been slain because they did not worship the image of the beast;
hence, I would agree with Charles that 14:13 "is a message for those
called to martyrdom in the immediately-impending persecution...."[36]

The major question facing the author of the Apocalypse is,
Why should the Christian continue to be willing to die at the hands
of Rome, who has become drunk from the blood of the saints (7:6)?
The question can be rephrased, Why should the Christian continue
to suffer and be willing to die for Christ who seems to be powerless?
The author answers this question, which he must have heard on numerous occasions, by appealing to the rewards reserved only for the
martyrs, those who "had been beheaded for their testimony to Jesus
and for the word of God, and who had not worshiped the beast or
its image and had not received its mark on their foreheads or hands"
(20:4 RSV). Only the martyrs will be resurrected during the first
resurrection, and only they will reign "with Christ a thousand years"
(20:4).

It is clear, therefore, that any attempt to understand the theology of the Apocalypse must acknowledge and attempt to comprehend
the ramifications of martyrdom in the early Church.[37] Although it
is difficult to be certain, I would agree with most commentators who
place the Apocalypse some time in the mid-90s during the persecution
of some Christians by Domitian (81-96 C.E.), who claimed that he
was both lord and god.[38] Yet, we must admit that the evidence for

Domitianic persecution is ambiguous and the author of the Apocalypse exaggerated the threat of martyrdom.

(5) Assurance and Exhortation

The attempt to understand the theology of the Apocalypse must be informed by each of the four factors discussed above: the Apocalypse must be read in light of its own time, it must be read in relation to the Jewish apocalypses that preceded and were contemporaneous with it, it must be read in terms of its own coherent unity, and it must be read with the recognition that it comes from a community not only facing martyrdom but also the threats of false teachings (e.g., the Nicolaitons [2:6] and "Jezebel" [2:20-23]).

The Apocalypse is the first full Christian apocalypse; yet it was preceded by Christian thoughts that were apocalyptic. Although Jesus was not a Jewish apocalyptist, he was influenced by Jewish apocalypticism. He probably inherited from Jewish apocalypticism the concept of two ages, the eschatological claim that God soon shall bring an end to all normal history, and the idea that God alone knows the hour of this divine intervention (Mark 13:32).[39] He possibly also inherited from Jewish apocalypticism the description of the future punishments for the unrighteous and the rewards for the righteous. Likewise, Paul shows that he was influenced by Jewish apocalypticism when he informed the Corinthians that he had ascended into the third heaven and into Paradise (2 Cor. 12), and when he warned the Thessalonians that Christ is going to return triumphant soon, riding on a cloud and accompanied by angels (1 Thes. 4).[40] Finally, the earliest gospel contains a chapter, the thirteenth, that is often called "the Synoptic Apocalypse."[41] This Markan tradition certainly influenced Matthew when he wrote chapters 24 and 25, and even Luke, when he compiled chapter 21.

There can be no doubt that the Apocalypse was preceded not only by Jewish apocalypses, but also by Christian apocalypticism. Moreover, unlike many writings that may have received their titles long after they had been composed, the Apocalypse commences with the following words: apokalupsis Iēsou Christou, "the Apocalypse of Jesus Christ," and continues by claiming that this "apocalypse" or revelation was given to John by God through his angel (Ap 1:1).

Earlier we saw that the major question being asked by the Christians behind the Apocalypse was, Why should we remain faithful to Christ, when it is obvious from what we see that the Romans are invincible, and the Emperor has the powers and authority of a god? The answer of the author of the Apocalypse is lucid: He exhorts his readers to remain faithful and persevere, because the present evil is to be terminated soon, because real and eternal power and authority comes from the world above and shall soon break majestically and triumphantly into the present. The author articulates his

position through pictorial descriptions of what is now happening in
the world above, forcing the reader to see another world and another age. The scenes are so graphic and dynamic that the reader
is transported to another place:

> After this I looked, and lo, in heaven an open door!
> And the first voice, which I had heard speaking to me like
> a trumpet, said, "Come up hither, and I will show you what
> must take place after this." At once I was in the Spirit,
> and lo, a throne stood in heaven, with one seated on the
> throne! And he who sat there appeared like jasper and
> carnelian, and round the throne was a rainbow that looked
> like an emerald. Round the throne were twenty-four thrones,
> and seated on the thrones were twenty-four elders, clad in
> white garments, with golden crowns upon their heads.
> From the throne issue flashes of lightning, and voices and
> peals of fire, which are the seven spirits of God; and be-
> fore the throne there is as it were a sea of glass, like crys-
> tal. [Ap. 4:1-6a RSV]

(6) The Way and Invitation

Two features in these verses are so significant for an understanding both of apocalypticism and of the Apocalypse that they should
be isolated and clarified. First, the author describes a way into
heaven--"an open door"--and quotes a divine command (the first
Greek verb is an aorist imperative): "Come up here, and I shall
show you what must happen after this" (4:1, cf. also TLevi 2:6).
Note that the way and the invitation is shared with the reader and
the congregation who hear the words; they are caught up into the
celestial journey. The reader and the congregation can, indeed are
prompted to, participate in the events. The subsequent hymns in
the Apocalypse symbolize the unifying of the holy ones; the earthly
faithful join with the celestial choruses in praising the Creator.

(7) Tranference and Redefinition

Second, the description is pictorially clear, allowing the reader
to be present in the precise place described. We need to observe
that when we think of a place that is well defined and picturesque
we imagine ourselves in that place phenomenologically observing what
is seen and participating in the dynamics of the events there.[42]
This power of transferring the reader from the world below to the
world above, and from the present age to the future age is one of
the most significant and essential features of apocalypticism. Any
definition of the essence of the apocalypses must include this phe-
nomenological dimension. It is typical of the apocalypses and of the
apocalyptic sections of literature influenced by apocalypticism; note,
for example, the Testament of Levi: "And I beheld a high moun-
tain, and I was on it" (2:5; Kee in OTP, vol. 1, p. 788).

Having transferred the reader from a finite world devoid of
meaning to another eternal world, the apocalyptist can now graph-
ically redefine power, [43] and descriptively explain time, eternity and
the blessings and punishments of the future. The verbs employed
to describe the future events are seldom subjunctives; they are usually in the past or present tense, denoting that the future events
have already begun, and that the results are assured.

The redefinition of power, which shifts the reader's view away
from the seemingly invincible might of Rome, is emphasized throughout the Apocalypse, and is especially clear in chapter five. A strong
(ischuros) angel proclaims in a loud voice, "Who is worthy to open
the scroll and break its seals?" (5:2). The account continues with
the report that no one was able to open the scroll, no one under
the earth, on the earth, or even in heaven (5:3). The seer then
weeps, perhaps reflecting the tears of those in his community, but
is commanded, "Do not weep" (5:5). The reason behind this exhortation is conveyed in past and present tenses: The Root of David
"has conquered (aorist)," and is able to open (aorist) the scroll
and its seal. Immediately the seer says he saw a Lamb who had
been slain--symbolic words to denote Jesus' martyrdom--but this
apparent weakness is a strength; indeed it is the reason the Lamb
alone is powerful and worthy to open the scroll. This fact, which
would have been very meaningful for those about to confront their
own martyrdom, is punctuated by poetry in a hymn, sung by the
celestial powers. The following chapters, 6-8, describe in past tenses
(aorists in 6:1, 3, 5, 7, 9, 12; 8:1) how the Lamb effortlessly opened
the seven seals on the scroll (cf. 5:1). In comparison to the Lamb,
therefore, all who are on earth as well as the angels in heaven are
powerless; moreover, the Lamb's majestic deeds are described as
having already been completed. These visions would have bolstered
the Christians, who faced death because they refused to acknowledge
the Roman Emperor as powerful and to confess that he is lord and
god.

The apocalyptist descriptively explains time, eternity and the
blessings and punishments of the future. Time is linear and teleo-
logical; it is moving in a direct line towards the end intended by
God. Hence, the seer sees the appearance of a new heaven and
a new earth, because the old heaven and earth have passed away
(21:1). The image here is highlighted by the depiction of the descent of a new Jerusalem (21:2-27), the holy city, and the bride
of the Lamb (21:2, 9f.). The descent of the new Jerusalem illustrates
the author's conviction that very soon God will dwell with mankind,
and that the suffering of the faithful is soon to be over. The seer
hears a loud voice from the throne: "Behold, the dwelling of God
is with men. He will dwell with them, and they shall be his people,
and God himself will be with them; he will wipe away every tear from
their eyes, and death shall be no more, neither shall there be mourning nor crying nor pain any more, for the former things have passed
away" (Ap 21:3f. RSV). These words clarify the assurance that the

suffering of the Christian is about to end, and that the fellowship
shared between mankind and God, once enjoyed in the beginning
in Eden (cf. Gen. 3:8f.), shall return at the end of time.

(8) Summary

The discussion above illustrates the proper means to study
the ancient writing called the Apocalypse of John, or simply, "the
Apocalypse." It is an apocalypse, heavily indebted to the earlier
Jewish apocalypses, but not directly dependent upon any one of them.
It was written out of and for a community facing martyrdom. The
exhortation to persevere is articulated through pictorial modes of
expression, lavishly illustrated with colorful language, and with verbs
that describe actions that are already completed, in actual process,
or soon to be accomplished. The power of the emperor is ephemeral;
the Lord God or Christ is pantokratōr, the All-Powerful, the Omni-
potent, a term--except for 2 Corinthians 6:18--found only in the
Apocalypse, and there no fewer than nine times (1:8, 4:8, 11:17,
15:3, 16:7, 16:14, 19:6, 19:15, 21:22). The future is breaking into
the present; Rome and Satan will be defeated and punished. The
martyrs will receive rich blessings and eternal rewards. A new heaven
and earth will appear, and God shall once again dwell with mankind.
And so at the end of the public reading of the apocalypse the congregation was probably led to say, "Amen. Come, Lord Jesus!" (22:20).

THE APOCALYPSE AND ITS IMPACT ON
SUBSEQUENT APOCALYPSES

The Apocalypse's profound and memorable message is conveyed
by brilliant images and events that make an indelible impression on
any reader. To what extent did this writing influence and shape
subsequent "Christian" apocalypses?

In an attempt to answer this question, we will exclude the
Jewish apocalypses, especially 3 Enoch, and the Merkabah, which
are now carefully examined by P. Alexander, I. Gruenwald, and
D. J. Halperin.[44] Our focus will be upon the "Christian" apocalypses
that date from the end of the first century C.E. to the end of the
tenth century C.E., or from the destruction of the Temple to the
threshold of the attempts, fueled by apocalyptic thought, to recover
Jerusalem through the Crusades.

(1) Problems

Numerous difficulties frustrate any attempt to assess the impact
of the Apocalypse on subsequent apocalypses. First, it is not easy
to apply consistently any definition of an apocalypse derived from
the study of Jewish apocalypses to the Christian apocalypses;[45] these

writings tend to resist the paradigms associated with the Jewish apocalypses. The alteration of both form and content becomes extreme
with the Christian apocalypses that postdate the fourth century.

Second, there are serious inconsistencies with regard to nomenclature in this field. For example, a reader of the eighth and tenth
volumes of the Ante-Nicene Fathers would logically conclude that
the Revelation of Paul is different from the Vision of Paul. In reality, these represent the same document with different names; the
differences in the translation stem from the different languages used
as a text base. Both entries in the Bibliography receive a warning
that these two titles represent one work (also see Guidelines). There
is as yet no commonly accepted nomenclature in the field of the Apocrypha and Pseudepigrapha of the New Testament; the present volume
attempts to establish some clarity regarding these titles and documents.

Third, the area of early Christian apocalypticism, in contrast
to Jewish apocalypticism, is virtually an uncharted field.[46] Some
of the obscurity is now being removed, thanks to the publications
by scholars, such as B. McGinn, in his Apocalyptic Spirituality and
especially his Visions of the End: Apocalyptic Traditions in the Middle Ages.[47] Fourth, it is difficult to decide where one should begin
and which documents should be included for examination. Fifth,
the date of the documents is not so much unknown as it is a subject
that has not attracted adequate and sufficient research; hence, we
are in the dark as to the date of most of the documents that we shall
soon be examining. Sixth, the documents obviously come from different periods representing a millennium of thought; to examine them
with understanding means that they should be, indeed must be, organized into coherent categories. Seventh, all of these problems
must be solved before we can adequately hope to obtain a reliable
understanding of each of the apocalypses, their place in history,
and the continuum of apocalypses.

Despite the obscurity of the early Christian apocalypses, it
has nevertheless become clear that these writings had a profound
impact on Christian history and thought. The importance of apocalyptic texts upon Byzantine and medieval history and thought has
been demonstrated recently by numerous scholars, especially N.
Cohn,[48] M. Reeves,[49] P.J. Alexander,[50] B. McGinn,[51] and E. Turdeanu.[52] At the outset, I wish to acknowledge my indebtedness
in what follows to these and many other distinguished scholars of
early Church history and of the early Middle Ages; I am much less
at home here than in the earliest Christian writings and in Early
Judaism.

(2) Criteria

The criteria I have used to ascertain whether or not the Apocalypse has influenced a subsequent apocalypse are the following: 1)

a quotation from the Apocalypse proves clear dependence; 2) the
utilization of a metaphor, a cluster of terms, concept, image, or pictorial scene unique to the Apocalypse signifies that there is either
direct or indirect influence; 3) the development of an idea peculiar
to the Apocalypse indicates some dependence. These criteria help
us to exclude other influences or dependences derived either from
other apocalypses and apocalyptic literature or from the living oral
traditions.

(3) Excluded Writings

I shall not include in my discussion the apocalypses preserved
in a fragmentary form in the Cologne Mani Codex since I am not persuaded that they are fragments from Christian apocalypses.[53] Likewise, I will not include writings that are not apocalypses even though
they have often been considered to be so or have been inaccurately
entitled an apocalypse; those to be omitted include the so-called Testament of Our Lord,[54] the Testament of Adam,[55] the History of the
Rechabites (which is sometimes called the Narrative or Apocalypse
of Zosimus),[56] the Apocalypse of Andrew and Paul,[57] the Assumption
of Mary,[58] the Apocalypse of Bartholomew,[59] and the Revelation of
Stephen.[60] Third, other writings that seem to be quasi-apocalyptic
but are not apocalypses have been excluded from the net that I have
cast over the first millennium C.E.; hence, I shall not discuss the
apocalyptic homilies, especially the Pseudo-Ephraem "Sermon on the
End of the World,"[61] the romances that have been confused as apocalypses,[62] the legends with apocalyptic tones such as the Legend
of Alexander,[63] and the apparent fragments of lost gospels with apocalyptic overtones, such as the so-called Questions of Bartholomew.[64]

(4) Included Writings

Fortunately there are numerous writings that appear to be
apocalypses and that can be organized into four interrelated groups:
the Jewish apocalypses that have been significantly expanded by
Christians, the Gnostic apocalypses, the early Christian apocryphal
apocalypses, and the early medieval Christian apocryphal apocalypses.

(5) Documents

a) Jewish Apocalypses Significantly Expanded by Christians.
While many of the Jewish apocalypses mentioned in the first portion
of this paper received intermittent Christian expansion or redaction,
other Jewish apocalypses and related documents have been so profoundly and fundamentally reworked by Christians that in their present form they are clearly Christian writings.[65] These rewritten Jewish apocalypses, now assembled for the first time in their full final
form in The Old Testament Pseudepigrapha, are as follows:[66]

1.	Testaments of the Twelve Patriarchs	(II B.C.E.; II-III C.E.)
2.	Ascension of Isaiah	(II B.C.E.; II C.E.)
3-4.	5, 6 Ezra	(4 Ezra: I C.E.; II-III C.E.)
5-9.	Christian Sibyllines	(Bk 3: II B.C.E., Bk. 4: I C.E., Bk 5:II C.E.; Bks 1, 2, 8, 6, 7;II C.E.)
10.	Apocalypse of Abraham	(I C.E.; II-X? C.E.)
11.	Ladder of Jacob	(I C.E.?; II? C.E.)
12.	Testament of Isaac	(TAb: I C.E.; I-V C.E.)
13.	Testament of Jacob	(TAb: I C.E.; II-V C.E.)

It is impressive, perhaps surprising, to observe that none of the Christian expansions or alterations to these earlier Jewish compositions unequivocally reflect influence from the Apocalypse. In attempting to assess the significance of this discovery we should perceive, on the one hand, that the expansions and additions were focused primarily upon the document being reworked, and, on the other hand, that the Apocalypse itself was a subject of considerable debate and did not make its way into the canon of the western Church[67] until a time that postdates the period in which almost all of these Christian expansions were added.

b) Gnostic Apocalypses. Among the codices discovered at Nag Hammadi are some writings that are titled an "apocalypse"; the most important of these, for our purposes, are those in codex V, tractate 2-5: the (Nag Hammadi) Apocalypse of Paul, the First Apocalypse of James, the Second Apocalypse of James, and the Apocalypse of Adam.[68] None of these so-called apocalypses have unquestionably been influenced by the Apocalypse. The Apocalypse of Adam (78) does mention a "mother" ("a virgin womb") and her son who fled to "a desert place" until the son "was nourished" and "received glory and power." This imagery is far too generic and widespread to confirm the possibility that the Apocalypse's vision of the woman who bears a child and flees into the wilderness, as pictured in the Apocalypse 12:1-6, has influenced the Apocalypse of Adam. Another apocalypse among the Nag Hammadi Codices, namely the (Nag Hammadi) Apocalypse of Peter (VII, 3), which may have been written in the third century C.E., also portrays no clear influence from the Apocalypse.

It comes as no surprise that the gnostic apocalypses do not betray significant or clear influences from the Apocalypse. The Apocalypse, and most other apocalypses, were written out of distress over present history, but the gnostic apocalypses are unconcerned with this world; rather, the gnostic apocalypses are almost totally preoccupied with personal salvation and revelations that will help the knower return to the original celestial abode. This marked difference between the non-gnostic apocalypses and the gnostic apocalypses have led some scholars, notably P. Vielhauer[69] and K. Rudolph[70] to argue--and I think persuasively--that the gnostic writings

just mentioned should not be considered examples of an "apocalypse."
It is difficult for me, therefore, to agree with F.T. Fallon, who claims
that these gnostic writings should be termed apocalypses.[71]

c) Early Christian Apocryphal Apocalypses. No fewer than
eight Christian apocalypses were written from about the time of the
Apocalypse until roughly the first "ecumenical" Christian Council
held at Nicaea in 325, following the conversion of the Roman Emperor
Constantine to Christianity. It is obvious that many passages in
the New Testament inspired the writing of apocalypses; for example,
Paul's account of being taken up into heaven and into paradise as
recorded in 2 Corinthians 12 eventually helped produce the Apocalypse of Paul. The injunctions about love found in 1 Corinthians
13 and in John 15:13 seem to have been the catalyst that caused
someone to compose the Apocalypse of Sedrach. The account of the
transfiguration of Jesus as found in Mark 9:2-8 (plus parallels and
2 Pet 1:18) invigorated the thoughts and imagination of at least two
writers, producing the First Revelation of John and the Apocalypse
of Peter. We would, therefore, tend to expect that the first and
greatest of the Christian apocalypses clearly influenced the following
writings:

1.	Didache XVI	(I-II C.E.)
2.	Hermas	(I-II C.E.)
3.	Apocalypse of Peter	(c. 135 C.E.)
4.	Book of Elchasai	(II C.E.)
5.	Apocalypse of Zechariah	(II-III C.E.?)
6.	Apocalypse of Elijah	(I-IV C.E.)
7.	Apocalypse of Sedrach	(II-IV C.E.)
8.	Apocalypse of Paul	(III-IV C.E.)

One of these apocalypses, the Apocalypse of Zechariah, is lost and
therefore cannot be assessed. Five others are not clearly influenced
by the Apocalypse, and one of them, the Shepherd of Hermas, is
an apocalypse only in form.[72] Two of these apocalypses, however,
have been influenced by the Apocalypse of John.

The author of the Apocalypse of Elijah shows in numerous passages that he (or she) knows and is familiar with the Apocalypse;
the two most impressive passages for this influence are at 1:9 and
2:31. In the Apocalypse of Elijah 1:9, it is probable that the thought
has been influenced by images found in Revelation 3:12, 7:3, and
7:16. These verses state or describe how the faithful will have the
Lord's name written upon them and will not hunger and thirst. These
passages were probably in the mind of the author of the Apocalypse
of Elijah when he stated that the Lord said, "I will write my name
upon their forehead and I will seal their right hand, and they will
not hunger or thirst" (1:9).[73]

In the next chapter (2:31) the author of the Apocalypse of
Elijah reveals that he probably has been influenced by the ideas

found in three passages in the Apocalypse: in 18:11, which describes the desolation of Babylon or Rome and the mourning of the merchants for her; in 9:6, which describes how people will at the end of time seek death and not be able to find it because death will flee from them; and in 6:16, which describes how all shall call upon the rocks to fall upon them. Obviously the author of the Apocalypse of Elijah was remembering the Apocalypse when he wrote the following: "In those days the cities of Egypt will groan for the voice of the one who sells and the one who buys will not be heard.... Those who are in Egypt ... will desire death, [but] death will flee and leave them ... they will run up to the rocks and leap off, saying 'fall upon us.' And still they will not die" (2:31-33).

The Apocalypse of Paul has also been clearly influenced by the Apocalypse. Some parallels between the Apocalypse of Paul and the Apocalypse are insignificant and too generic to warrant discussion (ApPaul 14--Ap 12:7; ApPaul 41--Ap 5:1), others are only possibly significant (ApPaul 12--Ap 7:9 and 22:4; ApPaul 16 and 18--Ap 16:7 and 19:2; ApPaul 31--Ap 3:16), others are probable (ApPaul 23--Ap 21:10-14), or extremely probable (ApPaul 14--Ap 4:10f.; ApPaul 21--Ap 20f.; ApPaul 44--Ap 4). Our attention will be focused exclusively upon this latter category. The Apocalypse of Paul, chapter 14, contains a mosaic of ideas and symbols found in the Apocalypse, especially 4:10f., with a description of the twenty-four elders who worship God and sing, "Worthy are you, our Lord and God" (cf. Apoc 5:8, 14; 11:16; 19:4). According to this section of the Apocalypse of Paul, Paul sees a righteous soul enter into heaven and subsequently be taken into paradise to wait "the day of resurrection"; the following sentence is full of ideas mined from the Apocalypse: "And after that I heard the voices of a thousand times a thousand angels and archangels and the cherubim and the twenty-four elders who sang hymns and glorified God and cried: Righteous art thou, O Lord, and righteous are thy judgments; there is no respect of persons with thee and though dost requite every man according to thy judgment" (ApPaul 14).[74]

In the Apocalypse of Paul, chapter 21, there is recorded the idea that "the first earth will be dissolved and this land of promise will then be shown," and the concept that "the Lord Jesus Christ" will "come with all his saints" and will reign "for a thousand years."[75] This cluster of ideas is unique; I have not found it in other apocalypses, although the thousand-year kingdom, according to McGinn, is "the third major element in patristic apocalyptic" thought. These ideas in the Apocalypse of Paul derive ultimately--if not directly-- from the Apocalypse, especially from chapters 20 and 21.

Finally the Apocalypse of Paul, chapter 44, reveals that the author was familiar with the Apocalypse, chapter 4, which contains a description of twenty-four elders before the throne of God and four living creatures around the throne. Notice how similar to the Apocalypse are the following passages: "And I looked and saw heaven

move as a tree shaken by the wind. And they suddenly threw themselves on their faces before the throne ... and I saw the 24 elders
and the 4 beasts worshipping God, and I saw the altar and the veil
and the throne, and all were rejoicing; and the smoke of a good
odour rose up beside the altar of the throne of God...." (ApPaul
44).[76] In attempting to assess the significance of the Apocalypse
for the author of the Apocalypse of Paul, it is wise to observe that
in chapter 21 he (or she) has directly quoted not only from 2 Corinthians 12:4 but also from Matthew 5:5.

     We have seen that very few of the seven extant early Chris-
tian apocalypses, sometimes called "the patristic apocalypses," were
influenced by the Apocalypse. The influence of the Apocalypse upon
these apocalypses could easily be exaggerated if we included for
consideration the obvious parallels that are also shared with the many
Jewish apocalypses now extant, but such a poor methodology would
blind us from perceiving the important point that only two of the
seven extant early Christian apocryphal apocalypses were clearly
influenced by the Apocalypse. How can we explain this observation?

     Perhaps the Apocalypse did not profoundly affect most of the
early Christian apocalypses because of the fluid nature of the canon
before the fourth century. Not only was the Apocalypse not yet
firmly established within the western canon, but also there is some
evidence suggesting that other apocalypses may have been considered
part of the canon, especially the Apocalypse of Paul, since it may
have been considered canonical by the compiler of the Muratorian
Canon, by Clement of Alexandria (according to Eusebius, H.E. 6.14.
1) and by Origen (according to Barhebraeus, Nomocanon 7. 9).[77]

     The apocryphal apocalypses can be contrasted with the earlier
Jewish apocalypses. For example, the Jewish apocalypses emphasize
the rewards in heaven for the righteous and often describe the ver-
dant nature of paradise; the Christian apocalypses provide full descriptions of the terrifying punishments in hell.[78] This preoccupation
with hell is especially pronounced in the Apocalypse of Peter, the
Apocalypse of Paul, and--among the early medieval apocalypses--
in the First Revelation of John and Apocalypse of Ezra, Vision of
Ezra, and Apocalypse of Mary, to which we will turn shortly. Also
in contrast to the Jewish apocalypses, the early Christian apocalypses
provide virtually no recital of history from the apocalyptic perspective.[79]

     d) Early Medieval Christian Apocryphal Apocalypses. From
the late fourth century until the tenth century, there is a continuum
of activity that either produced new apocalypses or so thoroughly
reworked earlier traditions or documents that they are now seen as
new compilations. Unfortunately, these apocalypses have never
been discussed adequately and are ignored in most of the discussions
of Christian apocalypticism. I would tend to classify as early medieval Christian apocryphal apocalypses at least the following thirteen
documents:

1.	Apocalypse of Thomas	(IV-V C.E.)
2.	1 Revelation of John	(V-VI C.E.)
3.	2 Revelation of John	(VI-VIII C.E.)
4.	3 Revelation of John	(pre-XI C.E.)
5.	Apocalypse of Ezra	(II-IX C.E.)
6.	Vision of Ezra	(IV-VII C.E.)
7.	Questions of Ezra	(VI-XI C.E.)
8.	Revelation of Ezra	(pre-IX C.E.)
9.	Seventh Vision of Daniel	(pre-VIII C.E.)
10.	Vision of Enoch	(pre-VIII C.E.)
11.	Apocalypse of Mary (or the Virgin)	(IX C.E.)
12.	Apocalypse of Daniel	(IX C.E.)
13.	Andreas Salos Apocalypse	(X C.E.)

At the outset, it is pertinent to report that the Second Revelation of John, the Questions of Ezra and the Revelation of Ezra are not precisely apocalypses; they are included in this list both because they evolve out of the apocalypses and share many of their features and because they are integral works in the cycle of documents related respectively to John and to Ezra.

Of the thirteen documents listed above, only three were clearly influenced by the Apocalypse. A. de Santos Otero reported incorrectly that the Apocalypse of Thomas was closely "dependent on the canonical Revelation of John" because it "apportions the events of the End into seven days." According to A. de Santos Otero, this literary device "clearly recalls the seven seals, the seven trumpets and the seven bowls of the Revelation of John (Rev. 5:1-8:2; 8:2-11; 16)."[80] There is, however, no clear link between the seven days and the use of seven in the Apocalypse. The author of the Apocalypse did not originate the significant symbolic meaning of the number seven; he inherited it from many traditions and any of these could likewise have influenced the author of the Apocalypse of Thomas. Of the early medieval Christian apocryphal apocalypses, only the First Revelation of John, the Apocalypse of Daniel and the Andreas Salos Apocalypse are clearly influenced by the Apocalypse.

Unlike the Apocalypse, the First Revelation of John is pseudepigraphically attributed to the apostle John, who is described as being "alone upon Mount Tabor." Obviously the author is attributing to John an experience he had during the so-called transfiguration. The author of the First Revelation of John clearly knew the Apocalypse and borrowed from it the description of the Lamb, who is depicted as having seven eyes and seven horns, who alone was able to open a book or scroll that was sealed with seven seals (cf. Ap 5:1-10). Note how thoroughly the Apocalypse has influenced the following section of the First Revelation of John, "And I looked, and saw a Lamb having seven eyes and seven horns. And again I heard a voice saying to me: I will bid the Lamb come before me, and will say, Who will open this book? And all the multitudes of the angels will answer, Give this book to the Lamb to open it."[81]

Subsequent to this account, the Lamb successively opens the seven
seals, but the effects are strikingly different from those according
to the Apocalypse; noticeably absent is the mention of the four horses
of the Apocalypse that are linked with the opening of the first four
seals and that have had such an impact on the art and literature of
the West. It is impressive, however, how little the Apocalypse has
influenced the First Revelation of John.[82] The author obviously
knew the Apocalypse but borrowed only the brief reference to the
Lamb and to the book or scroll with seven seals.[83]

In contrast to the First Revelation of John, the Apocalypse
of Daniel is profoundly influenced by numerous images and ideas
found in the Apocalypse. It seems to be built structurally and lin-
guistically upon the scene depicted in the Apocalypse 16-18. The
first four chapters of the Apocalypse of Daniel depict the "three
sons of Hagar" who lead an army against Byzantium in the great
war. It seems probable that this idea has been borrowed from the
Apocalypse 16:13-16, which describes three unclean spirits which
go forth to the great and final battle at Armageddon. Likewise,
the description of Babylon in the Apocalypse of Daniel seems to have
been borrowed directly from the description of the great harlot Babylon in the Apocalypse, chapters 16-18 (cf. ApDan 7:2, 5 and Ap
17:9; ApDan 7:2, 5, 11 and Ap 18:10, 16, 19). Many of these similarities are singled out briefly in the excellent introduction to the
Apocalypse of Daniel by G.T. Zervos in the new English edition of
the Pseudepigrapha,[84] but they warrant full and careful examination.
It seems safe to conclude that the Apocalypse of Daniel is more influenced by the Apocalypse than are any of the other apocalypses
we have examined; it should receive a full, separate study to discern the reason and extent of this unparalleled dependency.

The Andreas Salos Apocalypse is clearly influenced by the
Apocalypse, especially near the end in a cluster of images (cf. 868B-
873A). It is impossible to discern whether 872C is dependent upon
the Apocalypse because the reference to being inscribed "in the book
of life" could have been obtained from other writings, many of which
are not even apocalypses. It is possible that 868B may be dependent
upon the description of the fall of Rome as found in the Apocalypse
18:9-19, and even probable that 872C is influenced by the description
of the locusts with tails like scorpions who plague humankind, except
those who have the seal of God upon their foreheads, according to
the Apocalypse 9:10 and 4. It is clear, moreover, that 869B has
been obtained from the Apocalypse 20:7-8. This section of the Andreas Salos Apocalypse describes the coming of Satan or Antichrist,
who will "be loosed from the chains of Hades" and "will begin to
display his deceit, as John the Theologian says."[85] These ideas
are developed in the Apocalypse, chapter 20, and the expressed
acknowledgment of the source for the inspiration is unparalleled in
any of the apocalypses examined above.

(6) Summary

A historical synopsis is found in some classical Jewish apocalypses, especially Daniel 7-12, Jubilees 23, 4 Ezra, 2 Baruch, and
the Apocalypse of Abraham; however, this interest is lacking in the
early Christian apocryphal apocalypses.[86] A recital of historical
events, attempting especially to explain present crises, surfaces
again in four of the last five early medieval Christian apocalypses,
namely the Seventh Vision of Daniel, the Vision of Enoch, the Apocalypse of Daniel, and the Andreas Salos Apocalypse. Once again it is
necessary to emphasize that only three of the thirteen early medieval
Christian apocryphal apocalypses are clearly influenced by the Apocalypse. The significance of this fact needs to be assessed in light of
the observation that many of these apocalypses are directly influenced
by and sometimes paraphrase or quote from other books in the New
Testament, especially writings by Paul, the Gospel of Matthew, and
the Gospel of John.

CONCLUSION

In conclusion, I will focus upon three unresolved issues: the
significance of the Apocalypse for subsequent apocalypses, the continuum reflected by the Christian apocalypses, and the influence of
the Apocalypse itself and the subsequent apocalypses upon the great
classics of the fourteenth and seventeenth centuries.

(1) Significance

None of the thirteen Jewish apocalypses expanded by Christians
and none of the so-called gnostic "apocalypses" are clearly influenced
by the Apocalypse; moreover, of the twenty-one Christian apocryphal
apocalypses mentioned above only five have clearly been influenced
by the Apocalypse (Apocalypse of Elijah, Apocalypse of Paul, 1 Revelation of John, Apocalypse of Daniel, Andreas Salos Apocalypse).
It is surprising to observe that the Apocalypse had no direct influence upon three quarters (15 of the 20) of the Christian apocalypses
that postdate it. We are thereby confronted with a perplexing and
difficult question: Why were the early Christian apocalypses not profoundly influenced by the rich symbolism and memorable details found
in the Apocalypse, notably the pictorial representation of Jesus standing at the door of the heart and knocking, the galloping four horses
that inaugurate the eschatological end, the demonic beasts that come
up out of hell, the vivid descriptions of the harlot Rome, the millennial messianic reign and final defeat of Satan, the appearance of a
new heaven and a new earth, and finally the descent of the new
Jerusalem?

This is an exceedingly perplexing question and cannot be dismissed with the cavalier response that the author of an apocalypse

characteristically does not quote from or clearly depend upon other
documents. Many of the Christian apocalypses listed above do in
fact frequently depend upon the New Testament writings, especially
Paul's letters and the Gospels of Matthew and John. The question
cannot be easily dismissed by referring to the fact that the Apocalypse's peculiar historical period ceased to have paradigmatic significance. Certainly the Apocalypse was determined by its own peculiar
situation and was conditioned by the political and social forces of its
own day, especially the experience and threat of martyrdom. Even
so, the archaic historical dimension of the Apocalypse hardly explains
why this document had so little impact on subsequent Christian apocalypses. Perhaps the answer is to a certain extent related to the
ignorance of the Apocalypse or to its rejection from the canon of sacred scriptures. But, this answer would only apply to the state of
the canon in the West in the early centuries, and even in the West
there was early on a vivid interest in the Apocalypse. The search
for an answer to our question must include the perception of the
commentaries on and exegesis devoted to the Apocalypse especially
by Melito of Sardis, Victorinus of Pettau, Jerome, Augustine,[87] the
Venerable Bede, and Haimo of Auxerre.[88] The attempt to explain
away the question by referring to the demise of Christian apocalypticism[89] simply ignores the fact that the apocryphal apocalypses themselves pose this question and caricatures Christian theology by ignor-
ing the fundamental apocalyptic base of the Christian kerygma, and
the devotion to apocalypticism by such distant authors as Lactantius
in the fourth century and Joachim of Fiore in the twelfth. Finally,
I must confess, that the adequate answer to the problem presently
before us eludes me. The issues are exceedingly complex. As historians, we tend to ask more questions than we can answer. At
least the question has been clarified; future research by specialists
on the period from 200 to 1000 will help us comprehend why the Apocalypse did not more significantly affect the Christian apocryphal apocalypses that date from the first millennium C.E.

(2) The Continuum

     The study of apocalyptic thought has tended to be insular,
myopic and narrow. Some scholars have focused upon only one Jewish apocalypse, others have been content to seek the origins of Jewish apocalyptic thought, others attempting to prove the non-Jewish
nature of early Jewish apocalypticism have concentrated on the non-
Jewish "apocalypses" and related writings (see Part III). Many have
discussed apocalyptic thought as it appeared only in one period and
place, namely between 200 B.C.E. and 200 C.E. and in Jewish Palestine. Likewise, church historians and medievalists have recently
seen the continuing significance of apocalypticism, but they have not
known about the abundance of Christian apocryphal apocalypses; these
are organized and discussed above for the first time. There is a
great need to complete the excellent analytical studies with a synthesis. Perhaps the present study will help provide for such a synthesis

and for a recognition of the continuity of apocalypticism and the apocalypses.

The present work has looked only at the apocalypses; it must
be supplemented by an examination of the great commentaries and
homilies on Daniel and the Apocalypse by Hippolytus, Victorinus, and
Tyconius especially, and by the writings on the Antichrist, the apocalyptic legends, letters and histories, many of which are now collected
and assessed by McGinn in Visions of the End: Apocalyptic Traditions in the Middle Ages and in Apocalyptic Spirituality. Moreover,
this study needs to be set in a social context,90 and to be informed
by the continuing evidence of "prophets" who claimed to receive visions and revelations. Foremost among these apocalyptically inspired
prophets is the twelfth-century Calabrian prophet Joachim of Fiore,
who included in his triology an Exposition on the Apocalypse. Much
like the Righteous Teacher who founded the apocalyptic and Essene
community that produced the so-called Dead Sea Scrolls, to whom
alone God had disclosed "all the mysteries" of the prophets (1QpHab
7), Joachim of Fiore saw himself "as the exegete to whom God had
granted the gift of understanding the truth already revealed but
hidden in the Bible."91 Finally, a study of the influence of the the
Apocalypse must include an examination of its profound impact on
art.92

(3) The Influence

The continuum of Christian apocalypticism from the first century until at least the tenth century--and medieval specialists can
no doubt list other apocalypses and apocalyptic writings dating from
about the beginning of the crusades93 until the renaissance--should
help us to understand better some of the greatest classics of our
culture. In light of the early Christian apocalypses and the early
medieval Christian apocalypses, we should have a better understanding of the literary antecedents and possible influence upon the
seventeenth-century authors, especially John Bunyan and his Pilgrim's
Progress and John Milton and his Paradise Lost. Especially we should
better comprehend the medieval poet Dante, who in the fourteenth
century produced the magnificent Divina commedia. Perhaps a better understanding of Dante, his time and his masterpiece will evolve
from a critical examination of the literary antecedents of The Divine
Comedy.94 It seems relatively certain that many of these earlier
Christian apocalypses significantly influenced his magnum opus. I
think it is probable, for example, that the Apocalypse of Peter and
the Apocalypse of Paul95 directly influenced the Divine Comedy.

The preceding study intends to draw attention to the abundance
of apocalypses.96 Perhaps it will facilitate and encourages analyses
of these documents and synthetic studies.

NOTES

1. J.H. Charlesworth, ed. The Old Testament Pseudepigrapha, 2 vols. (Garden City, N.Y., 1983-1985). All translations are by me, unless otherwise specified. This essay was first read at the twelfth conference of The Center for Medieval and Renaissance Studies at Ohio State University in 1981; subsequently, it was presented to scholars in many universities and seminaries in South Africa. The lecture has been revised and expanded for publication.

2. D.M. Smith, "Johannine Christianity: Some Reflections on Its Character and Delineation," NTS 21 (1975) 222-48. For a reliable review of research on the Apocalypse, see O. Böcher, Die Johannesapokalypse (Erträge der Forschung 41; Darmstadt, 1975).

3. J.M. Ford, Revelation: Introduction, Translation and Commentary (The Anchor Bible; Garden City, N.Y., 1975).

4. E. Schüssler Fiorenza, Priester für Gott: Studien zum Herrschafts- und Priestermotiv in der Apokalypse (NTAbh n.F. 7; Münster, 1972); Fiorenza, The Apocalypse (Chicago, 1976). Also see her "Composition and Structure of the Book of Revelation," CBQ 39 (1977) 344-66, and the further works by her cited in note 2 of that article. I agree with Fiorenza that the Apocalypse should be seen as a literary unity, and I also agree that content is intrinsically related with form in search for the meaning of the Apocalypse, but I disagree with her that an analysis of this document "has to employ ... structuralist and structural or architectural analysis." CBQ 39 (1977) 344.

5. G. Mussies, The Morphology of Koine Greek as Used in the Apocalypse of St. John: A Study in Bilingualism (SuppNovT 27; Leiden, 1971).

6. N. Turner, Style (A Grammar of New Testament Greek by J.H. Moulton, Vol. 4; Edinburgh, 1976).

7. See the discussion below on the possible sources behind the Apocalypse. For a report on research on the Jewish apocalypses see the following: J.M. Schmidt, Die jüdische Apokalyptik: Die Geschichte ihrer Erforschung von den Anfängen bis zu den Textfunden von Qumran (Neukirchen-Vluyn, 1976[2]); J. Schreiner, Alttestamentlich-Jüdische Apokalyptik: Eine Einführung (Biblische Handbibliothek 6; Munich, 1969); K. Koch, Ratlos vor der Apokalyptik (Gütersloh, 1970; ET 1972); J. Barr, "Jewish Apocalyptic in Recent Scholarly Study," BJRULM 58 (1975) 9-35; J.H. Charlesworth, The Pseudepigrapha and Modern Research with a Supplement (SBL Septuagint and Cognate Studies 7S; Chico, Calif., 1981--contains full bibliography); G.W.E. Nickelsburg, Jewish Literature Between the Bible and the Mishnah (Philadelphia, 1981); C. Münchow, Ethik und Eschatologie: Ein Beitrag zum Verständnis der frühjüdischen Apokalyptik (Berlin, 1981); and C. Rowland, The Open Heaven: A Study of Apocalyptic in Judaism and Early Christianity (New York, 1982).

8. P.D. Hanson, The Dawn of Apocalyptic: The Historical and Sociological Roots of Jewish Apocalyptic Eschatology (Philadelphia, 1979, revised edition). Hanson's work has major strengths and severe weaknesses, among the latter is the failure to include

in his discussion the non-Jewish "apocalypses" (see Part III where these are listed), and the Jewish apocalypses. P.G.R. de Villiers in "Renaissance van die sosiologiese teksanalise" (Theologia Evangelica 15 [1982] 19-35) calls for a more nuanced, sensitive, and perceptive social analysis of early Judaism than is found in Hanson's book.

9. I would allow for more foreign influence upon the development of Jewish apocalyptic thought than Hanson has been willing to admit. See, for example, the important study by H.-D. Betz, "Zum Problem des religionsgeschichtlichen Verständnisses der Apokalyptik," ZTK 63 (1966) 391-409; ET in Apocalypticism, ed. R.W. Funk (JTC 6; New York, 1969) pp. 134-56. Also see A. Yarbro Collins, "The History-of-Religions Approach to Apocalypticism and the 'Angel of the Waters' (Rev 16:4-7)," CBQ 31 (1977) 367-81.

10. G. von Rad is well known for arguing that Jewish apocalypticism evolved out of the wisdom tradition. See his Theologie des Alten Testaments (Munich, 1960), vol. 2, pp. 314-28 (ET: vol. 2, pp. 301-15); and his Weisheit in Israel (Neukirchen, 1970), pp. 344-62 (ET: pp. 269-82). K. Koch in Ratlos vor der Apokalyptik (Gütersloh, 1970, pp. 40-46 [ET: pp. 42-47]) severely criticized von Rad. The initial rejection of von Rad's position, however, has waned. Discussions have turned away from a dialogue with him, and scholars now recognize that the apocalypses are influenced by the wisdom tradition and that apocalypticism and wisdom are considerably interrelated. See the insightful publications by J.Z. Smith, esp. his "Wisdom and Apocalyptic," in Religious Syncretism in Antiquity: Essays in Conversation with Geo Widengren, ed. B.A. Pearson (Missoula, Mont., 1975), pp. 131-56; repr. in Visionaries and Their Apocalypses, ed. P.D. Hanson (Philadelphia, London, 1983), pp. 101-20.

J.J. Collins correctly argues for the different perspectives of wisdom and apocalypticism, but also for the significantly shared features (a shared "cosmological conviction," an appeal to understanding more than obedience, and an emphasis on the cosmos); see his "Cosmos and Salvation: Jewish Wisdom and Apocalyptic in the Hellenistic Age," History of Religion 17 (1977) 121-42. See M.E. Stone's perceptive observations in "Lists of Revealed Things in the Apocalyptic Literature," in Magnalia Dei: The Mighty Acts of God; Essays in the Bible and Archaeology in Memory of G. Ernest Wright, eds. F.M. Cross, et al. (New York, 1976), pp. 414-52. Also see R.A. Coughenour, Enoch and Wisdom: A Study of the Wisdom Elements of Ethiopic Enoch (Ph.D. Ann Arbor, 1972); Coughenour, "The Wisdom Stance of Enoch's Redactor," JSJ 13 (1982) 47-56. Coughenour claims "that the key to the compilation (of 1 Enoch) is the wisdom stance of its final editor" (p. 47). The best discussion of this issue is now found in two articles by M.A. Knibb: "Apocalyptic and Wisdom in 4 Ezra," JSJ 13 (1982) 56-74 and "Prophecy and the Emergence of the Jewish Apocalypses," in Israel's Prophetic Heritage: Essays in Honour of Peter R. Ackroyd, eds. R.J. Coggins, A. Phillips and M.A. Knibb (Cambridge, 1982), pp. 155-80. See also M.E. Stone's cautions, speculations, and judicious observations on the origin of apocalypticism and the wisdom traditions in his Scriptures,

Sects and Visions: A Profile of Judaism from Ezra to the Jewish Revolts (Philadelphia, 1980), pp. 42-47. C. Rowland offers some cautions about relating too closely wisdom and apocalypticism; see his
The Open Heaven, pp. 203-08. A very helpful discussion is also
found in F. Schmidt's "'Traqué comme un loup': A propos du débat
actuel sur l'apocalyptique juive," Archives de Sciences Sociales des
Religions 53 (1982) 5-21.
        11. See D.M. Rhoads, Israel in Revolution: 6-74 C.E. (Phila-
delphia, 1976).
        12. See J.H. Charlesworth, "Jesus and Jehohanan: An Arch-
aeological Note on Crucifixion," The Expository Times 84 (1973) 147-
50.
        13. Many testaments are heavily influenced by apocalypticism;
hence, I have labeled the second group of texts in The Old Testament Pseudepigrapha "Testaments (often with Apocalyptic Sections)."
        14. The Treatise of Shem is not an apocalypse; it is included
here because it is parallel to the astronomical concerns of the apocalypses, especially in 1 Enoch 72-82. Not all these Jewish apocalypses
are Palestinian; 2 Enoch and the Sibylline Oracles are connected with
Egypt. The list of nineteen early Jewish apocalypses could be expanded easily, with the recovery of lost works like the Apocalypse
of Lamech, and with documents from Qumran, especially 4Q Visions
de 'Amran. In other words, this list of nineteen is not exhaustive.
        15. J.J. Collins, "Introduction: Towards the Morphology of
a Genre," Apocalypse: The Morphology of a Genre (Semeia 14; Missoula, Montana, 1979), p. 9. The excerpt is in italics in this book.
Also see Collins, "Excursus on the Apocalyptic Genre," in Daniel,
1-2 Maccabees (Old Testament Message 16; Wilmington, Delaware,
1981), pp. 130-45; and "The Apocalyptic Context of Christian Origins," Michigan Quarterly Review 22 (1983) 250-64.
        16. Collins, Apocalypse, p. 9. Collins' problems are first the
preoccupation with form, forcing him to divorce unduly the content
of an apocalypse from the form, and, second, the tension between
his admission that "no one apocalypse contains all the elements" (p.
8) and his struggle to demonstrate that a "few elements are constant"
(p. 9).
        17. For another recent attempt to define "apocalyptic litera-
ture," see J.G. Gammie, "The Classification, Stages of Growth, and
Changing Intentions in the Book of Daniel," JBL 95 (1976) 191-204.
I am also impressed with J.Z. Smith's observations on the character-
istics of apocalypticism in Religious Syncretism, pp. 154-56.
        18. H. Anderson, "A Future for Apocalyptic?" Biblical Studies:
Essays in Honor of William Barclay, eds. J.R. McKay and J.F. Miller
(Philadelphia, 1976), p. 57; emphasis is his. P. Hanson has articulated a somewhat similar definition of apocalyptic thought, which he
calls "apocalyptic eschatology." Hanson's methodology is attractive
because of the sensitivity he shows to social phenomena. See his
"Apocalypticism," IDBS, pp. 28-34; The Dawn of Apocalyptic, rev.
ed. (Philadelphia, 1979).
        19. G.F. Moore claimed the Apocrypha and Pseudepigrapha of
the Old Testament represented "the religion of the times outside the

schools"; he claimed that "inasmuch as these writings have never been" recognized by Judaism, "it is a fallacy of method for the historian to make them a primary source for the eschatology of Judaism, much more to contaminate its theology with them" (vol. 1, p. 127). Judaism in the First Centuries of the Christian Era: The Age of the Tannaim, 3 vols. (Cambridge, Mass., 1927-30).

20. E.g., W.D. Davies aptly states that "apocalyptic and Pharisaism ... were not alien to each other but often, if not always, enjoyed a congenial coexistence." Paul and Rabbinic Judaism (New York, 1967 edition), p. xi.

21. J.H. Charlesworth, "The Origin and Subsequent History of the Authors of the Dead Sea Scrolls: Four Transitional Phases Among the Qumran Essenes," RQ 38 (1980) 213-33.

22. See the voluminous works by J. Neusner, notably his Judaism: The Evidence of the Mishnah (Chicago, London, 1981); see esp. pp. 28-37. Also see J. Stiassny, "L'occultation de l'apocalyptique dans le rabbinisme," in Apocalypses et théologie de l'espérance, ed. L. Monloubou (Lectio Divina 95; Paris, 1977), pp. 179-203; A.J. Saldarini, "The Uses of Apocalyptic in the Mishna and Tosepta," CBQ 39 (1977) 396-409; and C. Rowland, The Open Heaven, pp. 269-348. An erudite overview of the "Sages of the Oral Law" is found in E.E. Urbach, The Sages: Their Concepts and Beliefs, 2 vols., trans. J. Abrahams (Jerusalem, 1979). N.N. Glatzer in "The Attitude to Rome in the Amoraic Period," (Proceedings of the Sixth World Congress of Jewish Studies [Jerusalem, 1975], vol. 2, pp. 9-19) argues that in the third-century school of Rabbi Yohanan bar Nappah "the classical concept of an activist, militant messianism was transformed into--or replaced by--a pacifist, distant, quiet hope" (p. 9).

23. A. Yarbro Collins correctly states, "In Revelation, Hermas and the Book of Elchasai, the seer apparently uses his own name" (p. 67). See her "The Early Christian Apocalypses," in Semeia 14, pp. 61-103. Also see J. Collins "Pseudonymity, Historical Reviews and the Genre of the Revelation of John," CBQ 39 (1977) 329-43.

24. To put this observation into perspective, it should be noted that the Apocalypse does not quote a single full verse from the Old Testament, but nonetheless is heavily dependent upon it; as D.M. Smith remarks, the Apocalypse is "literally quite inconceivable apart from the Old Testament." See Smith's "The Use of the Old Testament in the New," in The Use of the Old Testament in the New and Other Essays: Studies in Honor of William Franklin Stinespring (Durham, N.C., 1972), pp. 3-65; the quotation is from pp. 61f.

25. I wish to express appreciations to my doctoral students who in two separate seminars helped me to search for possible quotations or dependences.

26. P.M. Bogaert also sees the importance of studying the Apocalypse with the "deux apocalypses--soeurs attribuées à Baruch et à Esdras." The issue is not whether the Apocalypse was literarily dependent on one or both of these Jewish apocalypses; the major point is that all three of these apocalypses come from the decades following the burning of the Temple and the cessation of the cult. See Bogaert's

"La ruine de Jérusalem et les apocalypses juives après 70," in Apocalypses et théologie de l'espérance, pp. 123-41; and idem, "Les apocalypses contemporaines de Baruch, d'Esdras et de Jean," in L'Apocalypse johannique et l'Apocalyptique dans le Nouveau Testament (BETL
53; Gembloux, Belgium, 1980), pp. 47-68.

    27. R.H. Charles, The Revelation of St. John, 2 vols. (ICC;
Edinburgh, 1920).

    28. See notes 5 and 6 above.

    29. See the discussion on the recapitulation theory by A. Yar-
bro Collins in The Combat Myth in the Book of Revelation (Harvard
Dissertations in Religion 9; Missoula, Mont., 1976), pp. 8-13, and in
The Apocalypse (New Testament Messages 22; Wilmington, Del., 1979),
pp. xii-xiv.

    30. M. Dibelius thought that the hymns in the Apocalypse were
derived from the liturgy of the early Church; see his "Zur Formges-
chichte des Neuen Testaments," Theologische Rundschau 3 (1931)
220. J.J. O'Rourke in "The Hymns of the Apocalypse" (CBQ 30
[1968] 399-409) tried to show that "John borrowed consciously from
pre-existing liturgical sources when he composed his book, it would
seem almost certain that he did when he wrote Ap 1,4.5. 8b; 4,8b;
7,12.15-17; 11,15.17-18; 19,5.66-8" (p. 409). L. Thompson in "Cult
and Eschatology in the Apocalypse of John" (JR 49 [1969] 330-50)
argues that "the worship life of the early church was the model for
the seer in his presentation of cult and eschatology" (p. 350).

    31. K.-P. Jörns has argued that "die hymnischen Stücke der
Apc sowohl in ihrer jetzigen Gestalt als auch in ihrer Stellung im
Aufbau der Apc vom Verfasser der Apokalypse selbst stammen" (p.
178). See his Das hymnische Evangelium (Gütersloh, 1971).

    32. J.M. Court, Myth and History in the Book of Revelation
(Atlanta, 1979).

    33. The author of the seven letters is to be identified with
the author of the apocalypse itself, chapters 4-22. He probably composed these letters at a different time, because only in 3:21 is Jesus
depicted as seated on a throne (as in Hebrews) and because there
are a few linguistic features peculiar to chapters 1-3 (cf. Turner,
Style, pp. 146, 154).

    34. M. Kiddle, assisted by M.K. Ross, The Revelation of St.
John (New York, London, 1940 [?]), p. 60.

    35. G.R. Beasley-Murray, The Book of Revelation (The New
Century Bible; Greenwood, S.C., 1978), p. 227.

    36. Charles, Revelation, vol. 1, p. 370.

    37. See T. Baumeister, Die Anfänge der Theologie des Mar-
tyriums (Münsterische Beiträge zur Theologie 45; Münster, 1980),
esp. see pp. 211-28.

    38. See the careful study by D.L. Jones, "Christianity and
the Roman Imperial Cult," ANRW II. 23.2 (1980) 1023-54, esp. see
pp. 1033-35.

    39. I am persuaded that the attempts to attribute Mk. 13:32
to the early Church have failed (pace Perrin); early Galilean miracle
workers were called the "Son of God" (cf. G. Vermes, Jesus the Jew
[London, 1973], pp. 192-213). It is possible that Mk 13:32 derives
ultimately from Jesus or Jesus' own time.

40. See P. Benoit, "L'évolution du langage apocalyptique dans le corpus paulinien," in Apocalypses et théologie de l'espérance, pp. 299-335. Also see J.C. Beker, Paul the Apostle: The Triumph of God in Life and Thought (Philadelphia, 1980); Beker, Paul's Apocalyptic Gospel: The Coming Triumph of God (Philadelphia, 1982), and Baumeister, Die Anfänge, pp. 156-91. E. P. Sanders warns against identifying Paul's "pattern of religion" with any of the manifestations of religion in Palestinian Judaism, yet he admits a general similarity between Paul's view and apocalypticism. See Sanders' careful and detailed Paul and Palestinian Judaism: A Comparison of Patterns of Religion (Philadelphia, 1977). Also, see the Bibliography, 2.7, 2.29. Also see two chapters in Paul and Paulinism: Essays in Honour of C. K. Barrett, ed. M. D. Hooker and S. G. Wilson (London, 1982), namely J. M. Court, "Paul and the Apocalyptic Pattern" (pp. 57-66), and A. F. J. Klijn, "1 Thessalonians 4:13-18 and its Background in Apocalyptic Literature" (pp. 67-73). Finally, see H.-H. Schade, Apokalyptische Christologie bei Paulus (Göttinger Theologische Arbeiten 18; Göttingen, 1981).

41. H. C. Kee even sees Mark as the product of an early Christian apocalyptic group. See his Community of the New Age: Studies in Mark's Gospel (Philadelphia, 1977); for the social setting see pp. 77-105. Also see P. Patten, "The Form and Function of Parable in Select Apocalyptic Literature and Their Significance for Parables in the Gospel of Mark," NTS 29 (1983) 246-58.

42. M. Merleau-Ponty perceptively states that "I ... cannot conceive a perceptible place in which I am not myself present." See Merleau-Ponty, "The Primacy of Perception and Its Philosophical Consequences," The Primacy of Perception and Other Essays, ed. and trans. J. M. Edie (Evanston, Ill., 1964), part 1, ch. 2, pp. 12-27 [reprinted in Essential Writings, pp. 47-63, quotation is on p. 51].

43. I have been moving in the direction of acknowledging with J. Z. Smith that apocalypticism is a scribal and learned phenomenon. See Smith in Religious Syncretism in Antiquity, esp. pp. 140, 154-56.

44. See P. Alexander's introduction to and translation of 3 Enoch in The Old Testament Pseudepigrapha, vol. 1, pp. 223-315. Also see I. Gruenwald, Apocalyptic and Merkavah Mysticism (AGAJU 14; Leiden, 1980); and D.J. Halperin, The Merkabah in Rabbinic Literature (American Oriental Series 62; New Haven, Conn., 1980).

45. See the commentary by A. Yarbro Collins in Semeia 14, pp. 61-69.

46. The only earlier survey was H. Weinel's, "Die spätere christliche Apokalyptik," Eucharistērion [Gunkel Festschrift]. Göttingen, 1923; vol. 2, pp. 141-73.

47. B. McGinn, Apocalyptic Spirituality: Treatises and Letters of Lactantius Adso of Montier-en-der, Jochaim of Fiore, the Franciscan Spirituals, Savonarola (New York, 1979). B. McGinn, Visions of the End: Apocalyptic Traditions in the Middle Ages (Records of Civilization: Sources and Studies 96; New York, 1979). Also note the excellent bibliography on pp. 347-63.

48. N. Cohn, The Pursuit of the Millennium: Revolutionary

Millenarians and Mystical Anarchists of the Middle Ages (New York,
1970, revised and expanded edition).

    49. Esp. see M. Reeves, The Influence of Prophecy in the
Later Middle Ages: A Study of Joachimism (Oxford, 1969), and with
B. Hirsch-Reich, The Figurae of Joachim of Fiore (Oxford, 1972).
See also the important chapters in A. Williams (ed.), Prophecy and
Millenarianism: Essays in Honour of Marjorie Reeves (Burnt Hill,
Harlow, Essex, 1980), especially see M.W. Bloomfield, "Recent Schol-
arship on Joachim of Fiore and His Influence" (pp. 21-52); P.J. Alex-
ander, "The Diffusion of Byzantine Apocalypses in the Medieval West
and the Beginnings of Joachimism" (pp. 53-106); R. Bauckham, "The
Figurae of John of Patmos," (pp. 107-25); B. McGinn, "Symbolism in
the Thought of Joachim of Fiore," (pp. 143-64); F. Seibt, "Liber Fi-
gurarum XII and the Classical Ideal of Utopia," (pp. 257-66).

    50. P.J. Alexander, "Medieval Apocalypses as Historical
Sources, "American Historical Review 73 (1968) 1997-2018; The Oracle
of Baalbek: The Tiburtine Sibyl in Greek Dress (Washington, D.C.,
1967).

    51. See notes 46 and 47 above.

    52. See E. Turdeanu's "Dieu créa l'homme de huit éléments
et tira son nom des quatre coins du monde," Revue des Études Rou-
maines 13-14 (1974) 163-94. The medieval Bogomils' thought was
partly produced by the old apocalypses. See the discussion on the
Jewish origin of 2 Enoch by N.A. Meshchersky in his "On the Question
of the Source of the Slavonic Book of Enoch," Vizantiiskii Unemennik
24 (1964) 91-108 [Russian].

    53. See the handy Greek-English edition produced by R. Cam-
eron and A.J. Dewey titled The Cologne Mani Codex (Texts and Translations 15; Early Christian Literature Series 3; Missoula, Mont., 1979).

    54. See the bibliography below under Testamentum Domini
(Epistle of the Apostles).

    55. See the new texts and translations by S.E. Robinson,
The Testament of Adam (SBL Dissertation Series 52; Chico, Calif.,
1982).

    56. The History of the Rechabites is not an apocalypse; see
Charlesworth, The History of the Rechabites (Texts and Translations
17, Pseudepigrapha Series 10; Chico, Calif., 1982).

    57. See the following bibliography.

    58. See the following bibliography.

    59. See the following bibliography.

    60. See the following bibliography.

    61. For a translation see B. McGinn, Visions of the End, pp.
60f.

    62. See, for example, E.A. Wallis Budge, The Life and Ex-
ploits of Alexander the Great, 2 vols. (London, 1896; repr. New York,
London, 1968), esp. see vol. 1, pp. 259-353 [Ethiopic text] and vol.
2, pp. 437-553 [ET].

    63. See the introduction and translation in McGinn, Visions of
the End, pp. 56-59; also see p. 73.

    64. See the following bibliography.

    65. See Charlesworth, "Christian and Jewish Self-Definition in

Light of the Christian Additions to the Apocryphal Writings," Jewish and Christian Self-Definition: Aspects of Judaism in the Graeco-Roman Period, eds. E.P. Sanders, A.I. Baumgarten and A. Mendelson (Philadelphia, 1981), vol. 2, pp. 27-55, 310-15.

66. Underlining denotes the probable dates of the Jewish base. Also see the important discussions by V. MacDermot and the texts collected by her in The Cult of the Seer in the Ancient Middle East (Berkeley and Los Angeles, 1971).

67. The Apocalypse never became part of the Peshitta.

68. See the translations published under the general editorship of J.M. Robinson in The Nag Hammadi Library in English (New York, London, 1977). Also see F.T. Fallon, "The Gnostic Apocalypses," in Semeia 14, pp. 123-58.

69. P. Vielhauer in HSW. 2, pp. 581-600.

70. K. Rudolph, "Gnosis and Gnostizismus, ein Forschungsbericht," ThRu 34 (1969) 121-75, 181-231, 353-61.

71. F.T. Fallon in Semeia 14, p. 124.

72. K. Lake correctly reported "that though the form of the book is apocalyptic and visionary, its object is practical and ethical" (vol. 2, p. 2). See his Apostolic Fathers (LCL 25; London, Cambridge, Mass., 1913). J. Quasten was very impressed by the form of Hermas, stating that "Hermas belongs in reality to the apocryphal apocalypses" (vol. 1, p. 92). See his Patrology (Utrecht-Antwerp; Westminster, Md., 1963). See the discussion in Part III.

73. ET by O.S. Wintermute in The Old Testament Pseudepigrapha, vol. 1, pp. 736f.

74. Translated by H. Duensing and E. Best and published in HSW. 2, p. 767.

75. Translated by Duensing and Best in HSW. 2, p. 773.

76. Translated by Duensing and Best in HSW. 2, p. 787.

77. Biblical codices often preserve along with the canonical documents one or more of the extra-canonical workings. Codex Sinaiticus, for example, contains Hermas (or at least part of it; the ending is lost).

78. Among the classical Jewish apocalypses, the Apocalypse of Zephaniah stresses in an unparalleled way the tortures for the unrighteous in the future. McGinn (Visions of the End, pp. 148) judges that the preoccupation with the fate of the individual produces a new genre of literature, namely the visions.

79. Yarbro Collins states that, in contrast to the classical Jewish apocalypses, the early Christian apocalypses have a limited interest in the past. See her comments in Semeia 14, pp. 63, 64, and 67. As we shall see, this early characteristic of the Christian apocalypses shifts significantly after circa the sixth or seventh centuries, or at least before the eighth century C.E.

80. A. de Santos Otero in HSW. 2, p. 799.

81. Translation by A. Walker and published in ANF. 8, p. 584.

82. Other passages in The First Revelation of John are, of course, reminiscent of the Apocalypse. The description of the heavenly realm as being without night ("all is day") may come from Ap

21:25; but this idea is found in many apocalypses and apocalyptically
related documents (e.g., HistRech 12:1,8).

83. The Apocalypse depicts a <u>new</u> earth; The First Revelation
of John sees a <u>purified</u> earth. Those are two opposite alternatives
in the history of apocalypticism.

84. <u>The Old Testament Pseudepigrapha</u>; vol. 1, pp. 756-70.

85. See L. Rydén, "The Andreas Salos Apocalypse: Greek
Text, Translation, and Commentary," <u>Dumbarton Oaks Papers</u> 28
(1974) 199-261, the quotation is from p. 223.

86. See also A. Yarbro Collins in Semeia 14, p. 67.

87. Augustine, of course, de-apocalypticized the Apocalypse;
the millennial reign (Ap 20) was not a future event, but the present
Church. As P. Brown states, "The <u>City of God</u>, far from being a
book about flight from the world, is a book whose recurrent theme
is 'our business within this common mortal life' (de civ. <u>Dei</u>, XV, 21,
15); it is a book about being other-wordly in the world." <u>Augustine</u>
<u>of Hippo: A Biography</u> (Berkeley and Los Angeles, 1967, 1969), p.
324. The Council at Ephesus in 431 marked the triumph of Augustine's
interpretation of the millennium as the history of the Church; see F.
Rapp, "Apocalypse et mouvements populaires au moyen age," in <u>L'</u>
<u>Apocalyptique</u>, ed. M. Philoneneko (EHR 3; Paris, 1977), pp. 213-32.

88. See W. Kamlah, <u>Apocalypse und Geschichtstheologie: Die</u>
<u>Mittelalterliche Auslegung der Apokalypse vor Joachim von Fiore</u> (Ber-
lin, 1934; reprinted 1965).

89. The continuing interest in apocalypticism is reflected in
Christian circles by the abundance of reflection on the Antichrist,
especially the tracts by Adso of Monter-en-Der (X cent.), Peter Da-
mian (XI cent.), and Honorius Augustodunensis (XII cent.). These
and related issues are discussed in R.E. Lerner's "Refreshment of
the Saints: The Time After Antichrist as a Station for Earthly Progress in Medieval Thought," <u>Traditio</u> 32 (1976) 97-144; in H.D. Rauh's
<u>Das Bild des Antichrist im Mittelalter: Von Tyconius zum Deutschen</u>
<u>Symbolismus</u> (Beiträge zur Geschichte der Philosophie und Theologie
des Mittelalters n.F. 9; Aschendorff, 1979[2]); and in J.M. Rosenstiehl,
"Le portrait de l'Antichrist," <u>Pseudépigraphes</u>, ed. M. Philonenko;
pp. 45-60. Also, see the insightful comments by J.R. Mueller and
G.A. Robbins in "Vision of Ezra," in <u>The Old Testament Pseudepi-</u>
<u>grapha</u>, vol. 1, pp. 581-90.

90. Cohn claims to have "adequately indicated" the "social
composition of these sects and movements, and the social settings in
which they operated" (<u>The Pursuit of the Millennium</u> "Foreword,"
pages unnumbered). Cohn limited his study "to northern and central
Europe," and although his erudite book is a landmark in the field of
medieval apocalypticism, he incorrectly sees millenarianism as a characteristic of the "rootless poor" who employed the "phantasies" to in-
flame revolts. McGinn, with refreshingly more appreciation for apocalypticism, correctly attempted to show that it "could be used for a
variety of purposes, not only in criticism of the powers of this world,
but also in their behalf" (<u>Apocalyptic Spirituality</u>, p. 11). Years
ago, R.C. Petry drew attention to the social dimensions of apocalypticism and eschatology; see his <u>Christian Eschatology and Social</u>

Thought: A Historical Essay on the Social Implications of Some Se-
lected Aspects in Christian Eschatology to A.D. 1500 (New York,
1956).

91. McGinn, Apocalyptic Spirituality, p. 100.

92. See the illustrations in G. Quispell, The Secret Book of
Revelation (London, 1979).

93. This continuum is a key to understanding the motives of
people of action, like the crusaders, and explorers, notably Chris-
topher Columbus, who was a visionary influenced by Josephus (the
first-century C.E. Jewish historian and apologist) and Joachim. See
McGinn, Visions of the End, pp. 284f.

94. Perusals of monographs on Dante and the articles in Dante
Studies (formerly Dante Society Annual Report) disclose an appreciation of Dante's indebtedness to Virgil, Aquinas, Augustine, and the
Exodus and Sinai typology in the Bible, but nothing regarding his
dependence on the Christian apocryphal apocalypses. J.G. Demaray
in The Invention of Dante's "Commedia" (New Haven, 1974; p. 4)
correctly laments the confinement in commentaries on Dante to the
Latin canon. Present work on Dante has concentrated too heavily
on the poetry and literary structure of The Divine Comedy; we need
to shift again to an examination of its literary antecedents. See H.
Hatzfeld, "Modern Literary Scholarship as Reflected in Dante Criticism," American Critical Essays on The Divine Comedy, ed. R.J.
Clements (New York, 1967) pp. 195-219.

95. K. Kohler also made this claim in his Heaven and Hell in
Comparative Religion (New York, 1928), p. 93. J. Quasten in his
Patrology (Westminster, Md., 1962), vol. 1, p. 147, also judged that
Dante in Canto 2.28 "alludes to" the Apocalypse of Paul. Dante's
indebtedness to this apocalypse is affirmed by Ch. Maurer in HSW.
2, p. 667. See Th. Silverstein, "Did Dante Know the Vision of St.
Paul?" Harvard Studies and Notes in Philology and Literature 19
(1937) 231-47.

96. The notes have been selective. With Peter Brown (Augustine, p. 10) I expect "that the books and articles that I have included, will be like plants, which, when pulled up, will reveal the
full ramifications of the root-system of modern studies" on the continuum of the apocalypses. One will, of course, consult the publications cited in the Bibliography, especially "2. Apocalyptic."

PART III: THE CONTINUUM OF JEWISH AND
CHRISTIAN APOCALYPSES--TEXTS AND
ENGLISH TRANSLATIONS

One of the purposes of Part II was to draw attention to the vast number of unexamined apocalypses. Scholars' interest has been focused
upon either the early Jewish apocalypses and apocalyptic literature,
or upon the Apocalypse of John, or upon the apocalyptic passages
in the canonical texts, or upon some of the earliest Christian apocalypses and medieval apocalyptic writings. As B. McGinn states, this
preoccupation "has led to some neglect of the continuity of these traditions in later ages."[1] Yet even McGinn, who has made significant
contributions to the study of medieval apocalyptic thought, has not
included in his studies all the extant apocalypses. There is not only
a continuum of apocalypticism, but also a continuum of apocalypses;
yet both tend to remain unrecognized. The main reasons for this
myopia is our separation into specialties, the fact that the terrain is
unchartered, the predilection for an analytical study of the documents,
and the tendency to publish research in specialized periodicals that
are often extremely difficult to locate. The net has now been cast
and the apocalypses have been collected together for a proper synthesis.

DESCRIPTION OF AN APOCALYPSE

In order to compile the list of apocalypses I had to clarify my
own thinking on what distinguishes an apocalypse from another writing. An apocalypse cannot be defined; it can only be described.
An apocalypse, therefore, is a writing almost always in narrative
form, which employs personified mythological language and purports
to reveal something significantly new about the present and what is
soon to happen in the future, in terms of a visit, through vision or
audition, really or imaginatively, to the world above or the age to
come.

Apocalypses are revelatory writings; they represent a recog-
nizable literary genre, and usually reflect the literary form of the
Apocalypse of John. Their major characteristic is the eschatological
tone and correlative disenchantment with present meaningless history.
To be distinguished from the apocalypses is apocalypticism; the latter
refers not to a category of literature, but to a religious perspective,

which sees meaning, impossible in the present, as coming from the disclosure or revelation (apokalupsis Rev. 1:1) of an impending cosmic and dynamic action by God, an act so final that it divides all history, even perhaps ends it, and can be seen often rippling through present chaotic crises. Apocalypticism, therefore, can denote socioreligious phenomena.

The word "apocalyptic" is an adjective; it should not be used as a noun. Ironically, many scholars acknowledge this fact and then refer to "Jewish apocalyptic," when what is meant is either the Jewish apocalypses or Jewish apocalypticism. Much confusion has been caused by such imprecise nomenclature. As an adjective, "apocalyptic" can refer either to influences from apocalypticism or from one or more of the apocalypses. Careful and precise writing will clarify the meaning of the adjective.

EXCLUDED "APOCALYPSES"

Perhaps some apocalypses have been inadvertently missed; I apologize for the oversight, recognizing full well that this prolegomenous publication will be improved by others. Two groups of texts, however, have been removed by design from the following chart. First, the non-Jewish and non-Christian apocalyptic writings, some of which have been seen to be apocalypses, have not been listed. Among this group should be listed at least the following:

Egyptian[2]
  The Shipwrecked Sailor (c. 200 B.C.E.)
  Prince Satni and the Magic Book (c. 300 B.C.E.-100 C.E.)
  The Demotic Chronical (III-II B.C.E.)
  Potter's Oracle (IV-II B.C.E.)
  The Lamb to Bocchoris (? I C.E.)
  The Asclepius Apocalypse (before 200 C.E.)
  Poimandres (II C.E.?)
  Kore Kosmu (Maiden of the Cosmos) (II C.E.?)

Babylonian or Akkadian[3]
  Berossus (early Hellenistic)

Persian[4]
  Zand-ī Vohuman Yasn (Hellenistic)
  The Oracle of Hystaspes (II-I B.C.E.)
  Zāmāsp-Nāmak (?)
  Ard Viraf Nāmeh (? III B.C.E.-IX C.E.)
  Bundahis (?)
  Dēnkārt (?)

Greek and Latin[5]
  Plato's "Myth of Er" (IV B.C.E.)
  Cicero's Somnium Scripionis (I B.C.E.)

Plutarch's De genio Socratis (I/II C.E.)
Plutarch's De sera nominis vindicta (I/II C.E.)
Plutarch's De facie lunae (I/II C.E.)
Virgil's Fourth Eclogue (I B.C.E.)

These writings are considerably different from those listed below, and there is reason to suspect that not one of them is really an
apocalypse.

Also excluded from the following list are the late rabbinic or
medieval apocalyptically related writings, such as those recently examined by I. Gruenwald (Apocalyptic and Merkavah Mysticism; Leiden,
1980), D.J. Halperin (The Merkabah in Rabbinic Literature; New
Haven, Conn., 1980), and P. Schäfer (with M. Schlüter and H.G.
von Mutius, Synopse zur Hekhalot-Literatur [Texte und Studien zum
Antiken Judentum 2], Tübingen, 1981).

A LIST OF APOCALYPSES

The list is compiled to assist the study of these apocalypses.
It is simply a guide to apparently the best texts and translations.
Only English translations are listed, but if the work has not been
translated into English, another translation is cited. All abbreviations used in the columns are explained in alphabetical order immediately following the present list.

(1) Classical Jewish Apocalypses and Related Documents
(c. 200 B.C.E. to c. 135 C.E.)

			Text	ET
1.	Daniel 7-12	(II B.C.E.)	BHS	RSV
2.	1 Enoch	(II B.C.E.-I C.E.)	MAK	OTP
3.	Testament of Moses	(II B.C.E.-I C.E.)	RHC[1]	OTP
4.	Jubilees 23	(II B.C.E.)	RHC[2]	OTP
5.	Sibylline Oracle Book 3	(II B.C.E.)	JG	OTP
6.	Ascension of Isaiah 1:1- 3:12, 5:1-14 (= Martyr- dom of Isaiah)	(II B.C.E.)	RHC[3]	OTP
7.	Testaments of the Twelve Patriarchs (esp. TLevi 2-5, 14-18; TJudah 21- 24; TDan 5:7-13)	(II B.C.E.)	MdeJ	OTP
8.	Treatise of Shem	(I B.C.E.)	JHC[1]	OTP
9.	Sibylline Oracle Book 4	(I C.E.)	JG	OTP
10.	Testament of Abraham	(I-II C.E.)	MRJ	OTP
11.	4 Ezra	(I C.E.)	B/G	OTP
12.	2 Baruch	(I-II C.E.)	SD	OTP
13.	3 Baruch	(I-II C.E.)	JCP	OTP

			Text	ET
			Text	ET
14.	2 Enoch	(I C.E.)	AV	OTP
15.	Apocalypse of Abraham	(I-II C.E.)	NT	OTP
16.	Sibylline Oracle Book 5	(II C.E.)	JG	OTP
17.	Apocryphon of Ezekiel	(I B.C.E.-I C.E.)	AMD	OTP
18.	Apocalypse of Zephaniah	(I B.C.E.-I C.E.)	GS	OTP
19.	Apocalypse of Adam (?)	(I-IV C.E.)	BL	OTP

(2) Jewish Apocalypses Significantly Expanded by Christians
(underlining denotes the probable date of the Jewish base)[6]

			Text	ET
1.	Testaments of the Twelve	(II B.C.E.; II-		
		III C.E.)	MdeJ	OTP
2.	Ascension of Isaiah	(II B.C.E.; II C.E.)	RHC[3]	OTP
3.-	5, 6 Ezra	(4 Ezra: I C.E.; II-		
4.		III C.E.)	B/G	OTP
5.-	Christian Sibyllines	(Bk 3: II B.C.E.,		
9.		Bk 4: I C.E., Bk 5:		
		II C.E.; Bks 1, 2, 8,		
		6, 7: II C.E.)	JG	OTP
10.	Apocalypse of Abraham	(I C.E.; II-X		
		C.E.?)	NST	OTP
11.	Ladder of Jacob	(I C.E.?; II C.E.?)	NYP[1]	OTP
12.	Testament of Isaac	(TAb: I-II C.E.;		
		I-V C.E.)	KHK	OTP
13.	Testament of Jacob	(TAb: I-II C.E.;		
		II-V C.E.)	IG	OTP

(3) Gnostic "Apocalypses" in NH Codices 5 and 7

			Text	ET
1.	(Nag Hammadi) Apoca-			
	lypse of Paul	(II-III C.E.)	FE	JMR
2.	First Apocalypse of James	(II-III C.E.)	FE	JMR
3.	Second Apocalypse of			
	James	(II-III C.E.)	FE	JMR
4.	Apocalypse of Adam	(I-III C.E.)	FE	JMR
5.	(Nag Hammadi) Apoca-			
	lypse of Peter	(III C.E.)	FE	JMR

(4) Patristic Apocalypses or Early Christian Apocryphal Apocalypses

			Text	ET
1.	Didache XVI	(I-II C.E.)	KL	KL
2.	Hermas	(I-II C.E.)	KL	KL
3.	Apocalypse of Peter	(c. 135 C.E.)	HD	HSW
4.	Book of Elchasai	(II C.E.)	AH	HSW
5.	Apocalypse of Zechariah [lost]	(II-III C.E.?)		(WS)
6.	Apocalypse of Elijah	(I-IV C.E.)	GS	OTP
7.	Apocalypse of Sedrach	(II-IV C.E.)	OW	OTP
8.	Apocalypse of Paul	(III-IV C.E.)	AA1	ANT

(5) Early Medieval Christian Apocryphal Apocalypses

			Text	ET
1.	Apocalypse of Thomas	(IV-V C.E.)	B	ANT
2.	1 Revelation of John	(V-VI C.E.)	KT	AW
3.	2 Revelation of John	(VI-VIII C.E.)	FN	FN
4.	3 Revelation of John	(pre-XI C.E.)	Coptic Apoc.	Coptic Apoc.
5.	Apocalypse of Ezra	(II-IX C.E.)	OW	OTP
6.	Vision of Ezra	(IV-VII C.E.)	OW	OTP
7.	Questions of Ezra	(VI-XI C.E.)	NYP[2]	OTP
8.	Revelation of Ezra	(pre-IX C.E.)	GM	OTP
9.	Seventh Vision of Daniel	(pre-VIII C.E.)	SY	JI
10.	Vision of Enoch	(pre-VIII C.E.)	SY	JI
11.	Apocalypse of the Virgin (or Mary)	(IX C.E.)	AA1	Apoc. del NT
12.	Apocalypse of Daniel	(IX C.E.)	KB	OTP
13.	Andreas Salos Apocalypse	(X C.E.)	LR	LR

(6) Documents Often Considered to Be "Apocalypses"

		Text	ET
1.	"The Apocalypse of Bartholomew" (This work should be called The Book of Bartholomew.)	Coptic Apoc.	Coptic Apoc.
2.	"The Apocalypse of Zosimus" (This work should be called The History of the Rechabites.)	JHC[2]	OTP
3.	Revelation of Steven	SV	ANT
4.	Apocalypse of Philip	WS	WS

	Text	ET

5. "The Apocalypse of Andrew and Paul" (This
work should be called The Acts of Andrew
and Paul.)   GZ   FHH

This list again illustrates the confusion and misunderstanding
caused by misleading, inaccurate, even false titles. Scribes added
the title "Apocalypse" to many documents that are not apocalypses;
the Ancients did not define or describe what is meant by "apocalypse";
we no longer have the luxury of such ambivalence.

ABBREVIATIONS FOR THE LIST

AA1   M.R. James, Apocrypha Anecdota (T&S 2.3; Cam-
                            bridge, 1893; repr. 1967).
AH   A. Hilgenfeld, Novum testamentum extra canonum
                            receptum (Leipzig, 1881), vol. 3, pt. 2, pp.
                            227-40.
AMD   A.-M. Denis, Fragmenta pseudepigraphorum quae
                            supersunt graeca (PVTG 3; Leiden, 1970).
ANT   M.R. James, The Apocryphal New Testament (Ox-
                            ford, 1924; repr. 1926-1969).
Apocalypses   K. Tischendorf, Apocalypses Apocryphae: Mosis,
    Apocryphae   Esdrae, Pauli, item Mariae dormitio: Additis
                            Evangeliorum et actuum apocryphorum supple-
                            mentis (Leipzig, 1866; repr. 1966).
Apoc. del NT   M. Erbetta, Gli Apocrifi del Nuovo Testamento,
                            3 vols. (Turin, 1966-75).
AV   A. Vaillant, Le Livre des Secrets d'Hénoch:
                            Texte slave et traduction française (Paris,
                            1952; repr. 1976).
AW   A. Walker, "Revelation of John," ANF. 8, pp.
                            582-86.
B   R.J. Bidawid, "4 Esdras," Peshitta. Part 4,
                            fasc. 3 (Leiden, 1973) i-iv, 1-50. [Syr. text]
BHS   Biblia Hebraica Stuttgartensia, ed. R. Kittel et
                            al. (Stuttgart, 1977).
BL   A. Böhlig and P. Labib, Koptisch-gnostische
                            Apokalypsen aus Codex V von Nag Hammadi
                            im Koptischen Museum zu Alt-Kairo (Halle,
                            1963). Also see FE, below.
Coptic Apoc.   E.A. Wallis Budge, Coptic Apocrypha in the Dia-
                            lect of Upper Egypt, Edited with English Trans-
                            lations (London, 1913).
DPB   D.P. Bihlmeyer, "Un texte non interpolé de l'
                            Apocalypse de Thomas," RBen 28 (1911) 270-
                            82.
FE   The Facsimile Edition of the Nag Hammadi Codices
                            (Leiden, 1972-).

FHH   F. H. Hallock, "An Apocalypse of SS. Andrew
and Paul," Journal of the Society of Oriental
Research 13 (1929) 190-94.

FN   F. Nau, "Une deuxième apocalypse apocryphe
grecque de saint Jean," RB n.s. 11 (1914):
209-21. [Contains Gk. text and French translation.]

G   L. Gry, Les dires prophétiques d'Esdras, 2 vols.
(Paris, 1938).

GM   G. Mercati, Note di letteratura biblica e christiana antica (Studi e Testi 5; Rome, 1901).

GS   G. Steindorff, Die Apokalypse des Elias: Eine
Unbekannte Apokalypse und Bruchstücke der
Sophonias-Apokalypse: Koptische Text, Über-
setzung, Glossar (TU n.F. 2.3a; Leipzig, 1899).

GZ   G. Zoëga, Catalogus codicum copticorum (Rome,
1810; repr. 1973), pp. 230-35.

HD   H. Duensing, "Ein Stücke der urchristlichen Petrusapokalypse enthaltender Traktat der äthiopischen Pseudoklementinischen Literatur,"
ZNW 14 (1913) 65-78.

HSW   E. Hennecke, New Testament Apocrypha, eds. W.
Schneemelcher and R. McL. Wilson, 2 vols.
(Philadelphia, 1963, 1965).

IG   I. Guidi, "Il Testamento di Isacco e il Testamento
di Giaccobo," Rendiconti della Reale Accademia
dei Lincei, Classe di scienze morali, storiche
e filologiche. Ser. 5, vol. 9 (1900), pp. 157-
80, 223-64.

JCP   J.C. Picard, Apocalypsis Baruchi Graece (PVTG
2; Leiden, 1967), pp. 61-96.

JG   J. Geffcken, Die Oracula Sibyllina (GCS; Leipzig,
1902; repr. 1970).

JHC[1]   J.H. Charlesworth, "Die Schrift des Sem: Einführung, Text, und Übersetzung," ANRW
(Berlin, in press).

JHC[2]   J.H. Charlesworth, The History of the Rechabites
(SBL Texts and Translations 17; Pseudepi-
grapha Series 10; Chico, CA, 1982).

JI   J. Issaverdens, The Uncanonical Writings of the
Old Testament (Venice, 1901; repr. 1907, 1934).

JMR   J.M. Robinson (ed.), The Nag Hammadi Library
in English (New York, London, 1977).

KB   K. Berger, Die griechische Daniel-Diegese (Studia
Post-Biblica 27; Leiden, 1976).

KHK   K.H. Kuhn, "The Sahidic Version of the Testament of Isaac," JTS N.S. 8 (1957) 226-39.

KL   K. Lake, The Apostolic Fathers, 2 vols. (LCL;
Cambridge, Mass., 1912, 1913; repr. 1965).

LR   L. Rydén, "The Andreas Salos Apocalypse:
Greek Text, Translation, and Commentary,"
Dumbarton Oaks Papers 28 (1974) 199-261.

MAK   M.A. Knibb, The Ethiopic Book of Enoch: A
                     New Edition in the Light of the Aramaic Dead
                     Sea Fragments, 2 vols., with the assistance
                     of E. Ullendorff (Oxford, 1978).

MdeJ   M. de Jonge and H.W. Hollander, H.J. de Jonge,
                     Th. Korteweg, The Testaments of the Twelve
                     Patriarchs: A Critical Edition of the Greek
                     Text (PVTG 1.2; Leiden, 1978).

MRJ   M.R. James, The Testament of Abraham: The
                     Greek Text Now First Edited with an Intro-
                     duction and Notes (Cambridge, 1892) [The
                     Gk. text is reprinted in M.E. Stone, The Tes-
                     tament of Abraham: The Greek Recensions
                     (SBL Texts and Translations 2; Pseudepigrapha
                     Series 2; Missoula, Mont., 1972).]

NST   N.S. Tikhonravov, Pami͡atniki͡ otrechennoĭ russkoĭ
                     literatury (St. Petersburg, 1863), vol. 1, pp.
                     32-53.

NYP[1]   Not yet published, but cf. NST (vol. 1, pp. 91-
                     95) for an older edition of some texts.

NYP[2]   J.R. Mueller, ed., Documents in the Ezra Cycle
                     (SBL Texts and Translations; Pseudepigrapha
                     Series), in preparation.

OTP   Old Testament Pseudepigrapha, ed. J.H. Charles-
                     worth, 2 vols. (Garden City, N.Y., 1983-85).

OW   O. Wahl, ed., Apocalypsis Esdrae, Apocalypsis
                     Sedrach, Visio Beati Esdrae (PVTG 4) Leiden,
                     1977.

RHC[1]   R.H. Charles, The Assumption of Moses Trans-
                     lated from the Latin Sixth Century MS., The
                     Emended Text of Which Is Published Herewith,
                     Together with the Text in Its Restored and
                     Critically Emended Form (London, 1897).

RHC[2]   R.H. Charles, The Ethiopic Version of the He-
                     brew Book of Jubilees (Oxford, 1895).

RHC[3]   R.H. Charles, The Ascension of Isaiah, Translated
                     from the Ethiopic Version, Which, Together
                     with the New Greek Fragment, the Latin Ver-
                     sions and the Latin Translation of the Slavonic,
                     Is Here Published in Full (London, 1900).

RSV   Revised Standard Version.

SD   S. Dedering, "Apocalypse of Baruch," Peshiṭta
                     Part 4, fasc. 3 (Leiden, 1973), pp. i-iv, 1-50.

SV   S. Vanderlinden, "Revelatio S. Stephani," REByz
                     1 (1946): 178-217.

SY   S. Yovsepʿiancʿ, Collection of Uncanonical Writings
                     of the Old Testament (Venice, 1896). [Armenian
                     texts].

WS   W. Stokes, "The Evernew Tongue," Ériu 2 (1905)
                     96-162; 3 (1907) 34f. [text and ET]. Stokes
                     thought the Evernew Tongue, which is Philip

the Apostle, had quoted from a Latin work
titled the Apocalypse of Philip. R. Flower
agreed with Stokes in his Catalogue of Irish
Manuscripts in the British Museum (London,
1926) vol. 2, p. 557. M.R. James argued
that the lost Latin text was not an apocalypse,
but was perhaps, related to the Acts of Philip;
see his "Irish Apocrypha," JTS 20 (1919):
9-16, esp. p. 10. M. McNamara in The Apocrypha in the Irish Church (pp. 115-18) rightly
warns that "it is difficult to determine what
sources the author used" (p. 115). There is
no reason to assume the existence of an Apocalypse of Philip.

(WS)   W. Schneemelcher, "Later Apocalypses," in HSW.2,
pp. 752f. [Not a translation, but a good brief
introduction with bibliography.]

NOTES

1. B. McGinn, Visions of the End, p. 2. H. Schwartz in "The
End of the Beginning: Millenarian Studies, 1969-1975," (Religious
Studies Review 2 [1976] 1-15) sees a growing recognition of the continuity of apocalypticism. Even if this is an accurate assessment,
virtually no one is looking at all the extant apocalypses or perceiving the continuity of apocalypses.
2. See the valuable--albeit dated--insights by C. C. McCown
in "Hebrew and Egyptian Apocalyptic Literature," HTR 18 (1925)
357-411. Translations of the Egyptian "apocalypses":
    Shipwrecked Sailor
        ET: W.M. Flinders-Petrie, "The Shipwrecked Sailor," Egypt,
        ed. C. F. Horne (The Sacred Books and Early Literature
        of the East 2) New York, London, 1917, pp. 133-37.
    Prince Satni
        ET: G. Maspero, "Prince Satni and the Magic Book,"
        Egypt, pp. 431-53.
    Demotic Chronical
        ET: I know of no published ET. For the text see W.
        Spiegelberg, Die sogennante demotische Chronik des Pap.
        215 der bibliothèque nationale zu Paris. (Demotische
        Studien 7) Leipzig, 1914.
    Potter's Oracle
        ET: I also know of no published ET. For the text see
        L. Koenen, "Die Prophezeiungen des 'Töpfers,'" Zeit-
        schrift für Papyrologie und Epigraphik 2 (1968) 195-209.
    The Lamb to Bocchoris
        ET descrip. C. C. McCown, HTR 18 (1925) 392-94.
    The Asclepius Apocalypse
        ET: W. Scott, Hermetica. Oxford, 1924, vol. 1, pp.
        338-77.

Poimandres
> ET: W. Scott, Hermetica, vol. 1, pp. 114-33.

Kore Kosmou
> ET: W. Scott, Hermetica, vol. 1, pp. 456-533.

3. See the synthetic overview by A. K. Grayson and W. G. Lambert in "Akkadian Prophecies," Journal of Cuneiform Studies 18 (1964) 7-30; also see W. W. Hallo, "Akkadian Apocalypses," IEJ 16 (1966) 231-42. Translations of the Babylonian or Akkadian "apocalypses":

Berossus
> ET: I. P. Cory, Ancient Fragments, rev. by R. Hodges. London, 1876, pp. 51-69.

4. Esp. see the informed discussion by G. Widengren, Die Religionen Irans (Die Religionen der Menschheit 14; Stuttgart, 1965), pp. 199-215. Translations of the Persian "apocalypses":

Zand-ī Vohuman Yasn (also called Bahman Yašt)
> ET: B. T. Anklesaria, Zand i Vohuman Yasn. Bombay, 1957. [text, transliteration, ET]

Hystaspes
> ET: Lactantius' The Divine Institutes, trans. M. F. McDonald. Washington, D.C., 1964, pp. 518-21.

Žāmāsp-Namak
> ET: B. H. Bailey, "To the Zamasp-Namak." Bulletin of the School of Oriental Studies 6 (1930-32) 55-85, 581-600.

Arda Viraf Nāmeh
> ET: M. Haug, "The Book of Arda Viraf," Ancient Persia, ed. C. F. Horne (Sacred Books and Early Literature of the East 7) New York, London, 1917, pp. 185-207.

Bundahis
> ET: E. W. West, Pahlavi Texts. Oxford, 1880, pt. 1, pp. 2-151.

Dēnkart
> ET: E. W. West, Pahlavi Texts, part V: Marvels of Zorastrianism (The Sacred Books of the East 47) Oxford, 1897, pp. 3-130. I am grateful to Richard B. Vinson for helping me complete the bibliographical references to these "apocalypses."

5. See now H. Attridge's invaluable insights in "Greek and Latin Apocalypses," Semeia 14, pp. 159-86. Also, see the careful study of the cultural background of the Greek and Latin apocalypses by W. Burkert, Griechische Religion der archaischen und klassischen Epoche (Die Religionen der Menschheit 15; Stuttgart, Berlin, 1977); esp. see "Die Kunst der Seher" on pp. 180-84, and "Orakel" on pp. 184-90. Translations of the Greek and Latin apocalypses:

Myth of Er
> ET: P. Storey, The Republic (LCL) London, 1930; repr. 1961, vol. 6, pt. 2, pp. 490-519.

Somnium Scripionis
> ET: C. W. Keyes, De republica, De legibus (LCL) London, 1928; repr. 1966, pp. 260-83.

De genio Socratis
ET: P. de Lacy and B. Einarson, Plutarch's Moralia
(LCL) London, 1959, vol. 7, pp. 458-77.
De sera numisis vindicta
ET: P. de Lacy and B. Einarson, Plutarch's Moralia
(LCL) London, 1959, vol. 7, pp. 268-99.
De facie lunae
ET: H. Cheiniss and W. Helmbold, Plutarch's Moralia
(LCL) London, 1968, vol. 12, pp. 34-223.
Fourth Eclogue
ET: H. R. Fairclough, Virgil (LCL) London, 1947, vol.
1, pp. 28-33.

6. A bibliography for and brief introduction to the documents
(except Daniel) in (1) and (2) are published by J. H. Charlesworth,
The Pseudepigrapha and Modern Research with a Supplement (SBL
SCS 7S; Chico, Calif., 1981).

7. A bibliography on the Nag Hammadi codices is published by
D. M. Scholer, Nag Hammadi Bibliography 1948-1969 (Nag Hammadi
Studies 1), Leiden, 1971 [supplemented periodically in Novum Testamentum; also see in Part IV: Additional Bibliographical Publica-
tions].

PART IV: BIBLIOGRAPHY

GUIDELINES

I have tried to include all publications on the NTAP. Bibliographical entries have been checked by examining the publication itself, whenever possible, here at Duke University, by acquisitions through the Duke University Interlibrary Loan Department, and by visits to Princeton and New York City. When an entry remained apparently imprecise, inaccurate, or clearly incomplete, I have added an asterisk at the end of the entry. Relatively minor notes in reference works, like The Oxford Dictionary of the Christian Church, have not been included.

The documents are listed in alphabetical order, according to the name of the New Testament figure appearing in the title. The abbreviation for the document is given to the left of the main entry in the Table of Contents. Sections of documents, often cited as if they were separate writings, are listed also in alphabetical order; but they, of course, receive no number or abbreviation. Under the title of individual works I have also included documents related only to them or to similar traditions. Under cycles I have placed publications of works related to documents in the NTAP. It has been particularly difficult to discern if some publications relate to the document in the title of the publication or to another writing incorrectly receiving that title. It has been extremely difficult to be precise regarding publications related to works about Mary and about Pilate; hence, sometimes I have grouped such publications under the pseudonym and the cycle. Cross-references guide the reader to other sections of the bibliography.

All exotic scripts have been translated or transliterated. Brackets at the end of an entry clarify the language of the publication translated. Russian and Greek periodical titles are transliterated.

Many of the entries are editions of Syriac, Greek, Latin, Coptic, Slavic or other texts. Usually a concluding bracketed note clarifies this fact. The same procedure often follows an English translation; of course, this note is omitted if the title specifies this information. Notations are also added to annotate many entries. All these notations should assist the reader in locating with a modicum of time and effort texts, translations, and important discussions.

65

ADDITIONAL BIBLIOGRAPHICAL PUBLICATIONS

The present bibliography is designed to be complete on the
NTAP. It can be supplemented or updated in two ways. First, publications on the Nag Hammadi codices are listed in D. M. Scholer's
invaluable Nag Hammadi Bibliography 1948-1969 (NHS 1. Leiden, 1971)
and the annual supplements, each October, in Novum Testamentum.
In a letter of 14 March 1983 Scholer informed me, "I am currently
in the process of working on the manuscript for a second gnostic
bibliographic volume which will be entitled: Nag Hammadi Bibliography 1970-1981. It is my hope and expectation to have the manuscript to E. J. Brill prior to the end of 1983." Second, future publications on the NTAP should be listed in the major reference works
on recent publications; especially consult ETL, Internationale Zeit-
schriftenschau für Bibelwissenschaft und Grenzgebiete, New Testament
Abstracts, Elenchus Bibliographicus Biblicus (when it resumes publication), Bibliographia Internationalis Spiritualitatis, Bibliographia Patristica, Bibliographic Information Bank in Patristics ("patristics" is
defined broadly; published by Laval University, Quebec, Canada),
F. Stegmüller's Repertorium biblicum medii aevi, Coptic Bibliography
(Centro Italiano Microfiches, Piazza Apollodoro, 26, 00196 Roma), and
the American Theological Library Association's Religion Index One:
Periodicals. None of these reference works specializes on the NTAP;
hence, the importance of the present work.

ABBREVIATIONS

(1) Periodicals, Series, Encyclopedias, and Societies

AcOr	Acta orientalia
AION	Annali (dell') Istituto [Universitario] Orientale di Napoli
AJSLL	American Journal of Semitic Languages and Literatures
AJT	American Journal of Theology
ALW	Archiv für Liturgiewissenschaft
AmER	American Ecclesiastical Review
AnBoll	Analecta Bollandiana
ANRW	Haase, W., and H. Temporini, eds. Aufstieg und Neidergang der Römischen Welt. Berlin, New York, 1979–
Anton	Antonianum
ARS	Awle ryale Series
ArSocRel	Archives de sociologie religions

ARW	Archiv für Religionswissenschaft
ATANT	Abhandlungen zur Theologie des Alten und Neuen Testaments
ATR	Anglican Theological Review
Aug	Augustinianum
AusBR	Australian Biblical Review
BA	Biblical Archaeologist
BCO	Bibliotheca classica orientalis
BETL	Bibliotheca Ephemeridum Theologicarum Lovaniensium
BHT	Beiträge zur historischen Theologie
Bib	Biblica
BibSac	Bibliotheca Sacra
BibTB	Biblical Theology Bulletin
BIFAO	Bulletin de l'institut Français d'archéologie orientale
BiKi	Bibel und Kirche
BiLit	Bibel und Liturgie
BInstEstHel	Boletín del Instituto de Estudios Helénicos
BJRL	Bulletin of the John Rylands Library
BLE	Bulletin de littérature ecclésiastique
BO	Bibbia e Oriente
BSC	Bulletin de la Societé Copte
BTS	Bible et Terre Sainte
BW	Biblical World
BWANT	Beiträge zur Wissenschaft vom Alten und Neuen Testaments
ByZ	Byzantinische Zeitschrift
ByzNGrJ	Byzantinisch-Neugriechische Jahrbücher
BZ	Biblische Zeitschrift
BZNW	Beihefte zur Zeitschrift für die neutestamentliche Wissenschaft und die Kunde der älteren Kirche
CahJos	Cahiers de Joséphologie
CamHJ	Cambridge Historical Journal
CBQ	Catholic Biblical Quarterly
CiTom	Ciencia Tomista

CiuDios	Ciudad de Dios
CJT	Canadian Journal of Theology
ČOIDR	Čtenia v Imp. Obšestve Istorii i Drevnostej Rossij-skich pri Moskovskom Universitete (1845-1918) [in Russian]
CQR	Church Quarterly Review
CSCO	Corpus scriptorum christianorum orientalium
CTM	Concordia Theological Monthly
CW	Die christliche Welt
DACL	Cabrol, F., and H. Leclercq, eds. Dictionnaire d'Archéologie Chrétienne et de Liturgie. 15 vols. Paris, 1924-53.
DAFC	Alès, d'A., ed. Dictionnaire apologétique de la foi catholique. Paris, 1925.
DB	Vigouroux, F., ed. Dictionnaire de la Bible. 5 vols. Paris, 1895-1912.
DBSup	Pirot, L., et al, eds. Dictionnaire de la Bible, Supplements. Paris, 1928- .
Dictionnaire	Migne, J.-P. Dictionnaire des Apocryphes, ou collection de tous les livres apocryphes. 2 vols. Paris, 1856-58.
DowR	Downside Review
DSAM	Viller, M., et al., eds. Dictionnaire de spirit-ualité ascétique et mystique. Paris, 1932- .
DSEOC	Documents pour servir à l'étude des origins chré-tiennes, les Apocryphes du Nouveau Testa-ment
DThC	Vacant, A.; E. Mangenot; and É. Amann, eds. Dictionnaire de Théologie Catholique. 15 vols. Paris, 1930-1950.
DTT	Dansk teologisk Tidsskrift
EBib	Études bibliques
EC	Études classiques
ED	Euntes Docete
EE	Estudios Eclesiásticos
EJ	Eranos-Jahrbuch
EncCatt	Sansoni, G.C., ed. Enciclopedia Cattolica. 12 vols. Rome, 1948-54.
Enciclopedia de la Biblia	Gutiérrez-Larraya, J.A., ed. Enciclopedia de la Biblia. 6 vols. Barcelona, 1963.

EncRel	Gozzini, M., ed. Enciclopedia delle Religioni. 6 vols. Florence, 1970-76.
EncyJud	Roth, C., et al., eds. Encyclopedia Judaica. 16 vols. New York, 1971-72.
EphLitg	Ephemerides liturgicae
EphMar	Ephemerides Mariologicae
EstMar	Estudios Marianos
ETL	Ephemerides theologicae lovanienses
EvM	Evangelisches Missionsmagazin
EvT	Evangelische Theologie
Exp	Expositor
ExpT	Expository Times
Explor	Explor: A Journal of Theology
FRLANT	Forschungen zur Religion und Literatur des Alten und Neuen Testaments
GCS	Die griechischen christlichen Schriftsteller der ersten drei Jahrhunderte
GrigPal	Grēgorios ho Palamos. Dimēnaion Theologikon kai Ekklēsiastikon Periodikon Organon tēs Hieras Mētropoleōs Thessalōnikēs
GSAI	Giornale della Societá Asiatica Italiana
GSLI	Giornale Storico della Letteratura Italiana
HAW	Handbuch der Altertumswissenschaft
Hastings	Hastings, J., ed. A Dictionary of the Bible. 5 vols. New York, Edinburgh, 1898.
HeyJ	Heythrop Journal
HibJ	Hibbert Journal
HL	Das Heilige Land
HomPastR	Homiletic and Pastoral Review
HTR	Harvard Theological Review
HZ	Historische Zeitschrift
IDB	Buttrick, G.A., et al., eds. The Interpreter's Dictionary of the Bible. 4 vols. New York, 1962.
IDBS	Crim, K., et al., eds. The Interpreter's Dictionary of the Bible, Supplementary Volume. Nashville, 1976.
IER	Irish Ecclesiastical Record

Int	Interpretation
ITQ	Irish Theological Quarterly
IzvORJS	Izvestija Otdelenija Russkogo Jazych i Slovesnosti Imp. Akagemii Nauk (1896-1927)
JA	Journal asiatique
JAAR	Journal of the American Academy of Religion
JAC	Jahrbuch für Antike und Christentum
JAOS	Journal of the American Oriental Society
JBL	Journal of Biblical Literature
JBR	Journal of Bible and Religion
JEcuSt	Journal of Ecumenical Studies
JETS	Journal of the Evangelical Theological Society
JGO	Jahrbuch für Geschichte Osteuropas
JJS	Journal of Jewish Studies
JNES	Journal of Near Eastern Studies
JPhil	Journal of Philology
JPT	Jahrbücher für Protestantische Theologie
JQR	Jewish Quarterly Review
JRAS	Journal of the Royal Asiatic Society
JRel	Journal of Religion
JSNT	Journal for the Study of the New Testament
JSS	Journal of Semitic Studies
JTS	Journal of Theological Studies
KerDog	Kerygma und Dogma
KlT	Kleine Texte für Vorlesungen und Übungen
LA	Liber Annuus Studii Biblici Franciscani
LTK[2]	Buchberger, M., ed. Lexikon für Theologie und Kirche. 10 vols. Freiburg, 1930-38.[2]
LTK[3]	Buchberger, M.; J. Höfer; and K. Rahner, eds. Lexikon für Theologie und Kirche. 10 vols. Freiburg, 1957-67.[3]
LuthTJ	Lutheran Theological Journal
MJos	Mélanges de l'Université Saint-Joseph
NAKG	Nederlandsch Archief voor Kerkgeschiedenis
NCE	Catholic U. of America. New Catholic Encyclopedia. 17 vols. New York, London, 1967-79.

NedThT	Nederlandsch Theologisch Tijdschrift
NHS	Nag Hammadi Studies
NKZ	Neue Kirchliche Zeitschrift
NorTT	Norsk Teologisk Tidsskrift
NovT	Novum Testamentum
NovTSup	Novum Testamentum, Supplements
NRT	Nouvelle Revue Theologique
NTS	New Testament Studies
NZST	Neue Zeitschrift für Systematische Theologie
OCA	Orientalia christiana analecta
OCP	Orientalia christiana periodica
OLP	Orientalia Louvaniensia Periodica
OLZ	Orientalistische Literaturzeitung
Or	Orientalia
OrChr	Oriens christianus
OrSuec	Orientalia Suecana
OrSyr	L'Orient Syrien
OstkSt	Ostkirchliche Studien
PalCler	Palestra del Clero
Pauly-Wissowa	Wissowa, G., et al., eds. Paulys Real-Encyclopädie der classischen Altertums wissenschaft, neue Bearbeitung. Stuttgart [or Munich], 1893-1972.
PDP	Pamjatniki Drevnej Pic'mennosti i Iskusstva. [in Russian]
PG	Patrologia graeca, ed. J. Migne.
PO	Graffin, R., and F. Nau, eds. Patrologia Orientalis. Paris, 1907-1979. Vols. 1-39.
ProtKi	Protestantische Kirchenzeitung
RAC	Klauser, T., ed. Reallexikon für Antike und Christentum. Stuttgart, 1950- .
RazFe	Razón y Fe
RB	Revue biblique
RBelgPhH	Revue Belge de philologie et d'histoire
RBen	Revue bénédictine
RBSL	Revista Biblica con Sección Liturgica

REByz	Revue des études byzantines
RechBib	Recherches bibliques
RefTR	Reformed Theological Review
REG	Revue des études grecques
REJ	Revue des études juives
RES	Review of English Studies
RestQ	Restoration Quarterly
RevistB	Revista bíblica
RGG^3	Galling, K., et al., eds. Die Religion in Geschichte und Gegenwart, 3rd ed. 6 vols. plus index. Tübingen, 1957-65.
RHE	Revue d'histoire ecclésiastique
RHPR	Revue d'histoire et de philosophie religieuse
RHR	Revue de l'histoire des religions
ROC	Revue de l'Orient chrétien
RoTKan	Roczniki Teologiczno Kanoniczne
RPh	Revue de philologie, de littérature, et d'histoire anciennes
RPTK	Hauck, A. Realencyklopädie für protestantische Theologie und Kirche. 24 vols. Leipzig, 1896-1913.
RQ	Revue de Qumran
RQH	Revue des questions historiques
RSEHA	Revue semitique d'epigraphie et d'histoire ancienne
RSO	Rivista degli Studi Orientali
RSR	Recherches de science religieuse
RScRel	Revue des sciences religieuses
RTAM	Recherches de théologie ancienne et médiévale
RTP	Revue de théologie et de philosophie
RTQR	Revue de théologie et des questions religieuses
RuBi	Ruch Biblijny Liturgiezny
SacDoctr	Sacra Doctrina
Sacramentum Mundi	Rahner, K., et al., eds. Sacramentum Mundi: An Encyclopedia of Theology. 6 vols. New York, 1968-70.
SBL	Society of Biblical Literature

SBLDS	SBL Dissertation Series
SbORJS	Sbornik otdelenija russkago jazyka i slovesnosti Imperstorskoj Akademii Nauk
SBN	Studi Bizantini e Neoellenci
SBS	Stuttgarter Bibelstudien
SBT	Studies in Biblical Theology
SBU	Svensk Bibliskt Uppslagsverk
SC	Sources chrétiennes
ScCatt	Scuola Cattolica
SH	Studia Hierosolymitana
SHR	Studies in the History of Religions
SJT	Scottish Journal of Theology
SNTU	Studia zum Neuen Testament und seiner Umwelt
SOC	Studia Orientalia Christiana
SPAW	Sitzungsberichte der klg. preussischen Akademie der Wissenschaften zu Berlin
SS	Studia Sinaitica
ST	Studia Theologica
StCath	Studia Catholica
T&S	Texts and Studies
T + T	SBL Texts and Translations Series
TBei	Theologische Beiträge
ThBl	Theologische Blätter
ThEE	Martinos, A., ed. Thrēskeutike kai Ēthikē Enkuklopaideia. 12 vols. Athens, 1962-1968.
Theol	Theologie (Greek)
ThGl	Theologie und Glaube
ThJ	Theologisches Jahrbuch
ThRu	Theologische Rundschau
ThZ	Theologische Zeitschrift
TLZ	Theologische Literaturzeitung
TQ	Theologische Quartalschrift
TR	Theologische Revue
TRE	Krause, G., and G. Müller, eds. Theologische Realenzyklopädie. Berlin, 1977- .

TS	Theological Studies
TSK	Theologische Studien und Kritiken
TU	Texte und Untersuchungen
TVers	Theologische Versuche
UCHLS	The University of Chicago Historical and Linguistic Studies in the Literature Related to the New Testament
VC	Vigiliae christianae
VD	Verbum Domini
VT	Vetus Testamentum
WMANT	Wissenschaftliche Monographien zum Alten und Neuen Testament
WZKM	Wiener Zeitschrift für die Kunde des Morgenlandes
ZDMG	Zeitschrift der deutschen morgenländischen Gesellschaft
ZeichZt	Die Zeichen der Zeit. Evangelische Monatschrift für die Mitarbeiter der Kirche
ZHTh	Zeitschrift für historische Theologie
ZKG	Zeitschrift für Kirchengeschichte
ZKT	Zeitschrift für Katholische Theologie
ZKWKL	Zeitschrift für Kirchliche Wissenschaft und Kirchliches Leben
ZNW	Zeitschrift für die neutestamentliche Wissenschaft und die Kunde der älteren Kirche
ZPEB	Tenney, M.C., and S. Barabas, eds. The Zondervan Pictorial Encyclopedia of the Bible. 5 vols. Grand Rapids, Mich., 1975.
ZRGG	Zeitschrift für Religions- und Geistesgeschichte
ZRP	Zeitschrift für romanische Philologie
ZS	Zeitschrift für Semitistik und verwandte Gebiete
ZSlaw	Zeitschrift für Slawistik
ZTK	Zeitschrift für Theologie und Kirche
ZWT	Zeitschrift für Wissenschaftliche Theologie

(2) Books

AA 1	James, M.R., ed. Apocrypha Anecdota: A Collection of Thirteen Apocryphal Books and Fragments (T&S 2.3) Cambridge, 1893.

AA 2   James, M.R., ed. Apocrypha Anecdota, second
                        series (T&S 5.1) Cambridge, 1897.

AAA   Lipsius, R.A., and M. Bonnet. Acta Apostolorum
                        Apocrypha. 2 vols. Leipzig, 1891-1903; repr.
                        Hildesheim, 1959. [Revised and expanded edi-
                        tion of Tischendorf, Acta Apos. Apoc.]

Acta Apos. Apoc.   Tischendorf, K. von. Acta Apostolorum Apocry-
                        pha. Leipzig, 1851.

Actes Apocryphes   Bovon, F., ed. Les actes apocryphes des apô-
                        tres: Christianisme et monde païen (Publica-
                        tions de la faculté de théólogie de l'université
                        de Genève 4) Geneva, 1981.

Agrapha   Resch, A. Agrapha: Aussercanonische Schrift-
                        fragmente (TU, N.F. 15.3-4) Leipzig, 1906;
                        repr. Darmstadt, 1967.

ALNT   Wright, W., ed. and trans. Contributions to the
                        Apocryphal Literature of the New Testament,
                        collected and edited from Syriac manuscripts
                        in the British Museum. London, 1865.

Altslavischen   Santos Otero, A. de. Die handschriftliche Über-
Apok.   lieferung der altslavischen Apokryphen. 2
                        vols. (Patristische Texte und Studien 20, 23)
                        Berlin, New York, 1978, 1981.

ANF 8   Roberts, A., and J. Donaldson, eds. The Ante-
                        Nicene Fathers: Translations of the Writings
                        of the Fathers Down to A.D. 325. Vol. 8.
                        Edinburgh, 1868-1872; rev. and repr. Grand
                        Rapids, Mich., 1951.

ANT   James, M.R. The Apocryphal New Testament
                        Being the Apocryphal Gospels, Acts, Epistles,
                        and Apocalypses with Other Narratives and
                        Fragments. Oxford, 1924.

Apocalypses   Tischendorf, K. Apocalypses Apocryphae:
    Apocryphae   Mosis, Esdrae, Pauli, Iohannis, item Mariae
                        dormitio, additis Evangeliorum et actuum apoc-
                        ryphorum supplementis. Leipzig, 1866; repr.
                        Hildesheim, 1966.

Apoc. del NT   Erbetta, M. Gli Apocrifi del Nuovo Testamento.
                        4 vols. Turin, 1966-75.

Apoc. del NT   Moraldi, L. Apocrifi del Nuovo Testamento. 2
                        vols. (Classici delle Religioni, sezione 5) Turin,
                        1971.

ApocNT   Wake, W., and N. Lardner. The Apocryphal New
                        Testament. London [n.d.], repr. Mokelumne
                        Hill, Cal., 1970.

Apocryphal Gos-   Cowper, B.H. The Apocryphal Gospels and Other
  pels   Documents Relating to the History of Christ.
                      London, Edinburgh, 1867[2].

Apokryphen   Michaelis, W. Die Apokryphen Schriften zum
  Schriften   Neuen Testament (Sammlung Dieterich Band
                      129) Bremen, 1962.[3]

BHH   Reicke, B., and L. Rost, eds. Biblisch-histor-
                      isches Handwörterbuch. 3 vols. Göttingen,
                      1962-66.

Byways   Findlay, A.F. Byways in Early Christian Litera-
                      ture: Studies in Uncanonical Gospels and Acts.
                      Edinburgh, 1923.

CINTI   Klassen, W., and G.F. Snyder, eds. Current
                      Issues in New Testament Interpretation (Fest-
                      schrift O. Piper) New York, 1962.

Cod.Apoc.NT   Fabricius. J.A. Codex Apocryphus Novi Testa-
                      menti. 2 vols. Hamburg, 1703.

Coptic Apoc.   Budge, E.A.W. Coptic Apocrypha in the Dialect
                      of Upper Egypt. London, 1913.

Documents   Cartlidge, D.R., and D.L. Dungan. Documents
                      for the Study of the Gospels. Philadelphia,
                      1980.

En quête   Puech, H.-C. En quête de la Gnose; II: Sur
                      l'Évangile selon Thomas, Esquisse d'une in-
                      têrpretation systématique. (Bibliothèque des
                      Sciences Humaines) Paris, 1978.

EvApoc   Michel, C., and P. Peeters. Évangiles Apocry-
                      phes. 2 vols. (Texts et documents pour
                      l'étude historique du Christianisme 13, 18)
                      Paris, 1911-14.

Evangiles Apoc.   Amiot, F. Les Évangiles Apocryphes (Textes
                      pour l'histoire sacrée) Paris, 1952.

Evangelia   Tischendorf, K. von. Evangelia Apocrypha.
  Apocrypha   Leipzig, 1876; repr. Hildesheim, 1966.

Evangiles Apoc-   Variot, J. Les Évangiles Apocryphes. Paris,
  ryphes   1878.

Evangelios Apóc-   Santos Otero, A. de. Los Evangelios Apócrifos.
  rifos   Madrid, 1975.[3]

FAC   Lacau, M.P. Fragments D'Apocryphes Coptes
                      (Mémoires publiés par les Membres de L'Insti-
                      tut Français D'Archéologie Orientale du Caire
                      9) Cairo, 1904.

FGH   Jacoby, F. Die Fragmente der griechischen His-
                      toriker. Berlin, 1940-1943; repr. 1954.

GAL   Bardenhewer, O. Geschichte der altkirchlichen
                        Literatur. 4 vols. Freiburg im Breisgau,
                        1912-1924.

Gesch. altchrist.   Harnack, A. Geschichte der altchristlichen Lit-
    Lit.   teratur bis Eusebius. 2 vols., 4 parts. Leip-
                        zig, 1893-1904.

H^2 Hennecke, E., ed. Neutestamentliche Apokryphen.
                        Tübingen, 1924^2.

Handbuch,   Hennecke, E., ed. Handbuch zu den Neutesta-
    ed. Hennecke   mentlichen Apokryphen. 2 vols. Tübingen,
                        1904.

HS   Hennecke, E., and W. Schneemelcher, eds. Neu-
                        testamentliche Apokryphen in deutscher Über-
                        setzung. 2 vols. Tübingen, 1959-64^3.

HSW   Hennecke, E.; W. Schneemelcher; and R. McL.
                        Wilson, eds. New Testament Apocrypha. 2
                        vols. Philadelphia, 1963-65.

Intro. à la   Robert, A., and A. Feuillet, eds. Introduction
    Bible   à la Bible. 2 vols. Tournai, 1957-59.

Introduction   Koester, H. Introduction to the New Testament.
                        Vol. 1: History, Culture, and Religion of the
                        Hellenistic Age. Vol. 2: History and Litera-
                        ture of Early Christianity. Philadelphia, 1982.

JBC   Brown, R.E.; J.A. Fitzmyer; and R.E. Murphy,
                        eds. The Jerome Biblical Commentary. Engle-
                        wood Cliffs, N.J., 1968.

Koptische   von Lemm, O. Koptische Miscellen. eds. P. Na-
    Miscellen   gel and K. Kümmel. 2 vols. (Studia Byzan-
                        tina 10, 11) Leipzig, 1972. [Repr. from 1907-
                        1915 fascicles of Bulletin de l'Académie impér-
                        iale des sciences de St. Petersbourg.]

Les origines   Roncaglia, M. Histoire de l'église copte. 6 vols.
                        Vol. 1: Les origines du christianisme en
                        Egypte. Beirut, 1966.

Lost and Hostile   Baring-Gould, S. The Lost and Hostile Gospels:
    Gospels   An Essay on the Toledoth Jeschu, and the Pe-
                        trine and Pauline Gospels of the First Three
                        Centuries of Which Fragments Remain. Lon-
                        don, Edinburgh, 1874.

M. Smith Fest-   Neusner, J., ed. Christianity, Judaism and
    schrift   Other Greco-Roman Cults: Studies for Morton
                        Smith at Sixty. 4 parts. (Studies in Judaism
                        in Late Antiquity 12) Leiden, 1975.

NCCHS   Fuller, R.C. et al., eds. A New Catholic Com-
                        mentary on Holy Scripture. London, 1969.

Neutest. Apok.   Bauer, J.B. Die neutestamentlichen Apokryphen
                        (Die Welt der Bibel 21) Düsseldorf, 1968.

Neutest. Kanons   Zahn, T. Geschichte des neutestamentlichen
                        Kanons. 2 vols. Leipzig, 1888-92.

Nuwe-Test. Apok.   Müller, J.J. Nuwe-Testamentiese Apokriewe.
                        Pretoria, 1974.

Patrology   Quasten, J. Patrology. 3 vols. Utrecht-Antwerp,
                        1950-60.

PCB   Peake, A.S.; M. Black; and H.H. Rowley, eds.
                        Peake's Commentary on the Bible. London,
                        New York, 1962.

Pseud I   Fritz, K. von, ed. Pseudepigrapha I: Pseudo-
                        pythagorica, Lettres de Platon, Littérature
                        pseudépigraphe juive (Entretiens sur l'antiquité
                        classique 18) Geneva, 1972.

Pseudépigraphes   Philonenko, M., et al. Pseudépigraphes de l'An-
                        cien Testament et manuscrits de la Mer Morte
                        (Cahiers de la RHPR 41) Paris, 1967.

Repertorium   Stegmüller, F. Repertorium Biblicum Medii Aevi.
   Biblicum   Madrid, 1950 (vol. 1); 1976 (vol. 8).

SBL 1972 Seminar   McGaughy, L.C., ed. The Society of Biblical
   Papers   Literature One Hundred Eighth Annual Meet-
                        ing: Book of Seminar Papers, Friday-Tuesday,
                        1-5 September 1972, Century Plaza Hotel, Los
                        Angeles, CA. Missoula, Mont., 1972.

Vangeli Apocrifi   Bonaccorsi, P.G. Vangeli Apocrifi. Florence,
                        1948.

VTSup 28   Boer, P.A.H. de, ed. Congress Volume: Edin-
                        burgh 1974. (Supplements to VT 28) Leiden,
                        1975.

GENERAL:

1. STUDIES, TEXT EDITIONS, TRANSLATIONS

(See also 5.215)

1.1 Achelis, H. Das Christentum in den drei ersten Jahrhunderten. Leipzig, 1918.

1.2 Aescoly, A.Z. "Les noms magiques dans les apocryphes chrétiens des Ethiopiens," JA 220 (1932) 87-137.

1.3 Aland, K. "The Problem of Anonymity and Pseudonymity in Christian Literature of the First Two Centuries," JTS 12 (1961) 39-49; repr. SPCK Theological Collection 4 (London, 1965); German trans. "Das Problem der Anonymität und Pseudonymität in der christlichen Literatur der ersten beiden Jahrhunderte," Studien zur Überlieferung des Neuen Testaments und seines Textes (Arbeiten zur Neutestamentlichen Textforschung 2) Berlin, 1967. Pp. 24-34.

1.4 Altaner, B. "Augustinus und die neutestamentlichen Apokryphen, Sibyllinen und Sextusspruche," AnBoll 67 (1949) 236-48; repr. in Kleine Patristische Schriften (TU 83) Berlin, 1967. Pp. 204-15.

1.5 Altaner, B., and A. Stuiber. Patrologie. Freiburg, Basel, Vienna, 1966.[7] Pp. 117-44.

1.6 Amann, É. "Apocryphes du Nouveau Testament," DBSup.1. Cols. 460-533.

1.7 Amann, É. "Evangiles apocryphes," DThC.5. Cols. 1624-40.

1.8 Amiot, F. Les évangiles apocryphes (Textes pour l'histoire sacrée) Paris, 1952. [German trans. = 1.118]

1.9 Amiot, F. The Apocrypha of the New Testament. Collected and revised by H. Daniel-Rops and F. Amiot. London, 1955. [in Polish]

1.10   Andrews, H.T. An Introduction to the Apocryphal Books of
        the Old and New Testament, rev. and ed. C.F. Pfeiffer.
        Grand Rapids, 1964.

1.11   Angelov, B. Ancient Bulgarian Literature IX-XVIII V. Sofia,
        1922.* [in Polish]

1.12   Aranda, G. "Los Evangelios de la Infancia de Jesús," Scripta
        Theologica 10 (1978) 793-848.

1.13   Arens, F.J. De Evangeliorum Apocryphorum in canonicis usu
        historico, critico, exegetico. Göttingen, 1835.

1.14   Arnold, E. The Early Christians After the Death of the Apos-
        tles, Selected and Edited from All the Sources of the First
        Centuries. New York, 1970. [German original: 1926]

1.15   Asmussen, J.P. "Manikaeiske Jesus-tekster fra kinesisk Turk-
        estan," DTT 21 (1958) 129-45.

1.16   Bagatti, B. La chiesa primitiva apocrifa (II secolo). Saggio
        storico (Alla scoperta della Bibbia 13) Rome, 1981.

1.17   Bagatti, B. "Religiosità popolare dei giudeo-cristiani," Sac-
        Doctr 61 (1971) 33-49.

1.18   Bagatti, B., and F. García. La Vida de Jesús en los Apócri-
        fos del Nuevo Testamento (Cuadernos de Tierra Santa 10)
        Jerusalem, 1979. [Esp. included in the discussion are Prot-
        Jas, InfGosTh, GosTh, GosNic, GosPet, GosBart, PasMar.]

1.19   Bakker, A. "Christ an Angel?" ZNW 32 (1933) 255-65.

1.20   Balz, H.R. "Anonymität und Pseudepigraphie im Urchristen-
        tum: Überlegungen zum literarischen und theologischen
        Problem der urchristlichen und gemeinantiken Pseudepigraphie,"
        ZTK 66 (1969) 403-36.

1.21   Barbel, J. Christos Angelos: Die Anschauung von Christus
        als Bote und Engel in der gelehrten und volkstümlichen Lit-
        eratur des christlichen Altertums: Zugleich ein Beitrag zur
        Geschichte des Ursprungs und der Fortdauer des Arianis-
        mus. Bonn, 1941, 1964.[2]

1.22   Bardenhewer, O. Geschichte der altkirchlichen Literatur. 4
        vols. Freiburg im Breisgau, 1912-1924. [Vol. 1 of 1913[2],
        vol. 2 of 1914[2], vol. 3 of 1912, vol. 4 of 1924]

1.23   Bardsley, H.J. Reconstruction of Early Christian Documents.
        London, 1935.

1.24   Bardy, G.   "Apocryphes à tendance encratite," DSAM.1.   Cols.
        752-65.

1.25   Baring-Gould, S.   The Lost and Hostile Gospels: An Essay on
        the Toledoth Jeschu, and the Petrine and Pauline Gospels of
        the First Three Centuries of Which Fragments Remain.   Lon-
        don, Edinburgh, 1874.

1.26   Barkels, H.   Nieuw Testamentische Apocriefen.   2 vols. Ams-
        terdam, 1922.

1.27   Bartholmä, [?].   Übersetzung d. Apokryphen des Neuen Testa-
        ments.   Dinkelsbuhl, 1832.

1.28   Basarab, M.   "Cărtile anaginoscomena--bune de citit--in Bibliile
        româneşti," Studii Teologice 24 (1971) 59-69.   [in Rumanian]

1.29   Basser, A.   "Early Syriac Asceticism," DowR 88 (1970) 393-
        409.

1.30   Basset, R.   Les apocryphes éthiopiens traduits en Français.
        2 vols. Paris, 1893-1909.

1.31   Batiffol, P.   Anciennes littératures chrétiennes: La littérature
        grecque.   Paris, 1898. [See esp. pp. 35-41]

1.32   Batiffol, P.   "Évangiles apocryphes." DB.2. Cols. 2114-18.

1.33   Bauer, J.B.   Die neutestamentlichen Apokryphen (Die Welt der
        Bibel 21) Düsseldorf, 1968. [Spanish trans.: Los Apócrifos
        neotestamentarios, tr. J.M. Bernáldez (Actualidad Biblica 22)
        Madrid, 1971. French trans.: Les apocryphes du Nouveau
        Testament (Lire la Bible 37) Paris, 1973.]

1.34   Bauer, J.B.   "Die Entstehung apokrypher Evangelien," BiLit
        38 (1964) 268-71.

1.35   Bauer, W.   "Jesu irdische Erscheinung und Charakter," HS.
        1. Pp. 322-24.

1.36   Bauer, W.   "Jesus' Earthly Appearance and Character," HSW.
        1. Pp. 433-36.

1.37   Bauer, W.   Das Leben Jesu im Zeitalter der neutestamentlichen
        Apokryphen.   Tübingen, 1909; repr. Darmstadt, 1967.

1.38   Bauer, W.   Rechtgläubigkeit und Ketzerei im ältesten Chris-
        tentum.   (BHT 10) Tübingen, 1934, 1964^2. [ET: Orthodoxy
        and Heresy in Earliest Christianity, trans. by a team and
        edited by R.A. Kraft and G. Krodel. Philadelphia, 1971.

1.39   Baumstark, A. "Les apocryphes coptes," RB 3 (1906) 245-65.

1.40   Baumstark, A. Die Christlichen Literaturen des Orients. 2
        vols. Leipzig, 1911.

1.41   Baumstark, A. Geschichte der syrischen Literatur. Bonn,
        1922.

1.42   Beausobre, I. de. De Novi Foederis libris apocryphis disser-
        tatio. Berlin, 1734.

1.43   Beausobre, I. Essai critique de l'histoire de Manichée et du
        Manichéisme. Amsterdam, 1734. Pt. 1, pp. 335-407.

1.44   Beck, H.G. Kirche und theologische Literatur im byzantini-
        schen Reich. Munich, 1959.

1.45   Belser, J.E. "Die Apokryphen," Einleitung in das Neue Tes-
        tament. Freiburg, 1905. Pp. 789-871.

1.46   Berger, K. "Zur Frage des traditionsgeschichtlichen Wertes apok-
        rypher Gleichnisse," NovT 17 (1975) 58-76.

1.47   Beyschlag, K. "Das Jakobusmartyrium und seine Verwandten
        in der frühchristlichen Literatur," ZNW 56 (1965) 149-78.

1.48   Beyschlag, K. Die verborgene Überlieferung von Christus.
        Munich, 1969.

1.49   Bickel, E. Lehrbuch der Geschichte der römischen Literatur.
        Heidelberg, 1937.

1.50   Bieder, W. Die Vorstellung von der Höllenfahrt Jesu Christi.
        Zürich, 1949.

1.51   Bigaré, P. "Apocryphes du NT," Introduction à la Bible, ed.
        P. Grelot. Paris, 1977. Pp. 181-211.

1.52   Birch, A. Auctarium Codicis apocryphi Novi Testamenti Fab-
        riciani, I. Copenhagen, 1799, 1804.*

1.53   Bischoff, B. "Wendepunkte in der Geschichte der lateinischen
        Exegese im Frühmittelalter," Mittelalterliche Studien; ausge-
        wählte Aufsätze zur Schriftkunde und Literaturgeschichte.
        Stuttgart, 1966. Vol. 1. Pp. 205-73.

1.54   Black, M. "The Palestinian Syriac Gospel and the Diates-
        saron," OrChr 35 (1939) 101-11.

1.55   Blackman, E.C. Marcion and His Influence. London, 1948.

1.56   Blond, G. "Encratisme," DSAM. 4. Cols. 628-42.

1.57   Blond, G. "Les encratites et la vie mystique," Mystique et continence (Etudes carmelitaines). Bruges-Paris, 1951. Pp. 117-50.

1.58   Blond, G. "L'hérésie encratite vers la fin du IVe siècle," Sciences religieuses, Travaux et Recherches. Paris, 1944. Pp. 157-210.

1.59   Bolgiani, F. "La tradizione eresiologica sull' encratismo," Atti dell' Accademia delle Science [Turin] 91 (1956/57) 343-419; 96 (1966/67) 537-664.

1.60   Bonaccorsi, P.G. Vangeli apocrifi. Florence, 1948.

1.61   Buonaiuti, E. Detti extracanonici di Gesù. Rome, 1925.

1.62   Bonsirven, J., and C. Bigaré, "Apocryphes du Nouveau Testament," Intro. à la Bible. 2. Pp. 743-62.

1.63   Bonwetsch, N. "Die christliche vornicänische Litteratur in altslavischen Handschriften," Gesch.altchrist.Lit. 1.2. Pp. 896-917.

1.64   Borberg, K.F. Bibliothek der neutestamentlichen Apokryphen gesammelt Übersetz und erläutert. Stuttgart, 1841.

1.65   Bori, P.C. "La référence à la communauté de Jérusalem dans les sources chrétiennes orientales et occidentales jusqu'au Ve siècle," Istina 19 (1974) 31-48.

1.66   Bousset, W. "Zur Hadesfahrt Christi," ZNW 19 (1919-20) 50-66.

1.67   Bovon, F. "Evangiles canoniques et évangiles apocryphes: La naissance et l'enfance de Jesus," Bulletin des facultés catholiques de Lyon 58 (1980) 19-30.

1.68   Brockelmann, K., et al. Geschichte der christlichen Literaturen des Orients. Leipzig, 1907.

1.69   Brown, P. Religion and Society in the Age of St. Augustine. London, 1972.

1.70   Brown, R.E. "Christian Apocrypha," JBC. Pp. 543-46. [B. discusses ProtJas, Agrapha, GosTh, GosHeb, GosPet.]

1.71   Brox, N. Falsche Verfasserangaben: Zur Erklärung der frü-christlichen Pseudepigraphie (SBS 79) Stuttgart, 1975.

1.72   Brox, N. "Pseudo-Paulus and Pseudo-Ignatius: Einige Topoi
        altchristlicher Pseudepigraphie," VC 30 (1976) 181-88.

1.73   Brox, N. "Zum Problemstand in der Erforschung der altchrist-
        lichen Pseudepigraphie," Kairos 15 (1973) 10-23.

1.74   Bruce, F.F. Jesus and Christian Origins Outside the New
        Testament. Grand Rapids, 1974.

1.75   Brunet, G. Les Évangiles apocryphes, traduits et annotés
        d'après l'édition de J.C. Thilo. Suivis d'une notice sur les
        principaux livres apocryphes de l'Ancien Testament. Paris,
        1848, 1863^2. [HisJosCar, InfGos, ProtJas, InfGosth, Gos-
        BirMar, History of the Virgin, GosNic]

1.76   Bruns, J.E. The Forbidden Gospel: A "Fifth Gospel" Recon-
        structed from Authentic Ancient Sources That Gives an Un-
        orthodox Picture of Jesus and His Teachings. New York,
        1976.

1.77   Bruston, C. "La descente aux enfers selon les apôtres Pierre
        et Paul," RTQR (1905) 236-49, 438-56.

1.78   Bruston, C. La descente du Christ aux enfers d'après les
        apôtres et d'après l'Église. Paris, 1897.

1.79   Budge, E.A.W., ed. The Book of the Cave of Treasures: A
        History of the Patriarchs and Kings, Their Successors, from
        the Creation to the Crucifixion of Christ. London, 1927.

1.80   Budge, E.A.W., ed. Contendings of the Apostles, Being the
        Stories of the Lives and Martyrdoms and Deaths of the Twelve
        Apostles and Evangelists. 2 vols. London, New York, 1899-
        1901; repr. London, 1976.

1.81   Budge, E.A.W., ed. Coptic Apocrypha in the Dialect of Upper
        Egypt. London, 1913. [See M.R. James' review JTS 15 (1914)
        125-29.]

1.82   Budge, E.A.W., ed. Coptic Martyrdoms in the Dialect of Upper
        Egypt. London, 1914.

1.83   Budge, E.A.W., ed. Miscellaneous Texts in the Dialect of Upper
        Egypt, London, 1915.

1.84   Burghardt, W.J. "Literature of Christian Antiquity: 1975-
        1979," TS 41 (1980) 151-80. [reports on 31 projects in
        Patristics and related fields]

1.85   Burmester, O.H.E. "Egyptian Mythology in the Coptic Apoc-
        rypha," Or 7 (1938) 355-67.

1.86   Burrows, E. The Gospel of the Infancy and Other Biblical
       Essays, ed. F.F. Sutcliffe. New York, 1945.

1.87   Cabrol, F. "Descente du Christ aux enfers d'après la liturgie,"
       DACL. 4. Pp. 682-93.

1.88   Cameron, R., ed. The Other Gospels: Non-Canonical Gospel
       Texts. Philadelphia, 1982. [Includes reprints of transla-
       tions of the following: GosTh (from The Nag Hammadi Li-
       brary); GosEg, Papyrus Oxyrhynchus 840, Papyrus Egerton
       2, GosPet, GosHeb, AcJn, GosNaz, GosEb, ProtJas, InfGosTh,
       EpApos, AcPil (all from HSW).]

1.89   Campenhausen, H. von. Kirchliches Amt und geistliche Voll-
       macht in den ersten drei Jahrhunderten (BHT 14) Tübingen,
       1953.

1.90   Canal Sánchez, J.M. "S. José en los libros apócrifos del Nuevo
       Testamento: San Giuseppe nei primi 15 secoli," Estudios
       Josefinos 25 (1971) 123-49.

1.91   Carrey, M. "Nazareth dans les évangiles apocryphes," Le
       monde de la Bible 16 (1980) 44-47.

1.92   Cartlidge, D.R., and D.L. Dungan. Documents for the Study
       of the Gospels. Philadelphia, 1980.

1.93   Cartojan, N. Cartile populare in literatura romaneasca.   2
       vols. Bucharest, 1929-38.

1.94   Catch, M.M. see Gatch, M.M. (1.169a)

1.95   Cecchelli, C. Mater Christi. Rome, 1954.

1.96   Cerulli, E. "L'Oriente Christiano nell'unità delle sue tradi-
       zioni," (Lincei, Quaderni 62) Rome, 1964. Pp. 9-43.

1.97   Cerutti, F. "Note sul pensiero politico del cristianesimo antico
       (tratta dei vangeli apocrifi)," Ricerche Religiose [Rome] 20
       (1950) 20-34.

1.98   Chaine, J. "Descente aux enfers," DBSup. 2. Cols. 395-
       431.

1.99   Charles, R.H., and W.O.E. Oesterley. "Apocryphal Litera-
       ture," Encyclopaedia Britannica. Chicago, 1956. Vol. 2.
       Pp. 105-08.

1.100 Charlesworth, J.H. "Tatian's Dependence upon Apocryphal
       Traditions," HeyJ 15 (1974) 5-17.

1.101   Cheek, J.L. "The Apocrypha in Christian Scripture," JBR
        26 (1958) 207-12.

1.102   Chiappelli, A. Studi di antica letteratura cristiana. Turin,
        1887.

1.103   Chuedonius, [?]. Pseudo-Novum Testamentum, Exhibens Pseu-
        doevangelia, Acta, Epistolas, Apocalypses. Helmstädt, 1699.

1.104   Clemen, C. Niedergefahren zu den Toten. Giessen, 1900.

1.105   Clemens, R. Die geheimgehaltenen oder sogenannten Apokry-
        phen Evangelien. Stuttgart, 1850.

1.106   Conrady, L. Die Quelle der kanonischen Kindheitsgeschichten
        Jesus. Göttingen, 1900.

1.107   Costin, V. "L'écrit pseudépigraphique ... comme source de
        l'histoire du culte chrétien," Studii Teologice 17 (1965) 204-
        18.

1.108   Cotelier, J.B. Patres aevi apostolici. Paris, 1672.

1.109   Couard, L. Altchristlichen Sagen über das Leben Jesu und
        der Apostel. Gütersloh, 1909.

1.110   Cowper, B.H. The Apocryphal Gospels and Other Documents
        Relating to the History of Christ. London, 1867[2].

1.111   Craveri, M. I Vangeli apocrifi a curi di M. Craveri, con un
        Saggio di G. Pampaloni. Turin, 1969.

1.112   Cullmann, O. The Early Church: Studies in Early Christian
        History and Theology. Philadelphia, 1966.

1.113   Cullmann, O. Noël dans l'Église ancienne. Neuchâtel, 1949.

1.114   Cureton, W. Ancient Syriac Documents. London, 1863.

1.115   Dalmais, I.H. "Les apocryphes et l'imaginaire chrétien," BTS
        154 (1973) 12-20.

1.116   Dalmais, I.H. "A travers l'Égypte chrétienne sur les traces
        légendaires de la S. Famille," BTS 106 (1968) 8-15.

1.117   Daničić, Gj. "Two Apocryphal Gospels," Starine 6 (1872) 130-
        54. [in Serbo-Croatian]

1.118   Daniel-Rops, H. Die apocryphen Evangelien des Neuen Tes-
        taments. Zürich, 1956. [German trans. of texts collected
        in 1.8]

1.119 Daniélou, J. "Les douze apôtres et le zodiaque," VC 13 (1959)
       14-21.

1.120 Daniélou, J. "Judéo-Christianisme et Gnosticisme," RSR 54
       (1966) 272-96.

1.121 Daniélou, J. La théologie du judéo-christianisme. 3 vols.
       Paris, 1958. [ET: The Theology of Jewish Christianity.
       London, 1964 (= vol. 1 of A History of Early Christian Doc-
       trine Before the Council of Nicaea); Italian trans.: La teo-
       logia del giudeo-cristianesimo. Bologna, 1974]

1.122 Davies, S.L. The Revolt of the Widows: The Social World
       of the Apocryphal Acts. Carbondale, Ill., 1980.

1.123 Derouaux, W. "Littérature chrétienne antique et papyrologie,"
       NRT 62 (1935) 810-43.

1.124 Destefani, G. "I miracoli narrati dai vangeli apocrifi" Medi-
       cina e Morale 2 (1952) 95-104.

1.125 Dibelius, M. Geschichte der urchristlichen Literatur. Vol. 2:
       Apostolisches und Nachapostolisches. Berlin, Leipzig, 1926.

1.126 Dibelius, M. Jungfrauensohn und Krippenkind (1932) Botschaft
       und Geschichte I Tübingen, 1953. Pp. 1-78.

1.127 Dix, G. Jew and Greek: A Study in the Primitive Church.
       London, 1953.

1.128 Dobschütz, E. v. Christusbilder. Untersuchungen zur christ-
       lichen Legende (TU 18.1-2) Leipzig, 1899.

1.129 Dobschütz, E. v. "Der Roman in der altchristlichen Literatur,"
       Deutsche Rundschau 3 (1902) 87-106.

1.130 Dodds, E.R. Pagan and Christian in an Age of Anxiety. Cam-
       bridge, 1965.

1.131 Donehoo, J. de Q. The Apocryphal and Legendary Life of
       Christ, Being the Whole Body of Apocryphal Gospels and
       Other Extra Canonical Literature. London, 1903.

1.132 Dragojlovíc, D. "The Monastic 'Secret Book' in South Slavic
       Literature," Književna istorija 23 (1974) 509-16. [in Serbo-
       Croatian]

1.133 Drury, C. "Who's In, Who's Out," What About the New Tes-
       tament: Essays in Honour of Christopher Evans, eds. M.
       Hooker and C. Hickling. London, 1975. Pp. 223-33.

1.134 Dufourcq, A. De manichaeismo apud Latinos quinto sextoque
       saeculo atque de latinis apocryphis libris. Paris, 1900.

1.135 Dujčev, J. "Apocrypha byzantino-slavica: Une collection
       serbe d'exorcismes d'origine byzantine," Zbornik Filos.
       Fakulteta Univ. Beograd 9 (1967) 247-50.

1.136 Dumville, D.N. "Biblical Apocrypha and the Early Irish: A
       Preliminary Investigation," Proceedings of the Royal Irish
       Academy. 73C.8 (1973) 299-338.

1.137 Dunkerley, R. Beyond the Gospels. London, 1957.

1.138 Duriez, G. Les apocryphes dans le drame religieux en Alle-
       magne au moyen âge. Lille, 1914.

1.139 Duval, R. La littérature syriaque. Paris, 1899.

1.140 Edsman, C.M. Le baptême de feu. Leipzig, 1940.

1.141 Ehrhard, A.   Die altchristliche Literatur und ihre Erforschung
       seit 1880. Freiburg, 1894.

1.142 Ehrhard, A.   Die altchristliche Literatur und ihre Erforschung
       von 1884 bis 1900. Freiburg, 1900.

1.143 Ehrhard, A.   Uberlieferung und Bestand der hagiographischen
       und homiletischen Literatur der Griechischen Kirche von den
       Anfängen bis zum Ende des 16. Jahrhunderts. (TU 50-52)
       Leipzig, 1939-52.

1.144 Ehrhardt, A. The Apostolic Succession in the First Two Cen-
       turies of the Church. London, 1953.

1.145 Ellicott, C.J. Dissertation on Apocryphal Gospels. Cambridge,
       1856.

1.146 Enslin, M.S. "Apocrypha, NT," IDB. 1. Pp. 166-69.

1.147 Enslin, M.S. "The Christian Stories of Nativity," JBL 59
       (1940) 317-38.

1.148 Erbetta, M. Gli Apocrifi del Nuovo Testamento. 4 vols.
       Turin, 1966-1975.

1.149 Evans, E. The Apocrypha: Their Origin and Contents. Lon-
       don, 1939.

1.150 Eysinga, G. van den Bergh van. Indische Einflüsse auf evan-
       geliches Erzählungen (FRLANT 4) Göttingen, 1909^2.

1.151 Fabricius, J.A. Codex apocryphus Novi Testamenti. 2 vols.
       Hamburg, 1703, 1719^2.

1.152 Fabricius, L. Die Legende im Bild des ersten Jahrtausends
       der Kirche: Der Einfluss der Apokryphen und Pseudepi-
       graphen auf die altchristliche und byzantinische Kunst.
       Kassel, 1956.

1.153 Fehrle, E. Die kultische keuschheit im Altertum. Giessen, 1910.

1.154 Fields, W.C. The Christ in the Apocryphal Gospels. Southern
       Baptist Seminary Dissertation, 1950.

1.155 Findlay, A.F. Byways in Early Christian Literature: Studies
       in Uncanonical Gospels and Acts. Edinburgh, 1923.

1.156 Findlay, A.F. "Gospels (apocryphal)," A Dictionary of Christ
       and the Gospels, eds. J. Hastings, J.A. Selbie, J.C. Lam-
       bert. 2 vols. Edinburgh, 1906-1908. Vol. 1. Pp. 671-85.

1.157 Finegan, J., trans. Hidden Records of the Life of Jesus.
       Philadelphia, 1969.

1.158 Fitzmyer, J.A. An Introductory Bibliography for the Study
       of Scripture (Subsidia Biblica 3) Rome, 1981. [see esp.
       pp. 122-26]

1.159 Fontaine, J. La littérature latine chrétienne. Paris, 1970.
       [Italian trans.: La letturatura latina cristiana, Bologna,
       1973]

1.160 Foster, R.J. "The Apocrypha of the Old and New Testa-
       ments," NCCHS. Pp. 109-14.

1.161 Franko, I. Apocrypha and Legends (Codex apocryphus e
       manuscriptis ukraino-russicis collectus opera doctoris Joannis
       Franko) 5 vols. L'vov, 1896-1910. [in Russian]

1.162 Franko, I. "Beiträge aus dem Kirchenslavischen zu den Apok-
       ryphen des Neuen Testaments," ZNW 3 (1902) 146-55.

1.163 Freppel, [?] "On the Apocryphal Gospels," Trudy Kievskoj
       Duchovnoij Akademii 3 (1861) 381-418. [in Russian]*

1.164 Freyne, S. The World of the New Testament (New Testament
       Message 2) Wilmington, Del., 1980.

1.165 Frothingham, O.B. "Christ of the Apocryphal Gospels,"
       Chr. Exam. 53 (1852) 21ff.*

1.166 Fürst, J. "Untersuchungen zur 'Ephemeris' des Diktys von
       Kreta," Philologus 61 (1902) 407-20.

1.167 Gaiffier, B. de. "L''Historia Apocrypha' dans la légende
       dorée," AnBoll 91 (1973) 265-72.

1.168   Gancho, C.   "Apócrifos, Libros," Enciclopedia de la Biblia.
        1. Cols. 589-91.

1.169   Gärtner, B.E.   Apocryferna till NTet. Utgivna i samarbete
        med Svenska bibel sällskapet. Urval och översättning av.
        Stockholm, 1972.

1.169a Gatch, M.M.   "Two Uses of Apocrypha in Old English Homilies,"
        Church History 33 (1964) 379-91.

1.170   Geffcken, J.   Christliche Apokryphen. Tübingen, 1908.

1.171   Gero, S.   "Apocryphal Gospels: A Survey of Textual and
        Literary Problems," ANRW 2.25.4 (in preparation).

1.172   Gerstner, H.   Biblische Legenden. Gerabronn, 1971.

1.173   Ghedini, G.   "La lingua dei vangeli apocrifi greci," Studi
        dedicati alla memoria di P. Uboldi (Pubblicazione della Uni-
        versità Catt. del S. Cuore 16) Milan, 1937. Pp. 443-80.

1.174   Giblet, J.   "Pénitence: Apocryphes et pseudépigraphes,"
        DBSup. 7. Cols. 657-59.

1.175   Giles, J.A.   Codex Apocryphus Novi Testamenti. London,
        1852.

1.176   Glaser, N.   Apocrypha. Hamburg, 1614.

1.177   Goguel, M.   La foi à la resurrection de Jésus dans le chris-
        tianisme primitif. Paris, 1933.

1.178   González-Blanco, E.   Los Evangelios apócrifos. 3 vols. Ma-
        drid, 1934.

1.179   Goodspeed, E.J.   Modern Apocrypha. Boston, 1956.

1.180   Goodspeed, E.J.   New Chapters in New Testament Study.
        New York, 1937. Pp. 189-219.

1.181   Goodspeed, E.J.   Strange New Gospels. Chicago, 1931; repr.
        Freeport, N.Y., 1971.

1.181a Goppelt, L.   Christentum und Judentum im ersten und zweiten
        Jahrhundert. Gütersloh, 1950. [French trans.: Les ori-
        gines de l'Église: Christianisme et Judaïsme aux deux pre-
        miers siècles. Paris, 1961]

1.182   Goubert, P.   "L'arc éphésien de Sainte-Marie-Majeur et les
        évangiles apocryphes," Mélanges Eugène Tisserant (Studi e
        testi 232) Rome, 1964. Vol. 2.1. Pp. 187-215.

1.183   Grabar, B. The Apocrypha in Croatian Glagolitic Literature
        Before the Sixteenth Century with Special Consideration of
        Apocryphal Apostolic Works. Zagreb Dissertation, 1965.
        [in Serbo-Croatian]

1.184   Grabar, B. "From the Problems of the Slavic Apocrypha,"
        Makedonska Akademija na naukite i umetnostite, Simpozium
        lloo-godišnina od smrtta na Kiril Solunski. Skopje, 1970.
        Pp. 91-97. [in Serbo-Croatian]

1.185   Grabe, J.E. Spicilegium SS. patrum, ut et haereticorum,
        seculi post Christum natum I, II, et III. Oxford, 1714.[2]

1.186   Graf, G. Geschichte der christlichen arabischen Literatur.
        4 vols. (Studi e testi 118, 133, 146, 147, 172) Rome, 1944-
        53.

1.187   Grant, R.M. After the New Testament. Philadelphia, 1967.

1.188   Grant, R.M. "Apocrypa, New Testament," Encyclopaedia Bri-
        tannica. Chicago, 1970. Vol. 1. Pp. 115-19.

1.189   Grant, R.M. The Earliest Lives of Jesus. New York, 1961.

1.190   Grant, R.M. "The Heresy of Tatian," JTS 5 (1954) 62-68.

1.191   Grant, R.M. "New Testament Apocrypha," The New Ency-
        clopaedia Britannica. Chicago, 1974. Vol. 2. Pp. 973f.

1.192   Grant, R.M., and D.N. Freedman. The Secret Sayings of
        Jesus. Garden City, N.Y., 1960.

1.193   Gregersen, H.G. De apokryfiske evangelier til Ny Testamente
        med en efterslaet. Milan, 1886.

1.194   Gregoire, H. "Un nom mystique du Christ," Byzantion 2
        (1925) 449-53.

1.195   Grillmeier, A. "Der Gottessohn im Totenreich," ZKT 71 (1949)
        1-53, 184-203.

1.196   Grossouw, W. "De Apocriefen van het Oude en Nieuwe Tes-
        tament in de Koptische Letterkunde," StCath 10 (1933-34)
        334-46; 11 (1934-35) 19-36.

1.197   Grynaeus, J.J. Monumenta SS. Patrum orthodoxographa.
        Basel, 1568.

1.198   Grzegorz, Peradze. An Unknown Apocryphal Gospel Originat-
        ing from Monophysite Circles. Warsaw, 1935. [in Polish]

1.199   Gschwind, K. Die Niederfahrt Christi in die Unterwelt. Müns-
        ter, 1911.

1.200   Guidi, I. "Gli Atti apocrifi degli Apostoli nei testi copti,
        arabi ed etiopici," GSAI 2 (1888) 45ff.* [Italian trans. of
        works in 1.202-208]

1.201   Guidi, I. "Di alcune pergamene saidiche della Collezione Bor-
        giana," Rendiconti della Reale Accademia dei Lincei Ser. 5,
        vol. 2 (1893) 513-30. [Various Coptic fragments: Martyr-
        dom of Simon, son of Cleopas, AcJn, etc.]

1.202   Guidi, I. "Frammenti Copti. Nota Iª," Rendiconti della Reale
        Accademia dei Lincei Ser. 4, vol. 3.1 (1887) 47-63. [Var-
        ious Coptic fragments about Stephen, James the Greater,
        James the Lesser, Simon, Judas Thaddeus]

1.203   Guidi, I. "Frammenti Copti. Nota IIª," Rendiconti della
        Reale Accademia dei Lincei Ser. 4, vol. 3.2 (1887) 19-35.
        [Various Coptic fragments related to AcAn, AcPt, and
        Preaching of Philip]

1.204   Guidi, I. "Frammenti Copti. Nota IIIª," Rendiconti della Reale
        Accademia dei Lincei Ser. 4, vol. 3.2 (1887) 65-81. [Coptic
        fragments related to AcPl, AcPt, AcAnPL, AcJn, Acts of Si-
        mon and Theonoe]

1.205   Guidi, I. "Frammenti Copti. Nota IVª," Rendiconti della
        Reale Accademia dei Lincei Ser. 4, vol. 3.2 (1887) 177-90.
        [Coptic fragments of AcAn, BkBart, MartBart]

1.206   Guidi, I. "Frammenti Copti. Nota Vª," Rendiconti della Reale
        Accademia dei Lincei Ser. 4, vol. 3.2 (1887) 251-70. [Coptic
        fragments of AcJn, Pro]

1.207   Guidi, I. "Frammenti Copti. Nota VIª," Rendiconti della
        Reale Accademia dei Lincei Ser. 4, vol. 3.2 (1887) 368-84.
        [Coptic fragments of the Acts of Andrew and Philemon, and
        of a Coptic apocryphal gospel (see category 22)]

1.208   Guidi, I. "Frammenti Copti. Nota VIIª," Rendiconti della
        Reale Accademia Lincei Ser. 4, vol. 4 (1888) 60-70. [Coptic
        fragments related to unidentified apocrypha]

1.209   Günter, H. Die christliche Legende des Abendlandes. Leip-
        zig, 1910.

1.210   Gusmao, P. "La mediación en los apócrifos," EphMar 4 (1957)
        329-38.

1.211   Guthrie, D. "Acts and Epistles in Apocryphal Writings,"

Apostolic History and the Gospel (Fs. F.F. Bruce), ed. W.W. Gasque. Exeter, 1970. Pp. 328-45.

1.212   Haase, F. Apostel und Evangelisten in den orientalischen Überlieferungen (Neutestamentliche Abhandlungen 9) Münster, 1922.

1.213   Hasse, F. Literarkritische Untersuchungen zur orientalisch-apokryphen Evangelien-literatur. Leipzig, 1913.

1.214   Haenchen, E. "Neutestamentliche und gnostische Evangelien," Christentum und Gnosis, ed. W. Eltester (BZNW 37) Berlin, 1969. Pp. 19-45.

1.215   Hallock, F.H. "Coptic Apocrypha," JBL 52 (1933) 163-74.

1.216   Hallock, F.H. "Coptic Gnostic Writings," ATR 12 (1929) 145-54.

1.217   Hammerschmidt, E. "Das Pseudo-Apostolische Schriftum in äthiopischer Überlieferung," JSS 9 (1964) 114-21.

1.218   Harnack, A., ed. Apocrypha. Bonn, 1903. [contains GosPet, ApPet, PrePet, EpLao, 3Cor].

1.219   Harnack, A. Geschichte der altchristlichen Litteratur bis Eusebius. 2 vols. Leipzig, 1893-1904. [Apocryphal gospels: 1. Pp. 4f.; 1.2. Pp. 589-651; 2.2. Pp. 177-79.]

1.220   Harnack, A. Lehrbuch der Dogmengeschichte. Freiburg, 1886-1910[3]. [ET: History of Dogma, trans. N. Buchanan. 7 vols. New York, [1900]; repr. 1961; scattered references to various NT Apocrypha]

1.221   Harnack, A. Die Mission und Ausbreitung des Christentums in den ersten drei Jahrhunderten. 2 vols. Leipzig, 1924. [ET of second, enlarged and revised edition: The Mission and Expansion of Christianity in the First Three Centuries, trans. and ed. J. Moffatt. 2 vols. New York, 1908.]

1.222   Harrington, D.J. "The Reception of Walter Bauer's Orthodoxy and Heresy in Earliest Christianity During the Last Decade," HTR 73 (1980) 289-98.

1.223   Harris, J.R., ed. The Gospel of the Twelve Apostles Together with the Apocalypses of Each One of Them. Cambridge, 1900.

1.224   Henkey, C.H. "Apocrypha of the New Testament," NCE. 2. Pp. 404-14.

1.225   Hennecke, E., ed. Handbuch zu den Neutestamentlichen Apokryphen. Tübingen, 1904.

1.226 Hennecke, E., ed. Neutestamentliche Apokryphen. Tübingen,
       1924².

1.227 Hennecke, E., and W. Schneemelcher, eds. Neutestamentliche
       Apokryphen in deutscher Übersetzung. 2 vols. Tübingen,
       1959-64³.

1.228 Hennecke, E.; W. Schneemelcher; and R. McL. Wilson, eds.
       New Testament Apocrypha. 2 vols. Philadelphia, 1963-65.

1.229 Hennecke, E. "Zur christlichen Apokryphenliteratur," ZKG
       45 (1926) 309-15. [the discussion focuses on AcAn]

1.230 Hervieux, J. Ce que l'évangile ne dit pas. Paris, 1958.
       [German trans.: Was nicht im Evangelium steht. Aschaf-
       fenburg, 1959; Italian trans.: Ciò che il Vangelo non dice.
       Catania, 1960; ET: The New Testament Apocrypha (Twen-
       tieth Century Encyclopedia of Catholicism 72) New York,
       1960; Dutch trans.: Die apocriefe Evangeliën. Amsterdam,
       1963]

1.231 Hilgenfeld, A. Judentum und Judenchristentum: Eine Nach-
       lese zu der Ketzergeschichte des Urchristentums. Leipzig,
       1886; repr. Hildesheim, 1966².

1.232 Hilgenfeld, A. Die Ketzergeschichte des Urchristenthums ur-
       kundlich dargestellt. Leipzig, 1884.

1.233 Hilgenfeld, A. Novum Testamentum extra canonem receptum.
       Leipzig, 1866. Gk. and Lat. texts

1.234 Hoennicke, G. Das Judenchristentum im ersten und zweiten
       Jahrhundert. Berlin, 1908.

1.235 Hofmann, R.A. "Apokryphen des Neuen Testaments," RPTK
       1. Pp. 511-29.

1.236 Hofmann, R.A. "Apokryphen des Neuen Testamentes," RPTK.
       1. Pp. 653-70.

1.237 Hofmann, R.A. Das Leben Jesu nach den Apokryphen in Zu-
       sammenhang aus den Quellen Erzählt und wissenschaftlich
       Untersucht. Leipzig, 1851.

1.238 Holzmeister, U. "Relationes de miraculis Christi extra Evan-
       gelia canonica existentes," VD 21 (1941) 257-63.

1.239 Hone, W., ed. and tr. The Apocryphal New Testament: Be-
       ing all the Gospels, Epistles, and Other Pieces Now Extant;
       Attributed in the First Four Centuries to Jesus Christ, His
       Apostles, and Their Companions, and Not Included in the

New Testament by its Compilers. London, 1820; New York,
[1845].

1.240 Höpfl, H. Introductionis in sacros utriusque Testamenti libros: Compendium. Naples, Rome, 1943. Vol. 1. Pp.
200-16.

1.241 Hort, F.J.A. Judaistic Christianity. Cambridge, 1894.

1.242 Hoyer, J. Die apokryphischen Evangelien auch ein Beweis
für die Glaubwürdigkeit der Kanonischen. Halberstadt,
1898-99.

1.243 Ioannidis, V.C. "Apokrypha (KD)," ThEE 2. Pp. 1108-11.
[in modern Gk.]

1.244 Ittig, T. De haeresiarchis aevi apostolici et apostolico proximi.
Leipzig, 1690. [Suppl. De Pseudepigraphis Christi, Virginis
Mariae, et apostolorum]

1.245 Ivanov, J. Bogomil Books and Legends. Sofia, 1925. [in
Bulgarian]

1.246 Jacimirskij, A.I. "Apocrypha and Legends ... On the History
of the Apocrypha, Legends, and False Prayers in South
Slavic Manuscripts," IzvORJS 14.2 (1909) 103-59, 267-322;
15.1 (1910) 1-62. [in Russian]

1.247 Jacquier, E. Le Nouveau Testament dans l'église chrétienne.
2 vols. Paris, 1911-1913.

1.248 Jagić, V. Examples of the Old Croatian Language from Glagolitic and Cyrillic Literary Antiquities. 2 vols. Zagreb, 1864-
66. [in Serbo-Croatian]

1.249 Jagić, V. "New Contributions to the Literature of the Biblical
Apocrypha," Starine 5 (1873) 69-108. [in Serbo-Croatian]

1.250 Jagić, V. Slavische Beiträge zu den biblischen Apokryphen
(Denkschriften der Kaiserl. Akademie der Wissenschaften
in Wien 42) Vienna, 1893.

1.251 Jakubowski, W. "The Apocrypha in Rus'," Słownik starożyt-
ności słowiańskich [Warsaw] 1.1 (1961) 42-43. [in Polish]

1.252 James, M.R. "Apocrypha," Encyclopaedia Biblica, ed. T.K.
Cheyne and J.S. Black. New York, London, 1899-1903.
Vol. 1. Cols. 249-61.

1.253 James, M.R., ed. Apocrypha Anecdota: A Collection of Thirteen Apocryphal Books and Fragments (T&S 2.3) Cambridge,
1893; repr. Kraus, 1967.

1.254   James, M.R., ed. Apocrypha Anecdota, second series (T&S
        5.1) Cambridge, 1897; repr. Kraus, 1967. [contains cor-
        rections to Apocrypha Anecdota, "first series," esp. to VisPl,
        AcXanPol, ApVir; plus "Leucius and the Gospel of John,"
        which is on AcJn]

1.255   James, M.R. The Apocryphal New Testament: Being the
        Apocryphal Gospels, Acts, Epistles, and Apocalypses with
        other Narratives and Fragments. Oxford, 1924; repr. 1926-
        69.

1.256   James, M.R. "Bible Criticism and Study of NT Apocrypha,"
        Official Report of the Church Congress, Bradford, England
        Sept. 27-30, 1898. London, 1898. Pp. 234-39.

1.257   James, M.R. "Irish Apocrypha," JTS 20 (1919) 9-16.

1.258   James, M.R. "Notes on Apocrypha," JTS 7 (1906) 562-68; 16
        (1915) 403-13.

1.259   James, M.R. "Notes on Apocrypha II: Syriac Apocrypha in
        Ireland," JTS 11 (1910) 288-91.

1.260   James, M.R. "Some Coptic Apocrypha," JTS 18 (1917) 163-66.

1.261   James, M.R. "Some New Coptic Apocrypha," JTS 6 (1905)
        577-86.

1.262   Jannsens, J. De Hl. Maagd en Moeder Gods. Vol. 1: Het
        Dogma en den Apocriefen. Antwerp, 1926.

1.263   Janssens, Y. "Évangiles gnostiques," Archiv für Papyrusfor-
        schung 22/23 (1974) 229-47.

1.264   Jervell, J. "The Mighty Minority," ST 34 (1980) 13-38.

1.265   Johnson, S.E. "Stray Pieces of Early Christian Writing,"
        JNES 5 (1946) 40-54.

1.266   Jones, J. A New and Full Method of Settling the Canonical
        Authority of the New Testament. 3 vols. Oxford, 1726,
        1798[2].

1.267   Karrer, O. Altchristliche Erzählungen. Munich, 1967.

1.268   Katzenellenbogen, A. "The Separation of the Apostles,"
        Gazette des Beaux Arts 35 (1949) 81-98.

1.269   Kee, H.C. The Origins of Christianity: Sources and Docu-
        ments. Englewood Cliffs, N.J., 1973. [K. includes in his
        book selections from GosTh and AcTh.]

1.270 Kelly, J.N.D. Early Christian Creeds. New York, 1960.

1.271 Kerényi, K. Die Griechisch- orientalische Romanliteratur in
       religionsgeschichtlicher Beleuchtung. Tübingen, 1927;
       Darmstadt, 1962².

1.272 Kesich, V. "Christ's Temptation in the Apocryphal Gospels
       and Acts," St. Vladimir's Seminary Quarterly 5.4 (1962)
       3-9.

1.273 Klein, G. Die zwölf Apostel, Ursprung und Gehalt einer Idee,
       Göttingen, 1961.

1.274 Kleuker, J.F. Über die Apokryphen des Neuen Testaments.
       Hamburg, 1798.

1.275 Klijn, A.F.J. "Patristic Evidence for Jewish Christian and
       Aramaic Gospel Tradition," Text and Interpretation: Stud-
       ies in the New Testament presented to Matthew Black, eds.
       E. Best and R. McL. Wilson. Cambridge, 1979. Pp. 169-
       77. [includes discussion of GosHeb and GosEb]

1.276 Klijn, A.F.J. Seth in Jewish, Christian, and Gnostic Litera-
       ture (NovTSup 46) Leiden, 1977.

1.277 Kocsis, E. "Prophecy and Apocalypse in the New Testament,"
       Theológiai Szemle (1967) 7-12.* [in Hungarian]

1.278 Koep, L. Das himmlische Buch in Antike und Christentum.
       Bonn, 1952.

1.279 Koester, H. "Apocryphal and Canonical Gospels," HTR 73
       (1980) 105-30.

1.280 Koester, H. "GNOMAI DIAPHOROI: The Origin and Nature
       of Diversification in the History of Early Christianity," HTR
       58 (1965) 279-318; repr. Trajectories through Early Chris-
       tianity, eds. J.M. Robinson and H. Koester. Philadelphia,
       1971. Pp. 114-57; "GNOMAI DIAPHOROI: Ursprung und
       Wesen der Mannigfaltigkeit in der Geschichte des frühen
       Christentums," ZTK 65 (1968) 160-203.

1.281 Koester, H. Introduction to the New Testament. Vol. 1:
       History, Culture, and Religion of the Hellenistic Age. Vol.
       2: History and Literature of Early Christianity. Phila-
       delphia, 1982.

1.282 Kosack, W. Die Legende im Koptischen: Untersuchungen zur
       Volksliteratur Agyptens. Bonn, 1970.

1.283 Köstlin, R. "Die pseudonym. Literatur der ältesten Kirche,"
       Tüb. Jahrbb. (1851)*

1.284 Kozak, E. "Bibliographische Übersicht der biblisch-apokryphen
       Literatur bei den Slaven," JPT 18 (1892) 127-58.

1.285 Kretschmar, G. Studien zur frühchristlichen Trinitätstheologie
       (BHT 21) Tübingen, 1956.

1.286- Kretzenbacher, L. "Richterengel und Feuerstrom. Östliche
7   Apokryphen und Gegenwartslegenden um Jenseitsgeleite und
        Höllenstrafen," Zeitschrift für Volkskunde 59 (1963) 205-20.

1.288 Krogh Rasmussen, N., and H. Villadsen, "Nordiske oversaet-
       telser of patristisk litteratur I. Nytest. apokryfer (Versiones
       nordicae literaturae patristicae I. Apocrypha neotest)," Lu-
       men Kobenhavn 18 (1975) 73-97.*

1.289 Kroll, J. Beiträge zum Descensus ad Inferos. Königsberg,
       1922.

1.290 Kroll, J. Gott und Hölle: Der Mythos vom Descensuskampfe.
       Leipzig, Berlin, 1932.

1.291 Kropp, A.M. Ausgewählte Koptische Zaubertexte. 2 vols.
       Brussels, 1931.

1.292 Krüger, G. "A Decade of Research in Early Christian Litera-
       ture 1921-30," HTR 26 (1933) 143-321.

1.292a Krüger, G. Geschichte der altchristlichen Literatur in den
       ersten drei Jahrhunderten. Freiburg, 1895-98.

1.293 Lacau, M.P. Fragments d'Apocryphes Coptes (Mémoires pub-
       liés par les Membres de l'Institut Francais d'Archéologie
       Orientale du Caire 9) Cairo, 1904.

1.294 Lagarde, P.A. de. Libri Veteris Testamenti Apocryphi Syriace.
       Leipzig, 1861; repr. Osnabrück, 1972.

1.295 Langkammer, H.O. "The Suffering and Resurrection of Christ
       in Light of Apocryphal Literature," Roczniki Teologiczno-
       Kanoniczne 10 (1963) 43-50. [in Polish]

1.296 Laurentin, R. "Mythe et dogme dans les apocryphes" De prim-
       ordiis cultus mariani. Rome, 1970. Vol 4. Pp. 13-29.

1.297 Lavrov, P.A. "Apocryphal Texts," SbORJS 67 (1899) [in
       Russian]*

1.298 Lechler, G.V. Das apostolische und nachapostolische Zeitalter
       mit Rücksicht auf Unterschied und Einheit in Leben und
       Lehre. Leipzig, 1885³. [ET: The Apostolic and Post-
       Apostolic Times: Their Diversity and Unity in Life and
       Doctrine, trans. A.J.K. Davidson. Edinburgh, 1886]

1.299   Leclercq, H.   "Leucius Charinus," DACL. 8. Cols. 2982-86.

1.300   Lefort, L.T.   "Fragments d'apocryphes en copte-akhmimique,"
        Museon 52 (1939) 1-10, pl. 1-2.

1.301   Legasse, S.   "La légende juive des Apôtres et les rapports
        judéo-chrétiens dans le haut Moyen Age," BLE 75 (1974) 99-
        132.

1.302   Lemm, O. von. Koptische Miscellen, eds. P. Nagel and K.
        Kümmel, 2 vols. (Studia Byzantina 10,11) Leipzig, 1972.
        [repr. from 1907-1915 fascicles of Bulletin de l'Académie
        impériale des sciences de St. Petersbourg]

1.303   Lepin, M. Évangiles Canoniques et Évangiles Apocryphes.
        Paris, 1908³.

1.304   Levi Della Vida, G. "Leggende agiografiche cristiane nell'-
        Islam" Atti del Convegno internazionale sul tema: L'Oriente
        Cristiano nella Storia della Civiltà. Rome, 1964, Pp. 139-
        51.

1.305   Lewis, A.S. Apocrypha Syriaca (Studia Sinaitica 11) Cam-
        bridge, 1902.

1.306   Lietzmann, H. Geschichte der alten Kirche. I. Die Anfänge.
        Berlin, Leipzig, 1932.

1.307   Lightfoot, J.B.; M.R. James; H.B. Swete; et al. Excluded
        Books of the New Testament, with an introduction by J.A.
        Robinson. New York, London, 1927.

1.308   Linton, O. Das Problem der Urkirche in der neueren For-
        schung. Uppsala, 1932.

1.309   Lipsius, R.A. "Gospels, apocryphal," Dictionary of Christian
        Biography, eds. W. Smith and H. Wace. 4 vols. London,
        1877-87. Vol. 2. Pp. 700-17.

1.310   Lipsius, R.A., and M. Bonnet. Acta apostolorum apocrypha.
        2 vols. Leipzig, 1891-1903; repr. Hildesheim, 1959.

1.311   Lohse, E. "Ursprung und Prägung des christlichen Aposto-
        lates," ThZ 9 (1953) 259-75.

1.312   Longenecker, R.N. The Christology of Early Jewish Chris-
        tianity (SBT, 2nd series, 17) Naperville, Ill., 1970.

1.313   Loofs, F. "Christ's Descent into Hell," Transactions of the
        Third International Congress for the History of Religions
        II. Oxford, 1908. Pp. 290-301.

1.314 Lucius, E. Die Anfänge des Heiligenkults in der christlichen
       Kirche. Tübingen, 1904. [French trans: Les origines du
       culte des saints dans l'Eglise chrétienne. Paris, 1908.]

1.315 McCormick Gatch, M. see Gatch, M.M. (1.169a)

1.316 Macdonald, J., and A.J.B. Higgins, "The Beginnings of Chris-
       tianity According to the Samaritans: Introduction, Text,
       Translation, Notes, Commentary," NTS 18 (1971-72) 54-80.

1.317 MacMullen, R. Enemies of the Roman Order. Cambridge,
       Mass., 1966.

1.318 McNamara, M. The Apocrypha in the Irish Church. Dublin,
       1975.

1.319 McNeil, B. "Jesus and the Alphabet in Apocryphal Literature
       from the Second Century Onwards," JTS 27 (1976) 126-28.

1.320 Mahan, W.D. Historical Records Concerning Jesus the 'Christ'
       Messiah. Monrovia, California, 1943.

1.321 Malan, S.C. The Conflicts of the Holy Apostles: An Apocry-
       phal Book of the Early Church. London, 1871.

1.322 Malden, R.H. The Apocrypha. London, 1936.

1.323 Manns, F. Bibliographie du Judeo-Christianisme (Studium
       Biblicum Franciscanum Analecta 13) Jerusalem, 1979.

1.324 Manns, F. Essais sur le Judéo-Christianisme (Studium Bib-
       licum Franciscanum Analecta 12) Jerusalem, 1977.

1.325 Marsh, D.W., ed. The Lost Books of the New Testament, be-
       ing all the gospels, epistles, and other pieces now extant,
       attributed, in the four centuries to Jesus Christ, His apos-
       tles and their companions and not included in the New Tes-
       tament by its compilers. Jonestown, Pa., 1925. [First pub-
       lished in 1820 by W. Hone; reedited by J. Jones and W.
       Wake, and finally presented in 1925 by Marsh.]

1.326 Marsh-Edwards, J.C. "The Magi in Tradition and Art," IER
       85 (1956) 1-9.

1.327 Marsh-Edwards, J.C. "Our Debt to the Apocryphal Infancy
       Gospels," IER 105 (1966) 365-71.

1.328 Masser, A. Bibel, Apokryphen und Legenden. Geburt und
       Kindheit Jesu in der religiösen Epik des deutschen Mittel-
       alters. Cologne, 1969.

1.329 Mateo Argomaniz, J. La manifestación de la fe a través de
       las oraciones de los Hechos Apócrifos (Diss. lic. Studii Bib-
       lici Franciscani) Jerusalem, 1972.

1.330 Meinardus, O.F.A. In the Steps of the Holy Family from Beth-
       lehem to Upper Egypt. Cairo, 1963.

1.331 Merell, J. Ancient Christian Apocrypha. Prague, 1942. [in
       Czech]

1.332 Mescherskaja, E.N. "On the History of the Syriac Sources
       and Greek-Slavonic Versions of the Apocrypha," Palestinckii
       Sbornik 23 (86) (1971) 168-72. [in Russian]

1.333 Messina, G. "Lezioni apocrife nel Diatessaron persiano," Bib
       30 (1949) 10-27.

1.334 Metzger, B.M. "Apokryphen des Neuen Testaments," RGG[3].
       1. Cols. 473f.

1.335 Metzger, B.M. "Literary Forgeries and Canonical Pseudepi-
       grapha," JBL 91 (1972) 3-24.

1.336 Metzger, B.M. "New Testament Apocrypha," An Introduction
       to the Apocrypha. New York, 1957. Pp. 249-64.

1.337 Meyer, A. "Religiöse Pseudepigraphie als ethisch-psychologisch
       Problem," ZNW 35 (1936) 262-79.

1.338 Meyer, A., and W. Bauer, "Jesu Verwandtschaft," HS. 1.
       Pp. 312-21.

1.339 Meyer, A., and W. Bauer, "The Relatives of Jesus," HSW. 1.
       Pp. 418-32.

1.340 Michaelis, W. Die Apokryphen Schriften zum Neuen Testament
       (Sammlung Dieterich Band 129) Bremen, 1962[3].

1.341 Michaelis, W. Zur Engelchristologie im Urchristentum. Basel,
       1942.

1.342 Michel, C., and P. Peeters. Évangiles Apocryphes. 2 vols.
       (Textes et documents pour l'étude historique du Christian-
       isme 13, 18) Paris, 1911-14. [See M.R. James' review JTS
       13 (1912) 433-35; JTS 16 (1915) 268-73.]

1.343 Michl, J. "Apocrypha," Sacramentum Mundi. 1. Pp. 52-66.

1.344 Michl, J. "Apokryphe Evangelien," LTK[3]. 3. Cols. 1217-33.

1.345 Migne, J.-P. Dictionnaire des Apocryphes, ou collection de

tous les livres apocryphes. 2 vols. Paris, 1856-58. [Apoc-
ryphal gospels: Vol. 1. Cols. 961-72; Vol. 2. Cols. 231-
42]

1.346 Mingana, A. Catalogue of the Mingana Collection of Manu-
       scripts. Vol. 2: Christian Arabic Manuscripts and Addi-
       tional Syriac Manuscripts (Selly Oak Colleges Library) Cam-
       bridge, 1936.

1.347 Minissi, N. "La tradizione apocrifa e le origini del Bogomi-
       lismo," Ricerche slavistische 3 (1954) 97-113.

1.348 Moffatt, J. An Introduction to the Literature of the New Tes-
       tament. New York, 1911.

1.349 Moggridge, M.W. "Lost Gospels," Exp 12 (1880) 325-45.

1.350 Monneret de Villard, U. Le leggende orientali sui Magi evan-
       gelici. Rome, 1952.

1.351 Monnier, J. La descente aux enfers: Étude de pensée reli-
       gieuse, d'art et de littérature. Paris, 1905.

1.352 Montalverne, J. "A Literatura dos Judeo-cristiãos nos três
       primeiros séculos. Origem da Igreja da Circuncisão, ou
       Judeo-cristã," Theologica [Braga, Portugal] 6 (1971) 157-85.

1.353 Moraldi, L. Apocrifi del Nuovo Testamento. 2 vols. (Clas-
       sici delle Religioni, sezione 5) Turin, 1971.

1.354 Morino, C. Il ritorno al paradiso di Adamo in S. Ambrogio.
       Rome, 1952.

1.355 Movers, K. "Apokryphen und Apokryphenlitteratur," Kirch-
       enlexicon de Wetzer y Welte. Vol. 1.*

1.356 Mozley, J.R. "A New Text of the Story of the Cross," JTS
       31 (1929-30) 113-27.

1.357 Müller, J.J. Nuwe-Testamentiese Apokriewe. Pretoria, 1974.
       [Intro. to and trans. into Afrikaans of ProtJas, InfGTh,
       GPet, GosNic, AcJn, AcPl, AcPet, ApPet]

1.358 Munck, J. "Discours d'adieu dans le Nouveau Testament et
       dans la littérature biblique," Aux sources de la tradition
       chrétienne: Mélanges offerts à M. Maurice Goguel à l'oc-
       casion de son soixante-dixième anniversaire. Neuchâtel,
       1950. Pp. 155-70.

1.359 Murray, R. Symbols of Church and Kingdom: A Study in
       Early Syriac Tradition. Cambridge, 1975. [For an informed
       discussion of the Addai legend see esp. pp. 4-24]

1.360 Nagel, P. Die Motivierung der Askese in der alten Kirche und der Ursprung des Mönchtums (TU 95) Berlin, 1966. [Nagel includes in his discussion numerous NT apocryphal documents]

1.361 Nau, F. "Apocryphes," DAFC. 2. Cols. 174-76.

1.362 Naumow, A.E. The Apocrapha in the Church Slavic Literary System. Cracow, 1976. [in Polish]

1.363 Nautin, P. Lettres et écrivains chrétiens des IIe et IIIe siècles. Paris, 1961.

1.364 Neander, M. Apocrypha, hoc est Narrationes de Christo, Maria et Joseph, cognatione et familia Christi, extra biblia [Cathechesis Martini Lutheri parva graeco-latina] Basel, 1564.

1.365 Négrepelisse, P. de. Recherches sur les apocryphes du N.T.: Thèse historique et critique. Montauban, 1850.*

1.366 Nestle, E. De sancta Cruce: Ein Beitrag zur christlichen Legendengeschichte. Berlin, 1889.

1.367 Nestle, E. Novi Testamenti Graeci Supplementum. Leipzig, 1896.

1.368 Nicolas, M. Études sur les évangiles apocryphes. Paris, 1865.

1.369 Niemczyk, W. "The Extrabiblical Sources for the 'Life and Teaching of Jesus Christ,'" Rocznik Teologiczny 20 (1978) 109-24. [in Polish]

1.370 Nitzsch, C.I. De apocryphorum evangeliorum in explicandis canonicis usu et abusu. Vilebergae, 1808.

1.371 Nock, A.D. "The Apocryphal Gospels," JTS n.s. 11 (1960) 63-70.

1.372 Nola, A.M. di. "Apocrifi del Nuovo Testamento," EncRel. 1. Cols. 522-26.

1.373 Nola, A.M. di. "Atti ed epistole apocrifi degli Apostoli," EncRel. 1. Cols. 817-37.

1.374 Nola, A.M. di. "Evangeli apocrifi," EncRel. 2. Cols. 1347-86.

1.375 Nola, A.M. di. Vangeli apocrifi: Natività e infanzia (Biblioteca della Fenice 10). Milan, 1977.

1.376 Nostiz, O., and Tyciak, J. Die apokryphen Evangelien. Zurich, 1956.

104   IV. Bibliography

1.377 Novaković, S. "Apocrypha from the Printed Collections of
       Božidar Vuković," Starine 16 (1884) 57-76. [in Serbo-
       Croatian]

1.378 Novaković, S. "Apocrypha of One Serbian Cyrillic Collection
       of the Fourteenth Century," Starine 8 (1876) 36-74. [in
       Serbo-Croatian]

1.379 Novaković, S. "The Apocrypha of a Kiev Manuscript," Star-
       ine 16 (1884) 89-96. [in Serbo-Croatian]

1.380 Novaković, S. "Apocryphal Tales About the Death of the
       Virgin Mother and Other Apocryphal Details About the Vir-
       gin Mother," Starine 18 (1886) 188-208. [in Serbo-Croatian]

1.381 O Cuív, B. "Two Items from Irish Apocryphal Tradition,"
       Celtica 10 (1973) 87-113.

1.382 Oesterley, W.O.E. An Introduction to the Books of the Apoc-
       rypha. London, 1935.

1.383 Oesterley, W.O.E. Readings from the Apocrypha. London,
       1939.

1.384 Orr, J. New Testament Apocryphal Writings. London, 1903.

1.385 Overbeck, F. Über die Anfänge der patristischen Literatur.
       Basel, 1892; repr. Darmstadt, 1965.

1.386 Pantelakis, E. "The Beginnings of the Church's Works,"
       Theologia [Athens] 15 (1937) 323-39; 16 (1938) 5-31. [in
       Gk.]

1.387 Partyka, J.S. "The Apocrypha of the New Testament in the
       Plastic Arts," Znak 29 (1977) 531-34. [in Polish]

1.388 Pedicini, C. Demonologia e instaurazione del Regno di Dio nel
       pensiero dei più antichi cristiani. Naples, 1953.

1.389 Peeters, P., ed. Bibliotheca hagiographica orientalis (Subsi-
       dia Hagiographica 10) Brussels, 1910.

1.390 Peeters, P. Évangiles apocryphes (Textes et documents pour
       l'étude historique du christianisme) Paris, 1914.

1.391 Peinador, M. "Estudio sobre los Evangelios Apócrifos," Illus-
       tración del Clero 22 (1928) 86f., 101-04, 165-68, 198-202,
       211-16.

1.392 Penna, A. "Gli apocrifi del Nuovo Testamento," EncCatt. 1.
       Cols. 1629-33.

1.393 Peterson, E. Frühkirche, Judentum und Gnosis. Freiburg, 1959.

1.394 Piankoff, A. "La descente aux enfers dans les textes égyptiens et dans les apocryphes coptes," BSC 7 (1941) 33-46.

1.395 Pick, B. The Extra-Canonical Life of Christ: Being a Record of the Acts and Sayings of Jesus of Nazareth Drawn from Uninspired Sources. New York, London, 1903.

1.396 Pick, B. The Life of Jesus According to the Extra-canonical Sources. London, 1887.

1.397 Pines, S. "The Jewish-Christians of the Early Centuries of Christianity According to a New Source," Proceedings of the Israel Academy of Sciences and Humanities 2 (1966) 1-73. [see rev. by R.A. Kraft, JBL 86 (1967) 329-30.]

1.398 Pines, S. "Un texte judéo-chrétien adapté par un théologien musulman," Nouvelles chrétiennes d'Israël 2-3 (1966) 12-20.

1.399 Piontek, F. Die katholische Kirche und die häretischen Apostelgeschichten bis zum Ausgange des 6. Jahrhunderts. (Kirchenrechtliche Abhandlungen 6) Breslau, 1908.

1.400 Plummer, A. "The Apocryphal Gospels," ExpT 34 (1922-23) 373-76, 473f.

1.401 Pons, J. Recherches sur les apocryphes du nouveau Testament. Thèse historique et critique. Montauban, 1850.

1.402 Porfiryev, I.Y. "Apocryphal Sayings About New Testament People and Events in Manuscripts of the Solovetski Library," SbORJS 52 (1890). [in Russian]*

1.403 Porfiryev, I.Y. "Apocryphal Sayings About Old Testament People and Events in Manuscripts of the Solovetski Library," SbORJS 17 (1877). [in Russian]*

1.404 Potter, M.A. The Legendary Story of Christ's Childhood. New York, 1899.

1.405 Powell, C.H. "The Apocrypha and Pseudepigrapha," The Biblical Concept of Power. London, 1963. Pp. 44-59.

1.406 Preisendanz, K., ed. Papyri Graecae Magicae. 3 vols. Leipzig, Berlin, 1928; 2nd revised ed. by A. Henrichs, 1974.

1.407 Preuschen, E., ed. Antilegomena: Die Reste der ausserkanonischen Evangelien und urchristlichen Überlieferungen. Giessen, 1901, 1905^2. [Gk. and Lat. texts]

1.408 Prieur, J.M. "Les Évangiles apocryphes," Positions Luthér-
       iennes 24 (1976) 74-95.

1.409 Proctor, W.C. The Value of the Apocrypha. London, 1926.

1.410 Puech, A. Histoire de la littérature grecque chrétienne. 2
       vols. Paris, 1928.

1.411 Quasten, J. Patrology. 1. Pp. 106-57.

1.412 Quispel, G. "Mani et la tradition évangélique des judéo-
       chrétiens," RSR 60 (1972) 143-50.

1.413 Quispel, G., and R.M. Grant. "Note on the Petrine Apoc-
       rypha," VC 6 (1952) 31-32.

1.414 Ragot, A. "L'essénisme dans les apocryphes," Cahiers du
       Cercle Ernest Renan 20 (1972) 3-8.

1.415 Rauschen, G. Florilegium Patristicum, eds. Geyer-Zellinger-
       Rauschen. Bonn, 1905. [See esp. vol. 3]*

1.416 Raynold, [?]. Censura apocr. V. et N.T. Oppenh., 1611.*

1.417 Repp, F., "Untersuchungen zu den Apokryphen der Öster-
       reichischen Nationalbibliothek," Wiener Slavistisches Jahr-
       buch 6 (1957-58) 5-34; 7 (1959) 44-48; 10 (1963) 58-68.

1.418 Resch, A. Aussercanonische Paralleltexte zu den Evangelien:
       Textkritische und quellenkritische Grundlegungen (TU 10.1)
       Leipzig, 1893.

1.419 Resch, A. Aussercanonische Paralleltexte zu den Evangelien:
       Paralleltexte zu Johannes (TU 10.4) Leipzig, 1896.

1.420 Resch, A. Aussercanonische Paralleltexte zu den Evangelien:
       Paralleltexte zu Lucas (TU 10.3) Leipzig, 1895.

1.421 Resch, A. Aussercanonische Paralleltexte zu den Evangelien:
       Paralleltexte zu Matthaeus und Marcus (TU 10.2) Leipzig,
       1894.

1.422 "Research Groups in North America Studying Early Christian-
       ity," Second Century 1 (1981) 55-58.

1.423 Revillout, E. "Les Apocryphes Coptes," PO 2 (1907) 119-98;
       9 (1913) 57-140. [See M.R. James' review JTS 7 (1906)
       633f.]

1.424 Revillout, E. "Lettre à M. le Rédacteur du Journal Asiatique
       sur de nouveaux Évangiles apocryphes relatifs à la Vierge,"
       JA 2 (1903) 162-74.

1.425 Revillout, E. "La sage-femme Salomé d'après un apocryphe
       copte comparé aux fresques de Baouit et la princesse Salomé,
       fille du tétrarque Philippe, d'après le même document," JA
       5 (1905) 409-61.

1.426 Riddle, M.B. "Introductory Notice to Apocrypha of the New
       Testament," ANF. 8. Pp. 349-60.

1.427 Riesenfeld, H. "La descente dans la mort," Aux sources de
       la tradition chrétienne: Mélanges offerts à M. Maurice Go-
       guel à l'occasion de son soixante-dixième anniversaire. Neu-
       châtel, 1950.

1.428 Riesenfeld, H. "Nya testaments apokryfer," SBU 2 (1952)
       488-91.

1.429 Rist, M. "Pseudepigraphic Refutations of Marcionism," JRel
       22 (1942) 39-62.

1.430 Rist, M. "Pseudepigraphy and the Early Christians," Studies
       in New Testament and Early Christian Literature: Essays
       in Honor of Allen P. Wickgren, ed. D.E. Aune (NovTSup
       33) Leiden, 1972. Pp. 75-91.

1.431 Ritschl, A. Die Entstehung der altkatholische Kirche. Bonn,
       1850.

1.432 Roberts, A., and J. Donaldson, eds. The Ante-Nicene Fa-
       thers: Translations of the Writings of the Fathers Down to
       A.D. 325. Vol. 8. Edinburgh, 1868-1872; rev. and repr.
       Grand Rapids, Mich., 1951.

1.433 Robinson, F. Coptic Apocryphal Gospels: Translations To-
       gether with the Texts of Some of Them (T&S 4.2) Cambridge,
       1896.

1.434 Robson, J. "Stories of Jesus and Mary," Muslim World 40
       (1950) 236-43.

1.435 Roncaglia, M. "Les apocryphes chrétiens et la gnose," Les
       origines. Pp. 63-109.

1.436 Roncaglia, M. "La 'Praeparatio Evangelica' et les premiers
       contacts avec les idées chrétiennes," Les origines. Pp. 11-
       62.

1.437 Rost, C. Les Évangiles Apocryphes de l'enfance de Jésus-
       Christ avec une introduction sur les récits de Mattieu et
       de Luc. Montauban, 1894.

1.438 Rousseau, O. "La descente aux enfers, fondement sotériologique

du baptême chrétien," Mélanges Jules Lebreton (RSR 40)
Paris, 1952. Vol. 2. Pp. 273-97.

1.439 Rustafjaell, R. de. The Light of Egypt from Recently Dis-
       covered Predynastic and Early Christian Records. London,
       1909.

1.440 Ruts, C. De Apocriefen uit het Nieuw- Testament. Vol. 1:
       Evangeliën en Kerkstemmen. Brussels, 1927.

1.441 Ruwet, J. "Les 'Antilegomena' dans les oeuvres d'Origène,"
       Bib 23 (1942) 18-58.

1.442 Ruwet, J. "Les apocryphes dans les oeuvres d'Origène,"
       Bib 25 (1944) 143-66, 311-34. [see also 4.124]

1.443 Sadnik, L. "Das Schicksal der Apokryphen bei den Slaven,"
       Universitas 2 (1947) 1051-54.

1.444 Saintyves, P. "De la nature des évangiles apocryphes et de
       leur valeur hagiographique," RHR 106 (1932) 435-57.

1.445 Salmaslian, A. Bibliographie de L'Arménie. Erévan, 1969².

1.446 Santos Otero, A. de. Los Evangelios Apócrifos. Madrid,
       1975³.

1.447 Santos Otero, A. de. Die handschriftliche Überlieferung der
       altslavischen Apokryphen, 2 vols. (Patristische Texte und
       Studien 20, 23) Berlin, New York, 1978, 1981.

1.448 Santos Otero, A. de. "Das Problem der kirchen-slavischen
       Apokryphen," Zeitschrift fur Balkanologie 1 (1962) 123-32.

1.449 Scarabelli, L. I vangeli apocrifi ora per prima volta in nostra
       lingua tradotti. Bologna, 1867.

1.450 Schade, G. Wort im Versteck: Plädoyer für die Apokryphen.
       Berlin, 1969.

1.451 Schall, A. Zur äthiopischen Verskunst: Eine Studie über die
       Metra des Qenē auf Grund der Abhandlung 'al-Qenē laun min
       ās-špr al-Habašī'. Wiesbaden, 1961.

1.452 Schlatter, A. "Die Entwicklung des jüdischen Christentums
       zum Islam," EvM 62 (1918) 251-64.

1.453 Schmid, C.C.L. Corpus omnium veterum apocryphorum extra
       biblia. Hadamar, 1804.

1.454 Schmid, M. Die Darstellung der Geburt Christi in der bilden-
       den Kunst. Stuttgart, 1890.

1.455   Schmidt, C. "Übersicht über die vornicänische Literatur (ein-
        schliesslich der apokryphen) in koptischer Sprache," Gesch.
        altchrist. Lit. 1. Pp. 918-24.

1.456   Schmidt, J.A. Pseudo-Novum Testamentum exhibens Pseudo-
        Evangelia, Acta, Epistolas, Apocalypses. Helmstadt, 1699.

1.457   Schmidt, K.L. Kanonische und apokryphe Evangelien und
        Apostelgeschichten (ATANT 5) Basel, 1944.

1.458   Schneemelcher, W. "Bemerkungen zum Kirchenbegriff der
        apokryphen Evangelien," Gesammelte Aufsätze zum Neuen
        Testament und zur Patristik, ed. W. Bienert and K. Schä-
        ferdiek (Analekta Blatadōn 22) Thessalonica, 1974. Pp. 139-
        53. [Originally published in Ecclesia: Een Bundel opstellen
        aangeboden aan Prof. Dr. J. N. Bakhuizen van den Brink.
        Gravenhage, 1959. Pp. 18-32]

1.459   Schoeps, H.J. Aus frühchristlicher Zeit. Tübingen, 1950.

1.460   Schoeps, H.J. Theologie und Geschichte des Judenchristen-
        tums. Tübingen, 1949.

1.461   Scholer, D.M. Nag Hammadi Bibliography 1948-1969 (NHS 1)
        Leiden, 1971. [supplemented periodically in NovT]

1.462   Schonfield, H.J. Readings from the Apocryphal Gospels.
        London, 1940.

1.463   Schubert, K. "Versuchung oder Versucher? Der Teufel als
        Begriff oder Person in den Biblischen und ausserbiblischen
        Texten." BiLit 50 (1977) 104-07; cf. 600-03, 609, 793, 1657,
        1706, 1742, 1809, 1880.

1.464   Schwarz, F.J. De ev. impartiae Jesu verset ficto. Leipzig,
        1785.*

1.465   Schwegler, A. Das nachapostolische Zeitalter in den Haupt-
        momenten seiner Entwicklung. Tübingen, 1846.

1.466   Schweizer, E. Erniedrigung und Erhöhung bei Jesus und
        seinen Nachfolger (ATANT 28) Zurich, 1955.

1.467   Scobie, C.H.H. "Apocryphal New Testament," Dictionary of
        the Bible, ed. J. Hastings, rev. ed. F.C. Grant and H.H.
        Rowley. New York, 1963. Pp. 41-45.

1.468   Sedgwick, S.N. Story of the Apocrypha: A Series of Lec-
        tures on the Books and Times of the Apocrypha. London,
        1906.

1.469 Segal, J.B. Edessa: "The Blessed City." Oxford, 1970.
       [For a valuable discussion of the Addai legend see pp. 62-
       87.]

1.470 Siegmund, A. "Die Apokryphen-Literatur," Die Uberlieferung
       der Griechischen Christlichen Literatur (Abhandlungen der
       Bayerischen Benediktiner-Akademie 5) Munich, 1949. Pp.
       33-48.

1.471 Simon, M. Verus Israel: Études sur les relations entre Chré-
       tiens et Juifs dans l'empire romain (135-425). Paris, 1948;
       1964².

1.472 Siniscalco, P. "L'idea dell' eternità e della fine di Roma negli
       autori cristiani primitivi," Studi Romani 25 (1977) 1-26.

1.473 Sint, J.A. "Am Rande der vier Evangelien: Zu den Apokry-
       phen des NT," Bibel und Leben 1 (1960) 186-92.

1.474 Sint, J.A. Pseudonymität im Altertum: Ihre Formen und
       Gründe. Innsbruck, 1960.

1.475 Snell, B.J. The Value of the Apocrypha. London, 1905.

1.476 Sokolov, M.I. Apocryphal Apocalypse (Varucha: Drevnosti.
       Trudi Slavjanskoj Kommissii Imp. Moskovskogo Obšestva. 4).
       Moscow, 1907. [in Russian]

1.477 Spaetling, P.L. De Apostolicis, Pseudapostolicis, Apostolinis.
       Munich, 1947. [Dissertation]

1.478 Speranskij, M.N. "Slavic Apocryphal Gospels," The Work of
       the Eighth Archaeological Conference in Moscow, 1890. Mos-
       cow, 1895. Vol. 2. Pp. 38-172. [in Russian]

1.479 Speyer, W. "Fälschung, literarische," RAC. 7. Pp. 236-77.

1.480 Speyer, W. "Fälschung, pseudepigraphische freie Erfindung
       und 'echte religiöse Pseudepigraphie,'" Pseud I. Pp. 331-
       66. [See the comments by K. von Fritz, W. Speyer, M. Hen-
       gel, W. Burkert, and M. Smith, pp. 367-72.]

1.481 Speyer, W. Die literarische Fälschung im heidnischen, jüdi-
       schen und christlichen Altertum: Ein Versuch ihrer Deutung
       (HAW 1) Munich, 1971.

1.482 Speyer, W. "Religiöse Pseudepigraphie und literarische Fäl-
       schung im Altertum," JAC 8 (1965) 88-125.

1.483 Spinetoli, O. da. Introduzione ai Vangeli dell'infanzia. As-
       sisi, 1976.

1.484   Stählin, O. Die altchristliche griechische Literatur. Munich,
        1924.

1.485   Starowieyski, M. The Apocrypha of the New Testament. 2
        vols. (Studies and Monographs 106, 107) Lublin, 1980.
        [This Polish work is similar in format to HSW; but it includes
        more documents, a section on "The Apocrypha in Art," and
        an extensive bibliography.]

1.486   Starowieyski, M. "Apocryphal Gospels," Znak 29 (1977) 522-
        30. [in Polish]

1.487   Starowieyski, M. "Fragments of the Apocrypha," Znak 29
        (1977) 535-67. [in Polish]

1.488   Steffen, R. Jesu död. Urkunder och apokryfiska framställ-
        ningar. Stockholm, 1947.

1.489   Stegmüller, F. Repertorium biblicum Medii Aevi. Madrid,
        1950, 1976. Vols. 1, 8.

1.490   Stegmüller, O. "Sub tuum praesidium: Bemerkungen zur
        ältesten Überlieferung," ZKT 74 (1952) 76-82.

1.491   Steidle, B. Patrologia, seu Historia Litteraturae Ecclesiasticae.
        Freiburg, 1937. [See esp. pp. 277-84]

1.492   Stern, S.M. "Quotations from Apocryphal Gospels in ʿAbd Al-
        Jabbār," JTS 18 (1967) 34-57.

1.493   Stone, M.E. "The Apocryphal Literature in the Armenian Tra-
        dition," Israel Academy of Sciences and Humanities 4 (1969)
        59-78.

1.494   Stone, M.E. Armenian Apocrypha Relating to Patriarchs and
        Prophets. Jerusalem, 1982.

1.495   Stowe, C.E. Origin and History of the Books of the Bible.
        Hartford, 1867. Pp. 209-38.

1.496   Strecker, G. "Christentum und Judentum in den ersten beiden
        Jahrhunderten," EvT 16 (1956) 458-77.

1.497   Strecker, G. "Nachtrag," in Rechtgläubigkeit und Ketzerei
        im ältesten Christentum, by W. Bauer (BHT 10) Tübingen,
        1964. Pp. 243-314. [ET: "On the Problem of Jewish Chris-
        tianity," Appendix I in Orthodoxy and Heresy in Earliest
        Christianity, ed. R. Kraft and G. Krodel. Philadelphia,
        1971. Pp. 241-85]

1.498   Strohal, R. Old Croatian Apocryphal Tales and Legends,

Collected from Old Croatian Glagolitic Manuscripts from the
Fourteenth to the Eighteenth Centuries. BJelovaru, 1917.*

1.499 Stroker, W.D. "Examples of Pronouncement Stories in Early
       Christian Apocryphal Literature," Semeia 20 (1981) 133-41.

1.500 Stuiber, A. "Die christlichen Apocryphen Schriften," Altaner-
       Stuiber Patrologie. Freiburg, 1966. Pp. 117-44.

1.501 Surkau, H.W. Martyrium in jüdischen und frühchristlicher
       Zeit. Göttingen, 1938.

1.502 Svencickaja, I.S. Forbidden Gospels. Moscow, 1965. [in
       Russian]

1.503 Szefler, P. "The Apocrypha Concerning the Suffering and
       Resurrection of the Lord Christ," RoTKan 9 (1962) 75-105.
       [in Polish]

1.504 Szekely, S. Bibliotheca Apocrypha. Freiburg, 1913.

1.505 Talbert, C.H. "The Myth of a Descending-Ascending Redee-
       mer in Mediterranean Antiquity," NTS 22 (1976) 418-40.

1.506 Tappehorn, A. Ausserbiblische Nachrichten oder die Apocry-
       phen über die Geburt, Kindheit und das Lebensende Jesu
       und Maria. Paderborn-Munich, 1855.

1.507 Tasker, J.G. "Apocryphal Gospels," Hastings. 5. Pp. 420-
       38.

1.508 Tayec'i, E. Ankanon girk Nor ketakaranatz. 2 vols. Venice,
       1898-1904. [Arm. texts]

1.509 Thilo, J.C. Codex apocryphus Novi Testamenti. Leipzig,
       1832. [Gk. and Lat. texts]

1.510 Thomas, J. "Les ébionites baptistes," RHE 30 (1934) 257-96.

1.511 Thomas, J. Le mouvement baptiste en Palestine et Syrie.
       Gembloux, 1935.

1.512 Tichonravov, N.S. "Apocryphal Sayings," SbORJS 58 (1894)
       [in Russian]*

1.513 Tischendorf, K. Acta Apostolorum Apocrypha. Leipzig, 1851.
       [Gk. texts]

1.514 Tischendorf, K. "Additamenta ad Evangelia Apocrypha,"
       Apocalypses Apocryphae. Pp. LI-LXIV. [Gk. text]

1.515 Tischendorf, K. Apocalypses apocryphae Mosis, Esdrae, Pauli, Iohannis, item Mariae dormitio, additis Evangeliorum et Actuum apocryphorum supplementis. Leipzig, 1866. [Gk. and Lat. texts]

1.516 Tischendorf, K. Evangelia Apocrypha. Leipzig, 1876; repr. Hildesheim, 1966. [Gk. and Lat. texts]

1.517 Tischendorf, K. De evangeliorum apocryphorum origine et usu. Hagae Comitum, 1851.

1.518 Torm, F. Die Psychologie der Pseudonymität im Hinblick auf die Literatur des Urchristentums. Gütersloh, 1932.

1.519 Torres, M. "Breve introducción a los libros apócrifos," RevistB 12 (1950) 1-5.

1.520 Torrey, C.C. The Apocryphal Literature. New Haven, 1945; rev. ed. 1963.

1.521 Trenton, R.F. "References to Apocrypha, Pseudepigrapha, and Extrabiblical Literature as Noted in the Outer Margins of the Nestle-Aland New Testament," CTM 39 (1968) 328-32.

1.522 Tröger, K.W., ed. Gnosis und Neues Testament: Studien aus Religionswissenschaft und Theologie. Berlin, 1973.

1.523 Turdeanu, E. "Apocryphes bogomiles et apocryphes pseudo-bogomiles," RHR 138 (1950) 22-52, 176-218. [repr. in Apocryphes slaves et roumains de l'Ancien Testament (SVTP 5) Leiden, 1981. Pp. 1-74]

1.524 Turdeanu, E. "Les apocryphes slaves et roumains: Leur apport à la connaissance des apocryphes grecs," SBN 8 (1953) 47-52.

1.525 Turmel, J. La descente du Christ aux enfers. Paris, 1905.

1.526 Turner, H.E.W. The Pattern of Christian Truth: A Study in the Relations Between Orthodoxy and Heresy in the Early Church. Leipzig, 1954.

1.527 Tyloch, W. Literatura na świecie 12 (1974) 59-83.*

1.528 Variot, J. Les Évangiles apocryphes: Histoire littéraire, forme primitive, transformations. Paris, 1878.

1.529 Vassiliev, A. Anecdota graeco-byzantina. Moscow, 1893. [Gk. texts]

1.530 Vergote, J. "La littérature copte et sa diffusion," Atti del

Convegno internazionale sul tema: L'Oriente Cristiano nella
Storia della Civiltà. Rome, 1963. Pp. 103-17.

1.531 Vielhauer, P. Geschichte der urchristlichen Literatur: Ein-
       leitung in das Neue Testament, die Apokryphen und die
       Apostolischen Väter. Berlin, 1975; rev. ed. 1978. [V.
       gives special attention to the following documents: ApPet,
       GosTh, GosPet, GosNaz, GosEb, GosHeb, InfGosTh, AcPet,
       AcPl, AcAn, AcJn, AcTh, and the agrapha]

1.532 Vitti, A.M. "Apocryphorum de Magis enarrationes," VD 7
       (1927) 3-13.

1.533 Vitti, A.M. "De Christi resurrectione in Apocryphis," VD
       9 (1929) 103-11.

1.534 Vitti, A.M. "Desensus Christi ad infernos juxta I Pet., III,
       19-20; IV, 6 et juxta Apocrypha," VD 7 (1927) 111-18, 138-
       44, 171-81.

1.535 Vitti, A.M. "Evangelia Apocrypha," VD 3 (1923) 20-27.

1.536 Vitti, A.M. "I magi nella letteratura degli Apocrifi," Vita e
       Pensiero 18 (1928) 20-26.

1.537 Vranska, C. The Apocrypha Concerning the Virgin Mother
       in the Bulgarian Folk Song (Collection of the Bulgarian
       Academy of Sciences 34) Sofia, 1940. [in Bulgarian]

1.538 Waal, A. De "Die apokryphen Evangelien in der altchristlichen
       Kunst," Römische Quartalschrift 1 (1887) 173-77.

1.539 Waitz, H. "Apokryphen des Neuen Testamentes," RPTK. 23.
       Pp. 78-103.

1.540 Waitz, H. "Neue Untersuchungen über die sogen. judenchrist-
       lichen Evangelien," ZNW 36 (1937) 60-81. [W. discusses the
       GosHeb, GosEb, GosNaz]

1.541 Wake, W. The Forbidden Books of the Original New Testament.
       London, 1820.

1.542 Wake, W., and N. Lardner. The Apocryphal New Testament.
       London: n.d.; repr. Mokelumne Hill, California, 1970.

1.543 Walker, A. Apocryphal Gospels and Revelations. Edinburgh,
       1890.

1.544 Walker, A., tr. Readings from the Apocryphal Gospels. New
       York, 1940.

1.545   Walterscheid, J. Das Leben Jesu nach den neutestamentlichen
        Apokryphen. Düsseldorf, 1953.

1.546   Weiss-Liebesdorf, J.E. Christus und Apostelbilder: Der Ein-
        fluss der Apokryphen auf die ältesten Kunsttypen. Freiburg,
        1902.

1.547   Wessel, K. "Apokrypha," Reallexikon aus Byzantinischen Kunst
        1 (1972) 209-19.

1.548   Wessely, C. "Les plus anciens monuments du Christianisme
        écrits sur papyrus," PO 4 (1906) 105-209; 18 (1924) 341-
        509.

1.549   Wetter, G.P., Altchristliche Liturgien: Das christliche Myster-
        ium (FRLANT 13) Göttingen, 1921.

1.550   Wilkgren, A. "Luther and the 'New Testament Apocrypha,'"
        A Tribute to Arthur Vööbus: Studies in Early Christian
        Literature and its Environment, Primarily in the Syrian East,
        ed. R.H. Fischer. Chicago, 1977, Pp. 379-90.

1.551   Willard, R. Two Apocrypha in Old English Homilies. Leip-
        zig, 1935.

1.552   Wilson, R.McL. "Apocrypha, NT," IDBS. Pp. 34-36.

1.553   Wilson, R.McL. "Apocryphal New Testament," ZPEB. 1.
        Pp. 210-13.

1.554   Wilson, R.McL. "Apokryphen, II: Apokryphen des Neuen
        Testaments," TRE. 3. Pp. 316-62.

1.555   Wilson, R.McL. "The New Passion of Jesus in the Light of the
        New Testament and the Apocrypha," Neotestamentica et Sem-
        itica, eds. E.E. Ellis and M. Wilcox. Edinburgh, 1969. Pp.
        264-71. [see 1.397]

1.556   Winstedt, E.O. "Some Coptic Apocryphal Legends," JTS 9
        (1908) 372-86; 10 (1909) 389-412.

1.557   Wright, W. Apocryphal Acts of Apostles, Edited from Syriac
        Manuscripts in the British Museum and Other Libraries. 2
        vols. London, 1871; repr. Amsterdam, 1968. [Syr. texts
        and ET]

1.558   Wright, W. Contributions to the Apocryphal Literature of the
        New Testament, Collected and Edited from Syriac Manuscripts
        in the British Museum. London, 1865.

1.559   Yamauchi, E.M. Pre-Christian Gnosticism: A Survey of the

Proposed Evidences. Grand Rapids, 1973. [Y. includes
esp. a discussion of GosTh, AcTh]

1.560 Zahn, T. Geschichte des neutestamentliche Kanons. 2 vols.
Leipzig, 1888-92.

1.561 Zebelev, S.A. Canonical and Apocryphal Gospels. Petrograd,
1919. [in Russian]

1.562 Zruijewski, J. "Apostolische Paradosis und Pseudepigraphie,"
BZ N.F. 23 (1979) 161-71.

2. APOCALYPTIC LITERATURE

(See also 1.543.)

2.1   Amann, E. "Les Apocalypses Apocryphes," DBSup. 1. Cols.
525-33.

2.2   Audet, L. "L'influence de l'apocalyptique sur le pensée de
Jésus et de l'église primitive," Science et Esprit 25 (1973)
51-74.

2.3   Bardenhewer, O. "Apokryphe Apokalypsen," GAL. 1. Pp.
610-622.

2.4   Bauckham, R. "The Worship of Jesus in Apocalyptic Christianity," NTS 27 (1981) 322-41.

2.5   Bauer, J.B. "Apokryphe Apokalypsen," Neutest. Apok. Pp.
95-101.

2.6   Bauer, W. "Chiliasmus," RAC. 2. Cols. 1073-78.

2.7   Baumgarten, J. Paulus und die Apokalyptik (WMANT 44)
Neukirchen-Vluyn, 1975.

2.8   Beardslee, W.A. "New Testament Apocalyptic in Recent Interpretation," Int 25 (1971) 419-35.

2.9   Berger, K. Die Amen-Worte Jesu: Eine Untersuchung zum
Problem der Legitimation in apokalyptischer Rede (BZNW 39)
Berlin, 1970.

2.10   Berger K. "Hellenistisch-heidnische Prodigien und die Vor-
zeichen in der jüdischen und christlichen Apokalyptik,"
ANRW 2.23.2. Pp. 1428-69. [B. discusses relation of the
SibOr to observation of the prodigia]

2.11   Bietenhard, H. "The Millennial Hope in the Early Church,"
        SJT 6 (1953) 12-31.

2.12   Bietenhard, H. Das Tausendjährige Reich. Zürich, 1955[2].

2.13   Bonsirven, J., and C. Bigaré," Les épîtres et apocalypses
        apocryphes," Intro. à la Bible. 2. Pp. 760-62.

2.14   Burkitt, F. Jewish and Christian Apocalypses. London, 1914.

2.15   Collins, A. Yarbro. "The Early Christian Apocalypses," Apoc-
        alypse: The Morphology of a Genre. Semeia 14 (1979) 61-
        121.

2.16   Collins, A. Yarbro. "Early Christian Apocalyptic Literature,"
        ANRW 2.25.4 (in preparation).

2.17   Corsani, B. "L'Apocalittica: Fra Antico e Nuovo Testamento,"
        Protestantesimo 27 (1972) 15-22.

2.18   Daniélou, J. "La typologie millénariste de la semaine," VC
        2 (1948) 1-16.

2.19   Dinzelbacher, P. Vision und Visionsliteratur im Mittelalter
        (Monographien zur Geschichte des Mittelalters 23) Stuttgart,
        1981.

2.20   Dinzelbacher, P. "Die Visionen des Mittelalters. Ein geschi-
        chtlicher Umriss," ZRGG 30 (1978) 116-28.

2.21   Eppel, R. "Les tables de la Loi et les tables célestes," RHPR
        17 (1937) 401-12.

2.22   Erbetta, M. "Apocalissi," Apoc. del NT. 3. Pp. 149-73.

2.23   Ermoni, V. "Les phases successives de l'erreur millénariste,"
        RQH 70 (1901) 353-89.

2.24   Fanuli, A., ed. Gesù e l'apocalittica: Apocalittica e Apocalisse
        (Parole di Vita 25) Turin-Leumann, 1980. Pp. 323-480.

2.25   Giordano, O. "Il millenarismo orientale alla fine del II secolo,"
        Hélikon 3 (1963) 328-52.

2.26   Glasson, T.F. Jesus and the End of the World. Edinburgh,
        1980.

2.27   Glasson, T.F. "What is Apocalyptic?" NTS 27 (1980) 98-105.

2.28   Gry, L. Le millénarisme. Paris, 1904.

2.29   Gunther, J.J. St. Paul's Opponents and Their Background:
       A Study of Apocalyptic and Jewish Sectarian Teachings
       (NovTSup 35) Leiden, 1973.

2.30   Hadot, J. "Contestation socio-religieuse et apocalyptique dans
       le judéo-christianisme," ArSocRel 24 (1967) 34-47.

2.31   Hellholm, D. "The Problem of Apocalyptic Genre and the Apoc-
       alypse of John," SBL 1982 Seminar Papers, ed. K.H. Rich-
       ards. Chico, CA, 1982. Pp. 157-98.

2.32   Hellholm, D. Das Visionenbuch des Hermas als Apokalypse:
       Formgeschichtliche und texttheoretische Studien zu einer
       literarischen Gattung. Vol. 1: Methodologische Vorüber-
       legungen und makrostrukturelle Textanalyse. (Coniectanea
       Biblica, New Testament Series 13) Lund, 1980. [H. attempts
       to understand better the genre of apocalypse in earliest
       Christianity.]

2.33   Helmbold, A.K. "Apocalypses, Apocryphal," ZPEB. 1. P.
       204.

2.34   Himmelfarb, M. Tours of Hell: An Apocalyptic Form in Jew-
       ish and Christian Literature. Philadelphia, 1983. [H. dis-
       cusses ApPet, AcTh, ApPl, ApVir (Eth. and Gk.)]

2.35   Hooke, S.H. "The Myth and Ritual Pattern in Jewish and
       Christian Apocalyptic," The Siege Perilous. London, 1956.
       Pp. 124-43.

2.36   Hruby, K. "L'influence des apocalypses sur l'eschatologie
       judéo-chrétienne," OrSyr 11 (1966) 291-320.

2.37   Isenberg, S.R. "Millenarism in Greco-Roman Palestine," Re-
       ligion 4 (1974) 26-46.

2.38   James, M.R. "Two New Apocalypses," The Guardian 24 (24
       Nov. 1875).*

2.39   Jonge, M. de. "Jewish Expectations About the 'Messiah' Ac-
       cording to the Fourth Gospel," NTS 19 (1973) 246-70.

2.40   Jonge, M. de. "The Use of the Word 'Anointed' in the Time
       of Jesus," NovT 8 (1966) 132-48.

2.41   Jossa, G. La teologia della storia nel pensiero cristiano del
       secondo secolo. Naples, 1965.

2.42   Käsemann, E. "Zum Thema der urchristlichen Apokalyptik,"
       ZTK 59 (1962) 257-84; repr. in Exegetische Versuche und
       Besinnungen. Göttingen, 1965[2]. Vol. 2. Pp. 105-31.

[French trans.: "Sur le thème de l'apocalyptique chrétienne primitive," Essaís exégétiques. Neuchâtel, 1972. Pp. 159-226; ET: "On the Subject of Primitive Christian Apocalyptic," New Testament Questions of Today, trans. W.J. Montague. Philadelphia, 1969. Pp. 108-37.]

2.43   Koch, K. "Die Apokalyptik und ihre Zukunftserwartungen," Die Zeit Jesu, ed. H.J. Schultz (Kontexte 3) Stuttgart, 1966. Pp. 51-58. [ET: "Apocalyptic and Eschatology," Jesus in His Time, trans. B. Watchorn. Philadelphia, 1971. Pp. 57-65.

2.44   Kraft, R.A. "The Multiform Jewish Heritage of Early Christianity," M. Smith Festschrift. Part 3. Pp. 175-99.

2.45   Levin, A.G. The Tree of Life: Genesis 2:9 and 3:22-24 in Jewish, Gnostic and Early Christian Texts. Harvard Th.D., 1966.

2.46   Lohse, E. "Apokalyptik und Christologie," ZNW 62 (1971) 48-67; repr. Die Einheit des Neuen Testaments: Exegetische Studien zur Theologie des Neuen Testaments. Göttingen, 1973. Pp. 125-44.

2.47   Longenecker, R.N. The Christology of Early Jewish Christianity (SBT, 2nd series, 17) Naperville, Ill., 1970.

2.48   Michl, J. "Apokalypsen, apokryphe (AT/NT)," Sacramentum mundi. 1. Pp. 214-23.

2.49   Moraldi, L. "Apocalissi," Apoc. del NT. 2. Pp. 1789-1802.

2.50   Müller, U.B. Messias und Menschensohn in jüdischen Apokalypsen und in der Offenbarung des Johannes (Studien zum Neuen Testament 6) Gütersloh, 1972.

2.51   Nola, A.M. di. "Apocalissi cristiane apocrife," EncRel. 1. Cols. 504-16.

2.52   Nordio, M. "L'escatologia giudeo-cristiana in due steli di Khirbet Kilkis," BO 19 (1977) 263-72.

2.53   Perrin, N. "The Son of Man in Ancient Judaism and Primitive Christianity: A Suggestion," A Modern Pilgrimage in New Testament Christology. Philadelphia, 1974. Pp. 23-40.

2.54   Raurell, F. "Apocaliptica y Apocalipsis," Estudios Franciscanos 81 (1980) 183-207.

2.55   Rollins, W.G. "The New Testament and Apocalyptic," NTS 17 (1971) 454-76.

2.56   Rosenstiehl, J.-M. "Le portrait de l'Antichrist," Pseudépi-
       graphes. Pp. 45-60.

2.57   Ruppert, L. Jesus als der leidende Gerechte? Der Weg Jesu
       im Lichte eines alt-und zwischentestamentlichen Motivs (SBS
       59) Stuttgart, 1972.

2.58   Ruppert, L. Der leidende Gerechte: Eine motivgeschichtliche
       Untersuchung zum Alten Testament und zwischentestament-
       lichen Judentum (Forschung zur Bibel 5) Würzburg, 1972.

2.59   Ruppert, L. Der leidende Gerechte und seine Feinde: Eine
       Wortfelduntersuchung. Würzburg, 1973.

2.60   Schneemelcher, W. "Apocalyptic Prophecy of the Early Church:
       Introduction," HSW. 2. Pp. 684-89.

2.61   Schoeps, H.-J. "Ebionitische Apokalyptik im Neuen Testament,"
       ZNW 51 (1960) 33-46.

2.62   Simon, M. "Retour du Christ et reconstruction du Temple
       dans la pensée primitive," Aux sources de la tradition chré-
       tienne: Mélanges offerts à M. Maurice Goguel à l'occasion
       de son soixante-dixième anniversaire. Neuchâtel, 1950. Pp.
       247-57.

2.63   Snyder, G.F. "The Literalization of the Apocalyptic Form in
       the New Testament, Biblical Research 14 (1969) 5-18.

2.64   Sokolov, M.I. Apocryphal Apocalypse (Varucha: Drevnosti
       Trudi S Slavjanskoj Kommissii Imp. Moskovskogo Obŝestva
       4) Moscow, 1907. [in Russian]

2.65   Steinschneider, M. "Apocalypsen mit polemischer Tendenz,"
       ZDMG 28 (1874) 627-59; 29 (1875) 162-66.

2.66   Testa, E. "I fondamenti e i miti della speranza nella Chiesa
       madre," RevistB 23 (1975) 47-65.

2.67   Testa, E. "I Novissimi e la loro localizzazione nella Teologia
       ebraica e giudeo-cristiana," LA 26 (1976) 121-69.

2.68   Testa, P.E., et al. La distruzione di Gerusalemme del 70 nei
       suoi riflessi storico-letterari: Atti del V Convegno biblico
       francescano. Roma, 22-27 Settembre 1969 (Collectio Assi-
       siensis 8) Assisi, 1971.

2.69   Travis, S.H. "The Value of Apocalyptic," Tyndale Bulletin
       30 (1979) 53-76.

2.70   Vielhauer, P. "Apokalypsen und Verwandtes," HS. 2. Pp.
       405-27.

2.71   Vielhauer, P. "Apocalyptic," HSW. 2. Pp. 582-600.

2.72   Vielhauer, P. "Apokalyptik des Urchristentums," HS. 2.
       Pp. 428-54.

2.73   Vielhauer, P. "Apocalyptic in Early Christianity: 1. Intro-
       duction," HSW. 2. Pp. 608-42.

2.74   Weinel, H. "Die Apokalyptik des Urchristentums," H². Pp.
       298-302.

2.75   Weinel, H. "Die spätere christliche Apokalyptik," Eucharis-
       tērion: Studien zur Religion und Literatur des Alten und
       Neuen Testaments, ed. H. Schmidt (Hermann Gunkel Fs.)
       Göttingen, 1923. Pp. 140-73.

2.76   Wilder, A.N. "The Rhetoric of Ancient and Modern Apocalyp-
       tic," Int 25 (1971) 436-53.

2.77   Winstanley, E.W. "The Outlook of Early Christian Apocaly-
       pses," Exp 19 (1920) 161-84.

                    3. APOCRYPHAL ACTS

(See also 1.202-208, 211, 271, 272, 299, 456, 457, 524; 9.20.)

3.1   Achtemeier, P.J. "Jesus and the Disciples as Miracle Workers
       in the Apocryphal New Testament," Aspects of Religious
       Propaganda in Judaism and Early Christianity ed. E. Schüss-
       ler Fiorenza. Notre Dame, Ind., 1976. Pp. 149-86.

3.2   Amann, É. "Apocryphes du N.T.: Les actes apocryphes,"
       DBSup. 1. Cols. 488-514.

3.3   Bardenhewer, O. "Apokryphe Apostelgeschichten," GAL. 1.
       Pp. 547-96.

3.4   Batiffol, P. "Actes (apocryphes) des apôtres," DThC. 1.
       Cols. 354-57.

3.5   Bedjan, P., ed. Acta Martyrum et sanctorum Syriace. Paris,
       Leipzig, 1890; repr. Hildesheim, 1968.

3.6   Berger, K. "Jüdisch-hellenistische Missionsliteratur und Apok-
       ryphe Apostelakten," Kairos 17 (1975) 232-48.

3.7   Blumenthal, M. Formen und Motive in den apokryphen Apostel-
       geschichten (TU 48) Leipzig, 1933. Pp. 38-57.

3.8   Bonsirven, J., and C. Bigaré, "Les Actes apocryphes," Intro.
        à la Bible. 2. Pp. 757-60.

3.9   Bovon, F., ed. Les Actes apocryphes des apôtres: Chris-
        tianisme et monde païen (Publications de la faculté de thé-
        ologie de l'université de Genève 4) Geneva, 1981.

3.10   Budge, E.A.W., The Contendings of the Apostles, Being the
        Stories of the Lives and Martyrdoms and Deaths of the Twelve
        Apostles and Evangelists. 2 vols. London, New York, 1899-
        1901; repr. London, 1976.

3.11   Dallaeus, J. De pseudoepigraphis Apostolicis. Hardervici,
        1653.

3.12   Davies, S.L. The Revolt of the Widows: The Social World of
        the Apocryphal Acts. Carbondale, Ill., 1980.

3.13   Dritsas, L. "Some Rhythmical Prayers from the Gnostic Apoc-
        ryphal Acts," GrigPal 58 (1975) 372-89. [in modern Gk.]

3.14   Duchesne, L. "Les anciens recueils des légendes apostoliques,"
        Compte rendu du 3e Congrès scientifique internat. des Cath-
        oliques. Brussels, 1895. Pp. 67-79.

3.15   Fabricius, J.A. "Polycrates de Vita S. Timothei," Cod.Apoc.
        NT. 2. Pp. 812-14.

3.16   Findlay, A.F. "Apocryphal Acts of the Apostles," Byways.
        Pp. 179-207.

3.17   Geiger, [?]. "Sprachliche Bemerkungen zu Wright's Apocryphal
        Acts," ZDMG 26 (1872) 798-804.

3.18   Goulet, R. "Les vies de philosophes dans l'antiquité tardive
        et leur portée mystérique," Actes Apocryphes. Pp. 161-208.

3.19   Guidi, I. "Gli Atti apocrifi degli Apostoli nei testi copti,
        arabi ed etiopici," GSAI 2 (1888) 1-66. [Italian trans. of
        1.202-208]

3.20   Gutschmid, A. v. "Die Königsnamen in den apokryphen Apos-
        telgeschichten: Ein Beitrag zur Kenntnis des geschichtlichen
        Romans," Rheinisches Museum für Philologie 19 (1864) 161-
        83, 380-401.

3.21   Halkin, F. "Les Actes apocryphes de S. Héraclide de Chypre,
        disciple de l'apôtre Barnabé," AnBoll 82 (1964) 133-70.

3.22   Hamman, A. "'Sitz im Leben' des actes apocryphes du Nou-
        veau Testament," Studia Patristica. Vol. 8. Papers Pre-

sented to the Fourth International Congress on Patristic
Studies Held at Christ Church, Oxford, 1963. Part 2:
Patres Apostolici, Historica, Liturgica, Ascetica et Monastica,
ed. F.L. Cross. (TU 93) Berlin, 1966. Pp. 62-69.

3.23   Harnack, A. "Apostelgeschichten, Apokryphe," Gesch. alt-
        christ. Lit. 1. Pp. 116-23.

3.24   Harnack, A. "Zu den apokryphen Apostelgeschichten," Gesch.
        altchrist. Lit. 2.2. Pp. 169-77.

3.25   Hatch, W.H.P. "Three Hitherto Unpublished Leaves from a
        Manuscript of the Acta Apostolorum Apocrypha in Bohairic,"
        Coptic Studies in Honor of Walter Ewing Crum, ed. M. Mali-
        nine (Bulletin of the Byzantine Institute 2) Boston, 1950.
        Pp. 305-17.

3.26   Helm, R. Der Antike Roman. Berlin, 1948.

3.27   Hennecke, E. "Apostelgeschichten (Legenden): Zur Einlei-
        tung," Handbuch, ed. Hennecke. Pp. 351-58.

3.28   Hertling, L. "Literarisches zu den Apokryphen Apostelakten,"
        ZKT 49 (1925) 219-43.

3.29   Junod, E. "Actes Apocryphes et hérésie: Le jugement de
        Photius," Actes Apocryphes. Pp. 11-24.

3.30   Junod, E. "Origène, Eusèbe et la tradition sur la répartition
        des champs de mission des apôtres (Eusèbe, Histoire ecclés-
        iastique, III, 1, 1-3)," Actes Apocryphes. Pp. 233-48.

3.31   Junod, E. "Les vies de philosophes et les Actes apocryphes
        des apôtres poursuivent-ils un dessein similaire?" Actes
        Apocryphes. Pp. 209-19.

3.32   Kaestli, J-D. "Les principales orientations de la recherche sur
        les Actes apocryphes des apôtres," Actes Apocryphes. Pp.
        49-67.

3.33   Kaestli, J-D. "Les scènes d'attribution des champs de mission
        et de départ de l'apôtre dans les Actes apocryphes," Actes
        Apocryphes. Pp. 249-64.

3.34   Kaestli, J.-D. "L'utilisation des Actes apocryphes des apôtres
        dans le manichéisme," Gnosis and Gnosticism, ed. M. Krause
        (NHS 8) Leiden, 1977. Pp. 107-16.

3.35   Klijn, A.F.J. "The Apocryphal Acts of the Apostles," VC 37
        (1983) 193-99.

3.36   Kraemer, R.S. "The Conversion of Women to Ascetic Forms
        of Christianity," Signs 6 (1980) 298-307.

3.37   Krivocheine, B. "'Ho anuperēphanos Theos' St. Symeon the
        New Theologian and early Christian popular piety," Studia
        Patristica II, eds. K. Aland and F.L. Cross (TU 64) Berlin,
        1957. Pp. 485-94. [references to AcJn and AcXanPol]

3.38   Kurcikidze, C. The Georgian Versions of the Apocryphal
        Acts of the Apostles According to IX to XI Century Manu-
        scripts. Tbilissi, 1959. [only in Georgian; contains AcAnMth,
        AcJnPro, MartPhil, MartTh(AcTh)]

3.39   Lake, K., and J. de Zwann. "Acts of the Apostles (Apocry-
        phal)," Dictionary of the Apostolic Church, ed. J. Hastings.
        Edinburgh, 1926. Vol. 1. Pp. 29-39.

3.40   Leloir, L. "Rapports entre les versions arménienne et syria-
        que des Actes apocryphes des Apôtres," Symposium Syriacum
        1976 (OCA 205) Rome, 1978. Pp. 137-48.

3.41   Lemm, O. von. "Koptische apokryphe Apostelakten," Bulle-
        tin de l'Académie des Sciences de Saint Pétersbourg 10 (1892)
        354f. [see 1.302]

3.42   Lemm, O. von. "Koptische apokryphe Apostelakten," Mélanges
        asiatiques tirés du Bulletin Impériale des Sciences de Saint
        Pétersbourg 10 (1890) 99-171. [see 1.302]

3.43   Lewis, A.S. Acta Mythologica Apostolorum (Horae Semiticae
        3) London, 1904. [Arabic texts; ET in Horae Semiticae 4]

3.44   Lewis, A.S. The Mythological Acts of the Apostles (Arabic)
        (Horae Semiticae 4) London, 1904. [ET of Arabic texts in
        Horae Semiticae 3]

3.45   Lietz, H. "Der gnostisch-christliche Charakter der apokryphen
        Apostelgeschichten und-legenden im Anschluss an R.A. Lip-
        sius," ZWT 37 (1894) 34-57.

3.46   Lipsius, R.A., and M. Bonnet. Acta apostolorum apocrypha.
        2 vols. Leipzig, 1891-1903; repr. Hildesheim, 1959.

3.47   Lipsius, R.A. "Acts, Apocryphal," Dictionary of Christian
        Biography, eds. W. Smith and H. Wace. 4 vols. London,
        1877-87. Vol. 1. Pp. 17-32.

3.48   Lipsius, R.A. Die apokryphen Apostelgeschichten und Apostel-
        legenden. 2 vols. Brunswick, 1883-1890; repr. Amsterdam,
        1976.

3.49   Ljungvik, H. Studien zur Sprache der apokryphen Apostel-
        geschichten. (Uppsala Universitet Aarsskrift 8) Uppsala,
        1926.

3.50   Ludvikovsky, J. "The Greek Novel and the Apocryphal Acta
        Apostolorum," Listy Filologické (1925) 321-28. [in Czech]

3.51   Malan, S.C. The Conflicts of the Holy Apostles: An Apoc-
        ryphal Book of the Early Church. London, 1871.

3.52   Michaelis, W. "Einleitung in die Apokryphen Apostelgeschi-
        chten," Apokryphen Schriften. Pp. 216-21.

3.53   Migne, J.-P. "Apôtres. Ecrits attribués ou qui ont rapport
        aux apotres.," Dictionnaire 2. Cols. 111-38.

3.54   Morard, F. "Notes sur le recueil des Actes Apocryphes des
        Apôtres," RTP 31 (1981) 403-13.

3.55   Morard, F. "Souffrance et martyre dans les Actes apocryphes
        des apôtres," Actes Apocryphes. Pp. 95-108.

3.56   Nagel, P. "Die apokryphen Apostelakten des 2. und 3. Jahr-
        hunderts in der manichäischen Literatur: Ein Beitrag zur
        Frage nach den christlichen Elementen im Manichäismus,"
        Gnosis und Neues Testament: Studien aus Religionswissen-
        schaft und Theologie, ed. K.W. Tröger. Berlin, 1973. Pp.
        149-82.

3.57   Nola, A.M. di. "Atti ed epistole apocrifi degli Apostoli,"
        EncRel. 1. Cols. 817-37.

3.58   O'Conner, D.W. Peter in Rome: The Literary, Liturgical,
        and Archaeological Evidence. New York, 1969. [review by
        T.D. Barnes, JTS 21 (1970) 175-79]

3.59   Papenbrock, D. van, et al. Acta Sanctorum. 60 vols. Paris,
        Brussels, 1643-1887.

3.60   Perels, H.U. Besitzethik in den apokryphen Apostelgeschich-
        ten und in der zeitgenossischen christlichen Literatur. Hei-
        delberg, 1976.

3.61   Pfitzner, V.C. "Martyr and Hero: The Origin and Develop-
        ment of a Tradition in the Early Christian Martyr Acts,"
        LuthTJ 15 (1981) 9-17.

3.62   Pick, B. The Apocryphal Acts of Paul, Peter, John, Andrew
        and Thomas. London, 1909.

3.63   Piontek, F. Die katholische Kirche und die häretischen

Apostelgeschichten bis zum Ausgange des 6. Jahrhunderts
(Kirchengeschichtliche Abhandlungen 6) Breslau, 1908. Pp.
1-71.

3.64   Plümacher, E. "Apokryphe Apostelakten," Pauly-Wissowa.
        Supplementband 15. Cols. 11-70.

3.65   Poupon, G. "Les Actes apocryphes des apôtres de Lefèvre
        à Fabricius," Actes Apocryphes. Pp. 25-47.

3.66   Poupon, G. "L'accusation de magie dans les Actes apocryphes,"
        Actes Apocryphes. Pp. 71-93.

3.67   Redemarcher, L. "Die apokryph. Apostelakten und die Volk-
        sage," Zeitschrift für deutschen öster. Gymnasien (1909)
        pp. 673ff.*

3.68   Reitzenstein, R. Hellenistische Wundererzählungen. Berlin,
        1906; repr. Darmstadt, 1963.

3.69   Rohde, E. Der Griechische Roman und seine Vorläufer. Hilde-
        sheim, 1960.

3.70   Rostalski, F. "Die Gräzität der apokryphen Apostelgeschich-
        ten," Festschrift zur Jahrhundertfeier der Universtität Bres-
        lau. Breslau, 1911. Pp. 57-70.

3.71   Rostalski, F. Sprachliches zu den apokryphen Apostelges-
        chichten. 2 fasc. (Wissenschaftliche Beilage zum Jahres-
        bericht des Gymnasiums Myslowitz) Myslowitz, Upper Silesia,
        1909-10.

3.72   Schepfs, G. "Eine Würzburger lateinische Handschrift zu den
        apokryphen Apostelgeschichten," ZKG 8 (1886) 449-59.

3.73   Söder, R. Die apokryphen Apostelgeschichten und die roman-
        hafte Literatur der Antike (Würzburger Studien zur Alter-
        tumswissenschaft 3) Stuttgart, 1932; repr. Darmstadt, 1969.

3.74   Stemler, J.C. De vera fictaque certaminis apost. historia.
        Leipzig, 1767.*

3.75   Sturhahn, C.L. Die Christologie der apokryphen Apostelakten:
        Ein Beitrag zur Frühgeschichte des altchristlichen Dogmas.
        Diss. Heidelberg, 1951; Göttingen, 1952.

3.76   Tischendorf, K. "Additamenta ad acta apostolorum apocrypha,"
        Apocalypses Apocryphae. Pp. XLVII-L.

3.77   Tissot, Y. "Encratisme et Actes apocryphes," Actes Apocry-
        phes. Pp. 109-19.

3.78   Tsherakhian, K. Noncanonical Apostolic Books. Venice, 1904.
       [in Armenian; includes AcAn, AcAnMth, MartBart, AcJas,
       AcJnPro, MartPl, AcPetPl, MartPet, AcPhil, ApPl, AcTh]

3.79   Underwood, P.A. The Kariye Djami. 3 vols. New York,
       1966.

3.80   Verme, M. del. "L'apocrifo giudaico IV Maccabei e gli Atti
       dei Martiri Cristiani del II sècolo," Rivista di scienze teo-
       logiche N.S. 23 (1976) 287-302.

3.81   Vetter, P. "Die armenischen apokryphen Apostelakten," OrChr
       1 (1901) 217-39; 3 (1903) 16-55; 324-83.

3.82   Vetter, P. "Armenische Apostelakten," OrChr 1 (1901) 168-
       70.

3.83   Wright, W. Apocryphal Acts of the Apostles. Edited from
       Syriac Manuscripts in the British Museum and Other Li-
       braries. 2 vols. London, 1871; repr. Amsterdam, 1968.
       [Syr. texts and ET]

3.84   Zumstein, J. "Étude critique. Les Actes Apocryphes des
       Apôtres," RTP 31 (1981) 415-20.

                              4. CANON

(See also 1.3, 418-421, 441, 442; 5.33, 215.)

4.1   Aland, K. "Das Problem des neutestamentlichen Kanons,"
       NZST 4 (1962) 200-42.

4.2   Aland, K. The Problem of the New Testament Canon. London,
       1962.

4.3   Alexander, A. The Canon of the Old and New Testaments
       Ascertained. New York, 1826.

4.4   Altaner, B. "Augustinus und die neutestamentlichen Apokry-
       phen. Sibyllinen und Sextussprüche," AnBoll 67 (1949)
       236-48. [repr. in Kleine Patristische Schriften (TU 83)
       Berlin, 1967. Pp. 204-15]

4.5   Appel, N. Kanon und Kirche. Paderborn, [1964].

4.6   Appel, N. "New Testament Canon: Historical Process and
       Spirit's Witness," TS 32 (1971) 627-46.

4.7   Barr, J. Holy Scripture: Canon, Authority, Criticism. Phila-
        delphia, 1983.

4.8   Barucq, A., and H. Cazelles. "Le canon de livres inspirés,"
        Intro. à la Bible. 1. Pp. 31-57.

4.9   Batiffol, P. "L'Église naissante: Le canon du Nouveau Testa-
        ment," RB 12 (1903) 10-26, 226-233.

4.10   Bauer, J.B. "Apokryph und Kanonisch," Neutest. Apok.
        Pp. 9-13.

4.11   Beare, F.W. "Canon of the NT," IDB. 1. Pp. 520-32.

4.12   Best, E. "Scripture, Tradition and the Canon of the New
        Testament," BJRL 61 (1979) 258-89.

4.13   Bewer, J.A. The History of the New Testament Canon in the
        Syrian Church. Chicago, 1900.

4.14   Blackman, E.C. Marcion and His Influence. London, 1948.

4.15   Bleek, F. Einleitung in die heilige Schrift. Berlin, 1886⁵.
        [ET of an earlier edition: An Introduction to the New Tes-
        tament, tr. W. Urwick. Edinburgh, 1866². See esp. vol.
        2, pp. 233-89]

4.16   Braun, H. et al. Die Verbindlichkeit des Kanons. 1960.*

4.17   Brown, R.E. "The Canon of the New Testament," JBC. Pp.
        525-31.

4.18   Burkhardt, H. "Grenzen des Kanons: Motive und Masstäbe,"
        TBei 1 (1970) 153-60.

4.19   Burkhardt, H. "Motive und Masstäbe der Kanonbildung nach
        dem Canon Muratori," ThZ 30 (1974) 207-11.

4.20   Campenhausen, H. von. Die Enstehung der christlichen Bible.
        Tübingen, 1968. [ET: The Formation of the Christian
        Bible, trans. J.A. Baker. Philadelphia, 1972.]

4.21   Campenhausen, H. von. "Marcion et les origines du canon néo-
        testamentaire," Traduit par F. Benoit, RHPR 46 (1966)
        213-26.

4.22   Carroll, K.L. "The Earliest New Testament," BJRL 38 (1955)
        45-57.

4.23   Carroll, K.L. "The Expansion of the Pauline Corpus," JBL
        72 (1953) 230-37.

4.24   Carroll, K.L. "Toward a Commonly Received New Testament,"
        BJRL 44 (1962) 327-49.

4.25   Carroll, R.P. "Canonical Criticism: A Recent Trend in Bib-
        lical Studies?" ExpT 92 (1980) 73-78.

4.26   Chapman, G.C. Jr. "Ernst Käsemann, Hermann Diem, and
        the New Testament Canon," JAAR 36 (1968) 3-12.

4.27   Citrini, T. "Il problema del canone biblico: Un capitolo di
        teologia fondamentale," ScCatt 107 (1979) 549-90.

4.28   Collins, R.F. "The Matrix of the NT Canon," BibTB 7 (1977)
        51-59.

4.29   Corrodi, H. Versuch einer Beleuchtung der Geschichte des
        jüdischen und christlichen Bibelkanons. Halle, 1792.

4.30   Corssen, P. Monarchianische Prologe zu den vier Evangelien:
        Ein Beitrag zur Geschichte des Kanons (TU 15.1) Leipzig,
        1896.

4.31   Cosgrove, C.H. "Justin Martyr and the Emerging Christian
        Canon: Observations on the Purpose and Destination of
        the Dialogue with Trypho," VC 36 (1982) 209-32.

4.32   Cowley, R.W. "The Biblical Canon of the Ethiopian Orthodox
        Church Today [... of 81 Books]," OstkSt 23 (1974) 318-23.

4.33   Cullmann, O. "The Tradition, the Exegetical, Historical and
        Theological Problem," The Early Church: Historical and
        Theological Studies, ed. A.J.B. Higgins. Philadelphia,
        1956. Pp. 57-99.

4.34   Dahl, N.A. "Welche Ordnung der Paulusbriefe wird vom Mur-
        atorischen Kanon vorausgesetzt?" ZNW 52 (1961) 39-53.

4.35   Dayton, W.T. "Factors Promoting the Formation of the New
        Testament Canon," JETS 10 (1967) 28-35.

4.36   Dibelius, M. A Fresh Approach to the New Testament and
        Early Christian Literature. London, 1936; repr. Westport,
        Conn., 1979. [ET is a revised and expanded version of the
        German original]

4.37   Donner, T. "Some Thoughts on the History of the New Tes-
        tament Canon," Themelios 7 (1982) 23-27.

4.38   Dungan, D.L. "The New Testament Canon in Recent Study,"
        Int 29 (1975) 339-51.

4.39   Erbetta, M. Apoc. del NT. 1. Pp. 3-10, 14-39.

4.40   Ewald, P. Der Kanon des Neuen Testaments (Biblische Zeit
        und Streitfragen 2) Berlin, 1906.

4.41   Fairweather, E.R. "Scripture in Tradition," CJT 5 (1959) 7-
        14.

4.42   Farmer, W.R., and D. Farkasfalvy. The Formation of the
        New Testament Canon, An Ecumenical Approach. Ramsey,
        N.J., 1983. [Foreword by A. Outler]

4.43   Fascher, E. Einleitung in das Neue Testament. Tübingen,
        1931[7]. Pp. 450-588.

4.44   Ferris, G.H. The Formation of the New Testament. Phila-
        delphia, 1907.

4.45   Filson, F.V. Which Books Belong in the Bible? A Study of
        the Canon. Philadelphia, 1957.

4.46   Flessemann-van Leer, E. "Prinzipien der Sammlung und Auss-
        cheidung bei der Bildung des Kanons," ZTK 61 (1964) 404-
        20.

4.47   Foster, L. "The Earliest Collection of Paul's Letters," JETS
        10 (1967) 44-53.

4.48   Frank, I. Der Sinn der Kanonbildung: Eine historisch-
        theologische Untersuchung der Zeit vom I Clemensbrief bis
        Irenäus von Lyon (Freiburger Theologische Studien 90)
        Freiburg, 1971.

4.49   Fuchs, E. "Kanon und Kerygma: Ein Referat," ZTK 63
        (1966) 410-33.

4.50   Gaussen, L. The Canon of the Holy Scriptures, trans. E.N.
        Kirk. Boston, 1862.

4.51   Glasson, T.F. "Nestorian Canon and the Chinese Tablet,"
        ExpT 74 (1963) 260f.

4.52   Goodspeed, E.J. "The Canon of the New Testament," Inter-
        preters Bible: The Holy Scriptures in the King James and
        Revised Standard Versions, ed. G.A. Buttrick. 12 vols.
        New York, [1951-57]. Vol. 1. Pp. 63-71.

4.53   Goodspeed, E.J. Christianity Goes to Press. New York,
        1940.

4.54   Goodspeed, E.J. The Formation of the New Testament. Chi-
        cago, 1926.

4.55 Goodspeed, E.J. New Solutions of New Testament Problems. Chicago, 1927.

4.56 Grant, R.M. The Formation of the New Testament. New York, 1965.

4.57 Grant, R.M. A Historical Introduction to the New Testament. New York, 1963. Pp. 25-40.

4.58 Grant, R.M. "The New Testament Canon," Cambridge History of the Bible, eds. P.R. Ackroyd, et al. 3 vols. Cambridge, 1963-70. Vol. 1. Pp. 284-308.

4.59 Gregory, C.R. The Canon and Text of the New Testament. New York, 1907.

4.60 Grossheide, F.W. Some Early Lists of Books of the New Testament (Textus Minores 1). Leiden, 1948.

4.61 Guthrie, D. "Canon of the New Testament, The," ZPEB. 1. Pp. 731-45.

4.62 Hahn, F. "Die heilige Schrift als älteste christliche Tradition und als Kanon," EvT 40 (1980) 456-66.

4.63 Hanson, R.P.C. Origen's Doctrine of Tradition. London, 1954.

4.64 Häring, H. "Eine Kirche, eine Schrift--ein Evangelium?," BiKi 34 (1979) 122-32.

4.65 Harnack, A. Entstehung des Neuen Testaments und die wichtigsten Folgen der neuen Schöpfung. (Beiträge zur Einleitung in das Neue Testament 6) Leipzig, 1914. [ET: The Origin of the New Testament and the Most Important Consequences of the New Creation, trans. J.R. Wilkinson. London, 1925.]

4.66 Harnack, A. Gesch. altchrist. Lit. [scattered references throughout volumes]

4.67 Harnack, A. Das Neue Testament um das Jahre 200. Freiburg, 1889.

4.68 Harris, R.L. Inspiration and Canonicity of the Bible: An Historical and Exegetical Study. Grand Rapids, 1957.

4.69 Holtzmann, H.J. Die Entstehung des Neuen Testaments. Tübingen, 1906.

4.70 Höpfel, H. "Canonicité," DBSup. 1. Cols. 1022-45.

4.71   Hoskyns, E., and N. Davey. The Riddle of the New Testa-
       ment. New York, 1931.

4.72   Jacquier, E. "Préparation, formation et définition du canon
       du Nouveau Testament," Le Nouveau Testament dans l'église
       chrétienne. 2 vols. Paris, 1911-13. Vol. 1. Pp. 1-443.
       [vol. 1, 3rd ed.; vol. 2, 2nd ed.]

4.73   Joest, W. "Erwägungen zur kanonischen Bedeutung des Neuen
       Testaments," KerDog 12 (1966) 27-47.

4.74   Jones, J. A New and Full Method of Settling the Canonical
       Authority of the New Testament. 3 vols. London, 1726,
       1798[2].

4.75   Kalin, E. "The Inspired Community: A Glance at Canon His-
       tory," CTM 42 (1971) 541-49.

4.76   Käsemann, E. Das Neue Testament als Kanon: Dokumentation
       und kritische Analyse zur gegenwärtigen Diskussion. Göt-
       tingen, 1970.

4.77   Keck, L.E. "Is the New Testament a Field of Study? or,
       From Outler to Overbeck and Back," Second Century 1
       (1981) 19-35.

4.78   Kistemaker, S.J. "The Canon of the New Testament," JETS
       20 (1977) 3-14.

4.79   Knox, J. Marcion and the New Testament. Chicago, 1942.

4.80   Krötke, W. "Der neutestamentliche Kanon als Problem der
       Rede von Gott," TVers 9 (1977) 61-69.

4.81   Kümmel, W.G. "The Formation of the Canon of the New Tes-
       tament," Introduction to the New Testament, tr. H.C. Kee.
       Nashville, 1975. Pp. 475-510.

4.82   Lagrange, M.-J. Histoire ancienne du Canon du Nouveau Tes-
       tament. Paris, 1933.

4.83   Leipoldt, J. Geschichte des neutestamentlichen Kanons. 2
       vols. Leipzig, 1907-08.

4.84   Lietzmann, H. Das Muratorische Fragment und die Monarch-
       ianischen Prologe zu den Evangelien (KlT 1) Bonn, 1902.

4.85   Lietzmann, H. Wie wurden die Bücher des Neuen Testaments
       heilige Schrift? Tübingen, 1907; repr. Kleine Schriften
       (TU 68) Berlin, 1958. Pp. 15-98.

4.86   Lohse, E. "Die Einheit des Neuen Testaments als theologis-
       ches Problem: Uberlegungen zur Aufgabe einer Theologie
       des Neuen Testaments," EvT 35 (1975) 139-54.

4.87   Lohse, E. Entstehung des Neuen Testaments (Theologische
       Wissenschaft 4) Stuttgart, 1975.

4.88   Loisy, A. Histoire du canon du Nouveau Testament. Paris,
       1891.

4.89   Lønning, I. Kanon im Kanon: Zum dogmatischen Grundlagen-
       problem des neutestamentlichen Kanons (Forschungen zur
       Geschichte und Lehre des Protestantismus 10) Munich, Oslo,
       1972. [see also TLZ 102 (1977) 534f.; and TR 71 (1975)
       455-58]

4.90   Mangenot, E. "Canon du Nouveau Testament," DThC. 2.2.
       Cols. 1582-93.

4.91   Mangenot, E. "Canon du Nouveau Testament," DAFC. 1.
       Cols. 449-55.

4.92   Marxsen, W. "Kontingenz der Offenbarung oder (und?) Kon-
       tingenz des Kanons?" NZST 2 (1960) 355-64.

4.93   Marxsen, W. "Das Problem des neutestamentlichen Kanons aus
       der Sicht des Exegeten," NZST 2 (1960) 137-50.

4.94   Metzger, B.M. "Canon of the New Testament," Dictionary of
       the Bible, ed. J. Hastings, rev. ed. F.C. Grant and H.H.
       Rowley. New York, 1963. Pp. 123-27.

4.95   Michl, J. "Der neutestamentliche Kanon," LTK[3]. 5. Cols.
       1280-83.

4.96   Mitton, C.L. The Formation of the Pauline Corpus of Letters.
       London, 1955.

4.97   Moore, A.C. "Tradition and the New Testament Canon,"
       RefTR 16 (1957) 1-11.

4.98   Moore, E.C. The New Testament in the Christian Church.
       New York, 1904.

4.99   Morgan, R.L. Regula Veritatis: A Historical Investigation of
       the Canon of the Second Century. Union Theological Semi-
       nary in Virginia Ph.D., 1966.

4.100 Moule, C.F.D. "Collecting and Sifting the Documents," The
       Birth of the New Testament (Harper's New Testament Com-
       mentaries) San Francisco, 1982[3]. Pp. 235-69.

4.101 Müller, P.-G. "Destruktion des Kanons--Verlust der Mitte:
       Ein Kritisches Gespräch mit Siegfried Schulz," TR 73 (1977)
       177-86.

4.102 Murray, R. "How Did the Church Determine the Canon of
       Scripture?" HeyJ 11 (1970) 115-26.

4.103 Neuenzeit, P. "Canon of the Scriptures," Sacramentum Mundi.
       1. Pp. 252-57.

4.104 Nicol, T. The Four Gospels in the Earliest Church History.
       Edinburgh, 1908.

4.105 Nielsen, C.M. "Polycarp, Paul and the Scriptures," ATR 47
       (1965) 199-216.

4.106 Noack, B. "Jakobsbrevet som kanonisk Skrift," DTT 27
       (1964) 163-73.

4.107 Ohlig, K-H. Die theologische Begründung des neutestament-
       lichen Kanons in der alten Kirche. Düsseldorf, 1972.

4.108 Outler, A.C. "Methods and Aims in the Study of the Develop-
       ment of Catholic Christianity," Second Century 1 (1981) 7-
       17.

4.109 Oxford Society of Historical Theology. The New Testament in
       the Apostolic Fathers. Oxford, 1905.

4.110 Pedersen, S. "Die Kanonfrage als historisches und theolog-
       isches Problem," ST 31 (1977) 83-186.

4.111 Person, R.E. The Mode of Theological Decision Making at the
       Early Ecumenical Councils. An Inquiry into the Function of
       Scripture and Tradition at the Councils of Nicaea and Ephesus
       (Theologische Dissertationen 14) Basel, 1978.

4.112 Piper, J. "The Authority and Meaning of the Christian Canon:
       A Response to G. Sheppard on Canon Criticism," JETS 19
       (1976) 87-96.

4.113 Preus, J.A.O. "New Testament Canon in the Lutheran Dog-
       maticians," The Springfielder 25 (1961) 8-33.

4.114 Quasten, J. "Canon of the New Testament," Patrology. 1.
       Pp. 37, 144, 154, 306.

4.115 Quinn, J.D. "P 46, the Pauline Canon?" CBQ 36 (1974)
       379-85.

4.116 Ratschow, C.H. "Zur Frage der Begründung des neutestament-

lichen Kanons aus der Sicht des systematischen Theologen,"
NZST 2 (1960) 150-60.

4.117 Reuss, E. History of the Canon of the Holy Scriptures in the
       Christian Church, trans. and ed. D. Hunter. New York,
       1884².

4.118 Reuss, E. History of the Sacred Scriptures of the New Tes-
       tament, trans. E.L. Houghton. New York, 1884⁵.

4.119 Ricciotti, G. "Canone del Nuovo Testamento," EncCatt. 2.
       Cols. 1550f.

4.120 Ridderbos, H.N. The Authority of the New Testament Scrip-
       tures, trans. H. de Jongste. Philadelphia, 1963.

4.121 Riesenfeld, H. The Gospel Tradition and Its Beginning. Lon-
       don, 1957.

4.122 Roberts, J.H., and A.B. Du Toit. "The Canon of the New
       Testament," Guide to the New Testament, trans. D.R.
       Briggs. Pretoria, 1979. Vol. 1. Pp. 75-272.

4.123 Robinson, J.M. "Critical Inquiry into the Scriptural Bases
       of Confessional Hermeneutics," JEcuSt 3 (1966) 36-56.

4.124 Ruwet, J. "Clément d'Alexandrie: Canon des Écritures et
       Apocryphes," Bib 29 (1948) 77-99, 240-68, 391-408. [see
       also 1.442]

4.125 Sand, A. Kanon. Von den Anfängen bis zum Fragmentum
       Muratorianum. Freiburg, 1974.

4.126 Sanders, J.N. "The Literature and Canon of the New Tes-
       tament," PCB. Pp. 676-82.

4.127 Schneemelcher, W. "Die Entstehung des Kanons des Neuen
       Testaments und der christlichen Bibel," TRE. 6. Pp. 22-
       48.

4.128 Schneemelcher, W. "General Introduction," HSW. 1. Pp.
       21-68.

4.129 Schneemelcher, W. "Haupteinleitung," HS. 1. Pp. 1-38.

4.130 Schrage, W. "Die Frage nach der Mitte und dem Kanon im
       Kanon des NTs in der neueren Diskussion," Rechtfertigung:
       Festschrift für E. Käsemann, ed. J. Friedrich, W. Pöhlmann,
       and P. Stuhlmacher. Tübingen, Göttingen, 1976. Pp. 415-
       42.

4.131   Schroeder, F.   "History of New Testament Canon," NCE.   2.
        Pp. 391-96.

4.132   Sheppard, G.T.   "Canon Criticism: The Proposal of Brevard
        Childs and an Assessment for Evangelical Hermeneutics,"
        Studia Biblica et Theologica 4 (1974) 3-17.

4.133   Sickenberger, J.   "Der neutestamentliche Kanon," LTK². 5.
        Cols. 778f.

4.133a Simon, M.   "From Greek Hairesis to Christian Heresy," Early
        Christian Literature and the Classical Intellectual Tradition
        in honorem Robert M. Grant, eds. W.R. Schoedel and R.L.
        Wilkin (Théologique Historique 54) Paris, 1979. Pp. 101-16.

4.134   Smith, T.C.   "The Canon and the Authority of the Bible,"
        Perspectives in Religious Studies 1 (1974) 42-51.

4.135   Soucek, J.B.   "Einheit des Kanons: Einheit der Kirche,"
        ZeichZt 22 (1968) 219-25.

4.136   Souter, A.   The Text and Canon of the New Testament.   Lon-
        don, 1954 (rev. ed. by C.S.C. Williams).

4.137   Stanton, V.H.   "Canon," Hastings. 1. Pp. 348-50.

4.138   Stanton, V.H.   "New Testament Canon," Hastings. 3. Pp.
        529-42.

4.139   Starowieyski, M.   The Apocrypha of the New Testament.   2
        vols. (Studies and Monographs 106, 107) Lublin, 1980.
        Vol. 1. Pp. 626-34. [in Polish]

4.140   Strathmann, H.   "Die Krisis des Kanons in der Kirche,"
        ThBl 20 (1941) 295-310.

4.141   Sundberg, A.C., Jr.   "The Bible Canon and the Christian
        Doctrine of Inspiration," Int 29 (1975) 352-71.

4.142   Sundberg, A.C., Jr.   "Canon Muratori: A Fourth Century
        List," HTR 66 (1973) 1-41.

4.143   Sundberg, A.C., Jr.   "Canon of the NT," IDBS. Pp. 136-40.

4.144   Sundberg, A.C., Jr.   "Dependent Canonicity in Irenaeus and
        Tertullian," Studia Evangelica. Vol. 3: Papers Presented
        to the Second International Congress on New Testament
        Studies Held at Christ Church, Oxford, 1961.   Part 2:
        The New Testament Message, ed. F.L. Cross (TU 88) Ber-
        lin, 1964. Pp. 403-09.

4.145 Sundberg, A.C., Jr. "The Making of the New Testament Canon," Interpreter's One-Volume Commentary on the Bible, ed. C.M. Laymon. New York, 1971. Pp. 1216-24.

4.146 Sundberg, A.C., Jr. The Old Testament of the Early Church (Harvard Theological Studies 20) Cambridge, Mass., 1964.

4.147 Sundberg, A.C., Jr. "The Old Testament of the Early Church," HTR 51 (1958) 205-26.

4.148 Sundberg, A.C., Jr. "Towards a Revised History of the New Testament Canon," Studia Evangelica. Vol. 4: Papers Presented to the Third International Congress on New Testament Studies Held at Christ Church, Oxford, 1965. Part 1: The New Testament Scriptures, ed. F.L. Cross (TU 102) Berlin, 1968. Pp. 452-61.

4.149 Tenney, M.C. "The Canon of the Gospels," JETS 10 (1967) 36-43.

4.150 Theunis, F.J. "Omtrent Kanon en Schrift," Bijdragen 41 (1980) 64-87.

4.151 Tregelles, S.P., ed. Canon Muratorianus: The Earliest Catalogue of the Books of the New Testament. Oxford, 1867.

4.152 Ullmann, [?]. Zur Charakteristik d. kanon. und apokr.*

4.153 Unnik, W.C. van. "Hē kainē diathēkē--a Problem in the Early History of the Canon," Studia Patristica. Vol. 4: Papers Presented to the Third International Conference on Patristic Studies. Part 2: Biblica, Patres Apostolici, Historica, ed. F.L. Cross (TU 79) Berlin, 1961. Pp. 212-27.

4.154 Vielhauer, P. "Einleitung in das Neue Testament," ThRu 31 (1966) 193-231.

4.155 Vielhauer, P. Geschichte der urchristlichen Literatur: Einleitung in das Neue Testament, die Apokryphen und die Apostolischen Väter. Berlin, 1975; rev. ed. 1978. Pp. 774-86.

4.156 Vokes, F.E. "The Didache and the Canon of the New Testament," Studia Evangelica. Vol. 3: Papers Presented to the Second International Congress on New Testament Studies Held at Christ Church, Oxford, 1961. Part 2: The New Testament Message, ed. F.L. Cross (TU 88) Berlin, 1964. Pp. 427-36.

4.157 Wainwright, G. "New Testament as Canon," SJT 28 (1975) 551-71.

4.158   Wendt, K. "Der Kampf um den Kanon Heiliger Schriften in
        der äthiopischen Kirche der Reformen des XV Jahrhunderts,"
        JSS 9 (1964) 107-13.

4.159   Westcott, B.F. "Canon, IV. The History of the Canon of the
        NT," Dr. William Smith's Dictionary of the Bible, ed. H.B.
        Hackett. Boston, 1880. Pp. 368-76.

4.160   Westcott, B.F. A General Survey of the History of the Canon
        of the New Testament. London, 1896[7].

4.161   Wilson, R.McL. "'Thomas' and the Growth of the Gospels,"
        HTR 53 (1960) 231-50.

4.162   Wordsworth, C. On the Inspiration of the Holy Scripture:
        Or, On the Canon of the Old and New Testament. London,
        1851.

4.163   Zahn, T. Die bleibende Bedeutung des neutestamentlichen
        Kanons für die Kirche: Vortrag auf der Lutherischen Pas-
        toralkonferenz zu Leipzig June 1, 1898. Leipzig, 1899.

4.164   Zahn, T. Forschungen zur Geschichte des neutestamentlichen
        Kanons und der altchristlichen Literatur. 10 vols. Erlangen,
        1881-1929.

4.165   Zahn, T. Geschichte des neutestamentlichen Kanons. 2 vols.
        Leipzig, 1888-1892.

4.166   Zahn, T. Grundriss der Geschichte des neutestamentlichen
        Kanons. 2 vols. Leipzig, 1904[2].

4.167   Zarb, S.M. De historia canonis utriusque testamenti (Opus-
        cula Biblica Pontificii Instituti Angelici) Rome, 1934.

4.168   Zinkand, J.M. "The Canon of the Bible: Some Reasons for
        Contemporary Interest," JETS 10 (1967) 15-20.

5. AGRAPHA, FRAGMENTS OF UNKNOWN WORKS

(See also 1.61, 76, 88, 141, 142, 395, 418-421, 433, 444, 531; 21.69;
    95.207.)

5.1   Abbot, E.A. "The Logia of Behnesa or the New 'Sayings of
        Jesus,'" AJT 2 (1898) 1-27.

5.2   Amiot, F. "Les papyrus d'Oxyrhynque," Évangiles Apoc. Pp.
        43-45.

5.3   Andriessen, P. "A propos d'un agraphon cité par Hippolyte,"
        VC 2 (1948) 248f.

5.4   Asin y Palacios, M. "In opus cui titulus 'Logia et agrapha
        Domini Jesu apud moslemicos scriptores asceticos praesertim,
        usitata' animadversiones," RB 36 (1927) 76-83.

5.5   Asin y Palacios, M. "Logia et agrapha Domini Jesu apud Mos-
        lemos scriptores, asceticos praesertim usitata," PO 13 (1919)
        327-431; 19 (1926) 529-610. [Ar. text and French trans.]

5.6   Baarda, T. "2 Clement 12 and the Sayings of Jesus," Logia:
        Les Paroles de Jésus--The Sayings of Jesus. Mémorial
        Joseph Coppens, ed. J. Delobel. Leuven, 1982. Pp. 529-
        56.

5.7   Baker, A. "Justin's Agraphon in the Dialogue with Trypho,"
        JBL 87 (1968) 277-87.

5.8   Bammel, E. "Excerpts from a New Gospel?" NovT 10 (1968)
        1-9.

5.9   Barclay, W. "Gathering Up the Fragments," ExpT 69 (1957-
        58) 318f.

5.10   Bardenhewer, O. "Evangelienfragmente ohne Titel," GAL.
        1. Pp. 510-13.

5.11   Bardenhewer, O. "Sammlungen von Herrenworten," GAL. 1.
        Pp. 539-43.

5.12   Bartlet, V. "The Oxyrhynchus Sayings of Jesus," Contem-
        porary Review 87 (1905) 116-25.

5.13   Batiffol, P. "Les logia du papyrus de Behnesa," RB 6 (1897)
        501-15. [also in Congrès Scientifique des Catholiques II.
        Fribourg (Switz.), 1897. Pp. 103-17.]

5.14   Batiffol, P. "Nouveau fragments évangéliques de Behnesa,"
        RB 13 (1904) 481-93.

5.15   Bauer, J.B. "Agraphon 90 Resch," ZNW 62 (1971) 301-03.

5.16   Bauer, J.B. "Apokryphe Evangelien Synoptischen Typs,"
        Neutest. Apok. Pp. 15-17.

5.17   Bauer, J.B. "Unverbürgte Jesusworte," BiLit 54 (1981) 163-
        66.

5.18   Bauer, W. "Die Worte und Reden Jesu," Das Leben Jesu im
        Zeitalter der neutestamentlichen Apokryphen. Tübingen,
        1909. Pp. 377-415.

5.19   Baumstark, A. "Ausserkanonische Evangeliensplitter auf einem
        frühchristlichen Kleinkunstdenkmal?" OrChr 6 (1916) 49-64.

5.20   Bell, H.I. "The Gospel Fragments P. Egerton 2," HTR 42
        (1949) 53-63.

5.21   Bell, H.I., and T.C. Skeat. Fragments of an Unknown Gos-
        pel and Other Early Christian Papyri. London, 1935. [see
        review by M. Dibelius, Deutsche Literaturzeitung 57 (1936)
        cols. 3-11]

5.22   Bell, H.I., and T.C. Skeat. The New Gospel Fragments.
        London, 1935.

5.23   Bellinzoni, A.J. The Sayings of Jesus in the Writings of Jus-
        tin Martyr (NovTSup 17) Leiden, 1967.

5.24   Bellinzoni, A.J., Jr. "The Source of the Agraphon in Justin
        Martyr's Dialogue with Trypho 47:5," VC 17 (1963) 65-70.

5.25   Besson, E. Les logia Agrapha: Paroles du Christ qui ne se
        trouvent pas dans les Evangiles canoniques. Bihorel-lez-
        Rouen, 1923.*

5.26   Bickell, G. "Ein Papyrusfragment eines nichtkanonischen
        Evangeliums," ZKT 9 (1885) 489-504; 10 (1886) 208-10.

5.27   Bischoff, B. Sacris Erudiri 6 (1954) 189-91.*

5.28   Blau, L. "Das neue Evangelienfragment von Oxyrhynchos
        buch- und zaubergeschichtlich betrachtet nebst sonstigen
        Bemerkungen," ZNW 9 (1908) 204-15.

5.29   Bonaccorsi, P.G. "Frammenti di supposti antichi Vangeli nei
        Papiri Egiziani," Vangeli Apocrifi. 1. Pp. 30-48.

5.30   Bonaccorsi, P.G. "I Logia di Gesù," Vangeli Apocrifi. 1.
        Pp. 48-57.

5.31   Bonsirven, J., and C. Bigaré, "Les agrapha," Intro. à la
        Bible. 2. Pp. 747-49.

5.32   Bousset, W. Die Evangelienzitate Justins des Martyrers. Göt-
        tingen, 1891.

5.33   Braun, F.M. Pourquoi l'Église ne lit-elle que quatre Evan-
        giles? Liège, 1935.

5.34   Braun, F.M. "A propos d'un cinquième Évangile," La vie in-
        tellectuelle 34 (1935) 220-24. [Papyrus Egerton 2]

5.35   Brown, R.E. "Papyrus Fragments," JBC. Pp. 544f.

5.36   Bruce, F.F. "More Uncanonical Scriptures," Jesus and Chris-
        tian Origins Outside the New Testament. Grand Rapids,
        1974. Pp. 159-66.

5.37   Bruce, F.F. "'Unwritten' Sayings and Apocryphal Gospels,"
        Jesus and Christian Origins Outside the New Testament.
        Grand Rapids, 1974. Pp. 82-109.

5.38   Brun, L. "Nyfunne Evangelisfragmenter," NorTT 36 (1935)
        269-77. [Papyrus Egerton 2]

5.39   Bruston, C. Fragment d'un ancien recueil de paroles de Jésus.
        Paris, 1905.

5.40   Bruston, C. Les paroles de Jésus récemment découvertes en
        Égypte et remarques sur le texte du fragment de l'Évangile
        de Pierre. Paris, 1898.

5.41   Büchler, A. "The New 'Fragment of an Uncanonical Gospel,'"
        JQR 20 (1908) 330-46.

5.42   Buonaiuti, E. Detti extracanonici di Gesù. Rome, 1925.

5.43   Burrows, E. "Oxyrhynchus Logion (1907) V," JTS 28 (1927)
        186.

5.44   Cabrol, F. "Agrapha," DACL. 2. Cols. 979-84.

5.45   Cerfaux, L. "Parallèles canoniques et extra-canoniques de
        'l'Evangile inconnu,'" Muséon 49 (1936) 55-78.

5.46   Cerfaux, L. "Un nouvel évangile apocryphe," ETL 12 (1935)
        579-81. [Papyrus Egerton 2]

5.47   Cersoy, P. "Quelques remarques sur les logia de Benhesa
        [sic]," RB 7 (1898) 415-20.

5.48   Chiappelli, A. Studi di antica letteratura cristiana. Turin,
        1887. Pp. 1-19, 219-22.

5.49   Clemen, C. "Neugefundene Jesusworte?" CW 29 (1897) 702-05.

5.50   Cobern, C.M. "The Recently Discovered 'Sayings of Jesus'
        and the Oldest Leaf of the New Testament," Homiletic Re-
        view 34 (1897) 505-10.

5.51   Coleman-Norton, P.R. "An Amusing Agraphon," CBQ 12
        (1950) 439-49.

5.52   Couard, L. Altchristliche Sagen über das Leben Jesu und der
       Apostel. Gütersloh, 1908.

5.53   Crum, W.E. "Coptic Anecdota I. A Gnostic Fragment," JTS
       44 (1943) 176-79.

5.54   Deissmann, A. "Das angebliche Evangelienfragment von Kairo,"
       ARW 7 (1904) 387-92; repr. with slight alterations in Licht
       vom Osten. Tübingen, 1923⁴. Pp. 368-71. [ET: "The
       Supposed Fragment of a Gospel at Cairo," Light from the
       Ancient East, trans. L.R.M. Strachan. New York, 1927.
       Pp. 430-34]

5.55   Dibelius, M. "Auf der Spur eines unbekannten apokryphen
       Evangelien," CW 54 (1940) 221f.

5.56   Dodd, C.H. "A New Gospel," BJRL 20 (1936) 58-92.

5.57   Dodd, J.T. Sayings Ascribed to Our Lord by the Fathers
       and other Primitive Writers. London, 1874.

5.58   Donovan, J. The Logia in Ancient and Recent Literature.
       Cambridge, 1924.

5.59   Dunkerly, R. "The Oxyrhynchus Gospel Fragments," HTR
       23 (1930) 19-37.

5.60   Dunkerly, R. "The Muhammedan Agrapha," ExpT 39 (1927-
       28) 167-71, 230-34.

5.61   Dunkerly, R. The Unwritten Gospel, Ana and Agrapha of
       Jesus. London, 1925.

5.62   Eisler, R. "Un nouveau papyrus évangélique," Comptes ren-
       dus des séances de l'Académie des inscriptions et belles-
       lettres. Paris, 1935. Pp. 197-202.

5.63   Erbetta, M. "Agrapha," Apoc. del NT. 1. Pp. 83-96.

5.64   Erbetta, M. "Papiri con frammenti di antichi vangeli apocrifi,"
       Apoc. del NT. 1. Pp. 97-110.

5.65   Esser, G. "Die neu aufgefundenen 'Sprüche Jesu,'" Der Kath-
       olik 1 (1898) 26-43, 137-51.

5.66   Evelyn-White, H.G. "The Fourth Oxyrhynchus Saying," JTS
       14 (1913) 400-03.

5.67   Evelyn-White, H.G. "The Introduction to the Oxyrhynchus
       Sayings," JTS 13 (1912) 74-76.

5.68   Evelyn-White, H.G. The Sayings of Jesus from Oxyrhynchus:
        Edited with Introduction, Critical Apparatus and Commentary.
        Cambridge, 1920.

5.69   Evelyn-White, H.G. "The Second Oxyrhynchus Saying," JTS
        16 (1915) 246-50.

5.70   Filson, F.V. "New Greek and Coptic Gospel Manuscripts,"
        BA 24 (1961) 2-18.

5.71   Fisher, F.H. "The New Logia of Jesus," ExpT 9 (1897) 140-
        43.

5.72   Fitzmyer, J.A. "The Oxyrhynchus Logoi of Jesus and the
        Coptic Gospel According to Thomas," TS 20 (1959) 505-50.
        [repr. in Essays on the Semitic Background of the New
        Testatment. London, 1971; repr. Scholars Press, 1974.
        Pp. 355-433.]

5.73   Fonseca, L.G. da. "Agrapha," VD 2 (1922) 300-09.

5.74   Fonseca, L.G. da. "De novo Evangelio (?) recens invento,"
        VD 15 (1935) 94-96. [Papyrus Egerton 2]

5.75   Franke, H. "Ein fünftes Evangelium," HL 79 (1935) 112-15.
        [Papyrus Egerton 2]

5.76   Galizia, U. "Il papiro di Egerton 2," Aegyptus 36 (1956) 29-
        72, 178-234.

5.77   Garitte, G. "Les 'Logoi' d'Oxyrhynque et l'apocryphe copte
        dit 'Évangile de Thomas,'" Muséon 73 (1960) 151-72, 219-22.

5.78   Garitte, G. "Les 'Logoi' d'Oxyrhynque sont traduits du copte,"
        Muséon 73 (1960) 335-49.

5.79   Ghedini, G. "Nuovi frammenti della letteratura cristiana prim-
        itiva," ScCatt 63 (1935) 500-12. [Papyrus Egerton 2]

5.80   Glasson, T.F. "Carding and Spinning: Oxyrhynchus Papyrus
        No. 655," JTS N.S. 13 (1962) 331f.

5.81   Goguel, M. "Les fragments nouvellement découverts d'un Évan-
        gile du IIe. siècle," RHPR 15 (1935) 459-66. [Papyrus Eger-
        ton 2]

5.82   Goguel, M. "Les nouveaux fragments évangéliques de Lon-
        dres," RHR 113 (1936) 42-87.

5.83   Gomez, J.J. Logia o dichos del Señor extraevangélicos. Mur-
        cia, 1953.

5.84   Grant, R.M., and D.N. Freedman. The Secret Sayings of
       Jesus. Garden City, N.Y., 1960.

5.85   Greitemann, N. "Onze evangeliën in het licht van een belan-
       grijke papyrusvondst," Schild 17 (1935) 241-48.

5.86   Grenfell, B.P., and A.S. Hunt. Fragment of an Uncanonical
       Gospel from Oxyrhynchus. Oxford, 1908. [Gk. text and
       ET]

5.87   Grenfell, B.P., and A.S. Hunt. Logia Iesou: Sayings of Our
       Lord from an Early Greek Papyrus. London, 1897.

5.88   Grenfell, B.P., and A.S. Hunt. The Oxyrhynchus Papyri.
       6 vols. London, 1908.

5.89   Grenfell, B.P.; A.S. Hunt; and L.W. Drexel, eds. New Say-
       ings of Jesus and Fragment of a Lost Gospel from Oxyrhyn-
       chus. London, 1904. [Gk. text and ET]

5.90   Griffinhoofe, C.G. The Unwritten Sayings of Christ: Words
       of Our Lord Not Recorded in the Four Gospels, Including
       Those Recently Discovered. Cambridge, 1903.

5.91   Grobel, K. "Agrapha," Dictionary of the Bible, ed. J. Hast-
       ings, rev. ed. F.C. Grant and H.H. Rowley. New York,
       1963. Pp. 13-15.

5.92   Guillaumont, A. "Les logia d'Oxyrhynchos sont-ils traduits
       du copte?" Muséon 73 (1960) 325-33.

5.93   Guillaumont, A. "Nēsteuein ton Kosmon, (P. Oxy. 1, verso,
       1. 5-6)," BIFAO 61 (1962) 15-23.

5.94   Haacker, K. "Bemerkungen zum Freer-Logion," ZNW 63 (1972)
       125-29.

5.95   Harnack, A. "Ein neues Evangelienbruchstück," Preussische
       Jahrbücher 131 (1908) 201-10.

5.96   Harnack, A. "Einige Worte Jesu, die nicht in unseren Evan-
       gelien stehen," Erforschtes und Erlebtes. Giessen, 1923.
       Pp. 44-52.

5.97   Harnack, A. Das Evangelienfragment von Fajjûm (TU 5.4)
       Leipzig, 1889. Pp. 481-97.

5.98   Harnack, A. "Fajjumer Evangelienfragment (saec. III.),"
       Gesch. altchrist. Lit. 1. P. 6.

5.99   Harnack, A. Über die jüngst entdeckten Sprüche Jesu.

Freiburg, 1897. [ET: "The Recently Discovered Sayings of Jesus," Exp 5th series, 6 (1897) 321-40, 401-16.]

5.100   Harnack, A. "Über einige Worte Jesu, die nicht in den kanonischen Evangelien stehen, nebst einem Anhang über die ursprüngliche Gestalt des Vaterunsers," SPAW (1904) 170-208.

5.101   Harris, J.R. "The 'Logia' and the Gospels," Contemporary Review 72 (1897) 341-48.

5.102   Hautsch, E. Die Evangelienzitate des Origenes (TU 34/2) Leipzig, 1909.

5.103   Heer, M. "Pseudo-Cyprian Vom Lohn der Frommen und das Evangelium Justins," Römische Quartalschrift 28 (1914) 97-186.

5.104   Heinrici, G. "Die neuen Herrensprüche," TSK 78 (1905) 188-210.

5.105   Hennecke, E. "Versprengte Herrenworte," Handbuch, ed. Hennecke. Pp. 13-21.

5.106   Hennecke, E. "Gnostische und verwandte Evangelien," Handbuch, ed. Hennecke. Pp. 88-94.

5.107   Hennecke, E. "Versprengte Herrenworte," H^2. Pp. 32-38.

5.108   Hergessel, T. "Concerning the Apocryphal Words of Christ," RuBi 31 (1978) 28-35. [in Polish]

5.109   Hilgenfeld, A. "Kein neuentdecktes Evangelium," ZWT 29 (1886) 50-56.

5.110   Hilgenfeld, A. "Neue gnostische Logia Jesu," ZWT 47 (1903-04) 414-18, 567-73.

5.111   Hilgenfeld, A. "Die neuesten Logiafunde von Oxyrhynchus," ZWT 48 (1904-05) 343-53.

5.112   Hofius, O. "Das koptische Thomasevangelium und die Oxyrhynchus-Papyri, Nr. 1, 164 und 655," EvT 20 (1960) 21-42, 182-92.

5.113   Holzmeister, U. "Un loguion de Jesús," VD 21 (1941) 69-73.

5.114   Holzmeister, U. "Unbeachtete patristische Agrapha," ZKT 38 (1914) 113-43; 39 (1915) 98-118.

5.115   Horder, W.G. Newly Found Words of Jesus. London, 1904.

5.116 Hornschuh, M. "A Coptic Fragment," HSW. 2. Pp. 423-25.

5.117 Jackson, B. Twenty-five Agrapha. London, 1900.

5.118 Jacobs, J. "The New 'Logia,'" JQR 10 (1897-98) 185-90.

5.119 Jacobus, M.W. "The Newly Discovered 'Sayings of Jesus,'"
       Hartford Seminary Record 8 (1897) 5-17.

5.120 Jacoby, A. "Agrapha," ZNW 13 (1912) 161-64.

5.121 Jacoby, A. Ein neues Evangelienfragment. Strassburg, 1900.

5.122 Jacoby, A. "Zum Strassburger Evangelienfragment," Sphinx
       6 (1903) 132-42.

5.123 Jacquier, E. "Les sentences du Seigneur extracanoniques,"
       RB 15 (1918) 93-135.

5.124 James, M.R. "Agrapha," ANT. Pp. 33-37.

5.125 James, M.R. "The Fayoum Gospel-Fragment," ANT. P. 25.

5.126 James, M.R. "The New Sayings of Christ," Contemporary Re-
       view 72 (1897) 153-60, 163.

5.127 James, M.R. "Fragment of a Gospel: Oxyrhynchus Papyrus
       655," ANT. Pp. 28f.

5.128 James M.R. "Fragment of Another Gospel: Oxyrhynchus
       Papyri, Part V, 1908," ANT. Pp. 29f.

5.129 James, M.R. "The Oxyrhynchus Sayings of Jesus," ANT.
       Pp. 25-28.

5.130 James, M.R. "The Strasburg Papyrus," ANT. Pp. 30-32.

5.131 Jenkinson, J.H. The Unwritten Sayings of the Lord. London,
       1925.

5.132 Jeremias, J. "Freer-Logion," HS. 1. Pp. 125f.

5.133 Jeremias, J. "The Freer Logion: [Mk.] 16:14 W," HSW. 1.
       Pp. 188f.

5.134 Jeremias, J. "Isolated Sayings of the Lord," HSW. 1. Pp.
       85-90.

5.135 Jeremias, J. "The Saying of Jesus About the Bridge," ExpT
       69 (1957-58) 7-9.

5.136   Jeremias, J. Unbekannte Jesusworte. Gütersloh, 1963³. [ET:
        Unknown Sayings of Jesus, trans. R.H. Fuller. London,
        1964².]

5.137   Jeremias, J. "Versprengte Herrenworte," HS. 1. Pp. 52-55.

5.138   Jeremias, J. "Zur Überlieferungsgeschichte des Agraphon 'Die
        Welt ist eine Brücke,'" Nachrichten der Akademie der Wissen-
        schaften in Göttingen 4 (1953) 96-103.

5.139   Jeremias, J. "Der Zusammentstoss Jesu mit dem pharisäischen
        Oberpriester auf dem Tempelplatz: Zu Pap. Ox.
        V, 840," Coniectanea Neotestamentica 11 in honorem Antonii Fridrich-
        sen sexagenarii. Lund, Köpenhamn, 1947. Pp. 97-108.

5.140   Jeremias, J., and W. Schneemelcher. "Papyrusfragmente apok-
        rypher Evangelien," HS. 1. Pp. 56-74.

5.141   Jeremias, J., and W. Schneemelcher, "Papyrus Fragments of
        Apocryphal Gospels," HSW. 1. Pp. 91-116.

5.142   Johnson, S.E. "Stray Pieces of Early Christian Writing,"
        JNES 5 (1946) 40-54.

5.143   Karavidopoulos, J. "Ein Agraphon in einem liturgischen Text
        der griechischen Kirche," ZNW 62 (1971) 299f.

5.144   Karavidopoulos, J. "Ein ausserbiblisches Wort Jesu im Gebet
        des Euchelaion," Gregorias ho Palamas [Thessalonica] 54
        (1971) 291-94.

5.145   Klostermann, E., ed. Apocrypha II: Evangelien (KIT 8) Ber-
        lin, 1929³. ["Oxyrhyncuslogia," pp. 19-22; "Papyrusfrag-
        mente von Evangelien," pp. 23-26; Gk. texts]

5.146   Klostermann, E., ed. Apocrypha III: Agrapha, Slavische
        Josephusstücke, Oxyrhynchos-Fragment 1911 (KIT 11) Bonn,
        1911². Pp. 3-17. [Gk. and Lat. witnesses; also see "Ein
        neues Oxyrhynchusfragment," p. 26]

5.147   Klostermann, E. "Bruchstücke eines unbekannten Evangel-
        iums," TSK 106 (1934-35) 318-24. [Papyrus Egerton 2]

5.148   Klostermann, E. "Zu den Agrapha," ZNW 6 (1905) 104-06.

5.149   Köhler, K. "Das Agraphon bei Tertullianus, De Baptismo 20,"
        TSK 94 (1922) 169-73, 744-49.

5.150   Körner, J.G. De sermonibus Christi agraphoris. [?], 1776.*

5.151   Köster, H. "Die ausserkanonischen Herrenworte als Produkte
        der christlichen Gemeinde," ZNW 48 (1957) 220-35.

5.152   Kraft, B. Die Evangelienzitate des Heiligen Irenaeus. Frei-
        burg, 1924.

5.153   Kraft, R.A. "Oxyrhynchus Papyrus 655 Reconsidered," HTR
        54 (1961) 253-62.

5.154   Lacau, M.P. "Évangile(?) Apocryphe," FAC. Pp. 79-108.
        [Cop. text and French trans.; contains fragments of uniden-
        tified apocryphal documents; see CopNar]

5.155   Lacau, M.P. "Évangile(?) Apocryphe," FAC. Pp. 23-37.
        [Cop. text and French trans.; contains three fragments of
        unidentified apocryphal documents; see CopNar]

5.156   Lagrange, M.-J. "Deux nouveaux texts relatifs à l'évangile,"
        RB 44 (1935) 321-43. [Papyrus Egerton 2; probably derived
        from the four canonical gospels, esp. Jn]

5.157   Lagrange, M.-J. "Nouveau fragment non-canonique relatif à
        l'évangile," RB 5 (1908) 538-53.

5.158   Lagrange, M.-J. "La seconde parole d'Oxyrhynque," RB
        31 (1922) 427-33.

5.159   Lagrange, M.-J. "Une des paroles attribuées à Jésus," RB
        30 (1921) 233-37.

5.160   Lake, K. "The New Sayings of Jesus and the Synoptic Prob-
        lem," HibJ 3 (1904-05) 332-41.

5.161   Lane, W.L. "Agrapha," Encyclopedia of Christianity, eds.
        E.H. Palmer et al. Wilmington, Del., 1964- . Vol. 1.
        Pp. 105-12.

5.162   Lane, W.L. "A Critique of Purportedly Authentic Agrapha,"
        JETS 18 (1975) 29-35.

5.163   Leanza, S. I detti extracanonici di Gesù. Messina, 1977.

5.164   Lefort, L.T. "Fragments d'apocryphes en copte-akhminique,"
        Muséon 52 (1939) 1-10.

5.165   Lietzmann, H. "Ein apokryphes Evangelienfragment," ZNW
        22 (1923) 153f.

5.166   Lock, W. "Agrapha: Sayings of our Lord not Recorded in the
        Gospels," Exp 4th series, 9 (1894) 1-16, 97-109.

5.167   Lock, W. "The New Sayings of Jesus," CQR 58 (1904) 422-32.

5.168   Lock, W., and W. Sanday. Two Lectures on the 'Sayings of
        Jesus' Recently Discovered at Oxyrhynchus. Oxford, 1897.

5.169   Maas, A.J.   "The Newly Discovered 'Sayings of Jesus,'"
        American Catholic Quarterly Review 30 (1905) 253-67.

5.170   Mangenot, E.   "Agrapha," DThC.   1.   Cols. 625-27.

5.171   Margoliouth, D.S.   "Christ in Islam: Sayings Attributed to
        Christ by Mohammedan Writers," ExpT 5 (1893-94) 59, 107,
        177f., 503f., 561.

5.172   Marmorstein, A.   "Einige Bemerkungen zum Evangelienfrag-
        ment in Oxyrhynchus Papyri, vol. V. n. 840, 1907," ZNW
        15 (1914) 36-38.

5.173   Mayeda, G.   Das Leben-Jesu-Fragment Papyrus Egerton 2
        und seine Stellung in der urchristlichen Literaturgeschichte.
        Bern, 1946.

5.174   Mees, M.   "Formen, Strukturen und Gattungen ausserkanoni-
        scher Herrenworte," Aug 14 (1974) 459-88.

5.175   Menoud, P.H.   "Un nouvel évangile," RTP 23 (1935) 159-64.

5.176   Moraldi, L.   "Agrafa di Gesù," Apoc. del NT.   1.   Pp. 459-
        74.

5.177   Moraldi, L.   "Papiri frammentari," Apoc. del NT.   1.   Pp.
        421-51.

5.178   Moule, H.C.G.   "An Agraphon: The Secret of the Presence,"
        ExpT 11 (1899-1900) 507.

5.179   Nestle, E.   "Ein früher Agrapha--Sammler," ZNW 11 (1910)
        86f.

5.180   Nestle, E.   "Evangelien als Amulet am Halse und am Sofa,"
        ZNW 7 (1906) 96.

5.181   Nestle, E.   "Evangeliorum deperditorum fragmenta, dicta Sal-
        vatoris agrapha, alia," Novi Testamenti Graeci Supplementum.
        Leipzig, 1896.   Pp. 67-94.

5.182   The New Gospel Fragments.   London, 1955.   [two fragments
        and one small Gk. papyrus codex of an unknown gospel
        published by the British Museum]

5.183   Nock, A.D.   "The Apocryphal Gospels," JTS n.s. 11 (1960)
        63-70.

5.184   Noguer, N.   "Los dichos de Jesús llamados 'Logia' y 'Agrapha,'"
        RazFe 51 (1918) 19-29, 204-26.

5.185   Osborne, G.   "Note on Pap. Oxyrh. 655," JTS 32 (1930) 179.

5.186   Parker, P. "The 'Second' Saying from Oxyrhynchus," ATR
        22 (1940) 195-98.

5.187   Peeters, P. "Appendice: Jésus à l'école," EvApoc. 2. Pp.
        288-311.

5.188   Pick, B. Jesus in the Talmud: His Personality, His Disciples
        and His Sayings. Chicago, 1913.

5.189   Pick, B. Paralipomena: Remains of Gospels and Sayings of
        Christ. Chicago, 1908.

5.190   Pieper, K. "Ein neues Evangelium?" ThGl 27 (1935) 343-48.
        [Papyrus Egerton 2]

5.191   Preuschen, E. "Evangelienfragment," Antilegomena. Giessen,
        1905². Pp. 26, 152. [Ox. pap. 655; Gk. text]

5.192   Preuschen, E. "Das Evangelienfragment von Fajjûm," Antile-
        gomena. Giessen, 1905². Pp. 21f., 151. [Gk. text]

5.193   Preuschen, E. "Die Evangelienzitate Justins," Antilegomena.
        Giessen, 1905². Pp. 33-52, 156-72. [Gk. text]

5.194   Preuschen, E. "Herrenlose Herrnworte," Antilegomena. Gies-
        sen, 1905². Pp. 26-31, 152-55. [Gk. text]

5.195   Preuschen, E. "Logia Iēsou," Antilegomena. Giessen, 1905².
        Pp. 22-26, 151f. [Gk. text]

5.196   Preuschen, E. "Ein koptisches Evangelienfragment," Anti-
        legomena. Giessen, 1905². Pp. 115f. [Gk. text]

5.197   Preuschen, E. "Das neue Evangelienfragment von Oxyrhyn-
        chos," ZNW 9 (1908) 1-11.

5.198   Rawsley, H.D. Sayings of Jesus: Six Village Sermons on the
        Papyrus Fragment. London, 1897.

5.199   Redpath, H.A. "The So-called Logia and Their Relation to
        the Canonical Scriptures," Exp 6 (1897) 224-30.

5.200   Reinach, S. "Fragments d'un évangile manichéen," Revue
        Archéologique 22 (1913) 416-19.

5.201   Reitzenstein, R. "Ein Zitat aus den Logia Iesou," ZNW 6
        (1905) 203.

5.202   Resch, A. Agrapha: Aussercanonische Evangelienfragmente
        (TU 5.4) Leipzig, 1889.

5.203 Resch, A. Agrapha: Aussercanonische Schriftfragmente (TU
       N.F. 15.3-4) Leipzig, 1906; repr. Darmstadt, 1967.

5.204 Resch, A. Der Paulinismus und die Logia Jesu (TU 27) Leip-
       zig, 1904.

5.205 Riggenbach, E. "Das Wort Jesu im Gespräch mit dem pharisäi-
       schen Hohenpriester nach dem Oxyrhynchus Fragment V Nr.
       840," ZNW 25 (1926) 140-44.

5.206 Roberts, C.H. The Antiopolis Papyri I. London, 1950. P.
       17.

5.207 Roberts, C.H. Catalogue of the Greek and Latin Papyri in
       John Rylands Library. Vol. 3: Theological and Literary
       Texts. Manchester, 1938.

5.208 Roberts, C.H. "A Fragment of an Uncanonical Gospel," JTS
       47 (1946) 56f.

5.209 Robertson, A.T. The Christ of the Logia. New York, 1924.

5.210 Robertson, J.A. Sayings of Jesus of Nazareth. London,
       1920.

5.211 Ropes, J.H. "Agrapha," Hastings. 5. Pp. 343-52.

5.212 Ropes, J.H. "The So-called Agrapha," AJT 1 (1897) 758-76.

5.213 Ropes, J.H. Die Sprüche Jesu, die in den kanonischen Evan-
       gelien nicht überliefert sind (TU 14.2) Leipzig, 1896.

5.214 Rosenberg, A. Unbekannte Worte Jesu: Gesammelt und ein-
       geleitet. Munich, 1954.

5.215 Ruwet, J. "Les 'Agrapha' dans les oeuvres de Clément d'Alex-
       andrie," Bib 30 (1949) 133-60.

5.216 Sahlin, H. "Die Welt ist eine Brücke. Geht über sie hinüber-
       aber lasst euch nicht auf ihr nieder!" ZNW 47 (1956) 286f.

5.217 Santos Otero, A. de. "Agrapha," Evangelios Apócrifos. Pp.
       108-22. [Gk. texts and Spanish trans.]

5.218 Santos Otero, A. de. "Fragmentos Papiraceos," Evangelios
       Apócrifos. Pp. 76-107. [Gk. texts and Spanish trans.]

5.219 Savi, P. "Le fragment évangélique de Fayoûm," RB 1 (1892)
       321-44.

5.220 Savi, P. Studi critici del P. Paolo Savi, barnabita, raccolti
       e riordinati dal can. Fr. Polese. Siena, 1899. Pp. 123-45.

5.221   Schlisske, O. <u>Der Schatz im Schutthaufen: Der abenteuerliche</u>
        <u>Bericht von einer neuentdeckten Jesusgeschichte.</u> Stuttgart,
        1957.

5.222   Schmidt, C. "Ein vorirenäisches gnostisches Originalwerk in
        Koptischer Sprache," <u>SPAW</u> (1896) 839-47.

5.223   Schmidt, C. [a lengthy critique of A. Jacoby's <u>Ein neues</u>
        <u>Evangelienfragment</u>] <u>Göttingische Gelehrte Anzeigen</u> 6 (1900)
        481-506.

5.224   Schmidt, K.F.W., and J. Jeremias. "Ein bisher unbekanntes
        Evangelienfragment," <u>ThBl</u> 15 (1936) 34-45.

5.225   Schmidtke, A. <u>Neue Fragmente und Untersuchungen zu den</u>
        <u>judenchristlichen Evangelien: Ein Beitrag zur Literatur und</u>
        <u>Geschichte der Judenchristen.</u> (TU 37.1) Leipzig, 1911.

5.226   Schneemelcher, W. "Evangelienfragment des Strassburger
        koptischen Papyrus," HS. 1. Pp. 155-57.

5.227   Schneemelcher, W. "A Gospel Fragment from the Strasbourg
        Coptic Papyrus," HSW. 1. Pp. 227-30.

5.228   Schneemelcher, W., and J. Jeremias. "Sayings-Collections on
        Papyrus," HSW. 1. Pp. 97-113.

5.229   Schneemelcher, W., and J. Jeremias. "Spruchsammlungen auf
        Papyrus," HS. 1. Pp. 61-72.

5.230   Schneider, T. "Das prophetische 'Agraphon' der Epistola
        Apostolorum," <u>ZNW</u> 24 (1925) 151-54.

5.231   Scholz, A. von. "Zu den Logia Jesu," <u>TQ</u> 82 (1900) 1-22.

5.232   Schrage, W. "Evangelienzitate in den Oxyrhynchus-Logien
        und im koptischen Thomas-Evangelium," <u>Apophoreta: Fest-</u>
        <u>schrift für Ernst Haenchen</u>, ed. W. Eltester and F.H. Kettler
        (BZNW 30) Berlin, 1964. Pp. 251-68.

5.233   Schubart, W. "Das zweite Logion Oxyrhynchus Pap. IV 654,"
        <u>ZNW</u> 20 (1921) 215-23.

5.234   Schürer, E. "Fragment of an Uncanonical Gospel," <u>TLZ</u> 33
        (1908) 170-72.

5.235   Selbie, J.A. "'The Logia,'" <u>ExpT</u> 9 (1898) 548f.

5.236   Selbie, J.A. "The Oxyrhynchus Fragment," <u>ExpT</u> 9 (1897)
        221.

5.237   Selbie, J.A.   "The Recently Discovered Logia," ExpT 9 (1897)
        68f.

5.238   Semeria, G.   Le parole di Gesù recentemente scoperte e l'ultima
        fase della critica evangelica. Genoa, 1898.

5.239   Shahan, T.J.   "The Agrapha or 'Unwritten Sayings' of Our
        Lord," AmER 25 (1901) 458-73.

5.240   Smith, D.   Unwritten Sayings of Our Lord. New York, 1913.

5.241   Smothers, E.R.   "Un nouvel Évangile du deuxième siècle,"
        RSR 25 (1935) 358-62. [Papyrus Egerton 2]

5.242   Spiegelberg, W., and A. Jacoby.   "Zu dem Strassburger
        Evangelienfragment, eine Antikritik," Sphinx 4 (1901) 171-
        93.

5.243   Starowieyski, M.   The Apocrypha of the New Testament. 2
        vols. (Studies and Monographs 106, 107) Lublin, 1980.
        Vol. 1. Pp. 644-60. [in Polish]

5.244   Stegmüller, F.   Repertorium Biblicum. 1. Pp. 106f., 116; 8.
        Pp. 74-76, 89.

5.245   Stiglmayr, J.   "Die Agrapha bei Makarius von Agypten,"
        ThGl 5 (1913) 634-41.

5.246   Strack, L.   Jesus, die Häretiker und die Christen. Leipzig,
        1910.

5.247   Sulzbach, A.   "Zum Oxyrhynchus-Fragment," ZNW 9 (1908)
        175f.

5.248   Swete, H.B.   "The New Oxyrhynchus Sayings: A Tentative
        Interpretation," ExpT 15 (1904) 488-95.

5.249   Swete, H.B.   "The Oxyrhynchus Fragment," ExpT 8 (1897)
        544-50.

5.250   Swete, H.B.   Zwei neue Evangelienfragmente (KlT 31) Bonn,
        1924[2].

5.251   Taylor, C.   "The Oxyrhynchus and Other Agrapha," JTS 7
        (1906) 546-62.

5.252   Taylor, C.   The Oxyrhynchus Logia and the Apocryphal Gos-
        pels. Oxford, 1899.

5.253   Taylor, C.   The Oxyrhynchus Sayings of Jesus Found in 1903
        with the Sayings Called 'Logia' Found in 1897. Oxford, 1905.

5.254 Till, W. Die gnostischen Schriften des Koptischen Papyrus
        Berolinensis 8502 (TU 60) Berlin, 1955.

5.255 Tischendorf, K. "Additamenta ad Evangelia Apocrypha,"
        Apocalypses Apocryphae. Pp. LI-LXIV. [Gk. text]

5.256 Trabaud, H. "Les nouvelles paroles de Jésus," RTP 31 (1898)
        79-84.

5.257 Turner, C.H. "Adversaria Patristica. II. 'Let thine Alms
        Sweat in thy Hands,'" JTS 7 (1906) 593-95.

5.258 Uckeley, A. "Worte Jesu, die nicht in der Bibel stehen,"
        Biblische Zeit- und Streitfragen 7 (1911).*

5.259 Vaganay, L. "Agrapha," DBSup. 1. Cols. 159-98.

5.260 Vernon, B. "The Oxyrhynchus Sayings of Jesus in a New
        Light," Exp 48 (1922) 136-59.

5.261 Vogels, H.J. "Zum Agraphon 'ginesthe dokimoi trapezitai,'"
        BZ 8 (1910) 390.

5.262 Votaw, C.W. "The Newly Discovered 'Sayings of Jesus,'"
        BW 24 (1904) 261-77.

5.263 Votaw, C.W. "The Oxyrhynchus Sayings of Jesus in Relation
        to the Gospel-making Movement of the First and Second Cen-
        turies," JBL 24 (1905) 79-90.

5.264 Walls, A.F. "'Stone' and 'Wood' in Oxyrhynchus Papyrus I,"
        VC 16 (1962) 71-76.

5.265 Walsh, J. "Divine Call and Human Response: The Apocryphal
        Sayings of Jesus and his Apostles," Way 21 (1981) 225-32.

5.266 Warschauer, J. Jesus Saith: Studies in Some 'New Sayings'
        of Christ. London, 1905.

5.267 Weiss, J. "Neue Logia," ThRu 1 (1898) 227-36.

5.268 Wendland, P. Die urchristliche Literaturformen [Handbuch
        zum N.T. herausgegeben von H. Lietzmann. Vol. 1.3]
        Tübingen, 1912.

5.269 Wessely, K. "Fragments de collections de prétendues sentences
        de Jésus," PO 4 (1908) 151-72.

5.270 Wessely, K. "Über das Zeitalter des Wiener Evangelienpapyrus,"
        ZKT 11 (1887) 507-15.

5.271 Westcott, B.F. "On the Apocryphal Traditions of the Lord's

Words and Works," An Introduction to the Study of the Gospels. Cambridge, London, 1881⁶. Pp. 457-63.

5.272 Western, W. "The 'Puzzling Passage' in the Gospel Fragments," ExpT 48 (1936-37) 43.

5.273 White, W., Jr. "Agrapha," ZPEB. 1. P. 71.

5.274 Wilmart, A. Analecta Reginensia (Studi e testi 59) Rome, 1933.

5.275 Wilson, R.McL. "Further 'Unknown Sayings of Jesus,'" ExpT 69 (1957-58) 182.

5.276 Windisch, H. "Bruchstücke eines unbekannten Evangeliums," CW 49 (1935) 154-57. [Papyrus Egerton 2]

5.277 Workman, W.P. "Sayings of Jesus: A New Suggestion," ExpT 17 (1906) 191.

5.278 Wright, G.F. "The New 'Sayings of Jesus,'" BibSac 54 (1897) 759-70.

5.279 Wright, L.E. Alterations of the Words of Jesus. Oxford, 1952.

5.280 Wright, L.E. "The Oxyrhynchus Sayings of Jesus," JBL 65 (1946) 175-83.

5.281 Zahn, T. "Die jüngst gefundenen 'Aussprüche Jesu,'" Theologisches Litteraturblatt 18 (1897) 417-20, 425-31. [ET: "The Recently Discovered 'Logia of Jesus,'" Lutheran Church Review 1 (1898) 168-83]

5.282 Zahn, T. "Neue Funde aus der alten Kirche," NKZ 16 (1905) 94-105, 165-78.

5.283 Zahn, T. "Neue Bruchstücke nichtkanonischer Evangelien," NKZ 19 (1908) 371-86.

5.284 Zahn, T. "Über verlorene und wiederentdeckte Urevangelien," Neutest. Kanons. 2. Pp. 780-97.

MAJOR WORKS

6. ABBATON, ANGEL OF DEATH

6.1   Budge, E.A.W. Coptic Martyrdoms in the Dialect of Upper Egypt. London, 1914. Pp. 225-49 [Coptic text]; 474-93 [ET].

6.2   Erbetta, M. "L'Investitura di Abbaton, Angelo della Morte," Apoc. del NT. 3. Pp. 471-81. [Italian trans.]

6.3   Moraldi, L. "Abbatôn, angelo della morte," Apoc. del NT. 2. Pp. 1913-16.

7. PSEUDO-ABDIAS, APOSTOLIC HISTORIES OF

(See also entries under the names of the individual apostles.)

(See also 1.53; 9.8, 11.)

7.1   Amann, É. "Les remaniements postérieurs, le Pseudo-Abdias," DBSup. 1. Cols. 512-14.

7.2   Barre, L. de la. Historia christiana veterum patrum. Paris, 1583.

7.3   Erbetta, M. "Atti e Martirio di Pietro dello Ps. Abdia 1.I," Apoc. del NT. 2. Pp. 199-210.

7.4   Erbetta, M. "Gli Atti latini di Tommaso: I Miracoli e la Passione," Apoc. del NT. 2. Pp. 375-91.

7.5   Erbetta, M. "Giacomo di Zebedeo e la Passione latina," Apoc. del NT. 2. Pp. 543-48.

7.6   Erbetta, M. "Giacomo il Minore," Apoc. del NT. 2. Pp. 549-57.

7.7   Erbetta, M. "Il libro V dello Ps. Abdia," Apoc. del NT. 2.
       Pp. 111-29. [John]

7.8   Erbetta, M. "Libro X dello Ps. Abdia," Apoc. del NT. 2.
       Pp. 488-90. [Philip]

7.9   Erbetta, M. "La Passione di Bartolomeo," Apoc. del NT. 2.
       Pp. 581-88.

7.10   Erbetta, M. "La Passione di Paolo dello Ps. Abdia," Apoc. del
       NT. 2. Pp. 297-301.

7.11   Erbetta, M. "La Passione latina di Matteo," Apoc. del NT.
       2. Pp. 518-26.

7.12   Erbetta, M. "Simone e Giuda," Apoc. del NT. 2. Pp. 559-
       71.

7.13   Erbetta, M. "Le 'Virtutes Andreae' di Gregorio di Tours
       († 595) nella raccolta dello Ps. Abdia," Apoc. del NT. 2.
       Pp. 408-28.

7.14   Fabricius, J.A. "Acta Apostolorum Apocrypha, sive Historia
       Certaminis Apostolici, adscripta Abdiae," Cod. Apoc. NT.
       2. Pp. 387-742. [Book 1--Peter, 402-41; 2--Paul, 441-56;
       3--Andrew, 456-515; 4--James (maj), 516-31; 5--John, 531-
       90; 6--James, Simon, Jude, 591-636; 7--Matthew, 636-68;
       8--Bartholomew, 669-87; 9--Thomas, 687-736; 10--Philip,
       736-42]

7.15   Fabricius, J.A. "Marcellus de Conflictu (c) Petri et Simonis
       Magi," Cod. Apoc. NT. 2. Pp. 778-80.

7.16   Hess, J.-J. Geschichte und Schriften der Apostel Jesu. 4
       vols. Zürich, 1820-22.

7.17   James, M.R. "Apostolic History of Abdias," ANT. Pp. 462-
       69. [see also James' remarks under names of individual
       apostles]

7.18   Lami, J., De eruditione apostolorum. Florence, 1738.

7.19   Lazius, W. Abdiae episcopi babyloniae historia certaminis
       apostolorum. Basel, 1551. [Repr. Paris, 1560, 1571; Colonia,
       1566, 1569, 1575.]

7.20   Lipsius, R.A. Die apokryphen Apostelgeschichten und Apostel-
       legenden. 2 vols. Brunswick, 1883-1890; repr. Amsterdam,
       1976. Vol. 1. Pp. 117-78.

7.21   Martins, M. "Em torno do Pseudo-Abdius (De historia Certa-
       minis Apostoli libri X)," Brotéria 72 (1961) 428-38.

7.22   Migne, J.-P. "Abdias. (Histoire apostolique, ou Histoire du
        combat apostolique par Abdias, premier évêque de Babylone.),
        Dictionnaire. 2. Cols. 13-20.

7.23   Migne, J.-P. "André. (Histoire de saint André, d'après
        l'Histoire apostolique d'Abdias, lib. III.)," Dictionnaire. 2.
        Cols. 57-106.

7.24   Migne, J.-P. "Barthélemy. (Histoire de saint Barthélemy
        d'après l'Histoire apostolique d'Abdias, livre VIII).," Dic-
        tionnaire. 2. Cols. 149-59.

7.25   Migne, J.-P. "Histoire de saint Paul d'après l'Histoire apos-
        tolique d'Abdias, lib. II (597)," Dictionnaire. 2. Cols.
        657-64.

7.26   Migne, J.-P. "Histoire de saint Pierre d'après l'Histoire apos-
        tolique d'Abdias," Dictionnaire. 2. Cols. 695-716.

7.27   Migne, J.-P. "Jacques le Majeur. (Histoire de Jacques le
        Majeur, d'après l'Histoire apostolique d'Abdias, livre IV.),"
        Dictionnaire. 2. Cols. 265-76.

7.28   Migne, J.-P. "Jacques le Mineur. (Histoire de l'apôtre Jac-
        ques le Mineur, d'après l'Histoire apostolique d'Abdias, liv.
        VI.)," Dictionnaire. 2. Cols. 275-324. [also includes three
        liturgies of James]

7.29   Migne, J.-P. "Matthieu. (Histoire de saint Matthieu d'après
        l'Histoire apostolique d'Abdias, 1. VII.)," Dictionnaire 2.
        Cols. 549-84.

7.30   Migne, J.-P. "Simon et Jude, Apôtres. (La légende relative
        à ces saints apôtres fait partie du VIe libre de l'Histoire
        apostolique d'Abdias; elle est placée à la suite de celle de
        saint Jacques le Mineur.)," Dictionnaire. 2. Cols. 939-54.

7.31   Moraldi, L. "Memorie apostoliche di Abdia primo vescovo di
        Babilonia," Apoc. del NT. 2. Pp. 1431-1606.

7.32   Nausea, F. Anonymi Philalethi Eusebiani in vitas, miracula
        passionesque apostolorum rhapsodiae. Coloniae Agr., 1531.*

7.33   Neander, A. Geschichte der Pflanzung und Leitung der christ-
        lichen Kirche durch die Apostel. 2 vols. Hamburg, 1832-33.

7.34   Stegmüller, F. Repertorium Biblicum. 1. Pp. 164f.

7.35   Wilson, R.McL. "Abdias, Apostolic History of," ZPEB. 1.
        P. 7.

8. GOSPEL OF THE ADVERSARY OF THE
LAW AND THE PROPHETS

8.1   Hennecke, E. "Aus einer Markionitischen (?) Schrift," H^2.
      P. 65.

8.2   James, M.R. ANT. P. 20. [ET of quotation from Augustine]

8.3   Santos Otero, A. de. "Evangelio de los Adversarios de la Ley
      y de los Profetas," Evangelios Apócrifos. P. 67. [Gk. quo-
      tation from Augustine (Contra advers. Legis et Proph. II.
      3, 14) and Spanish trans.]

8.4   Stegmüller, F. Repertorium Biblicum. 1. P. 107; 8. P. 76.

9. ANDREW, ACTS OF; AND ANDREW CYCLE

(See also 1.203, 205, 284, 470, 531; 3.12, 53, 63, 77, 78; 5.116;
      7.13, 14, 23; 36.68.)

9.1   Amann, É. "Les Actes d'André," DBSup. 1. Cols. 504-08.

9.2   Amiot, F. "Actes d'André," Évangiles Apoc. Pp. 252-61.
      [French trans.]

9.3   Bardenhewer, O. "Die Akten des Andreas," GAL. 1. Pp.
      568-74.

9.4   Bardenhewer, O. "Das Andreas- und das Bartholomäusevan-
      gelium," GAL. 1. Pp. 538f.

9.5   Barns, J.W.B. "A Coptic Apocryphal Fragment in the Bod-
      leian Library," JTS N.S. 11 (1960) 70-76. [Cop. text and
      facsimile of a fourth century parchment fragment probably
      an extract from AcAn]

9.6   Bauer, J.B. "Die Andreasakten," Neutest. Apok. Pp. 75f.

9.7   Bertin, G.A., and A. Foulet. "The Acts of Andrew in Old
      French Verse: The Gardner Sage Library Fragment," Pub-
      lications of the Modern Language Association of America 81
      (1966) 451-54.

9.8   Bonnet, M., ed. Acta Andreae com laudatione contexta et
      Martyrium Andreae Graece: Passio Andreae Latine. (Sup-
      plementum Codicis Apocryphi 2) Paris, 1895. [repr. from
      AnBoll 13 (1894) 309-78]

9.9   Bonnet, M. "Acta Andreae Apostoli cum laudatione contexta,"
        AnBoll 13 (1894) 309-52. [Gk. text]

9.10   Bonnet, M., ed. "Ex actis Andreae," AAA. 2.1. Pp. XIVf.,
        38-45. [Intro. and Gk. text]

9.11   Bonnet, M., ed. "Gregorii Episcopi Turonensis Liber de
        Miraculis B. Andreae Apostoli," Monumenta Germaniae His-
        torica: Scriptorum rerum Merovingicarum. Hanover, 1885-
        [?]. Vol. 1. Pp. 821-46.

9.12   Bonnet, M., ed. "Martyrium Andreae Alterum," AAA. 2.1.
        Pp. 58-64. [Gk. text]

9.13   Bonnet, M., ed. "Martyrium Andreae Prius," AAA. 2.1.
        Pp. xv-xix, 46-57. [Intro. and Gk. text]

9.14   Bonnet, M. "Martyrium Sancti Apostoli Andreae," AnBoll 13
        (1894) 353-72. [Gk. text]

9.15   Bonnet, M. "La passion d'André en quelle langue a-t-elle
        été écrite?" ByZ 3 (1894) 458-69.

9.16   Bonnet, M., ed. "Passio sancti Andreae apostoli," AAA. 2.1.
        Pp. xi-xiv, 1-37. [Intro., Gk. and Lat. texts]

9.17   Bonnet, M. "Passio Sancti Andreae Apostoli," AnBoll 13
        (1894) 373-78. [Lat. text]

9.18   Bonsirven, J., and C. Bigaré, "Actes d'André," Intro. à la
        Bible. 2. P. 760.

9.19   Bonwetsch, N. "Acta Andreae," Gesch. altchrist. Lit. 1.
        P. 905.

9.20   Brooks, K.R. Andreas and the Fates of the Apostles. Lon-
        don, 1961.

9.21   Bruyne, D. de. "Nouveaux fragments des Actes de Pierre,
        de Paul, de Jean, d'André, et de l'Apocalypse d'Élie,"
        RBen 25 (1908) 149-60.

9.22   Deeleman, C.F.M. "Acta Andreae," Geloof en Vrijheid 46
        (1912) 541-77.

9.23   Dressel, A. Epiphanii opera edita ed inedita. Paris-Leipzig,
        1843. Pp. 44-83.

9.24   Dvornik, F. The Idea of Apostolicity in Byzantium and the
        Legend of the Apostle Andrew. (Dumbarton Oaks Studies
        4) Cambridge, Mass., 1958.

9.25   Dvornik, F. "L'idée de l'apostolicité à Byzance et la légende
        de l'apôtre André," Actes du X Congrès Inter. d'Études
        Byzantines 1955. Istanbul, 1975. Pp. 322-26.

9.26   Erbetta, M. "Gli Atti di Andrea," Apoc. del NT. 2. Pp.
        395-407.

9.27   Erbetta, M. "Due 'Martiri' di Andrea," Apoc. del NT. 2.
        Pp. 438-45.

9.28   Erbetta, M. "Il monaco Epiphanio, l'encomiaste o panegirista
        greco e i Menei," Apoc. del NT. 2. Pp. 446-49.

9.29   Erbetta, M. "La Passione di Andrea: Lettera spuria dei
        presbiteri e diaconi di Acaia," Apoc. del NT. 2. Pp. 429-
        37.

9.30   Fabricius, J.A. "Acta S. Andreae," Cod.Apoc.NT. 2. Pp.
        747-59.

9.31   Fabricius, J.A. "Evangelium S. Andreae," Cod.Apoc.NT. 1.
        Pp. 338f.

9.32   Flamion, J. Les Actes d'André et les textes apparentés. (Re-
        cueil de travaux d'histoire et de philologie 33) Louvain, 1911.
        [See M.R. James' review JTS 13 (1912) 433-37.]

9.33   Harnack, A. "Die Andreasakten," Gesch. altchrist. Lit. 1.
        Pp. 127f.

9.34   Harnack, A. "Die Johannes-, Andreas-, und Thomasacten,"
        Gesch. altchrist. Lit. 2.1. Pp. 541-49.

9.35   Hennecke, E. "Andreasakten," Handbuch, ed. Hennecke.
        Pp. 544-62.

9.36   Hennecke, E. "Andreasakten," H^2. Pp. 249-56.

9.37   Hennecke, E. "Zur christlichen Apokryphenliteratur," ZKG
        45 (1926) 309-15.

9.38   Hornschuh, M. "Acts of Andrew," HSW. 2. Pp. 390-425.

9.39   Hornschuh, M. "Andreasakten," HS. 2. Pp. 270-97.

9.40   Istomin, K. "From Slavo-Russian Manuscripts About the Apostle
        Andrew" Vestnik archeologii i istorii [izd. S.-Peterburgsk.
        Archeol. Instituta] 16 (1904) 233-280. [in Russian]

9.41   James, M.R. "Acts of Andrew," ANT. Pp. 337-63.

162   IV. Bibliography

9.42   James, M.R. "Fragmentary Story of Andrew," ANT. P. 473.

9.43   James, M.R. "On the Acts of Andrew," AA 2. Pp. xxix-xxxii.

9.44   Kuzmin, A.G. "Sayings About the Apostle Andrew and His
        Place in the First Chronicles," Letopisi i chroniki 1973.
        Moscow, 1974. Pp. 37-47. [in Russian]

9.45   Lemm, O. von. "Zu den Acten Andreas," Koptische Miscellen.
        Vol. 2. Pp. 175-83.

9.45a   Lewis, A.S. The Mythological Acts of the Apostles. (Horae
        Semiticae 4) London, 1904. Pp. 1-29. [ET of Arabic texts
        in Horae Semiticae 3]

9.45b   Lipsius, R.A. Die apokryphen Apostelgeschichten und Apos-
        tellegenden. 2 vols. Brunswick, 1883-1890; repr. Amster-
        dam, 1976. Vol. 1. Pp. 543-622.

9.46   Loewenwich, W. von. "Die Petrus-, Andreas-, Paulus-, und
        Thomas-Akten," Das Johannes-Verständnis im zweiten Jahr-
        hundert (BZNW 13) Giessen, 1932. Pp. 109-12.

9.47   Michaelis, W. "Andreas- Akten," Apokryphen Schriften. Pp.
        379-401. [German trans. of selected passages]

9.48   Moraldi, L. "Atti di sant'Andrea," Apoc. del NT. 2. Pp.
        1351-1429.

9.49   Moraldi, L. "Martirio di sant'Andrea apostolo," Apoc. del NT.
        2. Pp. 1354, 1396-1405.

9.50   Muryanov, M.F. "St. Andrew the Apostle in the Slavonic
        Chronicle," Palestinckiĭ Sbornik.*

9.51   Peterson, P.M. Andrew, Brother of Simon Peter: His History
        and His Legends. (NovTSup 1) Leiden, 1958.

9.52   Pick, B. The Apocryphal Acts of Paul, Peter, John, Andrew,
        and Thomas. London, 1909.

9.53   Prieur, J.-M. "La figure de l'apôtre dans les Actes apocry-
        phes d'André," Actes Apocryphes. Pp. 121-39.

9.54   Prieur, J.-M. "Les Actes apocryphes de l'apôtre André:
        Présentation des diverses traditions apocryphes et état de
        la question," ANRW 2.25.4 (in preparation).

9.55   Quispel, G. "An Unknown Fragment of the Acts of Andrew
        (Pap. Copt. Utrecht, 1)," VC 10 (1956) 129-48. [repr. in
        Gnostic Studies (Uitgaven van het Nederlands historisch-

archeologisch instituut te Ishtanbul 34) 2 vols. Istanbul, 1975. Vol. 2. Pp. 271-87]

9.56 Saussay, A. du, ed. Commentarius a Symeone Metaphrasta: Andreas Frater Simonis Petri seu de Gloria Andreae Apostoli Libri XII. Paris, 1656. Pp. 309-28.

9.57 Schmidt, C. "Acten des Andreas," Gesch. altchrist. Lit. 1. P. 920.

9.58 Schmidt, C. "Acten des Andreas und Bartholomäus," Gesch. altchrist. Lit. 1. P. 920.

9.59 Schultess, F. "Christlich-Palästinische Fragmente aus der Omajjaden-Moschee zu Damaskus," Abhandlungen der königlichen Gesellschaft der Wissenschaften zu Göttingen, Ph.-hist. Klasse n.F. 8.3 (1905) 108-19. [Syr. and Gk. texts]

9.60 Speranskij, M.N. Apocryphal Deeds of the Apostle Andrew in Slavo-Russian Works. Moscow, 1894. Vol. 15. Pp. 35-76. [in Russian]

9.61 Stegmüller, F. Repertorium Biblicum. 1. Pp. 108, 168-74; 8. Pp. 158-60.

9.62 Tarchnišvili, P.M. "Der Apostel Andreas," Geschichte der kirchlichen georgischen Literatur (Studi e Testi 185) Rome, 1955. Pp. 344f.

9.63 Tischendorf, K. "Acta Andreae," Acta Apos. Apoc. Pp. XL-XLVII, 105-31. [Intro. and Gk. text]

9.64 Walker, A. "Acts and Martyrdom of the Holy Apostle Andrew," ANF 8. Pp. 511-16. [ET]

9.65 Wilson, R. McL. "Andrew, Acts of," ZPEB. 1. Pp. 158f.

9.66 Woog, K.C. L'Epistola presbyterorum et diaconorum Achaiae de martyrio S. Andreae apostoli. Leipzig, 1747. [Gr. and Lat. texts]

10. ANDREW: ACTS OF ANDREW AND MATTHIAS

(See also 1.470; 3.38, 40, 53, 78; 9.51.)

10.1 Amann, É. "Actes d'André et de Mathias dans la ville des anthropophages," DBSup. 1. Cols. 508f.

10.2   Bauer, J.B. "Ein Papyrusfragment der 'Acta Andreae et Mat-
        thiae,' Pap. Graec. Vindob. 26227," Jahrbuch der Österreich-
        ischen Byzantinischen Gesellschaft 16 (1967) 34-38.

10.3   Blatt, F. Die lateinischen Bearbeitungen der 'Acta Andreae
        et Matthiae apud anthropophagos' mit sprachlichem Kommentar
        (BZNW 12) Giessen, 1930. [See M.R. James' review JTS 32
        (1931) 299f.]

10.4   Bonnet, M., ed. "Acta Andreae et Matthiae," AAA. 2.1.
        Pp. xix-xxiv, 65-116. [Intro. and Gk. text]

10.5   Bonwetsch, N. "Andreas und Matthäus," Gesch. altchrist.
        Lit. 1. P. 905.

10.6   Erbetta, M. "Gli Atti di Andrea e Matteo fra gli Antropofagi,"
        Apoc. del NT. 2. Pp. 493-505. [Italian trans.]

10.7   Flamion, J. Les actes d'André et les textes apparentés (Re-
        cueil de travaux d'histoire et de philologie 33) Louvain, 1911.

10.8   Franko, I. Apocrypha and Legends. L'vov, 1902. Vol. 3.
        Pp. 126-44. [in Russian]

10.9   Gil, J. "Sobre el texto de los 'Acta Andreae et Matthiae apud
        anthropophagos,'" Habis 6 (1975) 177-94.

10.10   Grabar, B. "Apocryphal Apostolic Works in Croatian Glagolithic
        Literature," Radovi Staroslavenskog Instituta 6 (1967) 109-61,
        186-200. [in Serbo-Croatian]

10.11   Grimm, J. Andreas und Elene. Cassel, 1840.

10.12   Harnack, A. "Die Acten des Matthäus," Gesch. altchrist. Lit.
        1. P. 139.

10.13   Harnack, A. Die Andreasacten," Gesch. altchrist. Lit. 1.
        Pp. 127f.

10.14   James, M.R. "Acts of Andrew and Matthias (Matthew)," ANT.
        Pp. 453-58.

10.15   Javorskij, J.A. New Manuscript Findings in the Field of An-
        cient Carpatho-Russian Writings. Prague, 1931. P. 103.
        [in Russian]

10.16   Lavrov, P.A. "Apocryphal Texts," SbORJS 67 (1899) 40-51.
        [in Russian]

10.17   Leloir, L. "La version arménienne des Actes apocryphes
        d'André et le Diatessaron," NTS 22 (1975) 127-39.

10.18   Lemm, O. von. Koptische Apokryphe Apostelacten (Mélanges
        asiatiques 10) St. Petersburg, 1890. Vol. 1. Pp. 148-66.
        [Coptic text and German trans.]

10.18a Lewis, A.S. The Mythological Acts of the Apostles. (Horae
        Semiticae 4) London, 1904. Pp. 126-39. [ET of Arabic
        Texts in Horae Semiticae 3]

10.18b Lipsius, R.A. Die apokryphen Apostelgeschichten und Apos-
        tellegenden. 2 vols. Brunswick, 1883-1890; repr. Amster-
        dam, 1976. Vol. 1. Pp. 547-54. [See also vol. 2.2; pp.
        258-69]

10.19   Löfstedt, B. "Zu den lateinischen Bearbeitungen der Acta
        Andreae et Matthiae apud anthropophagos," Habis 6 (1975)
        167-76.

10.20   Moraldi, L. "Atti di Andrea e Matteo nella città degli antro-
        pofagi," Apoc. del NT. 2. Pp. 1613-15.

10.21   Novaković, S. "Apocrypha of One Serbian Cyrillic Collection
        of the Fourteenth Century," Starine 8 (1876) 55-69.

10.22   Petrovskij, S.V. A Narration About an Apostolic Sermon on
        the Northeastern Shore of the Black Sea. Odessa, 1898.

10.23   Radermacher, L. "Zu den Acta Andreae et Matthiae," Wiener
        Studien 48 (1930) 108.

10.24   Reinach, S. "Les apôtres chez les anthropophages," Revue
        d'histoire et de littérature religieuses 9 (1904) 305-20.

10.25   Santos Otero, A. de. "Acta Andreae (et Matthiae)," Altslav-
        ischen Apok. 1. Pp. 69-83.

10.26   Schmidt, C. "Acten des Andreas und Matthäus in der Stadt
        der Menschenfresser," Gesch. altchrist. Lit. 1. P. 920.

10.27   Schneemelcher, W., and A. de Santos. "Acts of Andrew and
        Matthias Among the Cannibals," HSW. 2. P. 576.

10.28   Schultess, F. "Christlich-Palästinische Fragmente aus der
        Omajjaden-Moschee zu Damaskus," Abhandlungen der könig-
        lichen Gesellschaft der Wissenschaften zu Göttingen, Ph.-hist.
        Klasse n.F. 8.3 (1905) 86-93. [Syr. and Gk. texts]

10.29   Sedel'nikov, A. "An Ancient Kiev Legend About the Apostle
        Andrew," Slavia 3 (1924-25) 316-35. [in Russian]

10.30   Speranskij, M.N. Apocryphal Acts of the Apostle Andrew.
        Moscow, 1894. Pp. 35-76. [in Russian]

10.31   Speranskij, M.N.   "The Teaching of the Apostle Andrew,"
        ČOIDR (1889) 53-62. [in Russian]*

10.32   Stegmüller, F. Repertorium biblicum. 1. Pp. 173f.; 8. Pp.
        161f.

10.33   Stowe, C.E. Origin and History of the Books of the Bible.
        Hartford, 1867. Pp. 327-34.

10.34   Strohal, R. Ancient Croatian Apocrypha. Bjelovar, 1917.
        Pp. 43-47. [in Serbo-Croatian]

10.35   Syrku, P.A. "Manuscript Fragments of a Prolog," SbORJS
        64 (1899) 4-6. [in Russian]

10.36   Thilo, J.C., ed. Acta ss. Apostolorum Andreae et Matthiae
        Graece ex codd. Parisiensibus nunc primum edita. Halle,
        1846. [Gk. text]

10.37   Tischendorf, K. "Acta Andreae et Matthiae," Acta Apos.
        Apoc. Pp. XLVII-LIX, 132-166. [Intro. and Gk. text]

10.38   Tischendorf, K. "Ad Acta Andreae et Matthiae," Apocalypses
        Apocryphae. Pp. 139-41. [Gk. text]

10.39   Vasil'evskij, V. "The Pilgrimage of the Apostle Andrew into
        the Country of the Myrmidons," Žurnal Ministerstva Narodnago
        Prosveščenija. (1877). [in Russian]*

10.40   Walker, A. "Acts of Andrew and Matthias," ANF 8. Pp. 517-
        25. [ET]

10.41   Wilson, R.McL. "Andrew and Matthias (Matthew), Acts of,"
        ZPEB. 1. P. 159.

10.42   Wright, W. Apocryphal Acts of the Apostles Edited from Syr-
        iac Manuscripts in the British Museum and Other Libraries.
        London, 1871; repr. Amsterdam, 1968. Pp. 93-115. [Syr.
        text and ET]

11.   ANDREW: ACTS OF ANDREW AND PAUL

(See also 1.204; 9.51.)

11.1   Amann, É. "Actes de Paul et André," DBSup. 1. Cols.
        508f.

11.2   Erbetta, M. "Gli Atti di Andrea e Paolo e di Andrea e File-
         mone," Apoc. del NT. 2. Pp. 537f.

11.3   Hallock, F.H. "An Apocalypse of SS. Andrew and Paul,"
         Journal of the Society of Oriental Research 13 (1929) 190-94.

11.4   Jacques, X. "Les 'Actes d'André et de Paul,'" RSR 58 (1970)
         289-96.

11.5   Jacques, X. "Les deux fragments conservés des 'Actes d'
         André et de Paul' (Cod. Borg. Copt. 109, fasc. 132)," Or
         38 (1969) 187-213.

11.6   James, M.R. "The Acts of Andrew and Paul," ANT. Pp. 472-
         74.

11.7   Lemm, O von. Koptische Miscellen. Vol. 2. Pp. 61-69.

11.8   Lipsius, R.A. Die apokryphen Apostelgeschichten und Apostel-
         legenden. 2 vols. Brunswick, 1883-1890; repr. Amsterdam,
         1976. Vol. 1. Pp. 616f.

11.9   Moraldi, L. "Atti di Andrea, Paolo e Filemone," Apoc. del NT.
         2. Pp. 1616f.

11.10   Morenz, S. "Der Apostel Andreas als neos Sárapis," TLZ 72
         (1947) 295-97.

11.11   Schmidt, C. "Acten des Paulus und Andreas," Gesch. altchrist.
         Lit. 1. P. 920.

11.12   Schneemelcher, W., and A. de Santos. "The Acts of Andrew
         and Paul," HSW. 2. P. 576.

11.13   Stegmüller, F. Repertorium Biblicum. 1. P. 174; 8. Pp.
         162f.

11.14   Steindorff, G. Kurzer Abriss der Koptischen Grammatik.
         Berlin, 1921; repr. Hildesheim, 1964. Pp. *34-*47. [Cop-
         tic text]

11.15   Tischendorf, K. [Ex actis Pauli et Andreae a Zoega Sahidice
         repertis. Fragmentum ab E. Dulaurier versum,] Apocalypses
         Apocryphae. Pp. xlvii-xlix.

11.16   Wilson, R.McL. "Andrew and Paul, Acts of," ZPEB. 1. P.
         159.

11.17   Zoëga, G. Catalogus codicum copticorum. Rome, 1810; repr.
         Hildesheim, 1973. Pp. 230-35.

12. APOSTLES, EPISTLE OF THE

(See also the listings under TDom, which is related to or
a version of EpApos [cf. 12.27].)

(See also 1.88.)

12.1   Amann, E. "La lettre des apôtres," DBSup. 1. Cols. 523-
       25.

12.2   Amiot, F. "La Lettre des Apôtres," Évangiles Apoc. Pp. 275-
       85. [French trans.]

12.3   Bardenhewer, O. "Eine 'Epistola apostolorum,'" GAL. 1.
       Pp. 596-98.

12.4   Bauckham, R. "Synoptic Parousia Parables Again," NTS 29
       (1983) 129-34. [see esp. pp. 132f.]

12.5   Bauer, J.B. "Ein Rundschreiben der Elf Apostel," Neutest.
       Apok. Pp. 87f.

12.6   Bick, J. "Wiener Palimpseste," Sitzungsberichte der Wiener
       Akademie der Wissenschaften 159 (1908) 97-99 (with Plate
       IV).

12.7   Bonsirven, J., and C. Bigaré, "La lettre des Apôtres," Intro.
       à la Bible. 2. P. 761.

12.8   Daniélou, J. "Les traditions secrètes des Apôtres," EJ 31
       (1962) 199-215.

12.9   Delazer, J. "Disquisitio in argumentum Epistolae Apostolorum,"
       Anton 3 (1928) 369-406.

12.10 Delazer, J. "De tempore compositionis Epistolae Apostolorum,"
       Anton 4 (1929) 257-92, 387-430.

12.11 Duensing, H. "Epistula Apostolorum," HSW. 1. Pp. 189-227.

12.12 Duensing, H. "Epistula Apostolorum," HS. 1. Pp. 126-54.

12.13 Duensing, H., ed. Epistula Apostolorum: Nach dem äthiopi-
       schen und koptischen Texte. (KlT 152) Bonn, 1925. [See
       the review by C. Schmidt OLZ 28 (1925) Cols. 856-59]

12.14 Ehrhardt, A.A.T. "Judeo-Christians in Egypt, the Epistula
       Apostolorum, and the Gospel to the Hebrews," Studia Evan-
       gelica. Vol. 3: Papers Presented to the Second International

Congress on New Testament Studies Held at Christ Church, Oxford, 1961, ed. F.L. Cross (TU 88) Berlin, 1964. Pp. 360-84.

12.15 Eijk, A.H.G. van. "Only That can Rise Which has Previously Fallen," JTS 22 (1972) 517-31.

12.16 Erbetta, M. "L'Epistola degli Apostoli," Apoc. del NT. 3. Pp. 37-62.

12.17 Frank, I. "Epistula apostolorum," Der Sinn der Kanonbildung (Freiburger Theologische Studien 90) Freiburg, 1971. Pp. 100-11.

12.18 Gry, L. "La date de la parousie d'après l'Epistola Apostolorum," RB 49 (1940) 86-97.

12.19 Guerrier, L. "Un 'Testament de Notre-Seigneur et Sauveur Jésus-Christ' en Galilée," ROC 12 (1907) 1-8.

12.20 Guerrier, L., and S. Grébaut. "Le testament en Galilée de Notre-Seigneur Jésus-Christ," PO 9 (1913) 143-232. [Eth. text and French trans.]

12.21 Harnack, A. "Ein jüngst entdeckter Auferstehungsbericht," Theologische Studien: B. Weiss zum 70. Geburtstage dargebracht. Göttingen, 1897. Pp. 1-8.

12.22 Hauler, E. "Zu den neuen lateinischen Bruchstücken der Thomas-Apokalypse und eines apostolischen Sendschreibens in Codex Vindob. Nr 16," Wiener Studien 30 (1908) 308-40.

12.23 Hennecke, E. "Apostolisches Sendschreiben mit Zukunftsoffenbarungen des Auferstanden," H2. Pp. 146-50.

12.24 Hennecke, E. "Ein neuer Fund auf dem Gebiet der altchristlichen Literatur," NKZ 32 (1921) 244-57.

12.25 Hornschuh, M. "Das Gleichnis von den zehn Jungfrauen in der Epistula Apostolorum," ZKG 73 (1962) 1-8.

12.26 Hornschuh, M. Studien zur Epistula Apostolorum (Patristische Texte und Studien 5) Berlin, 1965.

12.27 James, M.R. "Epistle of the Apostles," ANT. Pp. 485-503.

12.28 James, M.R. "Epistola Apostolorum: A Possible Quotation," JTS 23 (1922) 56.

12.29 James, M.R. "The 'Epistula Apostolorum' in a New Text," JTS 12 (1911) 55f.

12.30 Lake, K. "The Epistola Apostolorum," HTR 14 (1921) 15-29.

12.31 Lietzmann, H. "Die Epistula Apostolorum," ZNW 20 (1921)
       173-76.

12.32 Michaelis, W. "Einleitung in die Apokryphen Briefe," Apokry-
       phen Schriften. Pp. 440-46.

12.33 Moraldi, L. "Lettera degli apostoli," Apoc. del NT. 2. Pp.
       1669-1702.

12.34 Overmeire, P. van. Livre que Jésus révéla à ses disciples:
       Etude sur l'apocryphe connu sous le nom d' 'Epistula Apos-
       tolorum'. Institut Catholique Dissertation, Paris, 1962.

12.35 Richardson, C.C. "New Solution to the Quartodeciman Riddle,"
       JTS 24 (1973) 74-84.

12.36 Santos Otero, A. de. "Quaestiones Apostolorum," Altslavi-
       schen Apok. 1. Pp. 210f.

12.37 Schmidt, C. "Eine bisher unbekannte altchristliche Schrift
       in koptischer Sprache," SPAW (1895) 705-11.

12.38 Schmidt, C. "Eine Epistola Apostolorum in koptischer und lat-
       einischer Überlieferung," SPAW (1908) 1047-56.

12.39 Schmidt, C. Gespräche Jesu mit seinen Jüngern nach der
       Auferstehung: Ein Katholish-Apostolisches Sendschreiben
       des 2. Jahrhunderts (TU 43) Leipzig, 1919; repr. Hildesheim,
       1967. [Coptic text and German trans.; see G. Bardy's re-
       view RB 30 (1921) 110-34; and that of H. Duensing, Göt-
       tingische Gelehrte Anzeigen 184 (1922) 241-52]

12.40 Schneider, T. "Das prophetische 'Agraphon' der Epistula
       Apostolorum," ZNW 24 (1925) 151-54.

12.41 Schumacher, H. "The Christology of the Epistola Apostolorum,"
       HomPastR 22 (1921-22) 1080-87, 1303-12.

12.42 Schumacher, H. "The Discovery of the Epistola Apostolorum,"
       HomPastR 22 (1921-22) 856-65.

12.43 Schumacher, H. "The Epistola Apostolorum and the 'Descensus
       ad Inferos,'" HomPastR 23 (1922-23) 13-21, 121-28.

12.44 Schumacher, H. "The Epistola Apostolorum and the New Tes-
       tament," HomPastR 22 (1921-22) 967-75.

12.45 Stegmüller, F. Repertorium Biblicum. 1. Pp. 159-61; 8.
       Pp. 152f.

12.46 Vitti, A. "De 'Epistula Apostolorum' Apocrypha," VD 3 (1923)
       367-73; 4 (1924) 210-18.

12.47 Walls, A.F. "The Montanist 'Catholic Epistle' and its New
       Testament Prototype," Studia Evangelica. Vol. 3: Papers
       Presented to the Second International Congress on New Tes-
       tament Studies Held at Christ Church, Oxford, 1961. Part
       2: The New Testament Message, ed. F.L. Cross (TU 88)
       Berlin, 1964. Pp. 437-46.

12.48 Wilson, R.McL. "Apostles, Epistle of the," ZPEB. 1. P.
       221.

12.49 Zwaan, J. de. "Date and Origin of the Epistle of the Eleven
       Apostles," Amicitiae Corollae, ed. H.G. Wood. London,
       1933. Pp. 344-55.

                      13. APOSTLES, MEMORIA OF

13.1   Alfaric, P. Les écritures manichéennes. Paris, 1919. Vol.
       2. Pp. 173-77.

13.2   Dufourcq, A. Étude sur les Gesta Martyrium romains. Paris,
       1910. Vol. 4. P. 162.

13.3   Fabricius, J.A. "Memoria Apostolorum," Cod.Apoc.NT. 2.
       P. 791.

13.4   Fabricius, J.A. "Memoria Apostolorum qua usi sunt Priscillian-
       istae," Cod.Apoc.NT. 2. Pp. 814f.

13.5   James, M.R. "Memoria of the Apostles," ANT. P. 21. [ET]

13.6   Mercati, G. Note di letteratura biblica e cristiana antica
       (Studi e Testi 5) Rome, 1901. P. 136.

13.7   Migne, J.-P. PL. 31. Col. 1213.

13.8   Puech, H.-C. "Die Memoria Apostolorum," HS. 1. Pp. 188-
       90.

13.9   Puech, H.-C. "The Memoria Apostolorum," HSW. 1. Pp.
       265-68.

13.10 Santos Otero, A. de. "Memoria de los Apóstoles," Evangelios
       Apócrifos. Pp. 68f. [Latin quotation from Orosius (= PL
       31,1213D) with Spanish trans.]

13.11   Schepss, G., ed. Priscilliani Quae Supersunt Maximam Partem
        Nuper Detexit (CSEL 18) Vienna, Prague, Leipzig, 1889. P.
        P. 154.

13.12   Stegmüller, F. Repertorium Biblicum. 8. P. 80.

                        14. BARNABAS, ACTS OF

(See also 3.53.)

14.1   Amann, É. "Les Actes de Barnabé," DBSup. 1. Col. 510.

14.2   Bonnet, M., ed. "Acta Barnabae," AAA. 2.2. Pp. xxviif.,
        292-302. [Intro. and Gk. text]

14.3   Bonwetsch, N. "Barnabas," Gesch. altchrist. Lit. 1. P.
        905.

14.4   Braunsberger, J. Der Apostel Barnabas, Sein Leben und der
        ihm beigelegte Brief. Mainz, 1876.

14.5   Eberta, M. "Atti e Martirio di Barnaba," Apoc. del NT. 2.
        Pp. 595-600.

14.6   Fabricius, J.A. "Johannes Marcus de Passione S. Barnabae,"
        Cod.Apoc.NT. 2. Pp. 781f.

14.7   Halkin, F. "Actes de Barnabé et Vie de saint Héraclide,"
        AnBoll 82 (1964) 408.

14.8   Harnack, A. "Die Barnabasacten," Gesch. altchrist. Lit.
        1. P. 139.

14.9   James, M.R. "Acts of Barnabas," ANT. P. 470.

14.10   Kalužnjackij, E. "Collections of the Njameskij Monastery,"
        SbORJS 83/2 (1907) 50-57. [in Russian]

14.11   Lipsius, R.A. Die apokryphen Apostelgeschichten und Apos-
        tellegenden. 2 vols. Brunswick, 1883-1890; repr. Amster-
        dam, 1976. Vol. 2.2. Pp. 270-320.

14.12   Migne, J.-P. "Barnabé," Dictionnaire. 2. Cols. 143-50.

14.13   Moraldi, L. "Atti e martirio dell' apostolo S. Barnaba,"
        Apoc. del NT. 2. Pp. 1620-22.

14.14 Papenbrock, D. van, et al. Acta Sanctorum. 60 vols. Paris,
       Brussels, 1643-1887. Vol. 2. Pp. 421-60.

14.15 Santos Otero, A. de. "Acta Barnabae," Altslavischen Apok.
       1. Pp. 136f.

14.16 Schneemelcher, W., and A. de Santos. "Acts of Barnabas,"
       HSW. 2. P. 578.

14.17 Schneemelcher, W., and A. de Santos. "Barnabasakten,"
       HS. 2. P. 404.

14.18 Stegmüller, F. Repertorium Biblicum. 1. Pp. 175f.; 8. P.
       163.

14.19 Tischendorf, K. "Acta Barnabae Auctore Marco," Acta Apos.
       Apoc. Pp. xxvi-xxxi, 64-74. [Intro. and Gk. text]

14.20 Walker, A. "The Acts of Barnabas," ANF 8. Pp. 493-96.
       [ET]

14.21 Wilson, R.McL. "Barnabas, Acts of," ZPEB. 1. P. 477.

15. BARNABAS, GOSPEL OF

The GosBarn, which is cited in the Gelasian Decree, is lost.
This work should not be confused with the later (14th-15th
century) Italian work by the same name--see Introduction.

15.1   Amann, É. "Évangile de Barnabé," DBSup. 1. Col. 480.

15.2   Fabricius, J.A. "Evangelium S. Barnabae," Cod.Apoc.NT.
       1. P. 341.

15.3   Harnack, A. "Evangelium Barnabae," Gesch. altchrist. Lit.
       1. P. 18.

15.4   Migne, J.-P. "Barnabé," Dictionnaire. 2. Cols. 139-43.

15.5   Santos Otero, A. de. "Evangelium Barnabae," Altslavischen
       Apok. 2. P. 60.

16. BARTHOLOMEW, BOOK OF THE RESURRECTION
OF CHRIST BY

(See also 1.205; 17.3, 9, 10, 12, 14, 15, 16, 24, 35.)

16.1   Budge, E.A.W.   "The Book of the Resurrection of Jesus Christ,
        by Bartholomew the Apostle," Coptic Apoc. Pp. 1-48, 179-
        231. [Coptic text and ET]

16.2   Dulaurier, E.   Fragment des révélations apocryphes de S.
        Barthélemy et de l'histoire des communautés religieuses
        fondées par S. Pakhome, traduit sur les textes copte-thébains
        inédits conservés à la bibliothèque du Roi (Orientalia varia
        13) Paris, 1835.

16.3   Erbetta, M.   "Il Libro della Resurrezione di Cristo dell'apostolo
        Bartolomeo," Apoc. del NT. 1.2. Pp. 301-19.

16.4   James, M.R.   "The Book of the Resurrection of Christ by
        Bartholomew the Apostle," ANT. Pp. 181-86.

16.5   Kroll, J.   Gott und Hölle: Der Mythos vom Descensuskampfe.
        Leipzig-Berlin, 1932. Pp. 77-82.

16.6   Lacau, P.   "Apocalypse de Barthélemy," FAC. Pp. 39-77.
        [Coptic text and French trans.]

16.7   Moraldi, L.   "Libro della risurrezione di Gesù," Apoc. del N.T.
        1. Pp. 801-05.

16.8   Reinach, S.   "Le livre de la Résurrection," Revue Archéologi-
        que 23 (1914) 123. [One paragraph remarks on Budge Livre
        de la Résurrection attributed to Barthélemy]

16.9   Rustafjaell, M.R.   The Light of Egypt from Recently Discovered
        Predynastic and Early Christian Records. London, 1909.
        [ET by W.E. Crum]

16.10   Schmidt, C.   "Apokalypse des Bartholomaeus gnostischen Ur-
        sprungs, sahidisch," Gesch. altchrist. Lit. 1. P. 919.
        [report on Coptic texts]

16.11   Schneemelcher, W.   "Apocalypse of Bartholomew," HSW. 2.
        P. 754. [not an apocalypse; cf. HSW. 1. Pp. 484-508]

16.12   Schneemelcher, W.   "Coptic Texts of Bartholomew," HSW. 1.
        Pp. 503-08.

16.13   Schneemelcher, W.   "Koptische Bartholomäus-Texte," HS. 1.
        Pp. 372-76.

16.14   Stegmüller, F.   Repertorium Biblicum. 1. P. 235. [see also
        his listings under GosBart]

16.15   Wilson, R.McL.   "Bartholomew the Apostle, Book of the Resur-
        rection of Christ by," ZPEB. 1. P. 480.

17. BARTHOLOMEW, GOSPEL OF
(Questions of Bartholomew)

Included here are the Revillout identification of several
Coptic fragments as GosBart and the subsequent responses
--see also the entries under CopNarr.

(See also 1.18, 284, 470; 16.2.)

17.1   Amann, É. "Évangile de Barthélemy," DBSup. 1. Cols.
        479f.

17.2   Bardenhewer, O. "Das Andreas- und das Bartholomäusevan-
        gelium," GAL. 1. Pp. 538f.

17.3   Baumstark, A. "Les apocryphes coptes," RB 3 (1906) 245-
        65. [B. discusses identification by Revillout of a series of
        Cop. fragments which he identified with GosBart]

17.4   Beeston, A.F.L. "The Quaestiones Bartholomae," JTS 25
        (1974) 124-27.

17.5   Bonwetsch, N. "Die apokryphen Fragen des Bartholomäus,"
        Nachrichten der Kgl. Gesellschaft der Wissenschaften zu
        Göttingen. Philologisch-historische Klasse. Göttingen,
        1897. P. 130.

17.6   Erbetta, M. "Il Vangelo di Bartolomeo," Apoc. del NT. 1.2.
        Pp. 288-300.

17.7   [No entry]

17.8   Fabricius, J.A. "Evangelium S. Bartholomaei," Cod.Apoc.NT.
        1. Pp. 341f.

17.9   Haase, F. "Zur Rekonstruktion des Bartholomäusevangeliums,"
        ZNW 16 (1915) 93-112. [H. discusses Revillout identification,
        see below]

17.10   Harnack, A., and C. Schmidt, "Ein koptisches Fragment einer
        Moses-Adam-Apocalypse," SPAW (1891) 1045-49. [H. and
        S. discuss Revillout identification, see below]

17.11   James, M.R. "Gospel of Bartholomew," ANT. Pp. 166-81.

17.12   James, M.R. "Some New Coptic Apocrypha," JTS 6 (1905-06)
        577-86; 7 (1906-07) 633f. [J. discusses Revillout identifi-
        cation, see below]

17.13   Kroll, J. Gott und Hölle: Der Mythos vom Descensuskampfe.
        Leipzig-Berlin, 1932. Pp. 71-77.

17.14   Kropp, A.M. Ausgewählte koptische Zaubertexte. Brussels,
        1931. Vol. 1. Pp. 79-81; Vol. 2. Pp. 249-51.

17.15   Lacau, M.P. "Évangile (?) Apocryphe," FAC. Pp. 23-37.
        [Cop. text and French trans. of fragments identified by
        Revillout as belonging to GosBart and by James as CopNar;
        see M.R. James' review JTS 7 (1906-07) 633f.]

17.16   Ladeuze, P. "Apocryphes évangéliques coptes: Pseudo-
        Gamaliel, Évangile de Barthélemy," RHE 7 (1906) 245-68.
        [L. discusses Revillout identification, see below]

17.17   Marsh, F.S. "A New Fragment of the Gospel (?) of Barthol-
        omew," JTS 23 (1922) 400f.

17.18   Migne, J.-P. "Barthélemy.," Dictionnaire 2. Cols. 159f.

17.19   Močul'skij, V.N. Traces of the Popular Bible in Slavic and
        Ancient Russian Writings. Odessa, 1893. Pp. 276-81. [in
        Russian]

17.20   Moraldi, L. "Vangelo di Bartolomeo," Apoc. del NT. 1. Pp.
        749-800.

17.21   Moricca, U. "Un nuovo testo dell' Evangelo di Bartolomeo,"
        RB 30 (1921) 481-516; 31 (1922) 20-30. [complete Lat. ver-
        sion]

17.22   Pirot, L. "Barthélemy (évangile)," DBSup. 1. Cols. 924-27.

17.23   Pypin, N.A. False and Dismissed Books of Ancient Russia.
        Petrograd, 1862. Vol. 3. Pp. 109-12. [in Russian]

17.24   Revillout, E. "Évangile de Saint Barthélemy," PO 2 (1907)
        185-98. [Cop. text and French trans. of a series of frag-
        ments R. identified as GosBart and James called CopNar]

17.25   Romeo, A. "Bartolomeo," EncCatt. 2. Cols. 916-20.

17.26   Santos Otero, A. de. "Evangelio de Bartolome," Evangelios
        Apócrifos. Pp. 536-72. [Gk. text and Spanish translation]

17.27   Santos Otero, A. de. "Evangelium Bartholomaei," Altslavischen
        Apok. 2. Pp. 56-59.

17.28   Scheidweiler, F. "Die Fragen des Bartholomäus," HS. 1.
        Pp. 360-72.

17.29 Scheidweiler, F. and W. Schneemelcher. "Bartholomäusevangelium," HS. 1. Pp. 359-76.

17.30 Scheidweiler, F., and W. Schneemelcher. "The Gospel of Bartholomew," HSW. 1. Pp. 484-508.

17.31 Speranskij, M.N. From the History Russo-Slavic .... Moscow, 1960. Pp. 90-93. [in Russian]

17.32 Stegmüller, F. Repertorium Biblicum. 1. Pp. 108-11; 8. Pp. 81f.

17.33 Tichonravov, N. "Bartholomew's Questions to the Virgin Mother," Pamjatniki Otrecěnno Russkoj Literatury. Petersburg, Moscow, 1863. Vol. 2. Pp. 18-22. [in Russian]

17.34 Vassiliev, A. "Quaestiones S. Bartholomaei apostoli," Anecdota Graeco-byzantina. Moscow, 1893. Vol. 1. Pp. 10-23.

17.35 Wilmart, A., and E. Tisserant. "Fragments grecs et latins de l'évangile de Barthélemy," RB 10 (1913) 160-90, 321-68.

17.36 Wilson, R.McL. "Bartholomew, Gospel (Questions) of," ZPEB. 1. Pp. 480f.

18. BARTHOLOMEW, MARTYRDOM OF; AND BARTHOLOMEW CYCLE

See also the entries on Bartholomew in PsAb. Most modern scholars identify the MartBart as a translation into Greek from the Latin of PsAb, Book 8.

(See also 1.205, 346; 3.53, 78; 7.9, 14, 24.)

18.1 Amann, É. "La Passion de Barthélemy," DBSup. 1. Cols. 509f.

18.2 Bonnet, M., ed. "Passio sancti Bartholomaei apostoli," AAA. 2.1. Pp. XXIV-XXVI, 128-150. [Intro., Gk. and Lat. texts]

18.3 Bonnet, M. "La Passion de S. Barthélemy en quelle langue a-t-ella été écrite?" AnBoll 14 (1895) 353-66.

18.4 Budge, E.A.W. Contendings of the Apostles. 2 vols. London, 1899-1901. Vol. 1. Pp. 93-100, 104-110. [Eth. text and ET]

18.5   Budge, E.A.W. "The Life of Saint Bartholomew. From the
        Ethiopic Synaxarium," Coptic Apoc. Pp. 49f.; 231f.

18.6   Erbetta, M. "Gli Atti armeni di Bartolomeo," Apoc. del NT.
        2. Pp. 589-91.

18.7   Historia armena originum christianae Religionis in Armenia,
        auctoribus S.S. Apostolis Bartholomaeo et Judas Thomas.
        Leipzig, 1705.

18.8   Lewis, A.S. "The Martyrdom of Saint Bartholomew," The
        Mythological Acts of the Apostles (Horae Semiticae 4) London,
        1904. Pp. 76-79. [ET of Arabic text in Horae Semiticae 3]

18.9   Lipsius, R.A. Die apokryphen Apostelgeschichten und Apos-
        tellegenden. 2 vols. Brunswick, 1883-90; repr. Amsterdam,
        1976. Vol. 2.2. Pp. 54-108. [Supplement, p. 130]

18.10   Migne, J.-P. "Barthélemy," Dictionnaire. 2. Cols. 160-62.

18.11   Moraldi, L. "Atti armeni di Bartolomeo," Apoc. del NT. 2.
        Pp. 1623f.

18.12   Mösinger, G. Vita et martyrion S. Bartholomaei apostoli.
        Innsbruck, 1877.

18.13   Schneemelcher, W., and A. de Santos. "Acts of Bartholomew,"
        HSW. 2. P. 577.

18.14   Schneemelcher, W., and A. de Santos. "Bartholomäusakten,"
        HS. 2. P. 404.

18.15   Söder, R. Die apokryphen Apostelgeschichten und die roman-
        hafte Literatur der Antike (Würzburger Studien zur Alter-
        tumswissenschaft 3) Stuttgart, 1932; repr. Darmstadt, 1969.
        P. 18.

18.16   Stegmüller, F. Repertorium Biblicum. 1. Pp. 178f.; 8. P.
        164.

18.17   Tischendorf, K. "Martyrium Bartholomaei," Acta Apos. Apoc.
        Pp. LXIX-LXX, 243-60. [Intro. and Gk. text]

18.18   Walker, A. "Martyrdom of the Holy and Glorious Apostle Bar-
        tholomew," ANF   8. Pp. 553-57. [ET]

19. CHRIST AND ABGARUS, LETTERS OF

The Abgar legend is developed in the AcThad--see also
the listings under that category.

(See also 1.359, 469; 57.52; 95.98.)

19.1   Abd Al-Masih, Y., "An Unedited Bohairic Letter of Abgar,"
        BIFAO 45 (1947) 65-80; 52 (1954) 13-43.

19.2   Alishan, L. Laboubnia, Lettre d'Abgar, ou Histoire de la
        Conversion des Édesséens par Laboubnia, écrivain contem-
        porain des apôtres. Venice, 1868.

19.3   Amiot, F. "Lettre d'Abgar d'Édesse à Jésus et réponse du
        Sauveur," Évangiles Apoc. P. 46.

19.4   Anderson, J.G.C. "Pontica," Journal of Hellenistic Studies
        20 (1900) 156-58.

19.5   Aufhauser, J.B., Antike Jesuszeugnisse (KlT 126) Leipzig,
        1913. Pp. 17-31.

19.6   Bardenhewer, O. GAL. 1. Pp. 498-622.

19.7   Bauer, J.B. Neutest. Apok. Pp. 79-81.

19.8   Bauer, W. "The Abgar Legend," HSW. 1. Pp. 437-44.

19.9   Bauer, W. "Abgarsage," HS. 1. Pp. 325-29.

19.10   Bauer, W., Rechtgläubigkeit und Ketzerei in ältesten Chris-
        tentum (BHT 10) Tübingen, 1934, 1964², Pp. 6-48. [ET:
        Orthodoxy and Heresy in Earliest Christianity. Philadelphia,
        1971. Pp. 1-43]

19.11   Bonnet-Maury, G. "La légende d'Abgar et de Thaddée et les
        missions chrétiennes à Édesse," RHR 16 (1887) 269-83.

19.12   Bonwetsch, N. "Der Briefwechsel Christi und Abgar's,"
        Gesch. altchrist. Lit. 1. P. 909.

19.13   Buffa, A. La légende d'Abgar et les origines de l'église d'
        Édesse: Étude historique et critique. Geneva, 1893.

19.14   Carrier, A. La légende d'Abgar dans "l'Histoire d'Arménie"
        de Moïse de Khoren. Paris, 1895.

19.15   Cartlidge, D.R., and D.L. Dungan, "Jesus' Medical Correspon-
        dence with King Abgar," Documents. P. 91. [ET]

19.16   Cartojan, N. Legenda lui Abgar în literatura veche român-
        eascâ. Bucharest, 1925.

19.17   Casson, L., and L.E. Hettich. Excavations at Nessana: Lit-
        erary Papyri. Princeton, 1950. Vol. 2. Pp. 143-47.

19.18   Considine, P., "Irish Versions of the Abgar Legend," Celtica
        10 (1973) 237-57.

19.19   Cowper, B.H. "The Correspondence Between Abgar and
        Jesus, etc.," Apocryphal Gospels. Pp. 217-20. [ET]

19.20   Cumont, F. "Nouvelles inscriptions du Pont," REG 15 (1902)
        326.

19.21   Cureton, W. Ancient Syriac Documents. London, 1863. Pp.
        5-23. [Syr. text and ET]

19.22   Dashian, J. "Der Briefwechsel Abgars und Christi nach der
        neuentdeckten Inschrift von Ephesus," Kurze bibliographi-
        sche Studien: Untersuchungen und Texte. Vienna, 1901.
        Vol. 2. Pp. 256-320.

19.23   Dashian, J. "Zur Abgar-Sage," WZKM 4 (1890) 17-34, 144-60,
        177-98.

19.24   Der Nersessian, S. "La légende d'Abgar d'après un rouleau
        illustré de la bibliothèque Pierpont Morgan a New York,"
        Études byzantines et arméniennes. Louvain, 1973. Pp.
        175-81.

19.25   Dobschütz, E. von. "Der Briefwechsel zwischen Abgar und
        Jesus," ZWT 43 (1900) 422-86.

19.26   Dobschütz, E. von. Christusbilder: Untersuchungen zur
        christlichen Legende. (TU 18) Leipzig, 1899. Pp. 102-96.

19.27   Drioton, E., "Un apocryphe anti-arien: La version copte de
        la correspondance d'Abgar, roi d'Edesse, avec Notre-
        Seigneur," ROC 20 (1915-17) 306-26, 337-73. [Cop. text]

19.28   Dujčev, I. Apokrypha byzantino-slavica: Miscellanea M. Bud-
        imir. Brigrade, 1967. Pp. 247ff.

19.29   Dujčev, I. Old Bulgarian Literature. Sofia, 1971. Vol. 1.
        Pp. 157-66. [in Bulgarian]

19.30   Duval, R. Histoire politique, religieuse, et littéraire d'Edesse
        jusqu'à la première croisade. Paris, 1892.

19.31   Duval, R., "Histoire politique, religieuse, et littéraire d'Edesse,"
        JA 18 (1891) 87-133, 201-78, 381-439; 19 (1892) 5-102.

19.32   Emine, J.R. "Leboubna d'Édesse: Histoire d'Abgar et de la
        Prédication de Thaddée. Trad. sur le manuscrit unique et
        inédit de la Bibliothèque Impériale de Paris," Collection des
        Historiens de l'Arménie. Paris, 1867-69.

19.33   Erbetta, M. "La Corrispondenza tra Abgar e Gesù," Apoc.
        del NT. 3. Pp. 77-84.

19.34   Fabricius, J.A. Cod.Apoc.NT. 1. Pp. 279-319.

19.35   Fuchs, J. "¿Jesucristo, escribió alguna vez?" RBSL 18
        (1956) 145f.

19.36   Galvin, R.J. "Addai and Mari Revisited: The State of the
        Question," EphLitg 87 (1973) 383-414.

19.37   Giversen, S. "Ad Abgarum: The Sahidic Version of the Let-
        ter to Abgar on a Wooden Tablet," AcOr 24 (1959) 71-82.

19.38   Gottheil, R.I.H. "An Arabic Version of the Abgar Legend,"
        Hebraica 7 (1890/91) 268-77. [Arabic text and ET]

19.39   Graf, G. Geschichte der christlichen arabischen Literatur
        (Studi e testi 118) Rome, 1944. Vol. 1. Pp. 237f.

19.40   Grébaut, S. "Les relations entre Abgar et Jésus," ROC 3
        (1918-19) 73-91, 190-203.

19.41   Grébaut, S. "Les trois appendices aux relations entre Abgar
        et Jésus," ROC 3 (1918-19) 352-60.

19.42   Guidi, I., ed. Chronica Minora (CSCO 1, 2) Ristampa, 1955.
        Vol. 1. Pp. 1-13; Vol. 2. Pp. 1-11.

19.43   Gutschmid, A. von. "Untersuchungen über die Geschichte des
        Königreiches Osroëne," Mémoires de l'Académie impériale des
        Sciences de Saint Petersbourg 35 (1887) 1-49.

19.44   Hallier, L. Untersuchungen über die Edessenische Chronik
        (TU 9) Leipzig, 1892.

19.45   Harnack, A. "Acta Edessena (Thaddäus-Geschichte)," Gesch.
        altchrist. Lit. 1. Pp. 533-40.

19.46   Howard, G., tr. The Teaching of Addai (SBL T&T 16 Early
        Christian Literature Series 4) Chico, Calif., 1981. [ET of
        G. Phillips' Syriac text which is also reproduced]

19.47   James, M.R. "Letters of Christ and Abgarus," ANT. Pp.
        476f.

19.48   Kozak, E. "Bibliographische Übersicht der biblisch-apokryphen
        Literatur bei den Südostslaven," JPT 18 (1892) 127-58.

19.49   Láscaris Comneno, E. "Apócrifa carta de Jesucristo," Oriente
        2 (1952) 33-36.

19.50 Leclercq, H. "Abgar, 'la légende,'" DACL. 1. Pp. 87-97.

19.51 Lipsius, A. Die Edessenische Abgarsage Kritisch Untersucht.
       Brunswick, 1880. [see also JPT 7 (1881) 187-92; 8 (1882)
       190-92]

19.52 Lipsius, R.A., ed. "Epistula Abgari," AAA. 1. Pp. 279-
       83. [Gk. text]

19.53 Martin, J.P.P. Les origines de l'église d'Édesse et des églises
       syriennes. Paris, 1889.

19.54 Matthes, K.C.A. Die Edessenische Abgarsage auf ihre Fort-
       bildung untersucht. Leipzig, 1882.

19.55 Melkonjan, G.G. "Armenian Version of the Syriac Legend
       About Abgar," Kratkie Soobšc. Instituta narodov Azii 86
       (1965) 45-50. [in Russian]

19.56 Michaelis, W. "Briefwechsel zwischen Jesus und König Abgar
       von Edessa," Apokryphen Schriften. Pp. 452-61.

19.57 Migne, J.-P. "Abgare. (Lettre d'Abgare à Jésus-Christ et
       réponse du Sauveur.)," Dictionnaire. 2. Cols. 19-26.

19.58 Moraldi, L. "Corrispondenza tra Abgar e Gesù," Apoc. del
       NT. 2. Pp. 1657-68.

19.59 Myslivec, J. "Die Abgaroslegende auf einer Ikone des 17.
       Jahrh.," Seminarium Kondakovianum 5 (1932) 185-90.

19.60 Nau, F. "Une inscription grecque d'Édesse: La lettre de
       N.S.J.C. à Abgar," ROC 3 (1918-19) 217-19.

19.61 Nirschl, J. Der Briefwechsel des Königs Abgar von Edessa
       mit Jesus in Jerusalem, oder die Abgarfrage. Mainz, 1896.

19.62 Nirschl, J. "Der Briefwechsel des Königs Abgar von Edessa
       mit Jesus in Jerusalem oder die Abgarfrage," Der Katholik
       2 (1896) 17-40, 97-114, 193-209, 322-45, 398-420.

19.63 Novaković, S. "Apocrypha from the Printed Collections of
       Božidar Vuković," Starine 16 (1884) 60-62. [in Serbo-
       Croatian]

19.64 Oppenheim, M. von, and F.H. von Gaertringen. "Höhlenin-
       schrift von Edessa mit dem Briefe Jesu an Abgar." SPAW
       (1914) 817-28.

19.65 Parisot, J. "Abgar," DThC. 1. Cols. 67-73.

19.66 Peppenmüller, R. "Griechische Papyrusfragmente der Doctrina
       Addai," VC 25 (1971) 289-301.

19.67 Petković, R. "The Legend of Abgar in the Frescoes of Ma-
       tejić," Prilozi za književnost, jezik, istoriju i folklor (1932)
       11-19. [in Serbo-Croatian]*

19.68 Phillips, G. The Doctrine of Addai, the Apostle, Now First
       Edited in a Complete Form in the Original Syriac. London,
       1876. [Syr. text and ET]

19.69 Picard, C. "Un texte nouveau de la correspondance entre
       Abgar d'Osroène et Jésus-Christ: Gravé sur une porte de
       ville, à Philippes (Macédoine)," Bulletin de Correspondance
       Hellenique 44 (1920) 41-69.

19.70 Pleyte, W., and A.A. Boeser. Manuscrits coptes du Musée
       d'antiquités des Pays-Bas à Leide. Leiden, 1897. Pp. 441-
       79. [Cop. text]

19.71 Porfirjev, I.Y. "Apocryphal Sayings About New Testament
       People and Events in Manuscripts of the Solovetski Library,"
       SbORJS 52 (1890) 61-74, 239-44, 250-53. [in Russian]

19.72 Pratten, B.P. "The Story Concerning the King of Edessa,"
       ANF. 8. Pp. 651-53.

19.73 Pypin, A.N. False and Dismissed Books of Ancient Russia.
       Petrograd, 1862. Pp. 150-53. [in Russian]

19.74 Rahner, H. "Abgar, König," LTK[3]. 1. Col. 43.

19.75 Runciman, S. "Some Remarks on the Image of Edessa," CamHJ
       13 (1931) 238-52.

19.76 Samuelian, P. Historisch-Kritische Abhandlung über das wun-
       dertätige ohne menschliche Kunst verfertigte Bild unseres
       Herrn und Heillandes, das er dem König Abgar von Armenien
       nebst einem Briefe nach Edessa gesandt hat. Vienna, 1847.

19.77 Santos Otero, A. de. "Correspondencia entre Jesus y Ab-
       garo," Evangelios Apócrifos. Pp. 662-69. [Gk. texts and
       Spanish trans.]

19.78 Santos Otero, A. de. "Epistula Abgari," Altslavischen Apok.
       1. Pp. 149-57.

19.79 Schamún, A. "Otro testimonio acerca de la imagen de Jesu-
       cristo enviada a Abgar V," RBSL 19 (1957) 209-12.

19.80 Scheurl, C. Utilitates Misse ... Epistola Abgari ad Jesum Salva-
       torem: Epistola responsiva ad Abgarum. Norimbergae, 1512.*

19.81   Schmidt, C. "Briefwechsel Abgar's mit Christus," Gesch.
        altchrist. Lit. 1. P. 919. [report on Cop. texts]

19.82   Schwartz, E. "Zur Abgarlegende," ZNW 4 (1903) 61-66.

19.83   Starowieyski, M. "Apocryphal Correspondence of King Abgar
        with Christ: Introduction, Translation from the Greek,
        Commentary," Studia Theologica Varsaviensia 15 (1977)
        177-200. [in Polish]

19.84   Stegmüller, F. Repertorium Biblicum. 1. Pp. 119-21; 8.
        Pp. 90-93.

19.85   Stülcken, A. "Abgarsage," Handbuch, ed. Hennecke. Pp.
        153-65.

19.86   Stülcken, A. HS. 1. Pp. 76-79.

19.87   Tixéront, J. Les Origines de l'Église d'Édesse et la Légende
        d'Abgar. Paris, 1888.

19.88   Tournebize, F. "Abgar V Aoukhâma, Le Noir," Dictionaire
        d'Histoire et de Géogr. Ecclés. Vol. 1. Pp. 113f.

19.89   Tournebize, F. "Étude sur la conversion de l'Arménie au
        Christianisme," ROC 1 (1907) 22-42.

19.90   Vellian, J. "The Anaphoral Structure of Addai and Mari Com-
        pared to the 'Berakhoth' Preceding the Shema in the Syna-
        gogue Morning Service," Muséon 85 (1972) 201-23.

19.91   Veselovskij, A. "Works on the History of the Development of
        Christian Legends," Žurnal ministerstva narodnago prosve-
        ščenija (1875). [in Russian]*

19.92   Vetter, P. Literarische Rundschau (1901).*

19.93   Vööbus, A. "Neue Angaben über die textgeschichtlichen
        Zustände in Edessa in den Jahren ca. 324-340," Papers of
        the Estonian Theological Society in Exile 2 (1951).*

19.94   Wake, W., and N. Lardner, "The Epistles of Jesus Christ and
        Abgarus, King of Edessa," ApocNT. Pp. 68f. [ET]

19.95   Wessely, K. "Abgar V ukhâmâ," LTK^2 1. Col. 30.

19.96   Wilson, R.McL. "Abgarus, Epistles of Christ and," ZPEB.
        1. P. 10.

19.97   Youtie, H.C. "A Gothenburg Papyrus and the Letter to Ab-
        gar," HTR 23 (1930) 299-302.

19.98 Youtie, H.C. "Gothenburg Papyrus 21 and the Coptic Version
       of the Letter to Abgar," HTR 24 (1931) 61-65.

19.99 Zahn, T. "Uber die Lehre des Addai," Forschungen zur
       Geschichte des neutestamentlichen Kanons und der altkirch-
       lichen Literatur. Erlangen, 1881. Pt. 1. Pp. 350-82.

                20. CHRIST, LETTER OF FROM HEAVEN

(See also 1.284.)

20.1   Amaducci, J.C. Anecdota litteraria ex mss. codicibus eruta I.
       Rome, 1773. Pp. 69-74. [Lat. text]

20.2   Ayuso Marazuela, T. "Un apócrifo español del siglo VI de
       probable origen judeo-cristiano," Sefarad 4 (1944) 3-39.

20.3   Bauer, J.B. "Ein vom Himmel gefallener Brief Christi,"
       Neutest. Apok. Pp. 81-84.

20.4   Bittner, M. Der vom Himmel gefallene Brief Christi in seinen
       morgenländischen Versionen und Rezensionen (Denkschriften
       der kaiserlichen Akademie der Wissenschaften Philosophisch-
       historische Klasse 51.1) Vienna, 1906.

20.5   Brunel, C. "Versions Espagnole, Provençale et Française de
       la Lettre du Christ Tombée du ciel," AnBoll 68 (1950) 381-
       96.

20.6   Casella, M. "La epistola di lu nostra Signuri," Atti della
       Reale Accademia delle scienze di Torino 50 (1914-15) 83-106.

20.7   Delehaye, H. "Un exemplaire de la lettre tombée du ciel,"
       RSR 18 (1928) 164-69.

20.8   Delehaye, H. "Note sur la Légende de la lettre du Christ tom-
       bée du ciel," Académie Royale de Belgique, Bulletin de Classe
       des Lettres. Brussels, 1899. Pp. 171-213; repr. Mélanges
       d'hagiographie grecque et latine (Subsidia Hagiographica 42)
       Brussels, 1966. Pp. 150-78.

20.9   Erbetta, M. "La Lettera della Domenica," Apoc. del NT. 3.
       Pp. 113-18.

20.10 Fabricius, J.A. Cod.Apoc.NT. 1. Pp. 309-13.

20.11 Gessler, J. "Een brief uit den hemel. Niederlandische en

andere versies van den Christusbrief," Philologischen Studien 7 (1936) 27-29.

20.12   Goodspeed, E.J.   "The Letter from Heaven," New Chapters
        in New Testament Study. New York, 1937. Pp. 191-96.

20.13   Graf, G.   "Der vom Himmel gefallene Brief Christi," ZS 6
        (1928) 10-23. [Arab. text and German trans.]

20.14   Halkin, F.   "Codex Huntingtonianus 583," AnBoll 90 (1972)
        288.

20.15   Hall, I.H.   "The Letter of Holy Sunday," JAOS 15 (1893) 122-
        37. [Syr. text and ET]

20.16   Khorrnn, I.F.   Dissertatio historico-theologica qua de libris et
        epistolis caelo et inferno delatis.... Helmastadii, 1725. Pp.
        24-28.*

20.17   Koníř, A.   "The Apocryphal 'Letter of Sunday' in Church
        Slavonic Literature," Listy filologické 41 (1914) 23-35, 104-
        11, 217-30. [in Czech]

20.18   Koníř, A.   "The Church Slavonic Recension of the Apocryphal
        'Letter of Sunday,'" Slavia 6 (1927-28) 398-34, 685-708. [in
        Czech]

20.19   Migne, J.-P.   "Jésus-Christ. (Ecrits attribués ou relatifs à
        Jésus-Christ.)," Dictionnaire. 2. Cols. 367-69.

20.20   Moraldi, L.   "Lettera del Signore nostro Gesù Cristo," Apoc.
        del NT. 2. Pp. 1703-18.

20.21   Murko, M.   "The Western 'Letter of Sunday' in South Slavic
        Literature," Festschrift v. Jagić. 1980. Pp. 706-10. [in
        Slovenian]*

20.22   Paul, K.   "A Few Words About the So-called Apocryphal 'Let-
        ter Sent from Heaven,'" Národnopisn. věstník českoslovanský
        12 (1917) 52-56. [in Czech]

20.23   Paul, K.   "The 'Letter Sent from Heaven' in Slavic Literatures,"
        Národnopisn. věstník českoslovanský 13 (1918) 78-80. [in
        Czech]

20.24   Pelaez, M.   "Redazioni italiane della pretesa lettera di Cristo
        pel riposo domenicale," Atti e memorie di Arcadia ser. 3, 2
        (1949).*

20.25   Priebsch, R.   "The Chief Sources of Some Anglo Saxon Hom-
        ilies," Otia Merseiana 1 (1899) 130-34.

20.26 Priebsch, R. "John Audelay's Poem on the Observance of
       Sunday and its Source," An English Miscellany Presented to
       Dr. Furnivall. Oxford, 1901. Pp. 397-407.

20.27 Priebsch, R. Letter from Heaven on the Observance of the
       Lord's Day. Oxford, 1936.

20.28 Pypin, A.N. "Sunday and the Letter of Sunday," Lĕtopis'zan-
       jatij Archeografičeskoj Kommissii 1862-63. St. Petersburg,
       1864. Vol. 2. Pp. 1-13. [in Russian Church Slavic]

20.29 Radcenko, K.F. "The Letter of Sunday According to the
       Philippopolis and Belgrade Manuscripts" Čtenija v istoričesk.
       obščestve Nestora Lĕtopisca 18 (1904) 1-21. [in Russian
       Church Slavic]

20.30 Renoir, E. "Christ (Lettre du) Tombée du ciel," DACL. 3.
       Cols. 1534-46.

20.31 Röhricht, R. "Ein 'Brief Christi,'" ZKG 11 (1890) 436-42,
       619.

20.32 Sachau, E. Verzeichnis der syrischen Handschriften der
       Königl. Bibliothek zu Berlin. Berlin, 1899. Pp. 278-81.

20.33 Santos Otero, A. de. "Der apokryphe sogennante Sonntags-
       brief," Studia Patristica. Vol. 3: Papers Presented to the
       Third International Conference on Patristic Studies, ed. F.L.
       Cross (TU 78) Berlin, 1961. Pp. 290-96.

20.34 Santos Otero, A. de. "La Carta del Domingo," Evangelios
       Apócrifos. Pp. 670-82. [Gk. text and Spanish trans.]

20.35 Santos Otero, A. de. "Epistula de die Dominica," Altslavischen
       Apok. 1. Pp. 158-69.

20.36 Scriptores Ecclesiastici Hispano-Latini veteris et medii aevi,
       facs. 3. Escorial, Spain, 1944.*

20.37 Sedel'nikov, A. "From the History of the 'Letter of Sunday.'
       The Jerusalem-Joachim Version Among the Russians and
       South Slavs," Slavia 11 (1932) 56-72, 274-94. [in Russian]

20.38 Stegmüller, F. Repertorium Biblicum. 1. Pp. 121-23; 8.
       Pp. 93-96.

20.39 Stumpf, A. "Historia Flagellantium praecipue in Thuringia,"
       Neue Mittheilungen aus dem Gebiet historisch-antiquarischer
       Forschungen 2 (1835) 1-37.

20.40 Tichonravov, N. Texts of Dismissed Russian Literature. Mos-
       cow, 1863. Vol. 2. Pp. 11-18, 314-22. [in Russian]

20.41   Tomar, M. Das aethiopische Briefbuch nach drei Handschriften
        Herausgegeben und Übersetzt. Leipzig, 1869.

20.42   Vassiliev, A. Anecdota Graeco-Byzantina. Moscow, 1893.
        Vol. 1. Pp. xiv-xx, 23-32. [Gk. text]

20.43   Veselovskij, A.N. "Works on the History of the Development
        of Christian Legend," Žurnal ministerstva narodnago pros-
        veščenija 184 (March, 1876) 50-116. [in Russian]

20.44   Vilinskij, S.G. "Bulgarian Texts of the 'Letter of Sunday,'"
        Lětopisa istoriko-filologičeskogo obščestva pri imp. Novoro-
        ssijckom Universitetě 10 (1902) 112-24. [in Russian]

20.45   Vilinskij, S.G. "The Cyrillo-Belozer Manuscript of the 'Letter
        of Sunday,'" Lětopis' istoriko-filologičeskago obščestva pri
        imper. Novorossijskom Universitetě 13 (1905) 1-22. [in Rus-
        sian]

20.46   Wattenbach, [?]. "Ueber erfundene Briefe in Handschriften
        des Mittelalters, besonders Teufelsbrief," SPAW (1812).

21. CLEMENTINES, PSEUDO-

        See also the works listed under PrePet and AcPet.

(See also 1.47, 53, 108; 24.41, 42.)

21.1   Amann, É. "Les romans pseudo-Clémentins," DBSup. 1.
        Cols. 514-18.

21.2   Amersfoort, J. van. "Traces of an Alexandrian Orphic Theog-
        ony in the Pseudo-Clementines," Studies in Gnosticism and
        Hellenistic Religions: Presented to Gilles Quispel on the
        Occasion of his 65th Birthday, eds. R. van den Broek and
        M. J. Vermaseren (Études préliminaires aux religions orien-
        tales dans l'Empire Romain 91) Leiden, 1981. Pp. 13-30.

21.3   [Archeografičeskaja Kommissija] Daily Readings of the Great
        'Menaea' (Nov. 23-25, 1917) Cols. 3317-36, 3356ff.* [in Rus-
        sian]

21.4   Arnold, G. Des h. Clementis von Rom Recognitiones in zehen
        Büchern. Berlin, 1702.

21.5   Baring-Gould, S. "The Clementine Gospels," Lost and Hostile
        Gospels. Pp. 193-218.

21.6   Bedjan, P., ed.   Acta martyrum et sanctorum Syriace.   7 vols.
       Paris, 1890-97.   Vol. 6.   Pp. 1-17.

21.7   Bergmann, J.   "Les éléments juifs dans les pseudo-clémentines,"
       REJ 46 (1903) 89-98.

21.8   Bigg, C.   "The Clementine Homilies," Studia biblica et eccles-
       iastica.   Oxford, 1890.   Vol. 2.   Pp. 157-93.

21.9   Boll, F.   "Das Eingangsstück der Ps.-Klementinen," ZNW 17
       (1916) 139-48.

21.10 Bousset, W.   "Die Geschichte eines Wiedererkennungsmär-
       chens," Nachrichten der Gesellschaft der Wissenschaft in
       Göttingen-Philologisch-historische Klasse (1916) 469-551.*

21.11 Bousset, W.   "Die Wiedererkennungs-Fabel in den pseudokle-
       mentinischen Schriften, den Menächmen des Plautus und
       Shakespeares Komödie der Irrungen," ZNW 5 (1904) 18-27.

21.12 Cadiou, R.   "Origène et les 'Reconnaissances Clémentines,'"
       RSR 20 (1930) 506-28.

21.13 Chapman, J.   "On the Date of the Clementines," ZNW 9 (1908)
       21-34, 147-59.

21.14 Chapman, J.   "Origen and the Date of Pseudo-Clement," JTS
       3 (1902) 436-41.

21.15 Cirillo, L.   "Le Pseudo-Clementine e il Vangelo di Barnaba
       della Biblioteca nazionale di Vienna," Asprenas 18 (1971) 333-
       36, cf. 495-99, 503f., 682, 799.

21.16 Cullmann, O.   "Die neuentdeckten Qumrantexte und das Juden-
       christentum der Pseudoklementinen," Neutestamentliche Stu-
       dien für Rudolf Bultmann zu Seinem 70 Geburtstag August
       20, 1954, ed. W. Eltester.   (BZNW 21)   Berlin, 1954.   Pp.
       35-51.

21.17 Cullmann, O.   Le problème littéraire et historique du roman
       pseudo-clémentin.   Étude sur le rapport entre le gnosticisme
       et le judéo-christianisme (Études d'histoire et de philosophie
       religieuses 23) Paris, 1930.

21.18 Dressel, A. R. M.   Clementinorum epitomae duae.   Leipzig,
       1859, 1873[2].

21.19 Dressel, A. R. M.   Clementis Romani quae feruntur Homiliae
       viginti nunc primum editae.   Göttingen, 1853.

21.20 Duensing, H.   "Ein Stück der urchristlichen Petrusapokalypse

enthaltender Traktat der äthiopischen pseudoklementinischen
Literatur," ZNW 14 (1913) 65-78.

21.21   Erbetta, M. "Le Pseudoclementine," Apoc. del NT. 2. Pp.
        211-36.

21.22   Fabricius, J.A. "Clementis Romani de Actis Petri," Cod.Apoc.
        NT. 2. Pp. 759-62.

21.23   Faivre, A. "Les fonctions ecclésiales dans les Ecrits Pseudo-
        Clémentins: Proposition de Lecture," RScRel 50 (1976) 97-
        111.

21.24   Frank, [?]. "Die evangelischen Citate in den Clementinischen
        Homilien," Studien der evangelischen Geistlichen Wirtembergs
        19 (1847) 144-95.*

21.25   Frankenberg, W. Die syrischen Clementinen mit griechischem
        Paralleltext: Eine Vorarbeit zu dem literargeschichtlichen
        Problem der Sammlung (TU 48.3) Leipzig, 1937.

21.26   Frankenberg, W. "Zum syrischen Text der Clementinen,"
        ZDMG 91 (1937) 577-604.

21.27   Franko, I. Apocrypha and Legends. L'vov, 1902. Vol. 3.
        Pp. 15-18, 238-46. [in Russian]

21.28   Franko, I. "Beiträge aus dem Kirchenslavischen zu den Apok-
        ryphen des Neuen Testamentes. I: Zu den Pseudoklemen-
        tinen," ZNW 3 (1902) 146-55.

21.29   Franko, I. "Saint Clement at Korsun," Zapysky naukovogo
        tovarystva im. Ševčenka 48 (1902) 45-144; 56 (1903) 145-80;
        59 (1904) 181-208; 60 (1904) 209-56; 66 (1905) 257-80; 68
        (1905) 281-310. [in Russian Church Slavic]

21.30   Frommberger, W. De Simone Mago, Pars prima: De origine
        Pseudo-Clementinorum. Breslau, 1886.

21.31   Gersdorf, E. G. S. Clementis Romani Recognitiones Rufino
        Aquilei. presb. interprete (Bibliotheca patrum ecclesiasticorum
        Latinorum selecta 1) Leipzig, 1838; repr. in PG, Vol. 1,
        Cols. 1201-1454.

21.32   Gibson, M.D. Recognitions of Clement (SS 5) London, 1896.
        [Ar. text and ET]

21.33   Grébaut, S. "Littérature éthiopienne pseudo-Clémentine,"
        ROC 12 (1907) 139-51; 15 (1910) 198-214, 307-23, 425-39;
        16 (1911) 72-81, 167-75, 225-33; 17 (1912) 16-31, 133-44,

244-52, 337-46; 18 (1913) 68-79; 19 (1914) 324-30; 20 (1915-17) 33-37, 424-30; 21 (1918-19) 246-52; 22 (1920-21) 22-28, 113-17, 395-400; 25 (1925) 22-31.

21.34 Harnack, A. "Die pseudoclementinischen Briefe De virginitate," Gesch. altchrist. Lit. 2.2. Pp. 133-35.

21.35 Harnack, A. "Pseudoclementinische Schriften," Gesch. altchrist. Lit. 1. Pp. 212-31.

21.36 Harnack, A. "Die pseudoklementischen Schriften," Gesch. altchrist. Lit. 2.2. Pp. 518-40.

21.37 Harris, J. R. "Notes on the Clementine Romances," JBL 40 (1921) 125-45.

21.38 Headlam, A. C. "The Clementine Literature," JTS 3 (1902) 41-58.

21.39 Heintze, W. Die Klemensromane und seine griechischen Quellen (TU 40.2) Leipzig, 1914.

21.40 Hilgenfeld, A. Die clementinischen Recognitionen und Homilien nach ihrem Ursprung und Inhalt dargestellt. Jena, 1848.

21.41 Hilgenfeld, A. Kritische Untersuchungen über die Evangelien Justin's, der clementinischen Homilien und Marcion's. Ein Beitrag zur Geschichte der ältesten Evangelien Literatur. Halle, 1850.

21.42 Hort, F. J. A. Notes Introductory to the Study of the Clementine Recognitions. A Course of Lectures. London, New York, 1901.

21.43 Irmscher, J. "Die Pseudo-Clementinen," HS. 2. Pp. 373-98.

21.44 Irmscher, J. "The Pseudo-Clementines," HSW. 2. Pp. 532-70.

21.45 Jacimirskij, A. I. "Apocrypha and Legends (V-VIII)," IzvORJS 14/3 (1909) 124-48. [in Russian]

21.46 Jones, F. S. "The Pseudo-Clementines: A History of Research," The Second Century 2 (1982) 1-33, 63-96.

21.47 Klijn, A. F. J. "The Pseudo-Clementines and the Apostolic Decree," NovT 10 (1968) 305-12.

21.48 Kline, L. L. "Harmonized Sayings of Jesus in the Pseudo-Clementine Homilies and Justin Martyr," ZNW 66 (1975) 223-41.

21.49 Kline, L.L. The Sayings of Jesus in the Pseudo-Clementine
       Homilies (SBLDS 14) Missoula, Mont., 1975.

21.50 Lagarde, P. de. Clementina. Leipzig, 1865.

21.51 Lagarde, P. de. Clementis Romani Recognitiones syriace.
       Leipzig, 1861.

21.52 Langen, J. Die Klemensromane. Ihre Entstehung und ihre
       Tendenzen aufs neue untersucht. Gotha, 1890.

21.53 Lavrov, P. "The Lives of the Kherson Saints in Greco-Slavic
       Writings," Pamjatniki christianskago Chersonesa II. Moscow,
       1911.* [in Russian]

21.54 Lehmann, J. Die Clementinischen Schriften mit besonderer
       Rücksicht auf ihr literarisches Verhältnis. Gotha, 1869.

21.55 Lipsius, R. A. Die Quellen der römischen Petrus-Sage Kritisch
       Untersucht. Kiel, 1872.

21.56 Maistre, [?]. St. Clément de Rome. 2 vols. Paris, 1883-84.*

21.57 Martyn, J. L. "Clementine Recognitions 1, 33-71, Jewish
       Christianity, and the Fourth Gospel," God's Christ and His
       People: Studies in Honor of Nils Alstrup Dahl, eds. J. Jer-
       vell and W. A. Meeks. Oslo, Bergen, Tromsö, 1977, Pp.
       265-95.

21.58 Martyn, J. L. The Gospel of John in Christian History: Es-
       says for Interpreters. New York, Ramsey, Toronto, 1978.
       Pp. 55-89.

21.59 Merx, A. Bardesanes von Edessa, nebst einer Untersuchung
       über das Verhältnis der clementinischen Recognitionen zu
       dem Buche der Gesetze der Länder. Halle, 1863.

21.60 Meyboom, H. U. De Clemens-Roman. Vol. 1: Synoptische
       Vertaling van den Tekst. Groningen, 1902.

21.61 Mingana, A. "A New Document on Clement of Rome, His Re-
       lations and His Interview with Simon Peter," Exp 8 (1914)
       227-42. [ET]

21.62 Mingana, A. "Some Early Judaeo-Christian Documents in the
       John Rylands Library," BJRL 4 (1917-18) 59-118. [ET, pp.
       66-76; Syr. text, pp. 90-108]

21.63 Molland, E. "La circoncision, le baptême et l'autorité du dé-
       cret apostolique (Actes XV, 28 sq.) dans les milieux judéo-
       chrétiens des pseudo-clémentines," ST 9 (1955) 1-39. [repr.

in Opuscula Patristica (Bibliotheca theologica Norvegica 2)
Oslo, 1970. Pp. 25-59]

21.64   Nau, F. "Clémentins (apocryphes)," DThC. 3. Cols. 201-
        23.

21.65   Nau, F. "Notes sur les Clémentines," Actes du XIVe congrès
        international des orientalistes, Alger 1905. Paris, 1906.
        Part 1, section 6. Pp. 24-38.

21.66   Nes, H. M. van. Het Nieuwe Testament in de Clementinen.
        Amsterdam, 1887.

21.67   Paschke, F. Die beiden griechischen Klementinen-Epitomen
        und ihre Anhänge. Überlieferungsgeschichtliche Vorarbeiten
        zu einer Neuausgabe der Texte (TU 90) Berlin, 1966.

21.68   Popov, A. Historico-Literary Review of Ancient Russian Po-
        lemical Compositions Against the Roman Catholics. Moscow,
        1875. Pp. 206-11. [in Russian; Fragment from the 'Epis-
        tolija na Rimljany' with the same contents as Codex slav.
        Wien Nr. 145 (9) fols. 371^v-374^v.]

21.69   Preuschen, E. "Evangelienzitate in den clementischen Homi-
        lien," Antilegomena. Giessen, 1905^2. Pp. 52-63, 172-82.
        [Gk. texts]

21.70   Puech, A. "Quelques observations sur les écrits Pseudo-
        Clémetins à propos du livre récent de Carl Schmidt,"
        RSR 10 (1930) 40-46.

21.71   Quarry, J. "Notes, Chiefly Critical, on the Clementine Hom-
        ilies and the Epistles Prefixed to Them," Hermathena 16
        (1890) 239-67; 17 (1891) 91-112; 18 (1892) 133-60; 19 (1893)
        287-300.

21.72   Quarry, J. "Notes, Chiefly Critical, on the Two Last Books
        of the Clementine Homilies," Hermathena 15 (1889) 67-104.

21.73   Quispel, G. "L'Évangile de Thomas et les Clémentines," VC
        12 (1958) 181-96. [repr. in Gnostic Studies (Uitgaven van
        het Nederlands historisch-archeologisch instituut te Ishtanbul
        34) 2 vols. Istanbul, 1975. Vol. 2 Pp. 17-29]

21.74   Rehm, B. "Bardesanes in den Pseudoclementinen," Philologus
        93 (1938) 218-47.

21.75   Rehm, B. "Clemens Romanus II (PsClementinen)," RAC. 3.
        Cols. 197-206.

21.76   Rehm, B. Die Pseudoklementinen. 2 vols. (GCS 42, 51) Ber-
        lin, 1953, 1965.

21.77   Rehm, B. "Zur Entstehung der pseudoclementinischen Schrif-
        ten," ZNW 37 (1938) 77-184.

21.78   Richardson, E. C. "The History of Clement," Presbyterian
        and Reformed Review 6 (1895) 108-13.

21.79   Rius-Camps, J. "Las Pseudoclementinas. Bases filológicas
        para una nueva interpretación," Revista Catalana de Teo-
        logía 1 (1976) 79-158.

21.80   Salač, A. "Philological Letters 7," Eunomia 3 (1959) 45ff.
        [in Czech]

21.81   Salles, A. "La diatribe anti-Paulinienne dans le 'Le Roman
        pseudo-Clémentin' et l'origine des 'Kérygmes de Pierre,'"
        RB 64 (1957) 516-51.

21.82   Salles, A. "Simon le Magicien ou Marcion," VC 12 (1958) 197-
        224.

21.83   Salmon, G. "Clementine Literature," Dictionary of Christian
        Biography, eds. W. Smith and H. Wace. 4 vols. London,
        1877-87. Vol. 1. Pp. 567-78.

21.84   Santos Otero, A. de. "Pseudo-Clementina," Altslavischen Apok.
        1. Pp. 140-46.

21.85   Schliemann, A. Die Clementinen nebst den verwandten Schrif-
        ten und der Ebionitismus. Hamburg, 1844. [see esp. pp.
        17-48]

21.86   Schliemann, A. Die clement. Recog. eine Überarbeitung der
        Clementinen. Kiel, 1843.

21.87   Schmidt, C. Studien zu den Pseudoklementinen (TU 46.1)
        Leipzig, 1929.

21.88   Schoeps, H. J. "Astrologisches im pseudoklementinischen
        Roman," VC 5 (1951) 88-100. [repr. in Studien zur unbe-
        kannten Religions- und Geistesgeschichte (Veröffentlichungen
        der Gesellschaft für Geistesgeschichte 3) Göttingen, 1963.
        Pp. 107-16]

21.89   Schoeps, H. J. "Das Judenchristentum in den Pseudoklemen-
        tinen," ZRGG 11 (1959) 72-77. [repr. in Studien zur unbe-
        kannten Religions- und Geistesgeschichte (Veröffentlichungen
        der Gesellschaft für Geistesgeschichte 3) Göttingen, 1963.
        Pp. 91-97]

21.90   Schoeps, H. J. "Iranisches in den Pseudoklementinen," ZNW
        51 (1960) 1-10. [repr. in Studien zur unbekannten Religions-

und Geistesgeschichte (Veröffentlichungen der Gesellschaft
für Geistesgeschichte 3) Göttingen, 1963. Pp. 98-106]

21.91 Schoeps, H.J. "Die Pseudoklementinen und das Urchristentum,"
       ZRGG 10 (1958) 3-15. [repr. in Studien zur unbekannten
       Religions- und Geistesgeschichte (Veröffentlichungen der
       Gesellschaft für Geistesgeschichte 3) Göttingen, 1963. Pp.
       80-90]

21.92 Schoeps, H. J. "Die Urgeschichte nach den Pseudoklemen-
       tinen," Aus frühchristlicher Zeit. Religionsgeschichtliche
       Untersuchungen. Tübingen, 1950. Pp. 1-37.

21.93 Schoeps, H. J. "Der Ursprung des Bösen und das Problem
       der Theodizee im pseudoklementinischen Roman," RSR 60
       (1972) 129-41.

21.94 Schwartz, E. "Unzeitgemässe Beobachtungen zu den Clemen-
       tinen," ZNW 31 (1932) 151-99.

21.95 Šestakov, S. "On the History of Texts on the Life of St.
       Clement Pope of Rome Who Suffered in Kherson," Vizantij-
       skij Vremennik 14 (1908) 215-26. [in Russian]

21.96 Siouville, A. Les homélies clémentines. Paris, 1933.

21.97 Snegarov, I. "Unpublished Old Greek Lives of the Saints.
       I: The Life of St. Clement of Rome," Godišnik na Duch.
       Akademija 'Kliment Ochridski' v Sofia 3.29 (1953/54) 151-59.
       [in Bulgarian]

21.98 Sobolevskij, A. "The Glagolithic Life of St. Clement the Pope
       (I-III)," IzvORJS 17/3 (1912) 216-22. [in Russian]

21.99 Sobolevskij, A. "The Lives of the Saints According to Ancient
       Russian Manuscripts," PDP 149 (1903) 1-6. [in Russian]

21.100 Sobolevskij, A. "The Miracle of St. Clement, Pope of Rome,"
       IzvORJS 6/1 (1901) 1-8. [in Russian]

21.101 Stegmüller, F. Repertorium Biblicum. 1. Pp. 179-82; 8.
       Pp. 164f.

21.102 Stötzel, A. "Die Darstellung der ältesten Kirchengeschichte
       nach den Pseudo-Clementinen," VC 36 (1982) 24-37.

21.103 Strecker, G. "Eine Evangelienharmonie bei Justin und Pseudo-
       klemens," NTS 24 (1978) 297-316.

21.104 Strecker, G. Das Judenchristentum in den Pseudoklementinen
       (TU 70) Berlin, 1958, 1981².

21.105 Uhlhorn, G. Die Homilien und Recognitionen des Clemens Ro-
       manus. Göttingen, 1854.

21.106 Ullmann, W. "The Significance of the 'Epistola Clementis' in
       the Pseudo-Clementines," JTS N.S. 11 (1960) 295-317.

21.107 Waitz, H. "Clementinen I," Pauly-Wissowa. 23. Pp. 312-16.

21.108 Waitz, H. "Die Lösung des pseudoclementinischen Problems?"
       ZKG 59 (1940) 304-41.

21.109 Waitz, H. Die Pseudoklementinen, Homilien und Rekognitionen:
       Eine quellenkritische Untersuchung (TU 10.4) Leipzig, 1904.

21.110 Waitz, H. "Die Pseudoklementinen und ihre Quellenschriften,"
       ZNW 28 (1929) 241-72.

21.111 Waitz, H., and H. Veil. "Auszüge aus den Pseudo-Clementinen,
       H². Pp. 151-63, 212-49.

21.112 Westcott, B. F. "The Gospel of the Clementine Homilies,"
       An Introduction to the Study of the Gospels. Cambridge,
       London, 1881⁶. Pp. 473-76.

22. COPTIC NARRATIVES OF THE
MINISTRY AND PASSION

This category represents James' attempt in ANT to order
a number of Coptic fragments Revillout (17.24) attributed
to GosBart.

(See also 17.3, 9, 10, 12, 14, 15, 16.)

22.1   Erbetta, M. "Frammenti copti concernenti soprattutto parti-
       colari del ministero e della passione di Cristo," Apoc. del
       NT. 1.2. Pp. 320-34.

22.2   James, M.R. "Coptic Narratives of the Ministry and the Pas-
       sion," ANT. Pp. 147-52.

22.3   Lacau, M.P. "Évangile (?) Apocryphe," FAC. Pp. 23-37,
       79-108. [Coptic texts and French trans.]

22.4   Moraldi, L. "Frammenti di testi copti," Apoc. del NT. 1.
       Pp. 387-419.

22.5   Revillout, E. "Les apocryphes coptes I," PO 2 (1907) 116-98.
       [Coptic texts and French trans.]

22.6 Robinson, F. Coptic Apocryphal Gospels: Translations Together with the Texts of Some of Them (T & S 4) Cambridge,
1896. Pp. 162-85; 235-45.

23. TESTAMENTUM DOMINI (EPISTLE OF
THE APOSTLES)

TDom is the name given to the Syr. version of EpApos to
which a prophecy concerning the signs of the end is often
prefixed--see also the entries under EpApos.

23.1 Amann, É. "Testament de Notre-Seigneur Jésus-Christ,"
DThC. 15. Cols. 194-200.

23.2 Arendzen, I.P. "A New Syriac Text of the Apocalyptic Part
of the Testament of the Lord," JTS 2 (1901) 401-11.

23.3 Arranz, M. "Les rôles dans l'assemblée chrétienne d'après
le Testamentum Domini," BiblEphLitg.*

23.4 Coquin, R.G. "Le Testamentum Domini: Problèmes de tradition textuelle," PO 5 (1914) 165-88.

23.5 Dib, S.D. "Les Versions Arabes du 'Testamentum Domini
Nostri Jesu Christi,'" ROC 10 (1905) 418-23.

23.6 Guerrier, L. "Un 'Testament de Notre-Seigneur et Sauveur
Jésus-Christ' en Galilée," ROC 12 (1907) 1-8.

23.7 Guerrier, L., and S. Grébaut. "Le testament en Galilée de
Notre-Seigneur Jésus-Christ," PO 9 (1913) 143-232. [Eth.
text and French trans.; see M.R. James' review JTS 14
(1913) 601-06]

23.8 Harnack, A. "Kirchenrechtliche Arbeiten Hippolyts," Gesch.
altchrist. Lit. 2.2. Pp. 501-17.

23.9 Rahmani, I.E. Testamentum Domini nostri Jesu Christi.
Mainz, 1899; repr. Hildesheim, 1968. [Syr. and Lat. texts]

23.10 Schmidt, C. "Eine Benutzung des Testamentum Domini nostri
Jesu Christi," Harnack-Ehrung. Leipzig, 1921. Pp. 263-67.

23.11 Stegmüller, F. Repertorium Biblicum. 1. P. 123; 8. P. 98.

23.12 Tabet, J. Testamentum Domini (Ve siècle) traduit en arabe
à partir de la version syriaque. Kaslik, 1975.

23.13   Vasile, C. "The Pseudepigraphic Text 'Testamentum Domini'
        as a Source for Christian Worship," Studii Theol. [Buchar-
        est] 17 (1965) 204-18. [in Rumanian]

                    24. EBIONITES, GOSPEL OF

The GosEb is known to us only by citations from Epiphan-
ius (Panarion 30); modern scholars have tried to identify
Origen's and Jerome's citations of the GosTw with the
GosEb--see also the listings under GosTw and Agrapha.

(See also 1.88, 275, 531, 540; 5.121, 122; 29.3, 27.)

24.1   Amann, É. "Évangile des Ébionites ou des douze âpotres,"
        DBSup. 1. Cols. 472f.

24.2   Bardenhewer, O. "Das Evangelium der Zwölf und das Ebion-
        itenevangelium," GAL. 1. Pp. 518-21.

24.3   Bauer, J.B. Neutest. Apok. Pp. 18-20.

24.4   Baumstark, A. "Les apocryphes coptes," RB 3 (1906) 245-65.

24.5   Bertrand, D.A. "L'Evangile des Ebionites: Une Harmonie
        évangélique antérieure au Diatessaron," NTS 26 (1980) 548-
        63.

24.6   Boismard, M.-É. "Évangile des Ebionites et problème synop-
        tique (Mc. 1, 2-6 et par.)," RB 73 (1966) 321-52.

24.7   Bonaccorsi, P.G. "Dal Vangelo degli Ebioniti," Vangeli Apoc-
        rifi. 1. Pp. 8-13.

24.8   Erbetta, M. "Vangelo degli Ebioniti," Apoc. del NT. 1.
        Pp. 132-36.

24.9   Fabbri, E. "El bautismo de Jesús en el 'Evangelio de los
        Hebreos' y en 'el de los Ebionitas,'" Revista de Teología 22
        (1956) 36-56. [see also Ciencia y Fe 6 (1956) 36-55]

24.10   Fabricius, J.A. "Ebionitarum Evangelium," Cod.Apoc.NT.
        1. Pp. 346-49. [P. 349 includes discussion of "Eneratitarum
        Evangelium"]

24.11   Fitzmyer, J.A. "The Qumrân Scrolls, the Ebionites and Their
        Literature," TS 16 (1955) 335-72. [repr. in Essays on the
        Semitic Background of the New Testament. London, 1971;
        repr. Missoula, Mont., 1974. Pp. 435-80.]

24.12 Gennaro, G. "Ebionite," EncCatt. 5. Col. 3.

24.13 Harnack, A. "Das Evangelium der zwölf Apostel (von Matth. angeblich niedergeschrieben) und andere Schriften der gnostischen Ebioniten," Gesch. altchrist. Lit. 1. Pp. 205-09.

24.14 Harnack, A. "Das Hebräer-und das Ebionitenevangelium [Ev. (der 12 Apostel durch) Matthäus]." Gesch. altchrist. Lit. 2.1. Pp. 625-51.

24.15 Hilgenfeld, A. Novum Testamentum extra canonem receptum. Leipzig, 1884[4]. [See esp. fasc. 4, pp. 32-38.]

24.16 Hirschberg, H. "Simon Bariona and the Ebionites," JBL 61 (1942) 171-91.

24.17 Howard, G. "The Gospel of the Ebionites," ANRW 2.25.4 (in preparation).

24.18 James, M.R. "The Gospel of the Ebionites," ANT. Pp. 8-10.

24.19 Klostermann, E., ed. "Ebionitenevangelium (Evangelium der Zwölf?)," Apocrypha II: Evangelien (KlT 8) Berlin, 1929[3]. Pp. 12-15. [Gk. witnesses]

24.20 Lake, D. "Ebionism, Ebionites (Gospel of the)," ZPEB. 2. P. 182.

24.21 Merkelbach, R. "Coniectura de fragmento Ev. Ebion. citato in Epiphanio, Haer 30, 13, 7," Studien zur Textgeschichte und Textkritik, ed. H. Dahlmann and R. Merkelbach. Cologne, 1959.*

24.22 Meyer, A. "Ebionitenevangelium: Evangelium der 12 Apostel," Handbuch, ed. Hennecke. Pp. 42-47.

24.23 Michaelis, W. "Ebioniten-Evangelium," Apokryphen Schriften. Pp. 128-30.

24.24 Migne, J.-P. "Ébionites," Dictionnaire. 2. Cols. 215f.

24.25 Moraldi, L. "Vangelo degli Ebioniti," Apoc. del NT. 1. Pp. 371-73.

24.26 Preuschen, E. "Reste des Evangeliums der Ebioniten," Antilegomena. Giessen, 1905[2]. Pp. 9-12, 141-43. [Gk. text]

24.27 Quispel, G. "Jewish-Christian Gospel Tradition," ATR Suppl. Ser. 3 (1974) 112-16.

24.28 Santos Otero, A. de. "Evangelio de los Doce o de los Ebionitas,"

Evangelios Apócrifos. Pp. 47-53. [reconstruction of Gk.
text with Spanish trans.]

24.29   Schmidtke, A. "Epiphanius über das Hebräerevangelium und
        seine Leser," Neue Fragmente und Untersuchungen zu den
        judenchristlichen Evangelien (TU 37.1) Leipzig, 1911. Pp.
        166-246.

24.30   Schoeps, H.J. "Ebionite Christianity," JTS N.S. 4 (1955) 219-
        24.

24.31   Schoeps, H.J. "Ebionitische Apokalyptik im NT," ZNW 51
        (1960) 101-11.

24.32   Schoeps, H.J. "Die ebionitische Wahrheit des Christentums,"
        ST 8 (1954) 43-50. [repr. in The Background of the New
        Testament and its Eschatology: Studies in Honor of C.H.
        Dodd, eds. W.D. Davies and D. Daube. Cambridge, 1956.
        Pp. 115-23]

24.33   Schoeps, H.J. "Handelt es sich wirklich um ebionitische Doc-
        umente," ZRGG 3 (1951) 322-36.

24.34   Schoeps, H.J. "Symmachusstudien: Der Bibelübersetzer Sym-
        machus als ebionitischer Theologe," Coniectanea Neotestamen-
        tica 6 (1942) 65-93.

24.35   Spiegelberg, W., and A. Jacoby. "Zu dem Strassburger Evan-
        gelienfragment, eine Antikritik," Sphinx 4 (1901) 171-93.

24.36   Stegmüller, F. Repertorium Biblicum. 1. P. 111 [see also
        p. 108]; 8. P. 82.

24.37   Strecker, G. "Ebioniten," RAC. 4. Pp. 487-500.

24.38   Teicher, J.L. "The Dead Sea Scroll Documents of the Jewish-
        Christian Sect of Ebionites," JJS 2 (1951) 65-77.

24.39   Vielhauer, P. "Das Ebionäerevangelium," HS. 1. Pp. 100-04.

24.40   Vielhauer, P. "The Gospel of the Ebionites," HSW. 1. Pp.
        153-58. [see also pp. 263f.]

24.41   Waitz, H. "Ebionäerevangelium oder Evangelium der Zwölf,"
        H[2]. Pp. 39-48.

24.42   Waitz, H. "Das Evangelium der zwölf Apostel (Ebionitenevan-
        gelium)," ZNW 13 (1912) 338-48; 14 (1913) 38-64, 117-32.

24.43   Wallach, L. "The Textual History of an Aramaic Proverb
        (Traces of the Ebionean Gospel)," JBL 60 (1941) 403-15.

24.44   Westcott, B.F. "The Gospel of the Ebionites," An Introduction
        to the Study of the Gospels. Cambridge, London, 1881[6].
        Pp. 471-73.

24.45   Zahn, T. "Koptische Fragmente eines apokryphen Evange-
        liums," NKZ 11 (1900) 361-70.

        25. EGYPTIANS, GOSPEL ACCORDING TO THE

(See also entries under Agrapha; and 1.88; 5.99, 121, 122, 242; 29.3,
        27, 56.)

25.1   Amann, É. "L'évangile des Égyptiens," DBSup. 1. Cols.
        475f.

25.2   Ambroggi, P. de. "Egiziani (Vangelo degli)," EncCatt. 5.
        Col. 181.

25.3   Bardenhewer, O. "Das Agypterevangelium," GAL. 1. Pp.
        521-24.

25.4   Baring-Gould, S. "The Gospel of the Egyptians," Lost and
        Hostile Gospels. Pp. 223-31.

25.5   Bauer, J.B. "Das Agypterevangelium," Neutest. Apok. Pp.
        27f.

25.6   Bolgiani, F. La tradizione eresiologica sull'encratismo. II.
        La confutazione di Clemente di Alessandria (Atti d. Acca-
        demia di Scienze di Torino 96) Turin, 1961.

25.7   Bonaccorsi, P.G. "Dal Vangelo secondo gli Egiziani," Vangeli
        Apocrifi. 1. Pp. 14-17.

25.8   Bonsirven, J., and C. Bigaré. "Évangile des Égyptiens,"
        Intro. à la Bible. 2. P. 751.

25.9   Deissmann, A. "Notiz über das Aegypter-Evangelium," TLZ
        26 (1901) Cols. 92f.

25.10   Emmerich, [?]. De evangelio secundum Hebraeos, Aegyptios
        atque Iustini martyrio. Argentoraci, 1807.*

25.11   Erbetta, M. "Il Vangelo degli Egiziani," Apoc. del NT. 1.
        Pp. 147-52.

25.12   Esser, G. "Die neuaufgefundenen 'Sprüche Jesu,'" Katholik
        1 (1898) 143.

25.13   Fabricius, J.A. "Evangelium Secundum (a) Aegyptios," Cod.
        Apoc.NT. 1. Pp. 335-37.

25.14   Harnack, A. "Agypterevangelium," Gesch. altchrist. Lit. 1.
        Pp. 12-14. [see also 2.1. Pp. 612-22]

25.15   Hennecke, E. "Aegypterevangelium," Handbuch, ed. Hennecke.
        Pp. 38-42.

25.16   Hennecke, E. "Aegypterevangelium," H^2. Pp. 55-59.

25.17   Hilgenfeld, A. Novum Testamentum extra canonem receptum.
        Leipzig, 1884^2. Fasc. 4, pp. 42-8.

25.18   Hornschuh, M. "Erwägungen zum 'Evangelium der Ägypter'
        insbesondere zur Bedeutung seines Titels," VC 18 (1954)
        6-13.

25.19   James, M.R. "The Gospel According to the Egyptians," ANT.
        Pp. 10-12.

25.20   Klostermann, E., ed. "Aegypterevangelium," Apocrypha II:
        Evangelien (KlT 8) Berlin, 1929^3. Pp. 15f. [Gk. witnesses]

25.21   Migne, J.-P. "Égyptiens (Évangile des)," Dictionnaire. 2.
        Cols. 1312f.

25.22   Migne, J.-P. "Égyptiens. (Évangile des Égyptiens)," Dic-
        tionnaire. 2. Cols. 217-20.

25.23   Moraldi, L. "Vangelo degli Egiziani," Apoc. del NT. 1.
        Pp. 383-85.

25.24   Nestle, E. Novum Testamentum Graece Supplementum. Stutt-
        gart, 1896. [see esp. pp. 72f.]

25.25   Preuschen, E. "Reste des Ägypterevangeliums," Antilegomena.
        Giessen, 1905^2. Pp. 2f., 135f. [Gk. text]

25.26   Resch, A. "Ägypterevangelium," Agrapha. Pp. 252-57, 371-
        75.

25.27   Santos Otero, A. de. "Evangelio de los Egipcios," Evangelios
        Apócrifos. Pp. 53-57. [reconstruction of Gk. text with
        Spanish trans.]

25.28   Schneckenburger, M. Über das Evangelium der Aegyptier.
        Bern, 1834.

25.29   Schneemelcher, W. "Ägypterevangelium," HS. 1. Pp. 109-17.

25.30   Schneemelcher, W.   "The Gospel of the Egyptians," HSW.   1.
        Pp. 166-78.

25.31   Stegmüller, F.   Repertorium Biblicum.   1.   P. 107; 8.   Pp.
        76-78.

25.32   Völter, D.   "Petrusevangelium oder Ägypterevangelium," ZNW
        6 (1905) 368-72.

25.33   Völter, D.   Petrusevangelium oder Agypterevangelium: Eine
        Frage bezüglich des neuentdeckten Evangelienfragments.
        Tübingen, 1893.

25.34   Wilson, R.McL.   "Egyptians, Gospel of the," ZPEB.   2.   Pp.
        258f.

25.35   Zahn, T.   "Das Agypterevangelium," Neutest. Kanons.   2.
        Pp. 628-42.

25.36   Zappala, M.   "L'encratismo di Giulio Cassiano e i suoi rapporti
        con il vangelo apocrifo secondo gli Egiziani," Studi Filosofici
        e Religiose 3 (1929) 4.

26.   ELCHASAI, BOOK OF

26.1   Brandt, W.   Elchasai, ein Religionsstifter und sein Werk.   Leip-
        zig, 1912.   [also see Harnack's review in TLZ 37 (1912) cols.
        683ff.]

26.2   Erbetta, M.   "Il Libro di Elcasai," Apoc. del NT.   3.   Pp.
        551-54.

26.3   Harnack, A.   Gesch. altchrist. Lit.   1.   Pp. 207-09.

26.4   Hilgenfeld, A.   Novum Testamentum extra canonem receptum.
        Leipzig, 1881.   Vol. 3.2.   Pp. 227-40.

26.5   Irmscher, J.   "The Book of Elchasai," HSW.   2.   Pp. 745-50.

26.6   Irmscher, J.   "Das Buch der Elchasai," HS.   2.   Pp. 529-32.

26.7   Klijn, A.F.J., and G.J. Reinink, "Elchasai and Mani," VC
        28 (1974) 277-89.

26.8   Köhler, W.   "Elkasaiten," RGG^2.   2.   Col. 303.

26.9   Levy, M.A.   "Bemerkung zu den arabischen Analekten des
        Herrn Prof. Hitzig," ZDMG 12 (1858) 712.

26.10   Moraldi, L. Apoc. del NT. 2. P. 1798.

26.11   Peterson, E. "Le traitement de la rage par les Elkésaïtes
        d'après Hippolyte," RSR 34 (1947) 232-38.

26.12   Ritschl, A. "Über die Sekte der Elkesaiten," ZHTh 23 (1853)
        573-94.

26.13   Schmidtke, A. Neue Fragmente und Untersuchungen zu den
        Judenchristlichen Evangelien (TU 37.1) Leipzig, 1911. Pp.
        228f.

26.14   Schoeps, H.J. "Elkesaiten," RGG3. 2. Col. 435.

26.15   Schoeps, H.J. "Gnostischer Ebionitismus: Die Elkesaiten,"
        Theologie und Geschichte des Judenchristentums. Tübingen,
        1949. Pp. 325-34.

26.16   Schulz, W. Dokumente der Gnosis. Jena, 1910. Pp. LXII-
        LXIV.

26.17   Strecker, G. "Elkesai," RAC. 5. Cols. 1171-86.

26.18   Thomas, J. Le mouvement baptiste en Palestine et Syrie.
        Gembloux, 1935.

26.19   Uhlhorn, G. "Elkesaiten," Pauly-Wissowa. 5. P. 34.

26.20   Waitz, H. "Das Buch des Elchasai," H2. Pp. 422-25.

26.21   Waitz, H. "Das Buch des Elchasai, das heilige Buch der ju-
        denchristlichen Sekte der Sobiai," Harnack-Ehrung. Leipzig,
        1921. Pp. 87-104.

27. EVE, GOSPEL OF

27.1   Bardenhewer, O. GAL. 1. P. 347.

27.2   Baring-Gould, S. "The Gospel of Eve," Lost and Hostile Gos-
        pels. Pp. 286-91.

27.3   Erbetta, M. "Il Vangelo di Eva," Apoc. del NT. 1. Pp.
        537f.

27.4   Fabricius, J.A. "Evangelium Evae," Cod. Apoc. NT. 1.
        Pp. 349f.

27.5   Fabricius, J.A. "Evangelium Evae," Codex Pseudepigraphus

Veteris Testamenti. Hamburg, 1722[2]. Vol. 1. Pp. 95f.
[Gk. witness of Epiphanius]

27.6   Fendt, L. Gnostische Mysterien: Ein Beitrag zur Geschichte
       des christlichen Gottesdienstes. Munich, 1922. Pp. 4-32.

27.7   Harnack, A. Gesch. altchrist. Lit. 1. P. 166.

27.8   Hennecke, E. "Evangelium der Eva," H[2]. P. 69.

27.9   Jonas, H. Gnosis und spätantiker Geist. Göttingen, 1964.
       Vol. 1. Pp. 139f.

27.10 Klostermann, E., ed. "Evangelium der Eva," Apocrypha II:
       Evangelien (KlT 8) Berlin, 1929[3]. P. 18. [Gk. witness]

27.11 Migne, J.-P. "Ève. (Évangile d'Ève.)," Dictionnaire. 2.
       Cols. 241-44.

27.12 Preuschen, E. "Ein Ophitisches Evangelium der Eva," Anti-
       legomena. Giessen, 1905[2]. Pp. 82f., 188. [Gk. text]

27.13 Puech, H.-C. "Evangelien unter dem Namen einer Person des
       Alten Testaments," HS. 1. Pp. 166-68.

27.14 Puech, H.-C. "Gospels Under the Name of an Old Testament
       Figure," HSW. 1. Pp. 241-43.

27.15 Santos Otero, A. de. "Evangelio de Eva," Evangelios Apócr-
       rifos. Pp. 71f. [Gk. quotations from Epiphanius, Adv.
       Haer 38.1, and Theodoret, Haeret. fabul. 1.15, with Span-
       ish trans.]

27.16 Stegmüller, F. Repertorium Biblicum. 1. P. 111; 8. P. 82.

27.17 Wilson, R.McL. "Eve, Gospel of," ZPEB. 2. Pp. 419f.

28. GAMALIEL, GOSPEL OF

(See also the entries under CopNar.)

28.1   Baumstark, A. "Un évangile de Gamaliel," RB 3 (1906) 253-
       59.

28.2   Clemen, C. "Notiz über ein neugefundenes Fragment einer
       bisher unbekannten Pilatuslegende," TSK 67 (1894) 757-68.

28.3   Erbetta, M. "Il Vangelo di Gamaliele," Apoc. del NT. 1.2.
        Pp. 344-66.

28.4   Giamberardini, G. L'immacolata concezione di Maria nella
        Chiesa egiziana. Cairo, 1953.

28.5   Giamberardini, G. La teologia assunzionistica nella Chiesa
        egiziana. Jerusalem, 1951.

28.6   Haase, F. Literarkritische Untersuchungen zur orient.-apokr.
        Evangelienliteratur. Leipzig, 1913. Pp. 20f.

28.7   James, M.R. ANT. Pp. 151f.

28.8   Lacau, P. FAC. P. 19.

28.9   Ladeuze, P. "Apocryphes évangéliques Coptes. Pseudo-
        Gamaliel; Évangile de Barthélemy," RHE 7 (1906) 245-68.

28.10   Migne, J.-P. Dictionnaire. 1. Col. 1101.

28.11   Mingana, A. "The Lament of the Virgin," Christian Documents
        in Syriac, Arabic, and Garshūni, Edited and Translated with
        a Critical Apparatus (Woodbrooke Studies 2) Cambridge,
        1928. Pp. 178-240. [Ar. texts and ET; repr. from BJRL
        12 (1928)]

28.12   Moraldi, L. "Vangelo di Gamaliele," Apoc. del NT. 1. Pp.
        655-82.

28.13   Oudenrijn, M.-A. van den. Gamaliel: Athiopische Texte zur
        Pilatus Literatur. (Spicilegium Friburgense; Texte zur Ges-
        chichte des Kirchlichen Lebens 4) Freiburg, 1959.

28.14   Oudenrijn, M.-A. van den. "Das 'Evangelium des Gamaliel,'"
        Schweizerische Kirchen-Zeitung 124 (1956) 403.

28.15   Oudenrijn, M.-A. van den. "The Gospel of Gamaliel," HSW.
        1. Pp. 508-10.

28.16   Revillout, E., ed. "Les apocryphes coptes I," PO 2 (1904)
        116-89.

28.17   Stegmüller, F. Repertorium Biblicum. 1. P. 112; 8. Pp.
        82f.

29. HEBREWS, GOSPEL OF THE

(See also the entries under Agrapha; and 1.53, 88, 100, 275, 412,
531.)

29.1   Adeney, W.A. "The Gospel According to the Hebrews," HibJ
        3 (1904) 11-117.

29.2   Amann, É. "Évangile selon les Hébreux," DBSup. 1. Cols.
        471f.

29.3   Ambroggi, P. de. "Ebrei (Vangelo secondo gli)," EncCatt.
        5. Cols. 25f.

29.4   Amiot, F. Évangiles Apoc. Pp. 37-39.

29.5   Bardenhewer, O. "Das Hebräerevangelium," GAL. 1. Pp.
        513-18.

29.6   Bardy, G. "St. Jérôme et l'Évangile selon les Hébreux,"
        Mélanges de science religieuse 3 (1946) 5-36.

29.7   Baring-Gould, S. "The Gospel of the Hebrews," Lost and
        Hostile Gospels. Pp. 119-92.

29.8   Barnes, A.S. "The Gospel According to the Hebrews," JTS
        6 (1905) 356-71.

29.9   Bauer, J.B. Neutest. Apok. Pp. 18f.

29.10   Bonaccorsi, P.G. "Dal Vangelo secondo gli Ebrei," Vangeli
        Apocrifi. 1. Pp. 2-7.

29.11   Bonsirven, J., and C. Bigaré. "Évangile selon les Hébreux,"
        Intro. à la Bible. 2. Pp. 750f.

29.12   Brock, S. "A Testimonium to the 'Gospel According to the
        Hebrews,'" NTS 18 (1971) 220-22.

29.13   Brown, R.E. "Gospel of the Hebrews," JBC. Pp. 545-46.

29.14   Burch, V. "The Gospel According to the Hebrews: Some
        New Matter Chiefly from Coptic Sources," JTS 21 (1920)
        310-15.

29.15   Christou, P. "Hebrews, Gospel according to," ThEE 5. Pp.
        310f. [in modern Gk.]

29.16   Chrzaszcz, J.   Die apokryphen Evangelien, insbesondere das
        Evangelium iuxta Hebraeos.   Gleiwitz, 1888.

29.17   Chrzaszcz, J.   De Evangelio secundum Hebraeos.   Cliviciis,
        1888.

29.18   Dibelius, M.   Der Brief der Jakobus.   Göttingen, 1956[8].   Pp.
        92-95.

29.19   Dodd, J.T.   "The Appearance of Jesus to James," Theology
        18 (1929) 189-97.

29.20   Dodd, J.T.   The Gospel According to the Hebrews.   London,
        1933.

29.21   Dunkerly, R.   "The Gospel According to the Hebrews," ExpT
        39 (1927-28) 437-42, 490-95.

29.22   Ehrhardt, A.A.T.   "Judaeo-Christians in Egypt, the Epistula
        Apostolorum and the Gospel to the Hebrews," Studia Evan-
        gelica.   Vol. 3:   Papers Presented to the Second Interna-
        tional Congress on New Testament Studies Held at Christ
        Church, Oxford, 1961, ed. F.L. Cross (TU 88) Berlin,
        1964.   Pp. 360-82.

29.23   Emmerich, [?].   De evangelio secundum Hebraeos, Aegyptios
        atque Iustini martyrio.   Argentoraci, 1807.*

29.24   Erbetta, M.   "Vangelo degli Ebrei," Apoc. del NT.   1.   Pp.
        114-31.

29.25   Fabbri, E.   "El bautismo de Jesús en el 'Evangelio de los
        Hebreos' y en 'el de los Ebionitas,'" Revista de Teologia
        22 (1956) 36-56.   [see also Ciencia y Fe 6 (1956) 36-55]

29.26   Fabricius, J.A.   "Evangelium Secundum Hebraeos," Cod.Apoc.
        NT.   1.   P. 351.

29.27   Findlay, A.F.   "Jewish-Christian Gospels," Byways.   Pp. 33-
        78.

29.28   Franck, F.   "Ueber das Evangelium der Hebräer," TSK 21
        (1848) 369-422.

29.29   Fries, S.A.   Det fjärdt Evangeliet och Ebreerevangeliet.   Stock-
        holm, 1898.

29.30   Gla, D.   Die Originalsprache des Matthäusevangeliums.   Pader-
        born, 1887.   Pp. 101-21.

29.31   Handmann, R.   Das Hebräer-Evangelium: Ein Beitrag zur

Geschichte und Kritik des hebräischen Matthäus (TU 3)
Leipzig, 1888.

29.32   Harnack, A. "Hebräer-Evangelium," Gesch. altchrist. Lit.
1. Pp. 6-10.

29.33   Harnack, A. "Das Hebräer- und das Ebioniterevangelium [Ev.
(der 12 Apostel durch) Matthäus]," Gesch. altchrist. Lit.
2.1. Pp. 625-51.

29.34   Hilgenfeld, A. "Das Hebräerevangelium in England," ZWT 27
(1884) 188-94.

29.35   Hilgenfeld, A. "Das Hebräerevangelium und sein neuster
Bearbeiter," ZWT 32 (1889) 280-302.

29.36   Hilgenfeld, A. Novum Testamentum extra Canonem receptum.
Leipzig, 1884^2. [See esp. fasc. 4, pp. 6-31.]

29.37   James, M.R. "The Gospel According to the Hebrews," ANT.
Pp. 1-8.

29.38   James, M.R. "Notes on Mr. Burch's Article 'The Gospel According to the Hebrews' (July 1920)," JTS 22 (1921) 160f.

29.39   Klijn, A.F.J. "The Question of the Rich Young Man in a
Jewish-Christian Gospel," NovT 8 (1966) 149-55.

29.40   Klostermann, E., ed. "Hebräerevangelium (Nazaräerevangelium)," Apocrypha II: Evangelien (KlT 8) Berlin, 1929^3.
Pp. 5-12. [Gk. and Lat. witnesses]

29.41   Lagrange, M.-J. "L'Évangile selon les Hébreux," RB 31 (1922)
161-81, 321-49.

29.42   Lagrange, M.-J. "Apocryphes du N.T.," RB 46 (1937) 282-
84.

29.43   Mees, M. "Petrus und Johannes nach ausgewählten Varianten
von P^{66} und S," BZ 15 (1971) 238-49.

29.44   Meyer, A. "Hebräerevangelium," Handbuch, ed. Hennecke.
Pp. 21-38.

29.45   Michaelis, W. "Hebräer-Evangelium," Apokryphen Schriften.
Pp. 130f.

29.46   Migne, J.-P. "Hébreux. (Évangile des Hébreux.)," Dictionnaire. 2. Cols. 247-52.

29.47   Moraldi, L. "Vangelo degli Ebrei e Nazarei," Apoc. del NT. 1.
Pp. 373-83.

29.48   Nestle, E. "Ein altdeutsches Bruchstück aus dem Hebräer-
        Evangelium," ZNW 10 (1909) 183f.

29.49   Nestle, E. "A Fragment of the Original Hebrew Gospel,"
        Exp 2 (1895) 309-15.

29.50   Nicholson, E.B. The Gospel According to the Hebrews: Its
        Fragments Translated and Annotated with a Critical Analysis
        of the External and Internal Evidence Relating to It. Lon-
        don, 1897.

29.51   Noesgen, K.F. ZKWKL (1889) 499-519, 561-78.*

29.52   Parker, P. "A Proto-Lukan Basis for the Gospel According
        to the Hebrews," JBL 59 (1940) 471-78.

29.53   Petrement, S. "Une suggestion de Simone Weil à propos
        d'Apocalypse XII," NTS 11 (1965) 291-96.

29.54   Preuschen, E. "Reste des Hebräerevangeliums," Antilegomena.
        Giessen, 1905². Pp. 3-9, 136-41. [Gk. text]

29.55   Quispel, G. "'The Gospel of Thomas' and the 'Gospel of the
        Hebrews,'" NTS 12 (1965) 371-82.

29.56   Quispel, G. "Das Hebräerevangelium im gnostischen Evangel-
        ium nach Maria," VC 11 (1957) 139-44.

29.57   Quispel, G. "Het Luikse 'Leven van Jesus' en het jodenchris-
        telijke 'Evangelie der Hebreër,'" De Nieuwe Taalgids 51 (1958)
        241-49.

29.58   Quispel, G. "Jewish-Christian Gospel Tradition," ATR 3
        (1974) 112-16.

29.59   Resch, A. "Hebräerevangelium," Agrapha. Pp. 215-52; 363-
        71.

29.60   Robinson, J.A. "Three Notes on the Gospel According to the
        Hebrews," Exp 5 (1897) 194-200. [Robinson argues against
        Harnack and claims that GosHeb is dependent on two of the
        canonical gospels]

29.61   Rouanet, A. Étude exégétique et critique de l'Évangile des
        Hébreux. Cahors, 1904.

29.62   Santos Otero, A. de. "Evangelio de los Hebreos," Evangelios
        Apócrifos. Pp. 29-47. [Gk. fragments with Spanish trans.]

29.63   Schade, L. "Hieronymus und das hebräische Matthäusoriginal,"
        BZ 6 (1908) 346-63.

29.64 Schmidtke, A. "Das Hebräerevangelium bei den griechischen
       Vätern bis Euseb.," Neue Fragmente und Untersuchungen
       zu den judenchristlichen Evangelien (TU 37.1) Leipzig,
       1911. Pp. 126-66. [see review M.J. Lagrange RB 21 (1912)
       587-89]

29.65 Schmidtke, A. "Zum Hebräerevangelium," ZNW 35 (1936) 24-
       44.

29.66 Schonfield, H.J. According to the Hebrews: New Translation
       of Jewish Life of Jesus (Toldoth Jeshu) with an Inquiry into
       Its Sources and Relationship to the First Gospel According
       to the Hebrews. London, 1937.

29.67 Starcky, J. "La quatrième demande du Pater," HTR 64 (1971)
       401-09.

29.68 Stegmüller, F. Repertorium Biblicum. 1. P. 112; 8. P. 83.

29.69 Strobel, August. "Die 'Keltische Katechese' des Cod. Vat.
       Regin. lat. 49 über das Hebräerevangelium," ZKG 76 (1965)
       148.

29.70 Variot, J. "Les Fragments de l'Évangile des Hébreux," Évan-
       giles Apocryphes. Pp. 331-78.

29.71 Vielhauer, P. "The Gospel of the Hebrews," HSW. 1. Pp.
       158-65.

29.72 Vielhauer, P. "Das Hebräerevangelium," HS. 1. Pp. 104-08.

29.73 Waitz, H. "Hebräerevangelium," H2. Pp. 48-55.

29.74 Waitz, H. "Neue Untersuchungen über die sogenannten juden-
       christlichen Evangelien," ZNW 36 (1937) 60-81.

29.75 Weber, C.F. Neue Untersuchungen über das Alter und Anse-
       hen des Evangeliums der Hebräer. Tübingen, 1806.

29.76 Westcott, B.F. "The Gospel According to the Hebrews," An
       Introduction to the Study of the Gospels. Cambridge, Lon-
       don, 1881⁶. Pp. 466-70.

29.77 Wilson, R. McL. "Hebrews, Gospel of," ZPEB. 3. Pp. 93f.

29.78 Zahn, T. "Das Hebräerevangelium," Neutest. Kanons. 2.
       Pp. 642-723. [Intro. and Gk. frag.; see also vol. 1, pp.
       776f.]

30. INFANCY, ARABIC GOSPEL OF THE

The greater part of this document is contained in the
Syriac History of the Virgin (cf. Budge, 30.8).

(See also the entries under Mary Cycle; and 1.12, 67, 75, 86, 105,
116, 147, 453, 484; 5.187; 96.73.)

30.1   Alvar, M. Libro de la infancia y muerte de Jesús (Edición
        y estudios: Clásicos Hispánicos 2.8) Madrid, 1965.

30.2   Amann, E. "L'évangile arabe de l'enfance," DBSup. 1.
        Cols. 485f.

30.3   Amiot, F. "Évangile Arabe de l'Enfance," Évangiles Apoc.
        Pp. 93-107. [French trans.]

30.4   Bauer, J.B. Neutest. Apok. Pp. 54f.

30.5   Baumstark, A. "Der Barnabasbrief bei den Syrern," OrChr
        n.s. 2 (1912) 235-40.

30.6   Bonaccorsi, P.G. "Dal 'Vangelo dell' Infanzia,'" Vangeli Apoc-
        rifi. 1. Pp. 232-59. [Lat. text and Italian trans.]

30.7   Bonsirven, J., and C. Bigaré. "Évangiles de l'Enfance,"
        Intro. à la Bible. 2. Pp. 754f.

30.8   Budge, E.A.W. The History of the Blessed Virgin Mary and
        the History of the Likeness of Christ. 2 vols. (Luzac's
        Semitic Text and Translation Series 4, 5) London, 1899;
        repr. New York, 1976. [Syr. text]

30.9   Burmester, K.H.S. "Fragments from an Arabic Version of Two
        Infancy Gospels," SOC 7 (1962) 103-14.

30.10   Cecchelli, C. Mater Christi. Rome, 1954. Vol. 3. Pp. 365-
        70.

30.11   Cosquin, E. "Un épisode d'un évangile syriaque et les contes
        de l'Inde: Le serpent ingrat, l'enfant roi et juge," RB
        28 (1919) 136-57.

30.12   Cowper, B.H. "The Arabic Gospel of the Infancy," Apocry-
        phal Gospels. Pp. 170-216. [ET]

30.13   Cowper, B.H. "The Arabic Gospel of the Infancy," The Great
        Rejected Books of the Biblical Apocrypha (The Sacred Books

and Early Literature of the East 14) New York, London,
1917. Pp. 296-324. [ET]

30.14 Cullmann, O. "Auszüge aus dem arabischen Kindheitsevangelium," HS. 1. Pp. 305f.

30.15 Cullmann, O. "Extracts from the Arabic Infancy Gospel,"
HSW. 1. Pp. 408f. [see also pp. 404f.]

30.16 Cullmann, O. "Story from the Arabic Infancy Gospel and the
Paris Manuscript of the Gospel of Thomas," HSW. 1. Pp.
400f.

30.17 Erbetta, M. "Il Vangelo arabo dell'Infanzia," Apoc. del NT.
1.2. Pp. 102-23.

30.18 Eysinga, G.A. van den Bergh van. Indische Einflüsse auf
evangelische Erzählungen (FRLANT 4) Ruprecht, 1909.

30.19 Fabricius, J.A. "Evangelium Infantiae ex Arabico translatum,"
Cod.Apoc.NT. 1. Pp. 168-212. [Lat. trans.]

30.20 Graf, G. Geschichte der christlichen arabischen Literatur
(Studi i testi 118) Rome, 1944. Vol. 1. Pp. 225-27.

30.21 Hofmann, J.C.K. Das Leben Jesu nach den Apokryphen in
Zusammenhang aus den Quellen Erzählt und wissenschaftlich
Untersucht. Leipzig, 1851. Pp. 144-265.

30.22 Hone, W. The Apocryphal New Testament. London, 1820;
New York, [1845]. Pp. 38-59 [American ed.].

30.23 James, M.R. "The Arabic Gospel of the Infancy," ANT. Pp.
80f.

30.24 Jones, J. A New and Full Method of Settling the Canonical
Authority of the New Testament. 3 vols. London, 1726,
1798². Vol. 2. Pp. 166-261.

30.25 Lafontaine-Dosogne, J. "Le cycle des Mages dans l'Évangile
arabe de l'Enfance du Christ à Florence," Mélanges d'isla-
mologie dédiés à la mémoire de A. Abel. Brussels, 1975.
Vol. 2. Pp. 287-94.

30.26 Lipsius, R.A. "Gospels, Apocryphal," Dictionary of Christian
Biography, eds. W. Smith and H. Wace. 4 vols. London,
1877-87. Vol. 2. Pp. 705f.

30.27 Messina, G. I magi a Betlemme e una predizione di Zoroastro.
Rome, 1933.

30.28   Migne, J.-P.   "Enfance. (Évangile de l'Enfance.)," Diction-
        naire. 1. Cols. 973-1008. [Intro. and French trans.]

30.29   Monneret de Villard, U. Le Leggende orientali sui magi evan-
        gelici (Studi e Testi 163) Rome, 1952.

30.30   Moraldi, L. "Vangelo arabo sull' infanzia del Salvatore,"
        Apoc. del NT. 1. Pp. 281-311.

30.31   Nola, A.M. di. Evangelo arabo dell' Infanzia. Parma, 1963.

30.32   Nola, A.M. di. Vangeli Apocrifi: Natività e Infanzia (Biblio-
        teca della Venice 10) Milan, 1977.

30.33   Peeters, P. "A propos de l'Évangile arabe de l'enfance. Le
        manuscrit de J. Golius," AnBoll 41 (1923) 132-34.

30.34   Peeters, P. "Le livre des miracles de notre-Seigneur, Maître
        et Sauveur Jésus-Christ," EvApoc. 2. Pp. i-xxix, 1-65.

30.35   Provera, M.E. Il Vangelo arabo dell' infanzia secondo il ms.
        Laurenziano orientale (n. 387) (Quaderni de La Terra Santa)
        Jerusalem, 1973.

30.36   Santos Otero, A. de. "Evangelio Arabe de la Infancia," Evan-
        gelios Apócrifos. Pp. 307-38. [Spanish trans.]

30.37   Schade, O. Narrationes de vita et conversatione B.M. Virginis
        et de pueritia et adolescentia Salvatoris. Halle, 1870.

30.38   Sike, H. Evangelium infantiae vel liber apocryphus de Infan-
        tia Salvatoris: Ex manuscripto edidit ac Latina versione et
        notis illustravit. Traiceti ad Rhenum, 1967.

30.39   Thilo, J.C. Codex Apocryphus Novi Testamenti. Leipzig,
        1832. Vol. 1. Pp. 63-158, XXVI-XLIV.

30.40   Tischendorf, C. "Evangelium infantiae. Ex arabico latine,"
        Evangelia Apocrypha. Pp. xlviii-liii, 181-209.

30.41   Variot, J. "L'Évangile arabe de l'Enfance," Évangiles Apocry-
        phes. Pp. 64-82.

30.42   Vitti, A.M. "Sancta Familia in Aegypto ubinam iuxta apocry-
        pha constiterit," VD 9 (1929) 3-13.

30.43   Waite, C.B. History of the Christian Religion. Chicago,
        1881. Pp. 147-76.

30.44   Walker, A. "The Arabic Gospel of the Infancy of the Saviour,"
        ANF 8. Pp. 405-15. [ET]

31. INFANCY, ARMENIAN GOSPEL OF THE

(See also the listings under Mary Cycle; and 1.12, 67, 75, 86, 105, 116, 147, 484; 5.187; 35.33; 96.73.)

31.1   Amiot, F. "Livre Arménien de l'Enfance," Évangiles Apoc. Pp. 81-93.

31.2   Bonsirven, J., and C. Bigaré, "Évangiles de L'enfance," Intro. à la Bible. 2. Pp. 754f.

31.3   Craveri, M. I Vangeli Apocrifi a curi di M. Craveri. Turin, 1969. Pp. 149ff.*

31.4   Cullmann, O. "Jüngere Kindheitsevangelien," HS. 1. P. 303.

31.5   Cullmann, O. "Later Infancy Gospels," HSW. 1. P. 405.

31.6   Erbetta, M. "Il Vangelo dell'Infanzia armeno," Apoc. del NT. 1.2. Pp. 124-85.

31.7   González-Blanco, E. Evangelios Apócrifos. Madrid, 1935. Vol. 2. Pp. 88-236.

31.8   James, M.R. "The Armenian Gospel of the Infancy," ANT. Pp. 83f.

31.9   Macler, F. Une "Nativité" (?) arméno-persane. Paris, 1925.

31.10 Moraldi, L. "Natività di Maria (Versione armena incompleta)," Apoc.del NT. 1. Pp. 89-94.

31.11 Peeters, P. "Le livre Arménien de l'enfance," EvApoc. 2. Pp. xxix-lvi, 67-286.

31.12 Santos Otero, A. de. "Evangelio Armenio de la Infancia." Evangelios Apócrifos. Pp. 359-65.

31.13 Tayec'i, E. Ankanon girkh nor Ketakaranatz. 2 vols. Venice, 1898-1904. [Arm. text]

32. INFANCY, LATIN GOSPEL OF THE

This work is a late compilation found in the Hereford MS and Arundel 404 MS, and is based on PsMt and ProtJas-- see the listings under those categories.

(See also 1.12, 53, 67, 75, 86, 105, 116, 147, 484; 96.73.)

32.1   Bonaccorsi, P.G. "Dal Vangelo Dell' Infanzia," Vangeli Apoc-
       rifi. 1. Pp. 232-59.

32.2   Bonsirven, J., and C. Bigaré. "Évangiles de l'Enfance,"
       Intro. à la Bible. 2. Pp. 754f.

32.3   Cartlidge, D.R., and D.L. Dungan. "The Birth of Jesus,"
       Documents. Pp. 104-06. [ET of the Arundel MS]

32.4   Cullmann, O. "Auszug aus dem lateinischen Kindheitsevan-
       gelium der Arundel-HS.," HS. 1. Pp. 309f. [see also p.
       304]

32.5   Cullmann, O. "Extract from the Latin Infancy Gospel in the
       Arundel Manuscript," HSW. 1. Pp. 431f. [see also pp.
       406f.]

32.6   Erbetta, M. "Liber de Infantia Salvatoris (Arundel 404-
       Hereford 0.3.9)," Apoc. del NT. 1.2. Pp. 206-17.

32.7   Ferri, S. "Nota al testo latino dell' 'Evangelium infantiae,'"
       Studi Mediolatini e Volgari 1 (1953) 119-25.

32.8   Gijsel, J. "Les 'Évangiles Latins de l'Enfance' de M.R. James:
       Manuscrits et Sources," AnBoll 94 (1976) 289-302.

32.9   James, M.R. Latin Infancy Gospels: A New Text with a
       Parallel Version from Irish. Cambridge, 1927.

32.10 James, M.R. "The New Infancy Gospel," Nation and Athenaeum
       (23 Oct. 1926) 110f., 377f.

32.11 James, M.R. "A New Piece of an Old Gospel?" Empire Review
       44 (1926) 318-25.

32.12 Kehl, A. "Der Stern der Magier," JAC 18 (1975) 69-80.

32.13 Lagrange, M.-J. "Un nouvel Évangile de l'Enfance édité par
       M. R. James," RB 37 (1928) 544-57.

32.14 Marsh-Edwards, J.C. "The Magi in Tradition and Art," IER
       85 (1956) 1-9.

32.15 Moraldi, L. "Dell'infanzia del Salvatore," Apoc. del NT. 1.
       Pp. 105-93.

32.16 Reinsch, R. Die Pseudo-Evangelien von Jesu und Maria's
       Kindheit in der roman. und german. Literatur. Halle, 1879.

32.17 Robinson, J.A. "M. R. James' 'Latin Infancy Gospels,'" JTS
       29 (1928) 205-07.

32.18 Santos Otero, A de. "Extractos del 'Liber de Infantia Salva-
       toris,'" Evangelios Apócrifos. Pp. 259-75. [Lat. text of
       Cod. Arundel 404 in BM and Spanish trans.]

32.19 Schade, O. Narrationes de vita et conversatione Beatae Ma-
       riae Virginis et de pueritia et adolescentia Salvatoris. Halle,
       1870.

              33. JAMES (THE GREATER), ACTS OF

(See also 1.202, 346; 3.78; 7.5, 14, 27.)

33.1   Berkey, M.L., Jr. "The Liber S. Jacobi...." Romania 76
       (1965) 77-103.*

33.2   Cuénod, J. "Jésus chez Zébédée," Revue Archéologique 13
       (1909) 120-22.

33.3   David, P. Études sur le Livre de Saint-Jacques attribué au
       pape Calixte II (Extrait du Bulletin des Études Portugaises
       10-13) Lisbon, 1946-49.

33.4   Diaz y Diaz, M.C. "Die spanische Jakobus-Legenda bei Isidor
       v. Sevilla," Historisches Jahrbuch 77 (1958) 467-72.

33.5   Ebersolt, J. Les Actes de Saint Jacques et les Actes d'Aquilas
       publiés d'après deux manuscrits grecs de la bibliothèque na-
       tionale. Paris, 1902.

33.6   Erbetta, M. "Gli Atti etiopici di Giacomo il Maggiore," Apoc.
       del NT. 2. Pp. 541-48.

33.7   Harnack, A. "Jacobus," Gesch. altchrist. Lit. 1. Pp. 905f.

33.8   James, M.R. ANT. P. 470.

33.8a Lipsius, R.A. Die apokryphen Apostelgeschichten und Apos-
       tellegenden. 2 vols. Brunswick, 1883-1890; repr. Amster-
       dam, 1976. Vol. 2.2. Pp. 201-28. [see also pp. 229-57)

33.9   Schmidt, C. "Acten des Jacobus," Gesch. altchrist. Lit. 1.
       P. 921.

33.10 Stegmüller, F. Repertorium Biblicum. 1. Pp. 185f; 8. Pp.
       166f.

33.11 Whitehill, W.M. <u>Liber Sancti Jacobi: Codex Calixtinus</u>. San-
       tiago, 1944.

34. JAMES (THE GREATER), ASCENT OF

34.1   James, M.R. "Ascents of James," <u>ANT</u>. Pp. 20f.

34.2   Santos Otero, A. de. "Ascensión de Santiago," <u>Evangelios
       Apócrifos</u>. Pp. 72f. [Gk. text from Epiphanius, <u>Adv.
       haer</u>. 26.2, 26.3 and 30.16]

34.3   Stegmüller, F. <u>Repertorium Biblicum</u>. 1. P. 116; 8. P. 89.

34.4   Wilson, R.McL. "James, Ascents of," <u>ZPEB</u>. 3. P. 396.

35. JAMES, PROTEVANGELIUM OF

This work is titled "The Birth of Mary" in the oldest
witnesses, but is not identical to the lost BirMar referred
to by Epiphanius (<u>Panarion</u> 26.12).

(See also the listings under Mary Cycle; and 1.12, 18, 53, 67, 75,
86, 88, 116, 213, 237, 284, 307, 324, 470, 484, 548; 44.13;
53.15; 96.73.)

35.1   Aldama, J.A. de. "Fragmentos de una versión latina del Pro-
       toevangelio de Santiago y una nueva adaptación de sus pri-
       meros capitulos," <u>Bib</u> 43 (1962) 57-74.

35.2   Aldama, J.A. de. "Un nuevo testigo indirecto del Protoevan-
       gelio de Santiago," <u>Studia Patristica</u> 12 (1975) 79-82.

35.3   Aldama, J.A. "Polyplousios dans le Protévangile de Jacques
       et l'Adversus haereses d'Irénée," <u>RSR</u> 50 (1962) 86-89.

35.4   Aldama, J.A. "El Protoevangelio de Santiago y sus problemas,"
       <u>EphMar</u> 12 (1962) 107-30.

35.5   Amann, É. "Le Protévangile de Jacques et ses remaniements,"
       <u>DBSup</u>. 1. Cols. 482f.

35.6   Amann, É., ed. <u>Le Protévangile de Jacques et ses remanie-
       ments latins: Introduction, textes, traduction et commentaire</u>.
       Paris, 1910. [see M.R. James' review <u>JTS</u> 12 (1911) 624-26]

35.7   Ambroggi, P. de., "Protovangelo di Giacomo," EncCatt. 6.
        Cols. 321f.

35.8   Amiot, F. "Le Protévangile de Jacques," Évangiles Apoc. Pp.
        47-64. [French trans.]

35.9   [Archeografičeskaja Kommissija], Daily Readings of the Great
        'Menaea' (Sept. 1-13, 1868) cols. 278-81; 352-63; (Dec. 25-
        31, 1912) cols. 2279-85. [in Russian]

35.10   Baldi, D. L'infanzia del Salvatore. Rome, 1925.

35.11   Bardenhewer, O. "Das Protevangelium Jacobi," GAL. 1.
        Pp. 533-37.

35.12   Bauer, J.B. Neutest. Apok. Pp. 47-52.

35.13   Berendts, A. Die handschriftliche Überlieferung der Zacharias-
        und Johannes-Apokryphen (TU N.F. 11 [=26].3) Leipzig,
        1904. Pp. 1-63.

35.14   Berendts, A. Studien über Zacharias-Apokryphen und
        Zacharias-Legenden. Leipzig, 1895. Pp. 71-80.

35.15   Birch, A. Auctarium codicis apocryphi N.T. Fabriciani. Co-
        penhagen, 1804. Vol. 1. Pp. 197-242. [Gk. text]

35.16   Birdsall, J.N. "A Second Georgian Recension of the Protevan-
        gelium Jacobi," Muséon 83 (1970) 49-72.

35.17   Bonaccorsi, P.G. "Il Protovangelo di Giacomo," Vangeli Apoc-
        rifi. 1. Pp. 58-109. [Gk. text and Italian trans.]

35.18   Bonsirven, J., and C. Bigaré. "Protévangile de Jacques,"
        Intro. à la Bible. 2. Pp. 751f.

35.19   Bonwetsch, N. "Protevangelium Jakobi," Gesch. altchrist. Lit.
        Pp. 909f.

35.20   Borberg, K.F. Bibliothek der neutestamentlichen Apokryphen
        gesammelt, übersetzt und erläutert. Stuttgart, 1841.

35.21   Bornhäuser, K. Die Geburts- und Kindheitsgeschichte Jesu.
        Leipzig, 1930.

35.22   Boslooper, T. "Jesus' Virgin Birth and Non-Christian 'Paral-
        lels,'" Religion and Life 26 (1955-57) 87-97.

35.23   Brown, R.E. "Protevangelium of James," JBC. P. 546.

35.24   Budge, E.A.W. The History of the Blessed Virgin Mary and

the History of the Likeness of Christ (Luzac's Semitic Text
and Translation Series 4, 5) London, 1899; repr. New York,
1976. [Syr. text]

35.25   Canal-Sánchez, J.M. "El libro apócrifo 'Nacimiento de Maria'
        del Pseudo-Yago en la Iglesia latina hasta el año 1000: Citas,
        versiones influjo en algunas pinturas y mosaicos," De pri-
        mordiis cultus mariani. Rome, 1970. Vol. 4. Pp. 295-326.

35.26   Canal-Sánchez, J.M. "Antiguas versiones latinas del Proto-
        evangelio de Santiago," EphMar 18 (1968) 431-73.

35.27   Cartlidge, D.R. and D.L. Dungan, "The Gospel of James,"
        Documents. Pp. 107-17. [ET]

35.28   Cecchelli, C. Mater Christi. Rome, 1954. Vol. 3. Pp. 303-
        30.

35.29   Chaine, M. Apocrypha de Beata Maria Virgine (CSCO 39-40;
        Scriptores Aethiopici 22-23) Louvain, 1955. Vol. 39 (22).
        Pp. 1-19; Vol. 40 (23). Pp. 1-16. [Eth. and Lat. texts]

35.30   Clemens, R. Die geheimgehaltenen oder sogenannten apokry-
        phen Evangelien. Stuttgart, 1850. Vol. 2. Pp. 5-88.

35.31   Conrady, L. "Das Protevangelium Jakob in neuer Beleuchti-
        gung," TSK 62 (1889) 728-84.

35.32   Conrady, L. Die Quelle der kanonischen Kindheitsgeschichten
        Jesus. Göttingen, 1900.

35.33   Conybeare, F.C. "Protevangelium Jacobi (From an Armenian
        Manuscript in the Library of the Mechitarists in Venice),"
        AJT 1 (1897) 424-42.

35.34   Cothenet, É. "Jacques (Protévangile de)," Catholicisme 6.23
        (1963) 259-62.

35.35   Cothenet, É. "Protévangile de Jacques," DBSup. 8. Cols.
        1374-84.

35.36   Cothenet, É. "Le Protévangile de Jacques: Origine, genre
        et signification d'un midrash chrétien sur la Nativité de
        Marie," ANRW 2.25.4 (in preparation).

35.37   Cowper, B.H. "The Gospel of James (Commonly Called the
        Protevangelium.)," Apocryphal Gospels. Pp. 1-26. [ET]

35.38   Cowper, B.H. "The Protevangelium or Gospel of James,"
        The Great Rejected Books of the Biblical Apocrypha (The
        Sacred Books and Early Literature of the East 14) New
        York, London, 1917. Pp. 238-52. [ET]

35.39 Cullmann, O. "Protevangelium des Jakobus," HS. 1. Pp.
277-90.

35.40 Cullmann, O. "The Protevangelium of James," HSW. 1. Pp.
370-88.

35.41 Demina, E.I. The Tichonravov Collection. 2 vols. Sofia,
1968, 1971. Vol. 1. Pp. 102-04; Vol. 2. Pp. 151-55.
[in Russian]

35.42 Ehrhard, A. Uberlieferung und Bestand der Hagiographischen
und Homiletischen Literatur der Griechischen Kirche von den
Anfängen bis zum Ende des 16. Jahrhunderts I (TU 50.1)
Leipzig, 1937. Pp. 57-69.

35.43 Emmi, B. "Tentativo d'interpretazione del dialogo tra Anna e
la serva nel Protovangelo di Giacomo," Studia Patristica 7
(1966) 184-93.

35.44 Enslin, M.S. "The Christian Stories of Nativity," JBL 59
(1940) 317-38.

35.45 Erbetta, M. "Il Protoevangelo di Giacomo," Apoc. del NT.
1.2. Pp. 7-43.

35.46 Erdmann, G. Die Vorgeschichten des Lukas und Matthäus-
Evangeliums. Berlin, 1932.

35.47 Fabricius, J.A. "Protevangelium Jacobi," Cod.Apoc.NT. 1.
Pp. 39-126. [Gk. text and Lat. trans.]

35.48 Fabricius, J.A. "S. Jacobi Minoris Protevangelium," Cod.Apoc.
NT. 1. Pp. 351f.

35.49 Ferri, S. "Nota sul testo latino dell' Evangelium Infantiae,"
Studi mediolatini e volgari 1 (1953) 119-25.

35.50 Feuillet, A. "Der Sieg der Frau nach dem Protoevangelium,"
Internationale Katholische Zeitschrift 7 (1978) 26-35.

35.51 Findlay, A.F. "Childhood Gospels," Byways. Pp. 148-70.

35.52 Franko, I. Apocrypha and Legends. L'vov, 1898. Vol. 2.
Pp. 36-59, 146-49, 153-59. [in Russian]

35.53 Fuchs, A. Konkordanz zum Protoevangelium des Jakobus
(SNTU 3) Linz, 1978.

35.54 Gaiffier, B. de. "Les sources de la passion de S. Eutrope de
Saintes dans le Liber Sancti Jacobi," AnBoll 69 (1951) 57-66.

35.55- Garitte, G. "Le 'Protévangile de Jacques' en géorgien,"
56   Muséon 70 (1957) 57-73, 233-65.

35.57 Garitte, G. "'Protevangelii Iacobi' versio arabica antiquior,"
      Muséon 86 (1973) 377-96.

35.58 Gijsel, J. "Het Protevangelium Iacobi in het Latijn," Anti-
      quité classique 50 (1981) 351-66.

35.59 Gjaurov, C. "Protevangelium of James," Godišnik na Sofijskija
      Universitet-Bogosl. Fak. 7 (1930) 125-401. [in Russian].

35.60 Graf, G. Geschichte der christlichen arabischen Literatur
      (Studi e Testi 118) Rome, 1944. Vol. 1. Pp. 224f.

35.61 Grenfell, B.P. An Alexandrian Erotic Fragment and Other
      Greek Papyri, Chiefly Ptolemaic. Oxford, 1896. Pp. 13-19.

35.62 Gribomont, J. "Couleur textuelle des Extraits Bibliques,"
      AnBoll 83 (1965) 402-10.

35.63 Grynaeus, J.J. Monumenta SS. Patrum Orthodoxographa.
      Basil, 1568. [Gk. text]

35.64 Harnack, A. "Das Buch des Jakobus (Proevang. Jacobi),"
      Gesch. altchrist. Lit. 1. Pp. 19-21.

35.65 Harnack, A. "Das Protevangelium des Jakobus," Gesch. alt-
      christ. Lit. 2.1. Pp. 598-603.

35.66 Heroldus, J. Orthodoxographa. Leipzig, 1555.

35.67 Istrin, V.M. On the Question About the Slavo-Russian Red-
      actions of the First Gospel of James. Odessa, 1900. [in
      Russian]

35.68 Jacimirskij, A.I. "Apocrypha and Legends ... IV," IzvORJS
      14.2 (1909) 294-311. [in Russian]

35.69 Jagić, V. "Analecta romana," Archiv für Slavische Philologie
      25 (1903) 36-47.

35.70 Jagić, V. "Critical Notes ...," IzvORJS 3.2 (1898) 315-38.
      [in Russian]

35.71 James, M.R. "Book of James, or Protevangelium," ANT. Pp.
      38-49.

35.72 Jones, J. A New and Full Method of Settling the Canonical
      Authority of the New Testament. 3 vols. London, 1726,
      1798[2]. [vol. 2 contains the Gk. text of ProtJas]

35.73 Kispaugh, M.J. The Feast of the Presentation of the Virgin
       Mary in the Temple: An Historical and Literary Study.
       Washington, 1941.

35.74 Klawek, A. "Das Motiv der Unbeweglichkeit der Natur im
       Protevangelium Iacobi," Collectanea Theologica 17 (1936)
       327-38.

35.75 Lavrov, P.A. "Apocryphal Texts ...," SbORJS 67 (1899) 52-
       69. [in Russian]

35.76 Lavrov, P.A. "Ochrid Manuscript of the First Gospel of James,"
       IzvORJS 6.1 (1901) 9-36. [in Russian]

35.77 Leclercq, H. "Apocryphes," DACL. 1. Cols. 2555-79.

35.78 Lehner, F.A. von. Die Marienverehrung in den ersten Jahr-
       hunderten. Stuttgart, 1886. Pp. 223-36.

35.79 Leipoldt, I. "Ein sahidisches Bruchstück des Jakobus-
       Protevangeliums," ZNW 6 (1905) 106f.

35.80 Lemme, L. Das Jakobus-Evangelium (Zeit-und Streitfragen
       des Glaubens 13, 11.12) Berlin-Lichterfelde, 1920.

35.81 Lewis, A.S. Apocrypha Syriaca: The Protoevangelium Iacobi
       and Transitus Mariae (Studia Sinaitica 11) Cambridge, 1902.

35.82 Lorber, J. Die Jugend Jesu: Das Jakobus-Evangelium vom
       Vater des Lichts auf neue kundgegeben. Bietigheim, 1936.

35.83 Lowe, M. "'Ioudaioi' of the Apocrypha: A Fresh Approach
       to the Gospels of James, Pseudo-Thomas, Peter and Nico-
       demus," NovT 23 (1981) 56-90.

35.84 Lützelberger, E.J. Das Protevangelium Jacobi, zwei Evan-
       gelien der Kindheit Jesu und die Akten des Pilatus. Nurem-
       berg, 1842.

35.85 Mehlmann, J. "Protoevangelium Jacobi, c. 21.2, in Liturgia
       citatum," VD 39 (1961) 50f.

35.86 Meyer, A. "Protevangelium des Jakobus," H². Pp. 84-93.

35.87 Meyer, A. "Protevangelium des Jakobus," Handbuch, ed.
       Hennecke. Pp. 106-31.

35.88 Michaelis, W. "Protevangelium des Jakobus," Apokryphen
       Schriften. Pp. 62-95.

35.89 Michel, C. "Protévangile de Jacques," EvApoc. 1. Pp. i-
       xviii, 1-51.

35.90   Migne, J.-P. "Jacques. (Protévangile de Saint Jacques le
        Mineur.)," Dictionnaire. 1. Cols. 1009-28. [Intro. and
        French trans.]

35.91   Mínguez Niño, F. El tema de la gruta según el Proto-evangelio
        de Santiago (Dis. lic. Studii Biblici Franciscani) Jerusalem,
        1972.

35.92   Moraldi, L. "Natività di Maria (o Protovangelo di Giacomo),"
        Apoc. del NT. 1. Pp. 61-87.

35.93   Müller, J.J. "Die Oer-evangelie van Jakobus," Nuwe-Test.
        Apok. Pp. 1-12. [Afrikaans trans.]

35.94   Neander, M. Apocrypha ... inserto etiam Protevangelio Jacobi
        Graece. Basel, 1564, 1567^2. [Gk. text and Lat. trans.]

35.95   Nestle, E. "Ein syrisches Bruchstück aus dem Protevangelium
        Iacobi," ZNW 3 (1902) 86f.

35.96   Nicola, A.M. di. Protevangelo di Giacomo. La natività di
        Maria. Parma, 1966.

35.97   Nola, A.M. di. Vangeli Apocrifi: Natività e Infanzia. (Bib-
        lioteca della Venice 10) Milan, 1977.

35.98   Novaković, S. "The Apocryphal Proto-Gospel of James,"
        Starine 10 (1878) 61-71. [in Russian]

35.99   Peretto, L.M. "Criteri d'impiego di alcune citazioni bibliche
        nel 'Protovangelo di Giacomo,'" De primordiis cultus mariani.
        Rome, 1970. Vol. 4. Pp. 273-93.

35.100 Peretto, L.M. "Espressioni del 'Protovangelo di Giacomo' nella
        eortologia mariana bizantina," De cultu Mariano saec. VI-XI,
        ed. C. Balić. Rome, 1972. Vol. 4. Pp. 65-80.

35.101 Peretto, L.M. "Influsso del Protovangelo di Giacomo nei secoli
        II-IV," Marianum 19 (1957) 59-78.

35.102 Peretto, L.M. La mariologia del Protovangelo di Giacomo.
        Rome, 1955.

35.103 Peretto, L.M. "Recenti ricerche sul Protoevangelo di Giacomo,"
        Marianum 24 (1962) 129-57.

35.104 Peretto, L.M. "Testi sacri nel Protovangelo di Giacomo,"
        RBSL 3 (1955) 174-78, 235-56.

35.105 Peretto, L.M. "La Vergine Maria nel pensiero di uno scrittore
        del secondo secolo (La mariologia del Protevangelo di Giacomo),"
        Marianum 16 (1954) 228-65.

35.106 Perler, O. "Das Protevangelium Jacobi nach dem PBodmer V," Freiburger Zeitschrift für Philosophie und Theologie 6 (1959) 23-25.

35.107 Peterson, H. Die Wunderbare Geburt des Heilands. Tübingen, 1909.

35.108 Pistelli, E. "Protevangelium Iacobi," Pubblicazioni della Società Italiana per la ricerca dei papiri. Florence, 1912. Vol. 1. Pp. 9-15.

35.109 Pistelli, E. Il Protevangelo di Jacopo: Prima Traduzione italiana con introduzione e note. Segue un appendice dallo Pseudo-Matteo. Lanciano, 1919.

35.110 Popov, A.N. "Bibliographical Materials ... 20," ČOIDR (1889) 7-24. [in Russian]*

35.111 Porfiryev, I.Y. "Apocryphal Sayings About New Testament People and Events in Manuscripts of the Solovetski Library," SbORJS 52 (1890) 10-13, 136-48. [in Russian]

35.112 Postel, S.I. Protevangelion. Basil, 1552.

35.113 Pypin, A.N. False and Dismissed Books of Ancient Russia. St. Petersburg, 1862. Pp. 78-80. [in Russian; Slav. text]

35.114 Quasten, J. "The Protoevangelium of James," Patrology. 1. Pp. 118-22.

35.115 Quecque, H. "Lk 1,34 in den alten Übersetzungen und im Protevangelium des Jakobus," Bib 44 (1963) 499-520.

35.116 Radovich, N. Un frammento slavo del Protovangelo di Giacomo (Biblioteca Enrico Damiani 2) Naples, 1968.

35.117 Rauschen, G. "Ex Protevangelio Iacobi capita selecta," Florilegium Patristicum. Bonn, 1905. Vol. 3. Pp. 59-68. [Gk. and Lat. texts]

35.118 Repp, F. "Untersuchungen zur alttschechischen Marienlegende," ZSlaw 4 (1959) 321-33.

35.119 Resch, A. Das Kindheitsevangelium nach Lukas und Matthäus. Leipzig, 1897.

35.120 Revillout, E. "Un nouvel apocryphe copte, le Livre de Jacques," JA 6 (1905) 113-20.

35.121 Robinson, F. Coptic apocryphal Gospels (T&S 4/2) Cambridge, 1896. [frag. Sahidic text and ET]

35.122 Roschini, G.M. "I fondamenti dogmatici del culto mariano nel 'Protovangelo di Giacomo,'" De primordiis cultus mariani. Rome, 1970. Vol. 4. Pp. 253-71.

35.123 Rotunno, C., and E. Bartoletti. Il Protoevangelio di Giacomo. Venice, 1950.

35.124 Santos Otero, A. de. "Protoevangelio de Santiago," Evangelios Apócrifos. Pp. 126-76. [Gk. text and Spanish trans.]

35.125 Santos Otero, A. de. "Protevangelium Jacobi," Altslavischen Apok. 2. Pp. 1-32.

35.126 Scheffczyk, L. Das Mariengeheimnis in Frömmigkeit und Lehre der Karolingerzeit. Leipzig, 1959.

35.127 Schoene, A. Eusebii Chronicon liber prior. Berolini, 1875. [see Appendix, pp. 177-239]

35.128 Schöne, H. "Palimpsestblätter des Protevangelium Iacobi in Cesena," Beiträge zur Geschichte der Wissenschaft, Kunst und Literatur in Westfalen, Alois Bömer zum 60 Geburtstag eds. H. Degering and W. Menn. Leipzig, 1928. Pp. 263-76.

35.129 Schonfield, H.J. The Lost Book of the Nativity of John. Edinburgh, 1930. [S. attempts to show that ProtJas is a source for the "Book of the Nativity of John"]

35.130 Smereka, W. "The Oldest Legend About the Mother of God," RuBi 16 (1963) 29-36. [in Polish]

35.131 Smid, H.R. Protevangelium Jacobi: A Commentary, trans. G.E. van Baaren-Pape (Apocrypha Novi Testamenti 1) Assen, 1965.

35.132 Speranskij, M.N. The History of Ancient Russian Literature. Moscow, 1920. Vol. 1. P. 260. [in Russian]

35.133 Speranskij, M.N. "Slavic Apocryphal Gospels," The Work of the Eighth Archaeological Conference in Moscow 1890. Moscow, 1895. Vol. 2. Pp. 56-73, 156-60. [in Russian]

35.134 Speranskij, M.N. "Variations on the First Gospel of James," ČOIDR (1889) I-XIV. [in Russian]*

35.135 Štefanič, V., et al. Croatian Literature. Zagreb, 1969. Pp. 142-45. [in Serbo-Croatian]

35.136 Stegmüller, F. Repertorium Biblicum. 1. Pp. 112-16; 8. Pp. 84-88.

35.137 Stempvoort, P.A. van. "De bronnen van het thema en de
stijl van het Protevangelium en de datering daarvan,"
NedThT 16 (1961) 18-34.

35.138 Stempvoort, P.A. van. "The Protevangelium Jacobi: The
Sources of its Theme and Style and Their Bearing on its
Date," Studia Evangelica. Vol. 3: Papers Presented to the
Second International Congress on New Testament Studies
Held at Christ Church, Oxford, 1961. Part 2: The Mes-
sage of the New Testament, ed. F.L. Cross (TU 88) Berlin,
1964. Pp. 410-26.

35.139 Strohal, R. Old Croatian Apocryphal Tales and Legends, Col-
lected from Old Croatian Glagolithic Manuscripts from the
Fourteenth to the Eighteenth Centuries. Bjelovar, 1917.
Pp. 6-11. [in Serbo-Croatian]

35.140 Strycker, É. de. La forme la plus ancienne du Protévangile
de Jacques: Recherches sur le PBodmer 5 avec une édition
critique du texte grec et une traduction annotée (Subsidia
hagiographie 33) Brussels, 1961.

35.141 Strycker, É. de. De griekse handschriften van het Protevan-
gelie van Jacobus: De Protevangelii Iacobi codicibus graecis.
Brussels, 1968.

35.142 Strycker, É. de. "Une métaphrase inédite du Protévangile
de Jacques," OLP 65 (1975) 163-84.

35.143 Strycker, E. de. "Le Protévangile de Jacques: Problèmes
critiques et exégétiques," Studia Evangelia. Vol. 3: Papers
Presented to the Second International Congress on New Testament Studies Held at Christ Church, Oxford, 1961. Part
2: The New Testament Message, ed. F.L. Cross (TU 88)
Berlin, 1964. Pp. 339-59.

35.144 Strycker, É. de. "Une version latine du Protévangile de
Jacques, avec des extraits de la Vulgate de Matthieu 1-2
et Luc 1-2," AnBoll 83 (1965) 365-410.

35.145 Strycker, É. de, and D. Harflinger. "Die griechischen Handschriften des Protevangeliums Jacobi," Griechische Kodiko-
logie und Textüberlieferung. Ein Sammelband. Darmstadt,
1980. Pp. 577-612.

35.146 Suckow, C.A. Protevangelium Jacobi ex codice ms. Venetiano
descripsit, prolegomenis, varietate lectionum, notis criticis
instructum edidit. Breslau, 1841. [Gk. text]

35.147 Sumcov, N.F. "Essays on the History of South Russian

228   IV. Bibliography

Apocryphal Sayings and Songs," Kievskaja Starina 19 (1887)
1-21. [in Russian]

35.148 Tayec'i, E. Ankanon girkh nor Ketakaranatz. 2 vols. Venice,
1898-1904. Pp. 237-50.* [Arm. text]

35.149 Thilo, C. Codex apocryphus Novi Testamenti. Leipzig, 1832.
Vol. 1. Pp. 159-273.

35.150 Tischendorf, K. "Protevangelium Iacobi," Evangelia Apocrypha.
Pp. xii-xxii, 1-50. [Gk. text]

35.151 Tischendorf, K. "Syriaca fragmenta protevangelii (capp.
XVII-XXV) e codice sexti saeculi," Apocalypses Apocryphae.
Pp. LI-LIII.

35.152 Vannutelli, P. Protoevangelium Iacobi synoptice. Rome, 1940.

35.153 Vannutelli, P. "Protoevangelium Iacobi synoptice," Synoptica
4 (1939) 1-64; 5 (1940) 65-96.

35.154 Variot, J. "Le Protévangile de Jacques," Évangiles Apocryphes. Pp. 37-43, 141-96.

35.155 Vattioni, F. "Frammento latino del Vangelo di Giacomo," Aug
17 (1977) 505-09.

35.156 Vetter, P. Literarische Rundschau (1901) 258f.*

35.157 Vranska, C. The Apocrypha Concerning the Virgin Mother
in the Bulgarian Folk Song (Collection of the Bulgarian
Academy of Sciences 34) Sofia, 1940. Pp. 30-36. [in Bul-
garian]

35.158 Walker, A. "The Protevangelium of James," ANF 8. Pp. 361-
67. [ET]

35.159 Wilson, R.McL. "James, Protevangelium of," ZPEB. 3. Pp.
401-03.

35.160 Wright, W. "The Protevangelium Jacobi," ALNT. Pp. D-Z,
1-5, 53-55. [Syr. text and ET]

35.161 Zahn, T. "Retractationes 4," NKZ 13 (1902) 19-22.

35.162 Zahn, T. "Das sogenannte Protevangelium des Jakobus,"
Neutest. Kanons. 2. Pp. 774-80. [see also vol. 1, pp.
914f.]

36.   JOHN, ACTS OF; AND JOHN CYCLE

(See also 1.88, 204, 254, 284, 346, 531, 548; 3.37, 40, 63, 77; 7.7,
     14.)

36.1   Amann, É. "Les Actes de Jean," DBSup. 1. Cols. 491-94.

36.2   Amiot, F. "Actes de Jean," Évangiles Apoc. Pp. 157-84.
        [French trans.]

36.3   [Archeografičeskaja Kommissija], Daily Readings of the Great
        'Menaea' 25 (Sept. 30, 1883). Cols. 1584-1660. [in Russian]

36.4   Bardenhewer, O. "Die Akten des Johannes," GAL. 1. Pp.
        574-79.

36.5   Bauer, J.B. "Die Johannesakten," Neutest. Apok. Pp. 60-64.

36.6   Beyschlag, K. Die verborgene Überlieferung von Christus.
        Munich, Hamburg, 1969. [see esp. pp. 88-116]

36.7   Bonnet, M., ed. "Acta Ioannis," AAA. 2.1. Pp. XXVI-
        XXXIII, 151-216. [Intro. and Gk. text]

36.8   Bonsirven, J., and C. Bigaré, "Actes de Jean," Intro. à la
        Bible. 2. P. 758.

36.9   Brekenridge, J.D. "Apocrypha of Early Christian Portraiture,"
        ByZ 67 (1974) 101-09.

36.10   Brioso y Candiani, M. "Sobre el 'Tanzhymnus' de Acta Johan-
        nis 94-6," Emérita 40 (1972) 31-45.

36.11   Brunklaus, F.A. De Joannes legende. Maastricht, 1969.

36.12   Bruyne, D. de. "Nouveaux fragments des Actes de Pierre,
        de Paul, de Jean, d'André, et de l'Apocalypse d'Elie,"
        RBen 25 (1908) 149-60.

36.13   Budge, E.A.W. "The Repose of Saint John the Evangelist and
        Apostle," Coptic Apoc. Pp. 51-58; 233-40.

36.14   Corsaro, F. Le Praxeis di Giovanni. Catania, 1968.

36.15   Corssen, P. Monarchianische Prologe zu den vier Evangelien:
        Ein Beitrag zur Geschichte des Kanons (TU 15.1) Leipzig,
        1896.

36.16   Crum, W.E. Catalogue of the Coptic Manuscripts in the British
        Museum London, 1905. P. 130. [Coptic frag. of AcJn]

36.17   Deeleman, C.F.M., "Acta Johannis," Geloof en Vrijheid 46
        (1912) 22ff., 123ff.*

36.18   Erbetta, M. "Gli Atti di Giovanni," Apoc. del NT. 2. Pp.
        29-67.

36.19   Esbroeck, M. van. "Les formes géorgiennes des Acta Iohannis,"
        AnBoll 93 (1975) 5-19.

36.20   Fabricius, J.A. "Acta Johannis," Cod.Apoc. NT. 2. Pp.
        765-67.

36.21   Fabricius, J.A. "Mellitus (a) de Passione Johannis Evangelis-
        tae," Cod.Apoc.NT. 2. Pp. 788-91.

36.22   Findlay, A.F. "The Acts of John," Byways. Pp. 208-37.

36.23   Franko, I. Apocrypha and Legends. L'vov, 1902. Vol. 3.
        Pp. 49-64. [in Russian]

36.24   Gamperl, J. Die Johannesakten: Eine literarkritische und
        geistesgeschichtliche Untersuchung. Vienna Dissertation,
        1965.

36.25   Goltz, E. Das Gebet in der ältesten Christenheit. Leipzig,
        1901.

36.26   Graf, G. Geschichte der christlichen arabischen Literatur
        (Studi e Testi 118) Rome, 1944. Vol. 1. Pp. 258-64.
        [Arab. and Eth. texts]

36.27   Grenfell, B.A., and A.S. Hunt. Oxyrhynchus Papyri. Lon-
        don, 1908. Vol. 6. Pp. 12-18. [Gk. text]

36.28   Grossouw, W. "Die apocriefen van het Oude en Nieuwe Tes-
        tament in de koptische letterkunde," StCath 10 (1933-34)
        334-46; 11 (1934-35) 19-36.

36.29   Guidi, I. "Di alcune Pergamene saidiche della collezione Bor-
        giana," Rendiconti della Reale Accademia dei Lincei Ser. 5,
        Vol. 2.7 (1893) 514ff. [fragments of Cop. version of AcJn]

36.30   Guidi, I. "Gli atti apocrifi degli Apostoli nei testi copti,
        arabi ed etiopici," Giornale della Società Asiatica Italiana
        2 (1888) 38-41. [Italian trans. of Coptic frag.]

36.31   Harnack, A. "Die Johannes-, Andreas-, und Thomasacten,"
        Gesch. altchrist. Lit. 2.1. Pp. 541-49.

36.32   Harnack, A. "Die Johannesacten," Gesch. altchrist. Lit. 1.
        Pp. 124-27.

36.33 Hennecke, E. "Johannesakten," H². Pp. 171-91.

36.34 Hilgenfeld, A. "Der gnostische und der kanonische Johannes
       über das Leben Jesu," ZWT 43 (1900) 1-61.

36.35 Jacimirskij, A.I. "Apocrypha and Legends ... VI-VIII,"
       IzvORJS 14 (1909) 114f. [in Russian]

36.36 Jagić, V. Examples of the Old Croatian Language from Glago-
       lithic and Cyrillic Literary Antiquities. Zagreb, 1866. Vol.
       2. Pp. 77-81. [in Serbo-Croatian]

36.37 James, M.R. "Actorum Iohannis a Leucio conscriptorum frag-
       mentum," AA 2. Pp. 1-25. [Gk. text and ET; see also pp.
       ix-xxviii]

36.38 James, M.R. "Acts of John," ANT. Pp. 228-70.

36.39 James, M.R. "Leucius and the Gospel of John," AA 2. Pp.
       144-53.

36.40 James, M.R. "Notes on Apocrypha," JTS 7 (1906) 562-68.
       [see esp. pp. 566-68]

36.41 Junod, É., and J.-D. Kaestli. Acta Iohannis (Corpus Chris-
       tianorum, Series Apocryphorum 1-2) 2 vols. Turnhout, 1983.

36.42 Junod, É., and J.-D. Kaestli. "Le dossier des Actes de Jean:
       Etat de la question et perspectives nouvelles," ANRW 2.25.4
       (in preparation).

36.43 Junod, É., and J.-D. Kaestli. "Un fragment grec inédit des
       Actes de Jean: La guérison des fils d'Antipatros à Smyrne,"
       Museum Helveticum 31 (1974) 96-104.

36.44 Junod, É., and J.-D. Kaestli. L'histoire des Actes apocryphes
       des apôtres du IIIe au IXe siècle: le cas des Actes de Jean
       (Cahiers de la Revue de Théologie et de Philosophie 7) Ge-
       neva, Lausanne, Neuchâtel, 1982.

36.45 Junod, É., and J.-D. Kaestli. "Les traits caractéristiques de
       la théologie des Actes de Jean," RTP 26 (1976) 125-45.

36.46 Katergian, J. Dormitio beati Johannis apostoli. Vienna, 1877.
       [Arm. version of AcJn and Lat. trans.]

36.47 Lacau, M.P. FAC. Pp. 79-108. [Some passages are similar
       to AcJn, cf. Guidi's work above]

36.48 Leipoldt, J. Agyptische Urkunden aus den königlichen Mu-
       seen zu Berlin (Koptische Urkunden 1) Berlin, 1904. Pp.
       173-75. [Coptic frag. of AcJn]

36.49 Lichačev, N.P. "The Pilgrimage of the Holy Apostle and Evan-
       gelist John the Theologian According to Illustrated Manu-
       scripts of the Fifteenth and Sixteenth Centuries," Izdanija
       obščestva ljubitelej drevnej pis' mennosti 130 (1911) 1-53,
       tab. 1-206, 11-82. [in Russian]

36.49a Lipsius, R.A. Die apokryphen Apostelgeschichten und Apos-
       tellegenden. 2 vols. Brunswick, 1883-1890; repr. Amster-
       dam, 1976. Vol. 1. Pp. 348-542.

36.50 Loewenich, W. von. "Die Johannesakten des Leucius," Das
       Johannes-Verständnis im zweiten Jahrhundert (BZNW 13)
       Giessen, 1932. Pp. 102-09.

36.51 McArthur, J.S. "The Words of the 'Hymn of Jesus,'" ExpT
       36 (1924-25) 136-38.

36.52 Malan, S.C., The Conflicts of the Holy Apostles. London,
       1871. Pp. 244-48. [Arm. text]

36.53 Michaelis, W. "Johannes-Akten," Apokryphen Schriften. Pp.
       223-68.

36.54 Milburn, R.L.P. "A Docetic Passage in Ovid's Fasti," JTS
       46 (1945) 68f.

36.55 Miller, R.H. "Liturgical Materials in the Acts of John,"
       Studia Patristica 13 (1975) 375-81.

36.56 Moraldi, L. "Atti di san Giovanni," Apoc. del NT. 2. Pp.
       1131-1212.

36.57 Müller, J.J. "Die Handelinge van Johannes," Nuwe-Test. Apok.
       Pp. 50-79. [Afrikaans trans.]

36.58 Pallas, D.J. "The Hymn of the Acts of John, Chapters 94-97,"
       Mélanges offerts à Octave et Melpo Merlier (Collection de
       l'Institut Français d'Athènes 93) Athens, 1956. Vol. 2.
       Pp. 221-64. [in modern Gk.]

36.59 Peterson, E. "Atti di Giovanni," EncCatt. 6. Cols. 510f.

36.60 Pick, B. The Apocryphal Acts of Paul, Peter, John, Andrew
       and Thomas. London, 1909.

36.61 Popov, G.V. "Illustrations of the 'Pilgrimage of the Theolo-
       gian John' in Miniature and [?] Paintings of the 15th Cen-
       tury," Trudy ODRL 22 (1966) 208-22. [in Russian]*

36.62 Pulver, M. "Jesu Reigen und Kreuzigung nach den Johannes-
       Akten," EJ (1942) 141-77. [ET: "Jesus' Round Dance and

Crucifixion According to the Acts of St. John," The Mysteries: Papers from the Eranos Yearbooks. New York, 1955. Pp. 169-193]

36.63 Santos Otero, A. de. "Acta Ioannis," Altslavischen Apok. 1. Pp. 97-123.

36.64 Schäferdiek, K. "The Acts of John," HSW. 2. Pp. 188-259.

36.65 Schäferdiek, K. "Johannesakten," HS. 2. 125-76.

36.66 Schimmelpfeng, G. "Johannesakten," Handbuch, ed. Hennecke. Pp. 492-543.

36.67 Schlier, H. "Das pathos Christi und die Kirche," Religionsgeschichtliche Untersuchungen zu den Ignatiusbriefen (BZNW 8) Giessen, 1929. Pp. 102-10.

36.68 Schlier, H. "Christus und die henōsis der Kirche," Religionsgeschichtliche Untersuchungen zu den Ignatiusbriefen (BZNW 8) Giessen, 1929. Pp. 97-102.

36.69 Sreznevskij, I. "Information and Notes About Little Known and Unknown Works," SbORJS 28 (1875) 393, 495-98. [in Russian]

36.70 Stead, G.C. "Conjectures on the Acts of John," JTS 32 (1981) 152f.

36.71 Stegmüller, F. Repertorium Biblicum. 1. Pp. 188-90; 8. Pp. 171f.

36.72 Tarchnišvili, P.M. "Johannes der Evangelist," Geschichte der kirchlichen georgischen Literatur (Studi e Testi 185) Rome, 1955. Pp. 341-43.

36.73 Thilo, J.C. Colliguntur et commentariis illustrantur fragmenta actuum S. Joannis a Leucio Charino conscriptorum. Halle, 1847.

36.74 Tischendorf, K. "Acta Ioannis," Acta Apos. Apoc. Pp. LXXIII-LXXVI, 266-76. [Intro. and Gk. text]

36.75 Unnik, W.C. van. "A Note on the Dance of Jesus in the 'Acts of John,'" VC 18 (1964) 1-5.

36.76 Vjazernskij, P.P. Publications of the Society of Lovers of Ancient Literature 23 (1878). [in Russian]*

36.77 Voigt, S. "Une accusation apocryphe contre l'apôtre Jean et son historicité possible," Studia Hierosolymitana in onore

del P. Bellarmino Bagatti, eds. E. Testa, I. Mancini, M.
Piccirillo (Studii Biblici Franciscani Collectio Maior 23)
Jerusalem, 1976. Pp. 278–88.

36.78 Walker, A. "Acts of the Holy Apostle and Evangelist John
the Theologian," ANF 8. Pp. 560–64. [ET]

36.79 Wessely, C. Studien zur Paleographie und Papyruskunde XV
(Griechische und Koptische Texte theologischen Inhalts 4)
Leipzig, 1914. Pp. 131f. [Cop. frag. of AcJn]

36.80 Wetter, G.P. Altchristliche Liturgien: Das Christliche Mysterium (FRLANT 13) Göttingen, 1921.

36.81 Wright, W. "An Account of the Decease of Saint John,"
Apocryphal Acts of the Apostles. London, 1871. Vol. 1.
Pp. 66–72 [Syr. text]; Vol. 2. Pp. 61–68 [ET].

36.82 Zahn, T. Acta Joannis, unter Benutzung von C. v. Tischendorf's Nachlass. Erlangen, 1880.

36.83 Zahn, T. "Über die Johannesakten des Leucius," Neutest.
Kanons. 2. Pp. 856–65. [Intro.]

36.84 Zahn, T. "Die Wanderungen des Apostels Johannes," NKZ
10 (1899) 191–218.

37. JOHN: ACTS OF JOHN BY PROCHORUS

This work borrows heavily from the earlier AcJn––see the
listings under AcJn and SyrAcJn.

(See also 1.206; 3.38, 78.)

37.1 Amfilochij Archimandrit. Paleographical Descriptions of Greek
Manuscripts ... 4 vols. Moscow, 1879–80. Vol. 3. Pp. 19–
26.* [in Russian]

37.2 Amfilochij Archimandrit, "The Pilgrimage, After the Ascension
of Our Lord Jesus Christ, of the Holy Apostle and Evangelist John, His Teaching and Death Transcribed by His Stu-
dent Prochorus," Izdanija obščestva ljubitelj drevnej pis'men-
nosti 31 (1878) Pp. 1–67. [in Russian]

37.3 Barre, L. de la. Historia christiana ... Paris, 1583.*

37.4 Barsukov, N. "Variations on the Pilgrimage of the Holy Apostle
and Evangelist John the Theologian," PDP 4 (1879) 97–139.

37.5 Bercic, I. An Old Church Slavonic Reader. Prague, 1864.
Pp. 36-38. [in Serbo-Croatian]

37.6 Bigne, M. de la. Bibliotheca Patrum. Paris, 1575. Vol. 2.*
[Lat. text]

37.7 Birch, A. Auctarium codicis apocryphi Novi Testamenti Fabriciani. Copenhagen, 1799, 1804. Vol. 1. Pp. 262-307.

37.8 Bonwetsch, N. "Die Acta Ioannis," Gesch. altchrist. Lit. 1.
P. 903.

37.9 Budge, E. A. W. Contendings of the Apostles. 2 vols. London, New York, 1899-1901; repr. London, 1976. Vol. 1.
Pp. 189-213; Vol. 2. Pp. 222-52.

37.10 Bulgakov, F. "The Life of the Theologian John in Manuscripts
of the 15th-16th Century in Comparison with Greek Texts
of 1022," PDP 3 (1878) 121-27. [in Russian]

37.11 Demina, E. I. The Tichonravov Collection. 2 vols. Sofia,
1968-71. Vol. 1. Pp. 93-96; Vol. 2. Pp. 81-88. [in Rus-
sian]

37.12 Erbetta, M. "Gli Atti di Giovanni dello Ps. Procoro," Apoc.
del NT. 2. Pp. 68-110.

37.13 Esbroeck, M. van. "Les Acta Iohannis traduits [en géorgien]
par Euthyme l'Hagiorite," Bedi Kartlisa 33 (1975) 73-109.

37.14 Fabricius, J. A. "Prochori Historia de S. Johanne Evange-
lista," Cod.Apoc.NT. 2. Pp. 815-18.

37.15 Grynaeus, J. J. Monumenta S. Patrum Orthodoxographa. 3
vols. Basel, 1569.

37.16 Halkin, F. "Le prologue inédit de Nicétas, Archevéque de
Thessalonique, aux Actes de l'Apôtre saint Jean," AnBoll
85 (1967) 16-20.

37.17 Hall, S. G. "Melito's Paschal Homily and the Acts of John,"
JTS NS 17 (1966) 95-98.

37.18 Hatch, W. H. P. "Three Hitherto Unpublished Leaves from a
Manuscript of the Acta Apostolorum Apocrypha in Bohairic,"
Coptic Studies in Honor of W. E. Crum, ed. M. Malinine
(Bulletin of the Byzantine Institute 2) Boston, 1950. Pp.
305-17. [ET]

37.19 Hollander, H. W. "The Influence of the Testaments of the
Twelve Patriarchs in the Early Church: Joseph as Model
in Prochorus' Acts of John," OLP 9 (1978) 75-81.

37.20   James, M. R.   ANT. P. 469.

37.21   Lewis, A. S.   "The Travels of John, Son of Zebedee," The
        Mythological Acts of the Apostles (Horae Semiticae 4) Lon-
        don, 1904. Pp. xxi-xxiv, 37-53. [ET of Ar. text in Horae
        Semiticae 3]

37.22   Lipsius, R. A.   Die apokryphen Apostelgeschichten und Apos-
        tellegenden. 2 vols. Brunswick, 1883-1890; repr. Amster-
        dam, 1976. Vol. 1. Pp. 355-408.

37.23   Migne, J.-P.   "Prochore. (Histoire de saint Jean l'Evangé-
        liste par Prochore.)," Dictionnaire. 2. Cols. 759-816.
        [Intro. and French trans.]

37.24   Mingarelli, G. L.   Aegyptiorum codicum reliquiae Venetiis in
        Bibliotheca Naniana asservatae. Bonn, 1785. [Cop. frag-
        ments]

37.25   Moraldi, L.   "Atti di Giovanni del Diacono Procoro," Apoc. del
        NT. 2. Pp. 1212-23.

37.26   Musikides, [?].   "Acta Johannis des Prochoros nach cod. 35
        des griech. Patriarchats von Jerusalem," Nea Sion. Jeru-
        salem, 1947. Pp. 245f.; 1948. Pp. 51-53, 121f.

37.27   Neander, M.   Cathechesis M. Lutheri parva, graecolatina....
        Basel, 1564. [Gk. and Lat. texts]

37.28   Popov, G. V.   "Illustrations of 'The Pilgrimage of the Theo-
        logian John' in Miniature and [?] Paintings of the 15th Cen-
        tury," Trudy ODRL 22 (1966) 208-22. [in Russian]

37.29   Schmidt, C.   "Leben des Johannes von Pseudo-Prochorus,"
        Gesch. altchrist. Lit. 1. P. 922.

37.30   Schneemelcher, W., and A. de Santos. HS. 2. Pp. 402f.

37.31   Schneemelcher, W., and A. de Santos. HSW. 2. P. 575.

37.32   Stegmüller, F.   Repertorium Biblicum. 1. Pp. 190-92; 8.
        Pp. 172f.

37.33   Vajs, J.   "Martyrii S. Georgii et periodorum S. Johannis apos-
        toli et evangelistae, fragmenta glagolitica," Slavorum litterae
        theologicae 3 (1907) 132-38.

37.34   Zahn, T.   Acta Joannis, unter Benutzung von C. v. Tischen-
        dorf's Nachlass. Erlangen, 1880.

38.   APOCRYPHAL GOSPEL OF JOHN

38.1   Bea, A.   "Inventio 'evangelii apocryphi S. Johannis,'" Bib 24
       (1943) 194f.   [announces a 14th cent. Arabic MS in the Bib-
       liotheca Ambrosiana that contains an "apocryphal gospel of
       John"]

38.2   Erbetta, M.   "Vangelo di Giovanni arabo," Apoc. del NT.   1.2.
       P. 225.

38.3   Esbroeck, M. van.   "A propos de l'Évangile apocryphe arabe
       attribué à Saint Jean," Mélanges de l'Université Saint-Joseph
       49 (1975-76) 597-603.

38.4   Galbiati, G.   "L'evangeliario apocrifo di S. Giovanni," Acca-
       demie e Biblioteche d'Italia 15 (1941) 378f.

38.5   Galbiati, G.   Iohannis Evangelium apocryphum Arabice.   2 vols.
       Milan, 1957.   [vol. 1 = facsimile]

38.6   Graf, G.   Geschichte der christlichen arabischen Literatur
       (Studi e Testi 118) Rome, 1944.   Vol. 1.   Pp. 236f.

38.7   Lindeskog, G.   "Kristologien i det apokryfiska Johannesevan-
       geliet," Teologinen Aikakauskirja 73 (1968) 249-62.

38.8   Löfgren, O.   Det apokryfiska Johannesevangeliet.   I översättn-
       ing från den enda Kanda arabiska handskriften i Ambrosiana.
       Med inledning och anmärkningar.   Stockholm, 1967.

38.9   Löfgren, O.   "Ergänzendes zum apokryphen Johannesevangelium,"
       Orientalia Suecana 10 (1961) 139-44.

38.10 Löfgren, O.   Fakta och dokument angaende det apokryfiska
       Johannes-evangeliet.   Uppsala, 1942.   [also published in
       Svensk exegetisk arsbok 7 (1942) 110-40]

38.11 Löfgren, O.   "Ein unbeachtetes apokryphes Evangelium," OLZ
       46 (1943) 153-59.

38.12 Löfgren, O.   "Zur Charakteristik des apokryphen Johannes-
       evangeliums," Orientalia Suecana 9 (1960) 107-30.

38.13 Penna, A.   "L'Evangelo arabo di Giovanni," Humanitas 14
       (1959) 622-67.

38.14 Peretto, L.M.   "Cristo e la Vergine nel Vangelo arabo di
       Giovanni," Marianum 25 (1963) 99-139.

38.15 Rompay, L. van. "Les manuscrits éthiopiens des 'Miracles de
       Jésus,'" AnBoll 93 (1975) 133–46.

38.16 Santos Otero, A. de. "Evangelio árabe del Ps. Juan," Evan-
       gelios Apócrifos. Pp. 23f.

38.17 Stegmüller, F. Repertorium Biblicum. 1. P. 129; 8. Pp.
       105f.

39. JOHN, BOOK OF

(See also 1.284.)

39.1   Benoist, I. Histoire des Albigeois. Paris, 1691. Vol. 1.
       Pp. 283–96.

39.2   Döllinger, J. Beiträge zur mittelalterlichen Sektengeschichte.
       Munich, 1890; repr. New York, [1960]. Vol. 2. P. 85.

39.3   Gonzalez-Blanco, E. Los Evangelios Apócrifos. Madrid, 1935.
       Vol. 2. Pp. 370–84. [Spanish trans.]

39.4   James, M.R. "Book of John the Evangelist," ANT. Pp. 187–
       93.

39.5   Migne, J.-P. "Livre de Saint Jean," Dictionnaire. 1. Cols.
       1155–68.

39.6   Stegmüller, F. Repertorium Biblicum. 1. Pp. 129f.; 8. P.
       106.

39.7   Thilo, J.C. Codex apocryphus Novi Testamenti. Leipzig,
       1832. Vol. 1. Pp. 884–96.

40. JOHN, 1 REVELATION OF
(APOKALYPSIS TOU HAGIOU IOANNOU TOU THEOLOGOU)

40.1   Angelov, B., and M. Genov. Ancient Bulgarian Literature.
       Sofia, 1922. [in Bulgarian]

40.2   Bonwetsch, N. Gesch. altchrist. Lit. Pp. 911f.

40.3   Ćorović, V. "The Apocryphal Apocalypse Concerning the
       Second Coming of Christ," Spomenik. Srpska Kralj. Akademija
       49 (1910) 41–45. [in Serbo-Croatian]

40.4 Erbetta, M. "La Prima Apocalisse Apocrifa di Giovanni," Apoc. del NT. 3. Pp. 409-14.

40.5 Fabricius, J.A. "S. Johannis Apocalypsis, diversa a Canonica," Cod.Apoc.NT. 2. Pp. 953-55.

40.6 Franko, I. Apocrypha and Legends. L'vov, 1906. Vol. 4. Pp. 258-64. [in Russian]

40.7 Harnack, A. "Johannes, Apokalypse, gefälschte," Gesch. altchrist. Lit. 1. P. 785.

40.8 Jagić, V. "New Contributions to the Literature of the Biblical Apocrypha," Starine 5 (1873) 74-79. [in Serbo-Croatian]

40.9 Migne, J.-P. "Jean (saint) l'Évangéliste. (Ecrits attribués ou qui se rapportent à saint Jean l'Evangéliste.)," Dictionnaire. 2. Cols. 325-64. [Neither 1RevJn, nor 2RevJn, nor 3RevJn is the "Prophecy of St. John on the End of the World"; cf. cols. 325f. Also see "Liturgy of St. John," cols. 358-64.]

40.10 [Miron]. "Essays on the History of South Russian Apocryphal Sayings and Songs," Kievskaja starina 47 (1894) 429f. [in Russian]

40.11 Močul'skij, V.I. Traces of the Popular Bible in Slavic and Ancient Russian Writings. Odessa, 1893. P. 198. [in Russian]

40.12 Moraldi, L. "Apocalisse di Giovanni," Apoc. del NT. 2. Pp. 1951-66.

40.13 Nau, F. "Une Didascalie de Notre-Seigneur Jésus-Christ," ROC 12 (1907) 245-48.

40.14 Novakovič, S. Examples of Literature. Belgrade, 1904³. Pp. 505-09. [in Serbo-Croatian]

40.15 Papakyriakos, S. "Apocalypsis apocrypha Joannis Theologi (graece)," Theologia 3 (1925) 217-23.

40.16 Parker, H.M. "The Scripture of the Author of the Revelation of John," Iliff Review 37 (1980) 35-51. [P. argues that the author of Rev. and his community held as sacred many apocryphal writings.]

40.17 Porfiryev, I.Y. "Apocryphal Sayings About New Testament People and Events in Manuscripts of the Solovetski Library," SbORJS 52 (1890) 311-26. [in Russian]

40.18 Pypin, A.N. False and Dismissed Books of Ancient Russia.
       St. Petersburg, 1862. Pp. 113-17. [in Russian]

40.19 Santos Otero, A. de. "Apocalypsis Ioannis," Altslavischen
       Apok. 1. Pp. 197-209.

40.20 Schneemelcher, W. "Apokalypsen des Johannes," HS. 2. P.
       535.

40.21 Schneemelcher, W. "Apocalypses of John," HSW. 2. P. 753.

40.22 Sreznevskij, I.I. "Ancient Slavic Texts," SbORJS 3 (1868)
       185-88, 406-16. [in Russian]

40.23 Stegmüller, F. Repertorium Biblicum. 1. P. 236f.; 8. P.
       206.

40.24 Thilo, J.C. Codex apocryphus Novi Testamenti. Leipzig,
       1832. Vol. 1. Pp. 884-86. [Lat. text]

40.25 Tichonravov, N.S. "Apocryphal Sayings," SbORJS 58/4
       (1894) 25-28. [in Russian]

40.26 Tichonravov, N. Texts of Dismissed Russian Literature.
       Moscow, 1863; repr. London, 1973. Vol. 2, pp. 174-212.
       [in Russian]

40.27 Tischendorf, K. von. "Apocalypsis Iohannis," Apocalypses
       Apocryphae. Pp. 70-94. [Gk. text]

40.28 Vassiliev, A. Anecdota graeco-byzantina. Moscow, 1893. Pp.
       317-22.

40.29 Walker, A. "Revelation of John," ANF 8. Pp. 582-86. [ET]

41. JOHN, 2 REVELATION OF
(A SECOND GREEK APOCRYPHAL APOCALYPSE OF JOHN)

(See also 40.1, 2, 3, 6, 8, 10, 11, 14, 17, 22, 25, 26.)

41.1   Erbetta, M. "Seconda Apocalisse Apocrifa di Giovanni,"
       Apoc. del NT. 3. P. 415.

41.2   Frey, J.B. "Seconde Apocalypse Apocryphe de Saint Jean,"
       DBSup. 1. Cols. 325f.

41.3   Moraldi, L. "Apocalisse di Giovanni," Apoc. del NT. 2. Pp.
       1951-55.

41.4   Nau, F. "Une deuxième apocalypse apocryphe grecque de S. Jean," RB 23 (1914) 209-21.

41.5   Popov, A.N. Description of the Manuscripts of the A. I. Chuldov Library. Moscow, 1872. Pp. 339-44. [in Russian]

41.6   Santos Otero, A. de. "Apocalypsis Ioannis," Altslavischen Apok. 1. Pp. 197-209.

41.7   Schneemelcher, W. "Apocalypses of John," HSW. 2. P. 753.

41.8   Stegmüller, F. Repertorium Biblicum. 1. Pp. 236f.

42. JOHN, 3 REVELATION OF
(THE MYSTERIES OF ST. JOHN AND THE HOLY VIRGIN)

42.1   Budge, E.A.W. "The Mysteries of Saint John and the Holy Virgin," Coptic Apoc. Pp. 59-74, 241-57. [Cop. text and ET]

42.2   Erbetta, M. "I Misteri di Giovanni, Apostolo e Vergine," Apoc. del NT. 3. Pp. 417-24.

42.3   Moraldi, L. "Apocalisse di Giovanni," Apoc. del NT. 2. Pp. 1951-55.

42.4   Schneemelcher, W. "Apokalypsen des Johannes," HS. 2. P. 535.

42.5   Schneemelcher, W. "Apocalypses of John," HSW. 2. P. 753.

42.6   Stegmüller, F. Repertorium Biblicum. 1. Pp. 236f.; 8. P. 206.

43. JOHN, SYRIAC HISTORY OF

(See also the listings under AcJnPro.)

43.1   Connolly, R.H. "The Diatessaron in the Syriac Acts of John," JTS 8 (1907) 571-81.

43.2   Connolly, R.H. "The Original Language of the Syriac Acts of John," JTS 8 (1907) 249-61.

43.3   James, M.R. ANT. Pp. 469f.

43.4   Klijn, A.F.J. "An Ancient Syriac Baptismal Liturgy in the
        Syriac Acts of John," NovT 6 (1963) 216-28.

43.5   Lewis, A.S. The Mythological Acts of the Apostles (Horae
        Semiticae 4) London, 1904. Pp. 157-71. [ET of Ar. text
        in Horae Semiticae 3]

43.6   Lipsius, R.A. Die apokryphen Apostelgeschichten und Apos-
        tellegenden. 2 vols. Brunswick, 1883-1890; repr. Amster-
        dam, 1976. Vol. 1. Pp. 431-41.

43.7   Macmunn, V.C. "The Menelaus Episode in the Syriac Acts of
        John," JTS 12 (1911) 463-65.

43.8   Stegmüller, F. Repertorium Biblicum. 1. P. 192; 8. P. 173.

43.9   Wright, W. "The History of John, the Son of Zebedee,"
        Apocryphal Acts of the Apostles. Vol. 1. Pp. 3-65 [Syr.
        text]; Vol. 2. Pp. 3-60 [ET].

44. JOHN THE BAPTIST CYCLE

See also articles and studies on John the Baptist traditions in the New Testament which make reference to the
apocryphal traditions.

44.1   Bagatti, B. "Antiche leggende sull' infanzia di S. Giovanni
        Battista," ED 30 (1977) 260-69.

44.2   Berendts, A. Die handschriftliche Uberlieferung der Zacha-
        rias- und Johannes-Apokryphen (TU 26.3) Leipzig, 1904.

44.3   Cullmann, O. "Extract from the Life of John According to
        Serapion." HSW. 1. 414-17.

44.4   Franko, I. Apocrypha and Legends. L'vov, 1898. Vol. 2.
        Pp. 317-26. [in Russian]

44.5   Garofalo, S. Con il Battista incontro a Cristo. Milan, 1981.

44.6   Mead, G.R.S. The Gnostic John the Baptizer. London, 1924.

44.7   Mingana, A. "A New Life of John the Baptist," BJRL 2
        (1927) 438-91. [see Woodbrooke Studies 1.4]

44.8   Nau, F. Histoire de Saint Jean-Baptiste attribuée à Saint
        Marc l'Évangéliste, ed. R. Griffin and F. Nau. (PO 43)
        Paris, 1908. Pp. 513-41.

44.9   Saller, J.S. Discoveries at St. John's Ain Karim 1941-1942.
        Jerusalem, 1946.

44.10   Santos Otero, A. de. "Descensus Ioannis Baptistae ad Inferos,"
        Altslavischen Apok. 2. Pp. 99-118.

44.11   Schonfield, H.J. The Lost Book of the Nativity of John.
        Edinburgh, 1929. [See M.R. James' review JTS 32 (1931)
        300f.]

44.12   Stegmüller, F. Repertorium Biblicum. 1. Pp. 126-29; 8.
        Pp. 104f.

44.13   Till, W.C. "Johannes der Täufer in der koptischen Literatur,"
        Mitteilungen des Deutschen Archäologischen Instituts 16
        (1958) 310-22.

44.14   Wall, H. "A Coptic Fragment Concerning the Childhood of
        John the Baptist," Revue d'Égyptologie 8 (1951) 207-14.

                45. JOSEPH OF ARIMATHEA, NARRATIVE OF

        This apocryphon is the story of Joseph of Arimathea pre-
        served in Gk. in which he requests the body of Jesus from
        Pilate (see also the entries under AcPil). Some confusion
        may result with the similarly attributed Lat. version of
        AVir (see also the entries under that heading and PasMar).

45.1   Birch, A. Auctarium Codicis N.T. Fabriciani. Hamburg,
        1804. Vol. 1. Pp. 183-85.

45.2   Bonwetsch, N. "Narratio de Iosepho Arimathiensi," Gesch.
        altchrist. Lit. 1. P. 910.

45.3   Carter, H.H. The Portuguese Book of Joseph of Arimathea.
        Chapel Hill, N.C., 1967.

45.4   Cowper, B.H. "The Story of Joseph," Apocryphal Gospels.
        Pp. 420-31. [ET]

45.5   Danicic, G. Starine 4 (1872) 149-54.* [Serb. text]

45.6   Erbetta, M. "La Dichiarazione di Giuseppe d'Arimatea,"
        Apoc. del NT. 1.2. Pp. 397-401.

45.7   Esbroeck, M. van. "L'histoire de l'Église de Lydda dans
        deux textes géorgiens," Bedi Kartlisa 35 (1977) 109-31.

45.8   James, M.R. "Story of Joseph of Arimathaea," ANT. Pp.
        161-65.

45.9   Kluge, T. "Die apokryphe Erzählung des Joseph von Arima-
        thäa über den Bau der ersten christlichen Kirche in Lydda,"
        OrChr 4 (1914) 24-38.

45.10   Martins, M. "A Eucaristia no. 'Livro de José de Arimateia' e
        na 'Demanda do Santo Graal,'" Itinerarium 21 (1975) 16-39.

45.11   Migne, J.-P. "Joseph d'Arimathie," Dictionnaire. 2. Cols.
        431-38.

45.12   Moraldi, L. "Narrazione di Giuseppe da Arimatea," Apoc. del
        NT. 1. Pp. 683-92.

45.13   Morenz, S. "Die Geschichte von Joseph...." OLZ 49 (1954)
        46ff.*

45.14   O'Gorman, R. "The Legend of Joseph of Arimathea and the
        Old French Epic 'Huon de Bordeaux,'" ZRP 80 (1964) 35-42.

45.15   Santos Otero, A. de. "Declaración de José de Arimatea,"
        Evangelios Apócrifos. Pp. 501-12. [Gk. text and Spanish
        trans.]

45.16   Starowieyski, M. "Apocryphon Joseph of Arimathea," RuBi
        28 (1975) 27-34.

45.17   Stegmüller, F. Repertorium Biblicum. 1. P. 148; 8. Pp.
        141f.

45.18   Tischendorf, C. "Narratio Iosephi Arimathiensis," Evangelia
        Apocrypha. Pp. LXXX 459-70. [Gk. text]

45.19   Variot, J. "La Narration de Joseph d'Arimathie," Évangiles
        Apocryphes. Pp. 125-31.

45.20   Walker, A. "The Narrative of Joseph," ANF 8. Pp. 468-71.
        [ET]

46. JOSEPH THE CARPENTER, HISTORY OF; AND JOSEPH CYCLE

(See also 1.75, 324.)

46.1   Amann, É. "Histoire de Joseph le Charpentier," DBSup. 1.
        Col. 484.

46.2   Amiot, F. "Histoire de Joseph le Charpentier," Évangiles Apoc.
       Pp. 107-12. [French trans.]

46.3   Bagatti, B. "Il culto di S. Giuseppe in Palestina," CahJos 19
       (1971) 564-75.

46.4   Battista, A., and B. Bagatti. Edizione critica del testo arabo
       della "Historia Iosephi fabri lignarii" e ricerche sulla sua
       origine (Studii Biblici Franciscani, Collectio Minor 20). Jeru-
       salem, 1978.

46.5   Bonsirven, J., and C. Bigaré, "Histoire de Joseph le Charpen-
       tier," Intro. à la Bible. 2. P. 754.

46.6   Canal-Sánchez, J.M. "S. José en los libros apócrifos del Nuevo
       Testamento: San Giuseppe nei primi 15 secoli," Estudios
       Josefinos 25 (1971) 123-49.

46.7   Cecchelli, C. Mater christi. Rome, 1954. Vol. 3. Pp. 416-21.

46.8   Cignelli, L. "Le Saint Joseph des judéo-chrétiens," CahJos
       28 (1980) 197-212.

46.9   Cowper, B.H. "The History of Joseph the Carpenter,"
       Apocryphal Gospels. Pp. 99-127. [ET]

46.10 Devos, P. "Une histoire de Joseph le Patriarche dans une
       oeuvre copte sur le chant de la Vierge," AnBoll 94 (1976)
       137-54.

46.11 Dusserre, J. "Les origines de la dévotion à St. Joseph,"
       CahJos 1 (1953) 33-38.

46.12 Erbetta, M. "La Storia del falegname Giuseppe," Apoc. del
       NT. 1.2. Pp. 186-205.

46.13 Fabricius, J.A. Cod.Apoc.NT. 2. Pp. 309-26. [Lat. trans.
       of Arabic text]

46.14 Gauthier, R. "La vierge Marie d'après l' 'Histoire de Joseph
       le Charpentier,'" De primordiis cultus mariani. Rome, 1970.
       Vol. 4. Pp. 353-69.

46.15 Giamberardini, G. "Joseph dans la tradition copte," CahJos
       17 (1969) 5-231.

46.16 Giamberardini, G. "San José en la tradicion egipcia," Tierra
       Santa 49 (1974) 70-78.

46.17 Giamberardini, G. "San Giuseppe nella tradizione copta,"
       Studia Orientalia Christiana Collectanea 2 (1957).*

246   IV. Bibliography

46.18   González-Blanco, E. Los Evangelios Apócrifos. Madrid, 1935.
        2. Vol. 2. Pp. [?].*

46.19   Graf, G. Geschichte der christlichen arabischen Literatur
        (Studi e Testi 118) Rome, 1944. Vol. 1. Pp. 234-36.

46.20   Hawthorne, G.F. "Joseph the Carpenter, History of," ZPEB.
        3. P. 696.

46.21   Hofmann, P.A. Das Leben Jesu nach den Apokryphen. Leip-
        zig, 1851. Pp. 263-88.

46.22   Holzmeister, U. De Sancto Joseph quaestiones biblicae. Rome,
        1945.

46.23   Höpfl, H. "Nonne hic est fabri filius?" Bib 4 (1923) 41-55.

46.24   James, M.R. "History of Joseph the Carpenter, or Death of
        Joseph," ANT. Pp. 84-86.

46.25   Khater, A. "Nouveaux fragments du Synaxaire arabe," Studia
        Orientalia Christiana Collectanea 10 (1965) 402-93.

46.26   Klameth, G. "Über der Herkunft der apokryphen 'Geschichte
        Josephs des Zimmermanns,'" Angelos 3 (1930) 6-31.

46.27   Lagarde, P. Aegyptiaca. Göttingen, 1883. [see esp. pp.
        1-37]

46.28   Leclercq, H. "La Littérature Apocryphe," DACL. 7. Cols.
        2659f.

46.29   Lefort, L.T. "A propos de 'l'histoire de Joseph le Charpen-
        tier,'" Muséon 66 (1953) 201-23. [Cop. text and French
        trans.]

46.30   McNeil, B. "Revelation 12:5 and the History of Joseph the
        Carpenter," Marianum 42 (1980) 126-28.

46.31   Manns, F. "Une aggadah judéo-chrétienne sur S. Joseph,"
        CahJos 26 (1978) 211-15.

46.32   Manns, F. "La prière de Joseph avant sa mort dans l'His-
        toire de Joseph le Charpentier," CahJos 26 (1978) 217-22.

46.33   Meyer, A., and W. Bauer. "Jesu Verwandtschaft," HS. 1.
        P. 320.

46.34   Meyer, A., and W. Bauer. "The Relatives of Jesus," HSW.
        1. P. 430.

46.35   Migne, J.-P.   "Joseph.   (Histoire de Joseph le Charpentier.)," Dictionnaire.   1.   Cols. 1027-44.   [Intro. and French trans.]

46.36   Moraldi, L.   "Storia di Guiseppe falegname," Apoc. del NT. 1.   Pp. 244f., 313-52.

46.37   Morenz, S.   Die Geschichte von Joseph dem Zimmermann (TU 56) Berlin, Leipzig, 1951.

46.38   Peeters, P.   "Histoire de Joseph le Charpentier," EvApoc. 1.   Pp. xxxiii-xl, 191-245.   [Arab.-Lat. text and Bohar. text]

46.39   Quatremère, E.   Recherches sur la langue et la littérature de l'Egypte.   Paris, 1808.

46.40   Revillout, E.   Apocryphes coptes du Nouveau Testament (Études égyptologiques 7), 1876.   Pp. 28-70.   [Sahid. and Bohar. texts]

46.41   Robinson, F.   "Bohairic Account of the Death of Joseph with Sahidic Fragments," Coptic Apocryphal Gospels (T&S 4.2) Cambridge, 1896.   Pp. 130-59, 220-35.   [Bohar. and Sahid. texts]

46.42   Roncaglia, M.   "St. Joseph dans la littérature manuscrite arabe chrétienne," CahJos 5 (1957) 261-64.

46.43   Rondet, H.   "Saint Joseph: Histoire et théologie," NRT 85 (1953) 113-40.

46.44   Salvoni, F.   "La storia di Giuseppe, il falegname," Ricerche Bibliche e Religiose 15 (1980) 228-37.

46.45   Sánchez, J.M.C.   "San José en los libros apocrifos del Nuevo Testamento," CahJos 19 (1971) 123-49.

46.46   Santos Otero, A. de.   "Historia de José el Carpintero," Evangelios Apócrifos.   Pp. 339-58.   [Spanish trans.]

46.47   Schmidt, C.   "Leben des Joseph," Gesch. altchrist. Lit.   1. P. 924.

46.48   Schmidt, C.   "Tod des Joseph," Gesch. altchrist. Lit.   1. P. 924.

46.49   Stegmüller, F.   Repertorium Biblicum.   1.   Pp. 130-32; 8. Pp. 110f.

46.50   Stern, L.   ZWT 26 (1883) 267-94.*

46.51   Testini, P. "Alle origini dell'iconografia di Giuseppe di Naz-
        areth," Rivista di Archeologia Cristiana 48 (1972) 271-347.

46.52   Thilo, J.C. Codex Apocryphus Novi Testamenti. Leipzig,
        1832. Vol. 1. Pp. 1-61, XV-XXVI. [Arabic text]

46.53   Tischendorf, C. "Historia Iosephi fabri lignarii," Evangelia
        Apocrypha. Pp. xxxii-xxxvi, 122-39. [Lat. trans.]

46.54   Variot, J. "L'histoire de Joseph le Charpentier," Évangiles
        Apocryphes. Pp. 83-92.

46.55   Walker, A. "The History of Joseph the Carpenter," ANF 8.
        Pp. 388-94. [ET]

46.56   Wallin, G. Historia Iosephi fabri lignarii: Liber apocryphus
        ex codice manuscripto Regiae Bibliothecae Parisiensis nunc
        primum arabice editus, nec non versione latina et notis il-
        lustratus. Lipsiae, 1772. [Arab. and Lat. texts]

46.57   Zoëga, G. Catalogus codicum copticorum manuscriptorum qui
        in Museo Borgiano Veletris adservantur. Rome, 1810.*

47. LENTULUS, LETTER OF

47.1   Amiot, F. Évangile, Vie et message du Christ. Paris, 1949.

47.2   Auletta, G. L'Aspetto di Gesù Cristo: Testimonianza e Leg-
        gende. Rome, 1948.

47.3   Brock, S.P. "A Syriac Version of the Letters of Lentulus and
        Pilate," OCP 35 (1969) 45-62.

47.4   Cowper, B.H. "The Letter of Lentulus," Apocryphal Gospels.
        Pp. 221-22. [ET]

47.5   Dobshütz, E. "Epistola Lentuli," Christusbilder: Untersuch-
        ungen zur christlichen Legende (TU N.F. 3) Leipzig, 1889.
        Pp. 308-30. [Lat. text]

47.6   Erbetta, M. "La Lettera di Lentulo," Apoc. del NT. 3. Pp.
        137f.

47.7   Fabricius, J.A. Cod.Apoc.NT. 1. Pp. 301f.

47.8   James, M.R. "Letter of Lentulus," ANT. Pp. 477f.

47.9   Migne, J.-P. "Lentulus. (Lettre de Publius-Lentulus.),"
        Dictionnaire. 2. Cols. 453-56.

47.10   Moraldi, L.   "Lettera di Lentulo," <u>Apoc. del NT</u>.   2.   Pp.
        1651-56.

47.11   Pedica, S.   <u>Il Volto Santo nei documenti della Chiesa</u>.   Turin,
        1960.

47.12   Stegmüller, F.   <u>Repertorium Biblicum</u>.   1.   P. 132; 8.   P. 112.

47.13   Wilson, R.McL.   "Lentulus, Epistle of," <u>ZPEB</u>.   3.   P. 909.

                48.   <u>MARK, ACTS OF</u>; AND MARK CYCLE

48.1   Bonwetsch, N.   "Marcus," <u>Gesch. altchrist. Lit</u>.   1.   P. 906.

48.2   Fabricius, J.A.   "Anonymi <u>Historia</u> S. Marci <u>Evangelistae</u>,"
        <u>Cod.Apoc.NT</u>.   2.   Pp. 780f.

48.3   Halkin, F.   "Actes inédits de Saint Marc," <u>AnBoll</u> 87 (1969)
        346-71.

48.4   Hatch, W.H.P.   "Three hitherto unpublished Leaves from a
        Manuscript of the Acta Apostolorum Apocrypha in Bohairic,"
        <u>Coptic Studies in Honor of W.E. Crum</u>, ed. M. Malinine
        (Bulletin of the Byzantine Institute 2) Boston, 1950.   Pp.
        305-17.

48.4a   Lewis, A.S.   <u>The Mythological Acts of the Apostles</u> (Horae
        Semiticae 4) London, 1904.   Pp. 147-51.   [ET of Ar. text
        in Horae Semiticae 3]

48.4b   Lipsius, R.A.   <u>Die apokryphen Apostelgeschichten und Apos-
        tellegenden</u>.   2 vols.   Brunswick, 1883-1890; repr. Amster-
        dam, 1976.   Vol. 2.2.   Pp. 321-53.

48.5   Migne, J.-P.   "Marc (saint)," <u>Dictionnaire</u>.   2.   Cols. 473-92.

48.6   Moraldi, L.   "Atti di san Marco," <u>Apoc. del NT</u>.   2.   Pp.
        1633f.

48.7   Stegmüller, F.   <u>Repertorium Biblicum</u>.   1.   Pp. 196f.; 8.   P.
        176.

49. MARY, BIRTH OF; AND MARY CYCLE

See also the listings under ProtJas and "Virgin."

(See also 1.380, 424, 537; 46.31; 96.18.)

49.1   Aranda, G. "Maria en los evangelios apócrifos coptos. Frag-
        mentos sahidicos de la vida de la Virgen," Scripta de Maria
        1 (1978) 115-26.

49.2   Bagatti, B. "De Beatae Mariae Virginis cultu in monumentis
        palaeochristianis Palaestinensibus," De Primordiis cultus
        mariani. Rome, 1970. Vol. 5. Pp. 1-20.

49.3   Bagatti, B. "Le origini della 'Tomba della Vergine' a Getse-
        mani," Rivista Biblica 11 (1963) 38-52.

49.4   Bagatti, B. "La verginità di Maria negli apocrifi del II-III
        secolo," Marianum 33 (1971) 281-92.

49.5   Balic, C. Testimonia de Assumptione B. Mariae Virginis in
        omnibus saeculis. Rome, 1948.

49.6   Bardenhewer, O. Mariä Verkündigung. Freiburg, 1905.

49.7   Barsov, E.V. "On the Influence of the Apocrypha on Liturgy
        and Icongraphy," Žurnal Ministertsva Narodnavo Prosveščenia.
        1885.*

49.8   Berendts, A. Studien über Zacharias-Apokryphen und Zach-
        arias-Legenden. Leipzig, 1895. Pp. 32-37.

49.9   Brändle, M. "Die älteste Marienlegende," Orientierung 22
        (1958) 235-37.

49.10   Brodsky, N.A. "L'iconographie oubliée de l'Arc Ephésien de
        Sainte Marie Majeure à Rome," Byzantion 31 (1961) 413-504.
        [with plates]

49.11   Budge, E.A.W. Legends of Our Lady Mary the Perpetual Vir-
        gin and Her Mother Hanna Translated from the Ethiopic Manu-
        scripts Collected by King Theodore of Makdala and Now in
        The British Museum. London, 1922. [Eth. texts and ET]

49.12   Budge, E.A.W. One Hundred and Ten Miracles of Our Lady,
        Translated from Ethiopic MSS. London, 1933.

49.13   Campenhausen, H. von. "Die Jungfrauengeburt in der Theo-
        logie der alten Kirche," KerDog 8 (1962) 1-26.

49.14 Capelle, B. "La fête de la Vierge à Jérusalem au Ve siècle," Museon 56 (1943) 1-33.

49.15 Cerulli, E. "Il codice di Leningrado del libro etiopico dei miracoli di Maria," Rendiconti della Reale Academie dei Lincei 20 (1965) 1f.

49.16 Chaîne, M., ed. Apocrypha de Beata Maria Virgine (CSCO 39-40; Scriptores Aethiopici 22-23) Louvain, 1955.

49.17 Chaîne, M. "Catéchèse attribuée à S. Basile de Césarée: Une lettre apocryphe de S. Luc," ROC 3 (1922-23) 150-59, 271-302. [This letter reputedly by Luke, the physician from Antioch, describes in particular the building of the first church, which was dedicated to Mary. Cop. text with French trans.]

49.18 Chaîne, M. "Le cycle de Marie dans les Apocryphes Éthiopiens," MJos 1 (1906) 189-96.

49.19 Clement, P. "Le sens chrétien et la maternité divine de Marie avant le conflit nestorien," ETL 4 (1928) 599-613.

49.20 Cothenet, E. "Marie dans les Apocryphes," Maria: Études sur la Ste Vierge. Paris, 1961. Vol. 6. Pp. 71-156.

49.21 Delius, W. Texte zur Geschichte der Marienverehrung und Marienverkündigung in der alten Kirche (KlT 178) Berlin, 1973³.

49.22 Erbetta, M. "Parole della Vergine a Giovanni XII," Apoc. del NT. 3. P. 141.

49.23 Esbroeck, M. van. "Généalogie de la Vierge," AnBoll 91 (1973) 347-58.

49.24 Fabricius, J.A. "De Epistola S. Mariae tributa ad Florentinos," Cod.Apoc.NT. 2. Pp. 851f.

49.25 Fabricius, J.A. "De Epistola S. Mariae tributa ad S. Ignatium," Cod.Apoc.NT. 2. Pp. 834-44.

49.26 Fabricius, J.A. "De Epistola S. Mariae tributa ad Messanenses," Cod.Apoc.NT. 2. Pp. 844-50.

49.27 Ferotin, M. Le liber mozarabicus sacramentorum et les manuscrits mozarabes. Paris, 1912. Pp. 786-95.

49.28 Frank, E.C.D. The History of the Blessed Virgin Mary: Its Apocryphal Basis and the Purpose of Its Composition. Melbourne Dissertation, 1974.

49.29 Garcia Castro, M. "Los apócrifos marianos," CiTom 77 (1950)
       145-75.

49.30 Genthe, F.W. Die Jungfrau Maria ihre Evangelien und ihre
       Wunder. Halle, 1852.

49.31 Gordillo, M. Mariologia Orientalis (Orientalia Christiana Ana-
       lecta 141) Rome, 1954.

49.32 Goubert, P. "L'Arc Éphésien de Sainte-Marie-Majeure et les
       évangiles apocryphes," Mélanges E. Tisserant (Studi e
       Testi 231-37) Rome, 1964. Vol. 2. Pp. 187-215.

49.33 Goubert, P. "Influence des évangiles apocryphes sur l'icono-
       graphie mariale (de Castelseprio à la Cappadocie)," Maria
       et Ecclesia (Acta Congressus Mariologici) London, Rome,
       1960. Pp. 147-64.

49.34 Grébaut, S. "La Prière de Marie au Golgotha," JA 226 (1935)
       273-86.

49.35 James, M.R. "The Birth of Mary," ANT. Pp. 19f.

49.36 Jannsens, A. De Hl. Maagd en Moeder Gods, Vol. 1. Het
       Dogma en den Apocriefen. Antwerpen, 1926.

49.37 Jugie, M. "Homélies mariales byzantines," PO 19 (1925) 344-
       87.

49.38 Kaufhold, W. Die Verkündigung an Maria nach Apokryphen
       in Literatur und Kunst. Freiburg Dissertation, 1942.

49.39 Kirpichnikov, A. "Sayings About the Life of the Virgin Mary
       and Their Expression in Medieval Art," Žurnal Ministerstva
       Narodnago Prosveščhenija. 1883. [in Russian]*

49.40 Kleinschmidt, B. Die heilige Anna. Ihre Verehrung in Ges-
       chichte, Kunst und Volkstum. Düsseldorf, 1930.

49.41 Kottackal, J. "The Life of Mary According to the Apocryphal
       Writings," Biblebhashyam 3 (1977) 303-12.

49.42 Lacau, P. FAC. P. 2 [Cop. texts]

49.43 Langevin, P.É. "Les écrits apocryphes du NT et la Vierge
       Marie," De primordiis cultus Mariani: Acta congressus
       Mariologici-Mariani in Lusitania anno 1967. Rome, 1970.
       Vol. 4. Pp. 233-52.

49.44 Lehner, F.A. von. Die Marienverehung in den ersten Jahr-
       hunderten. Stuttgart, 1886[2].

49.45 Liell, F. Die Darstellungen der allerseligsten Jungfrau und Gottesbärerin Maria auf den Kunstdenkmälern der Katakomben. Freiburg, 1887.

49.46 Mécérian, J. La Vierge Marie dans la littérature médievale de l'Arménie. Grégoire de Narek et Nersès de Lampron (Collection Arménologique 1) Beirut, 1954.

49.47 Migne, J.-P. "Joachim," Dictionnaire. 2. Cols. 399-402. ["Joachim" is the name given to Mary's father.]

49.48 Migne, J.-P. "Marie," Dictionnaire. 2. Cols. 499-542.

49.49 Moraldi, L. "Frammento copto sulla morte e risurrezione di Maria," Apoc. del NT. 1. Pp. 896-900.

49.50 Moraldi, L. "Il vangelo di Maria," Apoc. del NT. 1. Pp. 453-58. [Pap. Berolinensis 8502]

49.51 Muñoz Iglesias, S. "Los evangelios de la infancia y las infancias de los héroes," Estudios Bíblicos 16 (1957) 5-36.

49.52 Neubert, E. Marie dans l'Église anténicéene. Paris, 1908.

49.53 O'Carroll, M. THEOTOKOS: A Theological Encyclopedia of the Blessed Virgin Mary. Wilmington, Del., 1983.

49.54 Peretto, L.M. "La 'Natività' di Maria," Marianum 22 (1960) 176-96.

49.55 Plumpe, J.E. "Some Little-Known Early Witnesses to Mary's Virginitas in Partu," TS 9 (1948) 567-77.

49.56 Porfir'ev, I.Y. "Apocryphal Sayings About New Testament People and Events in Manuscripts of the Solovetski Library," SbORJS 52 (1890) 76-96, 170-79, 281-95. [in Russia]

49.57 Potter, M.A. The Legendary Story of Christ's Childhood. New York, 1899.

49.58 Puech, H.-Ch. "The 'Genna Marias,'" HSW. 1. Pp. 344f.

49.59 Puech, H.-C. "The Gospel According to Mary," HSW. 1. Pp. 340-44. [the work discussed is neither BirMar or GosBirMar]

49.60 Reinsch, R. Die Pseudo-Evangelien von Jesu und Maria's Kindheit in der roman. und german. Literatur. Halle, 1879.

49.61 Repp, F. "Untersuchungen zur alttschechischen Marienlegende," ZSlaw 4 (1959) 321-33.

49.62 Riviera, A. "La muerte de Maria en la tradición hasta la Edad Media (siglos I-VIII)," Estudios Marianos 9 (1950) 71-100.

49.63 Robson, J. "Stories of Jesus and Mary," Muslim World 40 (1950) 236-43. [John Rylands Lib. MS Arab nr. 664]

49.64 Rost, C. Les Evangiles apocryphes de l'enfance de Jésus-Christ avec une introduction sur les récits de Mathieu et de Luc. Thesis, Montauban, 1894.

49.65 Rush, A.C. "Mary's Holiness in the NT Apocrypha," AmER 133 (1955) 99-108.

49.66 Sacharov, V. "A Selection of Apocryphal Sayings About Mary Widespread in Ancient Russia," Christianskoe Ctenie (Mar/ Ap. 1888) 83-91. [in Russian]

49.67 Salgado, J.M. "La Présentation de Marie au Temple," PalCler 51 (1972) 469-74.

49.68 Santos Otero, A. de. "Libro sobre la Infancia del Salvador," Evangelios Apócrifos. Pp. 366-72. [Lat. text and Spanish translation]

49.69 Santos Otero, A. de. "Nacimiento de Maria (Genna Marias)," Evangelios Apócrifos. P. 70.

49.70 Schade, O. Narrationes de vita et conversatione B. M. V. et de pueritia et adolescentia Salvatoris. Halle, 1870.

49.71 Söll, G. "Haben das Heidentum und die Apokryphen die Marienverehrung illegitim beeinflusst?" Mariologische Studien 4 (1969) 25-33.

49.72 Spedaglieri, F. Maria nella Scrittura e nella tradizione della chiesa primitiva. Vol. 2: Studi e problemi. Parte 2: I privilegi della Madre di Dio Redentore. Rome, 1975.

49.73 Stegmüller, F. Repertorium Biblicum. 1. Pp. 133, 140; 8. Pp. 112, 124.

49.74 Tanguy, J. "L'Assomption de Notre Dame dans l'art," in Mémoires du Congr. Marial de Nantes. Nantes-Paris, 1925. Pp. 149-56.

49.75 Testa, E. "Cultus Marianus in textibus Nazarethanis primorum saeculorum," De Primordiis cultus Mariani: Acta congressus Mariologici-Mariani in Lusitania anno 1967 celebrati. Rome, 1970. Vol. 5. Pp. 21-34.

49.76 Testa, E. "De mutua relatione inter mariologiam Mahumetis et

mariologiam judeo-christianorum," De cultu mariano saec.
VI-XI apud varias nationes et secundum fontes islamicos.
Rome, 1972. Vol. 5. Pp. 403-32.

49.77   Testuz, M., ed. and tr. Nativité de Marie. (Papyrus Bod-
        mer 5) Cologny-Geneva, 1958. [Gk. and Fr. trans.]

49.78   Till, W. "Euangelion kata Mariam (Pap. Berlin 8502)," La
        parola del passato 1 (1946) 260-65. [appendix by G.P.
        Carratelli on P.Ryl. 463]

49.79   Till, W. Die gnostischen Schriften des koptischen Papyrus
        Berolinensis 8502 (TU 60.5) Berlin, 1955.

49.80   Trens, M. Vida y leyenda de la Virgen a través del arte
        español. Barcelona, 1954.

49.81   Turrado, L. "María en los Evangelios apócrifos," Cultura
        Biblica 11 (1954) 380-90.

49.82   Variot, J. "La Nativité de Marie," Évangiles Apocryphes.
        Pp. 60-63.

49.83   Venturi, A. La Madonna: Svolgimento artistico delle rappre-
        sentazioni della Vergine. Milan, 1900.

49.84   Vona, C. "Elementi apocrifi e populari nella omiletica mariana
        antica," ED 10 (1957) 51-64.

49.85   Wilson, R. McL. "Mary, Birth (or Descent) of," ZPEB. 4.
        P. 106.

50.   MARY, GOSPEL OF THE BIRTH OF

The GosBirMar, attributed to Jerome, is an amplification
of the early chapters of PsMt (see also the entries under
that heading). For entries on the Gospel of Mary in Pap.
Berolinensis 8502, see Mary Cycle.

(See also 1.12, 67, 75, 86, 105, 116, 147, 484; 32.9.)

50.1   Agius, T. A. "On Pseudo-Jerome, Epistle IX," JTS 24
        (1922) 176-83.

50.2   Amann, E. Le Protoévangile de Jacques et ses remaniements
        latins. Paris, 1910. Pp. 340-65. [Lat. text and French
        trans.]

50.3   Beyers, R. De Nativitate Mariae. Kritische voorstudie en
        tekstuitgave. Antwerp, 1980 .

50.4   Cowper, B. H. "The Gospel of the Nativity of Mary," Apoc-
        ryphal Gospels. Pp. 84-98. [ET]

50.5   Daniel-Rops, H. Les Évangiles de la Vierge. (Bibliothèque
        chrétienne d'histoire) Paris, 1948. [ET by Alastair Guinan,
        The Book of Mary. New York, 1960.]

50.6   Erbetta, M. "Il Libro della Natività di Maria," Apoc. del NT.
        1.2. Pp. 71-77.

50.7   Fabricius, J. A. "Evangelium de Nativitate S. Mariae," Cod.
        Apoc.NT. 1. Pp. 1-38. [Lat.]

50.8   Hone, W. The Apocryphal New Testament. London, 1820;
        New York, [1845]. Pp. 17-24 [Am. ed.].

50.9   James, M. R. "The Gospel of the Birth of Mary," ANT. P.
        79f.

50.10   Jones, J. A New and Full Method of Settling the Canonical
        Authority of the New Testament. 3 vols. London, 1726,
        1798^2. Vol. 2. Pp. 77-93. [see also pp. 130-65]

50.11   Lambot, C. "L'homélie du Pseudo-Jérôme sur l'assomption et
        l'Évangile de la Nativité de Marie d'après une lettre d'Hinc-
        mar," RBen 46 (1934) 265-82.

50.12   Lipsius, R. A. "Gospels, Apocryphal," Dictionary of Chris-
        tian Biography, eds. W. Smith and H. Wace. 4 vols. Lon-
        don, 1877-87. Vol. 2. Pp. 702f.

50.13   Migne, J.-P. "Naissance de la Vierge. (Évangile de la Nais-
        sance de la Vierge.)," Dictionnaire. 2. Cols. 635f. [short
        discussion, no trans.]

50.14   Migne, J.-P. "Nativité. (Évangile de la Nativité de Sainte
        Marie.)," Dictionnaire. 1. Cols. 1045-56. [Intro. and
        French trans.]

50.15   Moraldi, L. "Vangelo sulla nascita di Maria," Apoc. del NT.
        1. Pp. 95-104.

50.16   Morin, G. "Notes litergiques sur l'assomption," RBen 5 (1888)
        342-51. [see esp. p. 350]

50.17   Santos Otero, A. "Libro Sobre la Natividad de Maria," Evan-
        gelios Apócrifos. Pp. 243-58. [Lat. text and Spanish trans.]

50.18   Scheffczyk, L. Das Mariengeheimnis in Frömmigkeit und Lehre
        der Karolingerzeit. Leipzig, 1959.

50.19   Stegmüller, F. Repertorium Biblicum. 1. P. 133; 8. Pp.
        112-14.

50.20   Tischendorf, K. "Evangelium de nativitate Mariae," Evangelia
        Apocrypha. Pp. xxii-xxxi, 113-21. [Lat. text]

50.21   Wake, W., and N. Lardner. "The Gospel of the Birth of Mary,"
        ApocNT. Pp. 58-67. [ET]

50.22   Walker, A. "The Gospel of the Nativity of Mary," ANF   8.
        Pp. 384-87. [ET]

50.23   Wilson, R. McL. "Mary, Gospel of the Birth of," ZPEB.   4.
        P. 106.

51. MARY, PASSING OF
(= TRANSITUS MARIAE AND DORMITIONE MARIAE)

(See also the entries under AVir; and 1.18, 46, 284; 50.16.)

51.1   Amann, É. "Le Transitus Mariae," DBSup. 1. Cols. 483f.

51.2   Amiot, F. "Le Transitus Mariae," Évangiles Apoc. Pp. 112-
        34. [French trans.]

51.3   Arras, V. De Transitu Mariae apocrypha aethiopice. (CSCO;
        Scriptores Aethiopici 342-343) Louvain, 1973.

51.4   Bagatti, B. "Le due relazioni del 'Transitus Mariae,'" Mari-
        anum 32 (1970) 5-13.

51.5   Bagatti, B. "Ricerche sull'iconografia della Koimesis o Dorm-
        itio Mariae," LA 25 (1975) 225-53.

51.6   Bagatti, B. "Ricerche sulla Tradizione della morte della Ver-
        gine," SacDoctr 69-70 (1973) 185-214.

51.7   Bagatti, B. "S. Pietro nella Dormitio Mariae," BO 13 (1971)
        42-48.

51.8   Baldi, D. "La tradizione monumentale della dormizione a Ger-
        usalemme," Studia Mariana. Rome, 1948. Vol. 1. Pp. 129-
        158.

51.9   Balić, C. "Considerationes circa 'Transitus B. V. Mariae'
        Pseudo-Melitonis," De primordiis cultus mariani. Rome,
        1970. Vol. 4. Pp. 341-52.

51.10   Barsov, E. "The Dream of the Mother of God in a Striking
        National Version (of a Story)," ČOIDR 3 (1896). [in Rus-
        sian]*

51.11   Bonaccorsi, P.G. "Il Transito della Beata Vergine Maria,"
        Vangeli Apocrifi. 1. Pp. 260-89. [Gk. text and Italian
        trans.]

51.12   Bonsirven, J., and C. Bigaré. "Transitus Mariae," Intro. à
        la Bible. 2. P. 753.

51.13   Brou, D.L. "Restes de l'ancienne homélie sur la Dormition de
        l'archevêque Jean de Thessalonique dans le plus ancien anti-
        phonaire connu et le dernier Magnificat de la Vierge," ALW
        2 (1952) 84-93.

51.14   Cabrol, F. "Transitus Mariae," DACL. 1. Col. 2993.

51.15   Capelle, B. "Vestiges grecs et latins d'un antique 'Transitus'
        de la Vierge," AnBoll 67 (1949) 21-48.

51.16   Carli, L. "Le fonti del racconto della dormizione di Maria di
        Giovanni Tessalonicese," Marianum 2 (1940) 308-13.

51.17   Cerulli, E. "La festa etiopica del Patto di misericordia e le
        sue fonti nel greco 'Liber de Transitu,'" SBN 9 (1957) 53-
        71.

51.18   Chaine, M., ed. Apocrypha de Beata Maria Virgine (CSCO
        39-40; Scriptores Aethiopici 22-23) Louvain, 1955. [repr.
        of Scriptores Aethiopici series 1, vol. 7; Eth. and Lat.
        texts; see esp. vol. 39 (22) pp. 21-49 and vol. 40 (23) pp.
        17-42]

51.19   Chaine, M. "Le discours de Théodose, patriarche d'Alexandrie,
        sur la Dormition," ROC 29 (1933-34) 272-304.

51.20   Chaise, F. de la. "A l'origine des récits apocryphes du 'Trans-
        itus Mariae,'" EphMar 29 (1979) 77-90.

51.21   Daietsi, P.I. "Libellus de dormitione beatae virginis Mariae
        auct. Ps.-Nicodemo," Ankanon girkh Nor Ketakar anatz.
        Venice, 1898. Vol. 1. Pp. 452-78. [Arm. text]

51.22   Dalmais, I.H. "Les Apocryphes de la Dormition et l'ancienne
        liturgie de Jérusalem," Bible et Terre Sainte 179 (1976) 11-
        14.

51.23 D'Alsace, B. Le Tombeau de la Sainte Vierge à Jérusalem.
      Jerusalem, 1903.

51.24 Donahue, C. The Testament of Mary: The Gaelic Version of
      the Dormitio Mariae, Together with an Irish Latin Version
      (Fordham University Studies) New York, 1942. Pp. 8-70.

51.25 Enger, M. Iohannis apostoli de transitu beatae Mariae virginis
      liber. Eberfeld, 1854.

51.26 Esbroeck, M. van. "Apocryphes géorgiens de la Dormition,"
      AnBoll 91 (1973) 55-75.

51.27 Esbroeck, M. van. "Nouveaux apocryphes de la Dormition
      conservés en géorgien," AnBoll 90 (1972) 363-69.

51.28 Fabricius, J.A. "S. Johannis de Transitu S. Mariae," Cod.
      Apoc.NT. 1. P. 352.

51.29 Felicolo, C. "Il transito della Vergine secondo l'apocrifo la-
      tino," Terra Sancta 22 (1947) 137-44.

51.30 Franko, I. Apocrypha and Legends. L'vov, 1898. Vol. 3.
      Pp. 384-94. [in Russian]

51.31 Gabrielovich, E.P. Ephèse ou Jérusalem: Tombeau de la
      Sainte Vierge. Paris, 1897.

51.32 Gordillo, M. "La muerte de María, Madre de Dios, en la tra-
      dición de la Iglesia de Jérusalen," EstMar 9 (1950) 43-62.

51.33 Haibach-Reinisch, M. Ein neuer 'Transitus Mariae' des Pseudo-
      Melito. Rome, 1962.

51.34 Halkin, F. "Une légende byzantine de la Dormition: l'Epitomé
      du récit de Jean de Thessalonique," REByz 11 (1953) 156-64.

51.35 Jacimirskij, A.I. "Apocrypha and Legends ... V," IzvORJS
      14 (1909) 311-22. [in Russian]

51.36 Jugie, M. "Iohannis Archiepiscopi Thessalonicensis sermo de
      dormitione b. Mariae Virginis," PO 19.3 (1926) 375-431.

51.37 Kalužniacki, E. "Zur Geschichte der Wanderung des Traumes
      der Mutter Gottes," Archiv f. slavische Philologie 11 (1888)
      628-30.

51.38 Kirpicnikov, A. The Work of the Sixth Archaeological Confer-
      ence in Odessa. Odessa, 1888. Vol. 2. Pp. 191-250. [in
      Russian]

51.39   Kretzenbacher, L. "Südost-Uberlieferung zum apokryphen
        'Traum Mariens,'" Sitzungsberichte zu Bay. Akademie der
        Wissenschaft Phil.-hist. Klasse, Jahrg. 1975. Heft. 1.
        Munich, 1975.

51.40   Lagarde, P. de "Transitus b. Mariae Virginis," Aegyptiaca.
        Göttingen, 1883. Pp. 38-63.

51.41   Lausberg, H. "Zur literarischen Gestaltung des 'Transitus
        Beatae Mariae,'" Historiches Jahrbuch 72 (1953) 25-49.

51.42   Lemm, O. von. "Zu einer sahidischen Version der 'Dormitio
        Mariae,'" Koptische Miscellen. Pp. 335-39.

51.43   Leroy, L. "La Dormition de la Vierge," ROC 15 (1910) 162-72.

51.44   Lewis, A.S. Apocrypha Syriaca: The Protoevangelium Iacobi
        and Transitus Mariae (Studia Sinaitica 9) Cambridge, 1902.
        [Syr. texts and ET]

51.45   Manns, F. "La Mort de Marie dans le texte de la 'Dormition
        de Marie,'" Aug 19 (1979) 507-15.

51.46   Marocco, G. "Nuovi documenti sull'Assunzione del Medio Evo
        latino: due transitus dai codici latini 59 e 105 di Ivrea,"
        Marianum 12 (1950) 449-52.

51.47   Migne, J.-P. "Marie," Dictionnaire. 2. Cols. 503-42.

51.48   Migne, J.-P. "Méliton. (Livre du passage de la très-sainte
        Vierge Mère de Dieu.)," Dictionnaire. 2. Cols. 587-98.
        [French trans.]

51.49   Montagna, D. "Appunti critici sul 'Transitus Mariae' dello
        pseudo-Melitone," Marianum 27 (1965) 177-95.

51.50   Moraldi, L. "Morte di nostra signora sempre vergine teotoco
        Maria," Apoc. del NT. 1. Pp. 841-62.

51.51   Moraldi, L. "Transito Colbertiano," Apoc. del NT. 1. Pp.
        879-84.

51.52   Moraldi, L. "Transito della beata vergine Maria," Apoc. del
        NT. 1. Pp. 863-78.

51.53   Moraldi, L. "Transito R," Apoc. del NT. 1. Pp. 825-40.

51.54   Novaković, S. "Apocryphal Tales about the Death of the Vir-
        gin Mother and Other Apocryphal Details about the Virgin
        Mother," Starine 18 (1886) 188-208. [in Serbo-Croatian]

51.55 Novaković, S. Examples of Literature and Language. Bel-
       grade, 1904[3]. Pp. 502-04. [in Serbo-Croatian]

51.56 Penna, A. "Transito (Dormizione) di Maria," EncCatt. 12.
       Col. 432.

51.57 Petriceicu-Hasdeu, B. Cărtile poporane ale Românilor. Bu-
       charest, 1879. P. 398.

51.58 Plessis, J. Valeur historique des apocryphes de Transitu
       Mariae. Vannes, 1925.

51.59 Popov, A.N. "Bibliographical Materials Collected by A.N.
       Popov 2-3," ČOIDR (1880) 1-65. [in Russian]*

51.60 Popov, A.N. "Dormitio Deiparae--Bibliographical Material,"
       Chtenija 3 (1880) 9-65. [in Russian]

51.61 Porfiryev, I.Y. "Apocryphal Sayings About New Testament
       People and Events in Manuscripts of the Solovetski Library,"
       SbORJS 52 (1890) 76-96, 270-79, 281-95. [in Russian]

51.62 Pypin, A.N. False and Dismissed Books of Ancient Russia.
       Petrograd, 1862. Pp. 125-27. [in Russian]

51.63 Radčenko, K. Report on Studies with Manuscripts in the Li-
       braries of Moscow and Petersburg. Kiev, 1898. Pp. 18f.
       [in Russian]

51.64 Revillout, J.E. "Mort de la Vierge," PO 2 (1907) 175-80.

51.65 Rivière, J. "Le plus vieux transitus latin et son dérivé
       grec," RTAM (1936) 5-23.*

51.66 Rivière, J. "Rôle du démon au jugement particulier: Contri-
       bution à l'histoire des 'Transitus Mariae,'" BLE 48 (1947)
       49-56, 98-126.

51.67 Robinson, F. "Bohairic Accounts of the Falling Asleep of
       Mary with Sahidic Fragments," Coptic Apocryphal Gospels
       (T&S 4.2) Cambridge, 1896. Pp. 43-127. [Coptic texts
       and ET]

51.68 Rush, A.C. "Assumption Theology in the 'Transitus Mariae,'"
       AmER 123 (1950)*

51.69 Rush, A.C. "Little-known Testimonies to Peter's Primacy,"
       TS 11 (1950) 570-76.

51.70 Rush, A.C. "Mors Mariae, vita aeterna: An Insight into NT
       Apocrypha," AmER 142 (1960) 257-66.

51.71   Rush, A.C. "Scriptural Texts and the Assumption in the
        'Transitus Mariae,'" CBQ 12 (1950) 367-78.

51.72   Salazar, I.T. "Acta Dormitionis et Assumptionis b. Virginis
        Mariae Dei-Genetricis, Dominae Nostrae, ex Legendario Sego-
        biensi Ms. et aliis Breviariis," Martyrologium Hispanum.
        London, 1656. Vol. 4. Pp. 480-82.

51.73   Santos Otero, A. de. "Narración del Pseudo José de Arimatea,'
        Evangelios Apócrifos. Pp. 646-59. [Lat. text and Spanish
        translation]

51.74   Santos Otero, A. de. "Obdormitio Deiparae," Altslavischen
        Apok. 2. Pp. 161-95.

51.75   Santos Otero, A. de. "Somnus Deiparae," Altslavischen Apok.
        1. P. 196.

51.76   Schmidt, C. "Tod der Jungfrau Maria," Gesch. altchrist. Lit.
        1. Pp. 923f.

51.77   Seymour, D. "Irish Versions of the Transitus Mariae," JTS
        23 (1921-22) 36-41.

51.78   Sreznevskij, J. "Information and Notes About Little Known
        and Unknown Works," SbORJS 1 (1867) 61-76. [in Russian]

51.79   Stefanič, V., et al. Croatian Literature. Zagreb, 1969. Pp.
        149-53. [in Serbo-Croatian]

51.80   Stegmüller, F. Repertorium Biblicum. 1. Pp. 135-39; 8.
        Pp. 115-23.

51.81   Stojanović, L. Spomenik. Vol. 3. P. 194.

51.82   Tischendorf, K. "Iohannis liber de dormitione Mariae," Apoc-
        alypses Apocryphae. Pp. 95-112. [Gk. text]

51.83   Tischendorf, K. "Transitus Mariae. A," Apocalypses Aprocy-
        phae. Pp. 113-23. [Lat. text]

51.84   Tischendorf, K. "Transitus Mariae. B," Apocalypses Apoc-
        ryphae. Pp. 124-36. [Lat. text]

51.85   Vallecillo, M. "El 'Transitus Mariae' según el manuscrito Vat-
        icano O. R. 1982," Verdad y Vida 30 (1972) 187-260.

51.86   Veder, W.R. The Scaliger Paterikon. Vol. 1: Paleographic,
        Linguistic and Structural Description; Vol. 2: Text in Fac-
        simile, Transcription and Translation. Zug., 1976-1978.

51.87 Vetter, P. "Die armenische dormitio Mariae," TQ 84 (1902)
       421-49.

51.88 Voigt, S. "Une accusation apocryphe contre l'apôtre Jean et
       son historicité possible," SH 2 (Jerusalem, 1975) 278-88.

51.89 Vranska, C. The Apocrypha Concerning the Virgin Mother in
       the Bulgarian Folk Song (Collection of the Bulgarian Academy
       of Sciences 3-4). Sofia, 1940. Pp. 51-58. [in Bulgarian]

51.90 Walker, A. "The Book of John Concerning the Falling Asleep
       of Mary," ANF   8. Pp. 587-91. [ET]

51.91 Walker, A. "The Passing of Mary," ANF   8. Pp. 592-98.

51.92 Widding, O., and H. Bekker-Nielsen. "An Old Norse Trans-
       lation of the 'Transitus Mariae,'" Mediaeval Studies 23 (1961)
       324-33.

51.93 Willard, R. "The Testament of Mary: The Irish Account of
       the Death of the Virgin," RTAM 9 (1937) 341-61.

51.94 Willard, R. "La ville d'Agathê? Note sur le Transitus Mariae
       C," Échos d'Orient 38 (1939) 346-54.

51.95 Wratislaw-Mitrowic, L., and N. Okunev. "La dormition de la
       sainte Vierge dans la peinture médiévale orthodoxe,"
       Byzantino-Slavica 3 (1931) 134-73.

51.96 Wright, W. ALNT. Pp. KZ-ŠH (Syr.); 18-51 (ET); 59-63
       (notes).

51.97 Wright, W. "The Departure of my Lady Mary from this World,"
       Journal of Sacred Literature and Biblical Record 6 (1865)
       419-48; 7 (1865) 129-60. [Syr. text]

51.98 Zoega, G. "Transitus Mariae," Catlogus codicum copticorum
       manu scriptorum qui in Museo Borgiano Velitris adservantur.
       Rome, 1810. Pp. 223f.

52. MARY, QUESTIONS OF

52.1   Erbetta, M. "Le Questioni di Maria," Apoc. del NT. 1. P.
       292.

52.2   Fabricius, J.A. "Mariae Interrogationes Majores et Minores,"
       Cod.Apoc.NT. 1. P. 355.

52.3   James, M.R. "Lesser Questions of Mary," ANT. P. 20.

52.4   Liechtenhan, R. "Untersuchungen zur koptisch-gnostischen
        Litteratur," ZWT 44 (1901) 240.

52.5   Puech, H.-Ch. "Die Fragen Marias," HS. 1. Pp. 250f.

52.6   Puech, H.-Ch. "The Questions of Mary," HSW. 1. Pp. 338-
        40.

52.7   Stegmüller, F. Repertorium Biblicum. 1. P. 140; 8. P. 124.

53. PSEUDO-MATTHEW, GOSPEL OF

See also the entries listed under GosBirMar.

(See also 1.53, 86, 105, 116, 147, 319, 484; 35.26, 151; 46.31; 96.40,
73, 80.)

53.1   Amann, É. Le Protévangile de Jacques et ses remaniements
        latins. Paris, 1910. Pp. 272-339. [Lat. text and Fr.
        transl.]

53.2   Amiot, F. "Livre de la Naissance de la Bienheureuse Marie
        et de l'Enfance du Sauveur (Évangile du Pseudo-Matthieu),
        Evangiles Apoc. Pp. 65-79. [French translation]

53.3   Bishop, E.F.F. "Is Pontius Pilate's Aqueduct Referred to in
        the Qur'ân?" Muslim World 52 (1962) 189-93.

53.4   Bonaccorsi, P.G. "Lo Pseudo Matteo (Libro sulla nascita della
        Beata Maria e sull'infanzia del Salvatore)," Vangeli Apocrifi.
        1. Pp. 152-231. [Lat. text and Italian translation]

53.5   Bonsirven, J., and C. Bigaré, "Évangile du pseudo-Matthieu,"
        Intro. à la Bible. 2. P. 752.

53.6   Boulton, M.B.M. The Old French 'Évangile de l'Enfance': A
        Critical Edition. Diss. U. of Pennsylvania, 1976.

53.7   Caravaggi, G. Vangeli provenzali dell'Infanzia (Testi e manuali
        47) Modena, 1963.

53.8   Cartlidge, D.R., and D.L. Dungan. "The Gospel of Pseudo-
        Matthew," Documents. Pp. 98-103. [ET of selections]

53.9   Cowper, B.H. "The Gospel of Pseudo-Matthew," The Great

Rejected Books of the Biblical Apocrypha (The Sacred Books
and Early Literature of the East 14) New York, London,
1917. Pp. 261-95. [ET]

53.10 Cowper, B. H. "The Gospel of Pseudo-Matthew, or of the Infancy of Mary and of Jesus," Apocryphal Gospels. Pp. 27-
83. [ET]

53.11 Cullmann, O. "Auszüge aus dem Pseudo-Matthäusevangelium,"
HS. 1. Pp. 306-09. [see also pp. 303f.]

53.12 Cullmann, O. "Extracts from the Gospel of Pseudo-Matthew,"
HSW. 1. Pp. 410-12. [see also p. 406]

53.13 Erbetta, M. "Il Vangelo dello Ps. Matteo," Apoc. del NT.
1.2. Pp. 44-70.

53.14 Ferri, S. "Nota al testo latino dell' 'Evangelium infantiae,'"
Studi Mediolatini e Volgari 1 (1953) 119-25.

53.15 Franko, I. "The Apocryphal Gospel of Pseudo-Matthew and
Its Traces in Ukranian-Russian Literature," Zapysky nauko-
voho tovarystva im. sevcenka 35-36 (1900) 1-32. [in Ukrain-
ian]

53.16 Gijsel, J. Die unmittelbare Textüberlieferung des sog. Pseudo-
Matthäus (Verhandelingen van de Koninklijke Academie voor
wetenschappen, letteren en schone kunsten van België.
Klasse der Letteren 43) Brussels, 1981.

53.17 Gijsel, J. "Le problème de la contamination," NovT 18 (1976)
132-57.

53.18 González-Blanco, E. Los Evangelios apócrifos. Madrid, 1934.
1.*

53.19 Gousset, R. "Le boeuf et l'âne à la nativité du Christ,"
Mélanges d'archeologie et d'histoire 4 (1884) 332-44.

53.20 Hilgenfeld, A. Novum Testamentum extra canonem receptum.
Leipzig, 1866. Pp. 49f.

53.21 James, M.R. "The Liber de Infantia, or Gospel of Pseudo-
Matthew," ANT. Pp. 70-79.

53.22 Kate, R. ten. "Hrotsvits Maria und das Evangelium des
Pseudo-Matthäus," Classica et Mediaevalia 22 (1961) 195-204.

53.23 Lachs, S.T. "A 'Jesus Passage' in the Talmud Reexamined,"
JQR 59 (1969) 244-47.

266

53.24   Mazal, O. "Die Uberlieferung des 'Evangelium Pseudo-Matthaei' in der Admonter Riesenbibel," NovT 9 (1967) 61-78.

53.25   Michel, C. "Évangile du Pseudo-Matthieu," EvApoc. 1. Pp. xix-xxii, 53-159. [Lat. text and Fr. transl.]

53.26   Migne, J.-P. "Nativité. (Histoire de la Nativité de Marie et de l'Enfance du Sauveur.)," Dictionnaire. 1. Cols. 1057-88. [Preface by M. Brunet and French translation]

53.27   Migne, J.-P. PL. 30. Cols. 297-305. [Lat. text]

53.28   Moraldi, L. "Vangelo dello Pseudo Matteo," Apoc. del NT. 1. Pp. 195-239.

53.29   Nola, A.M. di. Evangelo apocrifo della Natività. Parma, 1963.

53.30   Peeters, P. EvApoc. 1. Pp. xiii-xviii.

53.31   Pistelli, E. Il Protevangelo di Jacopo: Prima Traduzione italiana con introduzione e note. Segue un'appendice dallo Pseudo-Matteo. Lanciano, 1919.

53.32   Repp, F. "Untersuchungen zur alttschechischen Marienlegende," ZSlaw 4 (1959) 321-33.

53.33   Santos Otero, A. de. "Evangelio del Pseudo Mateo," Evangelios Apócrifos. Pp. 177-242. [Lat. text and Spanish translation]

53.34   Schade, O. Narrationes de vita et conversatione Beatae Mariae Virginis et de pueritia et adolescentia Salvatoris. Halle, 1876.

53.35   Stegmüller, F. Repertorium Biblicum. 1. Pp. 141f.; 8. Pp. 125-28.

53.36   Thilo, J.C. Codex Apocryphus Novi Testamenti. Leipzig, 1832. Vol. 1. Pp. 319-36. [Lat. text]

53.37   Tischendorf, K. von. "Pseudo-Matthaei evangelium," Evangelia Apocrypha. Pp. xxii-xxxi, 51-112.

53.38   Tischendorf, K. von. "Ad Pseudo-Matthaei evangelium: Plura scripturae codicis D exempla proferuntur," Apocalypses Apocryphae. Pp. LVI-LX.

53.39   Variot, J. "L'Evangile du Pseudo-Mathieu," Évangiles Apocryphes. Pp. 51-59.

53.40   Walker, A. "The Gospel of Pseudo-Matthew," ANF 8. Pp. 368-83. [ET]

53.41   Wilson, R. McL. "Pseudo-Matthew, Gospel of," ZPEB. 4.
        Pp. 950f.

53.42   Wright, W. ALNT. Pp. 11-16 [Syr. text], 7-11 [ET].

                    54. MATTHEW, MARTYRDOM OF;
                         AND MATTHEW CYCLE

(See also 1.346; 7.11, 14, 29.)

54.1   [Archeografičeskaja Kommissija], Daily Readings of the Great
        'Menaea' (Nov. 16, 1910) cols. 2068-79; (Nov. 16-17, 1911)
        cols. 2639-45. [in Russian]

54.2   Atenolfi, T. "I testi della leggenda di S. Mt," Archivi 24
        (1957) 85-97.

54.3   Atenolfi, T. I testi meridionali degli Atti di S. Matteo l'Evan-
        gelista. Rome, 1958.

54.4   Bardenhewer, O. "Die Akten des Matthäus," GAL. 1. Pp.
        588f.

54.5   Bonnet, M. (ed.). "Martyrium Matthaei," AAA. 2.1. Pp.
        xxxiii-xxxv, 217-62. [Gk. and Lat. text]

54.6   Bonwetsch, N. "Matthäus," Gesch. altchrist. Lit. Pp. 906f.

54.7   Demina, E.I. The Tichonravov Collection. Sofia, 1971. Vol.
        2. Pp. 291-96. [in Russian]

54.8   Erbetta, M. "Gli Atti copti di Matteo a Kahanat," Apoc. del
        NT. 2. Pp. 506f.

54.9   Erbetta, M. "Il Martirio di Matteo in Persia," Apoc. del NT.
        2. Pp. 508f.

54.10   Erbetta, M. "Il Martirio di Matteo: La leggenda del Ponto,"
        Apoc. del NT. 2. Pp. 510-17.

54.11   Fabricius, J.A. "Anonymi Acta S. Matthiae," Cod.Apoc.NT.
        2. Pp. 782-84.

54.12   Franko, I. Apocrypha and Legends. L'vov, 1902. Vol. 3,
        Pp. 156-63. [in Russian]

54.13   Harnack, A. "Die Acten des Matthäus," Gesch. altchrist. Lit.
        1. P. 139.

54.14   James, M.R.   "The Martyrdom of Matthew," ANT.   Pp. 460-62.

54.14a Lewis, A.S.   The Mythological Acts of the Apostles (Horae
        Semiticae 4) London, 1904.   Pp. 100-12.   [ET of Ar. texts
        in Horae Semiticae 3]

54.15   Lipsius, R.A.   Die apokryphen Apostelgeschichten und Apos-
        tellegenden.   Brunswick, 1883-1890.   Vol. 2.2.   Pp. 109-41.

54.16   Moraldi, L.   "Martirio del santo apostolo Matteo," Apoc. del
        NT.   2.   Pp. 1635-38.

54.17   Santos Otero, A. de.   "Passio Matthaei," Altslavischen Apok.
        1.   Pp. 130-35.

54.18   Schmidt, C.   "Acten des Matthias," Gesch. altchrist. Lit.   1.
        P. 922.

54.19   Schneemelcher, W., and A. de Santos.   "Later Acts of Other
        Apostles," HSW.   2.   P. 577.

54.20   Schneemelcher, W., and A. de Santos.   "Spätere Akten an-
        deren Apostel," HS.   2.   P. 404.

54.21   Stegmüller, F.   Repertorium Biblicum.   1.   Pp. 197-200; 8.
        Pp. 176-80.

54.22   Tischendorf, K.   "Acta et Martyrium Matthaei," Acta Apos.
        Apoc.   Pp. LX-LXIII, 167-89.   [Intro. and Gk. text]

54.23   Vetter, P.   TQ 87 (1905) 610.*

54.24   Walker, A.   "Acts and Martyrdom of St. Matthew the Apostle,"
        ANF.   8.   Pp. 528-34.   [ET]

54.25   Wilson, R. McL.   "Matthew, Martyrdom of," ZPEB.   4.   Pp.
        138f.

55.   MATTHIAS, GOSPEL AND TRADITIONS OF

55.1   Amann, É.   "Évangile de Matthias," DBSup.   1.   Cols. 478f.

55.2   Bardenhewer, O.   "Das Matthias-, das Philippus- und das
        Thomasevangelium," GAL.   1.   Pp. 529-33.

55.3   Bonaccorsi, P. G.   "Dalle tradizioni di Mattia," Vangeli Apoc-
        rifi.   1.   Pp. 28-31.

55.4 Erbetta, M. "Il Vangelo e le Tradizioni di Mattia," Apoc. del
      NT. 1. Pp. 288-90.

55.5 Harnack, A. "Matthias-Evangelium resp.--Überlieferungen,"
      Gesch. altchrist. Lit. 1. Pp. 17f.; 2.1. Pp. 595-98.

55.6 Hennecke, E. Handbuch, ed. Hennecke. Pp. 90-92, 238-40.

55.7 Hennecke, E. "Matthiasüberlieferungen," H[2]. Pp. 139f.

55.8 James, M. R. "The Gospel or Traditions of Matthias," ANT.
      Pp. 12f.

55.9 Klostermann, E., ed. "Matthiasüberlieferungen," Apocrypha
      II: Evangelien (KlT 8) Berlin, 1929[3]. Pp. 16-18. [Gk.
      witnesses]

55.10 Migne, J.-P. "Matthias. (Ecrits attribués ou relatifs à Saint
      Matthias.)," Dictionnaire. 2. Cols. 543-50. [GosTradMth,
      col. 543; History of Matthias, cols. 543-50]

55.11 Moraldi, L. "Tradizione di Mattia," Apoc. del NT. 1. Pp.
      385f.

55.12 Preuschen, E. "Aus den Überlieferungen des Matthias," Anti-
      legomena. Giessen, 1905[2]. Pp. 13-15, 144f. [Gk. text]

55.13 Puech, H.-C. "Das Evangelium nach Matthias. Die Traditionen
      des Matthias," HS. 1. Pp. 224-28.

55.14 Puech, H.-C. "The Gospel According to Matthias. The Tra-
      ditions of Matthias," HSW. 1. Pp. 308-13.

55.15 Santos Otero, A. de. "Evangelio o Tradiciones de Matias,"
      Evangelios Apócrifos. Pp. 58-60. [Reconstruction of Gk.
      text with Spanish trans.]

55.16 Stegmüller, F. Reportorium Biblicum. 1. P. 143; 8. Pp.
      128f.

55.17 Zahn, T. "Das Evangelium und die Überlieferungen des Mat-
      thias," Neutest. Kanons. 2.2. Pp. 751-61.

56. NAZARAEANS, GOSPEL OF THE

(See also the entries under agrapha; and 1.53, 88, 531, 540.

56.1 Amann, E. "L'évangile des Nazaréens," DBSup. 1. Cols. 473f.

56.2   Amiot, F. Evangiles Apoc. Pp. 37-39.

56.3   Bauer, J.B. Neutest. Apok. Pp. 17f.

56.4   Bauer, J.B. "Sermo Peccati: Hieronymus und das Nazaräer-
        evangelium," BZ N.F. 4 (1960) 122-28.

56.5   Bonaccorsi, P.G. Vangeli Apocrifi. Pp. 2-7.

56.6   Drumwright, H.L. "Nazarenes, Gospel of the," ZPEB. 4.
        Pp. 387f.

56.7   Fabricius, J.A. "Evangelium Matthaei Hebraicum quo usi
        Nazaraei," Cod.Apoc.NT. 1. Pp. 355-70.

56.8   Klijn, A.F.J. "Jerome's Quotations from a Nazoraean Inter-
        pretation of Isaiah," Judéo-Christianisme. Recherches His-
        toriques et Théologiques offertes en Hommage à J. Daniélou.
        Paris, 1972. Pp. 241-55.

56.9   Klijn, A.F.J. "The Question of the Rich Young Man in a
        Jewish-Christian Gospel," NovT 8 (1966) 149-55.

56.10   Klostermann, E., ed. "Hebraeerevangelium (Nazaraeerevan-
        gelium)," Apocrypha II: Evangelien (KlT 8) Berlin, 1929³.
        Pp. 5-12. [Gk. and Lat. witnesses]

56.11   Mees, M. "Das Paradigma vom reichen Mann und seiner Beru-
        fung nach den Synoptikern und dem Nazaräerevangelium,"
        Vetera Christianorum 9 (1972) 245-65.

56.12   Michaelis, W. "Nazaräer-Evangelium," Apokryphen Schriften.
        Pp. 123-27.

56.13   Migne, J.-P. "Nazaréens. (Evangile des Nazaréens.)," Dic-
        tionnaire. 2. Cols. 635-38.

56.14   Moraldi, L. "Vangelo degli Ebrei e Nazarei," Apoc. del NT.
        1. Pp. 373-83.

56.15   Preuschen, E. "Evangelienzitate der Naassener," Antilegomena.
        Giessen, 1905². Pp. 12f., 143f. [Gk. text]

56.16   Schmidtke, A. "Die aramäische Matthäusbearbeitung der Na-
        zaräer im Urteil und Gebrauch der griechischen Väter,"
        Neue Fragmente und Untersuchungen zu den judenchrist-
        lichen Evangelien (TU 37.1) Leipzig, 1911. Pp. 41-126.

56.17   Stegmüller, F. Repertorium Biblicum. 8. P. 129.

56.18   Vielhauer, P. "The Gospel of the Nazaraeans," HSW. 1. Pp.
        139-53.

56.19 Vielhauer, P. "Das Nazaräerevangelium," HS. 1. Pp. 90-100.

56.20 Waitz, H. "Das Matthäusevangelium der Nazaräer (Nazaräer-
       evangelium)," H². Pp. 17-32.

57. NICODEMUS, GOSPEL OF

GosNic is often called the AcPil--see also the entries under
that heading.

(See also 1.18, 75, 284, 307, 470.)

57.1   Aitzetmüller, R. Milhanovic Homiliar [facsim. repr.] Graz,
       1957. Taf. 94b-99a; 116a-125a.

57.2   Allen, T.P. A Critical Edition of the Old English Gospel of
       Nicodemus. Rice Dissertation, 1968.

57.3   Amersbach, K. Ueber die Identität des Verfassers des Evan-
       gelium Nicodemi mit Heinrich Hesler. Konstanz, 1883.

57.4   Amiot, F. "Evangile de Nicodème ou Actes de Pilate," Evan-
       giles Apoc. Pp. 145-56. [French trans.]

57.5   [Archeografičeskaja Kommissija]. Daily Readings of the Great
       'Menaea'. (Nov. 13-15, 1899) cols. 1874-1905. [in Russian]

57.6   Augusti, J.C.G. Eusebii Emeseni quae supersunt opuscula
       graeca. Elberfeldi, 1829. Pp. 3-10.

57.7   Barabas, S. "Nicodemus, Gospel of," ZPEB. 4. P. 435.

57.8   Bauer, J.B. "Das Nikodemusevangelium oder die Pilatusakten,"
       Neutest. Apok. Pp. 55-58.

57.9   Bonsirven, J., and C. Bigaré. "Actes de Pilate ou Évangile
       de Nicodème," Intro. à la Bible. 2. Pp. 755f.

57.10 Bonwetsch, N. "Evangelium Nicodemi," Gesch. altchrist. Lit.
       1. Pp. 907-09.

57.11 Boor, H. de. "Stilbeobachtungen zu Heinrich von Hesler,"
       Kleine Schriften 1. Berlin, 1964. Pp. 1-20.

57.12 Brunn, G.L. Disquisitio historico-critica de indole, aetate et
       usu libri apocryphi vulgo inscripti "Evangelium Nicodemi."
       Berlin, 1794.

57.13 Bulgakov, F.I. "Sayings About the Lord's Passion," PDP 1
       (1878/79) 153-86. [in Russian]

57.14 Cazzaniga, I. "Osservazioni critiche al testo del 'prologo' del
       Vangelo di Nicodemo," Instituto Lombardo-Accademia di Sci-
       enze e Lettere, classe lettere 102 (1968) 535-48.

57.15 Chrétien (troubadour), André de Contance et un anonyme.
       Trois versions rimées de l'Evangile de Nicodème. New York,
       1968. [First printed in Paris, 1885]

57.16 Clark, E.G. "The York Plays and the Gospel of Nicodemus,"
       Publication of the Modern Language Association of America 43
       (1928) 153-61.

57.17 Cowper, B.H. "The Gospel of Nicodemus, or Acts of Pilate,"
       Apocryphal Gospels. Pp. 227-388. [ET]

57.18 Cowper, B.H. "The Gospels of Nicodemus," The Great Re-
       jected Books of the Biblical Apocrypha (The Sacred Books
       and Early Literature of the East 14) New York, London,
       1917. Pp. 325-402. [ET]

57.19 Crawford, S.J. The Gospel of Nicodemus. Edinburgh, 1927.

57.20 Daničić, G. "Two Apocryphal Gospels," Starine 4 (1872) 130-
       54. [in Serbo-Croatian]

57.21 Darley, A. Les Acta Salvatoris, un Evangile de la Passion et
       de la Résurrection et une mission apostolique en Aquitaine.
       Paris, 1913.

57.22 Erbetta, M. "Gli Atti di Pilato o il Vangelo di Nicodemo,"
       Apoc. del NT. 1.2. Pp. 231-87.

57.23 Fabricius, J.A. "Evangelium quod vulgo tribuitur S. Nicodemo,"
       Cod.Apoc.NT. 1. Pp. 213-98. [Lat. text]

57.24 Fau, G. "L'Évangile de Nicodème," Cahiers du Cercle Ernest-
       Renan. 25.99 (1977) 43-45.

57.25 Ford, A.E. L'Évangile de Nicodème: Les Versions courtes
       en ancien français et en prose. (Publications romanes et
       franc., 125) Geneva, 1973.

57.26 Ford, A.E.J. The Old French Prose Versions of the "Gospel
       of Nicodemus." University of Pennsylvania Ph.D., 1971.

57.27 Franko, I. Apocrypha and Legends. L'vov, 1898. Vol. 2.
       Pp. 252-357. [in Russian]

57.28   Ganka, V.   Čtenie Nikodemovo.   Prague, 1861.   [in Czech]

57.29   González-Blanco, E.   Los Evangelios Apócrifos.   Madrid, 1935.
        Vol. 2.   Pp. 236ff.

57.30   Grabar, B.   "Über das Problem der längeren Fassung des
        Nikodemusevangeliums in der älteren slavischen Literatur,"
        Mélanges I. Dujčev.   Paris, 1979.   Pp. 201-06.

57.31   Guasti, C.   Il Passio o Vangelo di Nicodemo volgarizzato nel
        buon secolo della lingua.   Bologna, 1862.

57.32   Hanka, V.   "Čtenie Nikodemovo [Cod. Prag Nar. Mus. IV.
        H.25]," Pojedn. Ucené Společnosti V, 11 (1860) 227-56.
        [in Czech]

57.33   Harnack, A.   "Die Acta Pilati = Ev. Nicodemi," Gesch. alt-
        christ. Lit.   2.1.   Pp. 603-12.   [see also vol. 1.   Pp. 21-
        24]

57.34   Hitchcock, D.R.   The Appeal of Adam to Lazarus in Hell
        (Slavistic Printings and Reprintings 302) The Hague, Paris,
        New York, 1979.   [H. claims that the Appeal of Adam, which
        is parallel to GosNic, is a Russian composition]

57.35   Hone, W.   The Apocryphal New Testament.   London, 1820;
        New York, [1845].   Pp. 63-91.   [Am. ed.].

57.36   Horstmann, C.   "Gregorius auf dem Steine aus Ms. Cotton.
        Cleop. DIX, nebst Beiträgen zum Evangelium Nicodemi,"
        Archiv für das Studium der neueren Sprachen und Litera-
        turen 57 ( ) 59-83.*

57.37   Jacimirskij, A.I.   "Apocrypha and Legends ... VI," IzvORJS
        14.3 (1909) 101-07.   [in Russian]

57.38   Jacobs, J.   "Een nieuw mnl. handschrift van het Evangelie
        van Nicodemus," Verslagen en Medeelingen der koninkl.
        vlaamsche Akad.   (1926) 546-51.*

57.39   Jagić, I.V.   "Critical Notes ... on the Slavic Translation of
        Apocryphal Sayings," IzvORJS 3.3 (1898) 793-822.   [in Rus-
        sian]

57.40   James, M.R.   "The Gospel of Nicodemus, or Acts of Pilate,"
        ANT.   Pp. 94-146.

57.41   Jones, J.   A New and Full Method of Settling the Canonical
        Authority of the New Testament.   3 vols.   London, 1726,
        1798². Vol. 2.   Pp. 262-353.

57.42 Karskij, E.F. "West Russian Collection of the Fifteenth Cen-
       tury," SbORJS 65.8 (1899) 9-12. [in Russian]

57.43 Knjazevskaja, O.A. and V.G. Demjanov, M.V. Ljapon. The
       Uspenskij Collection. Moscow, 1971. Pp. 358-68. [in Rus-
       sian]

57.44 Kraskovskij, J. Vizantijskij Vremennik 14 (1907) 246-75.
       [Arab. text]*

57.45 Kim, H.C. The Gospel of Nicodemus: Gesta Salvatoris; Ed-
       ited from the Codex Einsidlensis, Einsiedeln Stiftsbibliothek,
       MS 326 (Toronto Medieval Latin Texts 2). Toronto, 1973.

57.46 Lacau, M.P. "Évangile (?) Apocryphe," FAC. Pp. 13-22.
       [Cop. text and Fr. trans.; this frag. is related somehow to
       GosNic]

57.47 La Piana, G. "Le rappresentazioni sacre e la poesia ritmica
       dramatica nella letteratura bizantina dalle origini al seculo
       IX," Roma e l'Oriente 3 (1911/12) 36-44, 105-18, 392f.

57.48 Lindström, B. A Late Middle English Version of the Gospel
       of Nicodemus, Edited from British Museum Ms. Harley 149
       (Studia Anglica Upsaliensia 18) Uppsala dissertation, 1974.

57.49 Lorsbach, G.W. De vetusta Evang. Nic. interpr. germ. Herb.,
       1802.*

57.50 Lowe, M. "'Ioudaioi' of the Apocrypha: A Fresh Approach
       to the Gospels of James, Pseudo-Thomas, Peter and Nico-
       demus," NovT 23 (1981) 56-90.

57.51 Mareš, F.W. Anthology of Church Slavonic Texts of Western
       (Czech) Origin (Slavische Propylaen Texte in Neu- und Nach-
       drucken 127) Munich, 1979. Pp. 31-40.

57.52 Martins, M. "O Evangelho de Nicodemo e as Cartas de Abgar
       e de Pilatos nos 'Autos dos Apóstolos,'" Itinerarium 1 (1955)
       846-53.

57.53 Masser, A. Bibel- und Legendenepik des deutschen Mittelal-
       ters. Berlin, 1976. Pp. 112-24.

57.54 Masser, A. Dat Ewangelium Nicodemi van deme Lidende Vnses
       Heren Ihesu Christi. (Texte des späten Mittelalters und der
       frühen Neuzeit 29) Berlin, 1978. [contains the text of GosNic
       from Luneb. MS Theol. 2° 83 and Cod. Guelf. 430 Helmst.]

57.55 Maury, A. Nouvelles recherches sur l'époque à laquelle a été
       composé l'ouvrage connu sous le titre d'Évangile de Nicodème.
       Paris, 1850.

57.56 Michaelis, W. "Nikodemus-Evangelium," Apokryphen Schriften.
       Pp. 132-214. [Intro., German trans. and notes]

57.57 Migne, J.-P. "Nicodème (Evangile de Nicodème)," Dictionnaire.
       1. Cols. 1087-1138. [Intro. and French trans.]

57.58 Moraldi, L. "Memorie di Nicodemo," Apoc. del NT. 1. Pp.
       519-653.

57.59 Müller, J.J., "Die Evangelie van Nikodemus," Nuwe-Test. Apok.
       Pp. 26-49. [trans. into Afrikaans]

57.60 Münster, F. "Probabilien zur Leidengeschichte aus d. Evang.
       Nicod.;" Staudlin's Archiv 5. Pp. 317ff.*

57.61 Münster, F. Wahrscheinliche Zusätze zu Christi Leidensges-
       chichte nach Nicodemi Evangelium (Wissenschaftlichen Ver-
       handlungen des Seeländischen Conventes) Dinamarca, 1816.

57.62 Načov, N.A. "The Tives Manuscript," Sbornik za Narodini
       Umotvorenia: Navka i Knižnina 8 (1892) Pp. 400-02. [in Bul-
       garian]

57.63 Novaković, S. "Bulgarian Collection of Texts of the Last Cen-
       tury," Starine 6 (1874) 29, 45-47. [in Serbo-Croatian]

57.64 O'Ceallaigh, G.C. "Dating the Commentaries of Nicodemus,"
       HTR 56 (1963) 21-58.

57.65 Philippart, G. "Fragments palimpsestes latins du Vindobonen-
       sis 563 (Ve siècle?): Evangile selon S. Matthieu, Evangile
       de Nicodème, Evangile de l'Enfance selon Thomas," AnBoll
       90 (1972) 391-411.

57.66 Pickford, J.J. The Safegarde from Ship-wracke: Heavens
       Haven [and] Nicodemus, His Gospel. (English Recusant
       Literature, 1558-1640; v. 271) Ilkey, 1975.

57.67 Piontek, A. Die mhd. Ubersetzung des Nikodemus-Evangeliums
       in der Augsburger Hs. (Ms. 3) und in der Münchener Hs.
       (Cgm. 5018). Phil. Diss. Greifswald, 1909.

57.68 Polívka, G. "Descriptions and Excerpts," Starine 24 (1891)
       115-18, 124-29. [in Russian]

57.69 Polívka, J. "The Gospel of Nicodemus in Slavonic Literature,"
       Časopis Musea Král. Českého 64 (1890) 255-75; 65 (1891)
       535-68. [in Russian]

57.70 Popov, A.N. "Bibliographical Materials No. 15-19," COIDR
       (1889) 11, 28, 44-46. [in Russian]*

57.71 Porfiryev, I.Y. "Apocryphal Sayings About New Testament
       People and Events in Manuscripts of the Solovetski Library,"
       SbORJS 52 (1890) 21-36, 41-49, 164-97, 204-14. [in Russian]

57.72 Pypin, A.N. False and Dismissed Books of Ancient Russia.
       St. Petersburg, 1862. Pp. 91-109. [in Russian]

57.73 Quasten, J. "The Gospel of Nicodemus," Patrology. 1. Pp.
       115-18.

57.74 Reiss, E. "The Tradition of Moses in the Underworld and the
       York Plays of the Transfiguration and Harrowing," Mediavalia
       5 (1979) 141-64.

57.75 Santos Otero, A. de. "Descensus Ioannis Baptistae ad Inferos,"
       Altslavischen Apok. 2. Pp. 99-118.

57.76 Santos Otero, A. de. "Evangelium Nicodemi," Altslavischen
       Apok. 2. Pp. 61-98.

57.77 Santos Otero, A. de. "Actas de Pilato (o Evangelio de Nico-
       demo)," Evangelios Apócrifos. Pp. 396-471.

57.78 Scheidweiler, F. "The Gospel of Nicodemus: Acts of Pilate
       and Christ's Descent into Hell," HSW. 1. Pp. 444-81.

57.79 Scheidweiler, W. "Nikodemusevangelium: Pilatusakten und
       Höllenfahrt Christi," HS. 1. Pp. 330-58.

57.80 Schmidt, C. "Evangelium des Nicodemus," Gesch. altchrist.
       Lit. 1. Pp. 922f.

57.81 Sobolevskij, A.I. "Materials and Research ... IIIb," SbORJS
       88 (1910) 81-91. [in Russian]*

57.82 Speranskij, M.N. Izbornik v čest' T.D. Florinskogo. Kiev,
       1904. Pp. 39-63.

57.83 Speranskij, M.N. "Slavic Apocryphal Gospels," The Work of
       the Eighth Archaeological Conference in Moscow 1890. Mos-
       cow, 1895. Vol. 2. Pp. 92-133, 144-55. [in Russian]

57.84 Stefanič, V., et al. Croatian Literature. Zagreb, 1969. Pp.
       146-48, 154-58. [in Serbo-Croatian]

57.85 Stegmüller, F. Repertorium Biblicum. 1. Pp. 143, 148-53;
       8. Pp. 141-47. [listed as Acta Pilati V]

57.86 Steinhauser, M. Die mittelalterlichen hochdeutschen Hand-
       schriften des Nikodemusevangeliums: Prolegomena zu einer
       Edition. Innsbruck, 1975.

57.87 Stojanović, L. "Scripts from the Imperial Library in Beč,"
       Glasnik srpskog učenog društva 63 (1885) 89-120. [in
       Serbo-Croatian]

57.88 Sumcov, N.F. "Essays on the History of South-Russian Apoc-
       ryphal Sayings and Songs," Kievskaja Starina 19 (1887) 31-
       36. [in Russian]

57.89 Tupikov, N.M. "The Passion of Christ in a West Russian
       List of the Fifteenth Century," PDP 140 (1901) 1-85.

57.90 Vaillant, A. L'évangile de Nicodème: Texte slave et texte
       latin (Centre de Recherches d'Hist. et de Phil. de la IVe
       Section de l'École pratique des Hautes Études. 2. Hautes
       Etudes Orientales, 1) Paris, Geneva, 1968.

57.91 Vandoni, M., and T. Orlandi. Vangelo di Nicodemo (Testi e
       Documenti per lo Studio dell'Antichità 15) Milan-Varese, 1966.

57.92 Variot, J. "L'Évangile de Nicodème," Évangiles Apocryphes.
       Pp. 93-107, 233-328.

57.93 Vollmer, H. "Das Evangelium Nicodemi in deutscher Prosa,"
       Neue Texte zur Bibelverdeutschung des Mittelalters (= Bibel
       und deutsche Kultur 6). Potsdam, 1936. Pp. 200-29.

57.94 Waite, C.B. History of the Christian Religion. Chicago, 1881.
       Pp. 177-212.

57.95 Wake, W., and N. Lardner. "The Gospel of Nicodemus, Form-
       erly Called the Acts of Pontius Pilate," ApocNT. Pp. 69-
       105. [ET]

57.96 Walker, A. "The Gospel of Nicodemus," ANF 8. Pp. 416-58.
       [ET]

57.97 Westcott, A. The Gospels of Nicodemus and Kindred Docu-
       ments. Edinburgh, 1914.

57.98 Wülcker, R.P., Das Evangelium Nicodemi in der abendländischen
       Literatur. Paderborn, 1872.

             58. PAUL, ACTS OF; AND PAUL CYCLE

       The full AcPl contained, along with the Acts of Paul and
       Thecla, the MartPl and 3Cor--see also the listings under
       those categories.

(See also 1.204, 284, 470, 531; 3.12, 53; 7.14, 25; 74.14.)

58.1   Alfonsi, L. "Echi protrettici di un passo del papiro amburghese
       delle Praxeis Paulou," Aegyptus 30 (1950) 67-71.

58.2   Amann, É. "Les Actes de Paul," DBSup. 1. Cols. 494-96.

58.3   Amiot, F. "Actes de Paul," Évangiles Apoc. Pp. 226-51.
       [French trans.]

58.4   Aristarchès, S., ed. "Egkōmion eis tēn hagian prōtomartura
       Theklan," Phōtiou logoi kai homiliai. Constantinople, 1901.
       Vol. 2. [see esp. pp. 252-67]

58.5   Aubineau, M. "Le panégyrique de Thècle attribué à Jean
       Chrysostome: La fin retrouvée d'un texte mutilé," AnBoll
       93 (1975) 349-62.

58.6   Baker, A. "Early Syriac Asceticism," DowR 88 (1970) 393-409.

58.7   Bardenhewer, O. "Die Akten des Paulus," GAL. 1. Pp.
       554-61.

58.8   Bardenhewer, O. "Die Akten des Paulus und der Thekla,"
       GAL. 1. Pp. 561-64.

58.9   Barnikol, E. "Das Fehlen der Spanienreise, der vor- und nicht-
       paulinischen Romgemeinde und des paulin. 'Rombriefes' in
       den Paulusakten," ThJ 2 (1934) 103-14.

58.10 Bauer, J.B. "Die Paulusakten," Neutest. Apok. Pp. 71-75.

58.11 Baumstark, P. Die Petrus und Paulusakten in der litterari-
       schen Überlieferung der syrischen Kirche. Leipzig, 1902.

58.12 Baumstark, A. "Besprechungen ... Acta Pauli ... herausge-
       geben von Carl Schmidt," OrChr 34 (1937) 122-26.

58.13 Bedjan, P. ed. "L'histoire syriaque du bienheureux Apôtre
       Paul," Acta Martyrum et sanctorum Syriace. Paris, 1890-.
       Pp. 33f.

58.14 Berčić, I. Chrestomatia linguae verteroslovenicae. Prague,
       1859. Pp. 78-80.

58.15 Bonsirven, J., and C. Bigaré. "Actes de Paul," Intro. à la
       Bible. 2. Pp. 758f.

58.16 Bonwetsch, N. "Thekla," Geschich. altchrist. Lit. 1. Pp.
       904f.

58.17 Brox, N. "Pseudo-Paulus and Pseudo-Ignatius: Einige Topoi altchristlicher Pseudepigraphie," VC 30 (1976) 181-88.

58.18 Bruyne, D. de. "Nouveaux fragments des Actes de Pierre, de Paul, de Jean, d'André, et de l'Apocalypse d'Elie," RBen 25 (1908) 149-60.

58.19 Bulhart, V. "Nochmals Textkritisches," RBen 62 (1952) 297-99.

58.20 Capocci, V. "Sulla tradizione del martirio di S. Paolo alle Acque Salvie," Atti dello VIII° Congresso internazionale di Studi Bizantini II. Pp. 11-19.*

58.21 Claude D. Die byzantinische Stadt im 6. Jahrhundert. Munich, 1969.

58.22 Clemen, C. "Miszellen zu den Paulusakten," ZNW 5 (1904) 228-47.

58.23 Conybeare, F.C. "Acts of Paul and Thecla," The Armenian Apology and Acts of Apollonius and Other Monuments of Early Christianity. London, 1896². [Armenian text, Pp. 49-88]

58.24 Corssen, P. "Der Schluss der Paulusakten," ZNW 6 (1905) 317-38.

58.25 Corssen, P. "Die Urgestalt der Paulusakten," ZNW 4 (1903) 22-47.

58.26 Crum, W.E. "New Coptic Manuscripts in the John Rylands Library," BJRL 5 (1920) 497-503.

58.27 Dagron, G. "L'auteur des 'Actes' et des 'Miracles' de Sainte Thècle," AnBoll 92 (1974) 5-11.

58.28 Dagron, G. Vie et miracles de Sainte Thècle: Texte grec, traduction et commentaire (Subsidia Hagiographica 62) Brussels, 1978.

58.29 Davies, D.F. "Paul and Thecla," ATR 8 (1925-26) 331-44.

58.30 Deeleman, C.F.M. "Acta Pauli," Theologische Studiën 26 (1908) 1-44.

58.31 Deeleman, C.F.M. "Acta Pauli et Theclae," Theologische Studiën 26 (1908) 273-301.

58.32 Delehaye, H. "Les recueils antiques de miracles des saints," AnBoll 43 (1925) 5-85.

58.33   Deubner, L. De Incubatione capita quattuor. Leipzig, 1900.

58.34   Devos, P. "Actes de Thomas et Actes de Paul," AnBoll 69
        (1951) 119-30.

58.35   DeZwaan, J. "Een Papyrus van de 'Acta Pauli,'" NAKG (1938)
        48-57.*

58.36   Dölger, F.J. "Der heidnische Glaube an die Kraft des Für-
        bittgebetes für die vorzeitig Gestorbenen nach den Theklaak-
        ten," Antike und Christentum 2 (1930) 13-16.

58.37   Erbetta, M. "Gli Atti di Paolo," Apoc. del NT. 2. Pp. 243-
        88.

58.38   Erbetta, M. "Il Kerygma o Predicazione di Paolo," Apoc. del
        NT. 2. Pp. 302f.

58.39   Eyice, S. "Aga Thekla efsanesi ve sanat tarikinde Aga Thekla,"
        Anit (1962) 1-32.* [discusses Thecla in literature and art]

58.40   Fabricius, J.A. "Acta Pauli Apostoli," Cod.Apoc.NT. 2. Pp.
        791-94.

58.41   Fabricius, J.A. "Acta Pauli et Theclae (a)," Cod.Apoc.NT.
        2. Pp. 794-96.

58.42   Fabricius, J.A. "Evangelium S. Pauli," Cod.Apoc.NT. 1.
        Pp. 372f.

58.43   Fabricius, J.A. "S. Pauli Praedicatio," Cod.Apoc.NT. 2.
        Pp. 797-800.

58.44   Festugière, A.J. Collections grecques de miracles: Sainte
        Thècle, Saints Côme et Damien, Saints Cyr et Jean, Saint
        Georges. Paris, 1971.

58.45   Festugière, A.J. "Les énigmes de Ste Thècle," Comptes ren-
        dus. Paris, 1968. Pp. 52-63.

58.46   Findlay, A.F. "The Acts of Paul," Byways. Pp. 238-72.

58.47   Franko, I. Apocrypha and Legends. L'vov, 1902. Vol. 3.
        Pp. 33f., 45-47, 262f. [in Russian]

58.48   Gebhardt, O. von. Passio S. Theclae Virginis: Die lateinin-
        schen Ubersetzungen der Acta Pauli et Theclae (TU, N.F.
        7.2) Leipzig, 1902.

58.49   Goodspeed, E.J., ed. "The Book of Thekla," AJSLL 17 (1901)
        65-95.

58.50   Goodspeed, E.J.   The Book of Thekla (The University of Chicago Historical and Linguistic Studies in Literature Related to the New Testament 1) Chicago, 1901.   [Eth. text and ET]

58.51   Goodspeed, E.J.   "The Epistle of Pelagia," AJSLL 20 (1904) 95-108.

58.52   Grabar, B.   "Apostolic Apocryphal Works in Croatian Glagolitic Literature, 3," Radovi Staroslavenskog Instituta 7 (1972) 5-30.   [in Serbo-Croatian]

58.53   Grabe, J.E.   Spicilegium SS. patrum, ut et haereticorum, seculi post Christum natum I, II, et III.   Oxford, 1700.   Vol. 1.   Pp. 81-128.

58.54   Grant, R.M.   "The Description of Paul in the Acts of Paul and Thecla," VC 36 (1982) 1-4.

58.55   Grenfell, B.A., Hunt, A.S.   The Oxyrhynchos Papyri.   London, 1898.   Vol. 1.   Pp. 9f; Vol. 3.   P. 23.

58.56   Gribomont, J.   "Un document monastique sur papyrus," Studia Monastica 8 (1966) 385.

58.57   Gwynn, J.   "Thecla," A Dictionary of Christian Biography, eds. W. Smith and H. Wace.   London, 1877-87.   Vol. 4.   Pp. 882-96.

58.58   Halkin, F.   "Publications récentes de textes hagiographiques grecs, IV, 1946-1950," AnBoll 69 (1951) 388-403.

58.59   Harnack, A.   "Die Acta Pauli," Gresch. altchrist. Lit.   2.1.   Pp. 491-93.

58.60   Harnack, A.   "Die Acta Pauli et Theclae," Gesch. altchrist. Lit.   2.1.   Pp. 493-505.

58.61   Harnack, A.   "Die Acten des Paulus und der Thekla," Gesch. altchrist. Lit.   1.   Pp. 136-38.

58.62   Harnack, A.   Drei wenig beachtete cyprianische Schriften und die "Acta Pauli" (TU 19.3b).   Leipzig, 1899.   Pp. 1-34.

58.63   Harnack, A.   "Die Paulusacten," Gesch. altchrist. Lit.   1.   Pp. 128-31.

58.64   Harnack, A.   "Zu den Acta Pauli," Miscellen zu den Apostolischen Vätern, den Acta Pauli, Apelles, dem Muratorischen Fragment, den Pseudocyprianischen Schriften und Claudianus Mamertus (TU 5.3) Leipzig, 1900.   Pp. 100-06.

58.65 Hemmerdinger, B., "Evagrius Antiochenus--Euthaliana," JTS
       11 (1960) 349-55.

58.66 Holzhey, C. Die Thekla-Akten: Ihre Verbreitung und Beur-
       teilung in der Kirche (Veröffentlichungen aus dem Kirchen-
       historischen Seminar München 2.7). München, 1905.

58.67 Hone, W. The Apocryphal New Testament. London, 1820;
       New York, [1845]. Pp. 99-111 [Am. ed.].

58.68 Howe, E.M. "Interpretations of Paul in the Acts of Paul and
       Thecla," Pauline Studies: Essays Presented to Professor
       F.F. Bruce on His 70th Birthday, eds. D.A. Gagner and
       M.J. Harris. Exeter, Grand Rapids, 1980. Pp. 33-49.

58.69 Hug, W. "Quellengeschichtliche Studie zur Petrus-und Paulus-
       legende der Legenda Aurea," Historisches Jahrbuch 49 (1929)
       604-24.

58.70 Jagić, V. "Zur Berichtigung der altrussischen Texte," Ar-
       chiv für slavische Philologie 6 (1882) 232-38.

58.71 Jagić, V. Examples of Old Croatian. Vol. 2. Pp. 70-72.
       [in Serbo-Croatian]*

58.72 James, M.R. "Acts of Paul," ANT. Pp. 270-99.

58.73 James, M.R. "The Acts of Titus and the Acts of Paul," JTS
       6 (1905) 549-56.

58.74 James, M.R. "A Note on the Acta Pauli," JTS 6 (1905) 244-46.

58.75 Jones, J. A New and Full Method of Settling the Canonical
       Authority of the New Testament. 3 vols. London, 1726,
       1798². Vol. 1. Pp. 311-13, 387-411; Vol. 2. Pp. 353-86.
       [ET]

58.76 Kasser, R. "Acta Pauli 1959," RHPR 40 (1960) 45-57.

58.77 Kilpatrick, G.D., and C.H. Roberts. "The Acta Pauli: A
       New Fragment," JTS 47 (1946) 196-99.

58.78 Kurfess, A. "Zu dem Hamburger Papyrus der Praxeis Paulou,"
       ZNW 38 (1939) 164-70.

58.79 Lavagnini, B.S. "Tecla nella vasca delle foche e gli spetta-
       coli in acqua," Byzantion 33 (1963) 79-144.

58.80 Lipsius, R.A., ed. "Acta Pauli et Theclae," AAA. 1. Pp.
       XCIV-CVI, 235-72. [Intro. and Gk. text]

58.81 Lipsius, R.A. Die apokryphen Apostelgeschichten und Apos-
       tellegenden. Brunswick, 1883-1890. Vol. 2.1. Pp. 424-67.

58.82 Loewenich, W. von. "Die Petrus-, Andreas-, Paulus-, und
       Thomas-Akten," Das Johannes-Verständnis im zweiten Jahr-
       hundert (BZNW 13) Giessen, 1932. Pp. 109-12.

58.83 Loofs, F. Theophilus von Antiochien adversus Marcionem und
       die anderen theologischen Quellen bei Irenaeus (TU 46.2)
       Leipzig, 1930. Pp. 148-57.

58.84 MacDonald, D.R. "A Conjectural Emendation of 1Cor 15:31-32:
       Or the Case of the Misplaced Lion Fight," HTR 73 (1980)
       265-76.

58.85 MacDonald, D.R. The Legend and the Apostle: The Battle
       for Paul in Story and Canon. Philadelphia, 1983.

58.86 McHardy, W.D. "A Papyrus Fragment of the Acta Pauli,"
       ExpT 58 (1946-47) 279.

58.87 Metzger, B.M. "St. Paul and the Baptised Lion," Princeton
       Seminary Bulletin 39 (1945) 11-21.

58.88 Michaelis, W. "Paulus-Akten," Apokryphen Schriften. Pp.
       268-317.

58.89 Michel, A. "Compléments au dossier de Sainte Thècle," AnBoll
       93 (1975) 356-62.

58.90 Migne, J.-P. "Actes de saint Paul et de Thècle," Dictionnaire.
       2. Col. 656.

58.91 Migne, J.-P. "Paul," Dictionnaire. 2. Col. 1317.

58.92 Migne, J.-P. "Prédication de saint Paul," Dictionnaire. 2.
       Cols. 655f.

58.93 Migne, J.-P. "Thècle. (Actes de Sainte Thècle.)," Diction-
       naire. 2. Cols. 961-88. [Intro. and French trans.]

58.94 Moraldi, L. "Atti di san Paolo," Apoc. del NT. 2. Pp.
       1061-1130.

58.95 Morin, D.G. "L'homéliaire de Burchard de Würzburg: Con-
       tribution à la critique des sermons de saint Césaire d'Arles,"
       RBen 13 (1896) 97-111.

58.96 Müller, J.J. "Die Handelinge van Paulus," Nuwe-Test. Apok.
       Pp. 80-93. [trans. into Afrikaans]

58.97   Peeters, P. "Notes sur la légende des apôtres S. Pierre et
        S. Paul dans la littérature Syrienne," AnBoll 21 (1902) 121-
        40.

58.98   Peterson, E. "Die Acta Xanthippae et Polyxenae und die Paul-
        usakten, AnBoll 65 (1947) 57-60.

58.99   Peterson, E. "Einige Bemerkungen zum Hamburger Papyrus-
        Fragment der Acta Pauli," VC 3 (1949) 142-62.

58.100 Pick, B. The Apocryphal Acts of Paul, Peter, John, Andrew
        and Thomas. London, 1909.

58.101 Radermacher, L. Hippolytus und Thekla, Studien zur Ges-
        chichte von Legende und Kultus (Kaiserliche Akademie der
        Wissenschaften in Wien, philos.- hist. Kl., Sitzung. 182.3)
        Vienna, 1916.

58.102 Ramsay, W.M. "The Acts of Paul and Thekla," The Church
        in the Roman Empire Before A.D. 170. New York, 1893.
        Pp. 375-428.

58.103 Rey, A. Étude sur les 'Acta Pauli et Theclae' et la légende
        de Thecla. Paris, 1890.

58.104 Roberts, C.H. The Antinoopolis Papyri (Egypt Exploration
        Society 1.13) London, 1950. Pp. 26-28.

58.105 Rohde, J. "Pastoralbriefe und Acta Pauli," Studia Evangelica
        5 (TU 103, 1968). Pp. 303-10.

58.106 Rolffs, E. "Paulusakten," H². Pp. 191-212.

58.107 Rolffs, E. "Paulusakten," Handbuch, ed. Hennecke. Pp.
        358-95.

58.108 Rolffs, E. "Das Problem der Paulusakten," Harnack-Ehrung.
        Leipzig, 1921. Pp. 135-48.

58.109 Rordorf, W. "Die neronische Christenverfolgung im Spiegel
        der apokryphen Paulusakten," NTS 28 (1982) 365-74.

58.110 Šafařík, J.P. Texts of Glagolitic Literature. Prague, 1853.
        Pp. 58-61. [in Czech]

58.111 Sanders, H.A. "A Fragment of the Acta Pauli in the Michigan
        Collection," HTR 31 (1938) 73-90.

58.112 Sanders, H.A. "Three Theological Fragments," HTR 36
        (1943) 165-67.

58.113 Santos Otero, A. de. "Acta Pauli et Theclae," Altslavischen
Apok. 1. Pp. 43-51.

58.114 Scharpé, J., and F. Vyncke. The Bdinski Collection. Brugge,
1972. Pp. 72-87. [in Bulgarian]

58.115 Schlau, C. Die Acten des Paulus und der Thecla und die
ältere Thecla-Legende. Leipzig, 1877.

58.116 Schmidt, C. "Acta Pauli," Forschungen und Fortschritte 12
(1936) 352-54.

58.117 Schmidt, C., ed. Acta Pauli, aus der Heidelberger Koptischen
Papyrushandschrift Nr. 1. Leipzig, 1904; 1905^2; repr. Hildesheim, 1965. [Cop. text and German trans.]

58.118 Schmidt, C., ed. Praxeis Paulou: Acta Pauli nach dem Papyrus der Hamburger Staats- und Universitätsbibliothek,
unter Mitarbeit von W. Schubart. Hamburg, 1936. [see
the review by F. Halkin AnBoll 55 (1937) 354-57]

58.119 Schmidt, C. "Die alten Paulusakten in neuer Beleuchtung,"
Forschungen und Fortschritte 5 (1929) 266-68.

58.120 Schmidt, C. "Ein Berliner Fragment der alten Praxeis Paulou,"
SPAW (1931) 37-40.

58.121 Schmidt, C. "Ein neues Fragment der Heidelberger Acta Pauli,"
SPAW. (1909) 216-20. [Cop. text]

58.122 Schneemelcher, W. "Die Acta Pauli: Neue Funde und neue
Aufgaben," Gesammelte Aufsätze zum Neuen Testament und
zur Patristik, eds. W. Bienert and K. Schäferdiek (Analekta
Blatadōn 22) Thessaloniki, 1974. Pp. 182-203. [originally
published in TLZ 89 (1964) 241-54]

58.123 Schneemelcher, W. "Acts of Paul," HSW. 2. Pp. 322-90.

58.124 Schneemelcher, W. "Die Apostelgeschichte des Lukas und die
Acta Pauli," Gesammelte Aufsätze zum Neuen Testament und
zur Patristik, eds. W. Bienert and K. Schäferdiek (Analekta
Blatadōn 22) Thessaloniki, 1974. Pp. 204-22. [originally
published in Apophoreta: Festschrift fur Ernst Haenchen,
ed. W. Eltester. Berlin, 1964. Pp. 236-50.]

58.125 Schneemelcher, W. "Der getaufte Löwe in den Acta Pauli,"
Gesammelte Aufsätze zum Neuen Testament und zur Patristik,
eds. W. Bienert and K. Schäferdiek Analekta Blatadōn 22)
Thessaloniki, 1974. Pp. 223-39. [originally published in
Mullus: Festschrift Theodor Klauser, ed. A. Striber and

A. Hermann (Jahrbuch für Antike und Christentum 1)   Münster, 1964. Pp. 316-26]

58.126 Schneemelcher, W. "Paulus in der griechischen Kirche des zweiten Jahrhunderts," Gesammelte Aufsätze zum Neuen Testament und zur Patristik, eds. W. Bienert and K. Schäferdiek (Analekta Blatadōn 22) Thessaloniki, 1974. Pp. 154-81. [originally published in ZKG 75 (1964) 1-20]

58.127 Schneemelcher, W. "Paulusakten," HS. 2. Pp. 221-70.

58.128 Schwidt, K. Neue Funde zu den alten Praxeis Paulou. Berlin, 1929.

58.129 Souter, A. "The 'Acta Pauli' etc. in Tertullian," JTS 25 (1924) 292.

58.130 Sreznevskij, I. Texts of Ancient Russian Letters and Languages. St. Petersburg, 1863, 1882^2. Pp. 170f. [in Russian]

58.131 Sreznevskij, I. "Information and Notes About Little Known and Unknown Works," SbORJS 28 (1875) 499-503. [in Russian]

58.132 Staab, K. "Die alten Paulusakten in neuer Beleuchtung," Forschungen und Fortschritte 2 (1926) 266.

58.133 Stegmüller, F. Repertorium Biblicum. 1. Pp. 200-08; 8. Pp. 180f.

58.134 Stowe, C.E. Origin and History of the Books of the Bible. Hartford, 1867. Pp. 318-27.

58.135 Tischendorf, K. "Acta Pauli et Theclae," Acta Apos. Apoc. Pp. XXI-XXVI, 40-63. [Intro. and Gk. text]

58.136 Vouaux, L. Les Actes de Paul et ses Lettres apocryphes (Les apocryphes du nouveau testament) Paris, 1913. Pp. 146-228. [See M.R. James' review JTS 14 (1913) 604-06]

58.136a Vyncke, F.; J. Scharpé; and J. Goubert. Orientalia Gandensia 3 (1966) 45-89.*

58.137 Wake, W., and N. Lardner, "The Acts of Paul and Thecla," ApocNT. Pp. 113-30. [ET]

58.138 Walker, A. "Acts of Paul and Thecla," ANF   8. Pp. 487-92. [ET]

58.139 Wilmart, A. "Extraits d'Acta Pauli," RBen 27 (1910) 402-12.

58.140 Wilson, R.McL. "Paul, Acts of," ZPEB. 4. Pp. 622f.

58.141 Wohlenberg, G. "Die Bedeutung der Thekla- Akten für die
       neutestamentliche Forschung," ZKWKL 9 (1888) 363-82.

58.142 Wright, W. Apocryphal Acts of the Apostles. London, 1871.
       Vol. 1. Pp. 128-69 [Syr. text]; 2. Pp. 116-45 [ET]

58.143 Zahn, T. "Die Akten der Thekla und des Paulus," Neutest.
       Kanons. 2. Pp. 892-910. [see also 1. Pp. 783f.]

58.144 Zahn, T. "Die Paulusakten," Neutest. Kanons. 2. Pp. 865-
       91. [Intro.]

58.145 Zappalà, M., ed. Il romanzo di Paolo e Tecla. Milan, 1924.

       59. PAUL: GREEK ACTS OF PETER AND PAUL

       A slightly different version of this legend appears in Pass-
       PetPl--see also the listings under that category.

(See also 1.284, 470; 3.53, 78; 67.2, 67, 73, 88.)

59.1   Amann, É. "Les premiers remaniements des Actes de Pierre
       et des Actes de Paul," DBSup. 1. Cols. 498-501.

59.2   Assemani, S.E., and J.S. Assemani. Bibliothecae apostolicae
       vaticanae codicum manuscr. catalogus. Rome, 1959. Vol.
       3. P. 446.

59.3   Bardenhewer, O. "Die Akten des Petrus und des Paulus,"
       GAL. 1. Pp. 564-68.

59.4   Baumstark, A. Die Petrus- und Paulusakten in der literari-
       schen Überlieferung der syrischen Kirche. Leipzig, 1902.

59.5   Bedjan, P. Acta Martyrum et Sanctorum. Paris, 1890. Vol.
       1. Pp. 1-44.

59.6   Bonwetsch, N. "Acten des Petrus und Paulus," Gesch. alt-
       christ. Lit. 1. Pp. 903f.

59.7   Engberding, H. "Bemerkungen zu den äthiopischen 'Acta Pe-
       tri et Pauli,'" OrChr 41 (1957) 65f.

59.8   Erbetta, M. "Gli Atti di Pietro e Paolo dello Ps. Marcello,"
       Apoc. del NT. 2. Pp. 178-92.

59.9   Franko, I. Apocrypha and Legends. L'vov, 1902. Vol. 3.
       Pp. 20-25. [in Russian]

59.10 Graf, G. Geschichte der christlichen arabischen Literatur
       (Studi e Testi 118) Vatican, 1944. P. 263.

59.11 Guidi, I. "Bemerkungen zum ersten Bande der syrischen
       Acta Martyrum et Sanctorum," ZDMG 46 (1892) 744-58.
       [This work refers to the Syriac Acts of Peter and Paul.]

59.12 Haase, F. Apostel und Evangelisten in den orientalischen
       Überlieferungen (Neutestamentliche Abhandlungen 9) Münster,
       1922. P. 204.

59.13 Hilgenfeld, A. Novum Testamentum extra canonem receptum.
       Leipzig, 1884^2. vol. 4.2. Pp. 51-65.

59.14 James, M.R. ANT. Pp. 470f.

59.15 Lantschoot, A. van. "Contribution aux 'Actes de S. Pierre
       et de S. Paul,'" Muséon 68 (1955) 17-46, 219-33.

59.16 Lewis, A.S. The Mythological Acts of the Apostles (Horae
       Semiticae 4) London, 1904. Pp. 193-209. [ET of Ar. text
       in Horae Semiticae 3]

59.17 Lipsius, R.A., ed. "Acta Petri et Pauli," AAA. 1. Pp. 178-
       222. [Gk. text; see also pp. xiv-xciv (Introduction)]

59.18 Lipsius, R.A. Die apokryphen Apostelgeschichten und Apostel-
       legenden. 2 vols. Brunswick, 1883-1890; repr. Amsterdam,
       1976. Vol. 2.1. Pp. 1-423.

59.19 Lipsius, R.A. Die Quellen der römischen Petrus-Sage kritisch
       Untersucht. Kiel, 1872. Pp. 47-163.

59.20 Migne, J.-P. "Actes de Pierre et Paul," Dictionnaire. 2.
       Cols. 692-94.

59.21 Migne, J.-P. "Actes de saint Pierre et de saint Paul," Dic-
       tionnaire. 2. Cols. 715-32.

59.22 Mingana, A. Catalogue of the Mingana Collection of Manu-
       scripts, II: Christian Arabic Manuscripts. Cambridge,
       1936.

59.23 Moraldi, L. "Atti dei Beati Apostoli Pietro e Paolo dello Ps.-
       Marcello," Apoc. del NT. 2. Pp. 1041-1059.

59.24 Moraldi, L. "Atti di Pietro e Paolo," Apoc. del NT. 2. Pp.
       1640-44.

59.25   Popov, A.N.   "Bibliographical Materials 15:   Acts of the Apos-
        tles Peter and Paul," ČOIDR (1889) 1-41.   [in Russian]*

59.26   Santos Otero, A. de "Acta Petri et Pauli," Altslavischen Apok.
        1.   Pp. 60-66.

59.27   Schneemelcher, W., and A. de Santos.   HS.   2.   P. 402.

59.28   Schneemelcher, W., and A. de Santos.   HSW.   2.   P. 575.

59.29   Speranskij, M.N.   "Supplements and Notes," in A.N. Popov,
        "Bibliographical Materials 15," ČOIDR (1889) 42-52.   [in
        Russian]*

59.30   Stegmüller, F.   Repertorium biblicum.   1.   Pp. 222f.; 8.   P.
        192.

59.31   Thilo, J.C.   Acta Petri et Pauli.   2 vols.   Leipzig, 1837.
        [Gk. and Lat. Texts]

59.32   Tischendorf, K.   "Acta Petri et Pauli," Acta Apos. Apoc.   Pp.
        XIV-XXI, 1-39.   [Intro. and Gk. text]

59.33   Vetter, P.   "Die Akten der Apostel Petrus und Paulus," OrChr
        3 (1903) 16-55, 324-83.   [Armenian text with a Gk. retro-
        version]

59.34   Vetter, P.   "Die armenischen apokryphen Apostelgeschichten.
        I. Die Petrus- und Paulus-Akten," TQ 88 (1906) 161-86.
        [German trans. of an Armenian recension]

59.35   Walker, A.   "Acts of the Holy Apostles Peter and Paul," ANF
        8.   Pp. 477-86.   [ET]

59.36   Wilson, R.McL.   "Peter and Paul, Acts of," ZPEB.   4.   P.
        722.

60.   PAUL, APOCALYPSE OF

        The ApPl is often referred to as VisPl, the Latin version
        of the tradition--see also the listings under that category.

(see also 1.284; 2.34; 3.78.)

60.1   Amann, É.   "L'Apocalypse de Paul," DBSup.   1.   Cols. 528f.

60.2   Amiot, F.   "Apocalypse de Paul," Évangiles Apoc.   Pp. 295-
        331.   [French trans.]

60.3   Angelov, B. Ancient Bulgarian Literature of the Ninth-
        Eighteenth Centuries. Sofia, 1922. Pp. 224-38.

60.4   Bardenhewer, O. "Die Paulusapokalypse," GAL. 1. Pp. 615-
        20.

60.5   Barthélemy, A. Le livre d'Ardâ-Virâf. Paris, 1887.

60.6   Becher, E.J., A Contribution to the Comparative Study of the
        Medieval Visions of Heaven and Hell with Special Reference
        to the Middle-English Versions. Baltimore, 1899.

60.7   Bonsirven, J., and C. Bigaré. "L'Apocalypse de Paul," Intro.
        à la Bible. 2. P. 762.

60.8   Bonwetsch, N. "Apokalypse des Paulus," Gesch. altchrist. Lit.
        1. Pp. 910f.

60.9   Bousset, W. "Himmelreise," ARW 4 (1901) 234-6.

60.10   Budge, E.A.W. "The Apocalypse of Paul (incomplete)," Mis-
        cellaneous Texts. Oxford, 1915. Pp. 534-74 [text], 1043-
        1084 [ET], clxii-clxxiii [summary].

60.11   Casey, R.P. "The Apocalypse of Paul," JTS 34 (1933) 1-32.

60.12   Cumont, F. "Lucrèce et le symbolisme pythagoricien des en-
        fers," RPLHA 44 (1920) 229-40.

60.13   Demina, E.I. The Tichonravov Collection. Sofia, 1972. Vol.
        2. Pp. 248-55. [in Russian]

60.14   Dillmann, A. Nachrichten von der Akademie der Wissenschaf-
        ten in Göttingen. Göttingen, 1858. Pp. 185-99, 201-15,
        217-26.*

60.15   Duensing, H. "Apokalypse des Paulus," HS. 2. Pp. 536-67.

60.16   Duensing, H. "Apocalypse of Paul," HSW. 2. Pp. 755-98.

60.17   Dumaine, H. "Dimanche," DACL. 4. Cols. 858-994.

60.18   Du Pin, E. Nouvelle bibliothèque des auteurs ecclésiastiques.
        Paris, 1693.

60.19   Du Pin, E. Dissertation préliminaire ou prolégomènes sur la
        Bible. Paris, 1701. Vol. 2. P. 94.

60.20   Erbetta, M. "L'Apocalisse di Paolo," Apoc. del NT. 3. Pp.
        353-86.

60.21 Fabricius, J.A. "S. Pauli Anabatikon, Apocalypsis, & Visions,"
       Cod.Apoc.NT. 2. Pp. 943-53.

60.22 Fischer, B. "Impedimenta mundi fecerunt eos miseros," VC
       5 (1951) 84-87.

60.23 Franko, I. Apocrypha and Legends. L'vov. 1906. Vol. 4.
       Pp. 117-24. [in Russian]

60.24 Gaster, M. "Hebrew Visions of Hell and Paradise," JRAS 25
       (1893) 571-611.

60.25 Graf, A. Miti, leggende e superstizioni del medio evo. Turin,
       1892.

60.26 Harnack, A. "Paulus Apocalypse," Gesch. altchrist. Lit. 1.
       P. 788.

60.27 Hercigonja, E. "Glagolitic Version of the Complete Redaction
       of the Apocalypse of Paul from the Oxford Codex MS Can.
       Lit. 414," Radovi Staroslavenskog Instituta 6 (1967) 209-55.
       [in Russian]

60.28 Jacimirskij, A.I. An Account of Southern Slavic and Russian
       Manuscripts of Foreign Libraries. Vol. 1. St. Petersburg,
       1921. [in Russian]

60.29 Jacimirskij, A.I. "Insignificant Texts and Notes 17," IzvORJS
       4 (1899) 457-62. [in Russian]

60.30 Jagič, V. "How Bulgarian Was Written Two Hundred Years
       Ago," Starine 9 (1877) 151-71. [in Serbo-Croatian]

60.31 James, M.R. "Apocalypse of Paul," ANT. Pp. 525-55.

60.32 Jones, J. A New and Full Method of Settling the Canonical
       Authority of the New Testament. 3 vols. London, 1726,
       1798[2]. Vol. 1. Pp. 317-24.

60.33 Konusov, A.P., and V.F. Pokrovskaja. Description of the
       Manuscript Division of the USSR Library of the Academy of
       Sciences. Vol. 4. Moscow-Leningrad, 1951. [in Russian]

60.34 Kraeling, C.H. "The Apocalypse of Paul and the 'Iranisches
       Erlösungsmysterium,'" HTR 34 (1931) 209-11.

60.35 Kraus, C. Deutsche Gedichte des zwölften Jahrhunderts.
       Halle, 1894.

60.36 Landgraf, A. "Die Linderung der Höllenstrafen nach der Lehre
       der Frühscholastik," ZKT 60 (1936) 299-370.

60.37 Lejay, P. "Le sabbat juif et les poètes latins," Revue d'histoire
       et de littérature religeuses 8 (1903) 305-35.

60.38 Leloir, L. "L'Apocalypse de Paul selon sa teneur arménienne,"
       Revue des Études Arméniennes n.s. 14 (1980) 217-85.
       [French trans. of 4 Armenian versions; English summary
       on p. 542]

60.39 Lévi, I. "Le repos sabbatique des âmes damnées," REJ 25
       (1892) 1-13.

60.40 Lüdemann, G. Theologische Jahresberichte 12 (1892) 171-73;
       13 (1893) 171-81; 14 (1894) 185f.*

60.41 Matl, J. "Inferno e pene infernali nelle raffigurazioni popolari
       bulgare," Ricerche slavistiche 3 (1954) 114-23.

60.42 Merkle, S., "Die Sabbatruhe in der Hölle: Ein Beitrage zur
       Prudentiuserklärung und zur Geschichte der Apokryphen,"
       Römische Quartalschrift für Christliche Altertumskunde und
       Kirchengeschichte 9 (1895) 489-506.

60.43 Meyer, P. "La descente de Saint-Paul en enfer," Romania 24
       (1895) 357-75.

60.44 Migne, J.-P. "Apocalypse, Ascension et Vision de saint Paul,"
       Dictionnaire. 2. Cols. 653-55.

60.45 Moraldi, L. "Apocalisse di Paolo," Apoc. del NT. 2. Pp.
       1855-1911.

60.46 Myszor, W. "Apokalipsa Pawla," Studia theologica Varsavien-
       sia 10 (1972) 163-70. [also in RuBi 25 (1972) 22-29]

60.47 Načov, N.A. "The Tives Manuscript," Sbornik za Narodni
       Umotvorenia: Navka! Knižnina 9 (1893). Pp. 100-3.
       [in Bulgarian]

60.48 Novaković, S. Examples of Literature and Language. Belgrade,
       1904³. Pp. 510-13. [in Serbo-Croatian]

60.49 Nunassrantz, T. Die armenische Kirche in ihren Beziehungen
       zu den syrischen Kirchen (TU 11) Leipzig, 1885.

60.50 Perkins, J. "The Revelation of the Blessed Apostle Paul,
       Translated from an Ancient Syriac Manuscript," JAOS 8
       (1864) 183-212. [repr. Journal of Sacred Literature and
       Biblical Record 6 (1865) 372-401]

60.51 Polívka, G. "Descriptions and Excerpts ...," Starine 21
       (1889) 218-20. [in Serbo-Croatian]

60.52   Pypin, A.N. False and Dismissed Books of Ancient Russia.
        Petrograd, 1862. Pp. 129-33.

60.53   Ricciotti, G. "Apocalypses Pauli syriace," Or 2 (1933) 1-24,
        120-49. [Syr. text with Lat. trans.]

60.54   Ricciotti, G. L'apocalissi di Paolo Syriaca. 2 vols. Brescia,
        1932.

60.55   Ruegg, A. Die Jenseitsvorstellungen vor Dante. 2 vols.
        Einsiedlen-Köln, 1945.

60.56   Sacharov, V. Eschatological Sayings and Works in Ancient
        Russian Writings and Their Influence on National Spiritual
        Moods. Tula, 1879. Pp. 200-18. [in Russian]

60.57   Santos Otero, A. de. "Apocalypsis Pauli," Altslavischen Apok.
        1. Pp. 170-87.

60.58   Serruys, D. "Une source gnostique de l'Apocalypse de Paul,"
        RPLHA 35 (1911) 194-202.

60.59   Silverstein, T. "Dante and the Legend of the Mi'rāj: The
        Problem of Islamic Influence on the Christian Literature of
        the Other World," JNES 11 (1952) 89-110, 187-97.

60.60   Silverstein, T. "Dante and Vergil the Mystic," Harvard Stud-
        ies and Notes in Philology and Literature 14 (1932) 51-82.

60.61   Silverstein, T. "The Date of the 'Apocalypse of Paul,'"
        Mediaeval Studies 24 (1962) 335-48.

60.62   Silverstein, T. "The Graz and Zurich Apocalypse of St. Paul:
        An Independent Medieval Witness to the Greek" Medieval
        Learning and Literature: Essays Presented to R.W. Hunt,
        ed. J.J.G. Alexander and M.T. Gibson. Oxford, 1976.
        Pp. 166-80.

60.63   Stefanini-Gasparro, G. Studi di storia religiosa della tarda
        antichità. Messina, 1968. Pp. 93-107.

60.64   Stegmüller, F. Repertorium Biblicum 1. Pp. 240-45; 8.
        207-11.

60.65   Steindorff, G. Die Apokalypse des Elias: Eine unbekannte
        Apokalypse und Bruchstücke der Sophonias-Apokalypse (TU
        2.3) Leipzig, 1899.

60.66   Stowe, C.E. Origin and History of the Books of the Bible.
        Hartford, 1867. Pp. 499-508.

60.67   Strohal, R. Old Croatian Apocryphal Tales and Legends, Col-
         lected from Old Croatian Glagolithic Manuscripts from the
         Fourteenth to the Eighteenth Centuries. Bjelovar, 1917.
         Pp. 18-21, 32-36. [in Serbo-Croatian]

60.68   Tarchnišvili, P.M. "Der Apostel Paulus," Geschichte der
         kirchlichen georgischen Literatur (Studi e Testi 185) Rome,
         1955. P. 345.

60.69   Tichonravov, N. Texts of Dismissed Russian Literature.
         Moscow, 1863; repr. London, 1973. Vol. 2. Pp. 40-58.
         [in Russian]

60.70   Tischendorf, K. "Apocalypsis Pauli," Apocalypses Apocryphae.
         Pp. 34-69. [Gk. text]

60.71   Tischendorf, K. "Versuch einer vollständigen Einleitung in
         die Offenbarung des Johannes und die apokalyptische Lit-
         teratur überhaupt," TSK 24 (1851) 419-56.

60.72   Vetter, P. "Die armenische Paulusapokalypse," TQ 88 (1906)
         568-95; 89 (1907) 58-75.

60.73   Villari, P. Antiche leggende e tradizione che illustrano la Di-
         vina Commedia. Pesa, 1865.

60.74   Walker, A. "Revelation of Paul," ANF   8. Pp. 575-81. [ET]

60.75   Wieber, E. De Apocalypsis S. Pauli codicibus. Merpurgi
         Cattorum, 1904.

60.76   Wilson, R.McL. "Paul, Apocalypse of," ZPEB. 4. Pp. 623f.

60.77   Zingerle, P. "Die Apocalypse des Apostels Paulus," Viertel-
         jahrschrift für deutsch- und englisch-theologische Forschung
         und Kritik 4 (1871) 139-83.

61.   PAUL, CORRESPONDENCE BETWEEN SENECA AND

61.1   Amann, É. "Correspondance entre Sénèque et saint Paul,"
         DBSup. 1. Cols. 520-22.

61.2   Arnaud, E. "Sénèque le philosophe," RTQR 11 (1902) 64-75.

61.3   Aubertin, C. Étude critique sur les rapports supposés entre
         Sénèque et St. Paul. Paris, 1875. [contains an important
         bibliography]

61.4 Aubertin, C. Sénèque et St. Paul: Étude sur les rapports
     supposés entre le philosophe et l'apôtre. Paris, 1869.

61.5 Bardenhewer, O. "Die Briefwechsel zwischen Paulus und Sen-
     eca," GAL. 1. Pp. 606-10.

61.6 Barlow, C.W. Epistolae Senecae ad Paulum et Pauli ad Sene-
     cam quae vocantur (Papers and Monographs of the American
     Academy in Rome 10) Rome, 1938. [includes bibliography to
     1937]

61.7 Bauer, F.C. "Seneka und Paulus: Das Verhältnis des Stoiz-
     imus zum Christentum nach den Schriften Senecas," ZWT
     1 (1858) 161-246, 441-70.

61.8 Bauer, J.B. "Briefwechsel mit Seneca," Neutest. Apok. Pp.
     90-93.

61.9 Baumgarten, M. Lucius Annäus Seneca und das Christentum
     in der tiefgesunkenen antiken Weltzeit. Rostock, 1895.

61.10 Benoit, P. "Sénèque et S. Paul," RB 53 (1946) 7-35.

61.11 Bocciolini Palagi, L.B. Il carteggio apocrifo di Seneca e San
      Paolo: Introduzione, testo, commento (Accademia Toscana di
      Scienze e Lettere La Colombaria 46) Florence, 1978.

61.12 Boissier, L. "Sénèque et St. Paul," La religion romaine d'
      Auguste aux Antonins. Paris, 1884. Vol. 2. Pp. 52-104.

61.13 Bräutigam, L. "Seneca und das Christentum," Ethische Kultur
      4 (1896) 90f.

61.14 Codara, A. "Seneca filosofo e San Paolo," Rivista italiana di
      filosofia 12 (1897) 149-81, 341-64; 13 (1898) 26-41, 179-90.

61.15 Erbetta, M. "La Corrispondenza tra Seneca e Paolo," Apoc.
      del NT. 3. Pp. 85-92.

61.16 Fabricius, J.A. "Testimonia et Censurae de Epistolis Pauli
      et Senecae Amoebaeis," Cod.Apoc.NT. 2. Pp. 880-904.

61.17 Farel, P. "Pour Sénèque," RTQR 10 (1901) 342-57.

61.18 Fleury, A. St. Paul et Sénèque: Recherches sur les rapports
      du philosophe avec l'apôtre et sur l'infiltration du christianisme
      naissant à travers le paganisme. 2 vols. Paris, 1853.

61.19 Franceschini, E. "Un ignoto codice delle 'Epistolae Senecae
      et Pauli,'" Mélanges Joseph de Ghellinck, S.J. (Museum

Lessianum--Section Historique 13) Gembloux, 1951. Vol. 1.
Pp. 149-70.

61.20   Friedländer, L. "Der Philosoph Seneca," HZ 85 (1900) 193-
        249.

61.21   Harnack, A. "Der Briefwechsel zwischen Seneca und Paulus,"
        Gesch. altchrist. Lit. 2.2. Pp. 458f.

61.22   Harnack, A. "Paulus und Seneca, Briefe," Gesch. altchrist.
        Lit. 1. Pp. 763-65.

61.23   Haussleiter, J. "Literatur zu der Frage 'Seneca und das Chris-
        tentum," Jahresbericht über die Fortschritte der klassischen
        Altertumsurssenschaft 281 (1943) 172-76. [complete bibliog-
        raphy 1883-1938]

61.24   Herrmann, L. Sénèque et les premiers chrétiens (Collection
        Latomus 167) Brussels, 1979.

61.25   James, M.R. "The Correspondence of Paul and Seneca," ANT
        Pp. 480-84.

61.26   Kraus, F.X. "Der Briefwechsel Pauli mit Seneca: Ein Beitrag
        zur Apokryphenliteratur," TQ 49 (1867) 603-24.

61.27   Kreyher, J. L. Annaeus Seneca und seine Beziehungen zum
        Urchristentum. Berlin, 1887.

61.28   Kurfess, A. "The Apocryphal Correspondence Between Seneca
        and Paul," HSW. 2. Pp. 133-41.

61.29   Kurfess, A. "Der apokryphe Briefwechsel zwischen Seneca
        und Paulus," HS. 2. Pp. 84-89.

61.30   Kurfess, A. "Der Brand Roms und die Christenverfolgung
        im Jahre 64 n. Chr.," Mnemosyne 3, ser. 6 (1938) 261-72.

61.31   Kurfess, A. "Zu dem apokryphen Briefwechsel zwischen dem
        Philosophen Seneca und dem Apostel Paulus," Aevum 26
        (1952) 42-48.

61.32   Kurfess, A. "Zu Pseudo-Paulus ad Senecam," ZNW 35 (1936)
        307.

61.33   Kurfess, A. "Zum apokryphen Briefwechsel zwischen Seneca
        und Paulus," ThG1 29 (1937) 317-22.

61.34   Kurfess, A. "Zum apokryphen Briefwechsel zwischen Seneca
        und Paulus," TQ 119 (1938) 318-31.

61.35 Kurfess, A. "Zum apokryphen Briefwechsel zwischen Seneca und Paulus," ZRGG 2 (1949/50) 67-70.

61.36 Labriolle P. de. Le réaction païenne. Paris, 1934. Pp. 25-28.

61.37 Leclercq, H. "Sénèque et S. Paul," DACL. 15. Cols. 1193-98.

61.38 Liénard, E. "Alcuin et les Epistolae Senecae et Pauli," RBelgPhH 20 (1941) 589-98.

61.39 Liénard, E. "Sur la correspondance apocryphe de Sénèque et de Saint Paul," RBelgPhH 11 (1932) 5-23.

61.40 Lightfoot, J.B. St. Paul's Epistle to the Philippians. London, 1873³. Pp. 268-331.

61.41 Migne, J.-P. "Sénèque. (Correspondance de Saint Paul avec Sénèque.)," Dictionnaire. 2. Cols. 923-30, 1318f. [Intro. and French trans.]

61.42 Moraldi, L. "Corrispondenza tra Paolo e Seneca," Apoc. del NT. 2. Pp. 1730-32, 1749-55.

61.43 Pascal, C. "La falsa corrispondenza fra Seneca e S. Paolo," Rivista di filologia e d'instruzione classica 35 (1907) 33-42.

61.44 Pascal, C. "La falsa corrispondenza tra Seneca e Paolo," Letteratura latina medievale. Catania, 1909. Pp. 123-40.

61.45 Pink, K. "Die pseudo-paulinischen Briefe II," Bib 6 (1925) 179-200. [see esp. pp. 193-200]

61.46 Ribbeck, W. L. Annäus Seneca der Philosoph und sein Verhältnis zu Epikur, Plato und dem Christentum. Hannover, 1887.

61.47 Rubin, S. Die Ethik Senecas in ihrem Verhältnis zur älteren und mittleren Stoa. München, 1901.

61.48 Schanz, M. Geschichte der römischen Literatur. 4 vols. Munich, 1898-1920. Vol. 2. Pp. 414-17.

61.49 Schreiner, T. Seneca im Gegensatz zu Paulus: Ein Vergleich ihrer Welt- und Lebensanschauung. Diss. Tübingen, 1936.

61.50 Sevenster, J.N. Paul and Seneca (NovTSup 4) Leiden, 1961.

61.51 Stegmüller, F. Repertorium Biblicum. 1. Pp. 215f.; 8. P. 186.

61.52 Vouaux, L. "Correspondance entre Sénèque et Saint Paul,"
       Les Actes de Paul et ses Lettres apocryphes. (Les apocry-
       phes du nouveau testament) Paris, 1913. Pp. 332-69.

61.53 Wake, W., and N. Lardner, "The Epistles of Paul the Apostle
       to Seneca, with Seneca's to Paul," ApocNT. Pp. 107-13.
       [ET]

61.54 Westerburg, E. Der Ursprung der Sage, dass Seneca Christ
       gewesen sei: Eine Kritische Untersuchung nebst einer Re-
       zension des apokryphen Briefwechsels des Apostels Paulus
       mit Seneca. Berlin, 1881. [cf. Harnack's review TLZ 6
       (1881) 444-49]

61.55 Wilson, R.McL. "Paul and Seneca, Letters of," ZPEB. 4.
       P. 623.

61.56 Zahn, T. "Der Briefwechsel zwischen Seneca und Paulus,"
       Neutest. Kanons. 2. Pp. 612-21.

62. PAUL: EPISTLE OF PAUL TO
THE ALEXANDRIANS

62.1   Amann, É. "Epitre aux Alexandrins," DBSup. 1. Col. 520.

62.2   Bardenhewer, O. "Der Alexandrinerbrief," GAL. 1. Pp.
       600f.

62.3   Bonsirven, J., and C. Bigaré. "Epîtres de Paul," Intro. à
       la Bible. 2. P. 761.

62.4   Erbetta, M. "La Lettera agli Alessandrini," Apoc. del NT.
       3. Pp. 69f.

62.5   Harnack, A. "Der Laodicener- und Alexandrinerbrief des
       Paulus," Marcion: Das Evangelium vom Fremden Gott (TU
       45) Leipzig, 1924^2. Pp. 134-49.

62.6   Harnack, A. "Paulus, Apostel, angeblicher Brief an die Alex-
       andriner," Gesch. altchrist. Lit. 1. P. 33.

62.7   James, M.R. [A fragment, perhaps of an Epistle], ANT. Pp.
       479f.

62.8   Moraldi, L. "Lettera agli Alessandrini," Apoc. del NT. 2.
       Pp. 1723, 1739.

62.9   Pink, K. "Die pseudo-paulinischen Briefe II," Bib 6 (1925)
       179-200. [see esp. p. 193]

62.10   Schneemelcher, W.   "Brief des Paulus an die Alexandriner,"
        HS. 2. P. 55.

62.11   Schneemelcher, H.   "Letter of Paul to the Alexandrians,"
        HSW. 2. P. 91.

62.12   Stegmüller, F.   Repertorium Biblicum. 1. P. 210; 8. P. 182.

62.13   Vouaux, L.   "Épître aux Alexandrins," Les Actes de Paul et
        ses Lettres apocryphes. (Les apocryphes du nouveau testa-
        ment) Paris, 1913. Pp. 327-32.

62.14   Zahn, T.   "Der Brief an die Alexandriner," Neutest. Kanons.
        2. Pp. 586-92. [Intro. and Lat. text]

                63. PAUL, THIRD EPISTLE TO
                     THE CORINTHIANS

        Although 3Cor later circulated independently, it is actually
        a part of AcPl--see also the entries under that category.

(See also 1.218.)

63.1   Amann, É.   "La IIIe Épître aux Corinthiens," DBSup. 1.
        Cols. 518f.

63.2   Amiot, F.   "Séjour à Philippi. Correspondance avec les Corin-
        thiens," Évangiles Apoc. Pp. 243-47. [French trans.]

63.3   Asmussen, J.P.   "Der apokryphe dritte Korintherbrief in der
        armenischen Tradition," Aevum 48 (1974) 51-55.

63.4   Awkev, F.P., and L. Byron.   Grammar English and Armenian.
        Venice, 1813.

63.5   Bardenhewer, O.   "Der Briefwechsel zwischen Paulus und den
        Korinthern," GAL. 1. Pp. 601-06.

63.5a   Bauer, J.B.   "Ein dritter Korintherbrief," Neutest. Apok.
        Pp. 89f.

63.6   Berendts, A.   "Zur christologie des apokryphen dritten Kor-
        intherbriefs," Abhandlungen Akademie von Oettingen. Mu-
        nich, 1898. Pp. 1-28.

63.7   Boese, H.   "Uber eine bisher unbekannte Handschrift des

Briefwechsels zwischen Paulus und den Korinthern," ZNW
44 (1952) 66-76.

63.8   Bonsirven, J., and C. Bigaré. "Épîtres de Paul," Intro. à
        la Bible. 2. P. 761.

63.9   Bratke, E. "Ein zweiter lateinischer Text des apokryphen
        Briefwechsels zwischen dem Apostel Paulus und den Korin-
        thern," TLZ 17 (1892) 585-88. [Lat. text]

63.10   Bruyne, D. de. "Un nouveau manuscrit de la troisième lettre
        de S. Paul aux Corinthiens," RBen 25 (1908) 431-34.

63.11   Bruyne, D. de. "Un quatrième manuscrit latin de la corres-
        pondance apocryphe de S. Paul avec les Corinthiens," RBen
        45 (1933) 189-95.

63.12   Carrière, A., and S. Berger. "La correspondance apocryphe
        de S. Paul et les Corinthiens: Ancienne version latine et
        traduction du texte arménien," RTP 24 (1891) 333-51.

63.13   Ceriani, A.M. La correspondance apocryphe de Saint Paul
        et des Corinthiens. Paris, 1891. [Lat. text and French
        trans. of Arm. text]

63.14   Deeleman, C.F.M. "De apocriefe briefwisseling tusschen Paulus
        en de Corinthiërs," Theologische Studiën 27 (1909) 37-56.

63.15   Harnack, A. "Der gefälschte Briefwechsel der Korinther und
        des Apostels Paulus," Gesch. altchrist. Lit. 2.1. Pp. 506-
        08.

63.16   Harnack, A. "Der Korintherbrief," Apocrypha IV: Die apok-
        ryphen Briefe des Paulus an die Laodicener und Korinther
        (KlT 12) Berlin, 1931^2. Pp. 6-23. [Lat. text with Gk.
        retroversion]

63.17   Harnack, A. "Paulus, Apostel, angeblicher Brief an die Korin-
        ther als Antwort auf ein angebliches Schreiben der Korinther
        an ihn," Gesch. altchrist. Lit. 1. Pp. 37-39.

63.18   Harnack, A. "Untersuchungen über den apocryphen Brief-
        wechsel der Korinther mit dem Apostel Paulus," SPAW (1905)
        3-35.

63.19   James, M.R. ANT. Pp. 288-91.

63.20   Klijn, A.F.J. "The Apocryphal Correspondence between Paul
        and the Corinthians," VC 17 (1963) 2-23.

63.21   Loofs, F. Theophilus von Antiochien adversus Marcionem (TU
        44) Leipzig, 1930. Pp. 148-57.

63.22 Migne, J.-P. "IIIᵉ Epitre de Saint Paul aux Corinthiens,"
       Dictionnaire. 1. Cols. 1289-94.

63.23 Moraldi, L. "Lettera dei Corinzi a Paolo e di Paolo ai Corinzi,"
       Apoc. del NT. 2. Pp. 1723-30, 1740-48.

63.24 Penny, D.N. The Pseudo-Pauline Letters of the First Two
       Centuries. Diss. Emory, 1979.

63.25 Pink, K. "Die pseudo-paulinischen Briefe," Bib 6 (1925) 68-
       91, 179-200.

63.26 Rinck, W. Das Sendschreiben der Korinther an den Apostel
       Paulus und das dritte Sendschreiben Pauli an die Korinther.
       Heidelberg, 1823.

63.27 Rist, M. "Pseudepigraphic Refutations of Marcionism," JRel
       22 (1942) 36-62.

63.28 Rist, M. "III Corinthians as a Pseudepigraphic Refutation of
       Marcionism," Iliff Review 26 (1969) 49-58.

63.29 Schaeder, H.H. "Bardesanes von Edessa in der Überlieferung
       der griechischen und syrischen Kirche," ZKG 51 (1932)
       21-74.

63.30 Scharlemann, M.H. "Third Corinthians [with English tr. of
       text and bibliography]," CTM 26 (1955) 518-29.

63.31 Schmidt, C. "Der apokryphe Korintherbriefwechsel," Acta
       Pauli aus der Heidelberger Koptischen Papyrushandschrift
       n.I. Leipzig, 1904. Pp. 125-45. [Cop. text]

63.32 Stegmüller, F. Repertorium Biblicum. 1. Pp. 211-14; 8.
       Pp. 183f.

63.33 Testuz, M. "La correspondance apocryphe de S. Paul et des
       Corinthiens," RechBib 5 (1950) 217-23.

63.34 Testuz, M. "X: Correspondance apocryphe des Corinthiens
       et de l'apôtre Paul," Papyrus Bodmer X-XII, Cologne-Geneva,
       1959. Pp. 9-45. [Gk. text]

63.35 Vetter, P. "Der apokryphe dritte Korintherbrief," TQ 73
       (1890) 610-39.

63.36 Vetter, P. "Der apokryphe dritte Korintherbrief," Tübingen
       Universitätsschrift (1893-94) 41-52. [Arm. text]*

63.37 Vetter, P. Literarische Rundschau (1897) 36.*

63.38   Vetter, P. "Eine rabbinische Quelle des apokryphen dritten
        Korintherbrief," TQ 77 (1895) 622-33.

63.39   Vouaux, L. Les Actes de Paul et ses Lettres apocryphes
        (Les apocryphes du nouveau testament) Paris, 1913. Pp.
        248-75.

63.40   Whiston, W. Mosis Chorenensis historiae Armeniensis libri tres.
        London, 1736.

63.41   Wilkins, D. ed. Epistolae S. Pauli ad Corinthios. Amsterdam,
        1715.

63.42   Wilson, R.McL. "Corinthians, Third Epistle to The," ZPEB.
        1. P. 976.

63.43   Zahn, T. "Der apokryphe Briefwechsel zwischen Paulus und
        den Korinthern," Neutest. Kanons. 2. Pp. 592-611.
        [Intro. and German trans.]

63.44   Zohrab, P. La traduction arménienne de la Bible. Venice,
        1805.

64. PAUL: EPISTLE TO THE LAODICEANS

(See also 1.218.)

64.1   Amann, É. "Épître aux Laodicéens," DBSup. 1. 519f.

64.2   Anderson, C.P. "Who Wrote 'The Epistle from Laodicea?'"
        JBL 85 (1966) 436-40.

64.3   Anger, R. Uber den Laodicenerbrief: Eine biblisch-kritische
        Untersuchung (Beiträge zur historisch-kritischen Einleitung
        in das Alte und Neue Testament) Leipzig, 1843.

64.4   Bardenhewer, O. "Der Laodiceerbrief," GAL. 1. Pp. 598-
        600.

64.5   Belsheim, J. "Die Apostelgeschichte und die Offenbarung Jo-
        hannis in einer alten lateinischen Ubersetzung aus dem 'Gigas
        librorum,'" Christiana (1879) XIII A. 1.*

64.6   Blackman, E.C. "The Epistle to the Laodiceans," Marcion and
        His Influence. London, 1948. [see Appendix 4, Pp. 61f.]

64.7   Bonsirven, J., and C. Bigaré. "Épîtres de Paul," Intro. à
        la Bible. 2. P. 761.

64.8   Bonwetsch, N. "Laodiceerbrief," Gesch. altchrist. Lit. 1.
        P. 907.

64.9   Bratke, E. "Notiz zu einer arabischen Version des Laodicener-
        briefes," ZWT 37 (1894) 137f.

64.10   Ebied, R.Y. "A Triglot Volume of the Epistle to the Laodi-
        ceans, Psalm 151 and other Biblical Materials," Bib 47 (1966)
        243-54.

64.11   Erbetta, M. "La Lettera ai Laodiceni," Apoc. del NT. 3.
        Pp. 63-67.

64.12   Fabricius, J.A. "Testimonia et Censurae de Epistola Paulo
        adscripta ad Laodicenses," Cod.Apoc.NT. 2. Pp. 853-79.
        [Gk. and Lat.]

64.13   Fine, J.V.A. "Fedor Kuritsyn's 'Laodikijskoe poslanie' and
        the Heresy of Judaizers," Speculum 41 (1966) 500-04.

64.14   Freydank, D. "Der 'Laodicener Brief' (Laodikijskoe poslanie):
        Ein Beitrag zur Interpretation einer altrussischen Textes,"
        Slavistik 11 (1966) 98-108.

64.15   Goodspeed, E.J. "The Madrid MS of Laodiceans," AJT 8 (1904)
        536-38.

64.16   Goodspeed, E.J. "A Toledo Manuscript of Laodiceans," JBL
        23 (1904) 76-78.

64.17   Haney, J.V. "The Laodicean Epistle: Some Possible Sources,"
        American Slavic and East European Review 30 (1971) 832-42.

64.18   Harnack, A. "Der apokryphe Brief des Apostels Paulus an
        die Laodicener, eine Marcionitische Fälschung aus der 2.
        Hälfte des 2. Jahrhunderts," SPAW 27 (1923) 235-45.

64.19   Harnack, A. "Der Laodicener- und Alexandrinerbrief des
        Paulus," Marcion: Das Evangelium vom Fremden Gott (TU
        45) Leipzig, 1924[2]. Pp. 134-49.

64.20   Harnack, A. "Der Laodicenerbrief," Apocrypha IV: Die
        apokryphen Briefe des Paulus an die Laodicener und Kor-
        inther (KlT 12) Berlin, 1931[2]. Pp. 2-6. [Lat. text]

64.21   Harnack, A. "Paulus, Apostel, angeblicher Brief an die Lao-
        dicener," Gesch. altchrist. Lit. 1. Pp. 33-37.

64.22   Hermann, L. "L'Épître aux Laodiciens," Cahiers du Cercle
        Ernest-Renan 58 (1968) 1-16.

64.23   Jacquier, E. Le Nouveau Testament dans l'église chrétienne.
        2 vols. Paris, 1911-13. Vol. 1. Pp. 345-51.

64.24   James, M.R. "Epistle to the Laodiceans," ANT. Pp. 478-80.

64.25   Kämpfer, F. "Zur Interpretation des 'Laodicenischen Send-
        schreibens,'" JGO N.S. 16 (1968) 63-69.

64.26   Kauźniacki, A. Actus epistolaeque apostolorum palaeoslovenice
        ad fidem codicis Christinopolitani Saeculo XII Scripti. Vin-
        dobonae, 1896.

64.27   Kazakova, N.A., and J.S. Lur'e. Antifeudal Heretical Move-
        ments in Russia in the Fourteenth to the Beginning of the
        Sixteenth Centuries. Moscow-Leningrad, 1955. Pp. 256-76.
        [in Russian]

64.28   Knopf, R. "Laodicenerbrief," Handbuch, ed. Hennecke.
        P. 204.

64.29   Knopf, R., and G. Krüger. "Laodicenerbrief," H^2. Pp. 150f.

64.30   Knox, J. Marcion and the New Testament. Chicago, 1942.

64.31   Knox, J. Philemon Among the Letters of Paul: A New View
        of Its Place and Importance, rev. ed. New York, Nashville,
        1959. [On pp. 45-55 Knox discusses the "letter from Lao-
        dicea" (Col. 4:16) and suggests it refers to Philemon.]

64.32   Lightfoot, J.B. St. Paul's Epistles to the Colossians and to
        Philemon. London, 1886^8. Pp. 281-300.

64.33   Maier, J. "Zum jüdischen Hintergrund des sog. 'Laodiceni-
        schen Sendschreibens," JGO N.S. 17 (1969) 1-12.

64.34   Migne, J.-P. "Épître de Saint Paul aux Laodicéens," Diction-
        naire. 1. Cols. 1285-90.

64.35   Moraldi, L. "Lettera ai Laodicesi," Apoc. del NT. 2. Pp.
        1720-23, 1737f.

64.36   Nestle, E. "Ad Laodicenses," Novum Testamentum graece et
        latine. Stuttgart, 1951^{15}. P. xii.

64.37   Penny, D.N. The Pseudo-Pauline Letters of the First Two
        Centuries. Diss. Emory, 1979.

64.38   Pink, K. "Die pseudo-paulinischen Briefe II," Bib 6 (1925)
        179-200. [see esp. pp. 179-92]

64.39   Quispel, G. "De Brief aan de Laodicensen een Marcionitische
        vervalsing," NedThT 5 (1950) 43-46.

64.40 Ranke, E. Codex Fuldensis: Novum Testamentum latine in-
       terprete Hieronymo ex manuscripto Victoris Capuani. Mar-
       burg, 1868. Pp. 291f. [Lat. text]

64.41 Santos Otero, A. de. "Epistula Pauli ad Laodicenses," Alt-
       slavischen Apok. 1. Pp. 147f.

64.42 Schneemelcher, W. "The Epistle to the Laodiceans," HSW.
       2. Pp. 128-32.

64.43 Schneemelcher, W. "Der Laodicenerbrief," HS. 2. Pp. 80-84.

64.44 Schultz, W. "Epistola ad Laodicenses," ZWT 42 (1899) 36-39.
       [Lat. text]

64.45 Sîrbu, G. "Does the Epistle from the Apostle St. Paul to the
       Laodiceans Exist?" BCO 9 (1964) 169-74. [in Rumanian]

64.46 Stegmüller, F. Repertorium Biblicum. 1. Pp. 214f.; 8. Pp.
       184-86.

64.47 Stichel, R. "Zur Bedeutung des altrussischen 'Laodicenischen
       Sendschreibens,'" Zeitschrift für slavische Philologie 40
       (1978) 134f. [S. discusses relationship of EpLao to the late,
       Italian GosBarn]

64.48 Vaux, B.C. de. "L'Epitre aux Laodicéens en arabe," RB 5
       (1896) 221-25.

64.49 Voskresenskij, G. An Ancient Slavic Translation of the Apostle
       and Its Fortunes Prior to the XVth Century. Moscow, 1879.
       [in Russian]

64.50 Vouaux, L. "Épître aux Laodicéens," Les Actes de Paul et
       ses Lettres apocryphes. (Les apocryphes du nouveau testa-
       ment) Paris, 1913. Pp. 315-26.

64.51 Wake, W., and N. Lardner. "The Epistle of Paul the Apostle
       to the Laodiceans," Apoc.NT. Pp. 106f. [ET]

64.52 Weber, R., et al., eds. Biblia Sacra Iuxta Vulgatam Versionem.
       Stuttgart, 1969. Vol. 2. P. 1976.

64.53 Westcott, B.F. A General Survey of the History of the Canon
       of the New Testament. Cambridge, 1889[6]. P. 581.

64.54 Wilson, R.McL. "Laodiceans, Epistle to," ZPEB. 3. Pp.
       879f.

64.55 Zahn, T. "Der Brief an die Laodicener," Neutest. Kanons. 2.
       Pp. 566-85. [Intro. and Lat. text; see also Vol. 1. Pp.
       277-83]

65. PAUL, MARTYRDOM OF

MartPl is a subsection of AcPl--see also the entries under
that category.

(See also 3.41, 78; 7.10.)

65.1   Baumstark, A. Die Petrus- und Paulusakten in der literari-
        schen Uberlieferung der syrischen Kirche. Leipzig, 1902.
        Pp. 32-34.

65.2   Conybeare, F.C., ed. The Apology and Acts of Apollonius
        and Other Monuments of Early Christianity. London, 1894.

65.3   Erbetta, M. "La Passione di Paolo dello Ps. Lino," Apoc. del
        NT. 2. Pp. 289-96.

65.4   Fabricius, J.A. "Linus de Passione Petri(a) et Pauli," Cod.
        Apoc.NT. 2. Pp. 775f.

65.5   Hemmerdinger, B. "Euthaliana," JTS 11 (1960) 349-53.

65.5a   Lewis, A.S. The Mythological Acts of the Apostles (Horae
        Semiticae 4) London, 1904. Pp. 217-22. [ET of Ar. text
        in Horae Semiticae 3]

65.6   Lipsius, R.A., ed. "Passionis Pauli fragmentum," AAA. 1.
        Pp. 104-17. [Gk. and Lat. text]

65.7   Lipsius, R.A., ed. "Passio sancti Pauli apostoli," AAA. 1.
        Pp. 23-44. [Lat. text]

65.8   Migne, J.-P. "Passion de saint Paul," Dictionnaire. 2. Cols.
        665-74.

65.9   Moraldi, L. "Martirio di san Paolo apostolo," Apoc. del NT.
        2. Pp. 1125-30.

65.10   Nau, F. "La version syriaque inédite des martyres de S.
        Pierre, S. Paul et S. Luc d'après un manuscrit du dixième
        siècle," ROC 3 (1898) 39-57, 151-56.

65.11   Rordorf, W. "Die neronische Christenverfolgung im Spiegel
        der apokryphen Paulusakten," NTS 28 (1982) 365-74.

65.12   Schmidt, C. "Martyrium des Paulus," Gesch. altchrist. Lit.
        1. Pp. 921f.

65.13   Stegmüller, F. Repertorium Biblicum. 1. Pp. 208-10; 8. P.
        182.

65.14   Wilson, R.McL. "Paul, Passion of," ZPEB. 4. P. 624.

66. PAUL, VISION OF

VisPl is the title of the Latin version of ApPl--see also the
entries under that category.

(See also 1.254.)

66.1   Brandes, H. "Über die Quellen der mittelenglischen Versionen
        der Paulus-Vision," Englischen Studien 7 (1884) 34-65.

66.2   Brandes, H. Visio Sancti Pauli: Ein Beitrag zur Visions-
        litteratur mit einem deutschen und zwei lateinischen Texten.
        Halle, 1885.

66.3   Fabricius, J.A. "S. Pauli Anabatikon, Apocalypsis, & Visiones,"
        Cod.Apoc.NT. 2. Pp. 943-53.

66.4   Fischer, B. "Impedimenta mundi fecerunt eos miseros," VC
        5 (1951) 84-87.

66.5   Fritzsche, O. "Die latein. Visionen des M. Alt. bis zur Mitte
        des XII Jahrh.," Romanische Forschungen 3 (1887) 345f.

66.6   Graf, A. "A proposito della Visio Pauli," GSLI 11 (1888)
        344f.

66.7   Gutch, M.M. "Two Uses of Apocrypha in Old English Hom-
        ilies," Church History 33 (1965) 379-91.

66.8   Healey, A. di P., ed. The Old English Vision of St. Paul
        (Speculum Anniversary Monographs 2) Cambridge, Mass.,
        1978.

66.9   Healey, A. di P. The Vision of St. Paul. Diss., U. of To-
        ronto, 1973.

66.10   James, M.R. "On the Latin Version of the Visio Pauli," AA
        1. Pp. 1-42. [See also AA 2. P. 138]

66.11   Kastner, L.E. "The Vision of S. Paul by Anglo-Norman
        Trouvère Adam de Ross," Zeitschrift für französische Sprache
        und Literatur 29 (1905-06) 274-90.

66.12   Kastner, L.E. "Les visions françaises inédites de la descente
        de Saint Paul en enfer," Revue des langues romanes 48
        (1905) 385-95; 49 (1906) 49-62, 321-51, 427-49.

66.13   Mayor, J.E.B.   "Visio Pauli," JPhil 22 (1894) 187-97.

66.14   Migne, J.-P.   "Apocalypse, Ascension et Vision de saint Paul,"
        Dictionnarie.   2.   Cols. 653-55.

66.15   Olivar, A.   "'Liber Infernalis' o 'Visio Pauli,'" Sacris Erudiri
        18 (1967) 550-54.

66.16   Oliveras Caminal, J.   "Texto de la 'Visio S. Pauli' según el
        codice 28 de la Catedral de Barcelona," Scriptorium 1 (1946-
        47) 240-42.

66.17   Owen, D.D.R.   "The 'Vision of St. Paul':   The French and
        Provençal Versions and Their Sources," Romance Philology
        12 (1958) 33-51.

66.18   Polívka, G.   "Zur Visio S. Pauli," Archiv für slavische Phil-
        ologie 16 (1894) 611-16.

66.19   Šepelevič, L.   Studies on Dante I: The Apocryphal Vision of
        St. Paul.   2 vols.   Char'kov, 1891-92.   [in Russian]

66.20   Seymour, J.D.   "Irish Versions of the Vision of St. Paul,"
        JTS 24 (1922-23) 54-59.

66.21   Silverstein, T.   "Dante and the Visio Pauli," Modern Language
        Notes 47 (1932) 387-99.

66.22   Silverstein, T.   "Did Dante Know the Vision of St. Paul?"
        Harvard Studies and Notes in Philology and Literature 19
        (1937) 231-47.

66.23   Silverstein, T.   "The Source of a Provençal Version of the
        Vision of St. Paul," Speculum 8 (1933) 353-58.

66.24   Silverstein, T.   Visio Pauli: The History of the Apocalypse
        in Latin, Together with Nine Texts (Studies and Documents
        4) London, 1935.

66.25   Silverstein, T.   "The Vision of Saint Paul: New Links and
        Patterns in the Western Tradition," Archives d'histoire doc-
        trinale et littéraire du Moyen Age 34 (1959) 199-248.

66.26   Stegmüller, F.   Repertorium Biblicum.   1.   Pp. 241-45; 8.
        Pp. 207-11.

66.27   Turdeanu, E.   "La 'Vision de S. Paul' dans la tradition litté-
        raire des slaves orthodoxes," Die Welt der Slaven 1 (1956)
        401-30.

66.28   Tveitane, M.   "En Norrón Versjon au Visio Pauli," Acta

Universitatis Bergensis, Ser. Humaniorum litterarum 3
(1965) 8-13.

66.29 Williams, J.E.C. "Welsh Versions of 'Visio S. Pauli,'" Études
Celtiques 10 (1962) 109-26.

67. PETER, ACTS OF; AND PETER CYCLE

The full AcPet also contained MartPet, a version of which
circulated independently under the name of Linus; Petrine
material is also prominent in PsCl--see also the entries
listed under those categories.

(See also 1.203, 204, 413, 470, 531, 548; 3.12, 58, 63; 7.3, 14, 26;
36.68; 74.8.)

67.1 Amann, E. "Les Actes de Pierre," DBSup. 1. Cols. 496-501.

67.2 Ambroggi, P. de. "Apocrifi [Pietro Apostolo]," EncCatt. 9.
Cols. 1421-23.

67.3 Amiot, F. "Actes de Pierre," Evangiles Apoc. Pp. 185-225.
[French trans.]

67.4 Bardenhewer, O. "Die Akten des Petrus," GAL. 1. Pp.
550-54.

67.5 Bardsley, H.J. "The Derivation of the Acta from Early Acts
of Peter," JTS 16 (1915) 495-509.

67.6 Barnikol, E. "Die Eintragung des Paulus in die Petrusakten:
Spanienreise und Römerbrief des Paulus in den Petrusakten,"
ThJ 2 (1934) 153-57.

67.7 Barnikol, E. "Marcellus in den Petrusakten: Spanienreise
und Römerbrief des Paulus in den Petrusakten," ThJ 2
(1934) 158-64.

67.8 Barnikol, E. "Petrus vor dem Caesar? Ist der Präfekt in den
Petrusakten ursprünglich der Caesar?" ThJ 2 (1934) 115-22.

67.9 Barnikol, E. "Spanienreise und Römerbrief des Paulus in den
Petrusakten," ThJ 2 (1934) 1-12.

67.10 Barnikol, E. "Der späte Ursprung der Spanienreise des Paulus
in den Petrusakten und die frühe notwendige Umformung
des römischen Reiseplanes zum spanischen Reiseplan bei der

Gestaltung des sogenannte Römerbriefes im Corpus Paulinum,"
ThJ 2 (1934) 21-25.

67.11   Barnikol, E. "Die Urgestalt der Petrusakten: Spanienreise
        und Römerbrief des Paulus in den Petrusakten," ThJ 2
        (1934) 165f.

67.12   Bauer, J.B. "Die Petrusakten," Neutest. Apok. Pp. 64-71.

67.13   Baumstark, P. Die Petrus und Paulusakten in der litteraris-
        chen Überlieferung der syrischen Kirche. Leipzig, 1902.

67.14   Bonsirven, J., and C. Bigaré. "Actes de Pierre," Intro. à la
        Bible. 2. P. 759.

67.15   Bonwetsch, N. Gesch. altchrist. Lit. 1.2. Pp. 903f.

67.16   Bottomley, G. The Acts of St. Peter. London, 1933.

67.17   Bruyne, D. de. "Deux citations apocryphes de l'apôtre
        Pierre," JTS 34 (1933) 395-97.

67.18   Bruyne, D. de. "Nouveaux fragments des Actes de Pierre,
        de Paul, de Jean, d'André, et de l'Apocalypse d'Élie," RBen
        25 (1908) 149-60.

67.19   Cullmann, O. Saint Pierre, Disciple, Apôtre, Martyr. Neu-
        châtel, 1952. [ET: Peter: Disciple, Apostle, Martyr: A
        Historical and Theological Study. Philadelphia, 1962]

67.20   Daniélou, J. "Pierre dans le judéo-christianisme hétérodoxe,"
        San Pietro, Atti della XIX Settimana Biblica Italiana. Brescia,
        1967. Pp. 443-58.

67.21   Decroix, J. "Les apocryphes des actes de saint Pierre," BTS
        94 (1967) 6f.

67.22   Deeleman, C.F.M. "Acta Petri," Geloof en Vrijheid 44 (1910)
        193-244.

67.23   Dinkler, E. "Die Petrus-Rom-Frage," ThRu 27 (1959) 189-230,
        289-335.

67.24   Duchesne, L. "Les anciens recueils de légendes apostoliques,"
        Congrès scientifique international des catholiques. Brussels,
        1894. Pp. 67-79.

67.25   Erbes, C. "Ursprung und Umfang der Petrusakten," ZKG 32
        (1911) 161-85, 353-77, 497-530.

67.26   Erbetta, M. "Gli Atti di Pietro," Apoc. del NT. 2. Pp. 135-
        68.

67.27 Erbetta, M. "Atti di Pietro Inseriti nel Romanzo Pseudocle-
       mentino," Apoc. del NT. 2. Pp. 226-36.

67.28 Fabricius, J.A. "Acta S. Petri," Cod.Apoc.NT. 2. Pp. 801-
       05.

67.29 Fabricius, J.A. "Clementis Romani de Actis Petri," Cod.Apoc.
       NT. 2. Pp. 759-62.

67.30 Fabricius, J.A. "Epistola Petri ad Jacobum," Cod.Apoc.NT.
       2. Pp. 906-13. [Gk. and Lat. text]

67.31 Fabricius, J.A. "Historia Petri Persice Scripta Auctore Hier-
       onymo Xaverio, Soc. Jesu," Cod.Apoc.NT. 2. Pp. 828-30.

67.32 Ficker, G. Die Petrusakten: Beiträge zu ihrem Verständnis.
       Leipzig, 1903.

67.33 Ficker, G. "Petrusakten," Handbuch, ed. Hennecke. Pp.
       395-491.

67.34 Flamion, J. "Les Actes apocryphes de Pierre," RHE 9 (1908)
       233-54, 465-90; 10 (1909) 5-29, 215-77; 11 (1910) 5-28, 223-
       56, 447-70, 675-92; 12 (1911) 209-30, 437-50.

67.35 Grant, R.M. "Note on the Petrine Apocrypha," VC 6 (1952)
       31f.

67.36 Grenfell, B.A., and A.S. Hunt. The Oxyrhynchus Papyri.
       London, 1908. Vol. 4. Pp. 6-12. [Gk. text]

67.37 Harnack, A. "Petrus, Acten," Gesch. altchrist. Lit. 1.
       Pp. 131-36.

67.38 Harnack, A. "Die Petrusacten," Gesch. altchrist. Lit. 2.1.
       Pp. 549-60.

67.39 Heussi, K. Die römische Petrustradition in kritischer Sicht.
       Tübingen, 1955.

67.40 Hilgenfeld, A. "Die alten Actus Petri," ZWT 46 (1903) 322-41.

67.41 Hofstetter, K. "Das Petrusamt in der Kirche des 1.-2. Jahr-
       hunderts: Jerusalem-Rom," Begegnung der Christen: Studien
       evangelischer und katholischer Theologen, eds. M. Roesle
       and O. Cullmann. Frankfort, 1960. Pp. 375-89. [Fest-
       schrift O. Karrer]

67.42 Hug, W. "Quellengeschichtliche Studie zur Petrus- und Paul-
       uslegende der Legenda Aurea," Historisches Jahrbuch 49
       (1929) 604-24.

67.43   James, M.R.   "Acts of Peter," ANT. Pp. 300-36.

67.44   James, M.R.   "Leucius and the Gospel of John," AA   2. Pp.
        144-54. [James compares esp. AcPet with Jn and 1Jn.]

67.45   Javorskij, J.A.   "The Carpatho-russian Life of the Apostle
        Peter," IzvORJS 19 (1914) 75-98. [in Russian]

67.46   Klauser, T.   Die römische Petrustradition im Lichte der neuen
        Ausgrabungen unter der Peterskirche (Arbeitsgemeinschaft
        für Forschung des Landes Nordrhein-Westfalen 24) Cologne,
        1956.

67.47   Lipsius, R.A. ed.   "Actus Petri cum Simone," AAA. 1. Pp.
        44-103. [Lat. and Gk. texts; see also pp. lxxxixf.]

67.48   Lipsius, R.A.   Die apokryphen Apostelgeschichten und Apos-
        tellegenden. Brunswick, 1883-90. Vol. 2.1. Pp. 85-284.

67.49   Lipsius, R.A.   Die Quellen der römischen Petrus-Sage kritisch
        Untersucht. Kiel, 1872.

67.50   Loewenich, W. von.   "Die Petrus-, Andreas-, Paulus-, und
        Thomas-Akten," Das Johannes-Verständnis im zweiten Jahr-
        hundert (BZNW 13) Giessen, 1932. Pp. 109-12.

67.51   Lowe, J.   Saint Peter. Oxford, 1956.

67.52   McNeil, B.   "A Liturgical Source in Acts of Peter 38," VC
        33 (1979) 342-46.

67.53   Marco, A.A. de.   The Tomb of Saint Peter. Leiden, 1964.

67.54   Mariani, B.   "L'episodio del 'Quo Vadis' nella tradizione,"
        Studia Hierosolymitana in onore del P. Bellarmino Bagatti,
        eds. E. Testa, I. Mancini, M. Piccirillo. (Studii Biblici
        Franciscano Collectio Maior 23) Jerusalem, 1976. Pp. 333-46.

67.55   Mees, M.   "Das Petrusbild nach ausserkanonischen Zeugnissen,"
        ZRGG 27 (1975) 193-205.

67.56   Mees, M.   "Petrustradition im Zeugnis kanonischen und ausser-
        kanonischen Schrifttums," Aug 13 (1973) 185-203.

67.57   Michaelis, W.   "Petrus-Akten," Apokryphen Schriften. Pp.
        317-79. [German trans.]

67.58   Migne, J.-P.   "Actes de saint Pierre," Dictionnaire. 2. Cols.
        694-96.

67.59   Migne, J.-P.   "Épître de saint Pierre à saint Jacques," Dic-
        tionnaire. 2. Cols. 695f.

67.60 Migne, J.-P. "Liturgie ou sacrifice divin de l'apôtre saint Pierre (735)," Dictionnaire. 2. Cols. 731-48.

67.61 Miguel Sanz, T. La misericordia en los escritos apócrifos petrinos. Thesis, Studii Biblici Franciscani, 1973/74.

67.62 Minto, A. "P.S.I. 920: Cristo dorme nella barca di Pietro," Studi Calderini-Paribeni 2 (1957) 97-101.

67.63 Moraldi, L. "Atti di san Pietro," Apoc. del NT. 2. Pp. 963-1059.

67.64 Müller, J.J. "Die Handelinge van Petrus," Nuwe-Test. Apok. Pp. 94-127. [Afrikaans trans.]

67.65 Myszor, W. "The Acts of Peter," Studia Theologica Varsavien-sie 15 (1977) 169-75. [in Polish]

67.66 Nissen, T. "Die Petrusakten und ein bardesanitischer Dialog in der Aberkiosvita," ZNW 9 (1908) 190-203, 315-28.

67.67 Peeters, P. "Notes sur la légende des apôtres S. Pierre et S. Paul dans la littérature syrienne," AnBoll 21 (1902) 121-40.

67.68 Penna, A. S. Pietro. Brescia, 1954.

67.69 Pick, B. The Apocryphal Acts of Paul, Peter, John, Andrew and Thomas. London, 1909.

67.70 Poupon, G. "Les Actes de Pierre et leur remaniement," ANRW II.25.4 (in preparation)

67.71 Radčenko, K.F. "Notes About the Pergamum Collection of the 14th Century Vienna Court Library," IzvORJS 8 (1903) 180-96.

67.72 Rimoldi, A. L'Apostolo San Pietro, fondamento della Chiesa, principe degli Apostoli e ostiario celeste, nella Chiesa primi-tiva dalle origini al Concilio di Calcedonia (Analecta Gregor-iana 96) Rome, 1958.

67.73 Rimoldi, A. "L'apostolo S. Pietro nella letteratura apocrifa dei primi 6 secoli," Scuola Cattolica 83 (1955) 196-224.

67.74 Santos Otero, A. de. "Acta Petri," Altslavischen Apok. 1. Pp. 52-59.

67.75 Schmidt, C. Die alten Petrusakten im Zusammenhang der apok-ryphen Apostelliteratur, nebst einem neuentdeckten Fragment, Untersucht (TU 24.1) Leipzig, 1903. [see M.R. James' re-view JTS 5 (1904) 293-96]

67.76   Schmidt, C. "Studien zu den alten Petrusakten," ZKG 43
        (1924) 321-48; 45 (1927) 481-513.

67.77   Schmidt, C. "Zur Datierung der alten Petrusakten," ZNW
        29 (1930) 150-55.

67.78   Schmidt, D.H. The Peter Writings: Their Redactors and Their
        Relationships. Northwestern University, Diss. 1972.

67.79   Schneemelcher, W. "The Acts of Peter," HSW. 2. Pp. 259-
        322.

67.80   Schneemelcher, W. "Petrusakten," HS. 2. Pp. 177-21.

67.81   Smith, J.Z. "Birth Upside Down or Right Side Up?" History
        of Religions 9 (1969) 281-303.

67.82   Sotomayor, M. S. Pedro en la Iconografia paleocristiana. Gra-
        nada, 1962.

67.83   Speranskij, M.N. "Bibliographical Materials," ĈOIDR (1889)
        1-52.*

67.84   Stegmüller, F. Repertorium Biblicum. 1. Pp. 216f.; 8. 186f.

67.85   Stuhlfauth, G. Die apocryphen Petrusgeschichten in der alt-
        christlichen Kunst. Berlin, 1925.

67.86   Turner, C.H. "The Latin Acts of Peter," JTS 32 (1931) 119-
        33.

67.87   Vetter, P. "Die armenischen apokryphen Apostelakten," OrChr
        1 (1901) 217-39. [Arm. text]

67.88   Vouaux, L. Les Actes de Pierre: Introduction, textes, tra-
        duction et commentaire (Les Apocryphes du nouveau testa-
        ment) Paris, 1922. [Gk. text]

67.89   Waitz, H., and H. Veil. "Petrusakten," H². Pp. 212-49.

67.90   Wilson, R.McL. "Peter, Acts of," ZPEB. 4. P. 721.

67.91   Zahn, T. "Die gnostischen Akten des Petrus," Neutest. Kan-
        ons. 2.2. Pp. 832-55.

68. PETER, (SLAVONIC) ACTS OF

Along with the distinct AcPet(Slav) there exist many
Slavic translations of AcPet--see also the entries listed
under that category.

68.1   Archengel'skij, A.S. "On the History of Southern Slavic and
        Ancient Russian Apocryphal Literature," IzvORJS 4 (1899)
        101-47. [in Russian]

68.2   Erbetta, M. "Gli Atti di Pietro Slavi," Apoc. del NT. 2. Pp.
        535f.

68.3   Follieri, E. "L'originale greco di una leggenda in slavo su
        San Pietro," AnBoll 74 (1956) 115-30.

68.4   Franko, I. Apocrypha and Legends. L'vov, 1902. Vol. 3.
        Pp. 14f. [in Russian]

68.5   Franko, I. "Beiträge aus dem Kirchenslavischen zu den Apok-
        ryphen des Neuen Testamentes II: Zu den gnostischen
        Periodoi Petrou," ZNW 3 (1902) 315-35.

68.6   James, M.R. ANT. P. 474.

68.7   Močul'skij, V.N. "Life of the Apostle Peter," Trudy 10-go
        archeologiceskago s'ezda v Rigě. Moscow, 1896. [in Rus-
        sian]

68.8   Moraldi, L. "Gli atti slavi di Pietro," Apoc. del NT. 2. P.
        1639.

68.9   Radčenko, K.F. "Notes About the Pergamum Collection of the
        14th Century Vienna Court Library," IzvORJS 8 (1903) 199-
        211. [in Russian]

68.10   Santos, A. de. "Slavic Accounts of Peter," HSW. 2. Pp.
        573-75.

68.11   Santos, A. de. "Slavische Petrusberichte," HS. 2. Pp. 400-
        02.

68.12   Wilson, R.McL. "Peter, Slavonic Acts of," ZPEB. 4. P. 740.

69. PETER, ACTS OF ANDREW AND

        AcPetAn is a narrative continuation of AcAnMth and is
        based on the earlier AcAn--see also the listings under
        those categories.

(See also 1.470.)

69.1   Amann, É. "Actes des saints apôtres Pierre et André," DBSup.
        1. Col. 508.

316   IV. Bibliography

69.2   Bonnet, M., ed. "Acta Petri et Andreae," AAA. 2.1. Pp.
       XXIV, 117-27. [Intro. and Gk. text]

69.3   Bonwetsch, N. "Ein Beitrag zu den Akten des Petrus und
       Andreas," ZKG 5 (1882) 506-09.

69.4   Bonwetsch, N. "Petrus und Andreas," Gesch. altchrist. Lit.
       1. P. 905.

69.5   Erbetta, M. "Gli Atti di Pietro e Andrea," Apoc. del NT. 2.
       Pp. 529-34.

69.6   Grabar, B. "Apocryphal Apostolic Works in Croatian Glagolithic
       Literature," Radovi Staroslavenskog Instituta 6 (1967) 162-
       85, 200-06. [in Serbo-Croatian]

69.7   Harnack, A. "Die Andreasacten," Gesch. altchrist. Lit. 1.
       P. 127.

69.8   James, M.R. "Acts of Peter and Andrew," ANT. Pp. 458-60.

69.9   Lipsius, R.A. Die apokryphen Apostelgeschichten und Apos-
       tellegenden. 2 vols. Brunswick, 1883-1890; repr. Amster-
       dam, 1976. Vol. 1. Pp. 554-57.

69.10 Lipsius, R.A. "Zu den Acten des Petrus und Andreas,"
       JPT 9 (1883) 191.

69.11 Moraldi, L. "Atti dei santi apostoli Pietro e Andrea," Apoc.
       del NT. 2. Pp. 1618f.

69.12 Santos Otero, A. de. "Acta Petri et Andreae," Altslavischen
       Apok. 1. Pp. 67f.

69.13 Schneemelcher, W., and A. de Santos. "The Acts of the
       Apostles Peter and Andrew," HSW. 2. P. 576.

69.14 Schneemelcher, W., and A. de Santos. "Die Taten der Apos-
       tel Petrus und Andreas," HS. 2. P. 403.

69.15 Stegmüller, F. Repertorium Biblicum. 1. P. 222; 8. Pp.
       191f.

69.16 Tichonravov, N. Texts of Dismissed Russian Literature.
       Moscow, 1863; repr. London, 1973. Vol. 2. Pp. 5-10.
       [in Russian]

69.17 Tischendorf, K. von, "Acta Petri et Andreae," Apocalypses
       Apocryphae. Pp. 161-67. [Gk. text]

69.18 Walker, A. "Acts of Peter and Andrew," ANF 8. Pp. 526f.
       [ET]

69.19   Wilson, R.McL.   "Peter and Andrew, Acts of," ZPEB.   4.   Pp.
        721f.

                    70.   PETER, APOCALYPSE OF

(See also 1.120, 140, 218, 307, 531; 2.34; 67.2, 35.)

70.1   Amann, É.   "L'Apocalyse [sic.] de Pierre," DBSup.   1.
        Cols. 525-27.

70.2   Amiot, F.   "Apocalypse de Pierre," Évangiles Apoc.   Pp. 287-
        94.   [French trans.]

70.3   Baljon, J.M.S.   Het evangelie en de openbaring van Petrus,
        Textuigaaf.   Utrecht, 1896.

70.4   Bardenhewer, O.   "Die Petrusapokalypse," GAL.   1.   Pp. 610-
        15.

70.5   Bauckham, R.J.   "The Apocalypse of Peter: An Account of
        Research," ANRW 2.25.4 (in preparation)

70.6   Bauer, J.B.   "Die Petrus-Offenbarung," Neutest. Apok.   Pp.
        102-05.

70.7   Baumeister, T.   "Die Didache und die Petrusapokalypse," Die
        Anfänge der Theologie des Martyriums (Münsterische Beiträge
        zur Theologie 45) Münster, 1980.   Pp. 248-51.

70.8   Bonsirven, J., and C. Bigaré.   "L'Apocalypse de Pierre,"
        Intro. à la Bible.   2.   Pp. 761f.

70.9   Bouriant, U.   Mémoires publiées par les membres de la mission
        archéologique française au Caire.   9.   Paris, 1892.

70.10   Bratke, E.   "Handschriftliche Überlieferung und Bruchstücke
        der arabisch-äthiopischen Petrusapokalypse," ZWT 36 (1893)
        454-93.

70.11   Cabrol, F.   "La découverte du manuscrit d'Akhmîm: l'Evangile
        et l'Apocalypse de saint Pierre et le livre du prophète Enoch,"
        Revue des Facultés catholiques de l'Ouest (1893) 570-90.*

70.12   Chapius, P.   "L'Évangile et l'Apocalypse de Pierre," RTP 26
        (1893) 338-55.

70.13   Chiappelli, A.   "I frammenti ora scoperti d'un evangelio e
        d'un'apocalisse di Pietro," Nuova Antologia (1893) 212-38.*

70.14 Dieterich, A. Nekyia: Beiträge zur Erklärung der neuent-
       deckten Petrusapokalypse. Leipzig, 1893; repr. Berlin,
       1913.

70.15 Duensing, H. "Ein Stücke der urchristlichen Petrusapokalypse
       enthaltender Trakat der äthiopischen Pseudoklementinischen
       Literatur," ZNW 14 (1913) 65-78.

70.16 Erbetta, M. "L'Apocalisse di Pietro," Apoc. del NT. 3. Pp.
       209-33.

70.17 Fabricius, J.A. "Apocalypsis S. Petri," Cod.Apoc.NT. 2.
       Pp. 940-42.

70.18 Fiensy, D. "Lex Talionis in the Apocalypse of Peter," HTR
       76 (1983) 255-58.

70.19 Funk, X. "Fragmente des Evangeliums und der Apokalypse
       des Petrus," TQ 75 (1893) 255-63.

70.20 Gebhardt, O.L. von. Das Evangelium und die Apokalypse des
       Petrus. Leipzig, 1893.

70.21 Goguel, M. "A propos du texte nouveau de l'Apocalypse de
       Pierre," RHR 89 (1924) 191-209.

70.22 Grébaut, S. "Littérature éthiopienne pseudo-clémentine,"
       ROC 15 (1910) 198-214, 307-23, 425-39. [Eth. texts and
       French trans.; see also ROC 12 (1907) 139-45]

70.23 Harnack, A. Bruchstücke des Evangeliums und der Apokalypse
       des Petrus (TU 9.2) Leipzig, 1893.

70.24 Harnack, A. "Petrus, Apokalypse," Gesch. altchrist. Lit. 1.
       Pp. 29-33.

70.25 Harnack, A. "Die Petrus-Apokalypse," Gesch. altchrist. Lit.
       2.1. Pp. 470-72.

70.26 Harnack, A. "Die Petrusapokalypse in der alten abendlän-
       dischen Kirche," Eine bisher nicht erkannte Schrift des Pap-
       stes Sixtus II. vom Jahre 257/8. Zur Petrusapokalypse Pa-
       tristisches zu Luc. 16, 19 (TU 13.1) Leipzig, 1895. Pp. 71-
       73.

70.27 Harris, J.R. "The Odes of Solomon and the Apocalypse of
       Peter," ExpT 42 (1930) 21-23.

70.28 Hilgenfeld, A. Novum Testamentum extra canonem receptum.
       Leipzig, 1884. Pp. 71-74.

70.29 James, M.R. "Additional Notes on the Apocalypse of Peter," JTS 12 (1911) 157.

70.30 James, M.R. "Apocalypse of Peter," ANT. Pp. 505-21.

70.31 James, M.R. "A New Text of the Apocalypse of Peter," JTS 12 (1910) 36-54, 362-83, 573-83.

70.32 James, M.R. "The Rainer Fragment of the Apocalypse of Peter," JTS 32 (1931) 270-79.

70.33 James, M.R. "The Recovery of the Apocalypse of Peter," CQR 80 (1915) 1-36, 248.

70.34 Kaufmann, K.M. "Die Paradiesvision der Sog. Petrusapocalypse von Achmim-Panopolis und die urchristlichen Monumente," Congrès Scientifique des Catholiques X. Fribourg (Switz.), 1898. Pp. 100-12.

70.35 Klostermann, E., ed. Apocrypha I: Reste des Petrusevangeliums, der Petrusapokalypse und des Kerygma Petri (KlT 3) Berlin, 1933. Pp. 8-13. [Gk. text]

70.36 Kretzenbacher, L. "Richterengel und Feuerstrom: Östliche Apokryphen und Gegenwartslegenden um Jenseitsgeleite und Höllenstrafen," Zeltschrift für Volkskunde (1963) 205-20.*

70.37 Lagarde, P. Mittheilungen 4 (1891) 6.*

70.38 Lemm, O. "Bruchstück einer Petrusapokalypse," Koptische Miscellen. Pp. 107-12.

70.39 Lods, A. L'évangile et l'apocalypse de Pierre avec le texte grec du livre d'Hénoch. Paris, 1893.

70.40 Lods, A. Evangelii secundum Petrum et Petri apocalypseos quae supersunt. Paris, 1892.

70.41 Lüdemann, H. [Critical Comments on publications on GosPet and ApPet], Theologischer Jahresbericht 12 (1892) 171-73; 13 (1893) 171-83; 14 (1894) 185-91.

70.42 Marmorstein, A. "Jüdische Parallelen zur Petrusapokalypse," ZNW 10 (1909) 297-300.

70.43 Maurer, C., and H. Duensing. "Apocalypse of Peter," HSW. 2. Pp. 663-83.

70.44 Maurer, C., and H. Duensing. "Offenbarung des Petrus," HS. 2. Pp. 468-83.

70.45   Michaelis, W. "Petrus-Offenbarung," Apokryphen Schriften.
        Pp. 469-81. [German trans.]

70.46   Migne, J.-P. "Apocalypse de saint Pierre," Dictionnaire. 2.
        Col. 691.

70.47   Mingana, A. "Apocalypse of Peter," Woodbrooke Studies 3
        (1931) 93-450. [Arabic facsimile text and ET. This docu-
        ment is preserved in Arabic and is different from the ApPet,
        cf. HSW 2, p. 664, and the review of Mingana's publication
        by M.R. James in JTS 33 (1932) 311-13; this article is a
        reprint from BJRL 13, 14 (1929, 1930)]

70.48   Moraldi, L. "Apocalisse di Pietro," Apoc. del NT. 2. Pp.
        1803-54.

70.49   Müller, J.J. "Die Openbaring van Petrus," Nuwe-Test. Apoc.
        Pp. 128-31. [trans. into Afrikaans]

70.50   Petersen, E. "Des Martyrium des hl. Petrus nach der Petrus-
        Apokalypse," Frühkirche, Judentum und Gnosis: Studien
        und Untersuchungen. Freiburg, 1959. Pp. 88-91.

70.51   Petersen, E. "Die Taufe im Acherusischen See," VC 9 (1955)
        1-20.

70.52   Piccolomini, E. "Sul testo dei frammenti dell' Evangelio e dell'
        Apocalisse del Pseudo Pietro," Rendiconti della Reale Acca-
        demia dei Lincei. Classe di scienze morali, storiche e filo-
        logiche 8 (1899) 389-404.

70.53   Preuschen, E. "Reste der Petrusapokalypse," Antilegomena.
        Giessen, 1905[2]. Pp. 84-88, 188-92. [Gk. text]

70.54   Prümm, K. "De genuino Apocalypsis Petri textu: Examen
        testium iam notorum et novi fragmenti Raineriani," Bib 10
        (1929) 62-80.

70.55   Quispel, G., and R.M. Grant. "Note on the Petrine Apocrypha,"
        VC 6 (1952) 31f.

70.56   Robinson, J.A., and M.R. James. The Gospel According to
        Peter and the Revelation of Peter. London, 1892.[2]

70.57   Santos Otero, A. de. "Apocalypsis Petri," Altslavischen Apok.
        1. Pp. 212f.

70.58   Spitta, F. "Die Petrusapokalypse und der zweite Petrusbrief,"
        ZNW 12 (1911) 237-42.

70.59   Stegmüller, F. Repertorium Biblicum. 1. Pp. 245-47; 8. P.
        212.

70.60   Villamar, J.G.   El Apocalipsis de Pedro.   Thesis, Studii Bib-
        lici Franciscani, 1973-74.

70.61   Wabnitz, A.   "Les fragments de l'évangile et de l'apocalypse
        de Pierre," RTQR 2 (1893) 280-94, 353-70, 474-87.

70.62   Weinel, H.   "Offenbarung des Petrus," H². Pp. 314-27.

70.63   Weinel, H.   "Die Offenbarung des Petrus," Handbuch, ed.
        Hennecke.   Pp. 285-90.

70.64   Wessely, C.   "Les plus anciens monuments du Christianisme
        écrits sur papyrus," PO 18 (1924) 482.   [Gk. text]

70.65   Wilson, R.McL.   "Peter, Apocalypse of," ZPEB.   4.   Pp. 722f.

70.66   Zahn, T.   "Die Apokalypse des Petrus," Neutest. Kanons.   2.
        Pp. 810-20.   [Intro and Gk. frags; see also 1.307-10]

71.   PETER, GOSPEL OF

(See also 1.18, 88, 192, 218, 307, 531; 74.20.)

71.1   Amann, É.   "L'évangile de Pierre ou selon Pierre," DBSup.
        1.   Cols. 476f.

71.2   Ambroggi, P. de.   "Apocrifi di S. Pietro," EncCatt.   9.   Cols.
        1421-23.

71.3   Amiot, F.   "Évangile de Pierre," Évangiles Apoc.   Pp. 137-44.
        [French trans.]

71.4   Baljon, J.M.S.   Het evangelie en de openbaring van Petrus,
        Textuigaaf.   Utrecht, 1896.

71.5   Bardenhewer, O.   "Das Petrusevangelium," GAL.   1.   Pp.
        524-29.

71.6   Baring-Gould, S.   "The Gospel of St. Peter," Lost and Hostile
        Gospels.   Pp. 219-22.

71.7   Barnes, W.E.   "The Newly-Found Gospel in Relation to the
        Four," ExpT 15 (1893-94) 61-64.

71.8   Bauer, J.B.   "Das Petrusevangelium," Neutest. Apok.   Pp.
        20-27.

71.9   Bonaccorsi, P.G.   "Dal Vangelo di Pietro," Vangeli Apocrifi.
        1.   Pp. 16-29.

71.10   Bonsirven, J., and C. Bigaré, "Fragment de l'Evangile de
        Pierre," Intro. à la Bible. 2. Pp. 756f.

71.11   Bouriant, U. "Fragments du livre d'Enoch et de quelques
        écrits attribués à saint Pierre," Mémoires publiées par les
        membres de la Mission archéologique française au Caire 9.1.
        Paris, 1892. Pp. 137-42.

71.12   Brown, R.E. "Gospel of Peter," JBC. P. 546.

71.13   Bruston, C. Les paroles de Jésus récemment decouvertes en
        Egypte et remarques sur le texte du fragment de l'Évangile
        de Pierre. Paris, 1898.

71.14   Bruston, C. "De quelques passages obscurs de l'Évangile de
        Pierre," RTQR 2 (1893) 370-80.

71.15   Bruston, C. "De quelques textes difficiles de l'Évangile de
        Pierre," REG 10 (1897) 58-65.

71.16   Bruyne, D. de. "Deux citations apocryphes de l'Apôtre
        Pierre," JTS 34 (1933) 395-97.

71.17   Cabrol, F. "La découverte du manuscrit d'Akhmîm: L'Évan-
        gile et l'Apocalypse de saint Pierre et le livre du prophète
        Enoch," Revue des Facultés catholiques de l'Ouest (1893)
        570-90.*

71.18   Cartlidge, D.R., and D.L. Dungan. "The Gospel of Peter,"
        Documents. Pp. 83-86. [ET]

71.19   Cassels, W.R. The Gospel According to Peter: A Study by
        the Author of "Supernatural Religion." London, 1894.

71.20   Chapius, P. "L'Évangile et l'Apocalypse de Pierre," RTP 26
        (1893) 338-55.

71.21   Coles, R.A. "Fragments of an Apocryphal Gospel (?)," The
        Oxyrhynchus Papyri, vol. 41, ed. G.M. Browne. London,
        1972. Pp. 15f. [assigned to the "early third or possibly
        the late second century," this fragment is similar to, but not
        identical with the GosPet]

71.22   Cross, J.A. "The Akhmîm Fragment and the Fourth Gospel,"
        Exp 10 (1894) 320.

71.23   Denker, J. Die theologiegeschichtliche Stellung des Petrusevan-
        geliums: ein Beitrag zur Frühgeschichte des Doketismus.
        (Dissertation, Kiel 1972; Europ. Hochschulschr. 23, 36).
        Bern, 1975.

71.24 Dibelius, M. "Die alttestamentlichen Motiv in der Leidenges-
       chichte des Petrus- und des Johannes-evangeliums," Bot-
       schaft und Geschichte: Gesammelte Aufsätze. Tübingen,
       1953. Vol. 1. Pp. 221-47.

71.25 Ehrhard, A. Die altchristliche Literatur und ihr Erforschung
       von 1884-1900. Freiburg, 1900. Pt. 1. Pp. 127ff.

71.26 Erbetta, M. "Vangelo di Pietro," Apoc. del NT. 1. Pp. 137-
       45.

71.27 Fabricius, J.A. "Evangelium S. Petri," Cod.Apoc.NT. 1.
       Pp. 374-76.

71.28 Findlay, A.F. "The Gospel of Peter," Byways. Pp. 79-116.

71.29 Fuchs, A. Das Petrusevangelium (SNTU 2) Linz, 1978.

71.30 Funk, X. "Fragmente des Evangeliums und der Apokalypse
       des Petrus," TQ 75 (1893) 255-63.

71.31 Gardner-Smith, P. "The Date of the Gospel of Peter," JTS
       27 (1926) 401-07.

71.32 Gardner-Smith, P. "The Gospel of Peter," JTS 27 (1926)
       255-71.

71.33 Gebhardt, O. von. Das Evangelium und die Apokalypse des
       Petrus. Leipzig, 1893.

71.34 Grabe, J.E. Spicilegium SS. Patrum ut et Haereticorum seculi
       post Christum natum I, II, III. 2 vols. Oxford, 1714^2.
       Pp. 55-57.

71.35 Hale, E.E. The Apocryphal Gospel of Peter: A Fragment Re-
       cently Discovered in a Tomb in Upper Egypt. Boston, 1892.

71.36 Hall, I.H. "The Newly-discovered Apocryphal Gospel of Peter,"
       BW 1 (1893) 88-98.

71.37 Harnack, A. Bruchstücke des Evangeliums und der Apokalypse
       des Petrus (TU 9.2) Leipzig, 1893.

71.38 Harnack, A. "Das Evangelium nach Petrus," Gesch. altchrist.
       Lit. 2.1. Pp. 474f.

71.39 Harnack, A. "Petrusevangelium," Gesch. altchrist. Lit. 1.
       Pp. 10-12.

71.40 Harnack, A. "Das Petrusevangelium," Gesch. altchrist. Lit.
       2.1. Pp. 622-25.

71.41   Harris, J.R.   A Popular Account of the Newly-Recovered
        Gospel of Peter. London, 1893.

71.42   Harris, J.R.   "The Structure of the Gospel of Peter," Contem-
        porary Review 64 (1893) 212-36.

71.43   Hilgenfeld, A. von.   Novum Testamentum extra canonem recep-
        tum. Leipzig, 1884. Fasc. 4.2. Pp. 39-41.

71.44   Hilgenfeld, A.   "Das Petrusevangelium über Leiden und Aufer-
        stehung Jesu," ZWT 1 (1893) 439-54.

71.45   James, M.R.   "The Gospel of Peter," Official Report of the
        Church Congress, Norwick [England]. London, 1895. Pp.
        206-11.

71.46   James, M.R.   "Gospel of Peter," ANT. Pp. 90-94.

71.47   Johnson, B.A.   Empty Tomb Tradition in the Gospel of Peter.
        Harvard Th.D., 1966.

71.48   Kihn, H.   "Les découverts récents dans la patristique des
        deux premiers siècles," Compte rendu du troisième congrès
        scientifique des catholiques. Brussels, 1895. Pp. 190-98.

71.49   Klijn, A.F.J.   "Het Evangelia van Petrus en de Westerse tekst,"
        NedThT 15 (1960) 264-69.

71.50   Klostermann, E., ed.   Apocrypha I: Reste des Petrusevan-
        geliums, der Petrusapokalypse und des Kerygma Petri (KlT
        3) Berlin, 1933. Pp. 3-8. [Gk. text]

71.51   Koch, E.   "Das Petrusevangelium und unsere kanonischen
        Evangelien," Kirchliche Monatsschrift 15 (1896) 311-38.

71.52   Kunze, J.   Das neu aufgefundene Bruchstück des sog. Petru-
        sevangeliums übersetzt und beurteilt. Leipzig, 1893.

71.53   Lambiasi, F.   "I criteri di autenticità storica dei vangeli ap-
        plicati ad un apocrifo: Il vangelo di Pietro," BO 18 (1976)
        151-60.

71.54   Lods, A.   L'évangile et l'apocalypse de Pierre avec le texte
        grec du livre d'Hénoch. Paris, 1893.

71.55   Lods, A.   Evangelii secundum Petrum et Petri apocalypseos
        quae supersunt. Paris, 1892.

71.56   Lowe, M.   "'Ioudaioi' of the Apocrypha: A Fresh Approach
        to the Gospels of James, Pseudo-Thomas, Peter and Nico-
        demus," NovT 23 (1981) 56-90.

71.57 Lüdemann, H. [Critical Comments on publications on GosPet and ApPet], Theologischer Jahresbericht 12 (1892) 171-73; 13 (1893) 171-83; 14 (1894) 185-91.

71.58 Lührmann, D. "POx 2949: EvPt 3-5 in einer Handschrift des 2./3. Jahrhunderts," ZNW 72 (1981) 216-26.

71.59 Lundborg, M. Det sk. Petrusevangeliet, ett nyfunnet fragment ur en fornkristlig apokryf. Lund, 1893.

71.60 McCant, J.W. The Gospel of Peter: The Docetic Question Re-examined. Emory University, Ph.D., 1978.

71.61 McGifferd, A.C. "The Gospel of Peter," Papers of the American Society of Church History 6 (1894) 99-130.

71.62 MacPherson, J. "The Gospel of Peter," ExpT 5 (1894) 556-61.

71.63 Mallinckrodt, W. "De inhoud en de aard van het Pseudo-Petrus-Evangelie," Geloof en Vrijheid (1896) 33-109.*

71.64 Manchot, K. "Die neuen Petrus-fragmente," ProtKi 6 (1893) 126f.

71.65 Manen, W.C. van. Het Evangelie van Petrus, teckst en vertaling. Leiden, 1893.

71.66 Mara, M.G. Évangile de Pierre (SC 201) Paris, 1973. [Gk. text and French trans.]

71.67 Maurer, C. "The Gospel of Peter," HSW. 1. Pp. 179-87.

71.68 Maurer, C. "Petrusevangelium," HS. 1. Pp. 118-24.

71.69 Meunier, C. L'Évangile selon saint Pierre, traduction française avec notes. Paris, 1893.

71.70 Michaelis, W. "Petrus-Evangelium," Apokryphen Schriften. Pp. 45-61. [German trans.]

71.71 Migne, J.-P. "Évangile de saint Pierre," Dictionnaire. 2. Cols. 689-91.

71.72 Moraldi, L. "Vangelo di Pietro," Apoc. del NT. 1. Pp. 503-17.

71.73 Müller, J.J., "Die Evangelie van Petrus," Nuwe-Test. Apok. Pp. 21-25. [trans. into Afrikaans]

71.74 Perler, O. "L'Evangile de Pierre et Méliton de Sardes," RB 71 (1964) 584-90.

71.75   Piccolomini, E. "Sul testo dei frammenti dell' Evangelo e dell'
        Apocalissi del Pseudo Pietro," Rendiconti della Reale Acca-
        demia dei Lincei. Classe di scienze morali storiche e filo-
        logiche 8 (1899) 389-404.

71.76   Preuschen, E. "Reste des Petrusevangeliums," Antilegomena.
        Giessen, 1905². Pp. 15-20, 145-50. [Gk. text]

71.77   Rauschen, G. "Fragmentum evangelii secundum Petrum,"
        Florilegium Patristicum. Bonn, 1905. Vol. 3. Pp. 47-58.
        [Gk. and Lat. texts]

71.78   Robinson, J.A., and M.R. James. The Gospel According to
        Peter and the Revelation of Peter. London, 1892².

71.79   Sabatier, A. L'évangile de Pierre et les évangiles canoniques.
        Paris, 1893.

71.80   Santos Otero, A. de. "Evangelio de Pedro," Evangelios Apóc-
        rifos. Pp. 64-67; 375-93. [Gk. texts and Spanish trans.]

71.81   Schmidt, C. "Apokryphes Evang. des Petrus," Gesch. alt-
        christ. Lit. 1. P. 921.

71.82   Schubert, H. von. Die Komposition des pseudopetrinischen
        Evangelienfragments. Berlin, 1893.

71.83   Schubert, H. von. Das Petrusevangelium: Synoptische Tabelle
        nebst Übersetzung und kritischen Apparat. Berlin, 1893

71.84   Semeria, J.-B. "L'Evangile de Pierre," RB 3 (1894) 522-60.

71.85   Soden, H. von. "Das Petrusevangelium und die kanonischen
        Evangelien," ZTK 3 (1893) 52-92.

71.86   Stanton, V.H. "The 'Gospel of Peter': Its Early History and
        Character Considered in Relation to the History of the Rec-
        ognition in the Church of the Canonical Gospels," JTS 2
        (1901) 1-25.

71.87   Stegmüller, F. Repertorium Biblicum. 1. Pp. 143f.; 8. P.
        130.

71.88   Stocks, H. "Quellen zur Rekonstruktion des Petrusevange-
        liums," ZKG 34 (1913) 1-57.

71.89   Stocks, H. "Zum Petrusevangelium," NKZ 13 (1903) 276-314,
        515-42.

71.90   Stülcken, A. "Petrusevangelium," H². Pp. 59-63.

71.91   Stülcken, A. "Petrusevangelium," Handbuch, ed. Hennecke.
        Pp. 72-88.

71.92   Swete, H.B. The Apocryphal Gospel of Peter: The Greek
        Text of the Newly Discovered Fragment. London, 1893[2].

71.93   Swete, H.B. Euangelion kata Petron: The Akhmîm Fragment
        of the Apocryphal Gospel of St. Peter. London, 1893.

71.94   Turner, G.H. "The Gospel of Peter," JTS 14 (1913) 161-65.

71.95   Usener, H. Eine Spur des Petrusevangeliums (KlT 4) Leipzig,
        1913; repr. Osnabrück, 1965. [see also ZNW 3 (1902) 353-
        58]

71.96   Vaganay, L. L'Évangile de Pierre (Études Bibliques) Paris,
        1930. [see M.R. James' review JTS 32 (1931) 296-299]

71.97   Van de Sande Bakhuyzen. "Het fragment van het evangelie
        van Petrus," Verslagen en mededeel. d. Koninkl. Akad.
        van Wetensch. Afd. Letterkunde IIIR, IXD, (1893) 329-59.*

71.98   Völter, D. "Petrusevangelium oder Agypterevangelium," ZNW
        6 (1905) 368-72.

71.99   Völter, D. Petrusevangelium oder Agypterevangelium: Eine
        Frage bezüglich des neuentdeckten Evangelienfragments.
        Tübingen, 1893.

71.100 Wabnitz, A. "Les fragments de l'évangile et de l'apocalypse
        de Pierre," RTQR 2 (1893) 280-94, 353-70, 474-87.

71.101 Walter, N. "Eine vormatthäische Schilderung der Auferste-
        hung Jesu," NTS 19 (1972/73) 415-29. [see esp. 426-29]

71.102 Wessely, C. "Das Petrus-Evangelium und der mathematische
        Papyrus von Achmim," Studien zur Palaeographie und Papy-
        ruskunde 1 (1901) 37f.

71.103 Wilamowitz-Moellendorf, H. "Conjecturen zu den Petrus-
        Fragmenten," Index Scholarum von Göttingen. Sommer-
        semester, 1893.

71.104 Zahn, T. Das Evangelium des Petrus. Leipzig, 1893.

71.105 Zahn, T. "Das Evangelium des Petrus," Neutest. Kanons.
        2. Pp. 742-51. [Intro.]

72. PETER, MARTYRDOM OF

MartPet is a Latin text attributed to Linus which is based
on the martyrdom account in AcPet 30-41--see also the
entries under that category.

(See also 3.78; 7.3; 70.50.)

72.1   Bagatti, B. "La figura ed il martirio di S. Pietro secondo i
        giudeo-cristiani di Palestina," Pietro e Paulo nel XIX cen-
        tenario del Martirio a cura di P.L. Vannicelli e B. Mariani.
        Naples, 1969. Pp. 169-79.

72.2   Erbetta, M. "Ascensione di Isaia IV, 3 è la testimonianza più
        antica del martirio di Pietro?" ED 19 (1966) 427-36.

72.3   Erbetta, M. "La Passione di Pietro dello Ps. Lino," Apoc. del
        NT. 2. Pp. 169-77. [see also pp. 163-68]

72.4   Fabricius, J.A. "Linus de Passione Petri(a) et Pauli," Cod.
        Apoc.NT. 2. Pp. 775f.

72.5   James, M.R. ANT. Pp. 470. [see also pp. 330-36]

72.5a   Lewis, A.S. The Mythological Acts of the Apostles (Horae
        Semiticae 4) London, 1904. Pp. 210-16. [ET of Ar. text
        in Horae Semiticae 3]

72.6   Lipsius, R.A. Die apokryphen Apostelgeschichten und Apos-
        tellegenden. 2 vols. Brunswick, 1883-90; repr. Amsterdam,
        1976. Vol. 2.1. Pp. 91-93.

72.7   Lipsius, R.A., ed. "Martyrium beati Petri apostoli a Lino
        episcopo conscriptum," AAA. 1. Pp. 1-22. [Lat. text]

72.8   Migne, J.-P. "Lin.," Dictionnaire. 2. Cols. 459-70. ["Ré-
        cit de la passion de Saint Pierre, addressé aux Eglises de
        l'Orient par le bienheureux Lin (i.e. Linus), Pontife des
        Romains"]

72.9   Moraldi, L. "Martirio di san Pietro," Apoc. del NT. 2. Pp.
        1021-28.

72.10   Nau, F. "La version syriaque inédite des martyres de S.
        Pierre, S. Paul et S. Luc d'après un manuscrit du dixième
        siècle," ROC 3 (1898) 39-57, 151-56.

72.11   Nesbitt, C.F. "What did become of Peter?" JBR 27 (1959) 10-
        16.

72.12   Rimoldi, A.   "L'episcopato ed il martirio romano di S. Pietro
        nelle fonti letterarie dei primi tre secoli," ScCatt 95 (1967)
        495-521.

72.13   Salonius, A.H. (ed.)   Martyrium beati Petri apostoli a Lino
        episcopo Conscriptum. (Finska vetenskaps-societeten, Hel-
        singfors Commentationes humanarum litterarum 1.6) Helsinki,
        1926.

72.14   Schmidt, C.   "Martyrium des Petrus," Gesch. altchrist. Lit.
        1. P. 921.

72.15   Schneemelcher, W., and A. de Santos.   "Peter," HSW. 2.
        P. 570.

72.16   Schneemelcher, W., and A. de Santos.   "Petrus," HS. 2.
        P. 400.

72.17   Stegmüller, F.   Repertorium Biblicum. 1. Pp. 220-22; 8.
        Pp. 190f.

72.18   Vetter, P.   "Das gnostiche Martyrium Petri," OrChr 1 (1901)
        217-39. [Arm. text]

72.19   Wilson, R.McL.   "Peter, Passion of," ZPEB. 4. P. 732.

73.   PETER: PASSIONS OF PETER AND PAUL

        See also the entries under GkAcPetPl.

(See also 1.284, 470; 3.53, 78; 67.2, 67, 73, 88.)

73.1   Bardenhewer, O.   GAL. 1. Pp. 564-68.

73.2   Baron, R.   "'Le' manuscrit latin du Sinaï," Revue du Moyen
        Age Latin 10 (1954) 267-80.

73.3   Erbetta, M.   "Passione latina di Pietro e Paulo," Apoc. del.
        NT. 2. Pp. 193-98.

73.4   James, M.R.   "Acts and Passions of Peter and Paul," ANT.
        Pp. 470f.

73.5   Jacoby, A.   Recueil de travaux relatifs à la Philologie et à
        l'Archéologie égypt. et assyr. 24 (1902) 42-44.

73.6   Lefevre, R.   "Il sepolcro di Simon Mago all'Ariccia," L'Urbe
        N.S. 23.5 (1960) 14-20.

73.7   Lipsius, R.A., ed. "Passio apostolorum Petri et Pauli," <u>AAA</u>.
       1. Pp. 223-34 [Lat. text]

73.8   Lipsius, R.A., ed. "Passio sanctorum apostolorum Petri et
       Pauli," <u>AAA</u>. 1. Pp. 118-77. [Gk. and Lat. texts]

73.9   Lipsius, R.A. "Passiones Petri et Pauli graece ex codice
       Patmensi primum edidit," <u>JPT</u> 12 (1886) 86-106, 175f.

73.10 Schneemelcher, W., and A. de Santos. HS. 2. P. 402.

73.11 Schneemelcher, W., and A. de Santos. HSW. 2. P. 575.

73.12 Stegmüller, F. <u>Repertorium Biblicum</u>. 1. Pp. 223-25; 8.
       Pp. 192f.

73.13 Wilson, R.McL. "Peter and Paul, Passion of," <u>ZPEB</u>. 4. P.
       722.

74. PETER, PREACHING OF

Works on the <u>Kerygma Petrou</u>, known only by citation,
and the <u>Kerygmata Petrou</u>, posited as one of the sources
of PsCl, are cited here. For fuller discussions of Kerygmata Petrou, see works listed under PsCl.

(See also 1.47, 218; 24.41, 42; 67.35.)

74.1   Amann, É. "Le Kérygme de Pierre," <u>DBSup</u>. 1. Cols. 522f.

74.2   Bardenhewer, O. "Die Predigt des Petrus und die Predigt
       des Paulus," <u>GAL</u>. 1. Pp. 547-50.

74.3   Bazán, F.G. "Tres apuntes sobre la trascendencia divina en
       el lenguaje teológico del siglo II," <u>RevistB</u> 39 (1977) 223-42.

74.4   Betz, H.D. "Kerygmata Petrou," <u>Galatians</u> (Hermeneia) Phila-
       delphia, 1979. Pp. 331f.

74.5   Cullmann, O. "Ho opisō mou erchomenos," <u>Vorträge und Auf-
       sätze 1925-1962</u>. Tübingen, 1966. Pp. 169-75.

74.6   Dobschütz, E. von. <u>Das Kerygma Petri kritisch untersucht</u>.
       (TU 11.1) Leipzig, 1894.

74.7   Erbetta, M. "I Kerygmata Petru," <u>Apoc. del NT</u>. 2. Pp.
       211-14.

74.8   Erbetta, M. "La Predicazione Missionaria e la Dottrina di
       Pietro," Apoc. del NT. 2. Pp. 237-39.

74.9   Harnack, A. "Das Kerygma Petri," Gesch. altchrist. Lit.
       2.1. Pp. 472-74.

74.10 Harnack, A. "Petri Praedicatio," Gesch. altchrist. Lit. 1.
       Pp. 25-28.

74.11 Harnack, A. "Petrus, Kerygmata (judenchristliche)," Gesch.
       altchrist. Lit. 1. P. 788.

74.12 Hennecke, E. "Missionspredigt des Petrus," H². Pp. 143-46.

74.13 Hennecke, E. "Missionspredigt des Petrus," Handbuch, ed.
       Hennecke. Pp. 239-47.

74.14 Hilgenfeld, A. "Das Kerygma Petrou (kai Paulou)," ZWT 2
       (1893) 518-41. [Gk. text]

74.15 James, M.R. "The Preaching of Peter," ANT. Pp. 16-19.

74.16 Klostermann, E., ed. Apocrypha I: Reste des Petrusevan-
       geliums, der Petrusapokalypse und des Kerygma Petri (KlT
       3) Berlin, 1933. Pp. 13-16. [Gk. text]

74.16a Malherbe, A.J. "The Apologetic Theology of the 'Preaching
       of Peter,'" RestQ 13 (1970) 205-23.

74.16b Mara, M.G. "Il Kerygma Petrou," Studi e Materiali di Storia
       delle Religioni 38 (1967) 314-42.

74.17 Ménard, J.É. "Kérygmes de Pierre (Les)," Catholicisme 6.26
       (1966) 1419-21.

74.18 Migne, J.-P. "Prédication de saint Pierre," Dictionnaire. 2.
       Cols. 691f.

74.19 Nautin, P. "Les citations de la Prédication de Pierre dans
       Clément d'Alexandrie, Strom 6 v. 39-41," JTS 25 (1974) 98-
       105.

74.20 Paulsen, H. "Der Kerygma Petri und die urchristliche Apolo-
       getik," ZKG 88 (1977) 1-37.

74.21 Preuschen, E. "Reste des Kerugma Petrou," Antilegomena.
       Giessen, 1905². Pp. 88-91, 192-95. [Gk. text]

74.22 Reagan, J.N. The Preaching of Peter: The Beginning of
       Christian Apologetic. Chicago, 1923. [see M.R. James'
       review JTS 25 (1924) 184-89, 422]

74.23 Salles, A. "La diatribe anti-Paulinienne dans le 'Le Roman
       pseudo-Clémentin' et l'origine des 'Kérygmes de Pierre,'"
       RB 64 (1957) 516-51.

74.24 Salles, A. "Simon le Magicien ou Marcion," VC 12 (1958) 197-
       224.

74.25 Schneemelcher, W. "Das Kerygma Petrou," HS. 2. Pp. 58-
       63.

74.26 Schneemelcher, W. "The Kerygma Petrou," HSW. 2. Pp. 94-
       102.

74.27 Schoeps, H.J. "Bemerkungen zu Reinkarnationsvorstellungen
       der Gnosis," Numen 4 (1957) 228-32.

74.28 Seeberg, R. Die Apologie des Aristides. (Forschungen zur
       Geschichte des N.T. Kanons and der altkirchlichen Litera-
       tur 4.2) Leipzig, 1893. [See pp. 216-20]

74.29 Stegmüller, F. Repertorium Biblicum. 1. P. 218f.; 8. P.
       189.

74.30 Strecker, G. "Die Kerygmata Petrou," HS. 2. Pp. 63-80.

74.31 Strecker, G. "The Kerygmata Petrou," HSW. 2. Pp. 102-27.

74.32 Strecker, G. "Die Kerygmen des Petrus," Das Judenchristen-
       tum in den Pseudoklementinen (TU 70) Berlin, 1958. Pp.
       137-220.

74.33 Tarchnišvili, P.M. "Der Apostel Petrus," Geschichte der kirch-
       lichen georgischen Literatur (Studi e Testi 185) Rome, 1955.
       P. 343.

74.34 Wilson, R.McL. "Peter, Preaching of," ZPEB. 4. Pp. 732f.

74.35 Zahn, T. "Die Predigt des Petrus," Neutest. Kanons. 2. Pp.
       820-32, 881-84. [Zahn concludes that the Predigt Petrus--
       cf. Origen, Jn 13.17--dates from 90-100]

75. PHILIP, ACTS OF

The AcPhil contains MartPhil, a version of which circulated
independently--see also the entries under that category.

(See also 1.203, 346; 3.40, 53, 78; 7.8, 14.)

75.1   Amann, É. "Les Actes de Philippe," DBSup. 1. Col. 509.

75.2   [Archeografičeskaja Kommissija] Daily Readings of the Great
        'Menaea' (Nov. 13-15, 1899) cols. 1996-2002. [in Russian]

75.3   Bardenhewer, O. "Die Akten des Philippus," GAL. 1. Pp.
        584-88.

75.4   Batiffol, P. "Actus Sancti Philippi Apostoli," AnBoll 9 (1890)
        204-49.

75.5   Berger, K. "Jüdisch-Hellenistische Missionsliteratur und Apok-
        ryphe Apostelakten," Kairos 17 (1975) 4, 232-48.

75.6   Bonnet, M., ed. "Acta Philippi," AAA. 2.2. Pp. VII-XV,
        1-98. [Intro. and Gk. text; see M.R. James' review JTS
        5 (1904) 292.]

75.7   Bonwetsch, N. "Philippus," Gesch. altchrist. Lit. P. 906.

75.8   Bouvier, B., and F. Bovon. Les Actes de Philippe. In
        preparation.

75.9   Bovon, F. "Les Actes de Philippe: État de la question,"
        ANRW 2.25.4 (in preparation).

75.10   Demina, E.I. The Tichonravov Collection. Sofia, 1971. Vol.
        2. Pp. 286-90. [in Russian]

75.11   Erbetta, M. "Gli Atti di Filippo," Apoc. del NT. 2. Pp.
        453-87.

75.12   Fabricius, J.A. "Acta S. Philippi Apostoli," Cod.Apoc.NT.
        2. Pp. 806-10.

75.13   Flamion, J. "Les trois recensions du martyre de l'apôtre
        Philippe," Mélanges d'histoire offerts à Charles Moeller.
        Louvain, Paris, 1914. Pp. 215-25.

75.13a Franko, I. Apocrypha and Legends. L'vov, 1902. Vol. 3.
        Pp. 174-79. [in Russian]

75.14   Harnack, A. "Die Acten des Philippus," Gesch. altchrist. Lit.
        1. Pp. 138f.

75.15   James, M.R. "Acts of Philip," ANT. Pp. 439-53.

75.16   James, M.R. "On Supplements to the Acts of Philip," AA
        1. Pp. 158-63.

75.17   Kurfess, A. "Zu den Philippus-Akten," ZNW 44 (1952-53)
        145-51.

75.18   Lavrov, P.A.   "Apocryphal Texts," SbORJS 67 (1899) 129-35.
        [in Russian]

75.19   Lipsius, R.A.   Die apokryphen Apostelgeschichten und Apos-
        tellegenden. 2. vols. Brunswick, 1883-90; repr. Amster-
        dam, 1976. Vol. 2.2. Pp. 1-53.

75.20   Lipsius, R.A.   Ergänzungshelf. Braunschweig, 1890. [see
        esp. pp. 64-73]*

75.21   Lipsius, R.A.   "Zu den Akten des Philippus," JPT 17 (1891)
        459-73.

75.22   Migne, J.-P.   "Philippe (saint) (Écrits attribués ou relatifs à
        saint Philippe.)," Dictionnaire. 2. Cols. 679-90. [includes
        AcPhil, cols. 681-87; Book of Philip (pseudo-Abdias), cols.
        687-90 (French trans.)]

75.23   Moraldi, L.   "Atti di Filippo," Apoc. del NT. 2. Pp. 1625-32.

75.24   Peterson, E.   "Atti di Filippo," EncCatt. 5. Cols. 1311f.

75.25   Peterson, E.   "Die Häretiker der Philippus-Akten," ZNW 31
        (1932) 97-111.

75.26   Peterson, E.   "Die Philippus-Akten im armenischen Synaxar,"
        TQ 113 (1932) 289-98.

75.27   Peterson, E.   "Zum Messalianismus der Philippus-Akten,"
        OrChr 29 (1932) 172-79.

75.28   Petrovskij, S.V.   "The Historical Worth of Apocryphal Sayings
        About the Apostolic Sermon About Northeastern Black Sea
        Coast Materials," Zapiski Imp. Odesskogo obščestva istorii i
        drevnostej 21 (1898) 6-10. [in Russian]

75.29   Rougé, J.   "Tempête et littérature dans quelques textes chré-
        tiens," Nuovo Didaskaleion 12 (1962) 55-69.

75.30   Santos Otero, A. de.   "Acta Philippi," Altslavischen Apok. 1.
        Pp. 124-29.

75.31   Schmidt, C.   "Acten des Philippus," Gesch. altchrist. Lit. 1.
        P. 921.

75.32   Schneemelcher, W., and A. de Santos.   "Acts of Philip," HSW.
        2. P. 577.

75.33   Schneemelcher, W., and A. de Santos.   "Philippusakten," HS.
        2. P. 404.

75.34   Stegmüller, F. Repertorium Biblicum. 1. Pp. 225f; 8. Pp.
        193f.

75.35   Stölten, H.O. "Zur Philippuslegende," JPT 17 (1891) 149-60.

75.36   Tischendorf, K. von. "Acta Philippi," Acta Apos. Apoc. Pp.
        XXXI-XXXVIII, 75-94. [Intro. and Gk. text]

75.37   Tischendorf, K. von. "Acta Philippi in Hellade," Acta Apos.
        Apoc. Pp. XXVIII-XL, 95-104. [Intro. and Gk. text]

75.38   Tischendorf, K. von. "Ad Acta Philippi," Apocalypses Apoc-
        ryphae. Pp. 141-56. [Gk. text]

75.39   Walker, A. "The Acts of Philip," ANF   8. Pp. 497-510.
        [ET]

75.40   Wilson, R.McL. "Philip, Acts of," ZPEB. 4. P. 759.

75.41   Zahn, T. Forschungen zur Geschichte des neutestamentlichen
        Kanons. Leipzig, 1900.

76.   PHILIP, (SYRIAC) ACTS OF

(See also the entries under AcPhil.)

76.1   Wright, W. The Apocryphal Acts of the Apostles. Edited from
       Syriac Manuscripts. London, 1871. [Syr. text in vol. 1,
       pp. 73-99; ET in vol. 2, pp. 69-92]

77.   PHILIP, GOSPEL OF

77.1   Amann, É. "Évangile de Philippe," DBSup. 1. Col. 479.

77.2   Bardenhewer, O. "Das Matthias-, das Philippus- und das
       Thomasevangelium," GAL. 1. Pp. 529-33.

77.3   Baring-Gould, S. "The Gospel of St. Philip," Lost and Hos-
       tile Gospels. Pp. 293-98.

77.4   Bonaccorsi, P.G. "Frammento del Vangelo secondo Filippo,"
       Vangeli Apocrifi. 1. Pp. 30f.

77.5   Eisentraut, E. "Philippusevangelium," LTK[2]. 3. Col. 882.

77.6   Fabricius, J.A. "Evangelium S. Philippi," Cod.Apoc.NT. 1.
        Pp. 376f.

77.7   Harnack, A. "Philippus-Evangelium," Gesch. altchrist. Lit.
        1. Pp. 14f.

77.8   Harnack, A. "Das Philippusevangelium," Gesch. altchrist. Lit.
        2.1. Pp. 592f.

77.9   Hennecke, E. "Philippusevangelium," H^2. P. 69.

77.10   James, M.R. "Gospel of Philip," ANT. P. 12.

77.11   Klostermann, E., ed. "Philippusevangelium," Apocrypha II:
        Evangelien (KlT 8) Berlin, 1929^3. P. 18. [Gk. witness]

77.12   Michl, J. "Philippusevangelium," LTK^3. 3. Col. 1230.

77.13   Peterson, E. "Filippo (Il Vangelo di)," EncCatt. 5. Cols.
        1311f.

77.14   Preuschen, E. "Aus dem Evangelium des Philippus," Anti-
        legomena. Giessen, 1905^2. Pp. 15, 145. [Gk. text]

77.15   Puech, H.-Ch., "The Gospel of Philip," HSW. 1. Pp. 271-78.

77.16   Puech, H.-C. "Das Philippus-Evangelium," HS. 1. Pp. 194-
        99.

77.17   Santos Otero, A. de. "Evangelio de Felipe," Evangelios Apóc-
        rifos. Pp. 63f. [Gk. text from Epiphanius Haer. 26.13
        (= PG 41.352D-353A) with Spanish trans.]

77.18   Stegmüller, F. Repertorium Biblicum. 1. P. 144; 8. Pp.
        130-32. [Vol. 8 entry includes works on the Nag Hammadi
        GosPhil]

77.19   Wilson, R.McL. "Philip, Gospel of," ZPEB. 4. P. 759.

77.20   Zahn, T. "Apostel und Apostelschüler in der Provinz Asien,"
        Forschungen zur Geschichte des neutestamentlichen Kanons
        und der altchristlichen Literatur. 10 vols. Erlangen, 1881-
        1929. Vol. 6.1. Pp. 24-27.

77.21   Zahn, T. "Das Evangelium des Philippus," Neutest. Kanons.
        2. Pp. 761-68.

78. PHILIP, MARTYRDOM OF

See also entries listed under AcPhil and TransPhil.

(See also 3.38.)

78.1   Budge, E.A.W. Contendings of the Apostles. 2 vols. Lon-
       don, New York, 1899-1901; repr. London, 1976. Vol. 1.
       Pp. 135-39; Vol. 2. Pp. 156-62.

78.2   Erbetta, M. "Dai Viaggi dell'Apostolo Filippo," Apocrifi del NT.
       2. Pp. 476-85.

78.3   Franko, I. Apocrypha and Legends. L'vov, 1902. Vol. 3.
       Pp. 174-79. [in Russian]

78.4   Lewis, A.S. "The Martyrdom of Philip," The Mythological Acts
       of the Apostles (Horae Semiticae 4) London, 1904. Pp. 66-
       68. [ET of Arabic text in Horae Semiticae 3]

78.5   Stegmüller, F. Repertorium Biblicum. 1. Pp. 226f.; 8. P.
       195.

79. PHILIP, TRANSLATION OF

See also the entries listed under AcPhil and MartPhil.

79.1   James, M.R. "On Supplements to the Acts of Philip, Trans-
       latio Philippi," AA 1. Pp. 158-63.

80. PILATE, ACTS OF; AND PILATE CYCLE

AcPil is often called GosNic--see also the entries under
that category.

(See also 1.87, 88, 98, 195, 505; 28.21; 45.10; 87.2.)

80.1   Abbott, G.F. "The Report and Death of Pilate," JTS 4 (1903)
       83-86.

80.2   Amann, É. "Le cycle de Pilate," DBSup. 1. Cols. 486-88.

80.3   Amiot, F. "Évangile de Nicodème ou Actes de Pilate," Evan-
        giles Apoc. Pp. 145-56. [French trans.]

80.4   Bardenhewer, O. "Die Anfänge des Pilatusliteratur," GAL.
        1. Pp. 543-47.

80.5   Barnes, J.W.B. "Bodleian Fragments of a Sa'idic Version of
        the Acta Pilati," Coptic Studies in Honor of Walter Ewing
        Crum, ed. M. Malinine (Bulletin of the Byzantine Institute
        2) Boston, 1950. Pp. 245-50.

80.6   Barsov, E.V. "On the Influence of the Apocrypha on Liturgy
        and Icongraphy," Žurnal Ministerstva Narodnago Prosves-
        chenija (1885) 111ff. [in Russian]*

80.7   Bauer, J.B. "Das Nikodemusevangelium oder die Pilatusakten,"
        Neutest. Apok. Pp. 55-58.

80.8   Bieder, W. Die Vorstellung von der Höllenfahrt Jesu Christi.
        Zürich, 1949.

80.9   Birch, A. Auctarium codicis apocryphi Novi Testamenti Fabri-
        ciani. Copenhagen, 1804. Vol. 1. Pp. 1-154.

80.10   Bonsirven, J., and C. Bigaré. "Actes de Pilate ou Évangile
        de Nicodème," Intro. à la Bible. 2. Pp. 755f.

80.11   Bousset, W. "Zur Hadesfahrt Christi," ZNW 19 (1919-20)
        50-66.

80.12   Brock, S.P. "A Fragment of the Acts of Pilate in Christian
        Palestinian Aramaic," JTS 22 (1971) 157f.

80.13   Bruston, C. "La descente aux enfers selon les apôtres Pierre
        et Paul," RTQR (1905) 236-49; 438-56.*

80.14   Bruston, C. La descente du Christ aux enfers d'après les
        apôtres et d'après l'Église. Paris, 1897.

80.15   Cerulli, E. "La légende de l'empereur Tibère et de Pilate dans
        deux nouveaux documents éthiopiens," Byzantion 36 (1966)
        26-34.

80.16   Cerulli, E. "Tiberius and Pontius Pilate in Ethiopian Tradi-
        tion," Proceedings of the British Academy 59 (1973) 141-58.

80.17   Clemen, C. Niedergefahren zu den Toten. Giessen, 1900.

80.18   Clough, W.O. Gesta Pilati: The Reports, Letters, and Acts
        of Pontius Pilate, Procurator of Judea, With an Account of
        His Life and Death; Being a Translation and Compilation of

All the Writings Ascribed to Him, as Made to Tiberius Caesar, Emperor of Rome, Concerning the Life of Jesus, His Trial and Crucifixion. Indianapolis, 1880.

80.19   Conybeare, F.C. "Acta Pilati," Studia biblica et ecclesiastica. Oxford, 1896. Pp. 59-130.

80.20   Cowper, B.H. "The Gospel of Nicodemus, or Acts of Pilate," Apocryphal Gospels. Pp. 227-388. [ET]

80.21   Danicic, G. "Two Apocryphal Gospels," Starine 4 (1872) 130-49. [in Serbo-Croatian]

80.22   Darley, E. Les Acta Salvatoris: Un évangile de la passion et de la résurrection et une mission apostolique en Aquitaine. Paris, 1913.

80.23   Dobschütz, E. "Der Process Jesu nach den Acta Pilati," ZNW 3 (1902) 89-114.

80.24   Erbetta, M. "Gli Atti di Pilato o il Vangelo di Nicodemo," Apoc. del NT. 1.2. Pp. 231-87.

80.25   Franko, I. Apocrypha and Legends. L'vov, 1902. Vol. 3. Pp. 174-79. [in Russian]

80.26   Gatti, A. Il Processo di Gesù nei più antichi apocrifi della Passione. Jerusalem, 1975.

80.27   Gschwind, K. Die Niederfahrt Christi in die Unterwelt. Münster, 1911.

80.28   Harnack, A. "Acta Pilati, Descensus ad inferos (Evangelium Nicodemi)," Gesch. altchrist. Lit. 1. Pp. 21-24.

80.29   Harnack, A. "Die Acta Pilati = Ev. Nicodemi," Gesch. altchrist. Lit. 2.1. Pp. 603-12.

80.30   Harris, J.R. The Homeric Centones and the Acts of Pilate. London, 1898.

80.31   Hoffman, R.J. "Confluence in Early Christian and Gnostic Literature: The 'Descensus Christi ad Inferos' ('Acta Pilati' XVII-XXVII)," JSNT 10 (1981) 42-60.

80.32   James, M.R. "The Gospel of Nicodemus, or Acts of Pilate," ANT. Pp. 94-146.

80.33   Janashia, [?]. Description des mss. géorgiens du Musée d'État de Georgie. Tiflis, 1946.*

80.34   Javachishvili, I.A.   Sinis Mt's K'art'ul Xelnacert a Agceriloba.
        Tiflis, 1917.

80.35   Kroll, J.   Beiträge zum Descensus ad Infernos.   Königsberg,
        1922.

80.36   Kroll, J.   Gott und Hölle: Der Mythos vom Descensuskampfe.
        Leipzig-Berlin, 1932.   Pp. 83ff.

80.37   Lacau, P.   "Acta Pilati," Fragments.   Pp. 1-12.   [Coptic text
        and French trans.; see also pp. 13-22 for other Pilate ma-
        terial]

80.38   Lake, K.   "Texts from Mount Athos: Some Chapters of the
        Acta Pilati," Studia biblica et ecclesiastica 5 (1903) 152-63.

80.39   Lémonon, J.-P.   Pilate et le gouvernement de la Judée: Textes
        et monuments (EBib) Paris, 1981.

80.40   Lipsius, R.A.   Die Pilatus-Akten kritisch Untersucht.   Kiel,
        1871, 1886[2].

80.41   Loofs, F.   "Christ's Descent into Hell," Transactions of the
        Third International Congress for the History of Religions II.
        Oxford, 1908.   Pp. 290-301.

80.42   Lützelberger, E.J.   Das Protevangelium Jacobi, zwei Evange-
        lien der Kindheit Jesu und die Akten des Pilatus.   Nurem-
        berg, 1842.

80.43   MacNiocaill, G.   "Dha' leagan de scéal Phioláit," Celtica 7
        (1966) 205-13.

80.44   Mequitaristas, [?].   Ankanon girkh Nor Ketakar anatz I.
        Venice, 1898.   [Arm. text]*

80.45   Migne, J.-P.   "Hémorroïsse. (Lettre addressée à Pilate par la
        femme Hémorroisse.)," Dictionnaire.   2.   Cols. 253-56.   [The
        woman's name is "Veronique."]

80.46   Migne, J.-P.   "Pilate," Dictionnaire.   2.   Cols. 747-60.

80.47   Mingana, A.   "Martyrdom of Pilate," Woodbrooke Studies 2
        (1928) 241-332.   [Karshuni text and ET; repr. from BJRL
        12 (1928) 411-580]

80.48   Mommsen, T.   "Die Pilatus-Akten," ZNW 3 (1902) 198-205.

80.49   Monnier, J.   La descente aux enfers: Étude de pensée re-
        ligieuse, d'art et de litterature.   Paris, 1905.

80.50   Nersessian, S. der. <u>An American Version of the Homilies on</u>
        <u>the Harrowing of Hell</u>. Cambridge, Mass., 1954.

80.51   Oudenrijn, M.-A. van den. <u>Gamaliel: Athiopische Texte zur</u>
        <u>Pilatusliteratur</u> (Spicilegium Friburgense; Texte zur Geschichte
        des Kirchlichen Lebens 4) Freiburg, 1959. [Contains two
        apocryphal fragments, the <u>Marienlage</u> and <u>Martyrium Pilati</u>]

80.52   Pasquero, F. "Apocrifi di Pilato," <u>EncCatt</u>. 9. Cols. 1473-
        76.

80.53   Piankoff, A. "La descente aux enfers dans les textes égyptiens
        et dans les apocryphes coptes," <u>BSC</u> 7 (1941) 33-46.

80.54   Porfiryev, I.Y. "Apocryphal Sayings About New Testament
        People and Events in Manuscripts of the Solovetski Library,"
        <u>SbORJS</u> 52 (1890) 21ff.

80.55   Pypin, A. <u>False and Dismissed Books of Ancient Russia</u>. St.
        Petersburg, 1862. Pp. 91-103. [in Russian]

80.56   Quilliet, A. "Descente de Jésus aux enfers," <u>DThC</u> 4. Pp.
        565-619.

80.57   Rahmani, I.E. <u>Hypomnemata Domini nostri seu Acta Pilati</u>.
        (Studia Syriaca 2) Lebanon, 1908.

80.58   Revillout, E. "Acta Pilati," <u>PO</u> 9 (1913) 57-132. [Cop. text
        and French trans.]

80.59   Riesenfeld, H. "La descente dans la mort," <u>Aux sources de</u>
        la tradition chrétienne: <u>Mélanges offerts à M. Maurice Goguel</u>.
        Neuchâtel, 1950.

80.60   Rossi, F. <u>I papyri copti del museo Egizio di Torino</u>. Turin,
        1887. Vol. 1. Pp. 7-90; Vol. 2. Pp. 237ff.

80.61   Rousseau, O. "La descente aux enfers, fondement sotério-
        logique du baptême chrétien," <u>Mélanges Jules Lebreton</u>
        (Recherches de Science Religieuse 40) Paris, 1952. Vol. 2.
        Pp. 273-97.

80.62   Santos Otero, A. de. "Actas de Pilato (O Evangelio de Nico-
        demo)," <u>Evangelios Apócrifos</u>. Pp. 396-471. [Gk., Lat.
        texts and Spanish trans.; for other Pilate apocrypha see pp.
        472-535]

80.63   Santos Otero, A. de. "Pilato, Ciclo apócrifo de," <u>Enciclopedia</u>
        <u>de la Biblia</u>. 5. Cols. 1108f.

80.64   Santos Otero, A. de. "Sentencia de Pilato," <u>Evangelios Apóc-</u>
        <u>rifos</u>. Pp. 532-35. [Italian text and Spanish trans.]

80.65   Scheidweiler, F. "The Gospel of Nicodemus: Acts of Pilate
        and Christ's Descent into Hell," HSW. 1. Pp. 444-81.

80.66   Scheidweiler, W. "Nikodemusevangelium. Pilatusakten und
        Höllenfahrt Christi," HS. 1. Pp. 330-58.

80.67   Schmidt, C. "Exkurs II: Der Descensus ad infernos in der
        alten Kirche," Gespräche Jesu mit seinen Jüngern nach der
        Auferstehung (TU 3.13) Leipzig, 1919. Pp. 453-576.

80.68   Schmidt, K.W.C. Die Darstellung von Christi Höllenfahrt in
        den deutschen u.d. ihnen verwandten Spielen des Mittelal-
        ters. Diss. Marburg, 1915.

80.69   Schubert, H. von, Die Komposition des pseudopetrinischen
        Evangelienfragments. Berlin, 1893. Pp. 175-90.

80.70   Sedláček, J. Neue Pilatusakten, Besprochen und Übersetzt
        (Sitzungsberichte der böhm. Gesellsch. der Wiss.) Prague,
        1908.

80.71   Speyer, W. "Neue Pilatus-Apokryphen," VC 32 (1978) 53-59.

80.72   Stegmüller, F. Repertorium Biblicum. 1. Pp. 148-53; 8.
        Pp. 141-47.

80.73   Stojanovic, L. Glasnik 63 (1865) 89-120.*

80.74   Stülcken, A. "Pilatusakten," H^2. P. 77.

80.75   Stülcken, A. "Pilatusakten," Handbuch, ed. Hennecke. Pp.
        143-53.

80.76   Sutcliffe, E.F. "An Apocryphal Form of Pilate's Verdict,"
        CBQ 9 (1947) 436-41.

80.77   Thilo, J.C. Codex Apocryphus Novi Testamenti. Leipzig,
        1832. Pp. 487-795.

80.78   Tischendorf, K. "Acta Pilati," Evangelia Apocrypha. Pp.
        liv-lxxvi, 210-432. [Gk. text of both versions]

80.79   Tischendorf, K. [Ad Gesta Pilati Graece A: Dantur exempla
        scripturae e codice Monacensi nondum adhibitio], Apocalypses
        Apocryphae. Pp. LXI-LXIII. [Gk. text]

80.80   Tischendorf, K. "Gesta Pilati," Evangelia Apocrypha. Pp.
        liv-lxxvii, 333-88.

80.81   Tischendorf, K. Pilati circa Christum iudicio quid lucis affera-
        tur ex Acta Pilati. Leipzig, 1855.

80.82   Turmel, J.   La descente du Christi aux enfers.   Paris, 1905.

80.83   Vannutelli, P.   Actorum Pilati textus synoptici.   Rome, 1938.

80.84   Vannutelli, P.   "Actorum Pilati textus synoptici," Synoptica
        1 (1936) 1-13; 2 (1937) 65-128; 3 (1938) 129-44, 161-77,
        145-60.

80.85   Variot, J.   "L'Arrestation de Pilate," Évangiles Apocryphes.
        Pp. 120-22.

80.86   Vitti, A.M.   "Descensus Christi ad infernos juxta I Pet., III,
        19-20; IV, 6 et juxta Apocrypha," VD 7 (1927) 111-18, 138-
        44, 171-81.

80.87   Volkoff, O.V.   "Un saint oublié: Pilate," Bulletin de la So-
        ciété d'Archéologie Copte 20 (1969) 167-95.

80.88   Wake, W., and N. Lardner.   "The Gospel of Nicodemus, Form-
        erly Called the Acts of Pontius Pilate," Apoc. NT.   Pp. 69-
        105.   [ET]

80.89   Werner, D.   Pilatus: Untersuchungen zur metrischen latein-
        ischen Pilatus legende und kritische Textausgabe.   Cologne
        Dissertation, 1972.

80.90   Wilson, R.McL.   "Pilate, Acts of," ZPEB.   4.   Pp. 789f.

81. PILATE, DEATH OF

        See also the listings under RepParPil.

(See also 80.2, 4, 18, 37, 45.)

81.1   Cowper, B.H.   "The Death of Pilate," Apocryphal Gospels.
        Pp. 415-19.   [ET]

81.2   Dobschütz, E. von.   Christusbilder.   Untersuchungen zur
        christlichen Legende (TU 18.1-2) Leipzig, 1899.   Pp. 197-
        262.

81.3   Erbetta, M.   "La Morte di Pilato," Apoc. del NT.   1.2.   Pp.
        402-04.

81.4   González-Blanco, E.   Los Evangelios Apócrifos.   Madrid, 1934.
        Vol. 2.   Pp. 361-69.

81.5   James, M.R. "The Death of Pilate," ANT. Pp. 157-59.

81.6   Migne, J.-P. "Mort de Pilate qui condamna Jésus," Diction-
        naire. 1. Cols. 1177-80. [French trans.]

81.7   Moraldi, L. "Morte di Pilato che condannò Gesù," Apoc. del
        NT. 1. Pp. 721-24.

81.8   Polivka, G. Starine 24 (1892) 82-87. 112ff. [Bulg. text]*

81.9   Porfiryev, I.Y. "Apocryphal Sayings about New Testament
        People and Events in Manuscripts of the Solovetski Library,"
        SbORJS 52 (1890) 201f. [Russian text]

81.10   Santos Otero, A. de. "Muerte de Pilato," Evangelios Apó-
        crifos. Pp. 495-500. [Lat. text and Spanish trans.]

81.11   Stegmüller, F. Repertorium Biblicum. 1. P. 155; 8. P. 149.

81.12   Tischendorf, C. "Mors Pilati qui Iesum condemnavit," Evan-
        gelia Apocrypha. Pp. lxxixf., 456-58.

81.13   Variot, J. "La Mort de Pilate," Évangiles Apocryphes. Pp.
        122-24.

81.14   Walker, A. "The Death of Pilate, Who Condemned Jesus,"
        ANF 8. Pp. 466f. [ET]

82. PILATE: LETTER OF PILATE TO CLAUDIUS

This letter is included in the first Latin form of the
Descensus (see also the listings under AcPil), and was
originally part of AcPetPl 40-42--see also the listings under that category.

(See also 80.2, 4, 18, 37.)

82.1   Brock, S.P. "A Syriac Version of the Letters of Lentulus and
        Pilate," OCP 35 (1969) 57-61.

82.2   Cartlidge, D.R., and D.L. Dungan. "A Letter from Pilate to
        Claudius and The Trial of Pilate in Rome," Documents. Pp.
        87-90. [ET]

82.3   Erbetta, M. Apoc. del NT. 3. Pp. 131f.

82.4   James, M.R. "Letter of Pilate to Claudius," ANT. P. 146.

82.5   Michaelis, W. "Brief des Pontius Pilatus an Kaiser Klaudius,"
       Apokryphen Schriften. Pp. 446-52.

82.6   Scheidweiler, F. HS. 1. Pp. 353f.

82.7   Scheidweiler, F. HSW. 1. Pp. 476-78.

82.8   Stegmüller, F. Repertorium Biblicum. 1. P. 155; 8. Pp.
       149f.

82.9   Stülcken, A. "Brief des Pilatus an Claudius (Tiberius)," $\underline{H}^2$.
       Pp. 77f.

82.10 Tischendorf, C. "Pontius Pilatus Claudio regi suo salutem,"
       Evangelia Apocrypha. Pp. 413-16. [Lat. text]

83. PILATE: LETTERS OF PILATE AND HEROD

(See also 80.2, 4, 18, 37.)

83.1   Cowper, B.H. "Letters of Herod and Pilate," Apocryphal Gos-
       pels. Pp. 389-97. [ET]

83.2   Erbetta, M. "Corrispondenza tra Pilato ed Erode," Apoc. del
       NT. 3. Pp. 127-29.

83.3   James, M.R. "Epistolae Pilati et Herodis," AA 2. Pp. xlv-
       xlviii, 65-75. [Gk. text and ET]

83.4   James, M.R. "The Letter of Herod to Pilate," ANT. Pp.
       155f.

83.5   James, M.R. "The Letter of Pilate to Herod," ANT. P. 155.

83.6   Moraldi, L. "Lettere tra Pilato ed Erode," Apoc. del NT. 1.
       Pp. 703-06.

83.7   Rahmani, I.E. "Hypomnemata Domini Nostri seu acta Pilati,"
       Studia Syriaca 2 (1908) 32ff. [Syr. text and Lat. trans.]

83.8   Santos Otero, A. de. "Correspondencia entre Pilato y Herodes,"
       Evangelios Apócrifos. Pp. 484-89. [Gk. texts and Spanish
       trans.]

83.9   Speyer, W. "Der Tod der Salome [filiae Herodiae in Corre-
       spondentia apocr. Herodis et Pilati]," JAC 10 (1967) 176-80.

83.10 Stegmüller, F. Repertorium Biblicum. 1. Pp. 156f.; 8. P. 150.

83.11 Tischendorf, K. [De Herodis et Pilati epistulis], Apocalypses Apocryphae. P. LVI.

83.12 Variot, J. "Les Lettres de Pilate," Évangiles Apocryphes. Pp. 108-16. [French trans.]

83.13 Winter, P. "A Letter from Pontius Pilate," NovT 7 (1964) 37-43.

83.14 Winter, P. "Une lettre de Ponce-Pilate," Foi et Vie 62 (1963) 101-08.

83.15 Winter, P. "News from Pilate in Liverpool," Encounter 21 (1963) 68-70.

83.16 Wright, W. "The Letters of Herod and Pilate," ALNT. Pp. YZ-KD (Syr.), 12-17 (ET), 58f. (notes).

84. PILATE: LETTER OF PILATE TO TIBERIUS

See also the listings under LetTibPil.

(See also 1.470; 80.2, 4, 15, 16, 18, 37.)

84.1 Bauer, J.B. "Ein Schreiben des Pilatus an Tiberius," Neutest. Apok. Pp. 84-87.

84.2 Cowper, B.H. "The Epistle of Pontius Pilate," Apocryphal Gospels. Pp. 398-99. [ET]

84.3 Cowper, B.H. "Letter of Pilate to Tiberius," Apocryphal Gospels. P. 388. [ET]

84.4 Erbetta, M. "Lettera di Pilato a Tiberio," Apoc. del NT. 3. Pp. 130-33.

84.5 Fabricius, J.A. "Epistolae Duae Pilato tributae ad Tiberium Imperatorum," CodApocNT. 1. Pp. 298-302. [Lat.]

84.6 Gibson, M.D. Apocrypha Sinaitica (SS 5) London, 1896.

84.7 James, M.R. "Letter of Pilate to Tiberius," ANT. P. 153.

84.8 Javier, J. Historia Christi persice conscripta simulque multis

modis contaminata. [Lvgdvni Batavorvm, ex officina Elsevir-
iana] 1639.

84.9   Migne, J.-P. "Arrestation de Pilate (760)," Dictionnaire. 2.
        Cols. 751-54.

84.10   Migne, J.-P. "Pilate," Dictionnaire. 2. Cols. 757-60.

84.11   Moraldi, L. "Lettere tra Tiberio e Pilato," Apoc. del NT. 1.
        Pp. 707-09.

84.12   Santos Otero, A. de. "Carta de Poncio Pilato a Tiberio,"
        Evangelios Apócrifos. Pp. 472f. [Lat. text and Spanish
        trans.]

84.13   Stegmüller, F. Repertorium Biblicum. 1. Pp. 158f.; 8. P.
        151.

84.14   Thilo, J.C. Codex Apocryphus Novi Testamenti. Leipzig,
        1832. Pp. 801-03.

84.15   Tischendorf, C. "Epistola Pontii Pilati," Evangelia Apocrypha.
        Pp. lxxvii-lxxviii, 433f. [Lat. text]

84.16   Walker, A. "The Letter of Pontius Pilate Which He Wrote to
        the Roman Emperor, Concerning our Lord Jesus Christ,"
        ANF   8. P. 459. [ET]

85. PILATE: LETTER TO PILATE FROM TIBERIUS

See also the listings under LetPilTib.

(See also 80.2, 4, 15, 16, 18, 37.)

85.1   Birch, A. Auctarium codicis apocryphi N.T. fabriciani. Co-
        penhagen, 1804. Vol. 1. Pp. 172f.

85.2   Erbetta, M. "Lettera di Tiberio a Pilato," Apoc. del NT. 3.
        Pp. 125f.

85.3   James, M.R. "Epistola Tiberii ad Pilatum," AA 2. Pp. xlixf.,
        77-81. [Gk. text]

85.4   Santos Otero, A. de. "Carta de Tiberio a Pilato," Evangelios
        Apocrifos. Pp. 473-77. [Gk. text and Spanish trans.]

85.5   Stegmüller, F. Repertorium Biblicum. 1. Pp. 158f.; 8. P.
        151.

86. PILATE, REPORT AND PARADOSIS OF

See also the listings under DPil.

(See also 80.2, 4, 18, 37.)

86.1   Abbott, G.F. "The Report and Death of Pilate," JTS 4 (1903)
        83-86. [Gk. text]

86.2   Birch, A. Auctarium codicis apocryphi Novi Testamenti Fabri-
        ciani. Leipzig, 1804. Vol. 1. Pp. 161ff.

86.3   Cartlidge, D.R., and D.L. Dungan, "A Letter from Pilate to
        Claudius and The Trial of Pilate in Rome," Documents. Pp.
        87-90. [ET]

86.4   Cowper, B.H. "The Report of Pilate the Governor," Apocry-
        phal Gospels. Pp. 400-04. [ET]

86.5   Cowper, B.H. "The Report of Pontius Pilate," Apocryphal
        Gospels. Pp. 405-09. [ET]

86.6   Cowper, B.H. "The Trial and Condemnation of Pilate," Apoc-
        ryphal Gospels. Pp. 410-14. [ET]

86.7   Erbetta, M. "'Anafora' o Relazione di Pilato," Apoc. del NT.
        3. Pp. 119-21.

86.8   Erbetta, M. "'Paradosis' (= Consegna, Punizione) di Pilato,"
        Apoc. del NT. 3. Pp. 122-24.

86.9   Fabricius, J.A. CodApocNT. 3. Pp. 456ff.*

86.10   Gibson, M.D. Apocrypha Sinaitica. (SS 5) London, 1896.
        [Syr. and Arab. texts]

86.11   James, M.R. "Report of Pilate (Anaphora)," ANT. Pp. 153-
        55.

86.12   Migne, J.-P. "Pilate," Dictionnaire. 2. Cols. 751-58.

86.13   Moraldi, L. "Anafora di Pilato Governatore sul nostro padrone
        Gesù Cristo mandata a Cesare Augusto in Roma (Recensione
        greca 'A')," Apoc. del NT. 1. Pp. 710-13.

86.14   Moraldi, L. "Anafora di Ponzio Pilato Governatore della Giudea
        mandata a Tiberio Cesare in Roma (Recensione greca 'B'),"
        Apoc. del NT. 1. Pp. 714-16.

86.15   Moraldi, L.   "Paràdosi di Pilato," Apoc. del NT.   1.   Pp.
        717-20.

86.16   Porfiryev, I.Y.   "Apocryphal Sayings About New Testament
        People and Events in Manuscripts of the Solovetski Library,"
        SbORJS 52 (1890) 191ff.   [in Russian]

86.17   Santos Otero, A. de.   "Relación de Pilato (<<Anaphora>>),"
        Evangelios Apócrifos.   Pp. 477-84.   [Gk. text and Spanish
        trans.]

86.18   Santos Otero, A. de.   "Tradición de Pilato (<<Paradosis>>),"
        Evangelios Apócrifos.   Pp. 490-95.   [Gk. text and Spanish
        trans.]

86.19   Scheidweiler, F.   HS.   1.   Pp. 356-58.

86.20   Scheidweiler, F.   HSW.   1.   Pp. 481-84.

86.21   Stegmüller, F.   Repertorium Biblicum.   1.   Pp. 154, 157f.;
        8.   Pp. 148, 150f.

86.22   Thilo, J.C.   Codex Apocryphus Novi Testamenti.   Leipzig,
        1832.   Pp. 813ff.

86.23   Tischendorf, C.   "Anaphora Pilati: Graece A et B," Evan-
        gelia Apocrypha.   Pp. lxxviii-lxxvix, 435-49.

86.24   Tischendorf, C.   [Editionem Fabricianam libelli qui anaphora
        Pilatou inscribitur plurimis ac gravissimis vitiis de formatum
        esse ostenditur], Apocalypses Apocryphae.   Pp. LXIII-LXIV.

86.25   Tischendorf, C.   "Paradosis Pilati," Evangelia Apocrypha.
        Pp. lxxixf., 449-55.   [Gk. text]

86.26   Variot, J.   "La Relation de Pilate," Évangiles Apocryphes.
        Pp. 117-20.

86.27   Walker, A.   "The Giving Up of Pontius Pilate," ANF   8.   Pp.
        464f.   [ET]

86.28   Walker, A.   "The Report of Pilate the Procurator Concerning
        Our Lord Jesus Christ," ANF   8.   Pp. 460f.   [ET of first
        Gk. form]

86.29   Walker, A.   "The Report of Pontius Pilate, Procurator of Ju-
        daea," ANF   8.   Pp. 462f.   [ET of 2nd Gk. form]

87. SAVIOR, THE AVENGING OF THE

87.1   Cowper, B.H. "The Revenging of the Saviour," Apocryphal
       Gospels. Pp. 432-47. [ET]

87.2   Darley, E. Les actes du Sauveur, la lettre de Pilate, la mis-
       sion de Volussien, de Nathan; la Vindicte. Leurs origines
       et leurs transformations. Paris, 1919.

87.3   Darley, E. Les Acta Salvatoris, un Evangile de la passion et
       de la résurrection et une mission apostolique en Aquitaine.
       Paris, 1913.

87.4   Erbetta, M. "La Vendetta del Salvatore," Apoc. del NT. 1.2.
       Pp. 388-96.

87.5   González-Blanco, E. Evangelios Apócrifos. Madrid, 1934.
       Vol. 2. Pp. 343-60.

87.6   Goodwin, C. The Anglo-saxon Legends of St. Andrew and
       St. Veronica. Cambridge, 1851.

87.7   James, M.R. "The Vengeance or Avenging of the Saviour,"
       ANT. Pp. 159-61.

87.8   Migne, J.-P. "Vengeance du Sauveur," Dictionnaire. 1.
       Cols. 1169-78. [French trans.]

87.9   Moraldi, L. "Vendetta del Salvatore," Apoc. del NT. 1. Pp.
       736-47.

87.10 Santos Otero, A. de. "Venganza del Salvador (<<vindicta>>),"
       Evangelios Apócrifos. Pp. 512-32. [Lat. text and Spanish
       trans.]

87.11 Scheidweiler, F. HS. 1. P. 358.

87.12 Scheidweiler, F. HSW. 1. P. 484.

87.13 Tischendorf, C. "Incipit Vindicta Salvatoris," Evangelia
       Apocrypha. Pp. LXXXII, 471-86.

87.14 Variot, J. "La Vengeance du Sauveur," Évangiles Apocryphes.
       Pp. 131-38.

87.15 Walker, A. "The Avenging of the Saviour," ANF   8. Pp.
       472-76. [ET]

88. SIBYLLINE ORACLES

For further bibliography on the Jewish Sibyllines, see
J.H. Charlesworth, The Pseudepigrapha and Modern Re-
search with a Supplement (SCS 7S) Chico, CA, 1981.
Pp. 184-88, 300f.

(See also 2.10.)

88.1   Alexander, P.J. The Oracle of Baalbek: The Tiburtine Sibyl
        in Greek Dress (Dumbarton Oaks Studies 10) Washington,
        1967.

88.2   Alexandre, C. Oracula Sibyllina. 2 vols. Paris, 1841-53.
        [Gk. text, Lat. trans., and studies of all books and frags.]

88.3   Altaner, B. "Augustinus und die neutestamentlichen Apokry-
        phen, Sibyllinen und Sextusspruche," AnBoll 67 (1949) 236-
        48. [repr. in Kleine Patristische Schriften (TU 83) Berlin,
        1967. Pp. 204-15]

88.4   Altaner, B. "The Christian Sibyllines," Patrology. Pp. 91-93.

88.5   Amann, É. "Les livres sibyllins," DBSup. 1. Cols. 530-33.

88.6   Bauckham, R. "Synoptic Parousia Parables Again," NTS 29
        (1983) 129-34. [see esp. pp. 130f.]

88.7   Bauer, J.B. "Die Gottesmutter in den Oracula Sibyllina,"
        Marianum 18 (1956) 118-24.

88.8   Bauer, J.B. "(KAT) EPEIGOMENOIO CHRONOIO: Oracula
        Sibyllina 3,50 und 2,186," Hermes 83 (1955) 250-52. [repr.
        Scholia biblica et patristica. Graz, 1972. Pp. 145-48]

88.9   Bauer, J.B. "Die Messiasmutter in den Oracula Sibyllina,"
        Marialia. Excerpta Ephemeridis "Marianum" 18 (1956) 1-7.
        [repr. Scholia biblica et patristica. Graz, 1972. Pp. 149-
        57]

88.10   Bauer, J.B. "Oracula Sibyllina I 323ab," ZNW 47 (1956) 284f.
        [repr. Scholia biblica et patristica. Graz, 1972. Pp. 141-
        44]

88.11   Bauer, J.B. "Das Sprichwort der Orac. Sib. 3, 737," Rhein-
        isches Museum für Philologie 99 (1956) 95f.

88.12   Bertrand, D.A. "Les 'Oracles Sibyllins,'" Le baptême de

Jésus: Histoire de l'exégèse aux deux premiers siècles.
Tübingen, 1973. Pp. 52-55.

88.13 Bischoff, B. "Die lateinische Übersetzungen und Bearbeitungen
       aus den Oracula Sibyllina," Mélanges Joseph de Ghellinck,
       S.J. (Museum Lessianum--Section Historique 13) Gembloux,
       1951. Vol. 1. Pp. 121-47. [repr. Mittelalterliche Studien.
       Stuttgart, 1967. Vol. 1. Pp. 150-71]

88.14 Bouché-Leclercq, A. "Les oracles sibyllines," RHR 7 (1883)
       230-48; 8 (1883) 619-34; 9 (1884) 220-33.

88.15 Bousset, W. "Sibyl, Sibylline Books," The New Schaff-Herzog
       Encyclopedia of Religious Knowledge, ed. S.M. Jackson.
       Grand Rapids, Mich., 1950. Vol. 10. Pp. 396-400.

88.16 Bousset, W. "Sibyllen und Sibyllinische Bücher," RPTK. 18.
       Pp. 265-80.

88.17 Capizzi, C. "L'imperatore Anastasio I e la Sibilla Tiburtina,"
       OCP 36 (1970) 377-406.

88.18 Collins, J.J. "The Sibylline Oracles," The Old Testament
       Pseudepigrapha, ed. J.H. Charlesworth. Garden City, New
       York, 1983. Vol. 1. Pp. 317-472. [ET and intro. to the
       "14" books.]

88.19 Crönert, G. "Oraculorum Sybillinorum fragmentum," Symbolae
       Osloenses 5 (1927) 38ff.; 6 (1928) 57-59.

88.20 Dechent, H. Über das erste, zweite und elfte Buch der Sibyl-
       linischen Weissagungen. Frankfurt on the Main, 1873.

88.21 Delaunay, F. Moines et sibylles dans l'antiquité judéo-grecque.
       Paris, 1874.

88.22 Diels, H. Sibyllinische Blätter. Berlin, 1890.

88.23 Erbetta, M. "Gli Oracoli Sibillini Cristiani," Apoc. del NT.
       3. Pp. 486-540.

88.24 Ewald, H. Entstehung Inhalt und Werth der Sibyllinischen
       Bücher. Göttingen, 1858.

88.25 Fehr, E. Studia in Oracule Sibyllina. Uppsala, 1893.

88.26 Flusser, D. "An Early Jewish-Christian Document in the Ti-
       burtine Sibyl," Paganisme, Judaïsme, Christianisme. Paris,
       1978. Pp. 153-83.

88.27 Flusser, D. "A Quotation from the Ghathas in a Christian

Sibylline Oracle," Ex Orbe Religionum: Studia Geo Widengren. 2 vols. (SHR 21, 22) Leiden, 1972. Vol. 1. Pp.
172-75.

88.28 Frankowski, J. "The Sibylline Oracles," RuBi 26 (1973) 261-
70. [in Polish]

88.29 Friedlieb, J. Die Sibyllinischen Weissagungen. Leipzig, 1852.

88.30 Gallaei, S. Oracula Sibyllina: Ex veteribus codicibus emen-
data, ac restituta. Et commentariis diversorum illustrata,
opera et studio Servatii Galaei. Accedunt etiam Magica Zoro-
astris, Jovis, Apollinis, etc. Amsterdam, 1689.

88.31 Gancho, C. "Oráculos Sibilinos," Enciclopedia de la Biblia.
5. Cols. 667f.

88.32 Geffcken, J. "Christliche Sibyllinen," H^2. Pp. 399-422.

88.33 Geffcken, J. Komposition und Entstehungszeit der Oracula
Sibyllina (TU 23.1) Leipzig, 1902.

88.34 Geffcken, J., ed. Die Oracula Sibyllina (GCS 8) Leipzig,
1902. [Gk. text with intro. and notes]

88.35 Grant, F.C. "Sibyllinen," RGG^3. 6. Cols. 14f.

88.36 Guillaumin, M.-L. "Recherches sur les 'Oracula Sibyllina'
d'origine chrétienne," ANRW 2.25.4 (in preparation).

88.37 Harris, J.R. "Sibylline Oracles," Hastings. 5. Pp. 66-68.

88.38 Helmbold, A.K. "Sibylline Oracles," ZPEB. 5. P. 425.

88.39 Hoffmann, W. Wandel und Herkunft der Sibyllinischen Bücher
in Rom. Leipzig Dissertation, 1933.

88.40 James, M.R. "Second book of the Sibylline Oracles, 190-338,"
ANT. Pp. 521-24.

88.41 Jeanmaire, H. "Le règne de la Femme des derniers jours et
le rajeunissement du monde: Quelques remarques sur le
texte de Or. Sib. VIII: 190ff," Mélanges Cumont. Brussels,
1936. Vol. 2. Pp. 297-304.

88.42 Jeanmaire, H. La Sibylle et le Retour de l'Age d'Or. Paris,
1939.

88.43 Kampers, F. Die tiburtinische Sibylle im Mittelalter. 1894.*

88.44 Knox, J. "Sibylline Oracles," IDB. 4. P. 343.

88.45   Kurfess, A. "Ad Oracula Sibyllina," Symbolae Osloenses
        24 (1952) 54-77.

88.46   Kurfess, A. "Alte lateinische Sibyllinenverse," TQ 133 (1953)
        80-96.

88.47   Kurfess, A. "The Christian Sibyllines," HSW. 2. Pp. 703-
        45.

88.48   Kurfess, A. "Christliche Sibyllinen," HS. 2. Pp. 498-528.

88.49   Kurfess, A. "Horaz und die Sibyllinen," ZRGG 8 (1956) 253-
        56.

88.50   Kurfess, A. "Dies Irae. zum sogen. 2. Buch der Or. Sibyl.,"
        Historisches Jahrbuch 77 (1958) 328-38.

88.51   Kurfess, A. "Juvenal und die Sibylle," Judaica 10 (1954) 60-
        63. [also in Historisches Jahrbuch 76 (1957) 79-83]

88.52   Kurfess, A. "Das Mahngedicht des sogenannten Phokylides
        im zweiten Buch der Oracula Sibyllina," ZNW 38 (1939) 171-
        81.

88.53   Kurfess, A. "Oracula Sibyllina I/II," ZNW 40 (1941) 151-65.

88.54   Kurfess, A. "Sibyllarum carmina chromatico tenore modulata,"
        Aevum 26 (1952) 385-94.

88.55   Kurfess, A. "Die Sibylle in Augustins Gottesstaat," TQ 117
        (1936) 351-68.

88.56   Kurfess, A. Sibyllinische Weissagungen. Berlin, 1951.

88.57   Kurfess, A. "Vergil's 4. Ekloge und die christlichen Sibylli-
        nen," Gymnasium 62 (1955) 110f.

88.58   Kurfess, A. "Virgils vierte Ekloge und die Oracula Sibyllina,"
        Historisches Jahrbuch der Gorres Gesellschaft 73 (1954)
        120-27.

88.59   Kurfess, A. "Wie sind die Fragmenta der Oracula Sibyllina
        einzuordnen? Ein Beitrag zu ihrer Überlieferung," Aevum
        26 (1952) 228-35.

88.60   Kurfess, A. "Zu den Oracula Sibyllina," Colligere Fragmenta:
        Festschrift A. Dold. Beuron, 1952. Pp. 75-83.

88.61   Kurfess, A. "Zum V. Buch der Oracula Sibyllina," Rhein-
        isches Museum für Philologie 29 (1956) 225-41.

88.62   Lanchester, H.C.O. "Sibylline Oracles," Encyclopedia of Re-
        ligion and Ethics, ed. J. Hastings. Edinburgh, 1920. Vol.
        11. Pp. 496-500.

88.63   Leclercq, H. "Les 'Oracles Sibyllins,'" DACL. 12. Cols.
        2220-40.

88.64   Lieger, P. Christus im Munde der Sibylle. Vienna, 1911.
        [Gk. text and German trans.]

88.65   McClintock, J., and J. Strong. "Sibylline Oracles," Cyclo-
        paedia of Biblical, Theological and Ecclesiastical Literature,
        eds. J. McClintock and J. Strong. New York, 1969. Cols.
        723-26. [reprint of 1871-1881 ed.]

88.66   Michl, J. "Sibyllinen, Sibyllinische Orakel oder Bücher,"
        LTK³. Cols. 728f.

88.67   Migne, J.-P. "Sibylles," Dictionnaire. 2. Cols. 931-36.

88.68   Moffatt, J. "Sibylline Oracles," Dictionary of the Apostolic
        Church, ed. J. Hastings. Edinburgh, 1926. Vol. 2. Pp.
        477-90.

88.69   Momigliano, A. "La Portata Storica dei Vaticini sul Settimo Re
        nel Terzo Libro degli Oracoli Sibillini," Forma Futuri: Studi
        in Onore di Cardinale Michele Pellegrini. Turin, 1975. Pp.
        1077-84.

88.70   Moraldi, L. "Oracoli sibillini cristiani," Apoc. del NT. 2.
        Pp. 1849-54.

88.71   Nikiprowetzky, V. La Troisième Sibylle (Études Juives 9)
        Paris, 1970.

88.72   Nola, A.M. di. "Sibille," EncRel. 5. Cols. 1041-44.

88.73   Nola, A.M. di. "Sibillini, Libri," EncRel. 5. Cols. 1044f.

88.74   Nola, A.M. di. "Sibillini, Oracoli," EncRel. 5. Cols. 1045-
        50.

88.75   Oldenburger, E. De Oraculorum Sibyllinorum Elocutione.
        Rostochii, 1903.

88.76   Prüm, K. "Das Prophetenamt der Sibyllen in kirchlicher Lit-
        eratur," Scholastik 4 (1929) 54-77.

88.77   Prüm, K. "Sibyllen," LTK². 9. Cols. 525-28; LTK³. 9.
        Cols. 726f.

88.78 Quasten, J. "The Christian Sibylline Oracles," Patrology.
       1. Pp. 168-70.

88.79 Roncaglia, M. "Les 'Oracles Sibyllins' judéo-chrétiens," Les
       origines. Pp. 76-78.

88.80 Rordorf, W. "Die neronische Christenverfolgung im Spiegel
       der apokryphen Paulusakten," NTS 28 (1982) 365-74.

88.81 Rzach, A. Metrische Studien zu den Sibyllinischen Orakeln.
       Vienna, 1892.

88.82 Rzach, A. Oracula sibyllina. New York, 1891. [Gk. text]

88.83 Rzach, A. "Sibyllinische Orakel," Pauly-Wissowa. 2A. Cols.
       2073-2183.

88.84 Sackur, E. Sibyllinische Texte und Forschungen. Torino,
       1898; repr. 1976.

88.85 Stegmüller, F. Repertorium Biblicum. 1. Pp. 96-99; 8. Pp.
       57-59.

88.86 Stumfohl, H. "Zur Psychologie der Sibylle," ZRGG 23 (1971)
       84-103.

88.87 Terry, M.S. The Sibylline Oracles: Translated from the
       Greek into English Blank Verse. New York, 1899; repr.
       New York, 1973. [ET]

88.88 Thompson, B. "Patristic Use of the Sibylline Oracles," Re-
       view of Religion 16 (1952) 115-36.

88.89 Vielhauer, P. "The Sibyllines," HSW. 2. Pp. 600f.

88.90 Wolff, M.J. "Sibyllen and Sibyllinen," Archiv für Kultur-
       geschichte 24 (1934) 312-25.

89. STEPHEN, REVELATION OF

(See also 1.202.)

89.1 Abel, M. La légende apocryphe de saint Étienne. Jerusalem,
      1931.

89.2 Bardenhewer, O. "Die Stephanusapokalypse," GAL. 1. P.
      621.

89.3   Devreesse, R. "Une collection Hiérosolymitaine au Sinai," RB
        47 (1938) 556f.

89.4   Erbetta, M. "La Rivelazione di Stefano," Apoc. del NT. 3.
        Pp. 397-408.

89.5   Fabricius, J.A. "Apocalypsis S. Stephani, Protomartyris,"
        Cod.Apoc.NT. 2. Pp. 965f.

89.6   Franco, N. Roma e l'Oriente 1914. Pp. 289-307.*

89.7   Franko, I. "Beiträge aus dem Kirchenslavischen zu den neu-
        testamentlichen Apokryphen," ZNW 7 (1906) 151-71. [Ger-
        man trans. of Slavic text]

89.8   Harnack, A. "Stephanus, Apokalypse," Gesch. altchrist. Lit.
        1. P. 790.

89.9   James, M.R. "Revelation of Stephen," ANT. Pp. 564-68.

89.10   Lagrange, M.-J. St. Étienne et son sanctuaire à Jerusalem.
        Paris, 1894. Pp. 43-52.

89.11   Leclerq, H. DACL. 5. Cols. 641-44.

89.12   Martin, J. "Die 'revelatio Stephani' und Verwandtes," Histor-
        isches Jahrbuch 77 (1958) 419-33.

89.13   Mercier, B.-Ch. "L'Invention des reliques de Saint Étienne:
        Edition et traduction de la recension arménienne inédité,"
        ROC 30 (1936) 341-69. [Armenian text and Lat. trans.]

89.14   Migne, J.-P. "Étienne. (Apocalypse de saint Etienne.),"
        Dictionnaire. 2. Cols. 227-30.

89.15   Migne, J.-P. PL. 41. Cols. 805-15. [Lat. text]

89.16   Moraldi, L. Apoc. del NT. 2. P. 1799.

89.17   Nau, F. "Note sur quelques mss. latins de l'invention du
        corps de St. Étienne," ROC 12 (1907) 441-44.

89.18   Nau, F. "Sur les mots politikos et politeuomenos et sur plu-
        sieurs textes grecs relatifs à Saint Étienne," ROC 11 (1906)
        198-216.

89.19   Papadopulos-Kerameus. Analekta tēs Hierosolymitikes stachu-
        logias. St. Petersburg, 1898. Vol. 5. Pp. 25-53. [Gk.
        texts]

89.20   Schneemelcher, W. "Apocalypse of Stephen," HSW. 2. P. 754.

89.21   Schneemelcher, W. "Apokalypse des Stephanus," HS. 2. Pp.
        535f.

89.22   Schulthess, F. "Christlich-Palästinische Fragmente aus der
        Omajjaden-Moschee zu Damaskus," Abhandlungen der könig-
        lichen Gesellschaft der Wissenschaften zu Göttingen, Ph.-hist.
        Klasse N.F. 83 (1905) 102-06.

89.23   Stegmüller, F. Repertorium Biblicum. 1. Pp. 247f.; 8. Pp.
        213f.

89.24   Vailhé, S. "Les églises Saint-Étienne à Jérusalem," ROC 12
        (1907) 70-89.

89.25   Vanderlinden, S. "Revelatio S. Stephani," REByz 1 (1946)
        178-217.

89.26   White, W., Jr. "Stephen, Revelation of," ZPEB. 5. P. 517.

89.27   Winterfeld, P. von. "Revelatio sancti Stephani," ZNW 3 (1902)
        358.

90. THADDEUS, ACTS OF

The AcThad is built upon LetCAbg--see also the listings
under that category.

(See also 1.202; 95.98.)

90.1   Akinian, P.N. "Inquiries into the History of Armenian Lit-
        erature, Legends of Thaddeus," Handes Amsorya. Monat-
        schrift fur armenischen Philologie 83m (1969) 399-426; 84
        (1970) 1-34. [in Armenian]

90.2   Alishan, L. Laboubnia, Lettre d'Abgar, ou Histoire de la
        Conversion des Edesséens par Laboubnia, écrivain contem-
        porain des apôtres. Venice, 1868.

90.3   Amann, É. "Les Actes de Thaddée ou Actes d'Addaï," DBSup.
        1. Cols. 510-12.

90.4   Bardenhewer, O. "Die Thaddäuslegende," GAL. 1. Pp. 590-
        96.

90.5   Bonnet-Maury, G. "La légende d'Abgar et de Thaddée et les
        missions chrétiennes à Édesse," RHR 16 (1887) 269-85.

90.6   Broadribb, D. "La Apostolo (T)Addaj," Biblia Revuo 2 (1965)
        62-74.

90.7   Cureton, W. Ancient Syriac Documents. London, 1863. Pp.
        5-23. [Syr. text and ET]

90.8   Duval, R. La littérature syriaque. Paris, 1900². Pp. 102-18.

90.9   Emine, J.R. "Leboubna d'Édesse: Histoire d'Abgar et de la
        Prédication de Thaddée. Trad. sur le manuscrit unique et
        inédit de la Bibliothèque Impériale de Paris," Collection des
        historiens anciens et modernes de l'Arménie, ed. V. Langlois
        Paris, 1867-69. Vol. 1. Pp. 315-25.

90.10   Erbetta, M. "Gli Atti di Taddeo," Apoc. del NT. 2. Pp.
        575-78.

90.11   Esbroeck, M. van. "Le Roi Sanatrouk et l'apôtre Thaddée,"
        Revue des Études Arméniennes 9 (1972) 241-83.

90.12   Fabricius, J.A. "Evangelium Thaddaei," Cod.Apoc.NT. 1.
        P. 379.

90.13   Hagner, D.A. "Thaddeus, Acts of," ZPEB. 5. Pp. 713f.

90.14   Harnack, A. "Acta Edessena (Thaddäus-Geschichte)," Gesch.
        altchrist. Lit. 1. Pp. 533-40.

90.15   James, M.R. "Acts of Thaddaeus," ANT. Pp. 471f.

90.16   Lipsius, R.A. Die apokryphen Apostelgeschichten und Apos-
        tellegenden. 2 vols. Brunswick, 1883-1890; repr. Amster-
        dam, 1976. Vol. 2.2. Pp. 142-200.

90.17   Lipsius, R.A., ed. "Acta Thaddaei," AAA 1. Pp. CVI-CXI,
        273-78. [Intro. and Gk. text]

90.18   Moraldi, L. "Atti di Taddeo uno degli apostoli," Apoc. del NT.
        2. Pp. 1645-48.

90.19   Nestle, E. De Sancta Cruce: Ein Beitrag zur Christlichen
        Legendengeschichte. Berlin, 1889.

90.20   Perdrizet, P. "D'une gravure relative à la légende de S.
        Jude Thaddée," Seminarium Konda Kovianum 6 (1933) 67-72.

90.21   Phillips, G. The Doctrine of Addai, the Apostle, Now First
        Edited in a Complete Form in the Original Syriac. London,
        1876. [Syr. text and ET]

90.22   Schmid, G.M. Geschichte des Apostels Thaddaeus und der

Jungfrau Sanducht. (Zeitschrift für armenische Philologie
Bd. 1. H.1), Marburg, 1901.

90.23   Schmidt, C. "Acten des Judas Thaddäus," Gesch. altchrist.
        Lit. 1. P. 921.

90.24   Schneemelcher, W., and A. de Santos. "Acts of Thaddeus,"
        HSW. 2. P. 578.

90.25   Schneemelcher, W., and A. de Santos. "Thaddäusakten," HS.
        2. P. 404.

90.26   Stegmüller, F. Repertorium Biblicum. 1. P. 229; 8. P. 196.

90.27   Tischendorf, K. von. "Acta Thaddaei," Acta Apos. Apoc.
        Pp. LXXI-LXXIII, 261-65. [Intro. and Gk. text]

90.28   Vetter, P. "Rezensionen: Die armenischen Apokryphen,"
        TQ 87 (1905) 608-10. [Vetter reviews three books on
        Apocrypha extant in Armenian]

90.29   Walker, A. "Acts of the Holy Apostle Thaddeus," ANF 8.
        Pp. 558f. [ET]

90.30   Zahn, T. "Über die Lehre des Addai," Neutest. Kanons. 1.
        Pp. 350-82.

                    91.   THOMAS, ACTS OF

(See also 1.269, 284, 531, 559; 2.34; 3.38, 40, 53, 63, 77, 78; 7.4,
    14; 12.39; 95.348.)

91.1   Acta Apocrypha Armenica. Vienna, 1904. Pp. 369-427. [Arm.
        text]

91.2   Adam, A. Die Psalmen des Thomas und das Perlenlied als
        Zeugnisse vorchristlicher Gnosis (BZNW 24) Berlin, 1959.
        [see review by F.P. Ridolfini, RSO 37 (1962) 295-99]

91.3   Agouridis, S. "The Acts of Thomas: An Unpublished Modern
        Greek Manuscript," Deltíon Biblikōn Meletōn 1 (1971) 126-47.
        [in Modern Gk.]

91.4   Amann, É. "Les Actes de Thomas," DBSup. 1. Cols. 501-
        04.

91.5   Ambroggi, P. de. "Libri Apocrifi," EncCatt. 12. Col. 240.
        [refers to ApTh and AcTh]

91.6   Amfilochij Archimandrit. Paleografičeskoe opisanie. Moscow,
        1880. Vol. 2. Pp. 22-28.* [in Russian]

91.7   Amiot, F. "Actes de Thomas," Evangiles Apoc. Pp. 262-74.
        [French trans.]

91.8   [Archeografičeskaja Kommissija]. Daily Readings of the Great
        'Menaea' (4-18 October, 1874). Cols. 815-27.* [in Russian]

91.9   Baker, A. "Early Syriac Asceticism," DowR 88 (1970) 393-409.

91.10   Baluchatyj, S. "On the Apocryphal Acts of the Apostle
        Thomas," Sbornik statej v. čestb akademika A.I. Sobolevs-
        kogo. Leningrad, 1928 (Russian reprint series, IV, The
        Hague, 1965) Pp. 57-62. [in Russian]

91.11   Bardenhewer, O. "Die Akten des Thomas," GAL. 1. Pp.
        579-84.

91.12   Bauer, J.B. "Die Thomasakten," Neutest. Apok. Pp. 76-78.

91.13   Bauer, W., and R. Raabe. "Thomasakten," H^2. Pp. 256-89.

91.14   Bedjan, P. Acta Martyrum et Sanctorum. Paris, 1890-97.
        Vol. 3. Pp. 1-175. [Syr. text]

91.15   Bevan, A.A. The Hymn of the Soul, Contained in the Syriac
        Acts of St. Thomas (T&S 5.3) Cambridge, 1897.

91.16   Blond, G. "L'Encratisme dans les Actes apocryphes de
        Thomas," Recherches et travaux 1.2 (1946) 5-25.

91.17   Bonnet, M., ed. "Acta Thomae," AAA. 2.2. Pp. XV-XXVII,
        99-288. [Intro. and Gk. text]

91.18   Bonnet, M. Acta Thomae graece partim cum novis codicibus
        contulit, partim primus edidit, latine recensuit, praefatus
        est. Leipzig, 1883. Pp. 96-160. [Lat. text]

91.19   Bonnet, M. "Actes de S. Thomas apôtre. Le poème de l'âme.
        Version grecque remaniée par Nicétas de Thessalonique,"
        AnBoll 20 (1901) 159-64. [Gk. text]

91.20   Bonsirven, J., and C. Bigaré. "Actes de Thomas," Intro. à
        la Bible. 2. Pp. 759f.

91.21   Bonwetsch, N. "Acta Thomae," Gesch. altchrist. Lit. 1.
        Pp. 902f.

91.22   Bornkamm, G. "The Acts of Thomas," HSW. 2. Pp. 425-
        531.

91.23 Bornkamm, G. Mythos und Legende in den apokryphen Thom-
       asakten: Beiträge zur Geschichte der Gnosis und zur Vor-
       geschichte des Manichäismus (FRLANT 49) Göttingen, 1933.

91.24 Bornkamm, G. "Thomasakten," HS. 2. Pp. 297-372.

91.25 Bornkamm, G. "Die Thomas-Akten," Pauly-Wissowa. 6A.
       Cols. 320-23.

91.26 Botte, B. "L'Epiclèse dans les liturgies syriennes orientales,"
       Sacris Erudiri 6 (1954) 48-72.

91.27 Bousset, W. Hauptprobleme der Gnosis (FRLANT 10) Göttin-
       gen, 1907.

91.28 Bousset, W. "Manichäisches in den Thomasakten," ZNW 18
       (1917-18) 1-39.

91.29 Broadribb, D. "La Kanto pri la Perlo," Biblia Revuo 4.2
       (1968) 23-37.

91.30 Brock, S.P. "Early Syrian Ascetism," Numen 20 (1973) 1-19.

91.31 Brown, L.W. The Indian Christians of St. Thomas. Cam-
       bridge, 1956.

91.32 Budge, E.A.W., tr. Baralâm and Yĕwâsĕf: Being the Eth-
       iopic Version of a Christianized Recension of the Buddhist
       Legend of the Buddha and the Bodhisattva. Cambridge,
       1923.

91.33 Burch, V. "A Commentary on the Syriac Hymn of the Soul,"
       JTS 19 (1918) 145-61.

91.34 Burkitt, F.C. Theologisch Tijdschrift 39 (1905) 270-82.*

91.35 Burkitt, F.C. "Another Indication of the Syriac Origin of
       the Acts of Thomas," JTS 3 (1902) 94f.

91.36 Burkitt, F.C. Early Christianity Outside the Roman Empire.
       Cambridge, 1899. Pp. 63-89.

91.37 Burkitt, F.C. "Fragments of the Acts of Judas Thomas from
       the Sinaitic Palimpsest," Studia Sinaitica, IX: Select Nar-
       ratives. Syriac. Appendix VII. Pp. 23-44.

91.38 Burkitt, F.C. "The Name Habban in the Acts of Thomas,"
       JTS 2 (1901) 429.

91.39 Burkitt, F.C. "The Original Language of the Acts of Judas
       Thomas," JTS 1 (1900) 280-90.

91.40 Burkitt, F.C. "Sarbôg, Shuruppak," JTS 4 (1903) 125-27.

91.41 Canney, M.A. "The Life-giving Pearl," Journal of the Manchester University Egyptian and Oriental Society 15 (1930) 43-62.

91.42 Cartlidge, D.R., and D.L. Dungan. "The Acts of the Holy Apostle Thomas," Documents. Pp. 36-54. [summaries with ET]

91.43 Colpe, C. "Die Thomaspsalmen als chronologischer Fixpunkt in der Geschichte der orientalischen Gnosis," JAC 7 (1964) 77-93.

91.44 Connolly, R.H. "A Negative Golden Rule in the Syriac Acts of Thomas," JTS 36 (1935) 353-56.

91.45 Connolly, R.H. "The Original Language of the Syriac Acts of Thomas," JTS 8 (1907) 249-61.

91.46 Conybeare, F.C. "The Idea of Sleep in the 'Hymn of the Soul,'" JTS 6 (1905) 609f.

91.47 Conzelmann, H. "Zu Mythos, Mythologie und Formegeschichte, geprüft an der dritten Praxis der Thomas-Akten," ZNW 67 (1976) 111-22.

91.48 Culianou, I.R. "Erzählung und Mythos im 'Lied von der Perle,'" Kairos 21 (1979) 60-71.

91.49 Dahlmann, J., Die Thomas-Legende und die ältesten historischen Beziehungen des Christiantums zum fernen Osten. Freiburg, 1912.

91.50 Delaunay, J.A. "Rite et symbolique en Acta Thomas, vers. syr. I, 2a et ss.," Mémorial Jean de Menasce, eds. P. Gignoux and A. Tafazzoli. Louvain, 1974. Pp. 11-34.

91.51 Demina, E.I. The Tichonravov Collection. Sofia, 1971. Vol. 2. Pp. 89-94. [in Russian]

91.52 Devos, P. "Actes de Thomas et Actes de Paul," AnBoll 69 (1951) 119-30.

91.53 Devos, P. "Le miracle posthume de S. Thomas l'Apôtre," AnBoll 66 (1948) 231-76.

91.54 Dihle, A. "Neues zur Thomas-Tradition," JAC 6 (1963) 54-70.

91.55 Drijvers, H.J.W. Bardaisan of Edessa. Assen, 1966.

91.56 Duval, R. "Histoire politique, religieuse et littéraire d'Edesse,"
       JA 18 (1891) 87-133, 201-78, 381-439; 19 (1892) 5-102.

91.57 Enslin, M.S. "Thomas, Acts of," IDB. 4. Pp. 632-34.

91.58 Erbetta, M. "Gli Atti di Tommaso," Apoc. del NT. 2. Pp.
       307-74.

91.59 Fabricius, J. Cod. Apoc. NT. 2. Pp. 687-736, 819-28.

91.60 Falk, M. "L'histoire du mythe de la perle," Actes du XXIe
       Congrès International. Paris, 1948. Pp. 371-73

91.61 Farquahar, J.N. "The Apostle Thomas in Northern India,"
       BJRL 10 (1926) 80-111.

91.62 Farquahar, J.N. "The Apostle Thomas in South India," BJRL
       11 (1927) 20-50.

91.63 Farquahar, J.N., and G. Garitte. The Apostle Thomas in
       India According to the Acts of Thomas. (Syrian Churches
       Series 1) New York, 1972. [available at John XXIII Center,
       Fordham University]

91.64 Findlay, A.F. "The Acts of Thomas," Byways. Pp. 273-304.

91.65 Franko, I. Apocrypha and Legends. L'vov, 1902. Vol. 3.
       Pp. 91-111. [in Russian]

91.65a Garitte, G. "Le Martyre géorgien de l'apôtre Thomas,"
       Muséon 83 (1970) 497-532.

91.66 Garitte, G. "La Passion arménienne de S. Thomas l'Apôtre
       et son modèle grec," Muséon 84 (1971) 151-95.

91.67 Gerleman, G. "Bemerkungen zum Brautlied der Thomasakten,"
       Annual of the Swedish Theological Institute 9 (1973) 14-22.

91.68 Guillaume, A. "Actes de Thomas," École Pratique des Hautes
       Etudes, Sect. 5, Sciences Relig Annuaire 73 (1965) 147f.

91.69 Gutschmid, A. von. "Die Königsnamen in den apokryphen
       Apostelgeschichten," Rheinisches Museum für Philologie 19
       (1864) 161-83. [repr. Gutschmid, A. von. Kleine Schriften.
       Leipzig, 1890. Vol. 2. Pp. 332-64]

91.70 Haase, F. "Neue Bardesanesstudien," OrChr 12-14 (1925)
       129-40.

91.71 Haase, F. "Die Thomasakten und ihre Lieder," Zur bardesan-
       ischen Gnosis (TU 34) Leipzig, 1910. Pp. 50-67.

91.72 Halévy, J. "Cantique syriaque sur saint Thomas," RSEHA 16
       (1908) 85-94, 168-75.

91.73 Halkin, F. "Publications récentes de textes hagiographiques
       grecs IV (1946-50)," AnBoll 69 (1951) 388-403.

91.74 Hamman, A. "Le Sitz im Leben des Actes de Thomas," Studia
       Evangelica. Vol. 3: Papers Presented to the Second Inter-
       national Congress on New Testament Studies Held at Christ
       Church, Oxford, 1961. Part 2: The New Testament Mes-
       sage, ed. F.L. Cross (TU 88) Berlin, 1964. Pp. 383-89.

91.75 Harnack, A. "Die Johannes-, Andreas-, und Thomasacten,"
       Gesch altchrist. Lit. 2.1. Pp. 541-49.

91.76 Harnack, A. "Die Thomasacten," Gesch. altchrist. Lit. 1.
       Pp. 123f.

91.77 Harnack, A. "Zu den Thomasakten," Gesch. altchrist. Lit.
       2.2. P. 549.

91.78 Hilgenfeld, A. "Der Königssohn und die Perle," ZWT 47
       (1904) 229-341.

91.79 Hoffman, G. "Zwei Hymnen der Thomasakten," ZNW 4 (1903)
       273-309.

91.80 Jagić, V. "New Contributions to the Literature of Biblical
       Apocrypha," Starine 5 (1873) 96-108. [in Serbo-Croatian]

91.81 James, M.R. "Acts of Thomas," ANT. Pp. 364-438.

91.82 James, M.R. "Acta Thomae," AA 2. Pp. 27-63. [includes
       ET of "The Conflict of S. Thomas"; see also pp. xxxii-xliv]

91.83 Jansma, T. A Selection from the Acts of Judas Thomas (Se-
       mitic Study Series 1) Leiden, 1952. [Includes four short-
       ened and revised Acts, selected from W. Wright's Apocryphal
       Acts of the Apostles, London, 1871.]

91.84 Jonas, H. Gnosis und spätantiker Geist. Vol. 1: Die mytho-
       logische Gnosis (FRLANT 33) Berlin, 1954.

91.85 Joseph, T.K. "The Saint Thomas Traditions of South India,"
       Bulletin of the International Committee of Historical Science
       5 (1933) 560-69.

91.86 Kirylowicz, S. "Acta S. Thomas Apostoli, jako źródło histor-
       yczne," Elpis 5 (1931) 118-41. [in Polish]

91.87 Kirylowicz, S. "Historical Evidence Concerning Christianity

in India in Connection with the Apostolate of St. Thomas,"
Elpis 6 (1932) 280-318. [in Polish]

91.88 Klijn, A.F.J. The Acts of Thomas: Introduction, Text, Com-
       mentary. (NovTSup 5) Leiden, 1962.

91.89 Klijn, A.F.J. "Early Syriac Christianity--Gnostic?," Le ori-
       gini dello gnosticismo. Colloquio di Messina 13-18 Aprile
       1966, ed. U. Bianchi (SHR 12) Leiden, 1967. Pp. 515-79.

91.90 Klijn, A.F.J. Edessa, de Stad van de Apostel Thomas, Het
       oudste Christendom in Syrië. Baarn, 1962. [German trans.:
       Edessa, die Stadt des Apostels Thomas: Das älteste Chris-
       tentum in Syria, trans. M. Hornschuh (Neukirchener Studien-
       bücher 4) Giessen, 1965. Pp. 106-38.]

91.91 Klijn, A.F.J. "The Influence of Jewish Theology on the Odes
       of Solomon and the Acts of Thomas," Aspects du judéo-
       christianisme: Colloque de Strasbourg 23-25 avril 1964.
       Paris, 1965. [See also the discussion of Klijn's paper,
       pp. 177-79.]

91.92 Klijn, A.F.J. "The so-called Hymn of the Pearl (Acts of
       Thomas ch. 108-113)," VC 14 (1960) 153-64.

91.93 Klijn, A.F.J. "The Term 'Life' in Syriac Theology," SJT
       5 (1952) 390-97.

91.94 Kmosko, M. Liber Graduum (Patrologia Syriaca 1.3) Paris,
       1926.

91.95 Köbert, R. "Das Perlenlied," Or N.S. 38 (1969) 447-56.

91.96 Lake, K. "Texts from Mount Athos: A Fragment of the Acta
       Thomas," Studia biblica et ecclesiastica 5 (1903) 164-69.

91.97 Lavrov, P.A. "Apocryphal Texts," SbORJS 67 (1899) 136-43.
       [in Russian]

91.98 Lebeau, P. Le vin nouveau du Royaume: Étude exégetique
       et patristique sur la parole eschatologique de Jésus a la
       Cène. Paris, Brussels, 1966. Pp. 142-84.

91.99 Lévi, S. "Saint Thomas, Gondaphorès et Mazdeo," JA 9 (1897)
       27-42 [Arm. text]

91.100 Levi della Vida, G. Bardesane; Il dialogo delle leggi dei paesi:
       Introduzione, Traduzione e note. Rome, 1921.

91.101 Lewis, A.S. The Mythological Acts of the Apostles (Horae
       Semiticae 4) London, 1904. Pp. 80-99, 223-41. [ET of Ar.
       and Syr. texts in Horae Semiticae 3]

91.102 Lewis, A.S., ed. and tr. Select Narratives of Holy Women, from the Syro-Antiochene or Sinai Palimpsest as Written Above the Old Syriac Gospels by John Stylite, of Beth-mariqanan in A.D. 728. (Studia Sinaitica 9-10) London, 1900. [includes Syr. text and ET of seven frags. of AcTh]

91.103 Liechtenhan, R. "Die pseudepigraphe Literatur der Gnostiker: Die Acta Thomae," ZNW 3 (1902) 287-93.

91.104 Lipsius, R.A. Die apokryphen Apostelgeschichten und Apostellegenden. 2 vols. Brunswick, 1883-90; repr. Amsterdam, 1976. Vol. 1. Pp. 225-347.

91.105 Loewenich, W. von. "Die Petrus-, Andreas-, Paulus-, und Thomas-Akten," Das Johannes-Verständnis im zweiten Jahrhundert (BZNW 13) Giessen, 1932. Pp. 109-12.

91.106 Macke, K. Hymnen aus dem Zweiströmeland. Mainz, 1882. Pp. 246-56.

91.107 Macke, K. "Syrische Lieder gnostichen Ursprungs," TQ 56 (1874) 5-70.

91.108 Macler, F. Catalogue des manuscrits arméniens et géorgiens de la Bibliothèque Nationale. Paris, 1908. Pp. 48-54, 57-61. [Arm. text]

91.109 Malan, S.C. The Conflicts of the Holy Apostles. London, 1871. Pp. 187-220.

91.110 Margoliouth, D.S. "Some Problems in the 'Acta Thomae,'" Essays in Honor of G. Murray. London, 1936. Pp. 249-59.

91.111 Masing, U., and K. Rätsep. "Baarlam and Josaphat: Some Problems Connected with the Story of Baarlam and Josaphat, the Acts of Thomas, the Psalms of Thomas, and the Gospel of Thomas," Communio Viatorum 11 (1961) 29-36.

91.111a Medlycott, A.E. India and the Apostle Thomas: An Inquiry with a Critical Analysis of the Acta Thomae. London, 1905.

91.112 Ménard, J.É. "Le Chant de la Perle," RSR 42 (1968) 289-325.

91.113 Ménard, J.É. "La fonction sotériologique de la mémoire chez les Gnostiques," RScR 54 (1980) 298-310.

91.114 Merkelbach, R. "Der Seelenhymnus der Thomasakten und die Weihe Julians," Roman und Mysterium in der Antike, Beilage 1. Munich, Berlin, 1962. Pp. 299-325.

91.115 Merrill, E. H. "The Odes of Solomon and the Acts of Thomas: A Comparative Study," JETS 17 (1974) 231-34.

91.116 Michaelis, W. "Thomas-Akten," Apokryphen Schriften. Pp.
       402-38. [German trans. of selections]

91.117 Michel, O. "Zur Frage des Seslanliedes," ZNW 25 (1926) 312-
       13.

91.118 Migne, J.-P. "Thomas. (Histoire de Saint Thomas, d'après
       l'Histoire apostolique d'Abdias.)," Dictionnaire 2. Cols. 987-
       1046. [French trans.; includes French trans. of "Voyages
       et martyre de saint Thomas l'Apôtre," cols. 1015-46]

91.119 Mingana, A. Catalogue of the Mingana Collection of Manu-
       scripts II: Christian Arabic Manuscripts and Additional
       Syriac Manuscripts (Selly Oak Colleges Library) Cambridge,
       1936. Pp. 121f. [Arab. text of "an extensive portion of
       the AcTh. The date of the Kufic script is c. 830; and that
       makes it the oldest extant copy of AcTh in any language]

91.120 Mingana, A. "The Early Spread of Christianity in India,"
       BJRL 10 (1926) 435-514.

91.121 Monnaret de Villard, U. "La fiera di Batne e la traslazione
       di S. Tomaso a Edessa," Rendiconti della Accademia Nazionale
       dei Lincei Ser. 8. 6 (1951) 77-104.

91.122 Moraldi, L. "Atti di san Tomaso," Apoc. del NT. 2. Pp.
       1225-1350.

91.123 Müller, K. Die Ehelosigkeit aller Getauften in der alten Kirche.
       Tübingen, 1927.

91.124 Nau, F. Bardesane. Le livre des lois des pays. Paris, 1931.

91.125 Nöldeke, T. "Lied von der Seele," ZDMG 25 (1871) 676-79.

91.126 Novakovíc, S. "The Apocrypha of One Serbian-Cyrillic Col-
       lection of the Fourteenth Century," Starine 8 (1876) 69-74.
       [in Serbo-Croatian]

91.127 Ogle, M.B. "The Trance of the Lover and of the Saint,"
       Transactions and Proceedings of the American Philological
       Association 71 (1940) 296-301.

91.128 Omodeo, A. "I miti gnostici degli Atti di Tommaso," Parola
       del Passato 1 (1946) 321-37.

91.129 Pericoli Ridolfini, F. "I 'Salmi di Tommaso' e la gnosi giudeo-
       cristiana," RSO 38 (1962) 23-58.

91.130 Pick, B. The Apocryphal Acts of Paul, Peter, John, Andrew
       and Thomas. London, 1909.

91.131 Placid, R.P. "Les Syriens du Malabar," OrSyr 1 (1956) 375-
       424.

91.132 Poirier, P.-H. "L'Hymne de la Perle des Actes de Thomas:
       Étude de la tradition manuscrite," Symposium Syriacum 1976
       (OCA 205) Rome, 1978. Pp. 19-29.

91.133 Poirier, P.-H. L'Hymne de la Perle des Actes de Thomas.
       Introduction--Texte--Tradution--Commentaire (Homo Re-
       ligiosus 8) Louvain-la-Neuve, 1981.

91.134 Popov, A.N. "Bibliographical Materials 20," ČOIDR (1899)
       61-71. [in Russian]*

91.135 Preuschen, E. "Thomasakten," Handbuch, ed. Hennecke.
       Pp. 562-601.

91.136 Preuschen, E. Zwei gnostische Hymnen. Giessen, 1904.

91.137 Puech, H.C. Le manichéisme, son fondateur, sa doctrine.
       Paris, 1949.

91.138 Quispel, G. "Das Lied von der Perle," EJ 34 (1965) 9-32.
       [repr. in Gnostic Studies (Uitgaven van het Nederlands his-
       torisch-archeologisch instituut te Ishtanbul 34) 2 vols. Is-
       tanbul, 1975. Vol. 2. Pp. 122-41]

91.139 Quispel, G. Makarius, das Thomasevangelium und das Lied
       von der Perle (NovTSup 15) Leiden, 1967.

91.140 Quispel, G. "Makarius und das Lied von der Perle," Le ori-
       gini dello gnosticismo: Colloquio di Messina 13-18 Aprile
       1966, ed. U. Bianchi (SHR 12) Leiden, 1967. Pp. 625-44.

91.141 Radčenko, K.F. "Notes on Extant Manuscripts," IzvORJS 12
       (1907) 151, 154. [in Russian]

91.142 Reitzenstein, R. "Ein Gegenstück zu dem Seelenhymnus der
       Thomasakten," ZNW 21 (1922) 35-37.

91.143 Reitzenstein, R. Hellenistische Wundererzählungen. Leipzig,
       1906. [The second section of this monograph is devoted to
       the Hymn of the Pearl.]

91.144 Reitzenstein, R. Das iranische Erlösungsmysterium: Religion-
       sgeschichtliche Untersuchungen. Bonn, 1921. [see esp. p.
       113]

91.145 Resetar, M. Book of Many Arguments. Belgrade, 1926. Pp.
       43-47. [in Serbo-Croatian]

91.146 Rho, F. Intorno ai viaggi apostolici ed alla predicazione di
       S. Tomaso. Brescia, 1834.

91.147 Santos Otero, A. de. "Acta Thomae," Altslavischen Apok. 1.
       Pp. 84-96.

91.148 Schaeder, H.H. "Bardesanes von Edessa in der Überlieferung
       der griechischen und der syrischen Kirche," ZKG 51 (1932)
       21-74.

91.149 Schaeder, H.H. "Urform und Fortbildung des manichäischen
       Systems," Vorträge der bibliothek Warburg (1924-25) 65-157.*

91.150 Schaeder, H.H. "Zu C. Schmidt und H.J. Polotsky: Ein Mani-
       fund aus Agypten," Gnomon 9 (1933) 337-62.

91.151 Schmidt, M. "Bericht über das 2. Symposium Syriacum vom
       13-17 Sept. 1976 in Chantilly bei Paris," OrChr 61 (1977)
       231-35.

91.152 Schoedel, W.R. "The Hymn of the Pearl," Gnosticism: A
       Source Book of Heretical Writings from the Early Christian
       Period, ed. R.M. Grant. New York, 1961. Pp. 116-22.

91.153 Schöter, R. "Gedicht des Jakob von Sarug über den Palast
       den der Apostel Thomas in Indien baute," ZDMG 25 (1871)
       321-77.

91.154 Stegmüller, F. Repertorium Biblicum. 1. Pp. 230-32; 8.
       Pp. 197-99.

91.155 Tamila, D. "Acta Thomae Apocrypha," Rendiconti della Reale
       Accademia dei Lincei 5.12 (1920).*

91.156 Tarchnišvili, P.M. "Der Apostel Thomas," Geschichte der
       kirchlichen georgischen Literatur (Studi e Testi 185) Rome,
       1955. P. 344.

91.157 Thilo, C. Acta S. Thomae apostoli. Leipzig, 1823. [Gk.
       text]

91.158 Tischendorf, K. von. "Acta Thomae," Acta Apos. Apoc.
       Pp. LXII-LXVII, 190-234. [Intro. and Gk. text]

91.159 Tischendorf, K. von. "Ad Acta Thomae," Apocalypses Apocry-
       phae. Pp. 156-61. [Gk. text]

91.160 Tissot, Y. "Les actes de Thomas, exemple de recueil compo-
       site," Actes Apocryphes. Pp. 223-32.

91.161 Tissot, Y. "L'encratisme des Actes de Thomas," ANRW 2.25.4
       (in preparation).

91.162 Turner, C.H. "Priscillian and the Acts of Judas Thomas,"
JTS 7 (1906) 603-05.

91.163 Urbina, I.O. de. Patrologia Syriaca. Rome, 1965². Pp. 37-
41.

91.164 Vaeth, A. Der hlg. Thomas, der Apostel Indiens: Eine Untersuchung über den historischen Gehalt der Thomas-Legende.
Aachen, 1925.

91.165 Vetter, P. "Rezensionen: Die armenischen Apokryphen,"
TQ 87 (1905) 608-10.

91.166 Vööbus, A. History of Asceticism in the Syrian Orient (CSCO
184) Louvain, 1953.

91.167 Vööbus, A. "Liber Graduum," Papers of the Estonian Theological Society in Exile 7 (1954) 108-28.

91.168 Vööbus, A. "Neue Angaben uber die Textgeschichtlichen
Zustände in Edessa in den Jahren ca. 326-340," Papers of
the Estonian Theological Society in Exile 3 (1951) 33ff.*

91.169 Vööbus, A. "A Requirement for Admission to Baptism in the
Early Church," Papers of the Estonian Theological Society in
Exile 5 (1953) 49-58.

91.170 Walker, A. "Acts of the Holy Apostle Thomas," ANF 8. Pp.
535-49. [ET]

91.171 Wecker, O. "Christlicher Einfluss auf den Buddhismus?"
TQ 92 (1910) 538-65.

91.172 Wesendork, O.G. "Bardesanes und Mani," AcOr 10 (1932)
336-63.

91.173 Widengren, G. The Ascension of the Apostle and the Heavenly
Book (Uppsala Universitet Aarsskrift 7) Uppsala, 1950.

91.174 Widengren, G. The Great Vohu Manah and the Apostle of
God: Studies in Iranian and Manichaean Religion (Uppsala
Universitet Aarsskrift 5) Uppsala, 1945.

91.175 Widengren, G. "Der iranische Hintergrund der Gnosis,"
ZRGG 4 (1952) 97f.

91.176 Widengren, G. Mesopotamian Elements in Manichaeism (Uppsala
Universitet Aarsskrift 6) Uppsala, 1946.

91.177 Widengren, G. Muhammed, the Apostle of God, and his Ascension (Uppsala Universitet Aarsskrift) Uppsala, 1955.

91.178 Widengren, G. "Stand und Aufgabe der iranischen Religions-
       geschichte," Numen 1 (1954) 16-34; 2 (1955) 1-20.

91.179 Wilhelm, F. Deutsche Legenden und Legendare: Texte und
       Untersuchungen zu ihrer Geschichte im Mittelalter. Leipzig,
       1907.

91.180 Wilson, R. McL. "Thomas, Acts of," ZPEB. 5. 733f.

91.181 Wright, W. Apocryphal Acts of the Apostles: Edited from
       Syriac Manuscripts in the British Museum and Other Librar-
       ies, 2 vols. London, 1871. Vol. 1. Pp. 171-333 [Syr. text];
       Vol. 2. Pp. 146-298 [ET].

91.182 Zelzer, K. Die alten lateinischen Thomasakten (TU 122) Ber-
       lin, 1977.

91.183 Zelzer, K. "Zu den lateinischen Fassungen der Thomasakten,"
       Wiener Studien 84 (1971) 161-78; 85 (1972) 185-212.

91.184 Zelzer, K. "Zur Datierung und Verfasserfrage der lateinischen
       Thomasakten," Studia Patristica 12 (1975) 190-94.

92. THOMAS, MINOR ACTS OF

See also the entries under AcTh.

92.1   Ivšić, S. "Acta Thomae minora in slavischer Übersetzung,"
       Deuxième congrès international des études byzantines. Bel-
       grade, 1927. P. 185.

92.2   James, M.R. "Acta Thomae (Ex Cod. Brit. Mus. Add. 10,073,
       f. 128-53," AA 2. Pp. 27-45. [Gk. text]

92.3   James, M.R. ANT. P. 470.

93. THOMAS, APOCALYPSE OF

93.1   Ambroggi, P. de. "Libri Apocrifi," EncCatt. 12. Col. 240.

93.2   Bardenhewer, O. "Die Thomasapokalypse," GAL. 1. Pp.
       620f.

93.3   Bick, M.J. "Wiener Palimpseste," Sitzungsberichte der Wiener
       Akademie der Wissenschaften 159 (1908) 90-100.

93.4   Bihlmeyer, D.P. "Un texte non interpolé de l'Apocalypse de
        Thomas," RBen 28 (1911) 270-82.

93.5   Brunklaus, F.A. Het laatste testament; Het Evangelie van
        Judas; Het hooglied van Maria Magdalena; De openbaring
        van de apostel Thomas. Maastricht, 1969.

93.6   Bruyne, D. de. "Fragments retrouvés d'apocryphes priscil-
        lianistes," RBen 24 (1907) 318-35.

93.7   Dando, M. "L'Apocalypse de Thomas," CahJos 28.73 (1977)
        3-58.

93.8   Erbetta, M. L'Apocalisse di Tommaso," Apoc. del NT. 3.
        Pp. 387-95.

93.9   Förster, M. "A New Version of the Apocalypse of Thomas in
        Old English," Anglia 73 (1955) 6-36.

93.10   Frick, C. "Die Thomasapokalypse," ZNW 9 (1908) 172f.

93.11   Gatch, M.M. "Two Uses of Apocrypha in Old English Homilies,"
        Church History 33 (1965) 379-91.

93.12   Harnack, A. "Thomas, Apocalypse," Gesch. altchrist. Lit.
        1. P. 790.

93.13   Hauler, E. "Zu den neuen lateinischen Bruchstücken der
        Thomasapokalypse und eines apostolischen Sendschreibens
        im Cod. Vindob. Nr. 16," Wiener Studien 30 (1908) 308-40.

93.14   James, M.R. "Apocalypse of Thomas," ANT. Pp. 555-62.

93.15   James, M.R. "Notes on Apocrypha I: Revelatio Thomae,"
        JTS 11 (1910) 288-90.

93.16   James, M.R. "The Revalatio Thomae Again," JTS 11 (1910)
        569.

93.17   Moraldi, L. "Apocalisse di Tomaso," Apoc. del NT. 2. Pp.
        1939-50.

93.17a Morris, R. The Bickling Homilies. London, 1980. Pp. 91-95.

93.18   Santos Otero, A. de. "Apocalypse of Thomas," HSW. 2. Pp.
        798-803.

93.19   Santos Otero, A. de. "Thomasapokalypse," HS. 2. Pp. 568-
        72.

93.20   Seymour, J.D. "The Signs of Doomsday in the Saltair na Rann,"
        Proceedings of the Royal Irish Academy 36 (1921) 154-63.

93.21 Stegmüller, F. Repertorium Biblicum. 1. Pp. 248f.; 8. Pp.
       214f.

93.22 Wilhelm, F. "Epistula domini nostri Jhesu Christi ad Thomam
       discipulum suum," Deutsche Legenden und Legendare. Leip-
       zig, 1907. Pp. 40-42.

93.23 Wilson, R.McL. "Thomas, Apocalypse of," ZPEB. 5. P. 734.

              94. THOMAS, CONSUMMATION OF

       See also the listings under AcTh.

(See also 3.53.)

94.1   Bonnet, M. AAA. 2.2. Pp. 289f.

94.2   Stegmüller, F. Repertorium Biblicum. 1. P. 233; 8. Pp.
       200f. [also contains listings for Martyrdom of Thomas =
       Acts of Thomas 159-70.]

94.3   Tischendorf, K. von. "Consummatio Thomae," Acta Apos.
       Apoc. Pp. LXVIIIf., 235-42. [Intro. and Gk. text]

94.4   Walker, A. "Consummation of Thomas the Apostle," ANF   8.
       Pp. 550-52. [ET]

              95. THOMAS, GOSPEL OF

(See also 1.18, 88, 269, 470, 559; 5.106; 91.138.)

95.1   [Anonymous]. "El Evangelio de Tomás: Publicaciones y ac-
       tualidad periodistica," Cultura Bíblica 16 (1959) 371-73.

95.2   [Anonymous]. The Gospel According to Thomas. Santa Fe,
       1980.

95.3   [Anonymous]. "More About the Gospel of Thomas," Theology
       Digest 9 (1962) 180f.

95.4   [Anonymous]. "The New 'Sayings of Jesus': The Gospel Ac-
       cording to Thomas," The Sunday Times (London, Nov. 22,
       1959) 14f.

95.5   [Anonymous]. "Papiros de las sectas gnósticas contemporáneas
        del Cristianismo primitivo," Cultura Bíblica 14 (1957) 189f.

95.6   Adinolfi, M. "Le parabole della rete e del lievito nel Vangelo
        di Tommaso," Studii Biblici Franciscani Liber Annuus 13
        (1962-63) 33-52.

95.7   Akagi, T. The Literary Development of the Coptic Gospel of
        Thomas. Western Reserve University Ph.D., 1965.

95.8   Akagi, T. "A Proto-Thomas Hypothesis," Nihonno Shingaku
        [Theological Studies in Japan: Annual Report on Theology]
        (Japan Society of Christian Studies) 5 (1966) 26-37. [in
        Japanese]

95.9   Aland, K. Synopsis quattuor Evangeliorum: Locis parallelis
        evangeliorum apocryphorum et patrum adhibitis edidit. Stutt-
        gart, 1964. Pp. 517-30. [Lat., German and English trans-
        lations]

95.10   Albanese, C.L. "Inwardness: A Study of Some Gnostic
        Themes and Their Relation to Early Christianity With Spe-
        cific Reference to the Gospel According to Thomas," RTAM
        43 (1976) 64-88.

95.11   Amann, E. "Évangile de Thomas," DBSup. 1. Col. 478.

95.12   Arai, S. "The Gospel According to Thomas, with Special Em-
        phasis on its Relationship to the Canonical Gospels," Sheisho
        Kôza [Lectures on the Bible] 4 (1965) 365-86. [in Japanese;
        also in Early Christianity and Gnosticism, ed. S. Arai. Tokyo,
        1971. Pp. 240-56]

95.13   Arai, S. "The Gospel of Thomas: Logion 61, Concerning the
        Origin of the Conception of 'Homoousios,'" Kirisutokyô-Shigaku
        16 (1965) 69. [in Japanese]

95.14   Arai, S. "Jesus in the Gospel According to Thomas," Early
        Christianity and Gnosticism, ed. S. Arai. Tokyo, 1971.
        Pp. 257-72. [in Japanese; also in Christokyo Ronshu 10
        (1963) 57-74]

95.15   Arai, S. "On the Logion III of the Gospel According to
        Thomas," Journal of the History of Christianity 23 (1970)
        54f. [in Japanese]

95.16   Arai, S. "Thomas Tradition in the Early Church," Senkyô To
        Shingaku: Asano Junichi Hakase Kentei Ronbunshû [Evan-
        gelism and Theology: Essays in Honor of Dr. Junichi Asano],
        ed. N. Tajima et al. Tokyo, 1964. Pp. 246-72. [in Japan-
        ese; also in Early Christianity and Gnosticism, ed. S. Arai.
        Tokyo, 1971. Pp. 222-39]

95.17   Arthur, R.L.   The Gospel of Thomas and the Coptic New
        Testament.   Thesis, Graduate Theological Union, 1976.

95.18   Attridge, H.W.   "Greek Equivalents of Two Coptic Phrases:
        CG I, 1.65, 9-10 and CG II, 2.43.26," Bulletin of the Amer-
        ican Society of Papyrologists 18 (1981) 27-32.

95.19   Attridge, H.W.   "The Original Text of Gos. Thom., Saying
        30," Bulletin of the American Society of Papyrologists 16
        (1979) 153-57.

95.20   Baarda, T.   "Jezus Zeide: 'Weest Passanten.' Over betekenis
        en oorsprong van logion 42 in het Evangelie van Thomas,"
        Ad Interim (Festschrift for R. Schippers) Kampen, 1975.
        Pp. 113-40.

95.21   Bajusz, F., "Támas evangéliuma: 'Az ötödik evangélium,'"
        Református Egyház 7-8 (1960) 104-08.

95.22   Baker, A.   "Early Syriac Asceticism," DowR 88 (1970) 393-
        409.

95.23   Baker, A.   "Fasting to the World," JBL 84 (1965) 291-94.

95.24   Baker, A.   "The 'Gospel of Thomas' and the Diatessaron,"
        JTS 16 (1965) 449-54.

95.25   Baker, A.   "The 'Gospel of Thomas' and the Syriac 'Liber
        Graduum,'" NTS 12 (1965-66) 49-55.

95.26   Baker, A.   "Pseudo-Macarius and the Gospel of Thomas," VC
        18 (1964) 215-25.

95.27   Bammel, E.   "Rest and Rule," VC 23 (1969) 88-90.

95.28   Bartsch, H.-W.   "Das Thomas-Evangelium und die synoptischen
        Evangelien: Zu G. Quispels Bemerkungen zum Thomas-
        Evangelium," NTS 6 (1960) 249-61.

95.29   Bartsch, H.-W.   "Zur Veröffentlichung des 'Thomas Evangel-
        iums,'" Kirche in der Zeit 14 (1959) 193-95.

95.30   Bauer, J.B.   "Akta Jesu ord?" in Skriftfynden, ed. W.C. van
        Unnik.   Stockholm, 1962.*

95.31   Bauer, J.B.   "Arbeitsaufgaben am koptischen Thomasevange-
        lium," VC 15 (1961) 1-7.

95.32   Bauer, J.B.   "De agraphis genuinis evangelii secundum
        Thomam coptici," VD 37 (1959) 129-46.

95.33 Bauer, J.B. "De 'labore' Salvatoris (Evang. Thom. Log. 28.98.107)," VD 40 (1962) 123-30.

95.34 Bauer, J.B. "Echte Jesusworte," ThJ (1961) 108-50, 191-223.*

95.35 Bauer, J.B. "Das Jesuswort 'Wer mir nahe ist,'" TZ 15 (1959) 446-50. [repr. in Scholia Biblica et Patristica, ed. J.B. Bauer. Graz, 1972. Pp. 117-22.]

95.36 Bauer, J.B. Neutest. Apok. Pp. 30-40.

95.37 Bauer, J.B. Studien zum koptischen Thomasevangelium. Graz, 1962. [Habilitationsschrift]

95.38 Bauer, J.B. "The Synoptic Tradition in the Gospel of Thomas," Studia Evangelica. Vol. 3: Papers Presented to the Second International Congress on New Testament Studies Held at Christ College, Oxford, 1961. Part 2: The New Testament Message, ed. F.L. Cross (TU 88) Berlin, 1964. Pp. 314-17.

95.39 Bauer, J.B. "Das Thomasevangelium in der neuesten Fors- chung," Geheime Worte Jesu: Das Thomas-Evangelium, eds. R.M. Grant and D.N. Freedman. Frankfurt, 1960. Pp. 182-205.

95.40 Bauer, J.B. "Das Thomas-Evangelium von Nag Hammadi," Seelsorger 30 (1959) 416-22.

95.41 Bauer, J.B. "Zum koptischen Thomasevangelium," BZ 6 (1962) 283-88. [repr. in Scholia Biblica et Patristica, ed. J.B. Bauer. Graz, 1972. Pp. 123-30]

95.42 Beardslee, W.A. "Proverbs in the Gospel of Thomas," Studies in New Testament and Early Christian Literature: Essays in Honor of Allen P. Wikgren, ed. D.E. Aune. Leiden, 1972. Pp. 92-103.

95.43 Beare, F.W. "The Gospel According to Thomas: A Gnostic Manual," CJT 6 (1960) 102-12.

95.44 Beatrice, P.F. "Il significato di 'Evangile Thomas' 64 per la critica letteraria della parabola del banchetto (Mt. 22, 1-14/ Lc. 14, 15-24)," La parabola degli invitati al banchetto: Dagli evangelisti a Gesù, ed. J. Dupont. (Testi e ricerche di scienze religiose 14) Brescia, 1979. Pp. 237-77.

95.45 Bellet, P. "El Logion 50 del Evangelio de Tomás," Studia Papyrologica 8 (1969) 119-24.

95.46 Berveling, G. "La Evangelio Kopta laû Tomaso," Biblia Revuo 17 (1981) 3-19. [Esperanto trans.]

95.47 Best, E. "The Gospel of Thomas," Biblical Theology 10 (1960)
       1-10.

95.48 Birdsall, J.N. "Luke 12:16ff. and the Gospel of Thomas,"
       JTS 13 (1962) 332-36.

95.49 Bishop, E.F.F. "Passers-by: Sayings of Jesus," Muslim World
       50 (1960) 33f.

95.50 Bonaccorsi, P.G. "Frammento del Vangelo secondo Tommaso,"
       Vangeli Apocrifi. 1. Pp. 30f.

95.51 Brandon, S.G.F. "Thomas, Gospel of," A Dictionary of Com-
       parative Religion, ed. S.G.F. Brandon. London, New York,
       1970. P. 612.

95.52 Briscoe, H.L. A Comparison of the Parables in the Gospel
       According to Thomas and the Synoptic Gospels. Southwestern
       Baptist Theological Seminary Ph.D., 1965-66.

95.53 Brown, R.E. "Gospel of Thomas," JBC. P. 545.

95.54 Brown, R.E. "The Gospel of Thomas and St. John's Gospel,"
       NTS 9 (1963) 155-77.

95.55 Bruce, F.F. "The Gospel of Thomas," Faith and Thought 92
       (1961-62) 3-23.

95.56 Bruce, F.F. "The Gospel of Thomas," Jesus and Christian
       Origins Outside the New Testament. Grand Rapids, 1974.
       Pp. 110-58.

95.57 Bruce, F.F. "When is a Gospel Not a Gospel?" BJRL 45
       (1963) 319-39.

95.58 Bull, R.J. "Some Hints of an Independent Jewish-Christian
       Tradition in the Gospel of Thomas," Drew Gateway 30 (1960)
       168-73.

95.59 Cartlidge, D.R., and D.L. Dungan, "The Coptic Gospel of
       Thomas," Documents. Pp. 25-35. [ET]

95.60 Celada, B. "El evangelio de Tomás, con 'Palabras de Jesús'
       que pretenden ser anteriores y independientes de los Evan-
       gelios," Cultura Biblica 14 (1957) 408f.

95.61 Celada, B. "Más acerca del supuesto quinto Evangelio,"
       Cultura Biblica 16 (1959) 48-50.

95.62 Celada, B. "¿Se ha encontrado un quinto Evangelio?" Cultura
       Biblica 15 (1958) 366-75.

95.63   Cerfaux, L., and G. Garitte. "Les paraboles du royaume dans
        l''Évangile de Thomas,'" Muséon 70 (1957) 307-27.

95.64   Cerutti, M.V. "Note sul conoscere e l'essere conosciuti in
        alcuni testi paolini e gnostici," Rivista Biblica 29 (1981)
        69-77.

95.65   Chun, K.Y. "The Gospel of Thomas and the Parables of Jesus,"
        Yesu ŭi Piyu. Seoul, 1962. Pp. 225-50. [in Japanese]

95.66   Chun, K.Y. "The Gospel of Thomas and The Words of Jesus,"
        Kidokkyo Sasang 6 (1962) 6-14. [in Japanese]

95.67   Chun, K.Y. "The Jung Codex and the Gospel of Thomas,"
        Sinhak Yŏngu 6 (1960) 109-19. [in Japanese]

95.68   Church, F.F. The Secret to the Gospel of Thomas. Harvard
        University Ph.D., 1978.

95.69   Collins, J.J. "A Fifth Gospel?" America 101 (1959) 365-67.

95.70   Colpe, C. "Tuomaan evandeliumi," Teologinen Aikakauskirja
        65 (1960) 215-18.

95.71   Cornélis, É.M.J.M. "Quelques éléments pour une comparaison
        entre l'Evangile de Thomas et la notice d'Hippolyte sur les
        Naassènes," VC 15 (1961) 83-104.

95.72   Crossan, J.D. "Seed Parables of Jesus," JBL 92 (1973) 244-
        66. [re. Mk 4:3-8, 26-29, 30-32; Mt 13:3-8, 24-32; and
        GosTh]

95.73   Cullmann, O. "L'evangelo di Tommaso," Protestantesimo 15
        (1960) 145-52.

95.74   Cullmann, O. "The Gospel of Thomas," Theology Digest 9
        (1961) 175-80.

95.75   Cullmann, O. "Thomasevangelium," RGG[3]. 6. Pp. 865f.

95.76   Cullmann, O. "Das Thomasevangelium und die Frage nach
        dem Alter der in ihm enthaltenen Tradition," TLZ 85 (1960)
        321-34. [repr. in Vorträge und Aufsätze 1925-62, ed. K.
        Fröhlich. Tübingen, Zürich, 1966. Pp. 566-88; ET in Int
        16 (1962) 418-38.]

95.77   Cullmann, O. "Das Thomasevangelium und seine Bedeutung
        für die Erforschung der kanonischen Evangelien," Kirchen-
        blatt für die reformierte Schweiz 116 (1960) 306-10. [also
        in Universitas 15 (1960) 865-74; ET in HibJ 60 (1962) 116-
        24]

95.78   Cullmann, O., and H.-Ch. Puech. "The Great Discovery of
        the 'Gospel of Thomas,'" The Sunday Times (London, No-
        vember 15, 1959) 18.

95.79   Daniélou, J. "Un recueil inédit de paroles de Jésus?" Études
        302 (1959) 38-49.

95.80   Dart, J. "The Two Shall Become One," Theology Today 35
        (1978) 321-25.

95.81   Davies, S.L. The Gospel of Thomas and Christian Wisdom.
        New York, 1983.

95.82   Davies, S.L. "Thomas--The Fourth Synoptic Gospel," BA 46
        (1983) 6-9, 12-14.

95.83   Degge, E.H. A Computer-Generated Concordance of the Cop-
        tic Text of the Gospel According to Thomas. Houston, 1970.

95.84   Dehandschutter, B. "L'Évangile de Thomas comme collection
        de paroles de Jésus," Logia: Les paroles de Jésus (Memorial
        Joseph Coppens), ed. J. Delobel (BETL 59) Leiden, 1982.
        Pp. 507-15.

95.85   Dehandschutter, B. "L'Évangile selon Thomas: Témoin d'une
        tradition prélucanienne?" L'Évangile de Luc: Problèmes lit-
        téraires et théologiques, ed. F. Nierynck (BETL 32) Gem-
        bloux, 1973. Pp. 287-97.

95.86   Dehandschutter, B. "Le lieu d'origine de l'Évangile selon
        Thomas en Égypte," OLP 6 (1975) 125-31.

95.87   Dehandschutter, B. "La parabole de la perle (Mt 13:45-46)
        et l'Évangile selon Thomas," ETL 55 (1979) 243-65.

95.88   Dehandschutter, B. "La parabole des vignerons homicides
        (Mc XII 1-12) et l'évangile selon Thomas," L'Évangile selon
        Marc: Tradition et rédaction, ed. M. Sabbe. (BETL 34)
        Gembloux, 1974. Pp. 203-19.

95.89   Dehandschutter, B. "Les paraboles de l'Évangile selon Thomas:
        La parabole du trésor caché (log. 109)," ETL 47 (1971) 199-
        219.

95.90   Dehandschutter, B. "Het Thomasevangelie: Overzicht van
        het onderzoek," Licentiate dissertation, Université Catholique
        de Louvain, 1975.

95.91   DeLamotte, R.C. The Alien Christ. Washington, 1980.

95.92   Dembska, A., and W. Myszor. "Gnostic Gospels from Nag

Hammadi," Apokryfy Nowego Testamentu, ed. M. Starowieyski.
Lublin, 1980. Vol. 1. Pp. 119-37. [in Polish]

95.93 Dembska, A., and W. Myszor. "The Gospel of Thomas,"
       Teksty z Nag-Hammadi (Pisma Starochrześcijańskich Pisarzy
       20) Warsaw, 1979. Pp. 207-38. [in Polish]

95.94 Devos, P. [An untitled review of several articles] AnBoll 78
       (1960) 444-48.

95.95 Díez Macho, A. "El descubrimiento de 'nuevas palabras' de
       Jesucristo," Punta Europa 51 (1960) 47-65.

95.96 Doresse, J. Les livres secrets des Gnostiques d'Égypt. Vol.
       2: L'Evangile selon Thomas ou les paroles secrètes de Jésus.
       Paris, 1959.

95.97 Doresse, J. "Le problème des 'paroles secrètes de Jésus'
       ('L'Évangile de Thomas')," La Table Ronde 154 (1960) 120-
       28.

95.98 Drijvers, H.J.W. "Edessa und das jüdische Christentum,"
       VC 24 (1970) 4-33.

95.99 Durso, M.H. "The Gospel According to Thomas," The Bible
       Today 16 (1965) 1067-74.

95.100 Ehlers, B. "Kann das Thomasevangelium aus Edessa stammen?"
       NovT 12 (1970) 284-317.

95.101 Englezakis, B. "Thomas, Logion 30," NTS 25 (1978) 262-72.

95.102 Erbetta, M. "Il Vangelo di Tommaso," Apoc. del NT. 1. Pp.
       253-82.

95.103 Fabre-Luce, A. "L'Évangile selon Thomas," La Nouvelle Revue
       Française 8 (1960) 745-53.

95.104 Fabricius, J.A. "Evangelium S. Thomae," Cod.Apoc.NT. 1.
       P. 379f.

95.105 Fallon, F.T. "The Gospel of Thomas. A Forschungsbericht
       and Analysis," ANRW 2.25.4 (in preparation).

95.106 Fensham, F.C. "Die Evangelie van Thomas en sy Betekenis,"
       Tydskrif vir Letterkunde 3 (1965) 31-39.

95.107 Ferguson, J. "Gospel According to Thomas, The," An Illus-
       trated Encyclopedia of Mysticism and the Mystery Religions.
       London, 1976; New York, 1977. P. 69.

95.108 Fitzmyer, J.A. "The Oxyrhynchus Logoi of Jesus and the
       Coptic Gospel According to Thomas," TS 20 (1959) 505-60.
       [repr. in Essays on the Semitic Background of the New
       Testament. London, 1971; repr. Scholars Press, 1974. Pp.
       355-433]

95.109 Frend, W.H.C. "The Gospel of Thomas: Is Rehabilitation
       Possible?" JTS 18 (1967) 13-26.

95.110 Fuller, R.C. "The Two 'Gospels' of St. Thomas," The Tablet
       208 (1956) 549f.

95.111 Garitte, G. "Evangelium secundum Thomam latine," Synopsis
       Quattuor Evangeliorum: Locis parallelis evangeliorum apocry-
       phorum et patrum adhibitis, ed. K. Aland. Stuttgart, 1964.
       Pp. 517-30. [Lat. trans.]

95.112 Garitte, G. "Les 'Logoi' d'Oxyrhynque et l'apocryphe copte
       dit 'Évangile de Thomas,'" Muséon 73 (1960) 151-72, 219-22.

95.113 Garitte, G. "Les 'Logoi' d'Oxyrhynque sont traduits du copte,"
       Muséon 73 (1960) 335-49.

95.114 Garitte, G. "Le nouvel Évangile copte de Thomas," Académie
       Royale de Belgique; Bulletin de la Classe des Lettres et des
       Sciences morales et politiques 5. 50 (1964) 33-54.

95.115 Garitte, G. "Le premier volume de l'édition photographique
       des manuscrits gnostiques coptes et 'l'Évangile de Thomas,'"
       Muséon 70 (1957) 59-73.

95.116 Garitte, G., and L. Cerfaux. "Les paraboles du royaume dans
       l''Évangile de Thomas,'" Muséon 70 (1957) 307-27. [repr.
       in Recueil Lucien Cerfaux: Études d'Exégèse et d'Histoire
       Religieuse de Monseigneur Cerfaux Professeur à l'Université
       de Louvain réunies à l'occasion de son soixante-dixième an-
       niversaire (ETL Supplément 18) Gembloux, 1962. Vol. 3.
       Pp. 61-80]

95.117 Garofalo, S. "Un evangelio que no es evangelio: El 'Evan-
       gelio según Tomás' recientemente descubierto," Orbis Cath-
       olicus 4 (1961) 424-38.

95.118 Garofalo, S. "Das Thomasevangelium ist kein Evangelium:
       Der Chenoboskionfund als Quelle zur Erforschung der Gno-
       sis," Wort und Wahrheit 15 (1960) 364-71.

95.119 Gärtner, B. Ett nytt evangelium? Thomasevangeliets hemliga
       Jesusord. Stockholm, 1960.

95.120 Gärtner, B. The Theology of the Gospel According to Thomas,
       trans. E.J. Sharpe. New York, 1961.

95.121 Gärtner, B.E. "Thomasevangeliet," Apokryferna till Nya Tes-
       tamentet. Stockholm, 1972. Pp. 32-61.

95.122 Gärtner, B.E. "Tomasevangeliet," Svenskt Bibliskt Uppslag-
       sverk 2 (1963) 1250-52.

95.123 Giversen, S. "Questions and Answers in the Gospel According
       to Thomas: The Composition of pl. 81, 14-18 and pl. 83,
       14-27," AcOr 25 (1960) 332-38.

95.124 Giversen, S. Thomas Evangeliet. Copenhagen, 1959.

95.125 Giversen, S. "Tomasevangeliet [2]," Gads Danske Bibel Lex-
       sikon, ed. E. Nielsen and B. Noack. Copenhagen, 1966.
       Vol. 2. Pp. 1002f.

95.126 Glasson, T.F. "Carding and Spinning: Oxyrhynchus Papy-
       rus No. 655," JTS 13 (1962) 331f.

95.127 Glasson, T.F. "The Gospel of Thomas, Saying 3, and Deu-
       teronomy 30:11-14," ExpT 78 (1966/67) 151f.

95.128 Goodwin, C. "The Hidden Words of the Living Jesus, also
       Called the Gospel of Thomas," Yonsei Non-Chong 3 (1964)
       1-39. [in Japanese; English summary, p. 40]

95.129 Grant, R.M. "Notes on the Gospel of Thomas," VC 13 (1959)
       170-80.

95.130 Grant, R.M. "Two Gnostic Gospels," JBL 79 (1960) 1-11.

95.131 Grant, R.M., and D.N. Freedman. The Secret Sayings of
       Jesus; With an English Translation of the Gospel of Thomas
       by W.R. Schoedel. New York, 1960.

95.132 Gregor, D.B. "La intelekto de Jesuo," Biblia Revuo 17 (1981)
       39-60.

95.133 Greitemann, N. "Das Thomasevangelium," Wort und Wahrheit
       15 (1960) 64.

95.134 Grobel, K. "How Gnostic Is the Gospel of Thomas?" NTS 8
       (1962) 367-73.

95.135 Guey, J. "Comment le 'denier de César' de l'Évangile a-t-il
       pu devenir une pièce d'or," Bulletin de la Société française
       de Numismatique 15 (1960) 478f.

95.136 Guillaumont, A., et al., tr. The Gospel According to Thomas.
       Paris, Leiden, New York, 1959. [Copt. text and ET; French
       trans. L'Évangile selon Thomas: Texte copte etabli et trad.;

Spanish trans. El Evangelo según Tomás; Apocrifo-gnóstico;
Versión bilingüe copto-castellano: Texto copto establecido y
traducido]

95.137 Guillaumont, A. "Les Logia d'Oxyrhynchos sont-ils traduits
du copte?" Muséon 73 (1960) 325-33.

95.138 Guillaumont, A. "Nêsteuein ton Kosmon (P. Oxy. I, verso,
I.5-6)," BIFAO 61 (1962) 15-23.

95.139 Guillaumont, A. "Sémitismes dans les logia de Jésus retrouvés
à Nag-Hamâdi," JA 246 (1958) 113-23.

95.140 Guillaumont, A. "Les sémitismes dans l'Évangile selon Thomas:
Essai de classement," Studies in Gnosticism and Hellenistic
Religions: Presented to Gilles Quispel on the Occasion of
his 65th Birthday, eds. R. van den Broek and M.J. Vermas-
eren. (Études préliminaires aux religions orientales dans
l'Empire Romain 91) Leiden, 1981. Pp. 190-204.

95.141 Gunder, A. Anthropologie de l'Évangile selon Thomas. Strasbourg Ph.D., 1972.

95.142 Haardt, R. "Gibt es ein 'Fünftes Evangelium'? Der Fund von
Chenoboskion--eine Quelle zur Kenntnis neuer Jesusworte,"
Die Furche Nr. I (Vienna, January 2, 1960) 10.

95.143 Haardt, R. "Das koptische Thomasevangelium und die ausserbiblische Herrenworte," Der historische Jesus und der Christus unseres Glaubens: Eine Katholische Auseinandersetzung
mit den Folgen der Entmythologisierungstheorie, ed. K.
Schubert. Vienna, 1962. Pp. 257-87.

95.144 Haardt, R. "Zum subachmimischen Einfluss im Thomasevangelium," WZKM 57 (1961) 98f.

95.145 Haelst, J. van. "A propos du catalogue raisonné des papyrus
littéraires chrétiens d'Égypte, grecs et latins," Actes du X
Cong. Int. de Papyrologues. Warsaw, 1964. Pp. 215-25.

95.146 Haenchen, E. "Die Anthropologie des Thomas-Evangeliums,"
Neues Testament und christliche Existenz: Festschrift für
Herbert Braun, eds. H.D. Betz and L. Schottroff. Tübin-
gen, 1973. Pp. 207-27.

95.147 Haenchen, E. Die Botschaft des Thomas-Evangeliums (Theologische Bibliothek Töpelmann 6) Berlin, 1961.

95.148 Haenchen, E. "Literatur zum Thomasevangelium," ThRu 27
(1961) 147-78, 306-38.

95.149 Haenchen, E. "Spruch 68 des Thomasevangeliums," Muséon
       75 (1962) 19-29.

95.150 Haenchen, E. "Das Thomas-Evangelium," Synopsis Quattuor
       Evangeliorum: Locis parallelis evangeliorum apocryphorum
       et patrum adhibitis, ed. K. Aland. Stuttgart, 1964. Pp.
       517-30. [German trans.]

95.151 Hammer, R.J. "The Gospel of Thomas and the Historical
       Jesus," Seishogaku Ronshû 2 (1964) 108-24. [in Japanese]

95.152 Hammerschmidt, E. "Das Thomasevangelium und die Manichäer,"
       OrChr 46 (1962) 120-23.

95.153 Harl, M. "A propos des Logia de Jésus: Le sens du mot
       monachos," REG 73 (1960) 464-74.

95.154 Harnack, A. "Thomas-Evangelium," Gesch. altchrist. Lit.
       1. Pp. 15-17.

95.155 Higgins, A.J.B. "Non-Gnostic Sayings in the Gospel of
       Thomas," NovT 4 (1960) 292-306. [repr. in The Tradition
       About Jesus: Three Studies (SJT Occasional Papers 15)
       Edinburgh, 1969. Pp. 30-47]

95.156 Hoberman, B. "How Did the Gospel of Thomas Get its Name?"
       BA 46 (1983) 10f.

95.157 Hofius, O. "Das koptische Thomasevangelium und die
       Oxyrhynchus-Papyri Nr. 1, 654, und 655," EvT 20 (1960)
       21-42, 182-92.

95.158 Horman, J. "The Source of the Version of the Parable of the
       Sower in the Gospel of Thomas," NovT 21 (1979) 326-43.

95.159 Houghton, H.P. "The Coptic Gospel of Thomas," Aegyptus
       43 (1963) 107-40.

95.160 Hubaut, M. "La comparaison avec la version de Thomas,"
       La parabole des vignerons homicides (Cahiers de la Revue
       Biblique 16) Paris, 1976. Pp. 132-34.

95.161 Huisman, J.A. "Nachwort," VC 16 (1962) 152f. [comments on
       W. Krogmann's "Heiland, Tatian, und Thomasevangelium,"
       ZNW 51 (1960) 255-68]

95.162 Hunzinger, C.-H. "Aussersynoptisches Traditionsgut im
       Thomas-Evangelium," TLZ 85 (1960) 843-46.

95.163 Hunzinger, C.-H. "Unbekannte Gleichnisse Jesu aus dem
       Thomas-Evangelium," Judentum Urchristentum Kirche:

386   IV. Bibliography

Festschrift für Joachim Jeremias, ed. W. Eltester (BZNW 26)
Berlin, 1960. Pp. 209-20.

95.164 Ivanov, A. "Das neue apokryphe Evangelium von Thomas,"
Journal des Moskaeur Patriarchats 9 (1959) 72-74.

95.165 James, M.R. "The Gospel of Thomas," ANT. Pp. 14-16.

95.166 Janssens, Y. "Deux 'évangiles' gnostiques," Byzantion 35
[H. Grégoire Festschrift] (1965) 449-54.

95.167 Janssens, Y. "L'Évangile selon Thomas et son caractère
gnostique," Muséon 75 (1962) 301-25.

95.168 Janssens, Y. "Évangiles gnostiques," Archiv für Papyrusfor-
schung 22/23 (1974) 229-47.

95.169 Jones, G.V. "The Parables of the Gospel of Thomas," The
Art and Truth of the Parables: A Study in their Literary
Form and Modern Interpretation. London, 1964. Pp. 230-40.

95.170 Kaestli, J.-D. "L'Évangile de Thomas: Son importance pour
l'étude des paroles de Jésus et du gnosticisme chrétien,"
Etudes Théologiques et Religieuses 54 (1979) 375-96.

95.171 Karavidopoulos, I.D. The Gnostic Gospel of Thomas. Thes-
salonica, 1967. [in modern Gk.; Eng. summary, p. 67]

95.172 Kasser, R. "El evangelio según Santo Tomás," Pensamiento
Cristiano 8 (1960) 46-48.

95.173 Kasser, R. L'Évangile selon Thomas: Présentation et commentaire théologique. (Bibliothèque théologique) Neuchâtel, 1961.

95.174 Kee, H.C. "'Becoming a Child' in the Gospel of Thomas,"
JBL 82 (1963) 307-14.

95.175 Kim, Y.O. The Christological Problem in the Gospel According
to Thomas. Drew University Ph.D., 1965.

95.176 Kim, Y.O. "The Gospel of Thomas and the Historical Jesus,"
Northeast Asia Journal and Theology 2 (1969) 17-30.

95.177 Klijn, A.F.J. "Christianity in Edessa and the Gospel of
Thomas: On Barbara Ehlers, Kann das Thomasevangelium
aus Edessa stammen?" NovT 14 (1972) 70-77.

95.178 Klijn, A.F.J. Edessa, de Stad van de Apostel Thomas, Het
oudste Christendom in Syrië. Baarn, 1962. Pp. 64-83.
[German trans.: Edessa, die Stadt des Apostels Thomas:
Das älteste Christentum in Syria, trans. M. Hornschuh.
(Neukirchener Studienbücher 4) Giessen, 1965]

95.179 Klijn, A.F.J. "The 'Single One' in the Gospel of Thomas,"
       JBL 81 (1962) 271-78.

95.180 Klijn, A.F.J. "Das Thomasevangelium und das alt-syrische
       Christentum," VC 15 (1961) 146-59.

95.181 Klostermann, E., ed. "Thomasevangelium," Apocrypha II:
       Evangelien (KlT 8) Berlin, 1929³. P. 16. [Gk. witnesses]

95.182 Koester, H. "GNOMAI DIAPHOROI: The Origin and Nature
       of Diversification in the History of Early Christianity," HTR
       58 (1965) 279-318. [repr. Trajectories through Early Chris-
       tianity, eds. H. Koester and J.M. Robinson. Philadelphia,
       1971. Pp. 114-57; German trans. Tübingen, 1971]

95.183 Koester, H., and T. O. Lambdin. "The Gospel of Thomas
       (II,2)" Nag Hammadi Library in English, ed. J.M. Robinson.
       New York, London, 1977. Pp. 117-30.

95.184 Koester, H. "One Jesus and Four Primitive Gospels," HTR
       61 (1968) 203-47. [repr. Trajectories through Early Chris-
       tianity, eds. H. Koester and J.M. Robinson. Philadelphia,
       1971. Pp. 158-204; German trans. Tübingen, 1971]

95.185 Kosnetter, J. "Das Thomasevangelium und die Synoptiker,"
       Wissenschaft im Dienst des Glaubens: Festschrift für Abt
       Dr. Hermann Peichl, ed. J. Kisser et al. (Studien der Wie-
       ner Katholischen Akademie 4) Vienna, 1965. Pp. 29-49.

95.186 Kraft, R.A. "Oxyrhynchus Papyrus 655 Reconsidered," HTR
       54 (1961) 253-62.

95.187 Krogmann, W. "Heliand, Tatian und Thomasevangelium," ZNW
       51 (1960) 255-68.

95.188 Krogmann, W. "Heiland und Thomasevangelium," VC 18 (1964)
       65-73.

95.189 Kuhn, K.H. "Some Observations on the Coptic Gospel Accord-
       ing to Thomas," Muséon 73 (1960) 317-23.

95.190 Kunderewicz, C. "Evangelia wg [=wedlug]św. Tomasza,"
       Euhemer 4:3 [=16] (1960) 18-30.

95.191 Lagrand, J. "How was the Virgin Mary 'Like a Man' ('yk
       gbr')? A Note on Mt. 1:18b and Related Syriac Christian
       Texts," NovT 22 (1980) 97-107.

95.192 Lane, W.L. "Critique of Purportedly Authentic Agrapha,"
       JETS 18 (1975) 29-35.

388   IV. Bibliography

95.193 Laurentin, R. "L'Évangile selon Saint Thomas: Situation et
       mystifications," Études 343 (1975) 733-51.

95.194 Leipoldt, J. "Bemerkungen zur Übersetzung des Thomas-
       Evangeliums," TLZ 85 (1960) 795-98.

95.195 Leipoldt, J. Das Evangelium nach Thomas, Koptisch und
       Deutsch (TU 101) Berlin, 1967.

95.196 Leipoldt, J. "Ein neues Evangelium? Das koptische Thomas-
       evangelium, übersetzt und besprochen," TLZ 83 (1958) 481-
       96.

95.197 Leipoldt, J. "Zur Ideologie der frühen koptischen Kirche,"
       Bulletin de la Société d'Archéologie 17 (1963-64) 101-10.

95.198 Lemaire, A. "Has a Fifth Gospel Been Found?" Documenta
       3 (1960) 83f. [in Finnish]

95.199 Liébaert, J. "Les 'Odes de Salomon' et l''Évangile selon
       Thomas,'" Les enseignements moraux des Pères apostoliques
       (Recherches et Synthèses, Section de Morale 4). Gembloux,
       1970. Pp. 227-53.

95.200 Lincoln, B. "Thomas-Gospel and Thomas-Community: A New
       Approach to a Familiar Text," NovT 19 (1977) 65-76.

95.201 Lindemann, A. "Zur Gleichnisinterpretation im Thomas-
       Evangelium," ZNW 71 (1980) 214-43.

95.202 Lunt, H.G. "On the Apocryphal Gospel of St. Thomas,"
       Pristapni predavanja, prilozi i biblijografija na novite clenovi
       na Makedonskata Akademija na naukite i Umetnostite. Skopje,
       1970. Pp. 99-104.

95.203 McArthur, H.K. "The Dependence of the Gospel of Thomas
       on the Synoptics," ExpT 71 (1960) 286f.

95.204 McArthur, H.K. "The Gospel According to Thomas," New
       Testament Sidelights: Essays in Honor of A.C. Purdy, ed.
       H.K. McArthur. Hartford, 1960. Pp. 43-77.

95.205 McArthur, H.K. "Parable of the Mustard Seed," CBQ 33
       (1971) 198-210.

95.206 McCaughey, J.D. "Two Synoptic Parables in the Gospel of
       Thomas," AusBR 8 (1960) 24-28.

95.207 MacRae, G.W. "The Gospel of Thomas--Logia Iesou?" CBQ
       22 (1960) 56-71.

95.208 Marcovich, M. "Bedeutung der Motive des Volksglaubens für
        die Textinterpretation," Quaderni Urbinati di Cultura Clas-
        sica 8 (1969) 22-36.

95.209 Marcovich, M. "Textual Criticism on the Gospel of Thomas,"
        JTS 20 (1969) 53-74.

95.210 Masing, U., and K. Rätsep. "Baarlam and Josaphat: Some
        Problems Connected with the Story of Baarlam and Josaphat,
        the Acts of Thomas, the Psalms of Thomas, and the Gospel
        of Thomas," Communio Viatorum 4 (1961) 29-36.

95.211 Meerburg, P.P. De structuur van het koptische Evangelie
        naar Thomas. Maastricht, 1964.

95.212 Mees, M. "Einige Überlegungen zum Thomasevangelium,"
        Vetera Christianorum 2 (1965) 151-63.

95.213 Mees, M. "Thomasevangelium," Vetera Christianorum 4 (1967)
        215-24.

95.214 Ménard, J.É. "Beziehungen des Philippus- und des Thomas-
        Evangeliums zur syrischen Welt," Altes Testament, Frühju-
        dentum, Gnosis: Neue Studien zu "Gnosis und Bibel,"
        ed. K.-W. Tröger. Gütersloh, 1980. Pp. 317-25.

95.215 Ménard, J.É. "Connaissance de Dieu et quête du salut dans
        le logion 3 de l'Évangile selon Thomas," Gnosticisme et
        monde hellénistique: Les objectifs du Colloque de Louvain-
        la-Neuve (11-14 mars 1980), eds. J. Ries and J.-M. Sevrin.
        Louvain-la-Neuve, 1980. Pp. 131f.

95.216 Ménard, J.-É. L'Évangile selon Thomas (NHS 5) Leiden, 1975.

95.217 Ménard, J.-É. "L'Évangile selon Thomas," BTS 176 (1975)
        12-14.

95.218 Ménard, J.-É. "L'Évangile selon Thomas," Laval Théologique
        et Philosophique 30 (1974) 29-45, 133-71.

95.219 Ménard, J.-É. "L'Évangile selon Thomas et le Nouveau Testa-
        ment," Studii Montis Regii 9 (1966) 147-53.

95.220 Ménard, J.-É. "Le milieu syriaque de l'évangile selon Thomas
        et de l'évangile selon Philippe," RScRel 42 (1968) 261-66,
        358-61.

95.221 Ménard, J.-É. "Les origines de la gnose," RScRel 42 (1968)
        24-38.

95.222 Ménard, J.-É. "Les problèmes de l'Évangile selon Thomas,"

Essays on the Nag Hammadi Texts in Honour of Alexander
Böhlig, ed. M. Krause (NHS 3) Leiden, 1972. Pp. 59-73.

95.223 Ménard, J.-É. "Les problèmes de l'Évangile selon Thomas,"
Studia Patristica. Vol. 14. Papers Presented to the Sixth
International Conference on Patristic Studies held in Oxford
1971. Part 3: Tertullian, Origenism, Gnostica, Cappadocian
Fathers, Augustiniana, ed. E.A. Livingstone. (TU 117)
Berlin, 1976. Pp. 209-28.

95.224 Ménard, J.-É. "La Sagesse et le logion 3 de l'Évangile selon
Thomas," Studia Patristica. Vol. 10. Papers Presented to
the Fifth International Conference on Patristic Studies held
in Oxford, 1967. Part 1: Editiones, Critica, Philoloqica,
Biblica, Historica, Liturgica et Ascetica, ed. F.L. Cross.
(TU 107) Berlin, 1970. Pp. 137-40.

95.225 Ménard, J.-É. "Syrische Einflüsse auf die Evangelien nach
Thomas und Philippus," XVII Deutscher Orientalistentag
July 21-27, 1968 Würzburg; Part 2, ed. W. Voigt (ZDMG
Supp. 2) Wiesbaden, 1969. Pp. 385-91.

95.226 Ménard, J.-É. "Der syrische Synkretismus und das Thomasevangelium," Synkretismus im syrisch-persischen Kulturgebiet:
Bericht über ein Symposion in Rheinhausen bei Göttingen in
der Zeit vom 4. bis 8. Oktober 1971, ed. A. Dietrich. (Abhandlungen der Akademie der Wissenschaften in Göttingen,
Philologisch-Historische Klasse, 3d. Ser. 96) Göttingen,
1975. Pp. 65-79.

95.227 Ménard, J.-É. "Thomas, Gospel of," IDBS. Pp. 902-05.

95.228 Menestrina, G. "Matteo 5-7 e Luca 6:20-49 nell' Evangelo di
Tommaso," BO 18 (1976) 65-67.

95.229 Menestrina, G. "Le parabole nell' 'Evangelo di Tommaso' e
nei Sinottici," BO 17 (1975) 79-82.

95.230 Metzger, B.M. "The Gospel of Thomas," Synopsis Quattuor
Evangeliorum: Locis parallelis evangeliorum apocryphorum
et patrum adhibitis, ed. K. Aland. Stuttgart, 1964. Pp.
517-30. [ET]

95.231 Michaelis, W. "Das gnostische Thomasevangelium," Der Bund.
3 Jahrgang, Nr. 21 (January 15, 1960).

95.232 Michaelis, W. Das Thomas-Evangelium. (Calwer Hefte 34)
Stuttgart, 1960.

95.233 Miller, B.F. "A Study of the Theme of 'Kingdom': The Gospel According to Thomas, Logion 18," NovT 9 (1967) 52-60.

95.234 Moe, O. "Det nyfunne Thomas-evangelium," Tidsskrift for
       Teologi og Kirke 29 (1958) 217f.

95.235 Montefiore, H.W. "A Comparison of the Parables of the Gos-
       pel According to Thomas and of the Synoptic Gospels," NTS
       7 (1961) 220-48.

95.236 Moraldi, L. "Vangelo copto di Tomaso," Apoc. del NT. 1.
       Pp. 475-501.

95.237 Morard, F. "Encore quelques réflexions sur monachos," VC
       34 (1980) 395-401.

95.238 Morard, F. "Monachos, Moine: Histoire du terme grec jusqu'au
       4e siècle; Influences bibliques et gnostiques," Freiburger
       Zeitschrift fur Philosophie und Theologie 20 (1973) 332-411.
       [see esp. pp. 362-77]

95.239 Morard, F. "Monachos: Une importation sémitique en Egypte?
       Quelques aperçus nouveaux," Studia Patristica. Vol. 12.
       Papers presented to the Sixth International Conference on
       Patristic Studies held in Oxford 1971. Part 1: Inaugural
       Lecture, Editiones, Critica, Philologica, Biblica, Historica,
       ed. E.A. Livingstone (TU 115) Berlin, 1975. Pp. 242-46.

95.240 Moravcsik, G. "'Hund in der Krippe': Zur Geschichte eines
       griechischen Sprichwortes," Acta Antiqua 12 (1964) 77-86.

95.241 Moschonas, T.O. "Ta Logia tou Iēsou ē to Neon Apokruphon
       Evangelion Thōma," Pantainos 51 (1959) 330-32; 52 (1960)
       60f., 88-91, 120-22, 148f., 182-84. [in modern Gk]

95.242 Mueller, D. "Kingdom of Heaven or Kingdom of God?" VC 27
       (1973) 266-76.

95.243 Munck, J. "Bemerkungen zum koptischen Thomasevangelium,"
       ST 14 (1960) 130-47.

95.244 Muñoz Iglesias, S. "El Evangelio de Tomás y algunos aspectos
       de la cuestión sinóptica," Estudios Eclesiásticos 34 (1960)
       883-94.

95.245 Myszor, W. "The Gospel According to Thomas," Ślaskie studie
       historyczno-teologiczne 5 (1972) 19-42. [Polish trans.]

95.246 Nagel, P. "Erwägungen zum Thomas-Evangelium," Die Araber
       in der Alten Welt, ed. F. Altheim and R. Stiehl. Berlin,
       1969. Vol. 5, Part 2. Pp. 368-92.

95.247 Nagel, P. "Die Parabel vom klugen Fischer im Thomas-
       evangelium von Nag Hammadi," Beiträge zur Alten Geschichte

und deren Nachleben: Festschrift für Franz Altheim 6-10-
1968, eds. R. Stiehl and H.E. Stier. Berlin, 1969. Pp.
518-24.

95.248 Nations, A.L. A Critical Study of the Coptic Gospel According to Thomas. Vanderbilt University Ph.D., 1960.

95.249 Navarro Arias, R. "El Evangelio Según Tomás: Palabras
Secretas de Jesús Viviente," Christus 27 (1962) 869-75.

95.250 Neusner, J. "Zaccheus/Zakkai," HTR 57 (1964) 57-59.

95.251 O'Flynn, J.A. "The Gospel According to Thomas," ITQ 27
(1960) 65-69.

95.252 Penna, A. "Vangelo di Tommaso," EncCatt. 12. Col. 241.

95.253 Peretto, E. "Loghia del Signore e Vangelo di Tommaso,"
RevistB 24 (1976) 13-56.

95.254 Perkins, P. "Pronouncement Stories in the Gospel of Thomas,"
Semeia 20 (1981) 121-32.

95.255 Perrin, N. "Thomas and the Synoptic Gospels," Rediscovering
the Teaching of Jesus. New York, London, 1967. Pp. 253f.

95.256 Petersen, W.L. "The Parable of the Lost Sheep in the Gospel
of Thomas and the Synoptics," NovT 23 (1981) 128-47.

95.257 Piper, O.A. "The Gospel of Thomas," Princeton Seminary
Bulletin 53 (1959) 18-24.

95.258 Piper, O.A. "A New Gospel? Does the Gospel of Thomas, not
Long ago Discovered in Egypt, Warrant Inclusion in the New
Testament Canon?" The Christian Century 77 (1960) 96-99.

95.259 Poggi, G.; G. Quispel; and G. Saldarini. "Ecco i nuovi detti
attribuiti a Gesù scoperti in una giara dell' Alto Egitto,"
Oggi 15:44 (October 29, 1959) 20-24.

95.260 Poggi, G.; G. Quispel; and G. Saldarini. "The Gospel of St.
Thomas: The New Papyrus from Egypt," Revue Pazamaveb
117 (1959) 205-07, 254-58; 118 (1960) 24-26. [in Armenian]

95.261 Pokorný, P. The Gospel of Thomas: Translation with Commentary. Prague, 1981. [in Czech]

95.262 Preuschen, E. "Aus dem Thomasevangelium," Antilegomena.
Giessen, 1905². Pp. 21, 150. [Gk. text]

95.263 Prigent, P. "L'Évangile selon Thomas: État de la question,"
RHPR 39 (1959) 39-45.

95.264 Puech, H.-C. "Une collection des paroles de Jésus récemment
        découverte en Égypte: L''Évangile selon Thomas,'" RHR
        153 (1958) 129-33. [cf. Bulletin de la Société Ernst Renan
        6 (1957) 11-15; repr. En quête, pp. 33-57]

95.265 Puech, H.-C. "Une collection de paroles de Jésus récemment
        retrouvée: L'Évangile selon Thomas," Comptes rendus de
        l'Académie des Incriptions et Belles-Lettres. Paris, 1957.
        Pp. 146-67.

95.266 Puech, H.-C. "Doctrines ésotériques et thèmes gnostiques
        dans l' 'Evangile selon Thomas,'" Annuaire du Collège de
        France 62 (1962) 195-203; 63 (1963) 199-213; 64 (1964) 209-
        17; 65 (1965) 247-56; 66 (1966) 259-62; 67 (1967) 253-60; 68
        (1968) 285-97; 69 (1969) 269-83; 70 (1970) 273-88; 71 (1971)
        251-68. [repr. En quête, pp. 93-284]

95.267 Puech, H.-C. En quête de la Gnose; II: Sur l'Évangile selon
        Thomas, Esquisse d'une interprétation systématique. (Bibli-
        othèque des Sciences Humaines) Paris, 1978.

95.268 Puech, H.-C. "Explication de l'Évangile selon Thomas et
        recherches sur les Paroles de Jésus qui y sont réunies,"
        Annuaire du Collège de France 58 (1958) 233-39; 59 (1959)
        255-64; 60 (1960) 181; 61 (1961) 175-81. [repr. En quête,
        pp. 65-91]

95.269 Puech, H.-C. "The Gospel of Thomas," HSW. 1. Pp. 278-
        307.

95.270 Puech, H.-C. "Un logion de Jésus bandelette funéraire,"
        RHR 147 (1955) 126-29. [cf. Bulletin de la Société Ernest
        Renan 3 (1954) 6-9; repr. En quête, pp. 59-63]

95.271 Quecke, H. "Erhebet euch, Kinder des Lichtes," Muséon 76
        (1963) 27-55.

95.272 Quecke, H. "Het Evangelie volgens Thomas," Streven 13
        (1959-60) 401-24.

95.273 Quecke, H. "Das Evangelium nach Thomas übersetzt," ThJ
        (1961) 224-36.*

95.274 Quecke, H. "L'Évangile de Thomas: État des recherches,"
        La Venue du Messie: Messianisme et Eschatologie, ed. É.
        Massaux (RechBib 6) Brussels, 1962. Pp. 217-41.

95.275 Quecke, H. "'Sein Haus seines Königreiches': Zum Thomas-
        evangelium 85.9f.," Muséon 76 (1963) 47-53.

95.276 Quispel, G. "The Diatessaron and the Historical Jesus,"

Studi e Materiali di Storia delle Religioni 38 [Pincherle Fest-
schrift] (1967) 463-72.

95.277 Quispel, G. "L'Évangile de Thomas et les Clémentines," VC
        12 (1958) 181-96. [repr. in Gnostic Studies (Uitgaven van
        het Nederlands historisch-archeologisch instituut te Ishtanbul
        34) 2 vols. Istanbul, 1975. Vol. 2. Pp. 17-29]

95.278 Quispel, G. "L'Évangile selon Thomas et le Diatessaron,"
        VC 13 (1959) 87-117. [repr. in Gnostic Studies (Uitgaven
        van het Nederlands historisch-archeologisch instituut te
        Ishtanbul 34) 2 vols. Istanbul, 1975. Vol. 2. Pp. 31-55]

95.279 Quispel, G. "L'Évangile selon Thomas et le 'texte occidental'
        du Nouveau Testament," VC 14 (1960) 204-15.

95.280 Quispel, G. Het Evangelie van Thomas en de Nederlanden.
        Amsterdam, Brussels, 1971.

95.281 Quispel, G. "L'Évangile selon Thomas et les origines de
        l'ascèse chrétienne," Aspects du judéo-christianisme: Col-
        loque de Strasbourg 23-25 Avril 1964 (Bibliothèque des Cen-
        tres d'Études supérieures spécialisés) Paris, 1965. Pp. 35-
        51. [repr. Gnostic Studies (Uitgaven van het Nederlands
        historisch-archaeologisch instituut te Ishtanbul 34) 2 vols.
        Istanbul, 1975. Vol. 2. Pp. 98-112]

95.282 Quispel, G. "Gnosis and the New Sayings of Jesus," EJ 38
        (1969) 261-96. [repr. in Gnostic Studies (Uitgaven van het
        Nederlands historisch-archeologisch instituut te Ishtanbul 34)
        2 vols. Istanbul, 1975. Vol. 2. Pp. 180-209]

95.283 Quispel, G. "Gnosticism and the New Testament," VC 19
        (1965) 65-85.

95.284 Quispel, G. "The Gospel According to Thomas," The Listener
        and B.B.C. Television Review 63 (1960) 389f.

95.285 Quispel, G. "'The Gospel of Thomas' and the 'Gospel of the He-
        brews,'" NTS 12 (1965) 371-82.

95.286 Quispel, G. "The Gospel of Thomas and the New Testament,"
        VC 11 (1957) 189-207. [repr. in Gnostic Studies (Uitgaven
        van het Nederlands historisch-archeologisch instituut te Ish-
        tanbul, 34) 2 vols. Istanbul, 1975. Vol. 2. Pp. 3-16]

95.287 Quispel, G. "The Gospel of Thomas and the Western Text:
        A Reappraisal," Gnostic Studies (Uitgaven van het Nederlands
        historisch-archaeologisch instituut te Ishtanbul 34) 2 vols.
        Istanbul, 1975. Vol. 2. Pp. 56-69.

95.288 Quispel, G. "Der Heliand und das Thomasevangelium," VC
       16 (1962) 121-51. [repr. in Gnostic Studies (Uitgaven van
       het Nederlands historisch-archeologisch instituut te Ishtanbul
       34) 2 vols. Istanbul, 1975. Vol. 2. Pp. 70-97]

95.289 Quispel, G. "Jewish-Christian Gospel Tradition," Gospel Stud-
       ies in Honor of Sherman Elbridge Johnson, ed. M.H. Shep-
       herd, Jr. and E.C. Hobbs (ATR Supplementary Series 3)
       Evanston, 1974. Pp. 112-16. [re. Mt 13:47-50 and GosTh,
       Logion 8]

95.290 Quispel, G. "Jewish Influences on the 'Heliand,'" Religions in
       Antiquity: Essays in Memory of Erwin Ramsdell Goodenough,
       ed. J. Neusner (Sup Numen 14) Leiden, 1968. Pp. 244-50.

95.291 Quispel, G. "The Latin Tatian or the Gospel of Thomas in
       Limburg," JBL 88 (1969) 321-30. [repr. in Gnostic Studies
       (Uitgaven van het Nederlands historisch-archaeologisch insti-
       tuut te Ishtanbul 34) 2 vols. Istanbul, 1975. Vol. 2, pp.
       159-68]

95.292 Quispel, G. "Lindger en het evangelie van Thomas," Rondom
       het Woord 13 (1971) 207-18.

95.293 Quispel, G. "Het Luikse 'Leven van Jezus' en het joden-
       christelijke 'Evangelie der Hebreeën,'" De Nieuwe Taalgids
       51 (1958) 241-49.

95.294 Quispel, G. Makarius, das Thomasevangelium und das Lied
       von der Perle (NovTSup 15) Leiden, 1967.

95.295 Quispel, G. "Neugefundene Worte Jesu," Universitas 13 (1958)
       359-66.

95.296 Quispel, G. "Saint Augustin et l'Évangile selon Thomas,"
       Mélanges d'histoire des religions offerts à Henri-Charles
       Puech, eds. P. Lévy and E. Wolff. Paris, 1974. Pp. 375-
       78.

95.297 Quispel, G. "Some Remarks on the Diatessaron Haarense,"
       VC 25 (1971) 131-39.

95.298 Quispel, G. "Some Remarks on the Gospel of Thomas," NTS
       5 (1959) 276-90.

95.299 Quispel, G. "The Syrian Thomas and the Syrian Macarius,"
       VC 18 (1964) 226-35. [repr. in Gnostic Studies (Uitgaven
       van het Nederlands historisch-archaeologisch instituut te
       Ishtanbul 34) 2 vols. Istanbul, 1975. Vol. 2. Pp. 113-21.]

95.300 Quispel, G. Tatian and the Gospel of Thomas: Studies in
       the History of the Western Diatessaron. Leiden, 1975.

95.301 Quispel, G. "Tatianus Latinus," NedThT 21 (1967) 409-19.

95.302 Quispel, G. "Thomas, Het Evangelie van," Christelijke En-
       cyclopedie, ed. F.W. Grosheide and G.P. van Itterzon.
       Kampen, 1961. Vol. 6. P. 365.

95.303 Quispel, G. "Das Thomasevangelium und das Alte Testament,"
       Neotestamentica et Patristica: Eine Freundesgabe, Herrn
       Professor Dr. Oscar Cullman zu seinem 60. Geburtstag Über-
       reicht, ed. W.C. van Unnik (NovTSup 6) Leiden, 1962. Pp.
       243-48.

95.304 Quispel, G. "Unknown Sayings of Jesus," Universitas 2
       (1958-59) 123-30.

95.305 Quispel, G. "De Woorden van Jesus," Post Iucundam Iuventu-
       tem: Orgaan van het Utrechts Universiteitsfonds 22 (January
       1958).*

95.306 Refoulé, F. "L'Évangile de Thomas n'a pas servi à la rédaction
       des 4 évangiles," Informations Catholiques Internationales
       475 (1975) 21-23.

95.307 Reichelt, J. "Das 'Evangelium' nach Thomas," Im Lande der
       Bibel 8 (1962) 9-14.

95.308 Rengstorf, K.H. "Urchristliches Kerygma und 'gnostische'
       Interpretation in einigen Sprüchen des Thomasevangeliums,"
       Le origini dello gnosticismo: Colloquio di Messina 13-18
       Aprile 1966, ed. U. Bianchi (Sup Numen 12) Leiden, 1967.
       Pp. 563-74.

95.309 Richardson, C.C. "The Gospel of Thomas: Gnostic or En-
       cratite?" OCA 195 (1973) 65-75.

95.310 Rist, M. "The Fable of the Dog in the Manger in the Gospel
       of Thomas," Iliff Review 25 (1968) 13-25.

95.311 Roberts, C.H. "The Gospel of Thomas: Logion 30A," JTS
       21 (1970) 91f.

95.312 Robinson, J.M. "Interim Collations in Codex II and the Gos-
       pel of Thomas," Mélanges d'histoire des religions offerts à
       Henri-Charles Puech, eds. P. Lévy and E. Wolff. Paris,
       1974. Pp. 379-92.

95.313 Roques, R. "L''Évangile selon Thomas': Son édition critique
       et son identification," RHR 157 (1960) 187-218. [repr. in
       Structures théologiques de la gnose à Richard de Saint-Victor:
       Essais et analyses critiques (Bibliothèque de l'École des Hautes
       Études, Sections des Sciences Religieuses 72) Paris, 1962.
       Pp. 13-39]

95.314 Roques, R. "Gnosticisme et christianisme: L'Évangile selon Thomas," Irénikon 33 (1960) 29-40.

95.315 Rosa, G. de. "Un quinto vangelo? Il 'Vangelo secondo Tommaso,'" Civiltà Cattolica 3 (1960) 496-512.

95.316 Rudolph, K. "Gnosis und Gnostizismus: Ein Forschungsbericht," ThRu 34 (1969) 181-231.

95.317 Salvoni, F. "L'Evangelo secondo Tommaso," Ricerche Bibliche e Religiose 6 (1971) 177-205.

95.318 Santos Otero, A. de. "Evangelio de Tomas," Evangelios Apócrifos. Pp. 60-62.

95.319 Saunders, E.W. "A Trio of Thomas Logia," Biblical Research 8 (1963) 43-59.

95.320 Säve-Söderbergh, T., tr. Evangelium Veritatis och Thomasevangeliet. (Symbolae Biblicae Upsalienses 16) Uppsala, 1959.

95.321 Säve-Söderbergh, T. "Gnostic and Canonical Gospel Traditions (with special reference to the Gospel of Thomas)," Le origini dello gnosticismo: Colloquio di Messina 13-18 Aprile 1966, ed. U. Bianchi. (Sup Numen 12) Leiden, 1967. Pp. 552-62.

95.322 Schäfer, K.T. "Das neuentdeckte Thomasevangelium," Bibel und Leben 1 (1960) 62-74.

95.323 Schäfer, K.T. "Der Primat Petri und das Thomas-Evangelium," Die Kirche und ihre Amter und Stände: Festgabe seiner Eminenz dem hochwürdigsten Herrn Joseph Kardinal Frings, Erzbischof von Köln zum goldenen Priesterjubiläum am 10. August 1960 dargeboten, ed. W. Corsten et al. Cologne, 1960. Pp. 353-63.

95.324 Schenke, H.-M. "Thomasevangelium," BHH. 3. P. 1975.

95.325 Schippers, R. Het Evangelie van Thomas: Apocriefe woorden van Jezus. Kampen, 1960.

95.326 Schippers, R. "Het evangelie van Thomas een onafhankelijke traditie? Antwoord aan professor Quispel," Gereformeerd theologisch tijdschrift 61 (1961) 46-54.

95.327 Schippers, R. "The Mashal-character of the Parable of the Pearl," Studia Evangelica. Vol. 2: Papers Presented to the Second International Congress on New Testament Studies held at Christ Church, Oxford, 1961. Part 1: The New

Testament Scriptures, ed. F.L. Cross (TU 87) Berlin, 1964.
Pp. 236-41.

95.328 Schlatter, T. "Thomas, Evangelie van," Bijbelse Encyclopedie
met Handboek en Concordantie, ed. S.P. Dee and J. Schon-
veld. Baarn, 1969. Vol. 3. P. 275.

95.329 Schlatter, T. "Thomas-Evangelium," Calwer Bibellexikon, ed.
K. Gutbrod et al. Stuttgart, 1959. P. 1316; 1967^2. P.
1339.

95.330 Schmidt, K.O. Die geheimen Herren-Worte des Thomas-
Evangeliums: Wegweisungen Christi zur Selbstvollendung.
Pfullingen-Württ, 1966.

95.331 Schneemelcher, W., and J. Jeremias. "Sayings-Collections on
Papyrus," HSW. 1. Pp. 97-113.

95.332 Schneemelcher, W., and J. Jeremias. "Spruchsammlungen auf
Papyrus," HS. 1. Pp. 61-72.

95.333 Schnider, F. "Das Gleichnis vom verlorenen Schaf und seine
Redaktoren: Ein intertextueller Vergleich," Kairos 19 (1977)
146-54.

95.334 Schoedel, W.R. "The Gospel in the New Gospels," Dialog 6
(1967) 115-22. [an examination of the importance of the Nag
Hammadi gospels for the study of the canonical gospels]

95.335 Schoedel, W.R. "Naassene Themes in the Coptic Gospel of
Thomas," VC 14 (1960) 225-34.

95.336 Schoedel, W.R. "Parables in the Gospel of Thomas: Oral
Tradition or Gnostic Exegesis?" CTM 43 (1972) 548-60.

95.337 Schrage, W. "Evangelienzitate in den Oxyrhynchus-Logien
und im koptischen Thomas- Evangelium," Apophoreta:
Festschrift für Ernst Haenchen, ed. W. Eltester and F.H.
Kettler (BZNW 30) Berlin, 1964. Pp. 251-68.

95.338 Schrage, W. Das Verhältnis des Thomas-Evangeliums zur synoptischen Tradition und zu den koptischen Evangelienüberset-
zungen: Zugleich ein Beitrag zur gnostischen Synoptiker-
deutung (BZNW 29) Berlin, 1964.

95.339 Schürmann, H. "Das Thomasevangelium und das lukanische
Sondergut," BZ 7 (1963) 236-60. [repr. in Traditionsges-
chichtliche Untersuchungen zu den synoptischen Evangelien:
Beiträge (Kommentare und Beiträge zum Alten und Neuen
Testament) Düsseldorf, 1968. Pp. 228-47]

95.340 Sekiya, S. "Notes on the Gospel of Thomas," Seinangakuin Daigaku Shingakubu Kenkyû 10 (1960) 25-54. [in Japanese]

95.341 Sell, J. "Johannine Traditions in Logion 61 of the Gospel of Thomas," Perspectives in Religious Studies 7 (1980) 24-37.

95.342 Serrou, R. "Deux mille ans après, St. Thomas l'incrédule parle ...," Paris Match 1337 (January 11, 1975) 58f.

95.343 Sevenster, J.N. "Geeft den Keizer, wat des Keizers is, en Gode, Wat Gods is," NedThT 17 (1962/63) 21-31.

95.344 Sevenster, J.N. "Het evangelie naar Thomas en de synoptische evangeliën," Vox Theologica 32 (1961-62) 9-17.

95.345 Sevrin, J.-M. "L'Évangile selon Thomas: Paroles de Jésus et révélation gnostique," Revue Théologique de Louvain 8 (1977) 265-92.

95.346 Sheppard, J.B. A Study of the Parables Common to the Synoptic Gospels and the Coptic Gospel of Thomas. Emory University Ph.D., 1965.

95.347 Sieber, J.H. A Redactional Analysis of the Synoptic Gospels with Regard to the Question of the Sources of the Gospel According to Thomas. Claremont Graduate School Ph.D., 1966.

95.348 Smelik, K.A.D. "Aliquanta ipsius Sancti Thomas," VC 28 (1974) 290-94.

95.349 Smith, J.Z. "The Garments of Shame," History of Religions 5 (1965-66) 217-38. [repr. in Map is not Territory (Studies in Judaism in Late Antiquity 23) Leiden, 1978. Pp. 1-23]

95.350 Smyth, K. "Gnosticism in the 'Gospel According to Thomas,'" HibJ 1 (1960) 189-98.

95.351 Snodgrass, K.R. "The Parable of the Wicked Husbandmen: Is the Gospel of Thomas Version the Original?" NTS 21 (1974) 142-44.

95.352 Spadafora, F. "Tommaso (Vangelo di)," Dizionario Biblico, ed. F. Spadafora. Rome, 1963³. Pp. 602f.

95.353 Spivey, R.A. The Origin and Milieu of the Gospel According to Thomas. Yale University Ph.D., 1961.

95.354 Stead, G.C. "New Gospel Discoveries," Theology 62 (1959) 321-27.

95.355 Stead, G.C. "Some Reflections on the Gospel of Thomas,"
        Studia Evangelica. Vol. 3: Papers Presented to the Second
        International Congress on New Testament Studies Held at
        Christ Church, Oxford, 1961. Part 2: The New Testament
        Message, ed. F.L. Cross (TU 88) Berlin, 1964. Pp. 390-
        402.

95.356 Stegmüller, F. Repertorium Biblicum. 8. Pp. 133-35.

95.357 Strobel, A. "Textgeschichtliches zum Thomas-Logion 86 (Mt.
        8:20; Luke 9:58)," VC 17 (1963) 211-24.

95.358 Suarez, P. de. L'Évangile selon Thomas: Traduction, Présen-
        tation et Commentaires. Marsanne, 1975². [Coptic text and
        French trans.]

95.359 Summers, R. The Secret Sayings of the Living Jesus: Stud-
        ies in the Coptic Gospel According to Thomas. Waco, Texas,
        1968.

95.360 Taylor, R.E. "The 'Gospel of Thomas': Gnosticism and the
        New Testament," Christianity Today 4 (1959/60) 303-05.

95.361 Thieme, K. "Neues Evangelium? Zum Fund eines ägyptischen
        Textes," Hochland 52 (1959-60) 307-14.

95.362 Till, W.C. "Das Evangelium nach Thomas," Österreichische
        Hochschulzeitung 2 (1959) 2.

95.363 Till, W.C. "New Sayings of Jesus in the Recently Discovered
        Coptic 'Gospel of Thomas,'" BJRL 41 (1959) 446-58.

95.364 Trencsényi-Waldapfel, I. "Der Hund in der Krippe," Acta
        Orientalia (Budapest) 14 (1962) 139-43.

95.365 Trencsényi-Waldapfel, I. "Das Thomas-Evangelium aus Nag'
        Hammädi und Lukian von Samosata," Acta Orientalia (Buda-
        pest) 13 (1961) 131-33.

95.366 Trevijano Etcheverria, R. "La escatología del Evangelio de
        Tomás (Logion 3)," Salmanticensis 28 (1981) 415-41.

95.367 Trevijano Etcheverria, R. "Gnosticismo y hermenéutica (Evan-
        gelio de Tomás, Logion 1)," Salmanticensis 26 (1979) 51-74.

95.368 Tripp, D.H. "The Aim of the Gospel of Thomas," ExpT 92
        (1980) 41-44.

95.369 Trofimov, M.K. "From the Manuscript of Nag Hammadi,"
        Antič'nost' i Sovremenost' K 80-letija F.A. Petrovskogo.
        Moscow, 1972. Pp. 369-80. [in Russian]

95.370 Tröger, K.W. ed. Altes Testament-Früjudentum-Gnosis: Neue
        Studien zu Gnosis und Bibel. Gütersloh, 1980.

95.371 Trummer, P. "Thomas-Evangelium," Praktisches Bibellexikon,
        ed. A. Grabner-Haider. Freiburg, 1969. P. 1086.

95.372 Turner, H.E.W., and H. Montefiore. Thomas and the Evan-
        gelists (SBT 35) London, 1962.

95.373 Unnik, W. C. van. Newly Discovered Gnostic Writings: A
        Preliminary Survey of the Nag-Hammadi Find. (SBT 30)
        London, 1960. Pp. 46-57. [trans. of Openbaringen uit
        Egyptisch Zand]

95.374 Vielhauer, P. "Anapausis: Zum gnostischen Hintergrund des
        Thomasevangeliums," Apophoreta: Festschrift für Ernst
        Haenchen zu seinem siebzigsten Geburtstag am 10. Dezember
        1964, ed. W. Eltester and F.H. Kettler. (BZNW 30) Berlin,
        1964. Pp. 281-99. [repr. in Vielhauer, Aufsätze zum Neuen
        Testament (Theologische Bücherei 31) Munich, 1965. Pp.
        215-34]

95.375 Vielhauer, P. "Das Thomasevangelium," Geschichte der ur-
        christlichen Literatur: Einleitung in das Neue Testament,
        die Apokryphen und die Apostolischen Väter. Berlin, New
        York, 1975; rev. ed. 1978. Pp. 618-35.

95.376 Vogt, E. "Versio coptica 'Evangelii secundum Thomam,'" Bib
        38 (1957) 376.

95.377 Vrana, J. "Jesu li logiji Tomina evanđelja preuzeti iz kojeg
        kanonskog evanđelja?" Bogoslovska Smotra 46 (1976) 229-53.

95.378 Vrana, J. "'The Gospel of Thomas' and the Canonical Gospels,"
        Bogoslovska Smotra 45 (1975) 381-95. [in Serbo-Croatian]

95.379 Waller, E. "The Parable of the Leaven: A Sectarian Teaching
        and the Inclusion of Women," Union Seminary Quarterly Re-
        view 35 (1980) 99-109.

95.380 Walls, A.F. "The References to Apostles in the Gospel of
        Thomas," NTS 7 (1961) 266-70.

95.381 Walls, A.F. "'Stone' and 'Wood' in Oxyrhynchus Papyri I,"
        VC 16 (1962) 71-76.

95.382 Wautier, A. "L'Évangile selon Thomas: Introduction, version
        française et notes," Cahiers du Cercle Ernest-Renan 21
        (1973) 1-24.

95.383 Wautier, A. "Thomas, jumeau de Thaddée ou de Jésus?"
        Cahiers du Cercle Ernest-Renan 18 (1971) 66-68.

95.384 Wilson, R. McL. "The Coptic 'Gospel of Thomas,'" NTS 5
       (1958-59) 273-76.

95.385 Wilson, R. McL. "Further 'Unknown Sayings of Jesus,'"
       ExpT 69 (1957-58) 182.

95.386 Wilson, R. McL. "The Gospel of Thomas," ExpT 70 (1959)
       324f.

95.387 Wilson, R. McL. "The Gospel of Thomas," HSW. 1. Pp. 511-
       22.

95.388 Wilson, R. McL. "The Gospel of Thomas," Studia Evangelica.
       Vol. 3: Papers Presented to the Second International Con-
       gress on New Testament Studies held at Christ Church, Ox-
       ford, 1961. Part 2: The New Testament Message, ed. F.L.
       Cross. (TU 88) Berlin, 1964. Pp. 447-59.

95.389 Wilson, R. McL. "Light on Sayings of Jesus: Interpreting
       the 'Gospel of Thomas,'" Bible Translator 2 (1960) 132-35.

95.390 Wilson, R. McL. "Light on the Sayings of Jesus: Interpreting
       the 'Gospel of Thomas,'" The Daily Telegraph of Morning
       Post No. 32, 337 (Monday, April 6, 1959) 10.

95.391 Wilson, R. McL. "Nag Hammadi and the New Testament,"
       NTS 28 (1982) 289-302.

95.392 Wilson, R. McL. "Second Thoughts: The Gnostic Gospels from
       Nag Hammadi," ExpT 78 (1966) 36-41.

95.393 Wilson, R. McL. Studies in the Gospel of Thomas. London,
       1960.

95.394 Wilson, R. McL. "'Thomas' and the Growth of the Gospels,"
       HTR 53 (1960) 231-50.

95.395 Wilson, R. McL. "Thomas and the Synoptic Gospels," ExpT
       72 (1960) 36-39.

95.396 Wilson, R. McL. "Thomas, Gospel of," ZPEB. 5. Pp. 735f.

95.397 Wright, D.F. "Thomas, Gospel of," The New International
       Dictionary of the Christian Church, ed. J.D. Douglas.
       Grand Rapids, 1974. P. 971.

96. THOMAS, INFANCY GOSPEL OF

(See also 1.12, 18, 67, 75, 86, 88, 116, 147, 284, 327, 484, 531; 5.187.

96.1   Adrianova, V.P.   "The Gospel of Thomas in Ancient Ukrainian
       Literature," IzvORJS 14.2 (1909) 1-47. [in Russian]

96.2   Aitzetmüller, R.   Anzeiger für slavische Philologie 3 (1969)
       142-49.*

96.3   Amann, É.   "Évangile de Thomas," DBSup. 1. Cols. 485f.

96.4   Archangel'skij, A.S.   "On South Slavic History ...," IzvORJS
       4 (1899) 103-10. [in Russian]

96.5   Bagatti, B.   "Nota sul Vangelo di Tommaso Israelita," ED
       29 (1976) 482-89.

96.6   Bakšič, M.M.   From Old Serbian Literature. Belgrade, 1931[4].
       Pp. 93-95. [in Serbo-Croatian]

96.7   Bardenhewer, O.   "Das Matthias-, das Philippus- und das
       Thomasevangelium," GAL. 1. Pp. 529-33.

96.8   Bauer, J.B.   Neutest. Apok. Pp. 52-54.

96.9   Bock, E.   Urchristentum. Vol. 2: Kindheit und Jugend Jesu
       (Beiträge zur Geistesgeschichte der Menschheit, 2nd series)
       4 vols. Stuttgart, 1937-66.

96.10 Bonaccorsi, P.G.   "Lo Pseudo Tommaso (Racconti dell' infanzia
       del Signore di Tommaso filosofo israelita)," Vangeli Apocrifi.
       1. Pp. 110-51. [Gk. text and Italian trans.]

96.11 Bonsirven, J., and C. Bigaré.   "Évangiles de l'Enfance,"
       Intro. à la Bible. 2. Pp. 754f.

96.12 Bonwetsch, N.   "Evang. Thomae," Gesch. altchrist. Lit. 1.
       P. 910.

96.13 Borberg, K.F.   Bibliotek der neutestamentlichen Apocryphen
       gesammelt, übersetz und erläutert. Stuttgart, 1841. Pp.
       57-84.

96.14 Boulton, M.B.M.   The Old French 'Évangile de l'Enfance':
       A Critical Edition. University of Pennsylvania Diss., 1976.

96.15 Budge, E.A.W.   The History of the Blessed Virgin Mary and
       the History of the Likeness of Christ (Luzac's Semitic Text
       and Translation Series 4,5) 2 vols. London, 1899; repr.
       New York, 1976. Vol. 1. Pp. 217-22.

96.16 Burmeister, K.H.S.   "Fragments of an Arabic Version of Two
       Infancy Gospels," SOC Collectanea 7 (1962) 103-14. [Arab.
       Text]

96.17   Carney, J. "The Irish Gospel of Thomas: Text, Translation
        and Notes," Eriu 18 (1958) 1-43.

96.18   Carney, J. ed. The Poems of Blathmac, Son of Cú Brettan:
        Together with the Irish Gospel of Thomas and a Poem on the
        Virgin Mary. Dublin, 1964.

96.19   Cartlidge, D.R., and D.L. Dungan. "The Infancy Gospel of
        Thomas," Documents. Pp. 92-97. [ET]

96.20   Cecchelli, C. Mater Christi. Rome, 1954. Vol. 3. Pp. 351-
        62.

96.21   Clemens, R. Die geheimgehaltenen oder sogenannten apokry-
        phen Evangelien. Stuttgart, 1850. Vol. 2. Pp. 59-88.

96.22   Conrady, L. "Das Thomasevangelium: Ein wissenschaftlicher
        Kritischer Versuch," TSK 76 (1903) 377-459.

96.23   Cosquin, E. "Un épisode d'un évangile syriaque et les contes
        de l'Inde: Le serpent ingrat, l'enfant roi et juge," RB 16
        (1919) 136-57.

96.24   Cotelerius, J.B. Notae ad Constitutiones Apostolorum. 1724.
        Pp. 348ff. [Gk. and Lat. texts]*

96.25   Cowper, B.H. "The Gospel of Thomas," Apocryphal Gospels.
        Pp. 128-69. [ET]

96.26   Cowper, B.H. "The Gospel of Thomas," The Great Rejected
        Books of the Biblical Apocrypha (The Sacred Books and
        Early Literature of the East 14) New York, London, 1917.
        Pp. 253-60. [ET]

96.27   Cowper, B.H. "The Syriac Gospel of the Boyhood of Our
        Lord Jesus," Apocryphal Gospels. Pp. 448-56. [ET]

96.28   Cullmann, O. "The Infancy Story of Thomas," HSW. 1. Pp.
        388-401.

96.29   Cullmann, O. "Kindheitserzählung des Thomas," HS. 1. Pp.
        290-99.

96.30   Delatte, A. "Textes grecs inédits relatifs à l'histoire des re-
        ligions," Anecdota Atheniensia I. Bibliothèque de la Faculté
        de Philosophie et Lettres de l'Université de Liège 36 (1927)
        264-71. [Gk. and Lat. texts]

96.31   Dragomanov, M. "The Slavic Variants of One Gospel Legend,"
        Sbornik za narodni umotvorenija, nauka i knižnina 4 (1891)
        257-69. [in Bulgarian]

96.32 Dujcev, I. Natural Science in Medieval Bulgaria. Sofia, 1954.
       Pp. 182-85, 754. [in Bulgarian]

96.33 Erbetta, M. "Ta Paidika tu Kyriu (Ps. Tommaso)," Apoc. del
       NT. 1.2. Pp. 78-101.

96.34 Eysinga, G. van den Bergh. Indische Einflüsse auf evange-
       lische Erzählungen (FRLANT 4) Ruprecht, 1909. Pp. 63-67,
       90-96.

96.35 Fabricius, J.A. "Evangelium Infantiae Christi, Adscriptum
       Thomae Apostolo," Cod.Apoc.NT. 1. Pp. 127-67. [Gk.
       text and Lat. trans.]

96.36 Findlay, A.F. "Childhood Gospels," Byways. Pp. 170-78.

96.37 Fotinskij, O.A. On the Literary History of South Russian
       Apocrypha (Počaev-Žytomir 1896: Volynskij Istoriko-
       Archeologičeskij Sbornik, vyp. I). [in Russian]*

96.38 Franko, I. Apocrypha and Legends. L'vov, 1898. Vol. 2.
       Pp. 159-63, 169-72. [in Russian]

96.39 Fuchs, A. and F. Weissengruber. Konkordanz zum Thomas-
       evangelium: Version A and B (SNTU Ser. B. 4) Linz, 1978.

96.40 Garitte, G. "Le fragment géorgien de l''Évangile de Thomas,'"
       RHE 51 (1956) 513-20.

96.41 Gero, S. "The Infancy Gospel of Thomas: A Study of the
       Textual and Literary Problems," NovT 13 (1971) 46-80.

96.42 Gonzáles-Blanco, E. Los Evangelios Apócrifos. Madrid, 1935.
       Vol. 2. Pp. 5-41.

96.43 Grabar, B. "The Glagolitic Fragment of the Gospel of Pseudo-
       Thomas," Slovo 18 (1969) 213-31. [see also pp. 386-90; in
       Serbo-Croatian]

96.44 Grébaut, S. "Aperçu sur les miracles de Notre-Seigneur,"
       ROC 16 (1911) 255-65, 356-67.

96.45 Grébaut, S. "Les miracles de Jésus: Texte éthiopien publié
       et traduit," PO 12 (1918) 557-649; 14 (1921) 775-840; 17
       (1923) 787-854. [Eth. text and French trans.]

96.46 Harnack, A. "Das Thomasevangelium," Gesch. altchrist. Lit.
       2.1. Pp. 593-95.

96.47 Hayes, W. The Gospel According to Thomas. London, 1921.

96.48   Hofmann, J.C.K. Das Leben Jesu nach den Apokryphen in
        Zusammenhang aus den Quellen erzählt und wissenschaftlich
        untersucht. Leipzig, 1851. Pp. 144-265.

96.49   Iglesias, S.M. "Los Evangelios de la Infancia y las infancias
        de los héroes," EBib 16 (1957) 5-36.

96.50   Ivanov, J. Bogomil Books and Legends. Sofia, 1925. Pp.
        230-48. [in Bulgarian]

96.51   Jacimirskij, A.I. From Slavic Manuscripts ... (The University
        of Moscow: Historico-Philological Department) Moscow, 1899.
        Pp. 93-143. [in Russian]

96.52   James, M.R. "Gospel of Thomas," ANT. Pp. 49-70.

96.53   James, M.R. "The Gospel of Thomas," JTS 30 (1928) 51-54.

96.54   Lavrov, P.A. "Apocryphal Texts," SbORJS 67 (1899) 111-18.
        [in Russian]

96.55   Lipsius, R.A. Die apokryphen Apostelgeschichten und Apos-
        tellegenden. 2 vols. Brunswick, 1883-1890; repr. Amster-
        dam, 1976. Vol. 2. P. 24.

96.56   Lowe, M. "'Ioudaioi' of the Apocrypha: A Fresh Approach
        to the Gospels of James, Pseudo-Thomas, Peter and Nicode-
        mus," NovT 23 (1981) 56-90.

96.57   Lüdtke, W. "Die slavischen Texte des Thomas-Evangeliums,"
        ByzNGrJ 6 (1927) 490-508.

96.58   Lunt, H.G. "On the Apocryphal Gospel of St. Thomas,"
        Pristapni predavanja prilozi i bibliografija na novite clenovi
        na Makedonskata Akademija na naukite i umetnostite. Skopje,
        1970. Pp. 99-104.

96.59   Lunt, H.G. The Slavonic and East European Journal 12 (1968)
        488-90.*

96.60   McNamara, M. "Notes on the Irish Gospel of Thomas," ITQ
        38 (1971) 42-66.

96.61   McNeil, B. "Jesus and the Alphabet," JTS 27 (1976) 126-28.

96.62   Meyer, A. "Kindheitserzählung des Thomas," H². Pp. 93-102.

96.63   Meyer, A. "Kindheitserzählung des Thomas," Handbuch, ed.
        Hennecke. Pp. 132-42.

96.64 Michaelis, W. "Kindheitserzählung des Thomas," Apokryphen Schriften. Pp. 96-111.

96.65 Michel, C. "Évangile de Thomas," EvApoc. 1. Pp. xxiii-xxxii, 161-189.

96.66 Migne, J.-P. "Thomas. (Évangile de Thomas l'Israélite.)," Dictionnaire. 1. Cols. 1137-56. [Intro. and French trans.]

96.67 Milikset-Bek, L. Christianskij Vostok 6 (1917) 20.*

96.68 Mingarelli, G.L. Nuova raccolta d'opuscoli scientifici e filologici. Venice, 1764. Vol. 12. Pp. 73-155. [Gk. text]

96.69 Moraldi, L. "Vangelo di Tomaso," Apoc. del NT. 1. Pp. 247-79.

96.70 Müller, J.J. "Die Evangelie van Thomas," Nuwe-Test. Apok. Pp. 13-20. [Afrikaans trans.]

96.71 Noret, J. "Pour une édition de l'Évangile de l'Enfance selon Thomas," AnBoll 90 (1972) 412.

96.72 Novaković, S. "The Apocrypha of a Serbian-Cyrillic Collection of the Fourteenth Century," Starine 8 (1876) 48-55. [in Serbo-Croatian]

96.73 Patera, A. Časopis Musea Král. Ceského (1885) 114-26; (1889) 454-59.*

96.74 Peeters, P. Évangiles apocryphes II: L'Évangile de l'Enfance. Rédactions syriaques, arabe et arméniennes traduites et annotées par P.P. Paris, 1914.

96.75 Penna, A. "Vangelo di Tommaso," EncCatt. 12. Col. 241.

96.76 Philippart, G. "Fragments palimpsestes latins du Vindobonensis 563 (Ve siècle?): Évangile selon S. Matthieu, Évangile de Nicodème, Évangile de l'Enfance selon Thomas," AnBoll 90 (1972) 391-411.

96.77 Popov, A. An Account of Manuscripts and Catalogue of the Books of the Church Seal of the Library of A.I. Chludov. Moscow, 1872. Pp. 320-25. [in Russian]

96.78 Rompay, L. van. "De Ethiopische versie van het kindheidsevangelie volgens Thomas de Israëliet," L'enfant dans les civilisations orientales. Het kind in de Oosterse beschavingen, eds. A. Theodorides, P. Naster and J. Ries. Leuven, 1980. Pp. 119-32.

96.79 Rompay, L. van. "Les manuscrits éthiopiens des 'Miracles de Jésus,'" AnBoll 93 (1975) 133-46.

96.80 Šanidze, A. "A fragment of the Georgian version of the apocryphal 'Gospel of Thomas' and its incomprehensible passages," Stalinis sahelobis T'ibilisis sah. Universitetis Šromebi 18 (1941) 29-40. [in Russian]

96.81 Santos Otero, A. de. "Evangelio del Pseudo Tomás," Evangelios Apócrifos. Pp. 282-306. [Gk. text and Span. trans.]

96.82 Santos Otero, A. de. "Evangelium Thomae Infantiae," Altslavischen Apok. 2. Pp. 49-54.

96.83 Santos Otero, A. de. Das kirchenslavische Evangelium des Thomas (Patristische Texte und Studien 6) Berlin, 1967. [German trans.]

96.84 Schade, O. Narrationes de vita et conversatione B.M. Virginis et de pueritia et adolescentia Salvatoris. Halle, 1870.

96.85 Schmal, G. "Lk 2,41-52 und die Kindheitserzählung des Thomas 19,1-5; Ein Vergleich," Bibel und Leben 15 (1974) 249-58.

96.86 Speranskij, M.N. South Russian Texts of the Apocryphal Gospel of Thomas. Kiev, 1899. Pp. 169-90. [in Russian]

96.87 Speranskij, M.N. "Slavic Apocryphal Gospels," The Work of the Eighth Archaeological Conference in Moscow 1890. Moscow, 1895. Vol. 2. Pp. 73-92, 137-43. [in Russian]

96.88 Starowieyski, M. "On the Infancy of our Lord, the so-called Gospel of Thomas," Analecta Cracoviensia 4 (1972) 315-58. [in Polish]

96.89 Stegmüller, F. Repertorium Biblicum. 1. Pp. 145-47; 8. Pp. 136-39.

96.90 Thilo, J.C. Codex Apocryphus Novi Testamenti. Leipzig, 1832. Pp. 275-315.

96.91 Tischendorf, K. "Ad evangelium Thomae Graece A," Apocalypses Apocryphae. P. lxi.

96.92 Tischendorf, K. von. "Evangelium Thomae," Evangelia Apocrypha. Pp. xxxvi-xlviii, 140-80.

96.93 Tischendorf, K. [Thomae evangelium ex eodem codice Syriaco partim interprete Wrightio excribitur, partim cum nostris ricensionibus], Apocalypses Apocryphae. Pp. liii-lvi. [Gk. and Lat. texts]

96.94 Trofimov, M.K. "On the Method of the Study of Sources on
       the History of Early Christianity (for Example on the Litera-
       ture About the Gospel of Thomas)," Vestnik drevnei istorii
       1 (1970) 142-51. [in Russian]

96.95 Variot, J. "L'Évangile de Thomas l'Israélite," Évangiles Apoc-
       ryphes. Pp. 44-50, 197-232.

96.96 Walker, A. "The Gospel of Thomas," ANF 8. Pp. 395-404.
       [ET]

96.97 Wright, W. "The Gospel of Thomas the Israelite," ALNT.
       Pp. Y'-YW [Syr], 6-11 [ET], 55-58 [notes].

96.98 Zahn, T. "Das Evangelium des Thomas," Neutest. Kanons.
       2. Pp. 768-73. [Intro.]

97. TIMOTHY AND AQUILA, THE DIALOGUE OF; AND TIMOTHY CYCLE

97.1   Birdsall, J.N. "The Dialogue of Timothy and Aquila and the
       Early Harmonistic Traditions," NovT 22 (1980) 66-77.

97.2   Conybeare, F.C. ed. The Dialogue of Athanasius and Zac-
       chaeus, and of Timothy and Aquila (Anecdota Oxoniensia,
       Classical Series Part 8) Oxford, 1898.

97.3   Delehaye, H. "Les Actes de Saint Timothée," Anatolian Stud-
       ies Presented to William Hepburn Buckler, eds. W.M. Calder
       and J. Keil. Manchester, 1939. Pp. 77-84.

97.4   Globe, A. "The Dialogue of Timothy and Aquila as Witness
       to a Pre-Caesarean Text of the Gospels," NTS 29 (1983)
       233-46.

97.5   Goodspeed, E.J. "The Dialogue of Timothy and Aquila: Two
       Unpublished Manuscripts," JBL 24 (1905) 58-78.

97.6   Hoffmann, M. Der Dialog bei den christlichen Schriftstellern
       der ersten vier Jahrhunderte (TU 96) Berlin, 1966. [See
       esp. pp. 10, 163.]

97.7   Keil, J. "Zum Martyrium des heiligen Timotheus in Ephesus,"
       Jahreshefte des Österreichischen Archäologischen Instituts
       in Wien.*

97.7a Lipsius, R.A. Die apokryphen Apostelgeschichten und Apos-
       tellegenden. 2 vols. Brunswick, 1883-1890; repr. Amster-
       dam, 1976. Vol. 2.2. Pp. 372-400.

97.8   Mariès, L. [Important reviews of publications on DTimAq]
        Revue des Études Arméniennes 6 (1926) 185-328.

97.9   Robertson, R.G. "The Dialogue of Timothy and Aquila: The
        Need for a New Edition," VC 32 (1978) 276-88.

97.10   Stegmüller, F. Repertorium Biblicum. 1. Pp. 233f.; 8. P.
        201.

97.11   Tamilla, P. De Timothei Christiani et Aquilae Iudaici dialogo.
        Rome, 1901.

97.12   Usener, H. "Acta S. Timothei," Bonner Universitätsprogramm.
        Bonn, 1877.

97.13   Williams, A.L. "The Dialogue of Timothy and Aquila," Adver-
        sus Judaeos: A Bird's-eye View of Christian Apologiae un-
        til the Renaissance. Cambridge, Pp. 67-78.

                98. TITUS, EPISTLE OF; AND TITUS CYCLE

(See also 67.76.)

98.1   Bauer, J.B. "Ein Titusbrief," Neutest. Apok. Pp. 93f.

98.2   Bruyne, D. de. "Epistula Titi Discipuli Pauli, de Dispositione
        Sanctimonii," RBen 37 (1925) 47-72.

98.3   Bruyne, D. de. "Nouveaux fragments des Actes de Pierre,
        de Paul, de Jean, d'André et de l'Apocalypse d'Élie," RBen
        25 (1908) 149-60. [discusses the Elijah fragment in EpTit]

98.4   Bulhart, V. "Nochmals Textkritisches," RBen 62 (1952) 297-
        99.

98.5   Eckhart, [?] von. Commentarii de rebus Franciae orientalis.
        Vol. 2. Pp. 837-47.*

98.6   Erbetta, M. "L'Epistola di Tito, discepolo di Paolo, circa il
        modo di vivere nello stato di castità," Apoc. del NT. 3.
        Pp. 93-110.

98.7   Hagner, D.A. "Titus, Epistle of," ZPEB. 5. P. 761.

98.8   Halkin, F. "La légende crétoise de S. Tite," AnBoll 79 (1961)
        241-56.

98.9   Harnack, A. "Der Apokryphe Brief des Paulusschülers Titus
        'De dispositione Sanctimoni,'" SPAW 17 (1925) 180-213.

98.10 James, M.R. ANT. Pp. 265f.

98.11 James, M.R. The Lost Apocrypha of the Old Testament (TED)
       London, 1920. P. 55.

98.12 Koch, H. "Zu Ps.-Titus, De dispositione sanctimonii," ZNW
       32 (1933) 131-44.

98.12a Lipsius, R.A. Die apokryphen Apostelgeschichten und Apos-
       tellegenden. 2 vols. Brunswick, 1883-1890; repr. Amsterdam,
       1976. Vol. 2.2. Pp. 401-406.

98.13 Migne, J.-P. "Tite," Dictionnaire. 2. Cols. 1047f.

98.14 Moraldi, L. "Dall' epistola di Tito," Apoc. del NT. 2. Pp.
       1211f.

98.15 Moraldi, L. "Epistola di Tito Discepolo di Paolo," Apoc. del
       NT. 2. Pp. 1757-88.

98.16 Morin, D.G. "Un curieux inédit du IVe et Ve siècle: Le soi-
       disant évêque Asterius d'Ansedunum contre la peste des
       Agapètes," RBen 47 (1935) 101-113.

98.17 Morin, D.G. "L'homéliaire de Burchard de Würzburg: Contri-
       bution à la critique des sermons de saint Césaire d'Arles,"
       RBen 13 (1896) 97-111.

98.18 Santos Otero, A. de. "Der apokryphe Titusbrief," ZKG 74
       (1963) 1-14.

98.19 Santos Otero, A. de. "Der Pseudo-Titus-Brief," HS. 2. Pp.
       90-109.

98.20 Santos Otero, A. de. "The Pseudo-Titus Epistle," HSW. 2.
       Pp. 141-66.

98.21 Stegmüller, F. Repertorium Biblicum. 1. P. 234; 8. Pp.
       201f.

99. GOSPEL OF THE TWELVE APOSTLES

Modern scholars have tried to identify Origen's and Jerome's
citations of GosTw with the GosEb--see also the entries
under that category. Other works also referred to as
GosTw are included here for completeness.

99.1   Amann, É. "Évangile des Ébionites ou des douze apôtres,"
       DBSup. 1. Cols. 427f.

99.2   Bardenhewer, O. "Das Evangelium der Zwölf und das Ebion-
        itenevangelium," GAL. 1. Pp. 518-21.

99.3   Erbetta, M. "Il Vangelo dei dodici Apostoli con le loro singole
        Rivelazione," Apoc. del NT. 3. Pp. 431-40.

99.4   Fabricius, J.A. "Evangelium Duodecim Apostolorum," Cod.
        Apoc.NT. 1. Pp. 339f.

99.5   Harnack, A. "Das Evangelium der zwölf Apostel (von Matth.
        angeblich niedergeschrieben) und andere Schriften der gnos-
        tischen Ebioniten," Gesch. altchrist. Lit. 1. Pp. 205-09.

99.6   Harnack, A. "Das Hebräer- und das Ebionitenevangelium [Ev.
        (der 12 Apostel durch) Matthäus]," Gesch. altchrist. Lit.
        2.1. Pp. 625-51.

99.7   Harris, J. R. The Gospel of the Twelve Apostles Together
        with the Apocalypses of Each one of Them. Cambridge,
        1900. [see the review by E. Nestle, TLZ 25 (1900) 557-59]

99.8   Klostermann, E., ed. "Ebionitenevangelium (Evangelium der
        Zwölf?)," Apocrypha II: Evangelien (KlT 8) Berlin, 1929³.
        Pp. 12-15. [Gk. witnesses]

99.9   Lucchesi, E. "D'un soi-disant Évangile (apocryphe) des douze
        Apôtres a l'Évangile (canonique) selon saint Jean," Or 52
        (1983) 267.

99.10   Meyer, A. "Ebionitenevangelium: Evangelium der 12 Apostel,"
        Handbuch, ed. Hennecke. Pp. 42-47.

99.11   Migne, J.-P. "Apotres (Evangile des douze)," Dictionnaire.
        2. Col. 1311.

99.12   Ouseley, G.J.R. The Gospel of the Holy Twelve, known also
        as the Gospel of the Perfect Life. London, 1957.

99.13   Puech, H.-C. "Evangelien, Die der Gesamtheit der Apostel
        zugeschrieben werden," HS. 1. Pp. 186-88, 190f., 193.

99.14   Puech, H.-C. "Gospels Attributed to the Twelve as a Group,"
        HSW. 1. Pp. 263-65, 268f., 271.

99.15   Rahmani, I.E. Studia Syriaca IV. Rome, 1909. P. 78.
        [Kukean GTw]

99.16   Revillout, E. "Évangile des douze Apotres," PO 2 (1907) 123-
        84. [Supplement in PO 9 (1913) 133-40; Cop. text and
        French trans. of fragments R. identifies as GosTw and
        GosBart]

99.17 Revillout, E. "L'Évangile des XII Apôtres récemment décou-
       vert," RB 13 (1904) 167-87, 321-55.

99.18 Santos Otero, A. de. "Evangelio de los Doce o de los Ebion-
       itas," Evangelios Apócrifos. Pp. 47-53.

99.20 Schmidtke, A. "Epiphanius über das Hebräerevangelium und
       seine Leser," Neue Fragmente und Untersuchungen zu den
       judenchristlichen Evangelien (TU 37.1) Leipzig, 1911. Pp.
       173f. [Kukean GTw]

99.21 Stegmüller, F. Repertorium Biblicum. 1. P. 108; 8. Pp.
       79f.

99.22 Waitz, H. "Ebionäerevangelium oder der Zwölf," H². Pp.
       39-48.

99.23 Waitz, H. "Das Evangelium der zwölf Apostel (Ebionitenevan-
       gelium.)," ZNW 13 (1912) 338-48; 14 (1913) 38-64, 117-32.
       [see esp. 14 (1913) 46ff. for Kukean GTw]

99.24 Wilson, R. McL. "Apostles, Gospel of the Twelve," ZPEB.
       1. Pp. 221f.

99.25 Zahn, T. "Das Evangelium der Zwölf," Neutest. Kanons. 2.
       Pp. 724-42. [Intro. and Gk. frags.]

100. VIRGIN, APOCALYPSE OF

Works listed here refer to both the Gk. ApVir, which
describes her tour of hell, and the Eth. ApVir, which
is primarily dependent upon ApPl.

(See also 1.254, 284; 2.34.)

100.1 Bokadorov, N.K. "Legend About the Pilgrimage of the Mother
       of God Through Suffering," Festschrift T.D. Florinskij.
       Kiev, 1904. Pp. 39-94. [in Russian]

100.2 Buslaev, F. Historical Essays on Russian National Literature
       and Art. St. Petersburg, 1861. P. 437. [in Russian]

100.3 Dawkins, R.M. "A Cretan Apocalypse of the Virgin Mary,"
       Krēt. Chronika 2 (1948) 487-500. [in modern Gk.]

100.4 Delatte, A. Anecdota Atheniensia, Bibl. de la Faculté de
       Phil. et Lettres de l'Univ. de Liege. 1927. Vol. 1. Pp.
       272-88.*

100.5   Erbetta, M. "L'Apocalisse Etiopica della Vergine," Apoc. del
        NT. 3. Pp. 455-70.

100.6   Erbetta, M. "L'Apocalisse Greca della Vergine," Apoc. del NT.
        3. Pp. 447-54.

100.7   Gudzij, N.K. Anthology of Ancient Russian Literature of the
        11th-17th Centuries. Moscow, 1955. Pp. 92-98. [in Rus-
        sian]

100.8   Gudzij, N.K. The History of Ancient Russian Literature.
        Moscow, 1938. Pp. 48-52. [in Russian]

100.9   Jacimirskij, A.I. "Apocrypha and Legends ... V," IzvORJS
        14 (1909) 311-22. [in Russian]

100.10 James, M.R. "The Apocalypse of the Virgin," AA 1. Pp.
        109-26. [Gk. text; see also AA 2. P. 141]

100.11 James, M.R. "The Apocalypse of the Virgin," ANT. Pp.
        563f.

100.12 Kirpičnikov, A.I. "'Deity' in the East and West and Its Lit-
        erary Parallels," Žurnal ministerstva narodnago prosveš-
        čenija 2 (1893). [in Russian]*

100.13 Moraldi, L. "Apocalisse della vergine Maria," Apoc. del NT.
        1. Pp. 901-26.

100.14 Müller, L. "'Die Offenbarung der Gottesmutter über die
        Höllenstrafen' Theologischer Gehalt und dichterische Form,"
        Die Welt der Slaven 6 (1961) 26-39.

100.15 Pernot, H. "Descente de la Vierge aux enfers," REG 13
        (1900) 234-56.

100.16 Porfiryev, I.Y. "Apocryphal Sayings About New Testament
        People and Events in Manuscripts of the Solovetski Library,"
        SbORJS 52 (1890) 109f. [in Russian]*

100.17 Pypin, A.N. "Ancient Russian Literature II: Sayings About
        the Pilgrimage of the Mother of God Through Suffering,"
        Otečestvennyja zapiski 115 (1856) 335-60. [in Russian]

100.18 Pypin, A.N. False and Dismissed Books of Ancient Russia.
        St. Petersburg, 1862. Pp. 118-24. [in Russian]

100.19 Ruffini, M., ed. L'Apocalisse della Madre del Signore. Flor-
        ence, 1954.

100.20 Sacharov, V. Eschatological Works and Narrations in Ancient

Russian Writings and Their Influence on Popular Spiritual
Verse. Tula, 1879. Pp. 193-200. [in Russian]

100.21   Santos Otero, A. de. "Apocalypsis Deiparae," Altslavischen
Apok. 1. Pp. 188-95.

100.22   Schneemelcher, W. "Apocalypses of Mary," HSW. 2. Pp.
753f.

100.23   Schneemelcher, W. "Apokalypsen der Maria," HS. 2. P.
535.

100.24   Šepelevič, L. Essays From the History of Medieval Literature.
Vol. 1: Pilgrimage Through Suffering. Char'kov, 1890.
[in Russian]

100.25   Smirnov, I. "Apocryphal Sayings About the Mother of God
and Acts of the Holy Apostles," Pravoslavnoe obozrenie 4
(1873) 569-614. [in Russian]

100.26   Sreznevskij, I.I. Texts of Ancient Russian Literature. St.
Petersburg, 1882². Pp. 204-17. [in Russian]

100.27   Stegmüller, F. Repertorium Biblicum. 1. Pp. 238-40; 8.
Pp. 206f.

100.28   Tichonravov, N. Texts of Dismissed Russian Literature.
Moscow, 1863; repr. London, 1973. Vol. 2. Pp. 23-39.
[in Russian]

100.29   Tischendorf, K. [De quadam Mariae apocalypsi in variis
codicibus Graecis inventa], Apocalypses Apocryphae. Pp.
xxvii-xxx.

100.30   Trautmann, R. Altrussisches Lesebuch. Leipzig, 1949.
Part 1. Pp. 26-38.

100.31   Tshqonia, T. "Les anciennes recensions géorgiennes de
l'Apocalypsis Mariae," Moanbe de l'Institut des Manuscrits
de l'Acad. des Sc. de la RSS de Géorgie 1 (1959) 52-74.

100.32   Vranska, C. The Apocrypha Concerning the Virgin Mother
in the Bulgarian Folk Song (Collection of the Bulgarian
Academy of Sciences 34) Sofia, 1940. Pp. 58-64. [in
Bulgarian]

100.33   Wilson, R.McL. "Virgin, Apocalypses of the," ZPEB. 5.
P. 886.

101. VIRGIN, ASSUMPTION OF

See also the listings under PasMar.

(See also 50.11.)

101.1   Baldi, D., and A. Mosconi. "L'Assunzione di Maria SS. negli
         apocrifi," Studia Mariana I: Atti del congresso nazionale
         Mariano dei Frati Minori d'Italia, Roma 29 aprile--3 maggio,
         1947. Rome, 1948. Pp. 75-125.

101.2   Balić, C. Testimonia de Assumptione B. Mariae Virginis in
         omnibus saeculis. Rome, 1948.

101.3   Bonnet, M. "Bemerkungen über die älteste Himmelfahrt
         Mariä," ZWT 23 (1880) 222-47.

101.4   Bover, J.M. La asunción de María. Madrid, 1947. Pp. 155-
         197; 304-322.

101.5   Bover, P. "La asunción de María en el 'Transitus W' y en
         Juan de Thessalónica," EE 20 (1946) 415-36.

101.6   Brou, D.L. "Restes de l'ancienne homélie sur la Dormition
         de l'archevêque Jean de Thessalonique dans le plus ancien
         antiphonaire connu et le dernier Magnificat de la Vierge,"
         ALW 2 (1952) 84-93.

101.7   Budge, E.A.W., ed. and tr. The History of the Blessed
         Virgin Mary and the History of the Likeness of Christ
         which the Jews of Tiberias Made to Mock at. (Luzac's
         Semitic Text and Translation Series 4, 5) London, 1899;
         repr. New York, 1976. [Syr. texts and ET]

101.8   Capelle, D.B. "Les anciens récits de l'Assomption et Jean
         de Thessalonique," RTAM 12 (1940)*

101.9   Capelle, B. "L'assunzione e la Liturgia," Marianum 15 (1953)
         241-76.

101.10   Carli, M.-L. "Le fonti del racconto della dormizione di Maria
         di Giovanni Tessalonicese," Marianum 2 (1940) 308-13.

101.11   Carli, L. "Giovanni Tessalonicese e l'Assunzione di Maria,"
         Marianum 4 (1947) 1-9.

101.12   Carli, L. La morte e l'assunzione di Maria Sma. nelle omelie
         greche dei secoli VII-VIII. Rome, 1941.

101.13 Chaine, M., ed. Apocrypha de Beata Maria Virgine (CSCO
        39-40; Scriptores Aethiopici 22-23) Louvain, 1955. Vol.
        39 (22). Pp. 51-80; Vol. 40 (23). Pp. 43-68. [Eth. and
        Lat. texts]

101.14 Chaine, M. "Le discours de Théodose, patriarche d'Alexan-
        drie, sur la Dormition," ROC 29 (1933-34) 272-304.

101.15 Cignelli, L. "Il prototipo giudeo-cristiano degli apocrifi as-
        sunzionisti," ŠH (Jerusalem, 1976) 259-77, cf. 701,774.

101.16 Ciquello, P. "Récits apocryphes relatifs à la mort et à la
        assomption de la Sainte Vierge," Mémoire du Congrès Marial
        de Nantes. Paris, 1925. Pp. 51-58.

101.17 Duhr, J. "L'évolution iconographique de l'assomption," NRT
        68 (1946) 671-83.

101.18 Enger, M. Iohannis apostoli de transitu beatae Mariae vir-
        ginis liber. Eberfeld, 1854.

101.19 Erbetta, M. "Assunzione," Apoc. del NT. 1.2. Pp. 407-632.

101.20 Esbroeck, M. van "Les textes littéraires sur l'assomption avant
        le Xe siècle," Actes Apocryphes. Pp. 265-85.

101.21 Fabricius, J.A. "S. Johannis de Transitu S. Mariae," Cod.
        Apoc.NT. 1. P. 352.

101.22 Faller, O. "De priorum saeculorum silentio circa Assumptionem
        B. Mariae Virginis," Analecta Gregoriana 36 (1946) 44-59.

101.23 Feldburch, H. Die Himmelfahrt Mariä. Dusseldorf, 1951.

101.24 Gordillo, M. "La Asunción en los monumentos anteriores al
        concilio de Efeso," RazFe (1919).*

101.25 Halkin, F. "Une légende byzantine de la Dormition: l'Epi-
        tomé du récit de Jean de Thessalonique," REByz 11 (1953)
        156-64.

101.26 Heidit, L., and L. Pirot. "Assomption Tradition de Jérusa-
        lem," DBSupp. 1. Cols. 225-34.

101.27 James, M.R. "The Assumption of the Virgin," ANT. Pp.
        194-227.

101.28 Jugie, M. "La littérature apocryphe sur la mort et l'assomp-
        tion de Marie à partir de la seconde moitié du VIe siècle,"
        Échos d'Orient 29 (1930) 265-95.

101.29   Jugie, M. <u>La mort et l'assomption de la sainte Vierge</u> (Studi
         e Testi 114) Rome, 1944.

101.30   Jugie, M. "La morte et l'assomption de la sainte Vierge dans
         la tradition des cinq primiers siècles," <u>Échos d'Orient</u> 25
         (1926) 5-20, 129-43, 281-307; 26 (1927) 18-23, 385-92.

101.31   Jugie, M. "Le récit de l'histoire euthymiaque sur la mort et
         l'assomption de la S. Vierge," <u>Échos d'Orient</u> 25 (1926)
         385-92.

101.32   Lantschoot, A. van. "L'Assomption de la S. Vierge chez les
         Coptes," <u>Gregorianum</u> 27 (1946) 493-526.

101.33   LeHir, A. "De l'assomption de la sainte Vierge et des livres
         apocryphes qui s'y rapportent," <u>Études religieuses histor-
         iques et littéraires</u> (1866) 514-55.*

101.34   Moraldi, L. "Discorso di san Giovanni il Teologo sul riposo
         della santa teotoco," <u>Apoc. del NT</u>. 1. Pp. 885-95.

101.35   Odoardi, G. "Elementi leggendari nell'iconografia italiana
         dell'Assunta," <u>Città di vita</u> 3 (1948) 423-33.

101.36   Revillout, E. "Résurrection de la Vierge," <u>PO</u> 2 (1907) 181-
         84.

101.37   Rush, A.C. "The Assumption in the Apocrypha," <u>AmER</u> 116
         (1947) 5-31.

101.38   Salazar, I.T. "Acta Dormitionis et Assumptionis b. Virginis
         Mariae Dei-Genetricis, Dominae Nostrae, ex Legendario
         Segobiensi Ms. et aliis Breviariis," <u>Martyrologium Hispanum</u>.
         London, 1656. Vol. 4. Pp. 480-82.

101.39   Santos Otero, A. de. "Apócrifos Asuncionistas," <u>Evangelios
         Apócrifos</u>. Pp. 574-659.

101.40   Santos Otero, A. de. "Libro de Juan, Arzobispo de Tesa-
         lonica," <u>Evangelios Apócrifos</u>. Pp. 607-45. [Gk. text and
         Spanish trans.]

101.41   Stano, G. "L'assunzione negli apocrifi," <u>Città di vita</u> 3
         (1948) 408-17.

101.42   Stegmüller, F. <u>Repertorium Biblicum</u>. 1. Pp. 135-39; 8.
         Pp. 115-23.

101.43   Tischendorf, K. "Iohannis liber de dormitione Mariae,"
         <u>Apocalypses Apocryphae</u>. Pp. 95-112. [Gk. text]

101.44 Vasil'ev, A.V. Anedcota graeco-byzantina. Moscow, 1893.
        Pp. 125-34.

101.45 Vitti, A.M. "Libri apocrifi de assumptione B. Mariae Vir-
        ginis," VD 6 (1926) 225-34.

101.46 Walker, A. "The Book of John Concerning the Falling Asleep
        of Mary," ANF. 8. Pp. 587-91. [ET]

101.47 Weber, C.P. "Evodius, Homily of," ZPEB. 2. P. 421.

101.48 Wenger, A. L'assomption de la T. S. Vierge dans la tradition
        byzantine du VIe au Xe siècle. Paris, 1955.

101.49 Willard, R. "On Blickling Homily XIII: The Assumption of
        the Virgin. The Source and the Missing Passage," RES
        12 (1936) 1-17.

101.50 Wilmart, A. "Assumptio sanctae Mariae," Analecta Reginensia:
        Extraits des manuscrits latins de la reine Christine conserv-
        ées au Vatican (Studi e Testi 59) Rome, 1933. Pp. 323-57.

101.51 Wright, W. "The Obsequies of the Virgin," ALNT. Pp. NH-
        ŠH (Syr); 42-51 (ET); 59-63 (notes).

101.52 Wright, W. "Transitus Assumptio Virginis," ALNT. Pp.
        KZ-N' (Syr); 18-41 (ET); 59-63 (notes).

                    102. VIRGIN, COPTIC LIVES OF THE

        See also the entries under Mary Cycle.

(See also 16.12, 13.)

102.1   James, M.R. "Coptic Lives, etc., of the Virgin," ANT.
        Pp. 87-89.

102.2   Robinson, F. "Sahidic Fragments of the Life of the Virgin,"
        Coptic Apocryphal Gospels (T&S 4.2) Cambridge, 1896.
        Pp. 1-41. [Coptic text and ET]

            103. XANTHIPPE: ACTS OF XANTHIPPE AND
                              POLYXENA

(See also 1.254, 3.12, 37.)

103.1   Craigie, W.A. "The Acts of Xanthippe and Polyxena," ANF.
        10. Pp. 203-17. [ET]

103.2   James, M.R. ANT. Pp. 471, 475.

103.3   James, M.R. "Introduction to the Acts of Xanthippe and
        Polyxena; Acta Xanthippae et Polyxenae," AA. 1. Pp.
        43-85. [Gk. text; see also AA 2 Pp. 139f]

103.4   Lipsius, R.A. Die apokryphen Apostelgeschichten und Apos-
        tellegenden. 2 vols. Brunswick, 1883-90; repr. Amsterdam,
        1976. Vol. 2. Pp. 217-27.

103.5   Peterson, E. "Die Acta Xanthippae et Polyxenae und die
        Paulusakten," AnBoll 65 (1947) 57-60.

                    104. ZECHARIAH, APOCALYPSE OF

104.1   Bardenhewer, O. "Eine Zachariasapokalypse?" GAL. 1.
        Pp. 621f.

104.2   Berendts, A. Die handschriftliche Überlieferung der Zacha-
        rias und Johannes-Apokryphen (TU 26/3) Leipzig, 1904.

104.3   Berendts, A. Studien über Zacharias-Apokryphen und
        Zacharias-Legenden. Leipzig, 1895.

104.4   Dubois, J.-D. Études sur l'Apocryphe de Zacharie et sur
        les traditions concernant la mort de Zacharie. Diss. Oxford,
        Paris, 1978.

104.5   Erbetta, M. "Apocalisse di Zaccaria," Apoc. del NT. 3.
        P. 445.

104.6   James, M.R. The Lost Apocrypha of the Old Testament (TED)
        London, 1920. Pp. 74-77.

104.7   Migne, J.-P. "Zacharie," Dictionnaire. 2. Cols. 1309f.

104.8   Schneemelcher, W. "Apocalypse of Zechariah," HSW. 2. Pp.
        752f.

104.9   Schneemelcher, W. "Apokalypse des Zacharias," HS. 2.
        P. 534.

104.10 Stegmüller, F. Repertorium Biblicum. 1. P. 250; 8. P.
        216.

104.11   Wall, H.   "A Coptic Fragment concerning the Childhood of
            John the Baptist," Revue d'Egyptologie 8 (1951) 207-
            14.

AUTHOR INDEX

Compiled by M.J.H. Charlesworth

The numbers following names indicate the preceding pages. A name appearing more than once on a page is cited only once. It is difficult to bring order into the chaos that has characterized this area of research for over a century. Over the years, the names of Eastern European scholars were transliterated in more than one way; hence Trofimov is also Trofimova, Vasilief is also Vassiliev and Vasil'evskij (and perhaps Veselovskij).

Western European scholars also have used more than one form for their names. Some order is demanded; hence, for example, the famous Tischendorf is cited here as C. Tischendorf (not K. von). Struggles to systematize authors' names do not reflect evaluations of a scholar's stature. German names with ä, ö, and ü have been alphabetized as though spelled ae, oe, and ue, respectively.

It is not the responsibility of a bibliographer to make sweeping judgments. This index reflects years of trying to clarify forms or relationships; at times it was impossible to locate an article or book to verify spellings or identities.

Most additional problems can be solved by more research; we are convinced that Barnes may be the same person as Barns; they both have the same initials (J.W.B.). Such similarities, however, have sometimes proved to indicate different persons. Publishers have changed the name I attached to an article from J.H. to J. and even to H. Charlesworth. Scholars have erroneously referred to me as Professor Charles and Professor Worth. I know these discrepancies do not indicate different authors, but I am reticent to align spellings and initials of other names when I am not certain.

Obviously the team who worked on this bibliography attempted to locate a problematic publication and, when necessary, to transliterate names consistently. Occasionally we could not locate the articles or books and have discovered secondary references to them to be notoriously imprecise. When possible, different spellings of names are organized under the most appropriate one (cf. Starowieyski); other yet unresolved problems are the following:

Baker, A. (cf. Bakker, A.)
Capelle, B. (cf. Capelle, D.B.)
Carli, L. (cf. Carli, M.L.)
Fabriciani (cf. Fabricius, J.A.

and Fabricius, L.)
Martin, J. (cf. Martin, J.P.P.)
Petersen, E. (cf. Peterson, E.)

Quecke, H. (cf. Quecque, H.)
Robert, A. (cf. Roberts, A.)
Schoedel, W. (cf. Schoedel, W.R.)
Schultz W. (cf. Schulz, W.)
Sheppard, G. (cf. Sheppard, G.T.)
Smith, D. (cf. Smith, D.M. and Smith, M.)
Till, W. (cf. Till, W.C.)
Ullmann, W. (cf. Ullmann, [?])
Wessely, C. (cf. Wessely, K.)
Wickgren, A.P. (cf. Wikgren, A.P., and Wilkgren, A.)
Williams, A. (cf. Williams, A.L.)

The index is one map to the unexplored territory represented by the
entries above. The most important one is the first attempt to organize thousands of publications on the New Testament Apocrypha and
Pseudepigrapha in dozens of languages into a relationship.

Compiling this bibliography was far more complicated than preparing The Pseudepigrapha and Modern Research. Now, scholars
have a bibliographical guide to the Biblical Apocrypha and Pseudepigrapha, a new technical term.